P9-CDH-184

Get Updates and More on Nolo.com

Go to this book's companion page at:

www.nolo.com/back-of-book/GRN.html

When there's an important change to the law affecting this book, we'll post updates. You'll also find articles and other related materials.

More Resources from Nolo.com

Legal Forms, Books, & Software

Hundreds of do-it-yourself products—all written in plain English, approved, and updated by our in-house legal editors.

Legal Articles

Get informed with thousands of free articles on everyday legal topics. Our articles are accurate, up to date, and reader friendly.

Find a Lawyer

Want to talk to a lawyer? Use Nolo to find a lawyer who can help you with your case.

⚖ NOLO **The Trusted Name**
(but don't take our word for it)

"In Nolo you can trust."
THE NEW YORK TIMES

"Nolo is always there in a jam as the nation's premier publisher of do-it-yourself legal books."
NEWSWEEK

"Nolo publications…guide people simply through the how, when, where and why of the law."
THE WASHINGTON POST

"[Nolo's]…material is developed by experienced attorneys who have a knack for making complicated material accessible."
LIBRARY JOURNAL

"When it comes to self-help legal stuff, nobody does a better job than Nolo…"
USA TODAY

"The most prominent U.S. publisher of self-help legal aids."
TIME MAGAZINE

"Nolo is a pioneer in both consumer and business self-help books and software."
LOS ANGELES TIMES

14th Edition

How to Get a Green Card

Ilona Bray, J.D.

FOURTEENTH EDITION	JULY 2020
Editor	ILONA BRAY
Cover Design	SUSAN PUTNEY
Book Design	SUSAN PUTNEY
Proofreading	SUSAN CARLSON GREENE
Index	ACCESS POINTS INDEXING
Printing	BANG PRINTING

ISSN: 2371-9885 (print)
ISSN: 2371-9915 (online)
ISBN: 978-1-4133-2744-1 (pbk)
ISBN: 978-1-4133-2745-8 (ebook)

This book covers only United States law, unless it specifically states otherwise.

Copyright © 1993, 1996, 1998, 1999, 2003, and 2005 by Loida N. Lewis and Len Madlansacay. Copyright © 2006, 2008, 2010, 2012, 2014, 2016, 2018, and 2020 by Nolo. All rights reserved. The NOLO trademark is registered in the U.S. Patent and Trademark Office. Printed in the U.S.A.

No part of this publication may be reproduced, stored in a retrieval system, or transmitted in any form or by any means, electronic, mechanical, photocopying, recording, or otherwise without prior written permission. Reproduction prohibitions do not apply to the forms contained in this product when reproduced for personal use. For information on bulk purchases or corporate premium sales, please contact the Special Sales Department. Call 800-955-4775 or write to Nolo, 950 Parker Street, Berkeley, California 94710.

Please note

We know that accurate, plain-English legal information can help you solve many of your own legal problems. But this text is not a substitute for personalized advice from a knowledgeable lawyer. If you want the help of a trained professional—and we'll always point out situations in which we think that's a good idea—consult an attorney licensed to practice in your state.

R0458098904

Acknowledgments

The original authors of this book were Loida Nicolas Lewis and Len Madlansacay. Nolo thanks them for their efforts in producing a work of such ambitious scope, and one that has endured for many years.

Of course, massive and constant changes in immigration laws and practices have necessitated many rewrites and revisions of the original book.

For this edition, we owe tremendous debts of thanks to a number of highly skilled attorneys who offered their expertise in various areas of immigration law. First, we are grateful to Kyle A. Knapp, an Ohio-based immigration attorney, who thoroughly updated the contents of numerous chapters, based on his experience representing green-card seekers applying through family, employment, the diversity visa, and more. In addition, attorney Taylor Jameson, of Legal Services of Eastern Michigan, took on the challenge of updating the chapter concerning U visas. And Catherine Seitz, attorney and Legal Director of Immigration Institute of the Bay Area (IIBA) updated the chapter on refugees and asylees.

About the Author

Ilona Bray came to the practice of immigration law through her long interest in international human rights issues. Before joining Nolo as legal editor in charge of immigration, she ran a solo law practice and worked for nonprofit immigration agencies including the International Institute of the East Bay (Oakland) and the Northwest Immigrant Rights Project (Seattle). Ms. Bray was also an intern in the legal office at Amnesty International's International Secretariat in London. She received her Bachelor's degree in philosophy from Bryn Mawr College, and her law degree and a Master's degree in East Asian (Chinese) Studies from the University of Washington. Ms. Bray is a member of the American Immigration Lawyers Association (AILA). She has authored other books for Nolo, including *Fiancé & Marriage Visas: A Couple's Guide to U.S. Immigration* and *Becoming a U.S. Citizen: A Guide to the Law, Exam & Interview.*

Table of Contents

Your Immigration Companion

Are you a foreign-born person who's interested in making your home in the United States? If so, this book might be just the ticket to finding out whether you're eligible for permanent U.S. residence, also known as a "green card." A green card gives you the right to live and work in the United States your whole life, travel in and out of the country without too much hassle, sponsor certain family members to join you, and, if all goes well for a few years, apply for U.S. citizenship.

This book will help you learn the application procedures, fill out the various forms, and pick up tips for dealing with often-difficult government officials. We try to give you a realistic view of your immigration possibilities and guide you along the path—which could be a long one—to reaching your goals. And unlike many government publications, we'll warn you about what could go wrong, and what steps to take to avoid delays and problems. Immigrants to the United States have to face a huge and often unfriendly government bureaucracy. Often, it's not the law itself that gives immigrants problems, but dealing with government delays, mistakes, and inattention. So, it helps to have a friend like this book by your side.

However, some people won't get the help they need from this particular book, so read this chapter carefully before you continue!

A. Types of Green Cards We Cover

This book was designed to help the "average" person—for example, someone who doesn't have a million dollars to invest, isn't internationally famous, and hasn't received a job offer from a U.S. employer. That's why we've focused our discussion on the following types of green card opportunities:

- family-based green cards, available to close relatives and adopted children of U.S. citizens and permanent residents

- political asylum and refugee status, available to people fleeing certain types of persecution
- the visa lottery ("diversity visa"), available to people from certain countries with a minimum level of education who win a random drawing, and
- opportunities for people who have lived in the United States for ten years or more and are in removal proceedings ("cancellation of removal").

This book does *not* cover green cards through employment, investment, the amnesty programs of the 1980s and the followup "NACARA" program, religious workers, or other, more obscure categories. Nor does it cover temporary visas (distinct from green cards in that they expire, usually in a few years). Examples of temporary visas include student, business visitor, H-1B specialty worker, and J-1 exchange visitor visas. (For a quick overview of these temporary visas, see Chapter 3.)

> ⚠ **CAUTION**
> **Don't confuse green cards with U.S. citizenship.** The highest status you can obtain under the U.S. immigration laws is citizenship. However, with only a very few exceptions, you must get a green card before you can apply for citizenship. For example, an immigrant who marries a U.S. citizen can gain the immediate right to apply for a green card, but not yet to apply for U.S. citizenship.

B. How Much You Can Do Without a Lawyer

The advice given in this book is for simple, straightforward cases. In other words, it's for people who clearly meet the eligibility requirements laid out in this book and have the education and skills to understand and handle the application requirements.

Many tasks you can do yourself, such as filling in forms, collecting documents, and attending interviews. Still, even filling out immigration forms can be a challenge. You'll be dealing with a bureaucracy that loves paperwork, but isn't always friendly to someone who makes minor mistakes or submits inconsistent information. Hiring an attorney—who handles this type of paperwork every day and knows whom to call when things go wrong—can be well worth the expense, both for convenience and for your own peace of mind.

And if your case is more complex, you absolutely should hire a lawyer to advise or represent you. This might be the case if any of the following apply:

- You have been ordered to appear before an immigration judge for what are called "removal" proceedings because the immigration authorities do not believe that you have a legal reason to either enter or continue to stay in the United States.
- You have a criminal record.
- You have some other problems with your immigration paperwork; for example, you have submitted forged documents.
- The paperwork and technical requirements are too heavy; for example, you plan to apply for asylum, are feeling traumatized, and need to assemble a lot of evidence about conditions in your home country; or you are appealing some decision made in your case by immigration authorities.

Of course, the key is to get a really good, experienced attorney. See Chapter 24 for guidance in hiring and working with a lawyer.

C. Using This Book

You need not read every chapter in this book—only those helpful to your specific situation. Here is some guidance.

Read **Chapter 1** if you're interested in a summary of immigration trends and laws throughout history.

Everyone should read **Chapters 2, 3, and 4.** They describe the basic requirements for obtaining legal permission to stay in the United States.

Everyone should also read **Chapter 5.** It explains the general forms and procedures required for obtaining a green card and the annual numbered limits or quotas that may apply.

> **TIP**
> **This book doesn't provide blank forms, for good reason.** All the application forms you'll need—and we'll tell you exactly which ones they are—are either readily available for free (www.uscis.gov or www.state.gov) or will be mailed to you by the immigration authorities when the time is right. Some can be filled out online. The forms get revised frequently, so it's best for you to obtain the most up-to-date form straight from its source when you're ready to use it. We have, however, provided sample filled-in forms to illustrate our advice and show you what the form will look like.

Now you can choose and read the specific chapters that concern you. Look over the chapter headings for **Chapters 6 through 15, as well as 18 and 19**—and read the ones that make the most sense in your specific situation. For example, if you believe that you might qualify for a green card because you will be marrying or are already married to a U.S. citizen, read **Chapter 7.** It might refer you to other chapters you should read to get a more complete picture.

Each chapter contains samples of most of the forms you'll need to complete. In some cases, we've left out pages that are irrelevant to you (for example, those that professional preparers would need to fill out).

After reading about the various rules for specific types of immigrants, if you decide that you qualify to file for yourself or another person, read **Chapters 21 and 22**. These chapters will help you with filling out the necessary forms and getting them into the right hands.

If you lose your green card or need to renew or replace it, read **Chapter 23** to find out how to do so.

Some people will find that they don't qualify for U.S. immigration at all, or at least not yet—it's a complicated and narrow system. But the good news is that approximately one million people receive U.S. green cards every year.

CAUTION
Green cards come with certain limitations. It's not a completely secure status. For example, you can lose your right to your green card if you:
- commit a crime
- don't make your primary home in the United States
- forget to report your change of address to the immigration authorities
- involve yourself in terrorist or subversive activities, or
- otherwise violate the immigration laws.

Steps You Must Take to Keep Up to Date

This book was as up to date as we could make it on the day it was printed. However, immigration laws change frequently, and USCIS changes its fees, rules, forms, and procedures even more often—at times without telling anyone.

That's why you must take certain steps on your own to protect your rights and interests. In particular, be sure to do the following:

- Check the USCIS website before turning in any application, at www.uscis.gov/forms. Make sure the form you filled out is still the most up to date, and that the fee hasn't gone up.
- Check the companion page for this book at **www.nolo.com/back-of-book/GRN.html** Here you'll find legal updates, author blog postings, and other useful information. Also see whether we've published a later edition of this book, in which case you'll probably want to get that later edition.
- Listen to the news, particularly for changes by the U.S. Congress. But don't rush to USCIS to apply for something until you're sure it's final. A lot of laws in progress get reported on before the president has actually signed them.

Immigration Then and Now
America: A Nation of Immigrants

A. **America's Earliest Settlers**...6

    1. Forced Migration...6

    2. European Exodus...6

    3. Growth of the Continental U.S. 6

B. **Early Immigration Restrictions**...7

C. **Today's Immigration Laws**..8

    1. Preference for Skilled Workers..8

    2. Refugees and Political Asylum 8

    3. Amnesty for Undocumented Workers in the 1980s...................................9

    4. Immigration Acts From
       1990 to the Present..9

D. **Looking Forward** 10

To understand current immigration policy, it helps to know how it came about.

A. America's Earliest Settlers

Long before Cristóbal Colón—the Spanish name for Christopher Columbus—opened the Americas to the Europeans in 1492, the first inhabitants of what is now the United States were the Native American Indians, including the Eskimos. Other early settlers included the Vikings, in the northernmost part of North America, and the ancestors of today's Hawaiians.

From the 15th century onward, the continent became a magnet for explorers and colonists from Spain, Holland, France, and England. In 1620, the pilgrims landed in Massachusetts and founded their new Zion, free from the interference of the English government. Quakers settled in Pennsylvania. Maryland provided refuge for Catholics who had been persecuted in England.

Spanish Jews, who had settled in Brazil after being expelled from Spain, arrived in New York when the Portuguese took over the former Spanish colony and started the Brazilian inquisition. After the Scottish rebellion was crushed, people from Scotland left for the colonies.

Other immigrants came in groups and provided special skills to the new cities and settlements: Austrians from Salzburg made silk; Poles and Germans made tar, glass, and tools and built homes. Later, Italians came and raised grapes. New Jersey was settled by the Swedes; northern Pennsylvania attracted a large number of Germans.

1. Forced Migration

Not everyone who came to the New World did so of their own free will. Many crossed the ocean as indentured servants for landowners in the English colonies.

And as cotton became the most important product in the South, plantation owners turned to the inhuman trade of African people to create a huge and cheap workforce, while the businessmen of the North who conducted the slave trade found it highly profitable.

By the time the first census of the new republic was taken in 1790, two-thirds of its four million inhabitants were English-speaking, and the rest were from other nations. Of these, 698,000 were African Americans who lived in human bondage mostly in the South; another 59,000 were free.

Although the U.S. Congress amended the Constitution in 1808 to ban the importation of slaves, it took nearly half a century before the smuggling of human beings stopped.

2. European Exodus

Between 1820 and 1910, Europe experienced the greatest migration of people to the New World. During that time, at least 38 million Europeans arrived in the United States.

Several important events caused this great migration: the Napoleonic Wars; the political disturbances in Germany, Austria-Hungary, Greece, and Poland; the Potato Famine in Ireland; the religious persecutions of Protestants, Catholics, and Jews in Czarist Russia and other parts of Europe; and the Industrial Revolution, which produced thousands of unemployed workers and peasants.

3. Growth of the Continental U.S.

At the same time, the United States was expanding into the West and the Southwest all the way to the Pacific Coast. The country grew by purchase, such as the Louisiana Purchase from Napoleon I of France, which bought an expanse of land from the Mississippi to the Rocky Mountains, and the purchase of Florida from Spain. It grew by war, such as the one waged with Mexico for California and Texas, and the one with Britain in 1812, which ended with a treaty granting the United States parts of Canada. The nation grew by possession of Native Americans' ancestral lands, sometimes by treaty, sometimes by purchase, and all too often by outright massacre.

B. Early Immigration Restrictions

In California, the Gold Rush of 1849 brought people not only from all over America but also the Chinese from across the Pacific Ocean. Chinese workers provided cheap labor for the construction of the Union Pacific Railroad. However, they were not granted the right to become American citizens.

By 1882, there were approximately 300,000 low-wage Chinese laborers in America. These new workers became targets to Americans for antagonism and racial hatred. As a result, the Chinese Exclusion Act was passed in 1882, completely banning non-citizen Chinese from immigrating to the United States. This law remained in effect until 1943.

The Japanese then took the place of the Chinese in agriculture, domestic work, lumber mills, and salmon fisheries. These Japanese workers also were subjected to racial hatred. They were excluded from the United States in 1908 and prohibited from becoming U.S. citizens by the Immigration Act of 1924.

Also during this time, after America purchased the Philippines from Spain in 1898, Filipinos were able to immigrate. They concentrated mostly on the East Coast and Hawaii as laborers on farms and sugar plantations, and in fish canneries and logging camps. They too were excluded from citizenship by the immigration laws passed in 1924.

This great influx of people in the late 19th and early 20th centuries brought the passage of several restrictive immigration laws. At various times, the U.S. Congress forbade people it considered undesirable to enter—paupers, drunkards, anarchists, polygamists, and people of various specific national origins.

In 1917, Congress passed an Immigration Act to restrict the entry of immigrants, especially the flow of illiterate laborers from central and eastern Europe. No immigration was permitted to the United States from the Asiatic Barred Zone. In addition to China and Japan, this zone included India, Siam (Thailand), Indochina (Vietnam, Cambodia, and Laos), Afghanistan, parts of Siberia, Iran, and Arabia, and the islands of Java, Sumatra, Ceylon, Borneo, New Guinea, and Celebes.

After World War I, America faced economic depression and unemployment, and immigrants became the scapegoat. In 1921, a tight national-origins quota system was enacted as a temporary measure. Total immigration was limited to about 350,000 per year. Immigration from each country in a given year was limited to 3% of all nationals from that country who were living in the United States during the 1910 census.

This system was made permanent when the U.S. Congress approved the National Origins Act of 1924. Its purpose was "to arrest a trend toward a change in the fundamental composition of the American stock." Based on the ethnic composition of the United States as recorded in the 1920 census, it limited the entry of aliens from any one country to 2% of the number of their people living in the United States. In one stroke, the law reduced the total immigration of aliens from all countries to 150,000 per year.

The object of the law was not simply to limit immigration but to favor certain kinds of immigrants and keep out others. More immigrants were permitted from western Europe and fewer from southern and eastern Europe. The law totally excluded Asians. It was intended mainly to prohibit Chinese, Japanese, and Filipinos from acquiring U.S. citizenship.

After World War II, however, the door to immigration would again open—this time, to a few carefully selected groups of immigrants. A new category of naturalized Americans was admitted: thousands of alien soldiers who had served with the U.S. armed forces overseas during the war.

Congress also passed the War Brides Act in 1945 to facilitate the reunion of 118,000 alien spouses and children with members of the U.S. armed forces who had fought and married overseas.

The Displaced Persons Act of 1948 allowed 400,000 refugees admission to the U.S. over the next two years. Most of them had been displaced from Poland, Romania, Hungary, the Baltic area, the Ukraine, and Yugoslavia, and had been living in refugee camps in Germany, Italy, and Austria.

When the Iron Curtain fell on Eastern Europe, the Refugee Relief Act of 1953 allowed 214,000 refugees from Communist countries to be admitted into the United States. The anti-Soviet fighters from Hungary, after the suppression of their revolution in 1956, were paroled into the United States—that is, allowed to enter without a visa.

C. Today's Immigration Laws

When the Immigration and Nationality Act was passed in 1952, it wove all the existing immigration laws into one and formed a basic immigration law that's similar to the one we know now. (However, it was not until President Lyndon Johnson signed the 1965 amendments into law that the racially biased national origin quota was abolished.)

The amendments introduced two primary ways of becoming an immigrant: by family relationship and by the employment needs of the United States. The legislation established a preference system—giving priority to some groups of immigrants over others. For example, spouses and children of U.S. citizens had higher priority than their brothers and sisters. The law also provided a separate category for refugees.

Where to Find U.S. Immigration Laws

The entire set of immigration laws is now available online and at law libraries, in Title 8 of the U.S. Code. Occasionally in this book, we'll tell you where you can read a certain piece of the immigration laws by referring to the code section—for example, 8 U.S.C. § 1101.

However, immigration lawyers and government officials tend to use a separate numbering system for the same codes, preceded by the letters I.N.A., for "Immigration and Nationality Act," so when we include citations here we'll also give you the I.N.A. section reference. The I.N.A. is available on the USCIS website (www.uscis.gov) under "Laws."

---

1. Preference for Skilled Workers

In 1965, the laws were amended to allow skilled workers to move more easily to the United States. The departure of doctors, lawyers, engineers, scientists, teachers, accountants, nurses, and other professionals caused a "brain drain" not only in Europe, but also in Asia, the Pacific Rim, and developing countries.

This preference for skilled workers remains in effect. Although the laws allow a few unskilled workers to immigrate, the numbers are so limited that the category is useless for many people.

2. Refugees and Political Asylum

The end of the Vietnam War resulted in a flow of refugees from the Indochinese peninsula.

In 1980, Fidel Castro declared that the Port of Mariel was open to anyone who wanted to leave. Cuban refugees arrived on the shores of Florida by the thousands. These included some criminals and mentally ill people who had been forced by Castro to leave the jails and mental hospitals.

In response, the U.S. Congress passed the Refugee Act of 1980, which defined a "refugee" as someone who fears persecution in his or her home country because of religious or political beliefs, race, national origin, or ethnic identity. Based on this law, the U.S. admits a limited number of refugees annually. In the past, it has been tens of thousands per year, but the Trump administration has sharply reduced those numbers.

The U.S. also grants asylum to many who have fled persecution and made it to the U.S. on their own. This area of the law is in flux, however, as the Trump Administration, largely through use of executive orders, has sought to make asking for asylum far more difficult.

3. Amnesty for Undocumented Workers in the 1980s

The Immigration Reform and Control Act of 1986, more commonly known as the "Amnesty Law," benefited a large number of Mexicans and other aliens. Those who had entered and were living without legal status in the United States since January 1, 1982—more than two million aliens— were granted legal residency. Their spouses and children were also entitled to become permanent residents.

At the same time, the Amnesty Law attempted to control the future influx of undocumented aliens into the United States—and those controls still exist today. Any employer who hires or recruits an alien or who, for a fee, refers an alien to another employer without first verifying the alien's immigration status, is subject to a fine ranging from $200 to $10,000 for each undocumented alien employed.

4. Immigration Acts From 1990 to the Present

With the Immigration Act of 1990, the U.S. Congress approved its most comprehensive overhaul of immigration law since 1965.

This act provided for a huge increase of immigrants, up to 675,000 from 1995 forward. It aimed to attract immigrants who have the education, skills, or money to enhance the economic life of the country, while at the same time maintaining the immigration policy of family reunification. The law therefore makes it easier for scientists, engineers, inventors, and other highly skilled professionals to enter the United States. Millionaire entrepreneurs have their own immigrant classification.

Under the act, citizens of nations that have had little immigration to the United States for the past five years were allocated 50,000 immigrant visas yearly under the "lottery" system. Temporary protections (called TPS) were added for people fleeing war or natural disasters, such as earthquakes. Refugees from the civil war in El Salvador were the first beneficiaries.

Such provisions made the Immigration Act of 1990 the most humane legislation for immigrants in the past century. However, more recent changes again closed America's doors to many immigrants. These changes included 1996's Antiterrorism and Effective Death Penalty Act (AEDPA) and Illegal Immigration Reform and Immigrant Responsibility Act (IIRIRA).

A variety of legislative and regulatory changes were also added after the terrorist attacks of September 11, 2001, tightening controls on would-be immigrants as well as those who are already here.

The USA Patriot Act of 2002, for instance, expanded the definition of terrorism and increased the government's authority to detain and deport immigrants. Also in 2002, legislation established the new Department of Homeland Security (DHS), thus breaking the Immigration and Naturalization Service (INS) into three agencies under the DHS's control. These three new agencies include U.S. Citizenship and Immigration Services (USCIS), which took over the most public INS functions, such as deciding on applications for immigration benefits; Immigration and Customs Enforcement (ICE), which now handles enforcement of the immigration laws within the U.S. borders; and Customs and Border Protection (CBP), which handles U.S. border enforcement (including at land borders, airports, and seaports, and in interior areas near the border).

It's also important to remember the important role that federal court decisions can play in interpreting or even nullifying portions of the immigration laws and related federal laws. So, for example, the Supreme Court's 2013 decision in *U.S. v. Windsor* was a groundbreaking moment for same-sex binational couples. By striking down portions of the federal Defense of Marriage Act (DOMA), this decision removed the primary obstacle blocking rights to a green card, a fiancé visa (which leads to a green card), or various nonimmigrant visas for accompanying spouses, based on a same-sex relationship with a U.S. citizen or permanent resident. And the Supreme Court's 2015 decision in *Obergefell v. Hodges* further cemented these rights, with its ruling that the U.S.

Constitution guarantees a *nationwide* right to same-sex marriage. These changes further illustrate that U.S. immigration policy constantly shifts according to its needs and political will.

D. Looking Forward

Immigration law policies are a subject of ongoing congressional scrutiny, change, and then reverse change. With every shift in the presidential administration and the U.S. economy and sense of security (or insecurity), public attitudes toward immigrants shift as well.

By the time this book went to print in 2020, President Trump had issued countless executive orders limiting immigration—and many of these had either already been blocked or overturned or were still being contested in federal court. Only Congress has the power to actually change U.S. immigration law (as opposed to interpreting or enforcing it). Congress, however, has failed to act for years, though it regularly debates how to overhaul the U.S. immigration laws.

The opening lines of the Declaration of Independence of the United States of America, so eloquently written by Thomas Jefferson some 200 years ago, remain both an inspiration and a challenge:

We hold these truths to be self-evident, that all men are created equal, that they are endowed by their Creator with certain unalienable Rights, that among these are Life, Liberty, and the pursuit of Happiness.

All Ways to Get a Green Card

The official name for the green card is the Permanent Resident Card or Form I-551. It has been called a green card because, when it was first introduced in the 1940s, the color of the plastic identification card with the alien's photo, registration number, date of birth, and date and port of entry was green.

Over the years, the card's color has been, at various times, blue, white, and pink, but now it is green again.

Front of Green Card

Back of Green Card

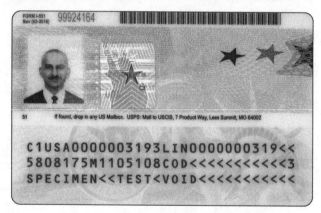

There are several ways a person can obtain a green card—that is, become a lawful permanent resident. The most popular ones are through family and work. The other ways include proving that you're fleeing from persecution, making large investments, and a few more obscure bases.

This book covers the green card categories most readily available to ordinary people, with an emphasis on family categories. However, this chapter will tell you a little about the other major green card categories, and where to go next if you're interested in them.

A. Family-Based Relationships

Recognizing that the family is important in the life of the nation, the U.S. Congress created ways for family members to be reunited with their relatives who are U.S. citizens or lawful permanent residents.

1. Related or Engaged to a U.S. Citizen

If you are the spouse (opposite sex or same sex), child, brother, sister, or parent of, or are engaged to be married to, a U.S. citizen, you can become a lawful permanent resident. The person to whom you're related or engaged must start the process by filing a petition with USCIS or the U.S. embassy in your country of residence.

If you are the widow or widower of a U.S. citizen and it was a good-faith marriage (not a sham to get a green card), you can petition for a green card for yourself, provided you file the application (Form I-360) within two years of the death of your spouse (unless your spouse had already filed a Form I-130 for you), you weren't legally separated at the time of death, and you haven't remarried.

2. Related to a Lawful Permanent Resident

If you are the spouse or unmarried child of a lawful permanent resident, you can obtain a green card—someday. First, the relative who has the green card must file a petition with USCIS. But you'll have to wait several years, until you reach the top of a waiting list, to apply for the actual green card.

3. Other Relatives

If you are the aunt, uncle, niece, nephew, cousin, grandmother, or grandfather of a U.S. citizen, or if you are the brother, sister, parent, or fiancé of someone who holds a green card, you do not qualify for a green card based on a "family relationship." Understandably, the U.S. Congress had to draw the line on what constitutes a family for the purpose of immigration.

 NEXT STEP

If you believe you qualify for a family-based green card, or are helping someone who does, here's where to go next: Readers who are engaged to U.S. citizens, see Chapter 6. Readers who are married to U.S. citizens or permanent residents, see Chapter 7. Readers who are parents of U.S. citizens, see Chapter 8. Readers who are children of U.S. citizens or permanent residents, see Chapter 9. For how to bring in an orphan child, see Chapter 10. Readers who are brothers or sisters of U.S. citizens, see Chapter 12.

B. Employment-Based Relationships

If you do not have a close family member who is a U.S. citizen or who holds a green card, you might be able to obtain a green card through a job offer from an employer in the United States—as either a priority or a nonpriority worker.

1. Priority Workers

Priority workers are people with extraordinary ability (such as an internationally known artist), outstanding professors and researchers, and multinational executives and managers. Another name for this category is "employment first preference."

Such highly skilled people have a relatively easy immigration process. Some do not even need a job offer, and none are required to go through the difficult labor certification process that other immigrating workers must pass, in which the Department of Labor determines that there are no qualified U.S. workers available and willing to do the same job.

2. Other Workers

Applicants who have been offered jobs that require graduate degrees in the arts or sciences or a profession (such as a law degree), or a master's degree in business administration (MBA), or a bachelor's degree plus five years of specialized experience are eligible for immigrant visas. This category is known as "employment second preference."

These applicants will first need certification from the Department of Labor saying that no qualified U.S. worker is available, willing, and able to do the job.

Also, ordinary professionals (without graduate degrees) and skilled or unskilled workers (factory workers, plumbers, domestic workers, carpenters, and the like) may apply for labor certification and a green card on the basis of a job offer. This category is known as "employment third preference."

SEE AN EXPERT

If you believe you qualify for any of these employment-based green cards, consult an experienced immigration attorney. As explained earlier, this book doesn't cover employment-based immigration. The employer who has offered you a job (and you must have a job offer in almost all categories described above) might have an attorney it works with regularly. In fact, the Department of Labor's labor certification rules require the employer to pay attorneys' fees and other costs.

Be Ready to Wait

It could take you a long time to become a permanent resident under some of the immigrant visa categories described in this chapter. Once you or your petitioner files the first petition form to set the process in motion, however, it might become difficult for you to come to the United States as a tourist or another nonimmigrant, or to have your status as a nonimmigrant extended. That's because, in order to obtain most nonimmigrant visas, you have to prove that you plan to return to your home country after your stay on the visa—and it's hard to prove permanent ties to your home country if you're simultaneously planning to leave it behind and get a U.S. green card.

The only groups who need not be concerned with this warning are diplomats (A visas), employees of international organizations (G visas), intra-company transferees (L-1 or L-2 visas), and workers in specialty occupations that require a bachelor's degree or its equivalent (H-1B visas).

- medical doctors who have been licensed in the United States and have worked and lived in the United States since January 1978
- former employees of the Panama Canal Zone
- retired officers or employees of certain international organizations who have lived in the United States for a certain time, plus their spouses and unmarried children
- foreign workers who have been employees of the U.S. consulate in Hong Kong for at least three years
- foreign children who have been declared dependent in juvenile courts in the United States, and
- international broadcasting employees.

All these people fall into a green card category known as "employment-based fourth preference."

 SEE AN EXPERT

If you believe you fit one of these categories, consult an experienced immigration attorney. Special immigrants are not covered in this book. Your employer-petitioner might be willing to hire an attorney for you.

C. Special Immigrants

Certain categories of people may obtain a green card by special laws—in addition to certain provisions of the Immigration Act of 1990—intended to benefit limited groups. These include, for example:

- priests, nuns, pastors, ministers, rabbis, imams, and other workers of recognized religious denominations
- former employees of the U.S. government, commended by the U.S. Secretary of State for having performed outstanding service to the government for at least 15 years

D. Entrepreneur Immigrants

An alien entrepreneur from any country who invests at least $1.8 million in a business (or $900,000 if the business is in an economically depressed area) and who employs at least ten U.S. citizens or lawful permanent residents is eligible for a green card. Each year, 10,000 immigrant visas are set aside for this millionaire immigrant category, which is designed to create employment. This category is also known as "employment-based fifth preference" or "EB-5."

SEE AN EXPERT

Are you financially able to qualify for a green card based on investment? If so, it's well worth hiring an experienced immigration attorney to help.

E. Asylum and Refugee Status

People who can prove that they fled their country based on past persecution or out of fear of future persecution owing to their race, religion, nationality, membership in a particular social group, or political opinion may apply for legal status as refugees (if they're outside the U.S.) or asylees (if they're already inside the U.S.).

A person who gains U.S. government approval as a refugee or an asylee can apply for permanent residence status later (more specifically, one year after being admitted to the United States as a refugee or one year after asylee status is granted).

NEXT STEP

For more information on applying for refugee or asylee status, see Chapter 13.

F. Diversity Visa Lottery

The Immigration Act of 1990 created a green card category to benefit people from countries that in recent years have sent the fewest numbers of immigrants to the United States. You can enter the lottery if you are a native of one of those countries and meet certain educational and other requirements. Because the winners are selected through a random drawing, the program is popularly known as the green card lottery. Its official name is the Diversity Immigrant Visa Lottery.

There are 50,000 winners selected each year. They are chosen by dividing the world into regions and allocating no more than 7% of the total green cards to each region.

However, even if you win the lottery, you still have to make it through the green card application process—and many people fail, because they're inadmissible or the government can't process their applications by the deadlines set by law.

NEXT STEP

For more information on applying for the visa lottery, and what to do if you win, see Chapter 11.

G. Amnesties

Once in a while, Congress gives blanket green card eligibility to people who have been living in the United States illegally.

The most recent amnesty was offered in the early 1980s. Although anti-immigrant commentators regularly complain that every new law that benefits immigrants is an "amnesty," there has been no actual amnesty offered since that time.

Some lawmakers have proposed bills offering an amnesty-like path to a green card in recent years, at least for "DREAMers," or those who were brought to the U.S. when young. Keep your eyes on the news and the Nolo website for updates, and beware of the many scammers urging immigrants to pay to submit an application when no such application exists.

CAUTION

Interested in learning more about a past or upcoming amnesty? Consult an experienced immigration attorney or a local nonprofit. Do not go to a USCIS office unless you want to risk deportation.

H. Private Bills

You might have heard of people who became permanent residents by means of a private bill passed by the U.S. Congress. However, such cases are rare. You must have very special circumstances—and very strong political ties—to get a private bill passed.

Look into the possibility of a private bill where the law is against you but your case has strong humanitarian factors. Private bills succeed when an injustice can be corrected only by a special act of the U.S. Congress.

1. What Is a Private Bill?

A private bill is the last resort of a desperate alien facing removal (deportation)—a special urging by high-level U.S. politicians to allow you to stay in the U.S. legally. Currently, very few private bills are filed on behalf of aliens. Fewer than 100 private bills have been successful during each of the past several years.

The successful ones tend to be people in unusually tragic situations, such as a family that came to the U.S. seeking cancer treatment for a child, only to have the father and mother of the child killed in a car wreck.

2. How a Private Bill Is Passed

A private bill must be sponsored by one or more members of the House of Representatives and one or more members of the Senate who urge that one individual be given special consideration in being allowed to become a permanent resident or get citizenship.

Like a law, a private bill has to be introduced in both houses of Congress. It then has to be recommended favorably by the Judiciary Committee to which it has been assigned in both houses, after having been favorably reported on by the Subcommittee on Immigration of both houses.

Both houses of Congress must approve the bill during a regular session. The president of the United States must then sign it into law.

Thus, if you are an alien facing deportation, you will have to go through the eye of a needle before getting your private bill passed by Congress and signed by the president. In short, hiring the best immigration lawyer in town will likely give you a better chance to obtain a green card than will the private bill route.

Short-Term Alternatives to a Green Card

As you know, this book is only about green cards—or, in legal-speak, U.S. permanent residence. However, you probably also know that many people who want U.S. green cards will never be able to get one. The green card categories are very limited, and the application process is hard to get through successfully. That's why this chapter will briefly tell you about some other—sometimes easier—ways to come to the United States, even if it's for a shorter time.

RESOURCE

Want to learn more about the ways to stay temporarily in the United States? See *U.S. Immigration Made Easy,* by Ilona Bray (Nolo).

A. How Do Foreign Nationals Enter the United States?

The basic rule is that most people may enter the United States only after receiving permission from the U.S. government, through the U.S. embassy or consulate in their own country. The permission or authority to enter the United States is called a "visa," and is stamped in your passport by the U.S. consul. A major exception is if you are eligible to enter under the Visa Waiver Program; see discussion in Section C, below.

If you enter the United States without permission, without a visa or a visa waiver, and without being examined by the immigration authorities, you are called an "undocumented alien" within the immigration laws and an "illegal alien" by the general public.

B. Types of Visas

There are two kinds of visas an alien can receive from the U.S. embassy or consulate: an immigrant visa and a nonimmigrant visa.

1. Immigrant Visas

Just to avoid confusion, we should mention that even those people who are in the process of getting a green card, as discussed in the rest of this book, must get a physical visa first if they'll be arriving from another country. They receive what is called an "immigrant visa." They receive the actual green card only after they have arrived in the United States and claimed their permanent residency. People who apply for their green cards from within the United States must also be allocated a visa number, although they'll never see or receive a physical visa.

2. Nonimmigrant Visas

Nonimmigrant visas are the main topic we'd like to introduce you to in this short chapter. A nonimmigrant visa gives you the ability to stay in the United States temporarily with limited rights. A visa that expires in a few years is probably your second choice, given that you're reading a book on green cards. However, a nonimmigrant visa might serve you in two different ways. First, it might allow you to legally visit the United States in order to decide whether you really want a green card, or to make a decision that will lead to your getting a green card. For example, a person might come to the U.S. on a tourist (B-2) visa to visit his or her U.S. citizen boyfriend or girlfriend, to find out whether getting married seems like a good idea.

Second, a nonimmigrant visa might be your only choice for the moment. If your research, using this book and other resources, leads you to believe that you don't qualify for a green card, then a nonimmigrant visa might allow you to at least live in the United States for a while, developing U.S. contacts or job skills, hoping that a green card opportunity will open up.

Unfortunately, nonimmigrant visas are not only short-term solutions, but they restrict your life in the United States in other ways. For example, a tourist visa (B-2) does not allow you to work. A student visa (F-1 or M-1) does not allow a student to stop studying in order to work. A temporary worker's visa (H-1B), given to a professional worker such as an accountant or engineer, does not authorize you to change employers without permission.

3. Nonimmigrant Visa Classifications

You will often hear visa classifications referred to in shorthand by a letter followed by a number. The following table summarizes the nonimmigrant visa classifications available.

Classification	Summary
A-1	Ambassadors, public ministers, consular officers, or career diplomats, and their immediate families
A-2	Other foreign government officials or employees, and their immediate families
A-3	Personal attendants, servants, or employees of A-1 and A-2 visa holders, and their immediate families
B-1	Temporary business visitors
B-2	Temporary pleasure visitors
C-1	Foreign travelers in immediate and continuous transit through the U.S.
D-1	Crewmembers (sea or air)
E-1	Treaty traders and their spouses or children
E-2	Treaty investors and their spouses or children
E-3	Australians who have at least a bachelor's degree or its equivalent, working in specialty occupations
F-1	Academic or language students
F-2	Spouses or children of F-1 visa holders
G-1	Designated principal resident representatives of foreign governments coming to the U.S. to work for an international organization, and their staff members and immediate families
G-2	Other representatives of foreign governments coming to the U.S. to work for an international organization, and their immediate families

Classification	Summary
G-3	Representatives of foreign governments and their immediate families, who would ordinarily qualify for G-1 or G-2 visas except that their governments are not members of an international organization
G-4	Officers or employees of international organizations, and their immediate families
G-5	Attendants, servants, and personal employees of G-1 through G-4 visa holders, and their immediate families
H-1B	Aliens working in specialty occupations requiring at least a bachelor's degree or its equivalent in on-the-job experience
H-2A	Temporary agricultural workers coming to the U.S. to fill positions for which a temporary shortage of American workers has been recognized by the U.S. Department of Agriculture
H-2B	Temporary workers of various kinds coming to the U.S. to perform temporary jobs for which there is a shortage of available qualified U.S. workers
H-3	Temporary trainees
H-4	Spouses or children of H-1A/B, H-2A/B, or H-3 visa holders
I	Representatives of the foreign press, coming to the U.S. to work solely in that capacity, and their immediate families
J-1	Exchange visitors coming to the U.S. to study, work, or train as part of an exchange program officially recognized by the U.S. Department of State
J-2	Spouses or children of J-1 visa holders
K-1	Fiancés and fiancées of U.S. citizens coming to the U.S. for the purpose of getting married
K-2	Children of K-1 visa holders
K-3	Spouses of U.S. citizens awaiting approval of their immigrant visa petition or the availability of a green card
K-4	Children of K-3 visa holders
L-1	Intracompany transferees who work as managers, executives, or persons with specialized knowledge

Class-ification	Summary
L-2	Spouses or children of L-1 visa holders
M-1	Vocational or other nonacademic students
M-2	Immediate families of M-1 visa holders
N	Children and parents of certain special immigrants
NATO-1	Principal permanent representatives of member states to NATO and its subsidiary bodies, who are residents in the U.S., and resident official staff members, secretaries general, assistant secretaries general, and executive secretaries of NATO, other permanent NATO officials of similar rank, or their immediate families
NATO-2	Other representatives to member states to NATO and its subsidiary bodies, including its advisers and technical experts of delegations, members of Immediate Article 3, 4 UST 1796 families; dependents of members of forces entering in accordance with the Status-of-Forces Agreement or in accordance with the Protocol on Status of International Military Headquarters; members of such a force if issued visas
NATO-3	Official clerical staff accompanying representatives of member states to NATO and its subsidiary bodies, and their immediate families
NATO-4	Officials of NATO other than those who can be classified as NATO-1, and their immediate families
NATO-5	Experts other than officials who can be classified as NATO-1, employed in missions on behalf of NATO, and their dependents
NATO-6	Members of civilian components accompanying forces entering in accordance with provisions of the NATO Status-of-Forces Agreement; members of civilian components attached to or employed by allied headquarters under the Protocol on Status of International Military Headquarters set up pursuant to the North Atlantic Treaty; and their dependents
NATO-7	Attendants, servants, or personal employees of NATO-1 through NATO-6 classes, and their immediate families

Class-ification	Summary
O-1	Aliens of extraordinary ability in the sciences, arts, education, business, or athletics
O-2	Support staff of O-1 visa holders
O-3	Spouses or children of O-1 or O-2 visa holders
P-1	Internationally recognized athletes and entertainers
P-2	Artists or entertainers in reciprocal exchange programs
P-3	Artists and entertainers coming to the U.S. to give culturally unique performances in a group
P-4	Spouses or children of P-1, P-2, or P-3 visa holders
Q-1	Participants in international cultural exchange programs
Q-2	Irish Peace Process Cultural and Training Program (Walsh Visas)
Q-3	Immediate family members of Q-1 visa holders
R-1	Aliens in religious occupations
R-2	Spouses or children of R-1 visa holders
S-5	Certain aliens supplying critical information relating to a criminal organization or enterprise
S-6	Certain aliens supplying critical information relating to terrorism
S-7	Immediate family members of S-5 and S-6 visa holders
T	Women and children who are in the United States because they are victims of trafficking, who are cooperating with law enforcement, and who fear extreme hardship (such as retribution) if returned home
TN	NAFTA professionals from Canada or Mexico
TD	Spouses and children of NAFTA professionals
U	Aliens who have been victims of crimes, have useful information about them, and have been helping U.S. law enforcement authorities with investigating and prosecuting these crimes.
V	Spouses and children of lawful permanent residents who have visa petitions that were filed for them prior to December 21, 2000, and who have been waiting for three years or more to qualify for a green card

4. Deferred Action for Childhood Arrivals

Until recently, another short-term alternative to a green card came not in the form of a visa, but as a special program to prevent deportation of people who came to the U.S. very young, and had attended school and otherwise made the U.S. their home. Instituted by President Obama, the DACA program's future now awaits a decision from the U.S. Supreme Court, following an unsuccessful attempt by President Trump to cancel it. At the time this book went to print, Congress also was considering various forms of legislation to avoid removal of DACA recipients (also called DREAMers, a name drawn from the title of long-promised Congressional legislation) but had still failed to come to an agreement.

5. Nonimmigrant U Visa Can Lead to a Green Card

One of the visas mentioned on our summary table bears further explanation. The U visa, for people who have been the victims of crimes in the U.S. and suffered as a result, and who are cooperating with law enforcement officials, can ultimately lead to a U.S. green card. For that reason, we cover it in Chapter 19 of this book.

C. Tourists Who Can Visit Without a Visa

The Visa Waiver Program (VWP) allows the citizens of certain countries—that the Department of State (DOS) chooses—to visit the United States for 90 days without first having a tourist visa stamped on their passports.

1. What You'll Need for VWP Travel

At the moment, 39 countries participate in the VWP. If you're from one of these countries, and wish to enter the U.S. without a tourist visa, you'll need to get these things first, before starting your trip:

- **A passport meeting U.S. government requirements.** This means an electronic passport with an integrated chip (e-passport) that is valid for six months past your expected stay in the United States.
- **A ticket for both your arrival to and departure from the United States.** Your arrival ticket needs to be with an airline or boat company that is authorized to carry VWP passengers. The exception is if you'll be entering via Canada or Mexico, in which case, no departure ticket is required.
- **Prior U.S. government authorization.** You'll do this through the Electronic System for Travel Authorization (ESTA), online at https://esta.cbp.dhs.gov. You can apply at any time prior to travel. There is a processing charge of $4 for electronic travel authorization. If your VWP application is approved, you'll need to pay an additional $10. The ESTA system requires use of a MasterCard, Visa, American Express, or Discover debit or credit card. You'll probably get an answer immediately, although it sometimes takes up to three days. Authorizations are generally valid for up to two years, or until your passport expires, whichever comes first. If you don't receive authorization, you'll need to apply for a nonimmigrant visa at a U.S. embassy or consulate.
- **Fee.** Travelers arriving at a land border (from Canada or Mexico) will be required to pay an entry fee.

CAUTION
Nationals of or visitors to countries with ties to terrorism cannot use the VWP. Congress passed changes to the VWP in December 2015 that prohibit

its use by nationals of or recent visitors to "high-risk" countries with ties to terrorism. These countries include Iraq, Libya, Somalia, Syria, Iran, Sudan, Yemen, and any other that the Department of Homeland Security (DHS) decides are of concern. Although none of these countries is currently a VWP member, nationals of a country on the terrorism watch list who carry the passport of another country that is on the VWP list would thus be excluded from VWP travel. There are minor exceptions, including for people performing military service in a country of concern, or based on law enforcement or national security interests. This isn't an outright prohibition on U.S. entry: People who cannot travel on the VWP can still apply for a visitor visa at the nearest U.S. embassy or consulate.

> **EXAMPLE:** You want to visit the United States for two months. If you live in a country that is included in the VWP, you first make sure your passport meets U.S. requirements, then get authorization to travel by filling out the online ESTA application, and then buy your round-trip plane ticket to the United States. You do not need to visit a U.S. consulate to get a tourist visa. You may, however, upon arrival in the U.S., be asked to show your departure ticket as evidence that you are simply visiting and that you will return to your country within the 90-day limit.

2. VWP-Eligible Countries

Under the Visa Waiver Program, citizens of the following countries who can present a machine-readable passport are exempted from getting visas before entering the United States:

Andorra	Denmark
Australia	Estonia
Austria	Finland
Belgium	France
Brunei	Germany
Chile	Great Britain (United Kingdom)
Czech Republic	Greece
Holland (Netherlands)	Norway
Hungary	Poland
Iceland	Portugal
Ireland	San Marino
Italy	Singapore
Japan	Slovakia
Latvia	Slovenia
Liechtenstein	South Korea
Lithuania	Spain
Luxembourg	Sweden
Malta	Switzerland
Monaco	Taiwan
New Zealand	

To be included in the Visa Waiver Program, the country must have:

- a very low rate of refusals of tourist visa applications, and
- few violations of U.S. immigration laws.

In short, countries whose citizens are least likely to stay too long or work illegally in the United States are most likely to be included in the Visa Waiver Program.

Disadvantages of Entering Without a Visa

There may be disadvantages to entering the U.S. under the Visa Waiver Program.

You cannot change your tourist status to another nonimmigrant status, such as that of student or temporary worker, nor can you request an extension of your 90-day stay.

With few exceptions, you also cannot change your status to a lawful permanent resident while staying in the United States.

In addition, should the border officials deny you entry into the United States for any reason, you have no right to appeal. Political refugees who are fleeing persecution and who apply for asylum in the United States are the sole exception. (See Chapter 13.)

D. The Importance of Staying Legal

If you enter the United States as a tourist, student, temporary worker, entertainer, or any other nonimmigrant category, your chances at a future green card depend on your maintaining your legal status and not violating the conditions of your stay in the United States. Do not overstay the limits of your visa. Do not work when you are not authorized to work. Do not change schools or employers without first requesting and receiving permission from the immigration authorities.

The consequences for breaking the rules controlling immigration can be quite serious: You could be detained in an immigration jail; removal proceedings could be started against you; and, if deported, you could be barred from returning to the United States for the next five years or more.

Even if you are not deported, if you overstay by 180 days (around six months) and then leave the United States, you will have to stay outside for three years before being admitted again. If you overstay by 12 months and then leave, the waiting period is ten years before you will be allowed to return. (See Chapter 4.)

More to the point, by staying within the law, you can make use of almost all the ways enumerated in this book to stay in the United States, as long as your current status is legal.

If you are running out of time on a permitted stay, one possibility is to apply to extend your stay (if you can show a good reason for needing more time) or change your status, for example from tourist to temporary worker. You can apply for extensions or changes of status only (in most cases) if your immigration status is legal, you are not overstaying a visa, and you have not worked illegally.

If, instead, you overstay, your visa will be automatically void—even if it is a multiple entry, indefinite visa. You will then be required to apply for a new visa at the consulate in your home country, unless you can prove "exceptional circumstances."

If there is some question in your case, or if you need to change status, you should seek professional advice from an immigration support group, a specialized clinic, or an experienced immigration lawyer. (See Chapter 24.) Do not depend on advice from your friends or relatives, or worse, information on the Internet.

E. How to Extend a Visitor Visa

Temporary business or tourist visitors—those who hold B-1 or B-2 visas—once admitted to the United States, can apply for an extension of stay. The basis can be business circumstances, family reasons, or any other good reason consistent with your visa.

For example, if a tourist decides to visit different locations or to spend more time with relatives, he or she can seek an extension. (See the USCIS website at www.uscis.gov for filing details and addresses; you may file electronically on the USCIS website or by mail.)

The application must include the following:

- Form I-539, Application to Extend/Change Nonimmigrant Status
- a copy of your Form I-94, which you (unless you're one of the few people who received a paper I-94 card when entering the U.S.) will need to download from the U.S. Customs and Border Protection (CBP) website at https://i94.cbp.dhs.gov
- a filing fee (currently $370) and a biometrics fee (currently $85) for the required fingerprint/photo appointment; either personal check or money order will be accepted

- a company letter or other supporting documentation stating the reason for the extension request—for example, more business consultations, ongoing medical reasons, extended family visit with a complete itinerary, or another reason
- evidence to show that the visit is temporary—particularly, evidence of continued overseas employment or residence and a return plane ticket, and
- evidence of financial support, such as a bank letter including amounts in accounts. You can also have a family member promise to support you, by filling out USCIS Form I-134, available at www.uscis.gov.

Also attach an itinerary or a letter explaining your reasons for requesting the extension.

The extension may not give you as much time as you'd like. Extensions of more than six months are rare. However, you are legally allowed to stay until USCIS makes a decision on your extension.

USCIS recommends that you file for an extension at least 45 days before the expiration date of your stay, which is shown on your Form I-94. If you are prone to procrastination, file the request for extension at least 15 days before the expiration date shown on your Form I-94.

F. Changing Your Reason for Staying

If you wish to request a change of status from one category to another or apply for a green card, be aware that applying for the change within the first three months after arriving in America could lead to USCIS denying your application based on the theory of "preconceived intent." Preconceived intent simply means that you lied about your reasons for coming to the United States.

For example, if you attempt to change your status from B-2 tourist to H-1B specialty worker soon after arriving in the United States, USCIS may conclude that you had the preconceived intent of working in the United States when you applied for a tourist visa from the U.S. embassy. Your failure to reveal your actual reason for going to the United States when you first requested a visa could be considered fraud.

A similar problem can arise for people who want to study in the U.S., but sensibly want to visit some schools and see whether they like them before going through the hassle of filling out application forms. You might think that the logical thing would be to come as a tourist and then, after choosing a school, apply for a change to student status.

However, logic and the immigration laws don't always match up. USCIS may deny this type of applicant's request to change status, saying that the person lied about his or her intention to be a tourist (the person's real, secret intention was to become a student).

Fortunately, this is one of the few immigration law traps that you can sometimes get around with advance planning. If, when applying for your tourist visa, you tell the consular official that you may wish to change to student status after looking around, then you can have a "prospective student" notation made in your tourist visa. After that, you'll be free to apply to change status without worrying that it will look like you lied.

G. What to Do If Your Application Is Denied

If USCIS denies your request for an extension of your stay in the U.S., you could contest the denial. However, this will require help from an experienced immigration lawyer. (See Chapter 24.)

It might be easier to leave the U.S. and apply for a new visa from overseas. This is far safer than staying in the U.S. illegally.

H. Tips on Filling Out Form I-539

Most of Form I-539 is self-explanatory; see the filled-in sample of Pages 1 to 4 below. However, on Part 4 of Form I-539, Additional Information, Questions 3 through 15 may act as time bombs if you answer "yes" to any one of them—that is, they may prove fatal to your application. (In the case of 14, however, you'll be okay if your employment was undertaken while you had a work permit (EAD) from USCIS.)

Do not lie and misrepresent your answer as no when the truthful answer is yes. But if you have to answer yes to any of these questions, it is best to consult with an immigration lawyer or another experienced immigration professional first.

EXAMPLE: The third question on this part of the form is: Are you, or any other person included on the application, an applicant for an immigrant visa? Answering "yes" is problematic, because it raises the possibility that you don't have the "nonimmigrant intent" required for a temporary U.S. stay—that is, that you are secretly looking for a way to stay in the U.S. until your green card comes through. Do not answer "no" if your U.S. citizen brother filed a relative I-130 petition for you, even if it was ten years ago, and your immigrant visa is still pending. In all probability, USCIS would find out your fraudulent answer, and you might never get your green card as a result.

Do Not Bring This Book With You

Because this book tells you how to stay and work legally in the United States, you should not have it—or any other book about immigrating to the U.S.—with you when you enter the United States on a tourist or other nonimmigrant visa.

If the border officials suspect that you are not a bona fide tourist, they may detain and question you at the airport or border about your purpose in coming to the United States.

For the same reason, you should not board the plane with a wedding dress, a stack of resumes, or letters from your Aunt Mary or cousin John stating that employment has been arranged for you as soon as you arrive in the United States. Should the border officials find such things when you land, you will not be admitted as a tourist; you may, in fact, be sent back to your home country without being allowed to set foot outside the airport or other port of entry in the United States.

If this happens, you will be unable to return to the U.S. for five years.

Sample Form I-539, Application to Extend/Change Nonimmigrant Status (page 1)

Application to Extend/Change Nonimmigrant Status

Department of Homeland Security
U.S. Citizenship and Immigration Services

**USCIS
Form I-539**

OMB No. 1615-0003
Expires 10/31/2021

For USCIS Use Only	Fee Stamp	Action Block
Returned		
Resubmitted		
Relocated / Received		
Sent		

Remarks:	☐ Granted	☐ Denied
	New Class _____	☐ Still within period of stay
	Dates: From ___/___/___	☐ S/D to: _____
	To ___/___/___	☐ Place under docket control
		☐ Applicant interviewed on _____

To be completed by an Attorney or Accredited Representative (if any).	☐ Select this box if Form G-28 is attached.	Attorney State Bar Number (if applicable)	Attorney or Accredited Representative USCIS Online Account Number (if any)

▶ **START HERE - Type or print in black ink.**

Part 1. Information About You

Your Full Name

1.a. Family Name (Last Name): Martino

1.b. Given Name (First Name): Tony

1.c. Middle Name: Fernando

2. Alien Registration Number (A-Number) (if any)
▶ A- [ ][ ][ ][ ][ ][ ][ ][ ]

3. USCIS Online Account Number (if any)
▶ [ ][ ][ ][ ][ ][ ][ ][ ][ ][ ][ ][ ]

U.S. Mailing Address

4.a. In Care Of Name (if any): Antero Martino

4.b. Street Number and Name: 3746 81st Street

4.c. ☒ Apt. ☐ Ste. ☐ Flr. 2D

4.d. City or Town: Jackson Heights

4.e. State: NY   **4.f.** ZIP Code: 11372

U.S. Physical Address

5.a. Street Number and Name: 3746 81st Street

5.b. ☒ Apt. ☐ Ste. ☐ Flr. 2D

5.c. City or Town: Jackson Heights

5.d. State: NY   **5.e.** ZIP Code: 11372

Other Information About You

6. Country of Birth
Philippines

7. Country of Citizenship or Nationality
Philippines

8. Date of Birth (mm/dd/yyyy): 08/02/1980

9. U.S. Social Security Number (if any)
▶ [ ][ ][ ][ ][ ][ ][ ][ ][ ]

10. Date of Last Arrival Into the United States (mm/dd/yyyy): 02/05/2019

Provide Information About Your Most Recent Entry Into the United States

11. Form I-94 Arrival-Departure Record Number
▶ | 3 | 3 | 4 | 5 | 3 | 3 | 9 | 0 | 9 | A | 1 |

12. Passport Number: TT1231237

Sample Form I-539 (page 2)

Part 1. Information about You (continued)

13. Travel Document Number [ ]

14.a. Country of Passport or Travel Document Issuance
Philippines

14.b. Passport or Travel Document Expiration Date (mm/dd/yyyy) 01/01/2025

15.a. Current Nonimmigrant Status (e.g. F-1 student, H-4 dependent, etc.)
B2 - TEMPORARY VISITOR FOR PLEASURE

15.b. Expiration Date (mm/dd/yyyy) 08/04/2019

16. ☐ Select this box if you were granted Duration of Status (D/S).

Part 2. Application Type

I am applying for (select **only one** box):

1. ☐ Reinstatement to student status.

2. ☒ An extension of stay in my current status.

3.a. ☐ A change of status.

3.b. New status and effective date of change (mm/dd/yyyy)

3.c. The change of status I am requesting is:

Number of people included in this application (select **only one** box):

4. ☒ I am the only applicant.

5.a. ☐ Members of my family are filing this application with me.

5.b. The total number of people (including me) in the application is: (Complete Form I-539A for each co-applicant.) 1

Part 3. Processing Information

1. I/We request that my/our current or requested status be extended until (mm/dd/yyyy): 02/03/2020

2.a. Is this application based on an extension or change of status already granted to your spouse, child, or parent? ☐ Yes ☒ No

2.b. If you answered "Yes" to **Item Number 2.a.**, provide USCIS Receipt Number. ▶ [ ]

3.a. Is this application based on a separate petition or application to provide your spouse, child, or parent an extension or change of status?
☐ Yes, filed with this Form I-539. ☐ No
☐ Yes, filed previously and pending with U.S. Citizenship and Immigration Services (USCIS).

3.b. If pending with USCIS, provide USCIS Receipt Number. ▶ [ ]

If the petition or application is pending with USCIS, also provide the following information:

4. First and Last Name of Petitioner or Applicant

5. Date Filed (mm/dd/yyyy)

Part 4. Additional Information About the Applicant

Provide Your Current Passport Information (if different from **Part 1.**)

1.a. Passport Number

1.b. Country of Passport Issuance

1.c. Passport Expiration Date (mm/dd/yyyy)

Physical Address Abroad

2.a. Street Number and Name 66 Felix Manolo St.

2.b. ☐ Apt. ☐ Ste. ☐ Flr.

2.c. City or Town Cubao, Quezon City

2.d. Province

2.e. Postal Code 1111

2.f. Country Philippines

Answer the following questions. If you answer "Yes" to any of the questions in **Item Numbers 3. - 15.**, use the space provided in **Part 8. Additional Information** to provide an explanation.

Sample Form I-539 (page 3)

Part 4. Additional Information About the Applicant (continued)

3. Are you, or any other individual included on the application, an applicant for an immigrant visa? ☐ Yes ☒ No

4. Has an immigrant petition **EVER** been filed for you or for any other individual included in this application? ☐ Yes ☒ No

5. Has Form I-485, Application to Register Permanent Residence or Adjust Status, **EVER** been filed by you or by any other individual included in this application? ☐ Yes ☒ No

6. Have you, or any other individual included in this application, **EVER** been arrested or convicted of any criminal offense since last entering the United States? ☐ Yes ☒ No

Have you, or any other individual included on the application, **EVER** ordered, incited, called for, committed, assisted, helped with, or otherwise participated in any of the following:

7.a. Acts involving torture or genocide? ☐ Yes ☒ No

7.b. Killing any person? ☐ Yes ☒ No

7.c. Intentionally and severely injuring any person? ☐ Yes ☒ No

7.d. Engaging in any kind of sexual contact or relations with any person who did not consent or was unable to consent, or was being forced or threatened? ☐ Yes ☒ No

7.e. Limiting or denying any person's ability to exercise religious beliefs? ☐ Yes ☒ No

Have you, or any other individual included on the application, **EVER**:

8.a. Served in, been a member of, assisted, or participated in any military unit, paramilitary unit, police unit, self-defense unit, vigilante unit, rebel group, guerrilla group, militia, insurgent organization, or any other armed group? ☐ Yes ☒ No

8.b. Worked, volunteered, or otherwise served in any prison, jail, prison camp, detention facility, labor camp, or any other situation that involved detaining persons? ☐ Yes ☒ No

9. Have you, or any other individual included in this application, **EVER** been a member of, assisted, or participated in any group, unit, or organization of any kind in which you or other persons used any type of weapon against any person or threatened to do so? ☐ Yes ☒ No

10. Have you, or any other individual included in this application, **EVER** assisted or participated in selling, providing, or transporting weapons to any person who, to your knowledge, used them against another person? ☐ Yes ☒ No

11. Have you, or any other individual included in this application, **EVER** received any type of military, paramilitary, or weapons training? ☐ Yes ☒ No

12. Have you, or any other individual included in this application, done anything that violated the terms of the nonimmigrant status you now hold? ☐ Yes ☒ No

13. Are you, or any other individual included in this application, now in removal proceedings? ☐ Yes ☒ No

If you answered "Yes" to **Item Number 13.**, provide the following information concerning the removal proceedings in the space provided in **Part 9. Additional Information**. Include the name of the individual in removal proceedings and information on jurisdiction, date proceedings began, and status of proceedings.

14. Have you, or any other individual included in this application, been employed in the United States since last admitted or granted an extension or change of status? ☐ Yes ☒ No

If you answered "No" to **Item Number 14.**, fully describe how you are supporting yourself in **Part 9. Additional Information**. Include documentary evidence of the source, amount, and basis for any income.

If you answered "Yes" to **Item Number 14.**, fully describe the employment in **Part 9. Additional Information**. Include the name of the individual employed, name and address of the employer, weekly income, and whether the employment was specifically authorized by USCIS.

15. Are you, or any other individual included in this application, currently or have you ever been a J-1 exchange visitor or a J-2 dependent of a J-1 exchange visitor? ☐ Yes ☒ No

If you answered "Yes" to **Item Number 15.**, you must provide the dates you maintained status as a J-1 exchange visitor or J-2 dependent in **Part 9. Additional Information**.

Sample Form I-539 (page 4)

Part 5. Public Benefits

Provide the requested information and submit documentation, as outlined in the Instructions.

1. Since obtaining the nonimmigrant status that you seek to extend or from which you seek to change, have you received, or are you currently certified to receive, any of the following public benefits? (select all that apply)

    ☐ Yes, I have received or I am currently certified to receive the following public benefits:

    ☐ Any Federal, State, local or tribal cash assistance for income maintenance

    ☐ Supplemental Security Income (SSI)

    ☐ Temporary Assistance for Needy Families (TANF)

    ☐ General Assistance (GA)

    ☐ Supplemental Nutrition Assistance Program (SNAP, formerly called "Food Stamps")

    ☐ Section 8 Housing Assistance under the Housing Choice Voucher Program

    ☐ Section 8 Project-Based Rental Assistance (including Moderate Rehabilitation)

    ☐ Public Housing under the Housing Act of 1937, 42 U.S.C. 1437 et seq.

    ☐ Federally-funded Medicaid

    ☒ No, I have not received any of the above listed public benefits.

    ☐ No, I am not certified to receive any of the above listed public benefits.

2. If you have received or are currently certified to receive any of the above public benefits provide information about the public benefits below. If you need extra space to complete this section, use the space provided in **Part 9. Additional Information.** Submit documentation as outlined in the Instructions.

    A. Type of Benefit

    n/a

    Agency That Granted The Benefit

    Date You Started Receiving the Benefit or if Certified, Date You Will Start Receiving the Benefit or Date Your Coverage Starts

    (mm/dd/yyyy)

    Date Benefit or Coverage Ended or Expires

    (mm/dd/yyyy)

B. Type of Benefit

Agency That Granted The Benefit

Date You Started Receiving the Benefit or if Certified, Date You Will Start Receiving the Benefit or Date Your Coverage Starts

(mm/dd/yyyy)

Date Benefit or Coverage Ended or Expires

(mm/dd/yyyy)

C. Type of Benefit

Agency That Granted The Benefit

Date You Started Receiving the Benefit or if Certified, Date You Will Start Receiving the Benefit or Date Your Coverage Starts

(mm/dd/yyyy)

Date Benefit or Coverage Ended or Expires

(mm/dd/yyyy)

D. Type of Benefit

Agency That Granted The Benefit

Date You Started Receiving the Benefit or if Certified, Date You Will Start Receiving the Benefit or Date Your Coverage Starts

(mm/dd/yyyy)

Date Benefit or Coverage Ended or Expires

(mm/dd/yyyy)

3. If you answered "Yes" to **Item Number 1.**, do any of the following apply to you? (select the applicable box). Provide the evidence listed in the Instructions if any of the following apply to you.

    ☐ I am enlisted in the Armed Forces, or am serving in active duty or in the Ready Reserve Component of the U.S. Armed Forces.

    ☐ I am the spouse or the child of an individual who is enlisted in the Armed Forces, or who is serving in active duty or in the Ready Reserve Component of the U.S. Armed Forces.

Sample Form I-539 (page 5)

Part 5. Public Benefits (continued)

☐ At the time I received the public benefits, I (or my spouse or parent) was enlisted in the Armed Forces, or was serving in active duty or in the Ready Reserve Component of the U.S. Armed Forces.

☐ At the time I received the public benefits, I was present in the United States in a status exempt from the public charge ground of inadmissibility.

☐ At the time I received the public benefits, I was present in the United States after being granted a waiver off the public charge ground of inadmissibility.

☐ I am a child currently residing abroad who entered the United States with a nonimmigrant visa to attend an N-600K, Application for Citizenship and Issuance of Certificate Under INA Section 322 interview.

☐ None of the above statements apply to me.

4.a. Have you received, applied for, or have been certified to receive federally-funded Medicaid in connection with any of the following (select all that apply) (Submit evidence as outlined in the Instructions):

☐ An emergency medical condition.

☐ For a service under the Individuals with Disabilities Education Act (IDEA).

☐ Other school-based benefits or services available up to the oldest age eligible for secondary education under state law.

☐ While you were under the of age 21.

☐ While you were pregnant or during the 60-day period following the last day of pregnancy.

☐ None of the above statements apply to me.

4.b. Provide the applicable dates:

From (mm/dd/yyyy) | n/a

To (mm/dd/yyyy) | n/a

Part 6. Applicant's Statement, Contact Information, Declaration, Certification and Signature

NOTE: Select the box for either **Item Number 1.a.** or **1.b.** If applicable, select the box for **Item Number 2.**

1.a. ☒ I can read and understand English, and I have read and understand every question and instruction on this application and my answer to every question.

1.b. ☐ The interpreter named in **Part 7.** read to me every question and instruction on this application and my answer to every question in

[   ],

a language in which I am fluent, and I understood everything.

2. ☐ At my request, the preparer named in **Part 8.**

[   ],

prepared this application for me based only upon information I provided or authorized.

Applicant's Contact Information

3. Applicant's Daytime Telephone Number

7155551212

4. Applicant's Mobile Telephone Number (if any)

9891237654

5. Applicant's Email Address (if any)

tonytourist@hotmail.com

Applicant's Certification

Copies of any documents I have submitted are exact photocopies of unaltered, original documents, and I understand that USCIS may require that I submit original documents to USCIS at a later date. Furthermore, I authorize the release of any information from any and all of my records that USCIS may need to determine my eligibility for the immigration benefit that I seek.

I furthermore authorize release of information contained in this application, in supporting documents, and in my USCIS records, to other entities and persons where necessary for the administration and enforcement of U.S. immigration law.

I understand that USCIS will require me to appear for an appointment to take my biometrics (fingerprints, photograph, and/or signature) and, at that time, I will be required to sign an oath reaffirming that:

1) I reviewed and understood all of the information contained in, and submitted with, my application; and

2) All of this information was complete, true, and correct at the time of filing.

I certify, under penalty of perjury, that all of the information in my application and any document submitted with it were provided or authorized by me, that I reviewed and understand all of the information contained in, and submitted with, my application and that all of this information is complete, true, and correct.

Sample Form I-539 (page 6)

Part 6. Applicant's Statement, Contact Information, Declaration, Certification and Signature (continued)

Federal Agency Disclosure and Authorizations

I authorize, as applicable, the Social Security Administration (SSA) to verify my Social Security number (to match my name, Social Security number, and date of birth with information in SSA records and provide the results of the match) to USCIS. I authorize SSA to provide explanatory information to USCIS as necessary.

I authorize, as applicable, the SSA, U.S. Department of Agriculture (USDA), U.S. Department of Health and Human Services (HHS), U.S. Department of Housing and Urban Development (HUD), and any other U.S. Government agency that has received and/or adjudicated a request for a public benefit, as defined in 8 CFR 212.21(b), submitted by me or on my behalf, and/or granted one or more public benefits to me, to disclose to USCIS that I have applied for, received, or have been certified to receive, a public benefit from such agency, including the type and amount of benefits, dates of receipt, and any other relevant information provided to the agency for the purpose of obtaining such public benefit, to the extent permitted by law. I also authorize SSA, USDA, HHS, HUD, and any other U.S. Government agency to provide any additional data and information to USCIS, to the extent permitted by law.

I authorize, as applicable, custodians of records and other sources of information pertaining to my request for or receipt of public benefits to release information regarding my request for and/or receipt of public benefits, upon the request of the investigator, special agent, or other duly accredited representative of any Federal agency authorized above, regardless of any previous agreement to the contrary.

I understand that the information released by records custodians and sources of information is for official use by the Federal Government, that the U.S. Government will use it only to review if I have received public benefits in regards to my eligibility for immigration benefits and to enforce immigration laws, and that the U.S. Government may disclose the information only as authorized by law.

Applicant's Signature

6.a. Applicant's Signature

➡ *Tony F. Martino*

6.b. Date of Signature (mm/dd/yyyy)   06/29/2020

NOTE TO ALL APPLICANTS: If you do not completely fill out this application or fail to submit required documents listed in the Instructions, USCIS may deny your application.

Part 7. Interpreter's Contact Information, Statement, Certification, and Signature

Provide the following information about the interpreter.

Interpreter's Full Name

1.a. Interpreter's Family Name (Last Name)

1.b. Interpreter's Given Name (First Name)

2. Interpreter's Business or Organization Name (if any)

Interpreter's Mailing Address

3.a. Street Number and Name

3.b. ☐ Apt. ☐ Ste. ☐ Flr.

3.c. City or Town

3.d. State

3.e. ZIP Code

3.f. Province

3.g. Postal Code

3.h. Country

Interpreter's Contact Information

4. Interpreter's Daytime Telephone Number

5. Interpreter's Mobile Telephone Number (if any)

6. Interpreter's Email Address (if any)

Interpreter's Certification

I certify, under penalty of perjury, that:

I am fluent in English and

which is the same language specified in **Part 6., Item Number 1.b.**, and I have read to this applicant in the identified language every question and instruction on this application and his or her answer to every question. The applicant informed me that he or she understands every instruction, question, and answer on the application, including the **Applicant's Declaration and Certification**, and has verified the accuracy of every answer.

Will Inadmissibility Bar You From Getting a Green Card?

The U.S. government has decided that people with certain histories or conditions are a risk to others and therefore should not be allowed to enter the country. These people are called "inadmissible." This chapter explains the conditions that make a person inadmissible— and whether there is any way under the bar of inadmissibility.

A. What Is Inadmissibility?

The U.S. government keeps a list of reasons that make a person unwelcome in the United States. The list includes affliction with various physical and mental disorders, commission of crimes, participation in terrorist or subversive activity, and more.

You may be judged inadmissible any time after you have filed an application for a green card, nonimmigrant visa, or other immigration status. Even a permanent resident who departs the United States for more than 180 days may be found inadmissible upon return.

If you are found inadmissible, your immigration application will probably be denied. Even if you manage to hide your inadmissibility long enough to receive a green card or visa and be admitted into the U.S., if the problem is discovered later— perhaps when you apply for U.S. citizenship—you can be removed or deported.

> **CAUTION**
>
> **The coronavirus pandemic has created a separate reason that people can be barred from the United States.** Through presidential proclamations, travelers cannot enter the U.S. after having spent 14 days or more in one of the countries with major outbreaks. Check the immigration legal updates at www.nolo.com for details on which countries and who is affected.

B. The Possibility of Waiving Inadmissibility

Not everyone who falls into one of the categories of inadmissibility is absolutely barred from getting a green card or otherwise entering the United States. Some grounds of inadmissibility may be legally excused, or "waived." Others may not.

Health Coverage Might Become Requirement for U.S. Immigrant Visa

In late 2019, Trump issued a proclamation forbidding immigrants who will "financially burden" the U.S. healthcare system from receiving immigrant visas or U.S. residence, unless they can show they'll have a U.S.-government–approved form of health insurance within 30 days of U.S. entry. When this book went to print, the matter was tied up in litigation and not in effect—and it might never be. Nevertheless, health coverage is something all visa applicants will be asked about and can be one of the many factors considered in making a public charge determination.

Below is a chart summarizing all the grounds of inadmissibility, whether or not a waiver is available, and the special conditions you must meet to get a waiver. (For more details, see I.N.A. § 212, 8 U.S.C. § 1182.)

C. Most Troublesome Grounds of Inadmissibility

Some of the grounds that have the most significant impact on green card applicants are summarized here.

1. Being Unable to Show Family Financial Support

All family-based immigrants seeking permanent residence must include with their application

Inadmissibility Summary

Ground of Inadmissibility	Waiver Available	Conditions of Waiver and/or Exceptions
Health Problems		
Communicable diseases, particularly clinically active tuberculosis. Note: HIV (AIDS) was once specifically listed as a ground of inadmissibility. However, in 2009, the Centers for Disease Control took it off the list of "communicable diseases of public health significance."	Yes	A waiver is available to a person who is an asylee or is the spouse, unmarried son or daughter, or the unmarried minor lawfully adopted child of a U.S. citizen or permanent resident, or of an alien who has been issued an immigrant visa; or to an individual who has a son or daughter who is a U.S. citizen; or to a permanent resident or an alien issued an immigrant visa, upon compliance with USCIS's terms and regulations.
Physical or mental disorders that threaten the property, welfare, or safety of the applicant or others.	Yes	Special conditions required by USCIS, at its discretion.
Drug abusers or addicts.	No	
Failure to show that the applicant has been vaccinated against certain vaccine-preventable diseases.	Yes	The applicant must show either that he or she subsequently received the vaccine, that the vaccine is medically inappropriate as certified by a civil surgeon, or that having the vaccine administered is contrary to the applicant's religious beliefs or moral convictions.
Criminal and Related Violations		
Commission of crimes involving moral turpitude.	Yes	Waivers are not available for commission of crimes such as attempted murder or conspiracy to commit murder, or for murder, torture, or drug crimes, or for people previously admitted as permanent residents, if they have been convicted of aggravated felony since such admission or if they have fewer than seven years of lawful continuous residence before deportation proceedings are initiated against them. Waivers for all other offenses are available only if the applicant is a spouse, parent, or child of a U.S. citizen or green cardholder; or the only criminal activity was prostitution; or the actions occurred more than 15 years before the application for a visa or green card is filed, and the alien shows that he or she is rehabilitated and is not a threat to U.S. security.
Convictions for two or more crimes.	Yes	
Prostitutes or procurers of prostitutes.	Yes	
Diplomats or others involved in serious criminal activity who have received immunity from prosecution.	Yes	
Human traffickers and their adult family members who benefited financially from trafficking in persons.	No	
Money launderers.	No	
Drug offenders.	No	However, there may be an exception for a first and only offense or for juvenile offenders. There's also a waiver for simple possession of less than 30 grams of marijuana.
Drug traffickers.	No	

Inadmissibility Summary (continued)		
Ground of Inadmissibility	**Waiver Available**	**Conditions of Waiver and/or Exceptions**
Immediate family members of drug traffickers who knowingly benefited from their illicit money within the last five years.	No	But note that the problem "washes out" after five years.
National Security and Human Rights Related Violations		
Spies, governmental saboteurs, violators of export or technology transfer laws.	No	
People intending to overthrow the U.S. government.	No	
Terrorists and members or representatives of foreign terrorist organizations.	No	
People whose entry would have adverse consequences for U.S. foreign policy.	No	But exceptions exist if the applicant is an official of a foreign government, or the applicant's activities or beliefs would normally be lawful in the U.S., under the Constitution.
Foreign government officials who carried out particularly severe violations of religious freedom.	No	
Involvement in population control policies including forced abortion or sterilization.	Yes	Does not apply to heads of state, heads of government, or cabinet level ministers. Waiver available if important to the U.S. national interest, with written notification and justification to Congress.
Involvement with coercive transplantation of human organs or bodily tissue, unless the foreign national has discontinued his or her involvement with, and support for, such practices.	Yes	Does not apply to heads of state, heads of government, or cabinet level ministers. Waiver available if important to the U.S. national interest, with written notification and justification to Congress.
Members of totalitarian parties.	Yes	An exception is made if the membership was involuntary, or is or was when the applicant was under 16 years old, by operation of law, or for purposes of obtaining employment, food rations, or other "essentials" of living. An exception is also possible for past membership if the membership ended at least two years prior to the application (five years if the party in control of a foreign state is considered a totalitarian dictatorship). If neither applies, a waiver is available for an immigrant who is the parent, spouse, son, daughter, brother, or sister of a U.S. citizen, or a spouse, son, or daughter of a permanent resident.
Participants in Nazi persecution, genocide, torture, extrajudicial killings, or the recruitment or use of child soldiers.	No	

Inadmissibility Summary (continued)

Ground of Inadmissibility	Waiver Available	Conditions of Waiver and/or Exceptions
Economic Grounds		
Any person who, in the opinion of a USCIS or a border or consular official, is likely to become a "public charge," that is, receive public assistance or welfare in the United States. The official can consider factors such as the person's age, health, family and work history, and previous use of public benefits.	No	However, the applicant may cure the ground of inadmissibility by overcoming the reasons for it possibly paying a public charge bond. Also, there's an exception for some applicant categories, most notably refugees or asylees, U visa holders, and VAWA self-petitioners who are adjusting status. (See I.N.A. § 209.)
Family-sponsored immigrants and employment-sponsored immigrants where a family member is the employment sponsor (or such a family member owns 5% of the petitioning business) and the sponsor has not executed an Affidavit of Support (Form I-864).	No	But an applicant may cure the ground of inadmissibility by subsequently satisfying affidavit of support requirements.
Nonimmigrant public benefit recipients (where the individual came as nonimmigrant and applied for benefits without being eligible or through fraud). Five-year bar to admissibility.	No	But ground of inadmissibility expires after five years.
Labor Certifications & Employment Qualifications		
People without approved labor certifications, if one is required in the category under which the green card application is made.	No	
Graduates of unaccredited medical schools, whether inside or outside of the U.S., immigrating to the U.S. in a second or third preference category based on their profession, who have not both passed the foreign medical graduates exam and shown proficiency in English.	No	Physicians qualifying as special immigrants who have been practicing medicine in the U.S. with a license since January 9, 1978, are not subject to this rule.
Uncertified foreign health care workers seeking entry based on clinical employment in their field (but not including physicians).	No	But applicant may show qualifications by submitting a certificate from the Commission on Graduates of Foreign Nursing Schools or the equivalent.
Immigration Violators		
People who entered in the U.S. without inspection by U.S. border authorities.	Yes	Available for certain battered women and children who came to the U.S. escaping such battery or who qualify as self-petitioners. Also available for some individuals who had visa petitions or labor certifications on file before January 14, 1998 or before April 30, 2001 if they were in the U.S. on December 21, 2000 ($1,000 penalty required for latter waiver). Does not apply to applicants outside of the U.S.; or to refugees and asylees adjusting status (see I.N.A. § 209).
People who were deported after a removal hearing and seek admission within ten years.	Yes	Discretionary with USCIS.

Inadmissibility Summary (continued)		
Ground of Inadmissibility	**Waiver Available**	**Conditions of Waiver and/or Exceptions**
People who have failed to attend removal (deportation) proceedings (unless they had reasonable cause for doing so). Five-year bar to reentry.	Yes	Discretionary with USCIS.
People who have been summarily excluded from the U.S. and again attempt to enter within five years.	Yes	Advance permission to apply for readmission. Discretionary with USCIS.
People who made misrepresentations during the immigration process.	Yes	The applicant must be the spouse or child of a U.S. citizen or green card holder. A waiver will be granted if the refusal of admission would cause extreme hardship to that relative. Discretionary with USCIS.
People who made a false claim to U.S. citizenship.	No	
Individuals subject to a final removal (deportation) order under the Immigration and Naturalization Act § 274C (Civil Document Fraud Proceedings).	Yes	Available to permanent residents who voluntarily left the U.S., and to those applying for permanent residence as immediate relatives or other family-based petitions if the fraud was committed solely to assist the person's spouse or child and provided that no fine was imposed as part of the previous civil proceeding.
Student visa abusers (persons who improperly obtain F-1 status to attend a public elementary school or adult education program, or transfer from a private to a public program except as permitted). Five-year bar to admissibility.	No	
Certain individuals twice removed (deported) or removed after aggravated felony. Twenty-year bar to admissibility for those twice deported.	Yes	Discretionary with USCIS (advance permission to apply for readmission).
Individuals unlawfully present (time counted only after April 1, 1997 and after the age of 18). Presence for 180–364 days results in three-year bar to admissibility. Presence for 365 or more days creates ten-year bar to admissibility. Bars kick in only when the individual departs the U.S. and seeks reentry.	Yes	A waiver is provided for an immigrant who has a U.S. citizen or permanent resident spouse or parent to whom refusal of the application would cause extreme hardship. There is also a complex body of law concerning when a person's presence will be considered "lawful," for example, if one has certain applications awaiting decisions by USCIS or is protected by battered spouse/child provisions of the immigration laws.
Individuals unlawfully present after previous immigration violations. (Applies to persons who were in the U.S. unlawfully for an aggregate period over one year, who subsequently reenter without being properly admitted. Also applies to anyone ordered removed who subsequently attempts entry without admission.)	No	A permanent ground of inadmissibility. However, after being gone for ten years, an applicant can apply for permission to reapply for admission.

Inadmissibility Summary (continued)		
Ground of Inadmissibility	Waiver Available	Conditions of Waiver and/or Exceptions
Stowaways.	No	
Smugglers of illegal aliens.	Yes	Waivable if the applicant was smuggling in people who were immediate family members at the time, and either is a permanent resident or is immigrating under a family-based visa petition as an immediate relative; the unmarried son or daughter of a U.S. citizen or permanent resident; or the spouse of a U.S. permanent resident.
Document Violations		
People without required current passports or visas.	No	Except limited circumstance waivers. Under new "summary removal" procedures, border officials may quickly deport people for five years who arrive without proper documents or make misrepresentations during the inspection process.
Draft Evasion and Ineligibility for Citizenship		
People who are permanently ineligible for U.S. citizenship.	No	
People who are draft evaders, unless they were U.S. citizens at the time of evasion or desertion.	No	
Miscellaneous Grounds		
Practicing polygamists.	No	
Guardians accompanying excludable aliens.	No	
International child abductors. (The exclusion does not apply if the applicant is a national of a country that signed the Hague Convention on International Child Abduction.)	No	
Unlawful voters (voting in violation of any federal, state, or local law or regulation).	No	
Former U.S. citizens who renounced citizenship to avoid taxation.	No	

an Affidavit of Support, on either Form I-864 or I-864-EZ, signed by their petitioner. This form helps satisfy the requirement that an immigrant show he or she is not likely to become a public charge (in other words, receive government assistance or welfare).

By filling out the form and attaching various documents, the petitioning U.S. citizen or permanent resident shows his or her earnings and savings, and promises to use that money to support the immigrant or to pay back any government agency that supplies need-based support to the immigrant. But not every petitioner earns enough to successfully show this.

Also, in 2020, both USCIS and the Department of State finalized new, parallel public charge rules. These shift the burden from the Affidavit of Support to the immigrant to show that he or she will not become a public charge, based on a totality of circumstances. Basically, the I-864 doesn't carry the weight it once did.

One of the more burdensome parts of the new regulations is that applicants will have to fill out a new application form, either USCIS Form I-944, Declaration of Self-Sufficiency (if applying in the U.S.) or DS-5540, Public Charge Questionnaire (if applying through an overseas consulate). Both forms request extensive financial information regarding the applicant rather than the U.S. petitioner; not just income and assets, but concerns like household size, debt, health coverage, and credit score. What's more, applicants who've lived in the U.S. face a new challenge: The U.S. government will consider use of non-cash benefits such as food stamps, Section 8 housing, or Medicaid in determining whether that person could become a public charge and is therefore inadmissible. When in doubt, the U.S. government might ask applicants to file a public charge bond (money that they'll lose if they eventually claim public assistance).

The I-864-EZ is a shorter, easier version of the form, which can be used only if you are the only person your petitioner is sponsoring, and your petitioner can meet the sponsorship requirements based solely upon his or her income (and nobody else's).

SKIP AHEAD
For a sample, filled-out Form I-864, see Chapter 17 of this book.

Living in the U.S.? Check Credit Score Now

In the past, having a good credit score in the U.S., which indicates how good one is at paying back debt, was mostly considered important for people in the process of applying for a loan or mortgage. Under the new public charge rules, however, it's become relevant for intending immigrants, too.

Any applicants seeking a green card while living in the U.S. (people "adjusting status") will, in filling out the newly required Form I-944 Declaration of Self-Sufficiency, be required to provide their score to USCIS, as well a copy of a recent credit report (issued within the last 12 months), if either can be obtained. And even if these don't exist, applicants will have to provide a document from a credit reporting company saying as much.

If you've been living in the U.S. and had a credit card, or took out any other loan, you're likely to have a credit report on file, whether you're aware of it or not.

The commentary to the new regulations points out that a high credit score and good report can help balance out negative factors, being "a positive factor that indicates a person is likely to be self-sufficient and support the household."

But it also says that a "lower credit score or negative credit history in the United States may indicate that a person's financial status is weak and that he or she may not be self-sufficient. Credit reports and credit scores provide information about a person's bill-paying history, loans, age of current accounts, current debts, as well as work, residences, lawsuits, arrests, collections, actions, outstanding debts, and bankruptcies in the United States."

Fortunately, there are steps you can and should take to find out what's in your credit report. You'll want to correct any errors and potentially improve your score before USCIS gets a look at it. See articles in the Debt Management section of Nolo.com for more information.

2020 Poverty Guidelines Chart for Immigrants

For the 48 Contiguous States, the District of Columbia, Puerto Rico, the U.S. Virgin Islands, Guam, and the Commonwealth of the Northern Mariana Islands:		
Sponsor's Household Size	100% of HHS Poverty Guidelines	125% of HHS Poverty Guidelines
	For sponsors on active duty in the U.S. armed forces who are petitioning for their spouse or child	*For all other sponsors*
2	$17,240	$21,550
3	$21,720	$27,150
4	$26,200	$32,750
5	$30,680	$38,350
6	$35,160	$43,950
7	$39,640	$49,550
8	$44,120	$55,150
	Add $4,480 for each additional person	**Add $5,600 for each additional person**

Alaska		
Sponsor's Household Size	100% of HHS Poverty Guidelines	125% of HHS Poverty Guidelines
	For sponsors on active duty in the U.S. armed forces who are petitioning for their spouse or child	*For all other sponsors*
2	$21,550	$26,937
3	$27,150	$33,937
4	$32,750	$40,937
5	$38,350	$47,937
6	$43,950	$54,937
7	$49,550	$61,937
8	$55,150	$68,937
	Add $5,600 for each additional person	**Add $7,000 for each additional person**

Hawaii		
Sponsor's Household Size	100% of HHS Poverty Guidelines	125% of HHS Poverty Guidelines
	For sponsors on active duty in the U.S. armed forces who are petitioning for their spouse or child	*For all other sponsors*
2	$19,830	$24,787
3	$24,980	$31,225
4	$30,130	$37,662
5	$35,280	$44,100
6	$40,430	$50,537
7	$45,580	$56,975
8	$50,730	$63,412
	Add $5,150 for each additional person	**Add $6,437 for each additional person**

Exceptions. There are limited exceptions to the Affidavit of Support requirement. If the immigrant will qualify for automatic U.S. citizenship upon becoming a permanent resident (discussed in Chapter 9), the I-864 is not necessary. Also, if the immigrant has already worked in the U.S. for 40 or more work quarters as defined by Social Security (about ten years), Form I-864 is not required. Moreover, the immigrant can count time worked by either a parent, while the immigrant was under the age of 18, or by a U.S. petitioning spouse, toward these 40 quarters.

Others who don't need to submit a Form I-864 include self-petitioning widows or widowers of U.S. citizens, and self-petitioning battered spouses or children (explained in later chapters).

If you're exempt from the Affidavit of Support requirement due to one of these exceptions, you should fill out Form I-864W instead of the regular Form I-864.

Sponsor's responsibilities. The government can rely on the I-864 to hold the sponsor responsible if the immigrant receives public benefits. And it is also enforceable by the immigrant family member against the sponsor for support.

Finally, it requires that the sponsor show income for a similar household size (including family and dependents) that is at least 125% of the federal Poverty Guidelines level. It goes down to 100% for sponsors who are on active duty in the U.S. armed forces and petitioning for a spouse or child. These Poverty Guidelines are revised annually; see the table above.

Your sponsor's income will need to meet the guidelines for the year when your Affidavit of Support is filed. Don't worry if the required income levels get raised later—it probably won't affect you. Your sponsor should include a copy of the current Poverty Guidelines with your affidavit, in order to remind the immigration authorities of the then-current income requirements. Also, be aware that one exception exists: If more than a year passes since the affidavit was submitted, the immigration

authorities can ask for proof of the sponsor's current income, in which case, they will judge it based on the most recent Poverty Guidelines.

The immigrant's income can also be added to the mix to help reach the Poverty Guidelines minimum, if the immigrant is already living with the petitioner in the U.S. and working legally at a job that will continue after getting the green card.

Who fills out the form. Family-based immigrants who file adjustment of status or immigrant visa applications are required to have Form I-864 filed by the person who is sponsoring their immigrant petition. However, if that family petitioner's income isn't high enough, another person—a joint sponsor—may add income if he or she meets the 125% income requirement for the household and is:

- a U.S. legal permanent resident or citizen
- over 18 years old
- living in the United States, and
- willing to be jointly liable.

The joint sponsor files a separate Affidavit of Support. The principal immigrant can have only one joint sponsor. However, if the joint sponsor's income is not sufficient to cover all the derivative beneficiaries (such as children), a second joint sponsor may be added. Two joint sponsors is the limit, however.

What if the primary petitioner can't find a joint sponsor to make up for an insufficient income and assets? Other people who live in the U.S. petitioner's household may also join their income to that of the primary sponsor to help reach the 125% level, but only if they are age 18 or older and agree to be jointly liable by filing Form I-864A, Contract Between Sponsor and Household Member. This is different than being a joint sponsor. It means that the person is literally living in the same house—perhaps is an older child or a parent—and is willing to have his or her income counted toward the household total and support the immigrants.

Using assets to meet the requirements. Personal assets of either the sponsor or the immigrant—such as property, bank account deposits, and personal property, such as automobiles (minus any outstanding debts)—may also be used to supplement the sponsor's income if the primary sponsor's actual income does not add up to 125% of the federal Poverty Guidelines income levels.

The sponsor or immigrant must show assets worth five times the difference between the Poverty Guidelines level and actual household income (or three times the difference for immediate relatives, for example husband and wife). The assets must be readily convertible to cash within one year. If using assets owned by the sponsor's household members or the immigrant, those people must submit a Form I-864A.

Immigrant's Story: Compensating for a Low Salary

Here is how Daniel, a U.S. citizen, can deal with his low income in sponsoring his Norwegian wife, Liv, and her twin boys from a previous marriage.

Daniel works as a youth counselor at a Seattle nonprofit, earning $30,000 a year. However, according to the 2020 Poverty Guidelines, Daniel will need an income of $32,750 or more to support a family of four—meaning he's $2,750 short. Liv plans to work in the U.S., but she is currently living in Norway, so that doesn't help.

Daniel could pick up a weekend job, to raise his income until Liv gets her green card (at which time no one would stop him from quitting). However, an easier solution is for him to declare his assets when filling out Form I-864. Because the value of assets must be divided by three for U.S. citizens sponsoring their spouses, Daniel will need $8,250 in assets to make up the shortfall.

Fortunately, Daniel has $9,000 in a money market account, so declaring this on his Form I-864 will be enough to help Liv and her children get approved for a green card. He'll need to remember to include a copy of a bank statement showing how much is in the account when he prepares the Form I-864.

SEE AN EXPERT

The requirements and paperwork burden of the affidavit are complicated and substantial. If you have questions about your eligibility or the scope of your legal responsibility, or are concerned that despite an adequate I-864 other factors could lead U.S. immigration authorities to conclude that you are a likely public charge, consult an experienced immigration attorney.

2. Being Stopped at the Border

Another law that has a drastic impact on individuals requesting to enter the United States is the summary exclusion law. This law empowers an inspector at the airport to exclude and deport you at your attempted entry to the U.S. if either of the following are true:

- The inspector thinks you are making a misrepresentation (lying) about practically anything connected to your right to enter the U.S.—such as your purpose in coming, intent to return, prior immigration history, or use of false documents.
- You do not have the proper documentation to support your entry to the U.S. in the category you are requesting.

If the inspector excludes you, you may not request entry for five years, unless a special waiver is granted. For this reason, it is extremely important to understand the terms of your requested status and not make any misrepresentations.

If the inspector looks likely to summarily exclude you, you may request withdrawing your application to enter the U.S., which will prevent having the five-year order on your record. The inspector might allow you to do this in some cases.

3. Being Barred From Returning After Past Unlawful U.S. Presence

Relatively new grounds of inadmissibility apply to people who were unlawfully present in the United States for 180 days (approximately six months) after

April 1, 1997, who subsequently left, and who now seek admission, for example through adjustment of status or by applying for an immigrant or nonimmigrant visa. Such people are subject to a three-year waiting period; the period is ten years if they were unlawfully present for 365 days after April 1, 1997. A waiver is available, as described in Section D4, below.

Some important exceptions help some applicants avoid this problem. For example, as long as you were under 18, your time in the U.S. doesn't count as unlawful presence. And people who have a bona fide pending asylum application or a pending application for adjustment of status are in the U.S. in perfectly lawful status. Also, battered spouses and children can get around the bars, if they can show a substantial connection between their unlawful presence and the abuse.

The worst-case scenario is for people who have lived in the United States illegally for more than one year and who then left or were deported but returned to the United States illegally (or were caught trying to). They can never get a green card. This is usually referred to as the "permanent bar." (Check with a lawyer before concluding that you're subject to the permanent bar, however—recent case law has carved out a few exceptions.) No waiver is available to the permanent bar for the first ten years.

4. Limitations on Who Can Adjust Status

The rules concerning adjustment of status—or getting your green card in the U.S. rather than at a U.S. consulate—are somewhat complicated. In general, if you entered the U.S. properly—by being inspected by a border official—and maintained your nonimmigrant status, you can probably get your green card without leaving the United States.

In addition, a "grandfather clause" helps a few people who happened to be in the United States when certain laws were changed (in particular, a law known as § 245(i)). Under the old laws, practically everyone had the right to stay in the United States to adjust their status, simply by

paying a $1,000 penalty fee. But under the newer laws, paying this fee is no longer an option except for those few people who had visa petitions filed on their behalf nearly two decades ago (see Chapter 16, Section A3 for details).

That means that many people who bypassed a border inspection are in a trap. If they stay in the United States, the fact that they entered illegally or committed certain other violations means that they're not allowed to adjust their status to permanent resident within the United States. But if they leave the United States and attempt to apply for their green card through an overseas consulate, they may well face a three- or ten-year bar to returning to the United States, as punishment for their unlawful stay.

If you believe you're in this trap, consult a lawyer to make sure and to see if you might qualify for a waiver of the three- or ten-year bar. Since 2013, a "stateside" or "provisional" waiver has allowed some people to avoid the trap by submitting a waiver application and receiving an answer BEFORE leaving the U.S. for their consular interview (as described in Section D5 of this chapter).

Note: All refugees or political asylees can stay in the U.S. to adjust status.

5. Having Committed Crimes Involving Alcohol or Drugs

Criminal grounds of inadmissibility are the number one factor making temporary visa applicants inadmissible, and they affect a lot of green card applicants, too. If you've committed any sort of crime, you can be found inadmissible, and should consult an experienced immigration attorney. Some attorneys specialize in analyzing the significance of criminal convictions in the immigration context.

However, if you've been convicted of a crime involving alcohol, you've got double trouble. Even if the crime itself doesn't make you inadmissible, USCIS can, and often does, argue that it's a sign that you have a physical or mental disorder associated with harmful behavior—in other words, that you're inadmissible on health, rather than criminal, grounds.

This is most often a problem for people with convictions for DUI or DWI (driving under the influence or driving while intoxicated). One DUI alone won't always create a problem, unless there were additional factors, such as someone having been injured, your license having been suspended, or your state treating the crime as a felony. But if USCIS sees a "significant criminal record of alcohol-related driving incidents," it will take a closer look. You may be required to undergo an additional examination by the doctor who filled out your medical report, or by more specialized doctors or psychiatrists.

DUIs aren't the only crime that can lead USCIS to find you inadmissible on health grounds. Crimes such as assaults or domestic violence where alcohol or drugs were contributing factors can lead to the same result. Again, see an attorney if this is an issue in your case—and remember that trying to hide crimes on your green card application will only get you in bigger trouble after the fingerprint or police report reveals them.

6. Suspected of Terrorist Activity

No one will be surprised to hear that the U.S. forbids people who are linked to terrorism to enter the country, and takes an extra hard look at applications from anyone whose government is thought to support terrorism. (The U.S.'s current four suspected countries are Iran, North Korea, Sudan, and Syria.) However, the terrorism-based inadmissibility grounds are broader than you might expect, and have the potential to exclude some people who wouldn't ordinarily be thought of as terrorists.

The inadmissibility grounds cover being a member of a terrorist organization, inciting others to participate in terrorism, persuading others to support terrorism, endorsing terrorism, raising funds for an organization that the U.S. considers terrorist in nature, and more. The support and fundraising prohibitions can be especially problematic for some people who have given money to organizations

that serve a mix of purposes or that have become established political parties despite a terrorist or guerrilla past.

No hard proof or court conviction is necessary—the U.S. government can exclude someone based on having "reasonable grounds to believe" that the person falls into one of the categories described above.

Also, the spouse or child of any immigrant found inadmissible based on the above provisions can be excluded if the immigrant's activities took place within the last five years. To get around this, the spouse or child will need to show that they were not aware of, nor could reasonably have been expected to know of, the activity.

Under Trump "Travel Ban," Certain Countries' Citizens May Be Denied U.S. Entry

Although not a ground of inadmissibility under federal law (the I.N.A.), citizens of certain countries may be denied U.S. entry simply because of their national origin. President Trump has signed various executive orders denying entry to visa holders from several Muslim-majority countries, with the stated purpose of reviewing U.S. visa-vetting procedures. Although immigration and civil rights advocates challenged these executive orders in several courts, they remain largely in force, owing to a U.S. Supreme Court decision.

At first, the ban barred nationals from the following countries from receiving an immigrant visa at a U.S. consulate abroad: Chad, Iran, Libya, North Korea, Somalia, Syria, and Yemen.

Then in early 2020, Trump issued a proclamation stopping U.S. consulates from issuing any immigrant visas for U.S. entry to nationals of Burma (Myanmar), Eritrea, Kyrgyzstan, and Nigeria. In addition, the proclamation suspends participation in the Diversity Visa Lottery for certain nationals of Sudan and Tanzania.

For more information about how the travel ban affects consular processing, see Chapter 17.

D. Reversing an Inadmissibility Finding

There are five ways to get past a finding that you are inadmissible:

- In the case of physical or mental illness only, you may be able to correct the condition.
- You can prove that you really don't fall into the category of inadmissibility USCIS believes you do.
- You can prove that the accusations of inadmissibility against you are false.
- You can apply for a waiver of inadmissibility.
- You can "wait out" the time period required by USCIS before reentering the U.S.

Each of these is discussed in some detail below. However, you'll most likely need an attorney's help.

1. Correcting Grounds of Inadmissibility

If you have had a physical or mental illness that is a ground of inadmissibility and you have been cured of the condition by the time you submit your green card application, or at least by the time a decision is made on it, you will no longer be considered inadmissible for that reason. For example, you may have been diagnosed with a clinically active and communicable case of tuberculosis ("TB") while awaiting a decision on your green card application. If you can show that you still test positive for TB on a skin test, but that the TB is latent and no longer infectious, you have "corrected" the ground of inadmissibility. If the condition is not cured by the time you apply, with certain illnesses you can still get a waiver of inadmissibility.

2. Proving That Inadmissibility Does Not Apply

Proving that inadmissibility does not apply in your case is a method used mainly to overcome criminal and ideological grounds of inadmissibility. When dealing with criminal grounds of inadmissibility, the immigration authorities will consider both the type of crime committed and the nature of the punishment to see whether your criminal activity constitutes a ground of inadmissibility.

For example, with some criminal activity, only actual convictions are grounds of inadmissibility. If you have been charged with a crime and the charges were then dropped, you may not be inadmissible.

Another example involves crimes of moral turpitude. Crimes of moral turpitude are those showing dishonesty or basically immoral conduct. Committing an act that is considered a crime of moral turpitude can make you inadmissible, even if you have not been convicted.

Crimes with no element of moral turpitude, however, are often not considered grounds of inadmissibility. Opinions may differ on which crimes are considered to involve moral turpitude and which are not.

Other factors that may work to your benefit are:

- expungement laws that remove the crime from your record (but don't assume this will take care of the problem)
- the length of the prison term
- how long ago the crime was committed
- the number of convictions in your background
- conditions of plea bargaining, and
- available pardons.

Sometimes, a conviction can be erased or vacated if you can show it was unlawfully obtained or you were not advised of its immigration consequences. In either case, you still need to disclose the criminal charge on your immigration application or petition.

Proving that a criminal ground of inadmissibility does not apply in your case is a complicated business. You need to have a firm grasp not only of immigration law, but also the technicalities of criminal law. If you have a criminal problem in your past, you may still be able to get a green card, but not without the help of an experienced immigration lawyer. (See Chapter 24.)

3. Proving That an Inadmissibility Finding Is Incorrect

If your green card or nonimmigrant visa application is denied because you are found inadmissible, you can try to prove that the finding of inadmissibility is incorrect. For example, if a USCIS medical examination shows that you have certain medical problems, you can present reports from other doctors stating that the first diagnosis was wrong and that you are free of the problem condition. If you are accused of lying on a visa application, you can present evidence proving you told the truth, or that any false statements were made unintentionally.

4. Applying for a Waiver

In many circumstances, you may be able to get a waiver of inadmissibility. By obtaining a waiver, you don't eliminate or disprove the ground of inadmissibility. Instead, you ask USCIS to overlook the problem and give you a green card or visa anyway.

For example, you can apply for a waiver if you can show that your being prevented from reentering the United States based on your 180 days or more of unlawful presence would cause extreme hardship to your U.S. citizen or permanent resident spouse or parent. (Note that having U.S. citizen children won't help here.)

The classic case of extreme hardship is if your spouse or parent is very ill, needs your care, and would suffer medically by joining you outside the United States. Note, however, that extreme hardship to you, the immigrant, does not count in this analysis.

All green card and visa application forms ask questions designed to find out whether any grounds of inadmissibility apply in your case. When the answers to the questions on these forms clearly show that you are inadmissible, you may be authorized to begin applying for a waiver immediately on filing your application. In most cases, however, the consulate or USCIS office insists on having your final visa or green card interview before ruling that you are inadmissible. If the USCIS office or consulate handling your case decides to wait until your final interview before finding you inadmissible, this will delay your ability to file for a waiver. This may delay your getting a green card or visa; waivers can take many months to process.

Once it is determined that a waiver is necessary, you will need to complete Form I-601 and pay a filing fee (currently $930). Note that if you file this with a U.S. consulate abroad, you will have to wait for the consulate to send your application to a USCIS office. The consulate cannot approve the waiver.

Once again, there are many technical factors that control whether or not a waiver of inadmissibility is granted. If you want to get one approved, you stand the best chance of success by hiring a good immigration lawyer.

5. New, Stateside Provisional Waiver for Applicants Facing Three- or Ten-Year Bar

As of March 4, 2013, green card seekers who were not eligible to adjust status in the U.S. and were afraid to leave for their consular interview because their past unlawful presence might block their return gained a new procedural option. Some of them can now submit a "provisional waiver" application, and hopefully have it approved, before leaving the United States. We'll provide detailed information here on what's involved—but because of the complexities of the process and the high rate of USCIS denials so far, we urge you to get an attorney's help with this task.

a. Who Is Eligible to Submit a Provisional/Stateside Waiver Application

Not everyone is eligible to use this new option. Applicants must be:

• **The beneficiary of an immigrant petition**—that is, eligible for an immigrant visa on some basis, whether it's family based, employment based, or through the Diversity Visa (DV) lottery. If a Form I-130 or Form I-140 application has been approved on your behalf or you've been selected for the DV lottery, you likely fit this criterion.

- **At least 17 years of age.** This doesn't really hurt anyone, because you cannot accrue unlawful presence in the U.S., and therefore don't need a waiver, until you're at least 18.
- **Physically present in the U.S. at the time of applying.**
- **Otherwise admissible to the United States.** In other words, you cannot separately ask for a waiver of any criminal, fraud, or other grounds of inadmissibility. In fact, if USCIS has any reason to believe that you are inadmissible on some ground other than unlawful presence, it will deny the provisional waiver. Furthermore, if the consular officer at your visa interview decides that you are otherwise inadmissible or are ineligible for the visa on some basis other than unlawful presence, the USCIS-approved provisional waiver will be automatically revoked.
- **Able to prove that, if not granted the waiver, their qualifying U.S. relatives will suffer extreme hardship as a result.** The list of qualifying relatives includes permanent resident and U.S. citizen's spouse or parents.

When the provisional waiver process was first implemented, denial rates were high, primarily due to criminal history issues. Applicants with even minor offenses on record, such as trespassing, shoplifting, or disorderly conduct were often denied the waiver. In response to protest by immigrant advocates, USCIS issued guidance to its officers in a January 2014 memo. It instructed officers not to deny a provisional waiver application if the criminal offense either 1) falls within the petty offense or youthful offender exception or 2) is not a crime of moral turpitude. (For definitions of "petty offense," "youthful offender exception," and "crime of moral turpitude," see I.N.A. § 212(a)(2).)

The provisional waiver process has gotten smoother since this memo, but applicants with arrests or convictions should take care to submit as much evidence as possible showing that their criminal past was relatively minor and would not render them inadmissible.

b. Timing of Filing Your Provisional, Stateside Waiver Application

If the U.S. petitioner hasn't already submitted the Form I-130 petition that starts the immigration process for a family member, he or she should indicate in Part 4 Question 62 that the immigrant will apply for an immigrant visa at a U.S. consulate abroad rather than adjusting status in the United States. (If the immigrant were legally allowed to adjust status in the U.S., you wouldn't have to bother with the provisional waiver in the first place.)

By doing so, you will alert USCIS that it needs to, upon approving the I-130, transfer the file to the National Visa Center (NVC) for further action and for transfer to the consulate. If the petitioner were to say on the I-130 that the immigrant will apply for adjustment of status in the U.S., you would then have to take extra steps to have the file transferred to the NVC. (This includes filing a Form I-824 and paying a filing fee, then waiting many months for action on the request.)

Only after USCIS approves the I-130 can you file your Provisional Waiver Application (on USCIS Form I-601A, available at www.uscis.gov/i-601a). You cannot submit the I-130 petition at the same time as ("concurrently" with) the waiver application.

USCIS will notify the National Visa Center (NVC) of the I-601A's approval. You will need to pay NVC any immigrant visa processing fee. (The NVC handles the case after USCIS approves the I-130 and schedules your immigrant visa interview at a U.S. embassy or consulate abroad.

If NVC goes ahead and schedules your visa appointment before USCIS has acted on the waiver request, you must quickly notify the consulate at which your appointment is scheduled to ask that your interview be postponed until USCIS has made a decision on your waiver application.

The DOS tries to schedule applicants for an immigrant visa interview within about two or three months of USCIS approving the waiver request and the applicant filing all the necessary visa forms and documents. Applicants can remain in the U.S. during this time period.

c. Fee for Provisional Waiver Application

DHS has set the fee for Form I-601A at $630. In addition, applicants under the age of 79 will need to pay the biometrics (fingerprinting) fee, currently $85. No fee waiver requests will be considered.

The biometrics requirement means the immigrant will be fingerprinted and the name and prints run through an FBI database to check for a criminal and immigration enforcement record. If there's a chance this will turn up negative information, consult a lawyer before going any further.

d. What to File for a Provisional Waiver Request

In addition to Form I-601A and the fee, you will need to provide proof of your eligibility, and documents showing that you merit the waiver as a matter of discretion. USCIS requires that you provide:

- ☐ a copy of the USCIS approval notice of your Form I-130 or I-140 visa petition or DV Program Selection
- ☐ an EOIR Administrative Closure order (if applicable because your case was in removal proceedings)
- ☐ proof of the U.S. citizen or lawful permanent resident status of your qualifying relative IF it is not the same person who filed the immigrant visa petition for you
- ☐ proof of your relationship to your qualifying relative IF it is not the same person who filed the immigrant visa petition for you

- ☐ documents showing that your qualifying relative (U.S. spouse or parent) would suffer extreme hardship if you were denied the U.S. visa, and
- ☐ a receipt showing that you have paid the DOS-required immigrant visa processing fee.

Wondering what extreme hardship is? USCIS gives a number of examples, including health concerns, financial, educational, and personal considerations, and other special factors. For example, if your elderly U.S. citizen parent depends upon you for care and would be unable to receive medical treatment abroad, you should submit evidence of this. If you're the primary earner in your family and your spouse can't work full time, that would be excellent to submit proof of. Decisions about what qualifies as extreme hardship are highly discretionary, however, so your best bet is to seek an attorney's assistance in preparing a convincing waiver application—one demonstrating that the hardship your qualifying family members would suffer if you were denied a visa is greater than just the natural sadness of separation if you were forced to leave the United States.

USCIS will not, in most cases, call applicants in for an interview on their provisional waiver request, since it would then have to transfer the file from its National Benefits Center to a local office.

e. If USCIS Deems Your Waiver Application Incomplete

USCIS will not necessarily deny a provisional waiver application that's missing some materials. Instead, it routinely sends out Requests for Evidence (RFEs) for applications that lack critical information related to issues like the qualifying relatives' extreme hardship, whether the applicant merits a favorable exercise of discretion, or on some other relevant topic. But USCIS can also simply deny an application outright, so do your best to submit a complete one the first time around.

Also, if you don't pay the correct fee, sign your application, or provide certain key bits of eligibility information, USCIS will return your entire application to you and you will have to refile.

f. Options After Denial of Provisional Waiver

Although you cannot appeal USCIS's denial of your stateside waiver request, you have a couple of options in this situation.

You can file a new I-601A and waiver application with USCIS, during the time that your case is still pending with the DOS. Of course, there is little point in doing this if you don't provide new or extra information to overcome USCIS's original reason for the denial. If you aren't already using an attorney, this would definitely be the time to consult one.

Another option is to go ahead and attend your consular interview, and then file the traditional waiver request on Form I-601 (Application for Waiver of Grounds of Inadmissibility) with USCIS. This, of course, risks your being unable to return to the U.S. for three or ten years if USCIS once again denies your waiver application, though it will be handled by a different USCIS officer this time around.

Should you worry that DHS agents will come knocking on your door in the U.S. to arrest you after an I-601A denial? According to U.S. government statements, "DHS also does not envision initiating removal proceedings against aliens whose Form I-601As are denied or withdrawn prior to final adjudication"—unless, that is, the person "has a criminal history, has committed fraud, or otherwise poses a threat to national security or public safety."

6. Remaining Outside the U.S. for the Required Amount of Time

If you're subject to a penalty requiring you to remain outside the U.S. for three or ten years before reentering—most likely because you stayed in the U.S. unlawfully—you don't have to wait for an immigration authority to tell you you're subject to the penalty to start the clock ticking on your time away.

For example, if you overstayed your tourist visa by more than 180 days but less than 365 days during a past visit to the U.S., you'll eventually be penalized by having to wait outside the U.S. for three years before reentering on any kind of visa. (That's the "three-year bar.") An unlawful stay of over 365 days gets you a ten-year bar.

If you stay in the U.S. and wait to receive your visa interview notice before you leave—and then at your interview, the consulate denies your request for a waiver of your unlawful stay—you'll be stuck outside the U.S. for three or ten years following your interview. That's why some immigrants prefer to leave the U.S. sooner, in order to start counting up the three years as soon as possible.

How Long You'll Have to Wait

Among the most common questions asked of immigration attorneys are ones concerning how long the immigration process takes, such as:

- "As a U.S. citizen, I filed the papers for my brother five years ago. Why is it taking so long for the U.S. Embassy in India to give him his immigrant visa?"
- "My ten-year-old daughter was born in Hawaii, where I was a graduate student. Since she is a U.S. citizen, when can I get a green card by having her claim me as her mother?"
- "Three years ago, based on my green card, I sponsored my wife, who comes from Mexico. She is still waiting for her green card. What is the problem?"

Such questions are often asked by people who might have expected some delay in getting their green cards, but who can't believe how many years it's taking.

There are numerous causes of common immigration delays. The first type of delay no one can escape. It's the operation of U.S. immigration law, defining when you become eligible for a green card. In the example of the mother of the U.S. citizen born in Hawaii, above, she'll need to wait until her child turns 21 to so much as start the immigration process.

Another common source of delay is simply the bureaucratic backup caused by an overworked government agency trying to deal with many thousands of applications every year. Even the amount of time you spend waiting for a decision on one application can be shocking—many months or years is normal. On top of that, the coronavirus pandemic has resulted in the closure to visitors of many U.S. government offices. Behind-the-scenes processing continues, but some parts of the application process can be done only in person. Expect ongoing delays even after offices reopen. Also a fair number of people wait months only to discover that their application got misplaced or lost in the paperwork shuffle. Although USCIS is perpetually launching efforts to fix these problems,

no one expects miracles. See Chapters 21 and 22 for tips on preventing and dealing with these delays.

Another type of delay is the security checks and double checks your name and fingerprints will be run through, sometimes more than once, during the application process. Although security checks were always part of the application process, they've become more rigorous since the terrorist attacks of September 11, 2001. For people with common names, this can create particular problems. Of course, if you've had any arrests or other history that you believe will raise questions in the immigration process, you should consult an attorney.

Then there is a type of delay that applies only to applicants in green card categories that have a yearly limit on how many are given out. For example, spouses of U.S. citizens don't have to worry, because as immediate relatives, the government can grant unlimited numbers of green cards to them, no matter how many apply. But spouses of U.S. permanent residents are less lucky. Their annual limit is 87,934, and far more spouses than that apply every year. Spouses of permanent residents have to wait, usually two years or more, until all the people who applied before them have gotten their green cards. After that, in technical terms, a "visa number" is said to become available, and they can continue their application for a green card.

TIP
"Visa" and "green card" can have similar meanings. When we're talking about numbers and quotas, the immigration laws always refer to "visas" rather than "green cards," for technical reasons. Part of the reason is that if you come from overseas, you don't become a permanent resident (green card holder) until you receive an "immigrant visa" and use it to enter the United States. But even if you're applying within the United States, you can't become a permanent resident until a "visa number" is allotted to you. So, when you hear about numbers and limits on "visas" in this discussion, assume it means your right to a green card, no matter where you're coming from or whether you use an actual, physical entry visa.

You'll face delays based on limited numbers of visas if you apply for a green card in any of the so-called "preference" categories (which we'll explain below). All the preference categories come with limits, or "quotas," on how many visas or green cards can be passed out in a year. And in every family preference category, the demand for green cards always seems to exceed the supply.

To make matters more complicated, no country is allowed to send more than 7% of all preference immigrants (or 25,620 people) to the United States in a year. That means that for certain countries with high rates of immigration to the United States—like Mexico, India, China, and the Philippines—the U.S. government sometimes has to start a separate—and longer—waiting list. This isn't discrimination so much as it is mathematics.

A. Immediate Relatives of U.S. Citizens: No Waiting

Immigrant visas are immediately available for one group of eligible aliens: immediate relatives of U.S. citizens. They have the highest priority in immigration law because of the congressional intent to encourage families of U.S. citizens to live together and stay together.

Members of this group have to wait only for as long as it takes various government offices to handle their applications. This averages from two to twelve months, depending on various factors, such as whether the immigrant is coming from another country or already lives legally in the United States, and how backed up the office serving his or her region is.

For purposes of immigration law, you are an immediate relative and eligible for an immigrant visa without waiting if you are:

- the husband or wife of a U.S. citizen
- the parent of a U.S. citizen, if the citizen is at least 21 years of age
- the unmarried child under 21 years of age (including stepchildren and children adopted before they reach the age of 16) of a U.S. citizen, or

- the widow or widower of a U.S. citizen (assuming you weren't legally separated at the time of death and haven't remarried since).

Although children of U.S. citizens must remain unmarried until they receive their visa, those approaching 21 do get some protection from a law called the Child Status Protection Act. As long as the initial I-130 petition was filed for them when they were under 21 years old, these immediate relative children never "age out," or lose their eligibility based on being too old. Previously, once an immediate relative child turned 21, he or she would automatically move into the less-favored preference category. Now, the child's age is frozen at whatever it was when the I-130 petition was filed, so the child stays in the immediate relative category.

EXAMPLE: The U.S. citizen father of Yasmeen, a 20-year-old girl, files an I-130 petition for her along with an application for adjustment of status to permanent resident. By the time of the interview, however, Yasmeen is 22 years old. Fortunately, under the CSPA, Yasmeen's age of 20 years old was permanently frozen or "locked in" when the petition was filed, so she is considered 20 years old for as long as it takes USCIS to approve her green card.

B. Relatives in Preference Categories: Longer Waits

In all family-based preference categories, petitions from U.S. citizens generally have higher priority than those of lawful permanent residents.

Family first preference: unmarried sons or daughters of U.S. citizens. This category is for children who are 21 years old or older and not married— meaning either single, divorced, or widowed. (A son or daughter who is under 21 years old and not married would be classified as an immediate relative.) A maximum of 23,400 immigrant visas are now available worldwide for the family first preference category. The current waiting period is approximately seven years, but 22 years if you're from Mexico and 13 years from the Philippines.

Family second preference: spouses and unmarried children of permanent residents. This category is divided into two parts, including:

- husbands and wives of lawful permanent residents and their unmarried children who are under 21 years old (Category 2A), and
- unmarried (meaning single, divorced, or widowed) sons or daughters (over 21 years old) of a lawful permanent resident (Category 2B, which waits somewhat longer than Category 2A).

A total of 114,200 immigrant visas worldwide are given to second preference immigrants. However, 77% (87,934) of the total is intended for the spouses and minor children of green card holders (2As), while 23% (26,266) of the total is meant for the unmarried children over 21 years of age (2Bs).

The typical wait in Category 2A is approximately two to three years. In Category 2B, the current wait is approximately seven years, except that applicants from Mexico wait about 22 years and applicants from the Philippines wait about 13 years.

Family third preference: married sons and daughters of U.S. citizens. What if a U.S. citizen's unmarried son or daughter (in the family first preference category) gets married before entering the U.S. as a lawful permanent resident? Or what if he or she is married already? Either way, the third preference category provides a solution, although the waits tend to be long. Only 23,400 visas worldwide are made available every year for married sons and daughters of U.S. citizens.

The current wait in the third preference category is approximately 12 years, except that applicants from Mexico and the Philippines wait as many as 21 years.

Family fourth preference: brothers and sisters of U.S. citizens. The brother or sister of a U.S. citizen has to wait until the U.S. sibling turns 21 years of age before a petition can be filed for the alien brother or sister. A total of 65,000 visas worldwide are available each year for this category. The waiting list is always very long, from 14 to 24 years.

C. Dealing With the Wait

If you belong to a preference category in which there are many hopeful immigrants waiting—for example, in Mexico, there are well over 750,000 brothers and sisters of U.S. citizens on file—you could have to wait several years for your immigrant visa number.

If, during these years, you want to come to the United States as a nonimmigrant—as a tourist, businessperson, student, or other category—be prepared for it to be more difficult for you to get that visa. Once a visa petition has been filed for you by a family member, the U.S. government figures you intend to come to the U.S. and stay permanently—which disqualifies you from most short-term visas.

You might be able to convince the U.S. consul that you will not remain illegally in the United States waiting for your immigrant visa to come up by demonstrating your ties to your home country. You are more likely to be able to show that you will not remain in the U.S. illegally if you are in a category requiring a wait of ten years or more, rather than one or two.

There are only a few exceptions to the general rule that nonimmigrants must convince the U.S. consul that they do not intend to stay permanently in the U.S. One is for people who qualify for certain temporary work statuses (H and L visas). Although they might have an approved I-130 petition by reason of their U.S. citizen spouse, child, parent, brother, or sister, or a lawful permanent resident spouse or parent, the U.S. embassy is supposed to issue them an H or L visa if they qualify for that nonimmigrant visa while waiting for a visa number to become available. Another is for spouses of U.S. citizens who might qualify for the newly expanded K visa (see Chapter 7).

D. Can You Predict How Long You'll Wait?

No one can tell you for certain how long you'll wait for a visa or green card. If you're an immediate relative, you'll get your best estimate from asking people who work in the office you're dealing with what the current expected application processing times are. Processing times for certain applications are also posted on USCIS's website at www.uscis.gov. Click "Check Processing Times." You choose the type of application or petition and the office or service center at which your case is pending. You'll be given a range of months for that type of case at that office.

If you are not in the immediate relative category, you should pay careful attention to the U.S. State Department's *Visa Bulletin* to track how long you're likely to spend on the waitlist; see the information about the Visa Cutoff Date in Section 2, below.

1. The Priority Date

The Priority Date is the date on which your relative began the process by filing a petition for you with USCIS (or INS, as it was formerly called).

The first notification of your Priority Date will be on the receipt notice that your relative gets, showing the date the petition was received and the fee paid to USCIS. That date will also be shown on your approval notice, which is the next piece of paper your relative will get from USCIS—and which is even more important to keep while you wait for your Priority Date to become current.

CAUTION

Your relative might wait several years for an answer on the initial I-130 petition. In 2004, USCIS announced a new policy on handling approvals and denials of Form I-130 petitions. Instead of reviewing all petitions in the order received, they began prioritizing those filed on behalf of people whose visas will be

available sooner. That means that if you're in a category with long waits, your U.S. citizen or resident relative could receive a receipt notice one year and the approval notice several years later, when it's almost time for you to immigrate. This practice won't add any delays to your overall wait—it's like having two sources of delay going on simultaneously. It will, however, add uncertainty to your life, since you won't know until the last minute whether the initial petition will be approved or denied.

The Department of State keeps careful count of how many immigrant visas are issued for each country in each preference category. If the quota has been reached in one category before the fiscal year is over (in October), the department will not issue any immigrant visas in that category for the rest of the fiscal year and will, in addition, state that visas are temporarily unavailable for that category, either for a particular country or worldwide.

October 1 of each year marks the beginning of another fiscal year for the federal government—and the count of the immigrant visas issued begins all over again for each country in each preference category.

2. Tracking Your Progress: Visa Cutoff Date

Each month, the Department of State issues a *Visa Bulletin*, which sets out the immigrant visa cutoff date of each visa preference, as a signal of who can move forward with their applications. See the sample below.

The State Department in fact publishes two charts each month: Final Action and Dates for Filing. The Final Action chart controls when you can actually receive your green card. The Dates for Filing chart controls when you can either submit an I-485 Application to Adjust Status from within the United States (see Chapter 16), if you already are here, or when you can start submitting your documents to the National Visa Center to prepare for consular processing (see Chapter 17). A layer of complexity on top of the two charts is that USCIS

Excerpt from *Visa Bulletin* for November 2019					
Family Sponsored	All Chargeability Areas Except Those Listed	CHINA-mainland born	INDIA	MEXICO	PHILIPPINES
F1	01MAR13	01MAR13	01MAR13	08AUG97	15SEP08
F2A	C	C	C	C	C
F2B	08JUL14	08JUL14	08JUL14	22AUG98	01OCT08
F3	15OCT07	15OCT07	15OCT07	22FEB96	01JUN98
F4	01JAN07	01JAN07	15OCT04	15DEC97	01SEP98

decides each month whether it will follow the Final Action or Dates for Filing chart and publishes the relevant chart in the Green Card section of its website (www.uscis.gov) under "Visa Availability & Priority Dates."

The bottom line is that these dates announce which Priority Dates in each category are receiving attention from the Department of State because people holding those numbers have become eligible or soon will be eligible for an immigrant visa. All applicants whose Priority Date falls before the applicable cutoff date will be given an appointment within a few months if they're overseas, or will be allowed to submit the next part of their application if they're in the U.S. and eligible to adjust status there. Anyone whose priority date falls after the cutoff date will have to wait.

EXAMPLE: You were born in Poland. Your brother, who is a naturalized U.S. citizen, filed a petition for you on May 1, 2006, which becomes your Priority Date.

You are in the fourth preference category. The *Visa Bulletin* of November 2019 says the State Department is processing siblings with a Priority Date on or before January 1, 2007. Your appointment for your immigrant visa is currently available. It doesn't matter that the dates don't match exactly. The point is that people whose visa petitions were filed later than yours are receiving visas, so you should too.

However, if you were from another country, the waiting period could be longer, as you can see in the chart above.

The cutoff dates announced in the *Visa Bulletin* might not change much from one month to the next—sometimes one week for one preference and two weeks for another preference. Or the date might not move at all for several months in your category. Be prepared to wait.

Get the latest *Visa Bulletin* at https://travel.state.gov by clicking on "U.S. Visas" and then "Check the Visa Bulletin." Pay special attention to the Priority Date and the cutoff date that apply to your visa application. The *Visa Bulletin* is normally available in each embassy or consulate, or in USCIS offices. You can also call the Department of State in Washington, DC, at 202-485-7699 for a recorded message that gives the cutoff dates for each preference category being processed that month.

As noted above, there's one more chart you will want to look at in order to move your application forward quickly, if you are not the immediate relative of a U.S. citizen and you are planning to adjust status while in the United States. It's called the "Adjustment of Status Filing Charts from the Visa Bulletin," found at www.uscis.gov/visabulletininfo. Here, you will find a date when you can submit your adjustment application and whether or not you can apply for a work permit in the meantime. That date might be BEFORE your priority date is actually current (though because you'll likely wait several months for an interview, it should be current by the time it matters). Only an immigrant legally in the U.S. on a valid, long-term visa (such as a student or employment visa) can obtain a green card through adjustment of status procedures, however. See Chapter 16 for more information about this process.

You can subscribe to an email service that will automatically send you the latest *Visa Bulletin* every month as it becomes available. Details about how to do this can be found at the bottom of the bulletin itself.

3. Some People Can Switch Preference Categories

A special rule applies to family-based immigrant visas, allowing you to hang onto your Priority Date if you change from one preference category to another.

If you belong to one family preference, and some event (marriage, divorce, death of spouse, or the simple passage of time) places you in a different preference category, your original Priority Date might remain unchanged. That means you won't lose much ground, because your place on the new waiting list will reflect the fact that your petition was filed long before many other people's.

The types of situations in which a family-based beneficiary who has undergone a change of circumstance can convert to another category without losing the original Priority Date include:

- Marriage of the son or daughter (over 21 years old) of U.S. citizen—moves down from first to third preference.
- Marriage of child (under 21 years old) of U.S. citizen—moves down from immediate relative to third preference.
- Divorce of child or adult son or daughter— moves up from third preference to immediate relative or first preference, depending on child's age at divorce.

- Naturalization of legal resident petitioner— 2A spouse and unmarried children under 21 move up from second preference to immediate relative and children age 21 or older move to first preference from category 2B.
- Child of lawful permanent resident reaching age 21 before Priority Date becomes current —drops from category 2A to category 2B of the second preference. However, if the child reaches age 21 after his or her Priority Date has become current but before actual approval for permanent residency, the child can retain 2A status as long as he or she applies within one year of the Priority Date having become current. (This represents a 2002 change in the law—formerly, such children would have also dropped into category 2B, simply by virtue of not having received their approval on time, and therefore had to wait longer.)

CAUTION
Some life changes make you ineligible for any visa at all. Not everyone who marries, divorces, or whose petitioning family member dies can switch to another preference category. You can switch only if, at the time, an existing category fits your new situation. So, for example, the child of a U.S. citizen who marries can switch to the third preference category. But the child of a lawful permanent resident who marries is out of luck, because there's no category for married children of permanent residents. Such issues are explained further in Section E, below.

4. Advise USCIS If You Can Upgrade

If you can switch to a better (faster) visa category— most likely because the person petitioning for you has gone from being a permanent resident to being a U.S. citizen—you'll need to let USCIS know.

Sample Request for Upgrade to USCIS

123 Central Avenue
Treesbird, VT 14235
April 14, 2020

Department of Homeland Security
U.S. Citizenship and Immigration Services
P.O. Box 648005
Lee's Summit, MO 64064

RE: I-130 UPGRADE REQUEST
    Petitioner: Samuel Thornburgh
    Beneficiary: Junyi Cho

Dear Sir/Madam:

I filed an I-130 visa petition for the above-named beneficiary on February 11, 2020, during which time I was a U.S. permanent resident. That petition is still pending.

Since filing the petition, however, I have become a naturalized U.S. citizen. A copy of my naturalization certificate is attached.

Please continue processing this case, but as an immediate relative petition. Thank you for your attention to this matter.

Very truly yours,
Samuel Thornburgh

Enclosed: Copy of naturalization certificate
        USCIS Receipt Notice

How you do that depends first on where your file is located at the time of change. If, for example, your Form I-130 petition is still pending at a USCIS service center, you'll want to send a letter titled "I-130 UPGRADE REQUEST" identifying you and the petitioner and explaining the situation (see the sample above). Also be sure to include a copy (not the original) of the petitioner's signed naturalization certificate, and the receipt notice showing the Priority Date.

If the I-130 petition has already been approved, and the beneficiary is living outside the U.S., you'll need to contact the National Visa Center. Its online instructions for that say to submit a question through its "Ask NVC" Web page, but attorneys have found this gets no results. Thus, a better option is to send a similar letter along with a copy of the petition approval notice (Form I-797) from USCIS, to:

    National Visa Center
    31 Rochester Avenue, Suite 100
    Portsmouth, NH 03801-2915

And if the beneficiary is living in the U.S. and is eligible to adjust status, you don't need to send a letter anywhere. You simply submit the full adjustment of status application (Form I-485, with supporting documents and fees) with a copy of the I-130 approval and the naturalization certificate.

These rules might sound hard to follow, but because they can make a big difference in how quickly your application is processed, it is worth your time to understand which rules apply to your situation.

Situations Where Children Are Protected From Switching Categories

The Child Status Protection Act of 2002 allows certain children of U.S. citizens and permanent residents to retain their original visa eligibility even if they turn 21 while they're waiting for the process to finish up. (Formerly, turning 21 would have automatically dropped them into a lower preference category and caused them to have to wait longer for their visa or green card.) Those who benefit include:

- Children of U.S. citizens—will retain immediate relative status even if they turn 21 at any time after a visa petition has been filed on their behalf.
- Children of lawful permanent residents—will retain 2A status if they turn 21 after their Priority Date has become current, so long as they file for a green card within one year of becoming current. (Technically, by filing for the green card the child "locks in" his or her age at 21 minus the number of days it took USCIS to approve the initial I-130 visa petition. However, given USCIS delays, that almost always shaves off enough months to keep the child's age, for immigration purposes, at less than 21.)

Immigrant Story: Uniting the Family

Here is how the quota system affected Giti and Meena, two young sisters from Afghanistan.

After waiting for more than ten years, their father was about to get a green card through his U.S. citizen brother. He planned to bring his wife and two children with him, as is allowed in this visa category (family fourth preference). What the family did not realize, however, was how their plans would be affected if either of the sisters married or turned 21 years old before they entered the U.S.

Just before the visa interview, Giti, who was 19 years old, married a man from their town in Afghanistan. Her eligibility for the green card was destroyed.

Meena, on the other hand, was unmarried but 21 years and 6 months old at the time of the family's interview. Her eligibility was not destroyed, because legal protections provided by the Child Status Protection Act allow her (and other children in the preference categories) to subtract from her age the amount of time it took USCIS to approve the visa petition. In this particular case, it had taken USCIS nine months to approve the petition (and then the family waited another ten years for the Priority Date to become current). So Meena is considered to have another three months before "aging out." Once her visa is approved, she needs to be sure that she enters the U.S. before she ages out.

What should the family do about Giti? Although it will take a long time, Giti's best bet is for one or both of her parents to learn English and become a U.S. citizen as soon as possible (this will normally take at least five years). Next, the parents will need to petition for her and her husband under the family third preference category. They'll wait approximately seven years before being allowed to immigrate to the United States.

Giti's father wonders whether Giti shouldn't just divorce the young man. However, that would be considered immigration fraud if done just to allow her to get a green card. If the immigration authorities found out about the fraud, it would destroy her eligibility for any green card in any category.

E. Revocation of a Petition or Application

Here is a bit of scary information, but it's better to know it than not to know: After a petition or application has been filed on behalf of an alien, it can be revoked or canceled—even if it has already been approved by the INS or USCIS.

One reason for revocation would be the potential immigrant's unintended "failure to prosecute" the petition. This can happen when your relative, the petitioner, has not informed USCIS about address changes, and so does not get notification that USCIS is ready for further processing of your case. If USCIS gets no response after repeated attempts to contact the petitioner, it will assume that you are no longer interested in going forward on the petition. USCIS then can revoke and cancel the petition! To avoid this, make sure USCIS always has the petitioner's updated address, and sign up for USCIS's automatic email/text alerts.

Another reason for revocation is a change in your circumstances that makes you no longer eligible for the visa. It can also be based on a discovery that you committed fraud, for example by pretending to be someone's relation when you really weren't.

USCIS will normally revoke a petition if, for example:

- The person who filed the petition decides to withdraw it and informs USCIS of this decision.
- The person who filed the petition dies; however, USCIS might decide not to revoke the petition if the law allows you to self petition (as it does for widows/widowers of U.S. citizens) or if it is convinced that there are "humanitarian reasons" not to do so.
- In a marriage case, the couple divorces or the marriage is annulled before the green card is approved.
- In a family second preference case, the unmarried son or daughter gets married before the green card is approved.

TIP
Don't let the NVC think you're no longer interested. The National Visa Center (NVC) has a one-year contact rule, which requires you to contact it within one year of notification that a visa has become available. If you do not, your visa application can be terminated. Avoid trouble by simply acting on your visa application and following the NVC instructions about steps to take before your interview is scheduled. If circumstances arise that require you to delay visa processing (for example, your parent is ill and requires you to provide home care before moving to the U.S.), send a letter or email to the NVC explaining the delay.

Special Rules for Widows and Widowers

If the beneficiary is the spouse of a U.S. citizen, the petition will be granted as long as the widowed beneficiary was not legally separated or divorced from the citizen at the time of death, applies within two years of the spouse's death, and has not remarried.

Consider this scenario: A permanent resident mother has brought all her children to the United States except her eldest son, who marries before she could petition for him. After five years, she becomes a U.S. citizen and immediately files a petition for her married son, still living in the foreign country. The petition is approved, but before the son and his family come to the United States, the mother dies. The petition is automatically revoked, and the son remains separated from his brothers and sisters, who have been living in the United States since their mother received her green card.

That application of the regulations seems cruel. It is precisely for such cases that the regulations have been somewhat liberalized. The beneficiary of a petition filed by a U.S. citizen or by a permanent resident who dies before the alien beneficiary could come to the United States is no longer in an entirely hopeless situation.

With a lawyer's help, you might be able to show the immigration authorities that for "humanitarian reasons" revocation would be inappropriate. There is, however, a catch: Because every immigrant to the United States must have a financial sponsor—that is, someone who promises to support the immigrant if he or she is unable to support him- or herself—you will need to find a substitute sponsor for the person who died. Only certain people can fill this substitute role, including your spouse, parent, mother-in-law, father-in-law, sibling, son, daughter, son-in-law, or daughter-in-law. As in the case of other sponsors, your sponsor must maintain an annual income equal to at least 125% of the federal Poverty Guidelines.

Fiancé(e) Visas

The fiancé visa (K-1) was designed to allow people who've become engaged to—but haven't yet married—a U.S. citizen to travel to the U.S. for the wedding. Your minor children can go with you to the U.S. If you marry within 90 days, you and your children can apply for green cards. Otherwise, you must leave the U.S. before the date indicated on your passport.

Unfortunately, this visa isn't available to the fiancés of U.S. permanent residents (green card holders).

A. Who Qualifies for a Fiancé Visa

To qualify for a fiancé visa, you must:
- intend to marry a U.S. citizen (see Section 1, below)
- have met your intended spouse in person within the last two years (though this can be waived based on cultural customs or extreme hardship; see Section 2, below), and
- be legally able to marry (see Section 3, below).

It's important to realize that a fiancé visa is not a green card. It's only a temporary, 90-day right to be in the United States. However, it's included in this book because it's an important first step towards getting a green card. After the immigrant has arrived in the United States and gotten married, he or she can file for a green card—through a process called "adjustment of status"—at a U.S.-based USCIS office. (Or, if the immigrant has no desire for a U.S. green card, he or she can simply return home before the fiancé visa runs out.)

1. You Must Intend to Marry a U.S. Citizen

Of course you want to get married—but how do you plan to prove that to the U.S. government? As part of your application, you'll have to supply documents that show your intention to get married. We'll talk more about this in the sections that discuss paperwork.

TIP

Make your wedding plans flexible. You can't know exactly how long it will take to get a fiancé visa, but you'll have to hold your wedding within 90 days of entering the United States. Before you sign any contracts for catering, photographic, or other services, discuss the situation with the service providers and build some flexibility into your contracts or agreements in case the date needs to change.

The person you plan to marry must be a citizen, not a permanent resident, of the United States. A U.S. citizen is someone who was either:
- born in the United States or its territories
- became a citizen through a process of application and testing (called "naturalization"), or
- acquired or derived citizenship through a family member (for more information, see Nolo's website at www.nolo.com; search for the article entitled "U.S. Citizenship by Birth or Through Parents").

2. You Must Have Met in Person Within the Last Two Years

To protect against sham marriages, the law requires that you and your fiancé have met in person within the last two years. Even a brief meeting could be enough. Perhaps the immigrant can visit the United States on a tourist visa. However, getting approval for a tourist visa might be difficult, because the U.S. consulate might believe that the immigrant actually intends to get married and apply for the green card right away—which would be a misuse of the tourist visa, and could amount to visa fraud. It will probably be easier for the U.S. citizen to visit the immigrant overseas.

If, however, you're from a country where prospective husbands and wives don't meet before the wedding, for religious or cultural reasons, this meeting will obviously be a greater hardship. In such cases, you can ask the immigration authorities to "waive" (overlook) the meeting requirement. You'll need letters from your religious leader, parents, or other relevant people, and other proof of the normal practices in your culture, to succeed with your request. Getting a lawyer's help would be a good idea here.

U.S. Citizen Petitioners Must Disclose Criminal Records

After Congressional concern that immigrating fiancés were particularly susceptible to domestic violence and abuse—particularly those whose engagements were arranged through marriage brokers (so-called "mail order brides")—Congress passed the International Marriage Brokers Regulation Act of 2005 (IMBRA).

As a result, the fiancé visa petition (Form I-129F) now asks *all* U.S. citizen petitioners whether they have a history of violent crime and crime relating to alcohol or controlled-substance abuse. In addition, Form I-129F now asks whether you and your fiancé or spouse met through an international marriage broker.

Many reputable online dating websites are exempt from IMBRA requirements and are not considered to be "mail order bride" services. A dating website or organization that does not serve mainly to provide international dating services between U.S. citizens and foreign residents and charges similar rates to both Americans and foreigners and men and women will not be considered "an international marriage broker" for IMBRA purposes. Nor will traditional nonprofit religious or cultural matchmaking services, as long as they otherwise comply with U.S. and local laws. If you did use a marriage broker, the immigrant will be asked, at the visa interview, whether the broker complied with legal requirements to collect information on the U.S. fiancé or spouse's criminal record and pass it to the immigrant.

---

3. You Must Be Legally Able to Marry

For most people, the requirement that you be legally able to marry won't pose any problems. However, if one of you is already married or too young to legally marry in the state or country where you plan to perform the wedding, or if the two of you are close relatives, such as cousins, and forbidden to marry in the state or country where you plan to hold the wedding, you might not qualify for a fiancé visa.

If possible, take steps to correct the problem—for example, obtain a divorce, figure out a different place to marry, or wait until you're older.

Same-sex couples saw a major hurdle removed when the U.S. Supreme Court issued its decision in *Obergefell v. Hodges*. As of June 26, 2015, same-sex couples can now marry in any U.S. state or territory. Before the *Obergefell* decision, same-sex marriage was permitted in only a minority of states. As a result, many same-sex couples needed to travel to another state in order to legally marry after the foreign fiancé's arrival in the United States. Keep in mind that a civil union or domestic partnership will not work for immigration purposes, and both opposite- and same-sex couples must legally marry in order for the foreign fiancé to eventually obtain a green card.

B. Quick View of the Fiancé Visa Application Process

Here's what to plan for on your path to a fiancé visa:

1. The U.S. citizen submits a fiancé petition to USCIS (on Form I-129F).
2. USCIS sends the U.S. citizen a receipt notice, after confirming that the application is complete, then (within months) a notice of its decision, hopefully approving the petition. (Occasionally, USCIS will call in the U.S. citizen petitioner for an interview before deciding on the petition.)

3. USCIS transfers the file to an intermediary called the National Visa Center (NVC), which then transfers it to the U.S. consulate serving the immigrant's country. The consulate instructs the immigrating fiancé on what documents to prepare.

4. The immigrating fiancé attends the interview, and if all goes well, is approved for a fiancé visa. The visa might need to be picked up on a separate day or might be mailed. The immigrant must use it to enter the U.S. within six months.

C. Detailed Instructions for the Fiancé Visa Application Process

Obtaining a fiancé visa—also called a K-1 visa—requires time, patience, and paperwork.

1. Documents Required for Fiancé Visa Petition

To start the process, the U.S. citizen must prepare or provide the following:

☐ Form I-129F, Petition for Alien Fiancé(e). (See the sample at the end of this chapter, done for the immigrant; get the latest one at www.uscis.gov/i-129f.)

☐ Separate passport-style color photographs of the U.S. citizen and the alien fiancé.

☐ Form G-1145 (optional, but useful so that you'll receive an email or text notification from USCIS when it has gotten your application; it's available at www.uscis.gov/g-1145).

☐ Proof of the U.S. fiancé's U.S. citizenship, such as a copy of a passport, birth certificate, or naturalization certificate (see Chapter 21, Section D3 for details).

☐ Proof that any previous marriages have been terminated by death, divorce, or annulment and proof of any name changes. Evidence of name changes may be found on a marriage certificate, divorce decree, or court order showing the name change.

Immigrant Story: Proving They'd Met

Doug, from Ireland, and Carol, a U.S. citizen, met online and exchanged emails for over a year before they decided to get married. However, Carol was living with her parents in Philadelphia while she finished her Ph.D. in medieval history, and her family was extremely protective. She knew they would have panicked at the idea of her so much as corresponding with a stranger online, much less marrying him.

So although Carol definitely wanted to meet Doug before the wedding, she decided a secret meeting would be best. When a history conference took her to Newark, New Jersey, she suggested to Doug that he meet her there. They stayed with friends of Carol's, had a great time, and reaffirmed their intention to marry.

Then came time to prove that they'd met the meeting requirement. Carol suddenly realized she had almost no proof of their meeting. She'd driven to Newark, hadn't paid for a hotel room, and had eaten either conference food or in her friends' kitchen the whole time. But after thinking harder, she realized she'd paid for gas with a credit card while in New Jersey, and registration materials from the conference. Plus, Carol's friends had taken a photo of the couple and posted it on social media during their trip. This, plus proof of Doug's plane ticket, was enough to satisfy the meeting requirement, and Doug was granted a fiancé visa.

☐ Proof that the U.S. citizen and the foreign-born fiancé have met each other within the past two years: photographs, plane tickets, letters, social media posts during the time you met, travel itineraries, hotel receipts, etc. This evidence will also help show that your relationship is genuine.

☐ If the U.S. citizen has ever been convicted of any violent crime, or a crime involving domestic violence or substance abuse (a more complete list is provided in the instructions to Form I-129F), certified copies of all police and court records showing the outcome (get a lawyer's help in this instance).

☐ Proof that the two of you intend to marry within 90 days after the foreign-born fiancé arrives in the U.S.: for example, emails, letters, online chat logs, telephone records, letter from the religious or civil authority who will officiate at the wedding, receipts or contracts for the wedding location or wedding expenses, such as flowers, food, music, and formal wear, and engagement or wedding announcement or invitation. It used to be that both the U.S. citizen and foreign-born fiancé had to submit signed statements about their relationship and intention to marry. Now, the U.S. citizen provides information about how the couple met in Form I-129F—but it's still advisable to provide additional statements about why you decided to marry (see sample at end of chapter).

☐ Filing fee (currently $535), either by credit card (fill out USCIS Form G-1450, Authorization for Credit Card Transactions), or by check or money order, payable to the U.S. Department of Homeland Security. (You do not, however, have to pay the fee if you're already married and filing Form I-129F after filing a Form I-130 in order to obtain a K-3 visa, as described in Chapter 7.)

two complete photocopies of everything, including the check or money order. This will be extremely important in the all-too-common event that USCIS misplaces the petition. Send one copy to the immigrating fiancé, for his or her records. The U.S. citizen should assemble the original package neatly, and preferably write a cover letter that lists, in bullet points, everything inside.

The petitioner should send the completed visa petition by certified mail, return receipt requested, to the appropriate USCIS lockbox. (See the USCIS website for contact details. As of this book's print date, all I-129F petitions were to be mailed to a Texas lockbox.) You *cannot* just walk the form into your local USCIS office.

It is also a good idea to file Form G-1145, asking USCIS to send you an email and/or text notification when your application has been accepted. (See sample at the end of this chapter.)

Once you have a receipt from USCIS, you can use the receipt number to sign up to receive automatic email updates that let you know whenever mail is sent regarding your application. Go to the USCIS website at www.uscis.gov and click "Check Case Status." Here, you can also sign up for a USCIS account, so as to register for automatic case status updates by email or text message.

TIP

Where did Form G-325A go? The most recent version of Form I-129F (dated 11/07/18) requests information about the petitioner's and the beneficiary's parents, previous marriages, and address and employment history. Previously, this information was submitted to USCIS on a separate biographical information form, Form G-325A— but it's no longer required with a fiancé visa application.

2. Where and How to Send the Fiancé Petition

Once the U.S. citizen petitioner has prepared everything on the above list, he or she should make

CAUTION

When's the most frustrating part of the process? Many K visa petitioners and beneficiaries report that it's the waiting period between when USCIS approves the Form I-129F petition and when the National Visa Center (NVC) takes further action and sends the case file to the U.S. embassy or consulate abroad. The NVC is notoriously slow and backlogged. USCIS advises that NVC case processing normally takes up to four weeks and you should wait until 30 days have elapsed before contacting it for further information. You can do so by calling 603-334-0700 or attempt an online inquiry via https://travel.state.gov (click "Get U.S. Visas" then "Immigrate" then "National Visa Center.")

What You'll Need for Your Consular Interview

It's never too early to begin gathering the necessary documents to bring with you to your scheduled interview at the U.S. embassy or consulate:

☐ the confirmation page and bar code, showing that you (and any accompanying family members) completed an online Form DS-160

☐ a current passport (unexpired for at least nine months after your intended entry to the U.S.) for yourself and for all of your unmarried children under 21 years of age, if they are coming with you or following you to the United States

☐ divorce or death certificates for any previous spouses of either you or the U.S. citizen, with English translations

☐ police clearance from all places you have lived for more than six months (except from the United States, where USCIS gathers the information)

☐ originals of all documents, copies of which were submitted by your U.S. citizen fiancé

with Form I-129F (see the sample at the end of this chapter) to confirm your relationship and show your eligibility for the visa

☐ two passport-style photographs of yourself and each of any children applying with you for a visa (see Chapter 21, Section E for detailed photo requirements)

☐ a report of your own medical examination and those of all children over 14 years of age to verify that you've had all your vaccinations and no one has a communicable disease. You will need to get this medical exam from a designated panel physician. For a list of panel physicians near you, visit https://travel.state.gov.

☐ Form I-134, Affidavit of Support, filled out by your U.S. citizen fiancé. (See the sample at the end of this chapter.)

Some U.S. embassies and consulates require additional documents. Check the State Department website for details.

3. Visa Petition Interviews

Although it does not happen often, it is possible that the U.S. citizen petitioner will be called in for an interview by a USCIS officer. He or she should bring all original documents to the interview. If the documents and the interview convince USCIS that true romance is behind the planned marriage, the petition will be approved and a Notice of Action, Form I-797, will be mailed to the U.S. citizen. The form will contain instructions for the next step to take—and might include a request for additional information or documentation.

4. U.S. Consulate Notified of Approval

After USCIS approves the Form I-129F petition, it will advise a processing unit called the National Visa Center (NVC). The NVC will send you, the

immigrating fiancé, a receipt number as well as information on what to do next.

You'll need to complete Form DS-160, Online Nonimmigrant Visa Application, prior to your visa interview. It's fairly straightforward, but you will need Internet access and at least a limited command of the English language. There is no paper version of the form (for which reason we do not supply a sample in this book).

By setting your location and nationality on the Bureau of Consular Affairs website, you can get the questions and guidance translated into your native language. You will, however, need to answer all questions in English. Each applicant for a K visa (including any accompanying children) will need to complete a separate Form DS-160, though you can complete the form for any of your children under age 16.

Make sure you record the Application ID that you are given once you first begin the online form. This will allow you to retrieve a saved DS-160 if you do not complete it or if the application "times out" due to issues such as a poor Internet connection.

You will be asked for personal information, such as any names used, date and place of birth, address, phone number and email, any national identification or other numbers, and passport information.

Also, you will need a recent and clear digital photograph of yourself to upload, and information on your U.S. travel plans. You will be asked for your expected date of U.S. arrival, names of any travel companions, previous U.S. travel history and contacts, family information, and work and educational history.

Although you don't need to print the application for submission, it's a good idea to keep a copy for your records. You WILL need a copy of the DS-160 confirmation page and bar code to bring to your interview at the U.S. embassy or consulate, which will allow the consular officer to upload your application.

While the procedure for interviewing for a K visa at a U.S. consulate or embassy is largely the same in all countries, some consulates do have slightly different requirements for people scheduling and attending interviews. For example, many consulates require K visa applicants to pay the application fee (currently $265) before the appointment is scheduled. You can likely do so by using a credit or debit card online or calling a telephone to provide banking information. Additionally, some consulates will permit the U.S. fiancé to attend the interview along with the immigrating fiancé, while others do not.

After the consulate or embassy nearest to you receives your case file from the NVC, it will send you instructions about how to proceed (including information about authorized medical examiners and how to obtain police records in your area). Many consulates will send an appointment letter. You will need to contact the consulate to reschedule if there is a conflict with the assigned interview date. However, some consulates will require you to schedule your own interview, using your receipt number and DS-160 bar code number. Check the consulate's website for its specific instructions about scheduling nonimmigrant or K visa interviews and any additional documentation required at the interview.

If you live far away from the consulate, you might want to arrive a couple of days before your actual interview. This will give you time to have the medical exam done and receive the results (if no doctors closer to your home were on the consulate's list). Also, check out the situation around the consulate itself. Often, there are long lines, so you'll need to arrive well before your appointment time and expect to be let in long after. Many prospective immigrants who have applied for a visa at a local consulate have posted their experiences online, so it's worth doing some homework.

5. Interview at the Embassy

On the date of your interview at the U.S. embassy or consulate, bring all the forms and documents listed in the consulate's instructions and under "What You'll Need for Your Consular Interview," above.

Form I-134. This form, called an Affidavit of Support, is used to show that you will not become a public charge (dependent on government support) while in the U.S., because your petitioner/sponsor has sufficient income and/or assets to support you. See the sample Form I-134 toward the end of this chapter (the latest is available at www.uscis.gov/i-134). Note that at one time, it was necessary to sign this form in front of a notary public, but no longer.

It's important to realize, however, that you'll need to prove you won't become a public charge at a later date, after you marry and apply for the green card in the United States. You will then need to submit a new Affidavit of Support on a different form, Form I-864, which comes with more demanding income requirements. Form I-134 sponsors need only show that their income is at least 100% of the federal Poverty Guidelines, while

I-864 sponsors must show that it reaches 125%. In support of this form, the citizen should add copies (as appropriate) of his or her:

- ☐ bank statements
- ☐ recent tax returns and W-2s
- ☐ employment verification (make this an original letter from the employer detailing salary, hours, and whether the position is temporary or permanent), and
- ☐ if necessary to bring the citizen's income above the Poverty Guidelines levels, documents showing the value of any of the following property, if owned: bonds and stocks, real estate, and mortgage information or life insurance.

Medical exam. The immigrating fiancé will also need to have a medical exam done. The fiancé can't just go to the family doctor, but will have to go to a clinic specified by the consulate. The doctor will do an exam, ask questions about medical history and drug and alcohol use, take X-rays, and withdraw blood. Although vaccinations are not required for K visa issuance, they will be required when you adjust your status to permanent resident. Embassies therefore encourage fiancés to fulfill the vaccination requirements at the time of the fiancé medical examination. The cost (including vaccines) is usually around $300, but varies by country.

Forms for children. Most of the forms and documents must be separately filled out for you and for any minor children who will also be going to the United States.

Security checks. Because of new and increased security procedures, it is unlikely that you will receive your visa on the same day as you attend your interview. It can take several weeks for the consulate to run security checks on you—and even longer if you come from a country that the United States suspects of supporting terrorism.

Approval. If the U.S. consular official is ultimately convinced that you and your U.S. citizen fiancé are truly engaged to be married and will marry upon your arrival in the United States, and that you aren't barred from entry for any of the reasons described in Chapter 4, your passport will be stamped with the K-1 visa. The passports of your accompanying minor children will be stamped with the K-2 visa, meaning that they are dependent upon you for their immigration status.

Questions to Expect at K-1 Visa Interview

At your interview, the consular officer will ask a few basic questions about you and your fiancé and about five to ten additional questions to test the validity of your relationship. On average, the entire K-1 visa interview takes 15 to 30 minutes.

Be prepared for questions about any previous marriages and about your or your fiancé's children. Make sure you know basic information about your fiancé including occupation, hometown, birthday, and names of close family members. Other sample questions about your relationship might include:

- "How long did you date before you got engaged?"
- "What types of activities do you like to do together?"
- "How many times have you met in person? Where and when?"
- "How are you communicating during the long-distance relationship? Is it difficult being apart?"
- "Have you met your fiancé's family? Has he or she met yours?"
- "When and where will the wedding be held?"
- "Do you have any plans for a honeymoon?"

TIP
If you're already married but are applying for a K-3 fiancé visa, most of the advice in this section regarding the visa interview applies to you, too. However, you won't have to worry about convincing anyone that you plan to get married. Your main task will simply be to show that your paperwork is in order, with the understanding that you will complete the green card application after you've arrived in the United States.

The fiancé visa is considered a nonimmigrant visa because you are simply promising to marry a U.S. citizen. You are not yet an immigrant.

6. At the Border

Once you receive your fiancé visa, you'll have six months to use it to enter the United States. At the U.S. port of entry, the border officer will examine the contents of your visa envelope and ask you a few questions. Be careful with this—if the officer spots a reason that you should not have been given the fiancé visa, he or she has the power to deny your entry right there. You would have no choice but to find a flight or another means of transport home. And you might not be allowed back for five years (unless the officer allows you to withdraw the application before it's officially denied, which is entirely at the officer's discretion).

Assuming all goes well, the border officer will stamp your passport with your K-1 fiancé visa status, and indicate in your passport the 90-day duration of your status.

7. Permission to Work in the U.S.

When you arrive in the United States, you can apply at once for an Employment Authorization card that will enable you to work legally. The proper paperwork to complete for this is Form I-765. (See the USCIS website for the latest version, www.uscis.gov/i-765.)

However, you'll have to submit your application to a USCIS service center, and the service centers are famous for delays of many months. Submitting this application might not be worth the effort since the maximum time the work permit will be good for is three months (based on the length of your fiancé visa). You might be better off getting married, then submitting your green card application together with an application for a work permit.

This allows you more time to work before the card expires (it will last for approximately one year).

D. How to Bring Your Children on a Fiancé Visa

Your unmarried children under age 21 are eligible to accompany you on your fiancé visa and apply for green cards after you're in the United States and you have gotten married. This includes biological as well as adopted children. All you have to do at the beginning of the fiancé visa application process is to include your children's names in Part 2 of the fiancé petition (Form I-129F). You, as the parent, can complete a Form DS-160 for any accompanying child under age 16.

Your children will probably be asked to attend your consular interview with you, although some consulates let younger children stay home. The technical name of their visa will be K-2. For the visa interview, they'll normally be asked to bring:

- ☐ DS-160 confirmation receipt
- ☐ birth certificate (original and photocopy, with English translation)
- ☐ police record (if the child is over age 16)
- ☐ passport (unless your country permits the child to be included on your passport)
- ☐ two photos, and
- ☐ medical exam results.

Even if your children don't accompany you when you first enter the U.S. as a fiancé, they can join you under the same visa for a year after yours was approved. Just make sure they remain unmarried and under the age of 21. They'll need to complete Forms DS-160 and schedule an interview. If they don't plan to immigrate with you, but want to attend your wedding, their other option is a visitor visa.

When it comes time to apply for green cards, you and your children will each have to submit a separate application, before each of your visas expires.

TIP
Don't let anyone tell you that your child needs to have been under 18 when you were married. Some USCIS officers get confused when dealing with K-2 applicants for adjustment of status, and expect them to meet the standards for stepchildren that apply to certain other applicants. The confusion is common enough that USCIS sent out a general reminder memo to all of its offices in 2007. The bottom line: So long as your K-2 child is under 21 (and unmarried), and you've gotten married to your U.S. citizen petitioner, the child can apply to adjust status and get a green card.

E. Marriage and After

It's a good idea to marry as soon as possible after you arrive. That will give you enough time to prepare and submit your application for adjustment of status before your fiancé visa expires, so that you remain in lawful fiancé status the whole time. (See Chapter 16 for more information about submitting your application for adjustment of status.) There could be delays in preparing the application that are out of your control. For example, your local government office could take several weeks to issue your official marriage certificate, which is a required document in your adjustment of status package—USCIS will not accept your application with just the initial "souvenir" certificate issued by civil and religious authorities.

You should definitely try to marry within 90 days of entering the U.S., that is, before your fiancé visa expires. You can wait until after the 90 days to submit your adjustment of status application, but you will be without any legal status from the time the 90 days expires until USCIS receives your application.

If something happens and you miss the 90-day deadline for getting married, you and your fiancé can still go ahead and get married and file for your adjustment of status. The difference is that you will have to also submit a Form I-130 (visa petition) along with its filing fee, currently $535.

CAUTION
What if, after coming to the U.S., you change your mind and decide not to get married? In that case, you should leave the U.S. before your 90 days on the fiancé visa are up.

If you fail to marry your U.S. citizen fiancé at all, USCIS can start removal (deportation) proceedings against you and all children who came with you on a fiancé visa.

If you enter the U.S. on a fiancé visa, you can adjust your status to permanent resident only if you marry your fiancé. If you marry someone else, you cannot adjust your status based on that other marriage—although you might be able to get a green card through consular processing. (Check Chapter 4 to see whether any grounds of inadmissibility might apply if you try to consular process, particularly the bar that is triggered if you were in the U.S. for more than 180 days after the expiration of your fiancé status.)

If you do marry your U.S. citizen fiancé within 90 days, there is one more important step you must take in order to get a green card. You must file for adjustment of status (see Chapter 16), for yourself and all your minor children who came on the fiancé visa.

CAUTION
Beware of the two-year time limit. Going through the adjustment of status procedure will give you and your minor children conditional permanent residence status, and you will acquire a green card that is valid for only two years. To make it a permanent green card after the two years, follow the procedures for conditional permanent residents, laid out in Chapter 7.

Sample Form G-1145, e-Notification of Application/Petition Acceptance

e-Notification of Application/Petition Acceptance

Department of Homeland Security
U.S. Citizenship and Immigration Services

USCIS
Form G-1145

What Is the Purpose of This Form?

Use this form to request an electronic notification (e-Notification) when U.S. Citizenship and Immigration Services accepts your immigration application. This service is available for applications filed at a USCIS Lockbox facility.

General Information

Complete the information below and clip this form to the first page of your application package. You will receive one e-mail and/or text message for each form you are filing.

We will send the e-Notification within 24 hours after we accept your application. Domestic customers will receive an e-mail and/or text message; overseas customers will only receive an e-mail. Undeliverable e-Notifications cannot be resent.

The e-mail or text message will display your receipt number and tell you how to get updated case status information. It will not include any personal information. The e-Notification does not grant any type of status or benefit; rather it is provided as a convenience to customers.

USCIS will also mail you a receipt notice (I-797C), which you will receive within 10 days after your application has been accepted; use this notice as proof of your pending application or petition.

USCIS Privacy Act Statement

AUTHORITIES: The information requested on this form is collected pursuant to section 103(a) of the Immigration and Nationality Act, as amended INA section 101, et seq.

PURPOSE: The primary purpose for providing the information on this form is to request an electronic notification when USCIS accepts immigration form. The information you provide will be used to send you a text and/or email message.

DISCLOSURE: The information you provide is voluntary. However, failure to provide the requested information may prevent USCIS from providing you a text and/or email message receipting your immigration form.

ROUTINE USES: The information provided on this form will be used by and disclosed to DHS personnel and contractors in accordance with approved routine uses, as described in the associated published system of records notices [**DHS/USCIS-007 - Benefits Information System and DHS/USCIS-001 - Alien File (A-File) and Central Index System (CIS),** which can be found at **www.dhs.gov/privacy**]. The information may also be made available, as appropriate for law enforcement purposes or in the interest of national security.

Complete this form and clip it on top of the first page of your immigration form(s).

Applicant/Petitioner Full Last Name	Applicant/Petitioner Full First Name	Applicant/Petitioner Full Middle Name
Beach	Sandra	Leah

Email Address	Mobile Phone Number (Text Message)
sandrab@email.com	+1 (212) 222-1212

Form G-1145 09/26/14 Y

Page 1 of 1

Sample Form I-129F, Petition for Alien Fiancé(e) (page 1)

Petition for Alien Fiancé(e)		**USCIS**
Department of Homeland Security		**Form I-129F**
U.S. Citizenship and Immigration Services		OMB No. 1615-0001
		Expires 11/30/2020

For USCIS Use Only	Fee Stamp	Action Block
Case ID Number		
A-Number		
G-28 Number		

☐ The petition is approved for status under Section 101(a)(15)(K). It is valid for 4 months and expires on:
_____

Extraordinary Circumstances Waiver
☐ Approved ☐ Denied   Reason _____

General Waiver
☐ Approved Reason
☐ Denied _____

Mandatory Waiver
☐ Approved Reason
☐ Denied _____

AMCON: _____
☐ Personal Interview ☐ Previously Forwarded
☐ Document Check ☐ Field Investigation

Initial Receipt	Relocated	Completed	Remarks
	Received	Approved	
Resubmitted	Sent	Returned	

IMBRA disclosure to the beneficiary required? ☐ Yes ☐ No

▶ **START HERE - Type or print in black ink.**

Part 1. Information About You

1. Alien Registration Number (A-Number) (if any)
▶ A- ☐☐☐☐☐☐☐☐☐

2. USCIS Online Account Number (if any)
▶ ☐☐☐☐☐☐☐☐☐☐☐☐

3. U.S. Social Security Number (if any)
▶ 1 2 3 4 5 6 7 8 9

Select **one** box below to indicate the classification you are requesting for your beneficiary:

4.a. ☒ Fiancé(e) (K-1 visa)

4.b. ☐ Spouse (K-3 visa)

5. If you are filing to classify your spouse as a K-3, have you filed Form I-130? ☐ Yes ☐ No

Your Full Name

6.a. Family Name (Last Name) Beach

6.b. Given Name (First Name) Sandra

6.c. Middle Name Leah

Other Names Used

Provide all other names you have ever used, including aliases, maiden name, and nicknames. If you need extra space to complete this section, use the space provided in **Part 8. Additional Information**

7.a. Family Name (Last Name)

7.b. Given Name (First Name)

7.c. Middle Name

Your Mailing Address

8.a. In Care Of Name

8.b. Street Number and Name 114 Fulton St.

8.c. ☒ Apt. ☐ Ste. ☐ Flr. 6E

8.d. City or Town New York

8.e. State NY **8.f.** ZIP Code 10038

8.g. Province

8.h. Postal Code

8.i. Country USA

8.j. Is your current mailing address the same as your physical address? ☒ Yes ☐ No

If you answered "No," provide your physical address in **Item Numbers 9.a. - 9.h.**

Sample Form I-129F, Petition for Alien Fiancé(e) (page 2)

Part 1. Information About You (continued)

Your Address History

Provide your physical addresses for the last five years, whether inside or outside the United States. Provide your current address first if it is different from your mailing address in **Item Numbers 8.a. - 8.i.** If you need extra space to complete this section, use the space provided in **Part 8. Additional Information**.

Physical Address 1

9.a. Street Number and Name

9.b. ☐ Apt. ☐ Ste. ☐ Flr.

9.c. City or Town

9.d. State [ ]   **9.e.** ZIP Code

9.f. Province

9.g. Postal Code

9.h. Country

10.a. Date From (mm/dd/yyyy)   03/01/2019

10.b. Date To (mm/dd/yyyy)   present

Physical Address 2

11.a. Street Number and Name   95 Myrtle Lane

11.b. ☐ Apt. ☐ Ste. ☐ Flr.

11.c. City or Town   Chicago

11.d. State   IL   **11.e.** ZIP Code   60176

11.f. Province

11.g. Postal Code

11.h. Country   USA

12.a. Date From (mm/dd/yyyy)   04/15/2013

12.b. Date To (mm/dd/yyyy)   02/28/2019

Your Employment History

Provide your employment history for the last five years, whether inside or outside the United States. Provide your current employment first. If you need extra space to complete this section, use the space provided in **Part 8. Additional Information**.

Employer 1

13. Full Name of Employer
Gotham City Plumbing

14.a. Street Number and Name   1234 Batwing Lane

14.b. ☐ Apt. ☐ Ste. ☐ Flr.

14.c. City or Town   New York

14.d. State   NY   **14.e.** ZIP Code   10039

14.f. Province

14.g. Postal Code

14.h. Country   USA

15. Your Occupation (specify)
Plumber

16.a. Employment Start Date (mm/dd/yyyy)   03/10/2019

16.b. Employment End Date (mm/dd/yyyy)   present

Employer 2

17. Full Name of Employer
Windy City Maintenance

18.a. Street Number and Name   5678 Main St.

18.b. ☐ Apt. ☐ Ste. ☐ Flr.

18.c. City or Town   Chicago

18.d. State   IL   **18.e.** ZIP Code   60175

18.f. Province

18.g. Postal Code

18.h. Country   USA

19. Your Occupation (specify)
Repair Technician

Sample Form I-129F, Petition for Alien Fiancé(e) (page 3)

Part 1. Information About You (continued)

20.a. Employment Start Date (mm/dd/yyyy)　　`05/01/2013`

20.b. Employment End Date (mm/dd/yyyy)　　`02/28/2019`

Other Information

21. Gender　　☐ Male　☒ Female

22. Date of Birth (mm/dd/yyyy)　`12/22/1992`

23. Marital Status
☒ Single　☐ Married　☐ Divorced　☐ Widowed

24. City/Town/Village of Birth
`Chicago`

25. Province or State of Birth
`IL`

26. Country of Birth
`USA`

Information About Your Parents

Parent 1's Information

27.a. Family Name (Last Name)　`Beach`

27.b. Given Name (First Name)　`Bradley`

27.c. Middle Name　`James`

28. Date of Birth (mm/dd/yyyy)　`05/29/1967`

29. Gender　☒ Male　☐ Female

30. Country of Birth
`USA`

31.a. City/Town/Village of Residence
`Chicago`

31.b. Country of Residence
`USA`

Parent 2's Information

32.a. Family Name (Last Name)　`Beach`

32.b. Given Name (First Name)　`Rebecca`

32.c. Middle Name　`Grace`

33. Date of Birth (mm/dd/yyyy)　`09/14/1968`

34. Gender　☐ Male　☒ Female

35. Country of Birth
`USA`

36.a. City/Town/Village of Residence
`Deceased`

36.b. Country of Residence
`Deceased`

37. Have you ever been previously married?
☐ Yes　☒ No

If you answered "Yes" to **Item Number 37.**, provide the names of each spouse and the date that each prior marriage ended in **Item Numbers 38.a. - 39.** If you need extra space to complete this section, use the space provided in **Part 8. Additional Information**.

Name of Previous Spouse

38.a. Family Name (Last Name)

38.b. Given Name (First Name)

38.c. Middle Name

39. Date Marriage Ended (mm/dd/yyyy)

Your Citizenship Information

You are a U.S. citizen through (select **only one** box):

40.a. ☒ Birth in the United States

40.b. ☐ Naturalization

40.c. ☐ U.S. citizen parents

41. Have you obtained a Certificate of Naturalization or a Certificate of Citizenship in your own name?
☐ Yes　☐ No

If you answered "Yes" to **Item Number 41.**, complete **Item Numbers 42.a. - 42.c.**

Sample Form I-129F, Petition for Alien Fiancé(e) (page 4)

Part 1. Information About You (continued)

42.a. Certificate Number

42.b. Place of Issuance

42.c. Date of Issuance (mm/dd/yyyy)

Additional Information

43. Have you ever filed Form I-129F for any other beneficiary? ☐ Yes ☒ No

If you answered "Yes" to **Item Number 43.**, provide the responses to **Item Number 44. - 46.** for each previous beneficiary. If you need to provide information for more than one beneficiary, use the space provided in **Part 8. Additional Information**.

44. A-Number (if any) ▶ A-

45.a. Family Name (Last Name)

45.b. Given Name (First Name)

45.c. Middle Name

46. Date of Filing (mm/dd/yyyy)

47. What action did USCIS take on Form I-129F (for example, approved, denied, revoked)?

48. Do you have any children under 18 years of age? ☐ Yes ☒ No

If you answered "Yes" to **Item Number 48.**, provide the ages for your children under 18 years of age in **Item Numbers 49.a. - 49.b.**

Provide the ages for your children under 18 years of age. If you need extra space to complete this section, use the space provided in **Part 8. Additional Information**.

49.a. Age

49.b. Age

Provide all U.S. states and foreign countries in which you have resided since your 18th birthday.

Residence 1

50.a. State IL

50.b. Country USA

Residence 2

51.a. State NY

51.b. Country USA

Part 2. Information About Your Beneficiary

1.a. Family Name (Last Name) Hollis

1.b. Given Name (First Name) Nigel

1.c. Middle Name Ian

2. A-Number (if any) ▶ A-

3. U.S. Social Security Number (if any) ▶

4. Date of Birth (mm/dd/yyyy) 09/26/1991

5. Gender ☒ Male ☐ Female

6. Marital Status ☐ Single ☐ Married ☒ Divorced ☐ Widowed

7. City/Town/Village of Birth West Mersea

8. Country of Birth United Kingdom

9. Country of Citizenship or Nationality United Kingdom

Other Names Used

Provide all other names you have ever used, including aliases, maiden name, and nicknames. If you need extra space to complete this section, use the space provided in **Part 8. Additional Information**.

10.a. Family Name (Last Name)

10.b. Given Name (First Name)

10.c. Middle Name

Sample Form I-129F, Petition for Alien Fiancé(e) (page 5)

Part 2. Information About Your Beneficiary (continued)

Mailing Address for Your Beneficiary

11.a. In Care Of Name

11.b. Street Number and Name
123 Limestone Way

11.c. ☐ Apt. ☐ Ste. ☐ Flr.

11.d. City or Town
Penzance

11.e. State

11.f. ZIP Code

11.g. Province
Cornwall

11.h. Postal Code
TR197NL

11.i. Country
United Kingdom

Your Beneficiary's Address History

Provide your beneficiary's physical addresses for the last five years, whether inside or outside the United States. Provide your beneficiary's current address first if it is different from the mailing address in **Item Numbers 11.a. - 11.i.** If you need extra space to complete this section, use the space provided in **Part 8. Additional Information.**

Beneficiary's Physical Address 1

12.a. Street Number and Name

12.b. ☐ Apt. ☐ Ste. ☐ Flr.

12.c. City or Town

12.d. State

12.e. ZIP Code

12.f. Province

12.g. Postal Code

12.h. Country

13.a. Date From (mm/dd/yyyy)
08/16/2011

13.b. Date To (mm/dd/yyyy)
present

Beneficiary's Physical Address 2

14.a. Street Number and Name

14.b. ☐ Apt. ☐ Ste. ☐ Flr.

14.c. City or Town

14.d. State

14.e. ZIP Code

14.f. Province

14.g. Postal Code

14.h. Country

15.a. Date From (mm/dd/yyyy)

15.b. Date To (mm/dd/yyyy)

Your Beneficiary's Employment History

Provide your employment history for the last five years, whether inside or outside the United States. Provide your current employment first. If you need extra space to complete this section, use the space provided in **Part 8. Additional Information.**

Beneficiary's Employer 1

16. Full Name of Employer
Ocean Engineering

17.a. Street Number and Name
999 Cliffside Walk

17.b. ☐ Apt. ☐ Ste. ☐ Flr.

17.c. City or Town
Penzance

17.d. State

17.e. ZIP Code

17.f. Province
Cornwall

17.g. Postal Code
TR197NL

17.h. Country
United Kingdom

18. Beneficiary's Occupation (specify)
Engineer

19.a. Employment Start Date (mm/dd/yyyy)
06/25/2009

19.b. Employment End Date (mm/dd/yyyy)
02/01/2019

Sample Form I-129F, Petition for Alien Fiancé(e) (page 6)

Part 2. Information About Your Beneficiary (continued)

Beneficiary's Employer 2

20. Full Name of Employer

21.a. Street Number and Name

21.b. ☐ Apt. ☐ Ste. ☐ Flr.

21.c. City or Town

21.d. State [ ] **21.e.** ZIP Code

21.f. Province

21.g. Postal Code

21.h. Country

22. Beneficiary's Occupation (specify)

23.a. Employment Start Date (mm/dd/yyyy)

23.b. Employment End Date (mm/dd/yyyy)

Information About Your Beneficiary's Parents

Parent 1's Information

24.a. Family Name (Last Name)   Hollis

24.b. Given Name (First Name)   John

24.c. Middle Name   Michael

25. Date of Birth (mm/dd/yyyy)   07/22/1968

26. Gender   ☒ Male ☐ Female

27. Country of Birth
United Kingdom

28.a. City/Town/Village of Residence
Deceased

28.b. Country of Residence
Deceased

Parent 2's Information

29.a. Family Name (Last Name)   Sanders

29.b. Given Name (First Name)   Margaret

29.c. Middle Name   Joan

30. Date of Birth (mm/dd/yyyy)   10/29/1971

31. Gender   ☐ Male ☒ Female

32. Country of Birth
United Kingdom

33.a. City/Town/Village of Residence
West Mersea

33.b. Country of Residence
United Kingdom

Other Information About Your Beneficiary

34. Has your beneficiary ever been previously married?

☒ Yes ☐ No

If you answered "Yes" to **Item Number 34.**, provide the names of each prior spouse and the date each prior marriage ended in **Item Numbers 35.a. - 36.** If you need to provide information for more than one spouse, use the space provided in **Part 8. Additional Information.**

Name of Previous Spouse

35.a. Family Name (Last Name)   Cunningham

35.b. Given Name (First Name)   Lauren

35.c. Middle Name   Barbara

36. Date Marriage Ended (mm/dd/yyyy)   06/06/2015

37. Has your beneficiary ever been in the United States?

☒ Yes ☐ No

If your beneficiary is currently in the United States, complete **Item Numbers 38.a. - 38.h.**

38.a. He or she last entered as a (for example, visitor, student, exchange alien, crewman, stowaway, temporary worker, without inspection):

38.b. I-94 Arrival-Departure Record Number
▶ [ ][ ][ ][ ][ ][ ][ ][ ][ ][ ][ ]

38.c. Date of Arrival (mm/dd/yyyy)

Sample Form I-129F, Petition for Alien Fiancé(e) (page 7)

Part 2. Information About Your Beneficiary (continued)

38.d. Date authorized stay expired or will expire as shown on Form I-94 or I-95 (mm/dd/yyyy) [ ]

38.e. Passport Number [ ]

38.f. Travel Document Number [ ]

38.g. Country of Issuance for Passport or Travel Document [ ]

38.h. Expiration Date for Passport or Travel Document (mm/dd/yyyy) [ ]

39. Does your beneficiary have any children? [ ] Yes [X] No

If you answered "Yes" to **Item Number 39.**, provide the following information about each child. If you need to provide information for more than one child, use the space provided in **Part 8. Additional Information**.

Children of Beneficiary

40.a. Family Name (Last Name) [ ]

40.b. Given Name (First Name) [ ]

40.c. Middle Name [ ]

41. Country of Birth [ ]

42. Date of Birth (mm/dd/yyyy) [ ]

43. Does this child reside with your beneficiary? [ ] Yes [ ] No

If the child does not reside with your beneficiary, provide the child's physical residence.

44.a. Street Number and Name [ ]

44.b. [ ] Apt. [ ] Ste. [ ] Flr. [ ]

44.c. City or Town [ ]

44.d. State [ ] **44.e.** ZIP Code [ ]

44.f. Province [ ]

44.g. Postal Code [ ]

44.h. Country [ ]

Address in the United States Where Your Beneficiary Intends to Live

45.a. Street Number and Name [114 Fulton St.]

45.b. [X] Apt. [ ] Ste. [ ] Flr. [6E]

45.c. City or Town [New York]

45.d. State [NY] **45.e.** ZIP Code [10038]

46. Daytime Telephone Number [2122221212]

Your Beneficiary's Physical Address Abroad

47.a. Street Number and Name [123 Limestone Way]

47.b. [ ] Apt. [ ] Ste. [ ] Flr. [ ]

47.c. City or Town [Penzance]

47.d. Province [Cornwall]

47.e. Postal Code [TR197NL]

47.f. Country [United Kingdom]

48. Daytime Telephone Number [1736222222]

Your Beneficiary's Name and Address in His or Her Native Alphabet

49.a. Family Name (Last Name) [Hollis]

49.b. Given Name (First Name) [Nigel]

49.c. Middle Name [Ian]

50.a. Street Number and Name [123 Limestone Way]

50.b. [ ] Apt. [ ] Ste. [ ] Flr. [ ]

50.c. City or Town [Penzance]

50.d. Province [Cornwall]

50.e. Postal Code [TR197NL]

50.f. Country [United Kingdom]

Sample Form I-129F, Petition for Alien Fiancé(e) (page 8)

Part 2. Information About Your Beneficiary (continued)

51. Is your fiancé(e) related to you?

☐ Yes ☒ No ☐ N/A, beneficiary is my spouse

52. Provide the nature and degree of relationship (for example, third cousin or maternal uncle).

[ ]

53. Have you and your fiancé(e) met in person during the two years immediately before filing this petition?

☒ Yes ☐ No ☐ N/A, beneficiary is my spouse

If you answered "Yes" to **Item Number 53.**, describe the circumstances of your in-person meeting in **Item Number 54.** Attach evidence to demonstrate that you were in each other's physical presence during the required two year period.

If you answered "No," explain your reasons for requesting an exemption from the in person meeting requirement in **Item Number 54.** and provide evidence that you should be exempt from this requirement. Refer to **Part 2., Item Numbers 53. - 54.** of the **Specific Instructions** section of the Instructions for additional information about the requirement to meet. If you need extra space to complete this section, use the space provided in **Part 8. Additional Information**.

54. I first met my fiancé in October 2018, while visiting a friend who has settled in England. Nigel went to New York to visit me in July 2019. I also visited Nigel in England in December 2019, when we became engaged.

International Marriage Broker (IMB) Information

55. Did you meet your beneficiary through the services of an IMB? ☐ Yes ☒ No

If you answered "Yes" to **Item Number 55.**, provide the IMB's contact information and Website information below. In addition, attach a copy of the signed, written consent form the IMB obtained from your beneficiary authorizing your beneficiary's personal contact information to be released to you.

56. IMB's Name (if any)

[ ]

57.a. Family Name of IMB (Last Name)

[ ]

57.b. Given Name of IMB (First Name)

[ ]

58. Organization Name of IMB

[ ]

59. Website of IMB

[ ]

60.a. Street Number and Name [ ]

60.b. ☐ Apt. ☐ Ste. ☐ Flr. [ ]

60.c. City or Town [ ]

60.d. Province [ ]

60.e. Postal Code [ ]

60.f. Country [ ]

61. Daytime Telephone Number [ ]

Consular Processing Information

Your beneficiary will apply for a visa abroad at the U.S. Embassy or U.S. Consulate at:

62.a. City or Town

London

62.b. Country

United Kingdom

Part 3. Other Information

Criminal Information

NOTE: These criminal information questions must be answered even if your records were sealed, cleared, or if anyone, including a judge, law enforcement officer, or attorney, told you that you no longer have a record. If you need extra space to complete this section, use the space provided in **Part 8. Additional Information**.

1. Have you **EVER** been subject to a temporary or permanent protection or restraining order (either civil or criminal)? ☐ Yes ☒ No

Have you EVER been arrested or convicted of any of the following crimes:

2.a. Domestic violence, sexual assault, child abuse, child neglect, dating violence, elder abuse, stalking or an attempt to commit any of these crimes? (See **Part 3. Other Information, Item Numbers 1. - 3.c.** of the Instructions for the full definition of the term "domestic violence.") ☐ Yes ☒ No

Sample Form I-129F, Petition for Alien Fiancé(e) (page 9)

<table>
<tr><td colspan="2">

Part 3. Other Information (continued)

2.b. Homicide, murder, manslaughter, rape, abusive sexual contact, sexual exploitation, incest, torture, trafficking, peonage, holding hostage, involuntary servitude, slave trade, kidnapping, abduction, unlawful criminal restraint, false imprisonment, or an attempt to commit any of these crimes? ☐ Yes ☒ No

2.c. Three or more arrests or convictions, not from a single act, for crimes relating to a controlled substance or alcohol? ☐ Yes ☒ No

NOTE: If you were ever arrested or convicted of any of the specified crimes, you must submit certified copies of all court and police records showing the charges and disposition for every arrest or conviction. You must do so even if your records were sealed, expunged, or otherwise cleared, and regardless of whether anyone, including a judge, law enforcement officer, or attorney, informed you that you no longer have a criminal record. If you need extra space to complete this section, use the space provided in **Part 8. Additional Information**.

If you have provided information about a conviction for a crime listed in **Item Numbers 2.a. - 2.c.** and you were being battered or subjected to extreme cruelty at the time of your conviction, select all of the following that apply to you:

3.a. ☐ I was acting in self-defense.

3.b. ☐ I violated a protection order issued for my own protection.

3.c. ☐ I committed, was arrested for, was convicted of, or pled guilty to a crime that did not result in serious bodily injury and there was a connection between the crime and me having been battered or subjected to extreme cruelty.

4.a. Have you ever been arrested, cited, charged, indicted, convicted, fined, or imprisoned for breaking or violating any law or ordinance in any country, excluding traffic violations (unless a traffic violation was alcohol- or drug-related or involved a fine of $500 or more)? ☐ Yes ☒ No

4.b. If the answer to **Item Number 4.a.** is "Yes," provide information about each of those arrests, citations, charges, indictments, convictions, fines, or imprisonments in the space below. If you were the subject of an order of protection or restraining order and believe you are the victim, please explain those circumstances and provide any evidence to support your claims. Include the dates and outcomes. If you need extra space to complete this section, use the space provided in **Part 8. Additional Information**.

_____

_____

</td><td>

Multiple Filer Waiver Request Information

Refer to **Part 3. Types of Waivers** in the **Specific Instructions** section of the Instructions for an explanation of the filing waivers.

Indicate which one of the following waivers you are requesting:

5.a. ☐ Multiple Filer, No Permanent Restraining Orders or Convictions for a Specified Offense **(General Waiver)**

5.b. ☐ Multiple Filer, Prior Permanent Restraining Orders or Criminal Conviction for Specified Offense **(Extraordinary Circumstances Waiver)**

5.c. ☐ Multiple Filer, Prior Permanent Restraining Order or Criminal Convictions for Specified Offense Resulting from Domestic Violence **(Mandatory Waiver)**

5.d. ☐ Not applicable, beneficiary is my spouse or I am not a multiple filer

Part 4. Biographic Information

1. Ethnicity (Select **only one** box)
☐ Hispanic or Latino
☒ Not Hispanic or Latino

2. Race (Select **all applicable** boxes)
☒ White
☐ Asian
☐ Black or African American
☐ American Indian or Alaska Native
☐ Native Hawaiian or Other Pacific Islander

3. Height   Feet [5]   Inches [4]

4. Weight   Pounds [1][2][2]

5. Eye Color (Select **only one** box)
☐ Black   ☐ Blue   ☒ Brown
☐ Gray   ☐ Green   ☐ Hazel
☐ Maroon   ☐ Pink   ☐ Unknown/Other

6. Hair Color (Select **only one** box)
☐ Bald (No hair)   ☐ Black   ☐ Blond
☒ Brown   ☐ Gray   ☐ Red
☐ Sandy   ☐ White   ☐ Unknown/Other

</td></tr>
</table>

Sample Form I-129F, Petition for Alien Fiancé(e) (page 10)

Part 5. Petitioner's Statement, Contact Information, Declaration, Certification, and Signature

NOTE: Read the **Penalties** section of the Form I-129F Instructions before completing this part.

Petitioner's Statement

NOTE: Select the box for either **Item Number 1.a.** or **1.b.** If applicable, select the box for **Item Number 2.**

1.a. ☒ I can read and understand English, and I have read and understand every question and instruction on this petition and my answer to every question.

1.b. ☐ The interpreter named in **Part 6.** read to me every question and instruction on this petition and my answer to every question in

[   ],

a language in which I am fluent, and I understood everything.

2. ☐ At my request, the preparer named in **Part 7.**,

[   ],

prepared this petition for me based only upon information I provided or authorized.

Petitioner's Contact Information

3. Petitioner's Daytime Telephone Number

[2122221212]

4. Petitioner's Mobile Telephone Number (if any)

[2122221212]

5. Petitioner's Email Address (if any)

[sandrab@email.com]

Petitioner's Declaration and Certification

Copies of any documents I have submitted are exact photocopies of unaltered, original documents, and I understand that USCIS may require that I submit original documents to USCIS at a later date. Furthermore, I authorize the release of any information from any and all of my records that USCIS may need to determine my eligibility for the immigration benefit that I seek.

I furthermore authorize release of information contained in this petition, in supporting documents, and in my USCIS records, to other entities and persons where necessary for the administration and enforcement of U.S. immigration law .

I understand that USCIS may require me to appear for an appointment to take my biometrics (fingerprints, photograph, and/or signature) and, at that time, if I am required to provide biometrics, I will be required to sign an oath reaffirming that:

1) I reviewed and understood all of the information contained in, and submitted with, my petition; and

2) All of this information was complete, true, and correct at the time of filing.

I certify, under penalty of perjury, that all of the information in my petition and any document submitted with it were provided or authorized by me, that I reviewed and understand all of the information contained in, and submitted with my petition, and that all of this information is complete, true, and correct.

Petitioner's Signature

6.a. Petitioner's Signature

➡ [*Sandra L. Beach*]

6.b. Date of Signature (mm/dd/yyyy) [02/01/2020]

NOTE TO ALL PETITIONERS: If you do not completely fill out this petition or fail to submit required documents listed in the Instructions, USCIS may deny your petition.

Part 6. Interpreter's Contact Information, Certification, and Signature

Provide the following information about the interpreter.

Interpreter's Full Name

1.a. Interpreter's Family Name (Last Name)

[   ]

1.b. Interpreter's Given Name (First Name)

[   ]

2. Interpreter's Business or Organization Name (if any)

[   ]

Interpreter's Mailing Address

3.a. Street Number and Name [   ]

3.b. ☐ Apt. ☐ Ste. ☐ Flr. [   ]

3.c. City or Town [   ]

3.d. State [   ] **3.e.** ZIP Code [   ]

3.f. Province [   ]

3.g. Postal Code [   ]

3.h. Country

[   ]

Sample Fiancé Meeting Statement—Attachment to Form I-129F

Filed by Sandra Beach on Behalf of Nigel Hollis

Part 2, Question 54

I met my fiancé 18 months ago, while visiting a college friend who has settled in England. My friend Carrie had been telling me for months that she wanted to introduce me to Nigel, because of our offbeat senses of humor and shared interest in long-distance swimming. I've had bad experiences with friends trying to set me up before, so I didn't take it very seriously. But when vacation plans took me to England, I let her arrange for me and Nigel to meet over lunch at a pub.

To my amazement, we clicked right away. We had a lot to talk about—he had completed an English Channel swim a few months before, and I'm hoping to swim the Channel next year. Both of us have built our lives around swimming, which sometimes leaves little time for other things, including relationships. We compared notes on training techniques, equipment, dealing with cold water, rip tides, and more.

Our lunch lasted all afternoon and into the evening. By the end of that evening, I considered Nigel a friend, and someone I could very easily fall in love with.

Nigel and I spent almost all my remaining week's vacation together. Poor Carrie joked that her plan had backfired, because I spent embarrassingly little time at her house. By the end of the week, we both knew this was headed toward a serious relationship.

Since then, Nigel and I have corresponded almost constantly by email, and call each other twice a week. During one long phone call, we decided to get married.

It was difficult deciding where we would live after marrying—Nigel has a beautiful cottage in Cornwall, and I could happily live in England. However, my mother is in poor health, and ever since my father passed away last year, she has relied on my help, so we agreed to make our home in New York.

As proof that Nigel and I are in love and plan to marry, I am attaching copies of his plane tickets to New York; photos of the two of us together; copies of our telephone bills and some of our emails; copies of catering and other contracts showing that the two of us plan to marry in July; and copies of our travel itinerary for New Zealand, where we will honeymoon.

Signed: _Sandra L. Beach_____
Sandra L. Beach

Date: _____2/1/20_____

Sample Form I-134, Affidavit of Support (page 1)

Affidavit of Support

Department of Homeland Security
U.S. Citizenship and Immigration Services

USCIS
Form I-134
OMB No. 1615-0014
Expires 02/28/2021

▶ **START HERE - Type or print in black ink.**

Part 1. Information About You (the Sponsor)

Your Full Name

1.a. Family Name (Last Name): Beach
1.b. Given Name (First Name): Sandra
1.c. Middle Name: Leah

Other Names Used

List all other names you have ever used, including aliases, maiden name, and nicknames. If you need extra space to complete this section, use the space provided in **Part 7. Additional Information**.

2.a. Family Name (Last Name):
2.b. Given Name (First Name):
2.c. Middle Name:

Sponsor's Mailing Address

3.a. In Care Of Name:
3.b. Street Number and Name: 114 Fulton Street
3.c. ☒ Apt. ☐ Ste. ☐ Flr. 6E
3.d. City or Town: New York
3.e. State: NY 3.f. ZIP Code: 10038
3.g. Province:
3.h. Postal Code:
3.i. Country: USA

4. Are your mailing address and physical address the same? ☒ Yes ☐ No

If you answered "No" to **Item Number 4.**, provide your physical address in **Item Numbers 5.a. - 5.h.**

Sponsor's Physical Address

5.a. Street Number and Name:
5.b. ☐ Apt. ☐ Ste. ☐ Flr.
5.c. City or Town:
5.d. State: 5.e. ZIP Code:
5.f. Province:
5.g. Postal Code:
5.h. Country:

Other Information

6. Date of Birth (mm/dd/yyyy): 12/22/1992
7.a. Town or City of Birth: Chicago
7.b. Country of Birth: USA
8. Alien Registration Number (A-Number) (if any) ▶ A-
9. U.S. Social Security Number (if any) ▶ 1 2 3 4 5 6 7 8 9
10. USCIS Online Account Number (if any) ▶

Citizenship or Residency or Status

If you are not a U.S. citizen based on your birth in the United States, or a non-citizen U.S. national based on your birth in American Samoa (including Swains Island), answer the following as appropriate:

11.a. ☐ I am a U.S. citizen through naturalization. My Certificate of Naturalization number is
11.b. ☐ I am a U.S. citizen through parent(s) or marriage. My Certificate of Citizenship number is

Form I-134 02/13/19

Page 1 of 8

Sample Form I-134, Affidavit of Support (page 2)

Part 1. Information About You (the Sponsor) (continued)

11.c. ☐ I derived my U.S. citizenship by another method. (Provide an explain in **Part 7. Additional Information**.)

11.d. ☐ I am a lawful permanent resident of the United States. My A-Number is

▶ A- ☐☐☐☐☐☐☐☐☐

11.e. ☐ I am a lawfully admitted nonimmigrant. My Form I-94, Arrival-Departure Record Number is

▶ ☐☐☐☐☐☐☐☐☐☐☐

12. I am ☐ years of age and have resided in the United States since (Date) (mm/dd/yyyy) ☐

Part 2. Information About the Beneficiary

This affidavit is executed on behalf of the following person:

1.a. Family Name (Last Name) `Hollis`

1.b. Given Name (First Name) `Nigel`

1.c. Middle Name `Ian`

2. Date of Birth (mm/dd/yyyy) `09/26/1991`

3. Gender ☒ Male ☐ Female

4. A-Number (if any) ▶ A- `9 8 7 6 5 4 3 2 1`

5. Country of Citizenship or Nationality `United Kingdom`

6. Marital Status
☐ Single or Single, Never Married
☐ Married
☒ Divorced
☐ Widowed
☐ Legally Separated
☐ Marriage Annulled
☐ Other ☐

7. Relationship to Sponsor `Fiance`

Beneficiary's Physical Address

8.a. Street Number and Name `123 Limestone Way`

8.b. ☐ Apt. ☐ Ste. ☐ Flr. ☐

8.c. City or Town `Penzance`

8.d. State ☐ **8.e.** ZIP Code ☐

8.f. Province `Cornwall`

8.g. Postal Code `TR197NL`

8.h. Country `United Kingdom`

Beneficiary's Spouse (accompanying or following to join beneficiary)

9.a. Family Name (Last Name) ☐

9.b. Given Name (First Name) ☐

9.c. Middle Name ☐

10. Date of Birth (mm/dd/yyyy) ☐

11. Gender ☐ Male ☐ Female

Beneficiary's Children

Child 1

12.a. Family Name (Last Name) ☐

12.b. Given Name (First Name) ☐

12.c. Middle Name ☐

13. Date of Birth (mm/dd/yyyy) ☐

14. Gender ☐ Male ☐ Female

Child 2

15.a. Family Name (Last Name) ☐

15.b. Given Name (First Name) ☐

15.c. Middle Name ☐

16. Date of Birth (mm/dd/yyyy) ☐

17. Gender ☐ Male ☐ Female

If you need additional space to complete this section, use the space provided in **Part 7. Additional Information**.

Sample Form I-134, Affidavit of Support (page 3)

Part 3. Other Information About the Sponsor

Employment Information

I am currently:

1.a. ☒ Employed as a/an   Plumber

1.a.1. Name of Employer (if applicable)

Gotham City Plumbing

1.b. ☐ Self employed as a/an

Current Employer Address (if employed)

2.a. Street Number and Name   1234 Batwing Lane

2.b. ☐ Apt.   ☐ Ste.   ☐ Flr.

2.c. City or Town   New York

2.d. State   NY   **2.e.** ZIP Code   10039

2.f. Province

2.g. Postal Code

2.h. Country   USA

Income and Asset Information

3. My annual income is $ 75,000

(If self-employed, I have attached a copy of my last income tax return or report of commercial rating concern which I certify to be true and correct to the best of my knowledge and belief. See Instructions for nature of evidence of net worth to be submitted.)

4. Balance of all my savings and checking accounts in United States-based financial institutions $ 10,500

5. Value of my other personal property $ 8,000

6. Market value of my stocks and bonds $ 0

I have listed my stocks and bonds in **Part 7. Additional Information** (or attached a list of them), which I certify to be true and correct to the best of my knowledge and belief.

7.a. I have life insurance in the sum of $

7.b. With a cash surrender value of $

Real Estate Information

8.a. I own real estate valued at $

8.b. I have mortgages or other debts amounting to $

My real estate is located at:

9.a. Street Number and Name

9.b. ☐ Apt.   ☐ Ste.   ☐ Flr.

9.c. City or Town

9.d. State   **9.e.** ZIP Code

Dependents' Information

The following persons are dependent upon me for support. If you need extra space to complete this section, use the space provided in **Part 7. Additional Information**.

10.a. Family Name (Last Name)

10.b. Given Name (First Name)

10.c. Middle Name

11. Relationship to Me:

12. Date of Birth (mm/dd/yyyy)

13. This person is:

☐ Wholly Dependent On Me For Support

☐ Partially Dependent On Me For Support

14.a. Family Name (Last Name)

14.b. Given Name (First Name)

14.c. Middle Name

15. Relationship to Me:

16. Date of Birth (mm/dd/yyyy)

Sample Form I-134, Affidavit of Support (page 4)

Part 3. Other Information About the Sponsor (continued)

17. This person is:

☐ Wholly Dependent On Me For Support

☐ Partially Dependent On Me For Support

18.a. Family Name (Last Name) [   ]

18.b. Given Name (First Name) [   ]

18.c. Middle Name [   ]

19. Relationship to Me: [   ]

20. Date of Birth (mm/dd/yyyy) [   ]

21. This person is:

☐ Wholly Dependent On Me For Support

☐ Partially Dependent On Me For Support

I have previously submitted affidavit(s) of support for the following person(s). (If none, write "None" in the space for name below.)

22.a. Family Name (Last Name) [   ]

22.b. Given Name (First Name) [   ]

22.c. Middle Name [   ]

23. Date Submitted (mm/dd/yyyy) [   ]

24.a. Family Name (Last Name) [   ]

24.b. Given Name (First Name) [   ]

24.c. Middle Name [   ]

25. Date Submitted (mm/dd/yyyy) [   ]

I have submitted a visa petition(s) to U.S. Citizenship and Immigration Services on behalf of the following persons. (If none, write "None" in the space for name below.)

26.a. Family Name (Last Name) [   ]

26.b. Given Name (First Name) [   ]

26.c. Middle Name [   ]

27. Relationship to Me: [   ]

28. Date of Birth (mm/dd/yyyy) [   ]

29. Date of Filing (mm/dd/yyyy) [   ]

30.a. Family Name (Last Name) [   ]

30.b. Given Name (First Name) [   ]

30.c. Middle Name [   ]

31. Relationship to Me: [   ]

32. Date of Birth (mm/dd/yyyy) [   ]

33. Date of Filing (mm/dd/yyyy) [   ]

34.a. Family Name (Last Name) [   ]

34.b. Given Name (First Name) [   ]

34.c. Middle Name [   ]

35. Relationship to Me: [   ]

36. Date of Birth (mm/dd/yyyy) [   ]

37. Date of Filing (mm/dd/yyyy) [   ]

38. I ☐ intend ☐ do not intend to make specific contributions to the support of the person(s) named in **Part 2**.

(If you select "intend," indicate the exact nature and duration of the contributions you intend to make in **Part 7. Additional Information.** For example, if you intend to furnish room and board, state for how long and, if money, state the amount in U.S. dollars and whether it is to be given in a lump sum, weekly or monthly, and for how long.)

Sample Form I-134, Affidavit of Support (page 5)

Part 4. Sponsor's Statement, Contact Information, Certification, and Signature

NOTE: Read the Penalties section of the Form I-134 Instructions before completing this part.

Sponsor's Statement

NOTE: Select the box for either **Item Number 1.a.** or **1.b.** If applicable, select the box for **Item Number 2.**

1.a. ☒ I can read and understand English, and I have read and understand every question and instruction on this affidavit and my answer to every question.

1.b. ☐ The interpreter named in **Part 5.** read to me every question and instruction on this affidavit and my answer to every question in

[   ] ,

a language in which I am fluent and I understood everything.

2. ☐ At my request, the preparer named in **Part 6.**,

[   ] ,

prepared this affidavit for me based only upon information I provided or authorized.

Sponsor's Contact Information

3. Sponsor's Daytime Telephone Number

[2122221212]

4. Sponsor's Mobile Telephone Number (if any)

[2122221212]

5. Sponsor's Email Address (if any)

[sandrab@email.com]

Sponsor's Certification

Copies of any documents I have submitted are exact photocopies of unaltered, original documents, and I understand that USCIS or the Department of State may require that I submit original documents to USCIS or the Department of State at a later date. Furthermore, I authorize the release of any information from any of my records that USCIS or the Department of State may need to determine my eligibility for the immigration benefit I seek.

I further authorize release of information contained in this affidavit, in supporting documents, and in my USCIS or the Department of State records to other entities and persons where necessary for the administration and enforcement of U.S. immigration laws.

I understand that USCIS may require me to appear for an appointment to take my biometrics (fingerprints, photograph, and/or signature) and, at that time, if I am required to provide biometrics, I will be required to sign an oath reaffirming that:

1) I reviewed and provided or authorized all of the information in my affidavit;

2) I understood all of the information contained in, and submitted with, my affidavit; and

3) All of this information was complete, true, and correct at the time of filing.

I certify, under penalty of perjury, that I provided or authorized all of the information in my affidavit, I understand all of the information contained in, and submitted with, my affidavit, and that all of this information is complete, true, and correct.

That this affidavit is made by me to assure the U.S. Government that the person named in **Part 2.** will not become a public charge in the United States.

That I am willing and able to receive, maintain, and support the person named in **Part 2.** I am ready and willing to deposit a bond, if necessary, to guarantee that such persons will not become a public charge during his or her stay in the United States, or to guarantee that the above named persons will maintain his or her nonimmigrant status, if admitted temporarily, and will depart prior to the expiration of his or her authorized stay in the United States.

That I understand that Form I-134 is an "undertaking" under section 213 of the Immigration and Nationality Act, and I may be sued if the persons named in **Part 2.** become a public charge after admission to the United States.

That I understand that Form I-134 may be made available to any Federal, State, or local agency that may receive an application from the persons named in **Part 2.** for Food Stamps, Supplemental Security Income, or Temporary Assistance to Needy Families.

That I understand that if the person named in **Part 2.** does apply for Food Stamps, Supplemental Security Income, or Temporary Assistance for Needy Families, my own income and assets may be considered in deciding the person's application. How long my income and assets may be attributed to the persons named in **Part 2.** is determined under the statutes and rules governing each specific program.

I acknowledge that I have read the section entitled **Sponsor and Beneficiary Liability** in the Instructions for this affidavit, and am aware of my responsibilities as a sponsor under the Social Security Act, as amended, and the Food Stamp Act, as amended.

Sponsor's Signature

6.a. Sponsor's Signature

[*Sandra L. Beach*]

6.b. Date of Signature (mm/dd/yyyy) [8/11/20]

Green Cards Through Marriage

Every year, thousands of immigrants fall in love with U.S. citizens or permanent residents. Some couples meet overseas, others meet when the foreign national is studying or traveling in the United States. In a few cases, both members of the couple are foreign born, but one becomes a U.S. citizen or permanent resident. No matter how it came about, your topmost priority right now might be to join up in the U.S. as soon as possible. This chapter will lay out the possibilities and help you decide the easiest, fastest way to achieve this.

> ! CAUTION
> **We're assuming that you plan to live in the United States.** If not, there's no point in applying for a green card now. You won't get one if the U.S. citizen or permanent resident can't show that he or she is, or soon will be, living and earning income in the U.S., and you'll lose the green card if you don't make the U.S. your home. If you're going to be living overseas for a while, wait until your plans change to apply for the green card.

A. Who Qualifies

You are eligible for a green card if you have entered into a bona fide (genuine), legal marriage with a U.S. citizen or lawful permanent resident. Bona fide means that the marriage is based on your desire to create a life together with your new spouse, not merely on your desire to obtain a green card. Legal means that it is valid and recognized by the laws of the state or country in which you live. It doesn't matter whether you hold the marriage ceremony in the United States or overseas, but you do need to abide by local laws—and obtain a document, such as a marriage certificate, to prove that you've done so.

Marriage to a U.S. citizen makes you an immediate relative and eligible to receive a green card just as soon as you can get through the application process.

Marriage to a U.S. permanent resident, unfortunately, will not yield such fast results. Your new spouse can file a visa petition for you right away, but then you'll be placed in category 2A of the family visa preferences and have to wait, probably two or three years, before a green card becomes available to you. Only after that waiting period is over and you've applied for your green card will you be legally permitted to live in the United States.

The Inconveniences of Marriages of Convenience

In the early 1980s, the U.S. government came to believe that as many as half the petitions based on marriage were fraudulent—in other words, entered into solely for the purpose of obtaining a green card. In 1986, the U.S. Congress passed a law called the Immigration Marriage Fraud Amendments, to eliminate as many "paper marriages" as possible.

U.S. citizens, permanent residents, and aliens who evade immigration laws by means of a fraudulent marriage can be charged with a federal crime. Those found guilty can be imprisoned for up to five years, fined up to $250,000, or both. In addition, permanent residents can be deported, as can those who are undocumented.

If you are even entertaining the idea of entering into a sham marriage, consider the following:

- Do you want to live with the possibility of being blackmailed emotionally, psychologically, and financially?
- Do you want to be prosecuted for a federal crime with a penalty of five years in prison, a fine of up to $250,000, or both?

If USCIS discovers that you have entered into a marriage or even helped someone else enter into a marriage to evade the immigration laws—or if you have submitted papers to USCIS based on such a marriage—you will almost certainly forever lose the possibility of getting a green card, no matter what relationships you may have in the future.

CAUTION

If the U.S. petitioner has a criminal record, see an attorney. Under the Adam Walsh Child Protection and Safety Act of 2006, U.S. citizens and lawful permanent residents who have been convicted of any "specified offense against a minor" are prohibited from filing a family-based immigrant petition on behalf of any beneficiary (whether a child or not). USCIS will run security checks on all petitions and may call the petitioner in for fingerprinting. If the petitioner has a conviction for one of the specified offenses against a minor, then the petition will not be approved unless USCIS determines that the U.S. petitioner poses no risk to the beneficiary.

B. Special Rules in Court Proceedings

Suppose that removal—formerly called deportation or exclusion—proceedings have been started against you, perhaps because the immigration authorities have found that you are out of status or that you entered the U.S. without the proper documentation. While the proceedings are pending, you marry a U.S. citizen. You are now potentially eligible to file your marriage-based petition and the application for adjustment of status with the judge.

However, because you married while removal proceedings were going on, your marital status is suspect. After all, you did get married with the "shotgun" of a possible removal order facing you. You, the newly married alien, will have to provide clear and convincing evidence showing that the marriage was entered into in good faith and not solely for the purpose of getting a green card, and that no fee or financial arrangements were given for filing the petition. (Don't worry about the money you might have paid an attorney or other person to help you prepare and submit the application, which doesn't count.)

You will have to clearly establish that you married to establish a life together—for love and with a real commitment—not simply to avoid removal from the United States. See Section D4, below, for more guidance on gathering this kind of evidence. Also seek help from an experienced immigration attorney.

Same-Sex Couples May Obtain Green Cards Through Marriage

On June 26, 2013, the U.S. Supreme Court in *U.S. v. Windsor* struck down major portions of the federal Defense of Marriage Act (DOMA), which had blocked U.S. spouses in same-sex marriages from filing immigration applications on behalf of their foreign spouses. Two years later, the Supreme Court went one step further in *Obergefell v. Hodges* and legalized same-sex marriage in all U.S. states and territories. As a result, it is now easier than ever for same-sex couples to get married in the U.S. and then apply for immigration benefits. The procedures for same-sex couples are exactly the same as described in this chapter and the rest of the book.

Same-sex couples who are not legally married (including in domestic partnerships and civil unions) will need to marry first in order for the foreign resident to receive a green card. This might seem difficult if the foreign resident's country does not recognize same-sex marriage and international travel to the U.S. or another country where same-sex marriage is legal is expensive. The best way to get around this is to use the K-1 fiancé visa to bring your partner to the U.S. for the purpose of getting married (see Chapter 6 for information on fiancé visas).

C. Quick View of the Marriage-Based Green Card Application Process

Let's start with the general concept: To get a marriage-based green card, the U.S. citizen or permanent resident spouse must begin the process by submitting (by mail) a "petition" (Form I-130). (You can't just walk this form into your local USCIS office.) This form serves to prove to the immigration authorities that you're legally married. After that petition is approved, you, the immigrant, complete your half of the process by submitting a green card application and attending an interview, usually with your spouse. Your application serves to prove not only that your marriage is technically legal, but that it's the "real thing," and that you're otherwise eligible for U.S. permanent residence.

However, the details of when and how all this happens depend on several things: first, whether you, the immigrant, are living overseas or in the United States; and second, whether your spouse is a U.S. citizen or a permanent resident. We'll briefly describe each possible situation separately. It will also depend on the procedures, practices, and scheduling backup at the embassy where you'll be receiving your visa eventually.

Immigrant living overseas, married to a U.S. citizen, Option 1 (immigrant visa). Under the traditional methods, the U.S. citizen mails the I-130 petition to a USCIS office (unless the citizen also lives overseas, in which case some consulates will accept the visa petition directly). After USCIS approves the visa petition, the immigrant goes through consular processing (fully described in Chapter 17), which involves sending in fees and paperwork and ultimately attending a visa interview at a U.S. consulate in the immigrant's home country. At the interview (which only the immigrant is required to attend), the immigrant is approved for a visa. He or she must then use the visa to enter the United States within six months to claim his or her permanent residence (or "conditional" residence, if you've been married less than two years at this time; see Section F for details). The entire process can take a year or longer.

Immigrant living overseas, married to a U.S. citizen, Option 2 (K-3 visa). Several years ago, obtaining a visa overseas based on marriage was taking almost two years, while obtaining a fiancé visa was taking about nine months. The discrepancy was due to the amount of time that it took USCIS to make a decision on the initial petitions (the I-130 and the I-129F). To address this unfair situation, a method was devised to allow the long-waiting spouses of U.S. citizens to enter the U.S. within the same time frame as a fiancé, by allowing spouses to enter the U.S. on a kind of fiancé visa for married people, called a K-3 visa.

However, the K-3 visa process hasn't been worthwhile for many years, for timing reasons. The K-3 visa often takes about the same amount of time to process as entry on a regular immigrant visa, yet it's not the end of the process. When you enter the U.S. using a K-3, you will still have to submit paperwork to USCIS in order to receive a temporary work permit, permission to travel outside the U.S., and finally a green card. With the trend as of late 2019 toward longer processing times for U.S. citizen spouse green cards (up to 15+ months for the I-130 petition alone), however, the K-3 visa could again be something to consider. An immigration attorney can tell you the latest processing timelines, so it's worth consulting with one if you are considering applying for a K-3 visa.

If you decide to use the K-3 method, the U.S. citizen starts the process by mailing a petition (Form I-130) to USCIS. However, as soon as the U.S. citizen receives a receipt notice from USCIS, he or she can submit a separate, fiancé petition (Form I-129F) to USCIS.

After USCIS approves the fiancé petition, the immigrant goes through consular processing (described later in this chapter), and attends an interview at a U.S. consulate. The consulate approves the immigrant for a K-3, or fiancé, visa. This does not mean that the immigrant has been approved for a green card; the K-3 visa simply allows the immigrant to enter the United States in order to apply for the green card there.

After entering the U.S., the immigrant can prepare and mail an adjustment of status application to USCIS. After several months, the immigrant and his or her spouse must attend an interview, at which the immigrant will be approved for permanent residence (or conditional residence if they've been married for less than two years at that time; see Section F for details).

! CAUTION
The traditional marriage visa procedure is certainly cheaper. At the time this book went to press, Option 1, the traditional consular processing method, cost $980 in filing fees, form review fees, and immigrant visa fees. In contrast, the K-3 visa and adjustment of status (Option 2) cost a total of $2,025 in filing fees and nonimmigrant visa fees. (Keep in mind, there are also other, miscellaneous expenses associated with all green card applications, such as fees for translating non-English documents, getting a medical exam from a USCIS-approved physician, and obtaining birth certificates and police records.)

Immigrant living overseas, married to a U.S. permanent resident. The U.S. permanent resident mails the visa petition to USCIS. It will stay there until close to the time the immigrant's Priority Date is current (see Chapter 5 for a discussion of Priority Dates). After it's approved, it will be sent to the National Visa Center for further processing, before being forwarded to the U.S. consulate where the immigrant will attend his or her interview.

At the interview at a U.S. consulate (which only the immigrant is required to attend), the immigrant is approved for a visa and must then enter the United States within six months to claim permanent residence.

Immigrant living in the United States, married to a U.S. citizen. Ideally, the U.S. citizen mails the I-130 petition together with the immigrant's green card application (adjustment of status packet complete with forms, photos, and the results of a medical exam; you also can submit the medical exam results later) to USCIS. The immigrant is sent a fingerprint appointment notice and later an interview appointment notice. Both husband and wife must attend the interview, which will be held at a local USCIS district office. At the interview, the immigrant is approved for permanent residence (or conditional residence, if they've been married less than two years at this time; see Section F for details). However, not all immigrants are eligible to use the adjustment of status procedure—in particular, those whose last entry into the U.S. was made without inspection and admission by a border official are not. See Chapter 16 for details. Also, applying within 90 days of arriving in the U.S. can raise questions about "preconceived intent" concerning your true plans when you came to this country. If you are in this situation, consult an immigration attorney.

Immigrant Story: Dealing With Entry Without Inspection

Carmela, from Costa Rica, won the green card lottery one year, and moved to San Diego, California. Her boyfriend Jorge, who missed Carmela terribly, made his way to Mexico and then crossed the border to join her. Jorge was unable to get a visa or another document allowing him to enter the U.S. legally, so he and some friends crossed the border at an unguarded spot—in immigration law lingo, without being "inspected and admitted."

Jorge and Carmela got married seven months later, and picked up a copy of this book. Carmela then filed a Form I-130 visa petition on Jorge's behalf. However, they also realized that Jorge would be ineligible to adjust status in the United States after his Priority Date became current (which they expected to take a few years).

What's more, Jorge realized, when it came time to get his green card at a U.S. consulate, he could be barred from returning for three years, because he'd already stayed in the U.S. unlawfully for more than 180 days—and that if he stayed another five months, he would be barred from returning for a whole ten years. (A waiver based on extreme hardship to family helps some people avoid this ten-year bar, but Jorge's situation presents no such extraordinary circumstances.)

Jorge decides to leave the United States before his unlawful presence has added up to one year. The good news is, he can work off the three-year bar on reentering as soon as he's out of the U.S. and while he's waiting for his Priority Date to become current.

Immigrant living in the United States, married to a U.S. permanent resident. The U.S. permanent resident mails the visa petition to USCIS. It will stay there until close to the time the immigrant's Priority Date (discussed in Chapter 5) is current. After it's approved, however, things can get complicated. The only way the immigrant can remain in the United States to adjust status (submit a green card application) is if he or she has either been living legally in the United States during all the intervening years (in which case the immigrant can adjust status as described in this book) or started the process when previous laws were in effect. (See Chapter 16 for details on who can adjust status.) The immigrant's alternative is to continue with the case at an overseas U.S. consulate, but if the immigrant has been living illegally in the U.S., this could result in a three- or ten-year bar on reentry (as explained in Chapter 4). See an attorney for a full personal analysis.

> CAUTION
>
> **Entering the U.S. without inspection causes problems.** Except in rare circumstances (described in Chapter 16), people who entered the United States surreptitiously (for example, by crossing the border away from an inspection point) do not have the right to adjust status—that is, apply for a green card—in the United States. Attempting to turn your application in to USCIS could get you deported. Your best course is to get help from an experienced immigration attorney in evaluating and completing your application.

D. Detailed Instructions for the Marriage-Based Green Card Application Process

Now we'll break the application process down into individual procedures, some of which will be covered here and others in the next chapters—we'll tell you exactly where to turn to for your situation.

Note: The legal term for the U.S. citizen or permanent resident who is signing immigration papers for an alien spouse is "petitioner." The legal term for the immigrating spouse is "beneficiary."

1. Beginning the Process: The I-130 Petition

No matter what the circumstances, the U.S. citizen or permanent resident must prepare and collect the following items that make up the visa petition:

- ☐ Form I-130, Petition for Alien Relative. (See the sample at the end of this chapter, and get the latest version at www.uscis.gov/i-130. If using the K-3 visa process, attach a statement indicating that you plan to file Form I-129F and adjust status in the United States. Form I-130 must be signed by the U.S. citizen or permanent resident spouse. It gives information about both the petitioner and beneficiary.)
- ☐ Form I-130A, Supplemental Information for Spouse Beneficiary. (See sample at the end of this chapter, and get the latest version at www.uscis.gov/i-130.) Form I-130A must be filled out and signed by the "beneficiary" (immigrant spouse).
- ☐ Form G-1145. This is optional, but filing it is a good idea, so that you'll receive an email and/or text notification from USCIS when your application has been accepted. Get it from www.uscis.gov/g-1145. Once USCIS sends you a receipt number, you can use that number to sign up to receive automatic email updates letting you know whenever mail is sent regarding your application.

> TIP
>
> **Form G-325A no longer needed.** In 2017, USCIS updated many forms (including the I-130 and I-130A) to include biographical information about both the petitioner and the beneficiary, such as places of employment and residence and information about height, weight, eye color, and skin color. As a result, applicants no longer need to submit Form G-325A, which asked many of the same questions.

TIP

How to sign up for automatic email updates:
Go to www.uscis.gov and click "Check Case Status" on the home page. Then under "Why sign up for an account?" click on "Sign Up" and follow the prompts. Creating an account with USCIS will allow you to view your immigration application history in one place and to receive email or text message updates about your case.

☐ Photos of the immigrant and the spouse (one each). These must be passport style, in color, and taken within 30 days before the filing. See Chapter 21 for more detailed photo requirements. Write your name in pencil on the back of the photo, in case it gets separated from your file.

☐ Proof that the American half of the couple (the "petitioner") is either a U.S. citizen or permanent resident. If a citizen, the petitioner should provide a copy of his or her passport, birth certificate, naturalization certificate (don't worry, it's legal to photocopy it for this purpose), or copy of Form FS-240 (Report of Birth Abroad of a Citizen of the United States, issued by a U.S. consulate). If a permanent resident, the person should provide a copy of his or her green card (front and back), passport stamp, or USCIS approval notice.

☐ Documents to prove that there is a valid marriage, including copies of the documents listed below:

• **Marriage certificate.** Submit the civil registry certificate and not the marriage license or the church certificate, unless your country accepts a church marriage certificate as an official document. Marriage by proxy, a cultural practice in certain countries, is not acceptable to the immigration authorities.

• **Previous marriages.** If either of you was previously married, attach proof of the termination of the previous marriage—a divorce decree, an annulment decree, or a death certificate. Some foreign divorces might not be recognized by USCIS. The law provides that at least one of the parties must be living in the place where the divorce was granted. In addition, if the divorcing pair is living in the U.S., they should obtain a divorce in a local court, not at their embassy.

☐ Filing fee (currently $535) in the form of a check, money order, or certified check payable to the U.S. Department of Homeland Security. You may also pay by credit card, by filling out Form G-1450, Authorization for Credit Card Transaction (www.uscis.gov/g-1450). Place it on top of the stack of papers you send USCIS.

See Chapter 21 for more detailed instructions on preparing these documents.

When you've completed and assembled all these items, make two complete copies of the entire packet for yourself and your spouse. What you'll do with it next depends on where you are living, how you entered the U.S. and whether you're eligible to adjust status here, your spouse's status, and where your spouse is living, as detailed on the summary chart later in this chapter. Look under "Where to Mail the Application" for filing addresses.

2. Option for Overseas Spouses of U.S. Citizens: The Fiancé Visa Petition (K-3)

If you've elected to use the fiancé visa option to get you into the United States in order to adjust status there, the U.S. citizen will also need to submit a separate petition, consisting of:

☐ Form I-129F, Petition for Alien Fiancé(e). (See the sample for married couples at the end of this chapter.) The most important thing to realize about this form is that it's usually used for people who haven't yet gotten married— who are, in fact, fiancés. Don't be thrown off by instructions or questions directed at people who aren't yet married.

☐ Proof that the U.S. half of the couple (the petitioner) is a U.S. citizen, such as a copy of his or her passport, birth certificate, naturalization certificate (don't worry, it's legal to photocopy it for this purpose), or copy of Form FS-240 (Report of Birth Abroad of a Citizen of the United States, issued by a U.S. consulate).

☐ Proof that the U.S. citizen spouse has already filed Form I-130, Petition for Alien Relative, with USCIS. Wait until USCIS sends a Form I-797 receipt notice, then photocopy this and send the copy.

☐ Photos of the immigrant and the spouse (one each). These must be in color, passport style, and taken within the 30 days before the filing.

As a K-3 applicant, your petitioner need not pay the usual fee for this petition.

When you've completed and assembled all these items, make two complete copies for each of your records. Then mail the completed package to the USCIS lockbox shown on the Form I-129F instructions.

3. Moving the Process Forward

After the U.S. citizen or permanent resident spouse has submitted Form I-130 (and possibly Form I-129F or an adjustment of status packet) to USCIS, it's time to start playing the waiting game.

See Chapter 5 for a full explanation of how long you're likely to wait, and why. Spouses of U.S. permanent residents should understand that years-long waits are caused by limitations on the number of green cards given out in their category every year.

The sooner the permanent resident spouses can apply for U.S. citizenship, the better. Once they become citizens, the immigrating spouses automatically become immediate relatives, and can proceed with the application for a green card. (You don't even have to file a new I-130 petition—it's enough to advise USCIS that the petitioner has

become a citizen, by sending a letter, including a copy of his or her naturalization certificate, to the last USCIS office you corresponded with. See Chapter 5 for a sample letter.)

If you will be consular processing, and if your spouse is a U.S. citizen, the current (late-2019) processing time for a decision on the Form I-130 is approximately seven to 15 months.

If you will not be consular processing, but instead will be filing to adjust status in the U.S., then as long as you send your I-485 and other documents for adjustment of status along with your I-130, you might get a decision sooner, because it will be handled by the same USCIS office as will handle your interview.

Check current processing times by going to www.uscis.gov. Click "Check Processing Times." If you're proceeding with the consular processing method, select I-130 for case type and the service center where your I-130 is being processed (shown on your receipt notice). If using adjustment of status, select I-485 for case type and the Field Office where you will be interviewed and then review the processing time for the I-485 application (since your I-130 will be processed simultaneously with your I-485).

If your application seems to be held up due to a simple bureaucratic delay, see Chapter 21 for instructions on prodding USCIS into taking action.

TIP

What if the U.S. petitioner dies? If your U.S. citizen spouse submitted an I-130 on your behalf but then died before it was approved, all you need to do is submit proof of the death to USCIS, and it will automatically convert the I-130 to an I-360 "self-petition." You will then be able to proceed with processing your case. If the U.S. citizen did not submit the I-130 before dying, you can "self-petition" by submitting Form I-360. The requirements for this are that you and your U.S. citizen spouse were married (and not legally separated) at the time of death, that you file the self-petition within two years of the death, and that you have not remarried.

Summary Chart: From Petition to Green Card Application		
Your situation	**Where to mail the application**	**What's next**
You're living overseas, and your spouse is a U.S. citizen living in the United States.	**Option 1: Standard procedure.** The petitioner either submits the I-130 petition online at uscis.gov or sends it via Priority Mail with a return receipt requested to the USCIS lockbox in either Dallas or Phoenix, depending on where you live. This office will forward it to the service center that serves your spouse's geographic region. Find the correct address and post office box on the USCIS website at www.uscis. gov/ i-130-addresses.	**Option 1: Standard procedure.** As soon as the petition is approved, you'll be able to apply for your immigrant visa and green card through an overseas U.S. consulate. (See Chapter 17.)
	Option 2: K-3 visa. Although you're married, you're allowed to use a special type of fiancé visa to get you into the United States, after which you must apply to adjust status in order to become a permanent resident. To take advantage of this option, send Form I-130 as detailed above, but as soon as you can prove that USCIS received it, also send Form I-129F to the USCIS office where the I-130 is pending.	**Option 2: K-3 fiancé visa procedure.** As soon as USCIS approves the Form I-129F fiancé petition, you will be able to apply for a nonimmigrant visa at an overseas consulate (see Chapter 6, Section C5 for instructions). (If your Form I-130 is approved before your consular interview for the K-3 visa, the consulate will prefer to continue processing your case so that you can enter the U.S. as a permanent resident rather than as a fiancé. You might need to make sure that the I-130 approval is forwarded to the consulate. After you enter the United States, it's time to apply for a green card through USCIS (see Chapter 16 for instructions on the adjustment of status application). To avoid USCIS confusion, you should, as soon as possible after entering the U.S., send a letter to the service center processing the Form I-130 saying that you are here and will be adjusting status. (Without such a letter, some service centers have been known to send the case to the overseas consulate for processing.)

Summary Chart: From Visa Petition To Green Card Application (continued)

Your situation	Where to mail the application	What's next
You're living overseas, and your spouse is a U.S. lawful permanent resident living in the United States.	The petitioner either submits the I-130 petition online at www.uscis.gov or sends it via Priority Mail with a return receipt requested to the USCIS lockbox in either Dallas or Phoenix, depending on where the petitioner lives. This office will forward it to the service center that serves this geographic region. Find the correct address and post office box at www.uscis.gov/i-130-addresses.	Approval of the I-130 petition will give you a Priority Date, but you'll have to wait until that date is current to apply for your green card. You'll need to wait overseas during that time, after which you'll apply for your immigrant visa and green card through a U.S. consulate. (See Chapter 17.)
You're presently in the U.S., and your spouse is a lawful permanent resident.	The petitioner either submits the I-130 petition online at www.uscis.gov or sends it via Priority Mail with a return receipt requested to the USCIS lockbox in either Dallas or Phoenix, depending on where the petitioner lives. This office will forward it to the service center that serves this geographic region. Find the correct address and post office box at www.uscis.gov/i-130-addresses.	Approval of the I-130 petition will give you a Priority Date, but you'll have to wait until that date is current to apply for your green card. Unless you have a separate visa to remain in the U.S. for those years, or will be eligible to adjust status in the U.S (see Chapter 16), you might have to leave soon to avoid the three- and ten-year time bars for having lived in the U.S. illegally.
You're presently in the U.S., and your spouse is a U.S. citizen. **Situation one:** You entered the U.S. without inspection.	See an immigration attorney for help—you might not be able to apply for a green card without leaving the United States, which could expose you to a three- or ten-year bar on returning; or you might qualify for a provisional waiver of unlawful presence, allowing you to safely leave for a consular interview and return.	
Situation two: You entered legally (with a visa or on a visa waiver, no matter if your expiration date passed), but did not misuse your visa to enter in order to get a green card.	You are eligible to adjust status in the United States. Submit your I-130 petition in combination with the immigrant's adjustment of status application (Form I-485 and supporting documents, described in Chapter 16). See an attorney if you have already or plan to marry and/or submit your application within 90 days of arriving in the United States.	Await fingerprinting and, later, an interview at your local USCIS office.

For the next step in the process, see the "What's next" column in the summary chart above. For most immigrants, the next step will involve either applying for a green card from outside the United States, through a process called consular processing (discussed in Chapter 17), or from inside the United States, through a process called adjustment of status (discussed in Chapter 16). However, a few unlucky immigrants will get stuck at this point, realizing that because of past illegal entries into the U.S. or other problems, their application cannot go forward. Such persons should consult with an experienced immigration attorney.

TIP
Regardless of whether you will be completing your application overseas or in the United States, come back to this chapter for a discussion of materials that only married couples need to prepare in advance of their interview. (See Section D.6, below.)

4. Advice for Spouses of Permanent Residents

You cannot apply for a green card as a second preference alien—that is, as the spouse of a green-card holder—until your Priority Date is current. The 2A category often has a wait of about two years, though it's been much shorter recently. U.S. permanent residents are usually eager to naturalize as soon as possible in order to speed up green card processing for their spouses and children.

Pay close attention to the *Visa Bulletin* (see Chapter 5 for a discussion on the *Visa Bulletin* and Priority Dates) when deciding whether the U.S. petitioner spouse should apply for U.S. citizenship before filing or proceeding with a pending Form I-130.

However, despite current favorable conditions for permanent resident spouses, keep in mind that if the date of your permitted stay in the U.S. expired or if you worked without authorization ("fell out of status"), you will not be able to apply for adjustment of status unless your U.S. spouse first becomes a U.S. citizen.

5. Advice for People Who Entered the U.S. Without Inspection

If you entered the U.S. without being met and inspected by an immigration officer ("EWI") you most likely won't be able to adjust status in the United States. There is a rare exception for people who are covered by an old law, the LIFE Act, which allowed otherwise ineligible applicants to adjust status by paying a $1,000 penalty. While most foreign citizens who EWI would love to simply pay a penalty to avoid leaving the U.S. and possibly facing a time bar before being allowed to return, it covers only people with a visa petition or labor certification on file before January 14, 1998; or those who were physically present in the U.S. on December 21, 2000 with a visa petition on file by April 30, 2001.

As time passes, fewer and fewer people are able to benefit from the provisions of the LIFE Act. The vast majority of people who EWI'd therefore cannot adjust status in the U.S. and will instead need to apply for a green card at a U.S. consulate abroad.

If you came to the U.S. as an EWI and your period of unlawful presence in the U.S. is less than 180 days, you should leave the U.S. immediately in order to avoid being barred from reentering for three years. If it's already too late and you've been time barred from applying for a U.S. immigration benefit, you might be able to benefit from a new waiver, the provisional waiver of unlawful presence. (For more on inadmissibility, and the provisional waiver, see Chapter 4.)

6. Documenting Your Bona Fide Marriage

Whether you are applying for adjustment of status or for an immigrant visa at a consulate abroad, start gathering documents for your green card interview. At the interview, you must present not only the standard information that every immigrant does, but also separate documents showing that you have a real, valid marriage. These might include:

☐ birth certificates for all children born to you and your U.S. spouse

☐ leases on apartments that you two have occupied, together with rent receipts or canceled checks

☐ hospital cards, union books, insurance policies, pay vouchers, joint bank account statements, utility bills, or charge cards containing both your names

☐ federal income tax returns, filed jointly, for the years that you have been married

☐ your wedding pictures, and

☐ any snapshots of the two of you together taken before the marriage and, more importantly, since the marriage, taken in different locations, and taken with different people or groups of people who might appear to know that the two of you are a couple.

**Immigrant Story: Provisional Waiver Provides Assurance That
Spousal Visa Applicant Can Promptly Reenter U.S.**

In 2008, Miguel, a citizen of Costa Rica, entered the U.S. at a remote point on the Mexican border, without being inspected by an immigration officer. He settled in the U.S. and began working without permission. In 2010, Miguel married Andrea, a U.S. citizen. In 2011, Andrea gave birth to their son, Paul.

When Miguel and Andrea married, they were surprised to learn that Miguel could not adjust status in the United States. Even worse, because Miguel had spent so much time in the U.S. illegally, he would not be eligible to apply for a green card at a consulate abroad until at least ten years after departing the U.S. unless he was granted a waiver based on extreme hardship to his qualifying relatives.

In 2012, Andrea was severely injured in a car accident and was no longer able to work or provide full-time care for Paul. Miguel worked long hours in order to support the family. He consulted with an immigration attorney, who told him that based on these hardships he might qualify for a waiver, but that he would still need to return to Costa Rica in order to apply—and if denied, he could be stuck outside the U.S. for ten years before continuing with the green-card application. Miguel decided not to risk being separated from his family for so long.

In March 2013, USCIS announced that people who entered without inspection could apply for a provisional, "stateside" waiver of unlawful presence before leaving the United States. This means that Miguel could learn whether or not the waiver was approved before returning to Costa Rica for his consular interview.

Andrea filed Form I-130 and indicated that Miguel would apply for a green card using consular processing. After USCIS approved the I-130, Miguel enlisted the help of an immigration attorney and applied for the provisional waiver (using Form I-601A and including evidence of Andrea's injuries and her inability to work and care for their son full time). Miguel also included a letter from Andrea's doctor explaining that Andrea could not receive adequate medical treatment in Costa Rica and paystubs and tax returns showing that he was the sole earner in their family.

Miguel's provisional waiver application was approved. After submitting paperwork to the consulate in San Jose, Costa Rica, he received an interview date. At the interview, Miguel's immigrant visa was approved and about a week later, he received his passport and visa allowing him to reenter the U.S. as a legal permanent resident.

Collect and make copies of as many of these documents as possible. If you and your spouse have married for love, you will eventually prevail. Nevertheless, you still have to present the required documentary proof.

E. Bringing Your Children

People immigrating through marriage are often allowed to bring their children with them, even if the children are from a previous marriage or relationship. For immigration purposes, your children must be unmarried and under the age of 21 to immigrate at the same time as you. (Options for older or married children are discussed in Chapter 9.)

However, the exact rules and procedures for having your children immigrate with you depend on whether your U.S. spouse is a permanent resident or a citizen.

1. If You're Marrying a U.S. Citizen

If you're marrying a U.S. citizen, each of your children must separately qualify as an "immediate relative" of your spouse in order to immigrate with you.

To qualify as an immediate relative, your child can either be:

- the natural child of the U.S. citizen (if born out of wedlock to a U.S. citizen father, the father must have either legitimated the child while the child was under 18 and living in his custody, or demonstrated a bona fide relationship, through financial or other support), or
- the stepchild of the U.S. citizen, meaning it's legally your (the immigrant's) child, whether by birth or adoption, and you married the U.S. citizen before the child reached the age of 18.

Your spouse will need to submit a separate petition (Form I-130) for each one of these immediate-relative children, preferably in the same packet as the petition for you, the immigrant. (If you have no choice but to submit the petitions separately, write a letter to accompany the later petitions, explaining that you'd like the cases joined together.)

If you're also using a fiancé visa for U.S. entry, your spouse must additionally fill out a separate Form I-129F fiancé petition for each child.

2. If You're Marrying a U.S. Permanent Resident

If you're marrying a permanent resident, your children (natural or adopted) who are unmarried and under age 21 are considered "derivative beneficiaries." As a practical matter, this means that, at least at the beginning, your children won't need a separate petition in order to be included in your immigration process—your spouse must simply fill in the blanks on Form I-130 where it asks for the children's names. Unlike many other applicants, your children won't need to prove that your spouse is their parent or stepparent.

Your children will be given the same Priority Date as you, and most likely get a visa at the same time (provided they remain unmarried and under the age of 21). If they marry, they lose their chance to immigrate as beneficiaries. If they turn 21 before the Priority Date becomes current, they risk dropping into a separate visa category (2B) and having to wait longer for their Priority Date to become current in that category. Under the Child Status Protection Act, however, this situation is sometimes taken care of, because they get to subtract from their age the amount of time that they were waiting for USCIS to decide on the I-130.

EXAMPLE: Maria was 17 years old when her mother, Luisa, married a U.S. permanent resident, who immediately filed a petition for Luisa (which included Maria). Because USCIS knew that it would be approximately five years before the Priority Date became current in that category, USCIS waited three years and seven months to approve the petition. Under the old law, if the Priority Date was still not current when Maria turned 21 (four years after the petition was submitted), she would "age out" and immediately fall into the 2B category with a longer wait. Under the Child Status Protection Act, however, Maria gets to take into account the three years and seven months that she waited for the I-130 to be approved, so Maria will not "age out" until she is 24 years and seven months old. If her Priority Date still is not current at that point, she will drop into the 2B category.

3. Final Phases of Children's Green Card Application

After the I-130 petition has been approved and you and your children are ready to submit your paperwork for your green cards, each child must submit his or her own application, whether to the U.S. consulate overseas or to a U.S. immigration office. These applications are discussed in Chapters 16 and 17.

As a practical matter, however, you can help your child fill out the forms online, and even sign them if the child is too young (just write next to your signature, "by [*your name*], the child's [*mother or father*]."

F. If Your Marriage Is Less Than Two Years Old

If you become a U.S. resident within two years of the date you were married, whether you were granted your green card through adjustment of status or consular processing, your green card is only conditional—in other words, it expires in another two years. You are considered a "conditional permanent resident."

It seems contradictory to be both "permanent" and "conditional" at the same time, but it actually makes sense in this situation. This is because once you remove the conditional basis, your two years of conditional residence will count as unconditional or permanent residence for naturalization (citizenship) and other purposes.

To receive a green card without conditions that will be valid for more than two years, you could wait until you have been married at least two years before becoming a permanent resident. In fact, if you're overseas, this might mean delaying your date of entry to the United States—because even after you get your immigrant visa from the consulate, you're not a permanent resident until you go through a U.S. port of entry. If your marriage is already two years old at the time your permanent residence is granted, you are a full-fledged permanent resident and do not need to file papers to remove any conditions.

However, most people go ahead and become permanent residents, then wait two years minus 90 days and request the removal of the conditional status. Your foreign-born sons or daughters who might have been petitioned by your spouse must likewise apply for removal of their conditional statuses.

> (!) **CAUTION**
>
> **The timing of your request is crucial.** Mark on your calendar the third month before your second anniversary of becoming a conditional permanent resident, and get your application in before your residence expires. USCIS might send you a reminder, but keep track on your own, just in case (especially if you've changed addresses).

> **EXAMPLE:** Your date of admission as a conditional permanent resident was December 7, 2019, the date printed on your conditional green card. The second anniversary of your conditional permanent residence is December 7, 2021. And 90 days (three months) before the second anniversary of December 7, 2021 is September 7, 2021. Therefore, you must file for the removal of the conditional status any time after September 7, 2021 and before December 7, 2021.

1. Forms Required for Removal of Conditions

Within the 90 days before the second anniversary of your conditional permanent residence, you must submit the following:

☐ Form I-751, Petition to Remove the Conditions on Residence, signed by both husband and wife (see the sample at the end of this chapter, and get the latest version from www.uscis.gov/i-751), or by the alien spouse alone, if seeking a waiver, and

☐ the application fee (currently $590, which includes the biometrics fee) in the form of a money order or personal check, payable to U.S. Department of Homeland Security.

You must also present evidence of a true marriage. To do this, submit copies of as many of the following documents as possible (from within the past two years):

☐ your federal and state income taxes for the last two years (assuming they were filed as "married, filing jointly")

☐ title to house or condo or co-op, or any other real property showing joint ownership

☐ lease to your apartment showing joint tenancy since the time of marriage

☐ telephone or electric and gas bills showing both your names

☐ bank books or statements showing evidence of a joint checking or savings account; to prevent identity theft, you are allowed to partially black out the account numbers

☐ registration and title documents, with both names, of cars or any personal property

☐ insurance policies taken by husband or wife and showing the other as the beneficiary of any insurance benefits

☐ birth certificate of any child born of the marriage, showing both parents' names

☐ current letters from both husband and wife's employer on the company letterhead, stating present job and salary and the name of a person to be notified in case of emergency, if that person is your spouse

☐ current will showing one spouse as the beneficiary of the other's estate, and

☐ a minimum of two sworn statements from people who know that you are married. The letter writer could be your friend, relative, coworker, neighbor, or anyone else who knows that you are married. The person should give his or her own contact information—address and telephone number—and explain how he or she knows the two of you, and knows that you have a real marriage. It's helpful if the person can mention specific times and places at which you appeared as a married couple.

These documents should be sent by Priority Mail to the USCIS lockbox in either Dallas or Phoenix, depending on where you live. This office will forward it to the service center that serves your geographic region. (See the USCIS website for the address and P.O. box.) You might receive a notice for an interview, or your petition might be approved without one. If you receive a notice for an interview, we recommend that you have an attorney review your case prior to the interview.

While you're waiting for a decision, however, the receipt notice that you get from the USCIS service center will be your only proof that you are legally in the United States. Your stay will remain legal until a decision is made on your Form I-751, but the receipt notice normally expires in 18 months. As long as your receipt notice has not expired, you can use it in combination with your expired green card to prove your right to work and to return from foreign travel. If you travel, however, the border officials will likely take your expired green card and put a stamp in your passport.

In any case, with or without an interview, your green card becomes permanent only when UCIS decides to approve your joint petition.

TIP

What if 18 months have gone by and you still haven't gotten a USCIS decision on your I-751 application? Although you're technically still legal, it will be hard to prove that to anyone. The best thing to do is call the Customer Contact Center at 800-375-5283. They might be able to find out what's happening, and make an appointment at a local office, where you can get a stamp in your passport showing your conditional resident status.

2. If Your Spouse Does Not Sign the Joint Petition

If your spouse will not or cannot sign the joint petition, do not despair. Where certain circumstances are beyond your control, USCIS allows you, as the conditional permanent resident alien, to file without your spouse's signature.

You must fill out the same form, Form I-751, Petition to Remove the Conditions on Residence, and mail it with the same fee. However, you must also request one of the waivers described on the form. These waivers cover situations where:

- your spouse died
- you were the victim of battery or domestic abuse
- your marriage was valid when it occurred but is now legally terminated (you divorced or got an annulment), or
- you would suffer extreme hardship if removed.

These waivers require the assistance of an experienced immigration attorney. (See Chapter 24 for tips on finding a good one.)

3. People Married Two Years or More

If the original date of your admission as a permanent resident is more than two years after your marriage, you are not considered a conditional permanent resident. You are a full-fledged permanent resident and not subject to the conditions on residence.

EXAMPLE: You married a permanent resident on February 14, 2015, and a petition was filed on your behalf shortly thereafter in the second preference category. However, your visa number was not immediately available, and you had to wait a few years. You finally received your green card and were admitted as a permanent—not conditional—resident on July 4, 2019, more than two years after your date of marriage.

G. If You Marry Again

If your marriage ends in divorce or annulment after you receive your permanent green card, and then you marry another foreign-born person, it will be difficult for you to sponsor your new spouse for a green card.

To obtain permanent residence for your alien spouse during the first five years after you received your green card through marriage, you'll have to show by "clear and convincing evidence" that your first marriage—the one by which you got your green card—was not fraudulent and was entered into in good faith. (See I.N.A. § 204(a)(2)(A); 8 U.S.C. § 1154(a)(2)(A).) Again, this means showing you got married because you wanted to establish a life together, not just to get a green card.

In addition to the other proof required (see Section D, above), you will be asked to explain:

- why and when you got the previous divorce
- how long you lived with your first spouse
- how, when, and where you met your intended spouse, and
- facts about your courtship.

However, after you have been a green card holder for five years—the number of years required for naturalization—you can file a petition for your second spouse without providing such evidence.

Again, Congress provided this restriction because a number of alien couples had obtained green cards fraudulently. One of them would marry either a

U.S. citizen or a permanent resident. After getting the immigrant visa, the marriage to the citizen or permanent resident would be ended by divorce or annulment. The immigrant, then in possession of a valid green card, would then marry the original boyfriend, girlfriend, or spouse to give that person a green card, too.

H. Common Questions About Marriage and Immigration

The answers to most immigration questions depend on timing and the specific history of those involved, so it is difficult to give one correct response in solving a problem. There are, however, a number of questions that are asked over and over.

1. Before Marriage

Q: My boyfriend, who is a U.S. citizen, is getting a divorce soon. Can he file a petition now for me to get a green card?

A: No—because he has not yet legally ended his previous marriage, he cannot marry you now. He can marry you as soon as his previous divorce petition is finalized and file a petition once you receive a marriage certificate.

Q: I intend to marry a U.S. citizen, but because work obligations will require us to live in different states for a while, we will not be living together for the first six months or so after we're married. Can she file for me to get a green card?

A: Yes. But you will have to prove to the USCIS examiner that your marriage is true and not a sham. Good evidence of that would be ticket stubs from visits to one another; telephone bills, emails, texts, and instant messages showing frequent contact; stubs from social events you attended together such as movies, theater performances, and meals; copies of joint bank accounts; and bills bearing both of your names.

2. After Marriage

Q: I entered the U.S. with another name. Now I am married to a U.S. citizen using my real name. Can I get my green card?

A: Yes. But you might need to request that the misrepresentation be waived, or forgiven, before USCIS will approve your case. You should see a lawyer in this case.

Q: I have a minor child living with me in the U.S. and two more young children now living outside the U.S. Can I get green cards for all of them?

A: Yes—if your U.S. citizen spouse files separate petitions for them. If your spouse is a permanent resident, not a citizen, he or she can simply include the children on your visa petition.

Q: What will happen if my marriage legally ends before the conditional status of my green card is removed?

A: A conditional resident can file an application for a waiver with USCIS. However, because there are complicated matters of proof, it is best to consult an experienced immigration lawyer for help.

Sample Form I-130, Petition for Alien Relative (page 1)

Petition for Alien Relative

Department of Homeland Security
U.S. Citizenship and Immigration Services

**USCIS
Form I-130**

OMB No. 1615-0012
Expires 02/28/2021

For USCIS Use Only	Fee Stamp	Action Stamp

A-Number
A-

Initial Receipt

Resubmitted

Relocated	Section of Law/Visa Category
Received	☐ 201(b) Spouse - IR-1/CR-1 ☐ 203(a)(1) Unm. S/D - F1-1 ☐ 203(a)(2)(B) Unm. S/D - F2-4
Sent	☐ 201(b) Child - IR-2/CR-2 ☐ 203(a)(2)(A) Spouse - F2-1 ☐ 203(a)(3) Married S/D - F3-1
Completed	☐ 201(b) Parent - IR-5 ☐ 203(a)(2)(A) Child - F2-2 ☐ 203(a)(4) Brother/Sister - F4-1

Approved	Petition was filed on (Priority Date mm/dd/yyyy):	☐ Field Investigation ☐ Personal Interview ☐ 204(a)(2)(A) Resolved
Returned	PDR request granted/denied - New priority date (mm/dd/yyyy):	☐ Previously Forwarded ☐ Pet. A-File Reviewed ☐ I-485 Filed Simultaneously ☐ 203(g) Resolved ☐ Ben. A-File Reviewed ☐ 204(g) Resolved
Remarks		

At which USCIS office (e.g., NBC, VSC, LOS, CRO) was Form I-130 adjudicated? _____

To be completed by an attorney or accredited representative (if any).

☐ Select this box if Form G-28 is attached.

Volag Number (if any)

Attorney State Bar Number (if applicable)

Attorney or Accredited Representative USCIS Online Account Number (if any)

▶ **START HERE - Type or print in black ink.**

If you need extra space to complete any section of this petition, use the space provided in **Part 9. Additional Information.**
Complete and submit as many copies of Part 9., as necessary, with your petition.

Part 1. Relationship (You are the Petitioner. Your relative is the Beneficiary)

1. I am filing this petition for my (Select **only one** box):
   ☒ Spouse ☐ Parent ☐ Brother/Sister ☐ Child

2. If you are filing this petition for your child or parent, select the box that describes your relationship (Select **only one** box):
   ☐ Child was born to parents who were married to each other at the time of the child's birth
   ☐ Stepchild/Stepparent
   ☐ Child was born to parents who were not married to each other at the time of the child's birth
   ☐ Child was adopted (not an Orphan or Hague Convention adoptee)

3. If the beneficiary is your brother/sister, are you related by adoption? ☐ Yes ☒ No

4. Did you gain lawful permanent resident status or citizenship through adoption? ☐ Yes ☒ No

Part 2. Information About You (Petitioner)

1. Alien Registration Number (A-Number) (if any)
   ▶ A-

2. USCIS Online Account Number (if any)
   ▶

3. U.S. Social Security Number (if any)
   ▶ 7 5 6 9 1 0 6 3 7

Your Full Name

4.a. Family Name (Last Name) NGUYEN

4.b. Given Name (First Name) Teo

4.c. Middle Name Thanh

Sample Form I-130, Petition for Alien Relative (page 2)

Part 2. Information About You (Petitioner) (continued)

Other Names Used (if any)

Provide all other names you have ever used, including aliases, maiden name, and nicknames.

5.a. Family Name (Last Name)

5.b. Given Name (First Name)

5.c. Middle Name

Other Information

6. City/Town/Village of Birth

Portland

7. Country of Birth

USA

8. Date of Birth (mm/dd/yyyy) 04/12/1993

9. Sex ☒ Male ☐ Female

Mailing Address

10.a. In Care Of Name

10.b. Street Number and Name 1640 Lincoln Park

10.c. ☐ Apt. ☐ Ste. ☐ Flr.

10.d. City or Town Salem

10.e. State OR **10.f.** ZIP Code 97006

10.g. Province

10.h. Postal Code

10.i. Country

USA

11. Is your current mailing address the same as your physical address? ☒ Yes ☐ No

If you answered "No" to **Item Number 11.**, provide information on your physical address in **Item Numbers 12.a. - 13.b.**

Address History

Provide your physical addresses for the last five years, whether inside or outside the United States. Provide your current address first if it is different from your mailing address in **Item Numbers 10.a. - 10.i.**

Physical Address 1

12.a. Street Number and Name

12.b. ☐ Apt. ☐ Ste. ☐ Flr.

12.c. City or Town

12.d. State **12.e.** ZIP Code

12.f. Province

12.g. Postal Code

12.h. Country

13.a. Date From (mm/dd/yyyy) 05/01/2017

13.b. Date To (mm/dd/yyyy) present

Physical Address 2

14.a. Street Number and Name 2010 River Street

14.b. ☒ Apt. ☐ Ste. ☐ Flr. 2

14.c. City or Town Beaverton

14.d. State OR **14.e.** ZIP Code 97009

14.f. Province

14.g. Postal Code

14.h. Country

USA

15.a. Date From (mm/dd/yyyy) 02/10/2012

15.b. Date To (mm/dd/yyyy) 04/30/2017

Your Marital Information

16. How many times have you been married? ▶ 1

17. Current Marital Status

☐ Single, Never Married ☒ Married ☐ Divorced

☐ Widowed ☐ Separated ☐ Annulled

Sample Form I-130, Petition for Alien Relative (page 3)

Part 2. Information About You (Petitioner) (continued)

18. Date of Current Marriage (if currently married) (mm/dd/yyyy)

05/22/2019

Place of Your Current Marriage (if married)

19.a. City or Town — Salem

19.b. State — OR

19.c. Province

19.d. Country — USA

Names of All Your Spouses (if any)

Provide information on your current spouse (if currently married) first and then list all your prior spouses (if any).

Spouse 1

20.a. Family Name (Last Name) — NGUYEN

20.b. Given Name (First Name) — Lea

20.c. Middle Name — Nadres

21. Date Marriage Ended (mm/dd/yyyy) — n/a

Spouse 2

22.a. Family Name (Last Name)

22.b. Given Name (First Name)

22.c. Middle Name

23. Date Marriage Ended (mm/dd/yyyy)

Information About Your Parents

Parent 1's Information

Full Name of Parent 1

24.a. Family Name (Last Name) — Nguyen

24.b. Given Name (First Name) — Thanh

24.c. Middle Name

25. Date of Birth (mm/dd/yyyy) — 09/14/1967

26. Sex — ☒ Male ☐ Female

27. Country of Birth — Vietnam

28. City/Town/Village of Residence — Salem

29. Country of Residence — USA

Parent 2's Information

Full Name of Parent 2

30.a. Family Name (Last Name) — Nguyen

30.b. Given Name (First Name) — Thao

30.c. Middle Name

31. Date of Birth (mm/dd/yyyy) — 03/09/1970

32. Sex — ☐ Male ☒ Female

33. Country of Birth — Vietnam

34. City/Town/Village of Residence — Salem

35. Country of Residence — USA

Additional Information About You (Petitioner)

36. I am a (Select **only one** box):

☒ U.S. Citizen ☐ Lawful Permanent Resident

If you are a U.S. citizen, complete Item Number 37.

37. My citizenship was acquired through (Select **only one** box):

☒ Birth in the United States

☐ Naturalization

☐ Parents

38. Have you obtained a Certificate of Naturalization or a Certificate of Citizenship? ☐ Yes ☐ No

If you answered "Yes" to **Item Number 38.**, complete the following:

39.a. Certificate Number

39.b. Place of Issuance

39.c. Date of Issuance (mm/dd/yyyy)

Sample Form I-130, Petition for Alien Relative (page 4)

Part 2. Information About You (Petitioner) (continued)

If you are a lawful permanent resident, complete **Item Numbers 40.a. - 41.**

40.a. Class of Admission

40.b. Date of Admission (mm/dd/yyyy)

Place of Admission

40.c. City or Town

40.d State

41. Did you gain lawful permanent resident status through marriage to a U.S. citizen or lawful permanent resident?
☐ Yes ☐ No

Employment History

Provide your employment history for the last five years, whether inside or outside the United States. Provide your current employment first. If you are currently unemployed, type or print "Unemployed" in **Item Number 42.**

Employer 1

42. Name of Employer/Company
Gem Electronics

43.a. Street Number and Name
1400 Main Street

43.b. ☐ Apt. ☒ Ste. ☐ Flr. 1000

43.c. City or Town
Salem

43.d. State OR **43.e.** ZIP Code 97006

43.f. Province

43.g. Postal Code

43.h. Country
USA

44. Your Occupation
Electrical Engineer

45.a. Date From (mm/dd/yyyy)
05/01/2012

45.b. Date To (mm/dd/yyyy)
present

Employer 2

46. Name of Employer/Company

47.a. Street Number and Name

47.b. ☐ Apt. ☐ Ste. ☐ Flr.

47.c. City or Town

47.d. State **47.e.** ZIP Code

47.f. Province

47.g. Postal Code

47.h. Country

48. Your Occupation

49.a. Date From (mm/dd/yyyy)

49.b. Date To (mm/dd/yyyy)

Part 3. Biographic Information

NOTE: Provide the biographic information about you, the petitioner.

1. Ethnicity (Select **only one** box)
☐ Hispanic or Latino
☒ Not Hispanic or Latino

2. Race (Select **all applicable** boxes)
☐ White
☒ Asian
☐ Black or African American
☐ American Indian or Alaska Native
☐ Native Hawaiian or Other Pacific Islander

3. Height Feet 5 Inches 10

4. Weight Pounds 1 3 5

5. Eye Color (Select **only one** box)
☐ Black ☐ Blue ☒ Brown
☐ Gray ☐ Green ☐ Hazel
☐ Maroon ☐ Pink ☐ Unknown/Other

Sample Form I-130, Petition for Alien Relative (page 5)

Part 3. Biographic Information (continued)

6. Hair Color (Select **only one** box)

- [ ] Bald (No hair)
- [x] Black
- [ ] Blond
- [ ] Brown
- [ ] Gray
- [ ] Red
- [ ] Sandy
- [ ] White
- [ ] Unknown/Other

Part 4. Information About Beneficiary

1. Alien Registration Number (A-Number) (if any)

   ▶ A- ☐☐☐☐☐☐☐☐☐

2. USCIS Online Account Number (if any)

   ▶ ☐☐☐☐☐☐☐☐☐☐☐☐

3. U.S. Social Security Number (if any)

   ▶ ☐☐☐☐☐☐☐☐☐

Beneficiary's Full Name

4.a. Family Name (Last Name) — NGUYEN

4.b. Given Name (First Name) — Lea

4.c. Middle Name — Nadres

Other Names Used (if any)

Provide all other names the beneficiary has ever used, including aliases, maiden name, and nicknames.

5.a. Family Name (Last Name) — Nadres

5.b. Given Name (First Name) — Lea

5.c. Middle Name — Maria

Other Information About Beneficiary

6. City/Town/Village of Birth — Quezon City

7. Country of Birth — Philippines

8. Date of Birth (mm/dd/yyyy) — 07/18/1991

9. Sex — [ ] Male [x] Female

10. Has anyone else ever filed a petition for the beneficiary?

    [ ] Yes [x] No [ ] Unknown

    NOTE: Select "Unknown" *only* if you do not know, and the beneficiary also does not know, if anyone else has ever filed a petition for the beneficiary.

Beneficiary's Physical Address

If the beneficiary lives outside the United States in a home without a street number or name, leave **Item Numbers 11.a.** and **11.b.** blank.

11.a. Street Number and Name — 100 Roxon Avenue

11.b. [x] Apt. [ ] Ste. [ ] Flr. — 22

11.c. City or Town — Quezon City

11.d. State — ____ 11.e. ZIP Code — ____

11.f. Province — Metro Manila

11.g. Postal Code — 1109

11.h. Country — Philippines

Other Address and Contact Information

Provide the address in the United States where the beneficiary intends to live, if different from **Item Numbers 11.a. - 11.h.** If the address is the same, type or print "SAME" in **Item Number 12.a.**

12.a Street Number and Name — 1640 Lincoln Park

12.b. [ ] Apt. [ ] Ste. [ ] Flr. — ____

12.c. City or Town — Salem

12.d. State — OR 12.e. ZIP Code — 97006

Provide the beneficiary's address outside the United States, if different from **Item Numbers 11.a. - 11.h.** If the address is the same, type or print "SAME" in **Item Number 13.a.**

13.a. Street Number and Name — SAME

13.b. [ ] Apt. [ ] Ste. [ ] Flr. — ____

13.c. City or Town — ____

13.d. Province — ____

13.e. Postal Code — ____

13.f. Country — ____

14. Daytime Telephone Number (if any) — ____

Sample Form I-130, Petition for Alien Relative (page 6)

Part 4. Information About Beneficiary (continued)	

15. Mobile Telephone Number (if any)

6326265401239

16. Email Address (if any)

lea@email.com

Beneficiary's Marital Information

17. How many times has the beneficiary been married?

▶ 1

18. Current Marital Status

☐ Single, Never Married ☒ Married ☐ Divorced

☐ Widowed ☐ Separated ☐ Annulled

19. Date of Current Marriage (if currently married) (mm/dd/yyyy)

05/22/2019

Place of Beneficiary's Current Marriage (if married)

20.a. City or Town — Salem

20.b. State — OR

20.c. Province

20.d. Country

USA

Names of Beneficiary's Spouses (if any)

Provide information on the beneficiary's current spouse (if currently married) first and then list all the beneficiary's prior spouses (if any).

Spouse 1

21.a. Family Name (Last Name) — Nguyen

21.b. Given Name (First Name) — Teo

21.c. Middle Name — Thanh

22. Date Marriage Ended (mm/dd/yyyy)

Spouse 2

23.a. Family Name (Last Name)

23.b. Given Name (First Name)

23.c. Middle Name

24. Date Marriage Ended (mm/dd/yyyy)

Information About Beneficiary's Family

Provide information about the beneficiary's spouse and children.

Person 1

25.a. Family Name (Last Name) — Nguyen

25.b. Given Name (First Name) — Teo

25.c. Middle Name — Thanh

26. Relationship — Spouse

27. Date of Birth (mm/dd/yyyy) — 04/12/1993

28. Country of Birth

USA

Person 2

29.a. Family Name (Last Name)

29.b. Given Name (First Name)

29.c. Middle Name

30. Relationship

31. Date of Birth (mm/dd/yyyy)

32. Country of Birth

Person 3

33.a. Family Name (Last Name)

33.b. Given Name (First Name)

33.c. Middle Name

34. Relationship

35. Date of Birth (mm/dd/yyyy)

36. Country of Birth

Sample Form I-130, Petition for Alien Relative (page 7)

Part 4. Information About Beneficiary (continued)

Person 4

37.a. Family Name (Last Name)

37.b. Given Name (First Name)

37.c. Middle Name

38. Relationship

39. Date of Birth (mm/dd/yyyy)

40. Country of Birth

Person 5

41.a. Family Name (Last Name)

41.b. Given Name (First Name)

41.c. Middle Name

42. Relationship

43. Date of Birth (mm/dd/yyyy)

44. Country of Birth

Beneficiary's Entry Information

45. Was the beneficiary **EVER** in the United States? ☒ Yes ☐ No

If the beneficiary is currently in the United States, complete **Items Numbers 46.a. - 46.d.**

46.a. He or she arrived as a (Class of Admission):

46.b. Form I-94 Arrival-Departure Record Number ▶

46.c. Date of Arrival (mm/dd/yyyy)

46.d. Date authorized stay expired, or will expire, as shown on Form I-94 or Form I-95 (mm/dd/yyyy) or type or print "D/S" for Duration of Status

47. Passport Number

D1346466

48. Travel Document Number

49. Country of Issuance for Passport or Travel Document

Philippines

50. Expiration Date for Passport or Travel Document (mm/dd/yyyy) 05/10/2027

Beneficiary's Employment Information

Provide the beneficiary's current employment information (if applicable), even if they are employed outside of the United States. If the beneficiary is currently unemployed, type or print "Unemployed" in **Item Number 51.a.**

51.a. Name of Current Employer (if applicable)

Unemployed

51.b. Street Number and Name

51.c. ☐ Apt. ☐ Ste. ☐ Flr.

51.d. City or Town

51.e. State   **51.f.** ZIP Code

51.g. Province

51.h. Postal Code

51.i. Country

52. Date Employment Began (mm/dd/yyyy)

Additional Information About Beneficiary

53. Was the beneficiary **EVER** in immigration proceedings? ☐ Yes ☒ No

54. If you answered "Yes," select the type of proceedings and provide the location and date of the proceedings.

☐ Removal ☐ Exclusion/Deportation
☐ Rescission ☐ Other Judicial Proceedings

55.a. City or Town

55.b. State

56. Date (mm/dd/yyyy)

Sample Form I-130, Petition for Alien Relative (page 8)

Part 4. Information About Beneficiary (continued)

If the beneficiary's native written language does not use Roman letters, type or print his or her name and foreign address in their native written language.

57.a. Family Name (Last Name)

57.b. Given Name (First Name)

57.c. Middle Name

58.a. Street Number and Name

58.b. ☐ Apt. ☐ Ste. ☐ Flr.

58.c. City or Town

58.d. Province

58.e. Postal Code

58.f. Country

If filing for your spouse, provide the last address at which you physically lived together. If you never lived together, type or print, "Never lived together" in Item Number 59.a.

59.a. Street Number and Name — Never lived together

59.b. ☐ Apt. ☐ Ste. ☐ Flr.

59.c. City or Town

59.d. State **59.e.** ZIP Code

59.f. Province

59.g. Postal Code

59.h. Country

60.a. Date From (mm/dd/yyyy)

60.b. Date To (mm/dd/yyyy)

The beneficiary is in the United States and will apply for adjustment of status to that of a lawful permanent resident at the U.S. Citizenship and Immigration Services (USCIS) office in:

61.a. City or Town

61.b. State

The beneficiary will not apply for adjustment of status in the United States, but he or she will apply for an immigrant visa abroad at the U.S. Embassy or U.S. Consulate in:

62.a. City or Town — Manila

62.b. Province

62.c. Country — Philippines

NOTE: Choosing a U.S. Embassy or U.S. Consulate outside the country of the beneficiary's last residence does not guarantee that it will accept the beneficiary's case for processing. In these situations, the designated U.S. Embassy or U.S. Consulate has discretion over whether or not to accept the beneficiary's case.

Part 5. Other Information

1. Have you **EVER** previously filed a petition for this beneficiary or any other alien? ☐ Yes ☒ No

If you answered "Yes," provide the name, place, date of filing, and the result.

2.a. Family Name (Last Name)

2.b. Given Name (First Name)

2.c. Middle Name

3.a. City or Town

3.b. State

4. Date Filed (mm/dd/yyyy)

5. Result (for example, approved, denied, withdrawn)

If you are also submitting separate petitions for other relatives, provide the names of and your relationship to each relative.

Relative 1

6.a. Family Name (Last Name)

6.b. Given Name (First Name)

6.c. Middle Name

7. Relationship

Sample Form I-130, Petition for Alien Relative (page 9)

Part 5. Other Information (continued)	

Relative 2

8.a. Family Name
(Last Name)

8.b. Given Name
(First Name)

8.c. Middle Name

9. Relationship

WARNING: USCIS investigates the claimed relationships and verifies the validity of documents you submit. If you falsify a family relationship to obtain a visa, USCIS may seek to have you criminally prosecuted.

PENAL TIES: By law , you may be imprisoned for up to 5 years or fined $250,000, or both, for entering into a marriage contract in order to evade any U.S. immigration law. In addition, you may be fined up to $10,000 and imprisoned for up to 5 years, or both, for knowingly and willfully falsifying or concealing a material fact or using any false document in submitting this petition.

Part 6. Petitioner's Statement, Contact Information, Declaration, and Signature

NOTE: Read the **Penalties** section of the Form I-130 Instructions before completing this part.

Petitioner's Statement

NOTE: Select the box for either **Item Number 1.a.** or **1.b.** If applicable, select the box for **Item Number 2.**

1.a. ☒ I can read and understand English, and I have read and understand every question and instruction on this petition and my answer to every question.

1.b. ☐ The interpreter named in **Part 7.** read to me every question and instruction on this petition and my answer to every question in

_____ ,

a language in which I am fluent. I understood all of this information as interpreted.

2. ☐ At my request, the preparer named in **Part 8.**,

_____ ,

prepared this petition for me based only upon information I provided or authorized.

Petitioner's Contact Information

3. Petitioner's Daytime Telephone Number

503-555-1493

4. Petitioner's Mobile Telephone Number (if any)

5. Petitioner's Email Address (if any)

teo@email.com

Petitioner's Declaration and Certification

Copies of any documents I have submitted are exact photocopies of unaltered, original documents, and I understand that USCIS may require that I submit original documents to USCIS at a later date. Furthermore, I authorize the release of any information from any of my records that USCIS may need to determine my eligibility for the immigration benefit I seek.

I further authorize release of information contained in this petition, in supporting documents, and in my USCIS records to other entities and persons where necessary for the administration and enforcement of U.S. immigration laws.

I understand that USCIS may require me to appear for an appointment to take my biometrics (fingerprints, photograph, and/or signature) and, at that time, if I am required to provide biometrics, I will be required to sign an oath reaffirming that:

   1) I provided or authorized all of the information contained in, and submitted with, my petition;

   2) I reviewed and understood all of the information in, and submitted with, my petition; and

   3) All of this information was complete, true, and correct at the time of filing.

I certify, under penalty of perjury, that all of the information in my petition and any document submitted with it were provided or authorized by me, that I reviewed and understand all of the information contained in, and submitted with, my petition, and that all of this information is complete, true, and correct.

Petitioner's Signature

6.a. Petitioner's Signature (sign in ink)

➡ *Teo Thanh Nguyen*

6.b. Date of Signature (mm/dd/yyyy)   02/01/2020

NOTE TO ALL PETITIONERS: If you do not completely fill out this petition or fail to submit required documents listed in the Instructions, USCIS may deny your petition.

Sample Form I-130A, Supplemental Information for Spouse Beneficiary (page 1)

Supplemental Information for Spouse Beneficiary		**USCIS**
Department of Homeland Security		**Form I-130A**
U.S. Citizenship and Immigration Services		OMB No. 1615-0012
		Expires 02/28/2021

To be completed by an attorney or accredited representative (if any).

☐ Select this box if Form G-28 is attached.

Volag Number (if any)

Attorney State Bar Number (if applicable)

Attorney or Accredited Representative USCIS Online Account Number (if any)

▶ **START HERE - Type or print in black ink.**

The purpose of this form is to collect additional information for a spouse beneficiary of Form I-130, Petition for Alien Relative. If your spouse is a U.S. citizen, lawful permanent resident, or non-citizen U.S. national who is filing Form I-130 on your behalf, you must complete and sign Form I-130A, Supplemental Information for Spouse Beneficiary, and submit it with the Form I-130 filed by your spouse. If you reside overseas, you still must complete Form I-130A, but you do not need to sign the form.

Part 1. Information About You (Spouse Beneficiary)

1. Alien Registration Number (A-Number) (if any)
   ▶ A-

2. USCIS Online Account Number (if any)
   ▶

Your Full Name

3.a. Family Name (Last Name) — NGUYEN

3.b. Given Name (First Name) — Lea

3.c. Middle Name — Nadres

Address History

Provide your physical addresses for the last five years, whether inside or outside the United States. Provide your current address first. If you need extra space to complete this section, use the space provided in **Part 7. Additional Information**.

Physical Address 1

4.a. Street Number and Name — 100 Roxon Avenue

4.b. ☒ Apt. ☐ Ste. ☐ Flr. — 22

4.c. City or Town — Quezon City

4.d. State — 4.e. ZIP Code —

4.f. Province — Metro Manila

4.g. Postal Code — 1109

4.h. Country — Philippines

5.a. Date From (mm/dd/yyyy) — 05/01/2019

5.b. Date To (mm/dd/yyyy) — PRESENT

Physical Address 2

6.a. Street Number and Name — 13 Dao Street, Valle Zende

6.b. ☐ Apt. ☐ Ste. ☐ Flr. —

6.c. City or Town — Metro Manila

6.d. State — 6.e. ZIP Code —

6.f. Province —

6.g. Postal Code — 1109

6.h. Country — Philippines

7.a. Date From (mm/dd/yyyy) — 07/18/1993

7.b. Date To (mm/dd/yyyy) — 04/30/2019

Last Physical Address Outside the United States

Provide your last address outside the United States of more than one year (even if listed above).

8.a. Street Number and Name — 13 Dao Street, Valle Zende

8.b. ☐ Apt. ☐ Ste. ☐ Flr. —

8.c. City or Town — Metro Manila

8.d. Province —

8.e. Postal Code — 1109

8.f. Country — Philippines

Sample Form I-130A, Supplemental Information for Spouse Beneficiary (page 2)

Part 1. Information About You (The Spouse Beneficiary)

9.a. Date From (mm/dd/yyyy) `07/18/1993`

9.b. Date To (mm/dd/yyyy) `05/31/2016`

Information About Parent 1

Full Name of Parent 1

10.a. Family Name (Maiden Name) `Pebet`

10.b. Given Name (First Name) `Antero`

10.c. Middle Name

11. Date of Birth (mm/dd/yyyy) `11/23/1970`

12. Sex ☒ Male ☐ Female

13. City/Town/Village of Birth `Manila`

14. Country of Birth `Philippines`

15. City/Town/Village of Residence `Manila`

16. Country of Residence `Philippines`

Information About Parent 2

Full Name of Parent 2

17.a. Family Name (Last Name) `Martino`

17.b. Given Name (First Name) `Flores`

17.c. Middle Name

18. Date of Birth (mm/dd/yyyy) `05/02/1972`

19. Sex ☐ Male ☒ Female

20. City/Town/Village of Birth `Quezon City`

21. Country of Birth `Philippines`

22. City/Town/Village of Residence `Manila`

23. Country of Residence `Philippines`

Part 2. Information About Your Employment

Provide your employment history for the last five years, whether inside or outside the United States. Provide your current employment first. If you are currently unemployed, type or print "Unemployed" in **Item Number 1.** below. If you need extra space to complete this section, use the space provided in **Part 7. Additional Information**.

Employment History

Employer 1

1. Name of Employer/Company `Unemployed`

2.a. Street Number and Name

2.b. ☐ Apt. ☐ Ste. ☐ Flr.

2.c. City or Town

2.d. State   **2.e.** ZIP Code

2.f. Province

2.g. Postal Code

2.h. Country

3. Your Occupation

4.a. Date From (mm/dd/yyyy)

4.b. Date To (mm/dd/yyyy)

Employer 2

5. Name of Employer/Company

6.a. Street Number and Name

6.b. ☐ Apt. ☐ Ste. ☐ Flr.

6.c. City or Town

6.d. State   **6.e.** ZIP Code

6.f. Province

6.g. Postal Code

6.h. Country

Sample Form I-130A, Supplemental Information for Spouse Beneficiary (page 3)

Part 2. Information About Your Employment (continued)

7. Your Occupation

8.a. Date From (mm/dd/yyyy)

8.b. Date To (mm/dd/yyyy)

Part 3. Information About Your Employment Outside the United States

Provide your last occupation outside the United States if not shown above. If you never worked outside the United States, provide this information in the space provided in **Part 7. Additional Information**.

1. Name of Employer/Company

   n/a

2.a. Street Number and Name

2.b. ☐ Apt. ☐ Ste. ☐ Flr.

2.c. City or Town

2.d. State   2.e. ZIP Code

2.f. Province

2.g. Postal Code

2.h. Country

3. Your Occupation

4.a. Date From (mm/dd/yyyy)

4.b. Date To (mm/dd/yyyy)

Part 4. Spouse Beneficiary's Statement, Contact Information, Certification, and Signature

NOTE: Read the **Penalties** section of the Form I-130 and Form I-130A Instructions before completing this part.

Spouse Beneficiary's Statement

NOTE: Select the box for either **Item Number 1.a.** or **1.b.** If applicable, select the box for **Item Number 2.**

1.a. ☒ I can read and understand English, and I have read and understand every question and instruction on this form and my answer to every question.

1.b. ☐ The interpreter named in **Part 5.** read to me every question and instruction on this form and my answer to every question in

   a language in which I am fluent, and I understood everything.

2. ☐ At my request, the preparer name in **Part 6.**,

   prepared this form for me based only upon information I provided or authorized.

Spouse Beneficiary's Contact Information

3. Spouse Beneficiary's Daytime Telephone Number

4. Spouse Beneficiary's Mobile Telephone Number (if any)

   6326265401

5. Spouse Beneficiary's Email Address (if any)

   lea@email.com

Spouse Beneficiary's Certification

Copies of any documents I have submitted are exact photocopies of unaltered, original documents, and I understand that USCIS may require that I submit original documents to USCIS at a later date. Furthermore, I authorize the release of any information from any of my records that USCIS may need to determine my eligibility for the immigration benefit I seek.

I further authorize release of information contained in this form, in supporting documents, and in my USCIS records to other entities and persons where necessary for the administration and enforcement of U.S. immigration laws.

I certify, under penalty of perjury, that I provided or authorized all of the information in this form, I understand all of the information contained in, and submitted with, my form, and that all of this information is complete, true, and correct.

Spouse Beneficiary's Signature

6.a. Spouse Beneficiary's Signature (sign in ink)

   ➡ *Lea Nadres Nguyen*

6.b. Date of Signature (mm/dd/yyyy)   02/01/2020

NOTE TO ALL SPOUSE BENEFICIARIES: If you do not completely fill out this form or fail to submit required documents listed in the Instructions, USCIS may deny the Form I-130 filed on your behalf.

Sample Form I-129F, Petition for Alien Fiancé(e) (as used by married couple) (page 1)

Petition for Alien Fiancé(e)		**USCIS**
Department of Homeland Security		**Form I-129F**
U.S. Citizenship and Immigration Services		OMB No. 1615-0001
		Expires 11/30/2020

For USCIS Use Only	Fee Stamp	Action Block
Case ID Number		
A-Number		
G-28 Number		

☐ The petition is approved for status under Section 101(a)(15)(K). It is valid for 4 months and expires on: _____

Extraordinary Circumstances Waiver
☐ Approved ☐ Denied   Reason

General Waiver	Mandatory Waiver	AMCON: _____
☐ Approved Reason	☐ Approved Reason	☐ Personal Interview ☐ Previously Forwarded
☐ Denied _____	☐ Denied _____	☐ Document Check ☐ Field Investigation

Initial Receipt	Relocated	Completed	Remarks	IMBRA disclosure to the beneficiary required?
	Received	Approved		
Resubmitted	Sent	Returned		☐ Yes ☐ No

▶ **START HERE - Type or print in black ink.**

Part 1. Information About You

1. Alien Registration Number (A-Number) (if any)
▶ A- ☐☐☐☐☐☐☐☐☐

2. USCIS Online Account Number (if any)
▶ ☐☐☐☐☐☐☐☐☐☐

3. U.S. Social Security Number (if any)
▶ 1 2 3 4 5 6 7 8 9

Select **one** box below to indicate the classification you are requesting for your beneficiary:

4.a. ☐ Fiancé(e) (K-1 visa)

4.b. ☒ Spouse (K-3 visa)

5. If you are filing to classify your spouse as a K-3, have you filed Form I-130? ☒ Yes ☐ No

Your Full Name

6.a. Family Name (Last Name) | Anderson
6.b. Given Name (First Name) | Christa
6.c. Middle Name | Lee

Other Names Used

Provide all other names you have ever used, including aliases, maiden name, and nicknames. If you need extra space to complete this section, use the space provided in **Part 8. Additional Information**

7.a. Family Name (Last Name) |
7.b. Given Name (First Name) |
7.c. Middle Name |

Your Mailing Address

8.a. In Care Of Name |
8.b. Street Number and Name | 123 4th Street
8.c. ☒ Apt. ☐ Ste. ☐ Flr. | 2
8.d. City or Town | San Diego
8.e. State | CA   **8.f.** ZIP Code | 92120
8.g. Province |
8.h. Postal Code |
8.i. Country | USA
8.j. Is your current mailing address the same as your physical address? ☒ Yes ☐ No

If you answered "No," provide your physical address in **Item Numbers 9.a. - 9.h.**

Sample Form I-129F, Petition for Alien Fiancé(e) (as used by married couple) (page 2)

Part 1. Information About You (continued)

Your Address History

Provide your physical addresses for the last five years, whether inside or outside the United States. Provide your current address first if it is different from your mailing address in **Item Numbers 8.a. - 8.i.** If you need extra space to complete this section, use the space provided in **Part 8. Additional Information**.

Physical Address 1

9.a. Street Number and Name

9.b. ☐ Apt. ☐ Ste. ☐ Flr.

9.c. City or Town

9.d. State   **9.e.** ZIP Code

9.f. Province

9.g. Postal Code

9.h. Country

10.a. Date From (mm/dd/yyyy) 06/01/2011

10.b. Date To (mm/dd/yyyy) present

Physical Address 2

11.a. Street Number and Name

11.b. ☐ Apt. ☐ Ste. ☐ Flr.

11.c. City or Town

11.d. State   **11.e.** ZIP Code

11.f. Province

11.g. Postal Code

11.h. Country

12.a. Date From (mm/dd/yyyy)

12.b. Date To (mm/dd/yyyy)

Your Employment History

Provide your employment history for the last five years, whether inside or outside the United States. Provide your current employment first. If you need extra space to complete this section, use the space provided in **Part 8. Additional Information**.

Employer 1

13. Full Name of Employer San Diego Zoo

14.a. Street Number and Name 2920 Zoo Drive

14.b. ☐ Apt. ☐ Ste. ☐ Flr.

14.c. City or Town San Diego

14.d. State CA   **14.e.** ZIP Code 92112

14.f. Province

14.g. Postal Code

14.h. Country USA

15. Your Occupation (specify) Zookeeper

16.a. Employment Start Date (mm/dd/yyyy) 05/15/2011

16.b. Employment End Date (mm/dd/yyyy) present

Employer 2

17. Full Name of Employer

18.a. Street Number and Name

18.b. ☐ Apt. ☐ Ste. ☐ Flr.

18.c. City or Town

18.d. State   **18.e.** ZIP Code

18.f. Province

18.g. Postal Code

18.h. Country

19. Your Occupation (specify)

Sample Form I-129F, Petition for Alien Fiancé(e) (as used by married couple) (page 3)

Part 1. Information About You (continued)

20.a. Employment Start Date (mm/dd/yyyy) [ ]

20.b. Employment End Date (mm/dd/yyyy) [ ]

Other Information

21. Gender ☐ Male ☒ Female

22. Date of Birth (mm/dd/yyyy) [04/18/1991]

23. Marital Status
☐ Single ☒ Married ☐ Divorced ☐ Widowed

24. City/Town/Village of Birth [Portland]

25. Province or State of Birth [Oregon]

26. Country of Birth [USA]

Information About Your Parents

Parent 1's Information

27.a. Family Name (Last Name) [Anderson]

27.b. Given Name (First Name) [Mark]

27.c. Middle Name [James]

28. Date of Birth (mm/dd/yyyy) [01/19/1957]

29. Gender ☒ Male ☐ Female

30. Country of Birth [USA]

31.a. City/Town/Village of Residence [Deceased]

31.b. Country of Residence [Deceased]

Parent 2's Information

32.a. Family Name (Last Name) [Anderson]

32.b. Given Name (First Name) [Karen]

32.c. Middle Name [Julia]

33. Date of Birth (mm/dd/yyyy) [09/16/1958]

34. Gender ☐ Male ☒ Female

35. Country of Birth [USA]

36.a. City/Town/Village of Residence [Portland]

36.b. Country of Residence [USA]

37. Have you ever been previously married? ☐ Yes ☒ No

If you answered "Yes" to **Item Number 37.**, provide the names of each spouse and the date that each prior marriage ended in **Item Numbers 38.a. - 39.** If you need extra space to complete this section, use the space provided in **Part 8. Additional Information**.

Name of Previous Spouse

38.a. Family Name (Last Name) [ ]

38.b. Given Name (First Name) [ ]

38.c. Middle Name [ ]

39. Date Marriage Ended (mm/dd/yyyy) [ ]

Your Citizenship Information

You are a U.S. citizen through (select **only one** box):

40.a. ☒ Birth in the United States

40.b. ☐ Naturalization

40.c. ☐ U.S. citizen parents

41. Have you obtained a Certificate of Naturalization or a Certificate of Citizenship in your own name? ☐ Yes ☒ No

If you answered "Yes" to **Item Number 41.**, complete **Item Numbers 42.a. - 42.c.**

Sample Form I-129F, Petition for Alien Fiancé(e) (as used by married couple) (page 4)

Part 1. Information About You (continued)

42.a. Certificate Number

42.b. Place of Issuance

42.c. Date of Issuance (mm/dd/yyyy)

Additional Information

43. Have you ever filed Form I-129F for any other beneficiary? ☐ Yes ☒ No

If you answered "Yes" to **Item Number 43.**, provide the responses to **Item Number 44. - 46.** for each previous beneficiary. If you need to provide information for more than one beneficiary, use the space provided in **Part 8. Additional Information**.

44. A-Number (if any) ▶ A-

45.a. Family Name (Last Name)

45.b. Given Name (First Name)

45.c. Middle Name

46. Date of Filing (mm/dd/yyyy)

47. What action did USCIS take on Form I-129F (for example, approved, denied, revoked)?

48. Do you have any children under 18 years of age? ☐ Yes ☒ No

If you answered "Yes" to **Item Number 48.**, provide the ages for your children under 18 years of age in **Item Numbers 49.a. - 49.b.**

Provide the ages for your children under 18 years of age. If you need extra space to complete this section, use the space provided in **Part 8. Additional Information**.

49.a. Age

49.b. Age

Provide all U.S. states and foreign countries in which you have resided since your 18th birthday.

Residence 1

50.a. State OR

50.b. Country USA

Residence 2

51.a. State CA

51.b. Country USA

Part 2. Information About Your Beneficiary

1.a. Family Name (Last Name) Cuevas

1.b. Given Name (First Name) Bernardo

1.c. Middle Name Cristobal

2. A-Number (if any) ▶ A-

3. U.S. Social Security Number (if any) ▶

4. Date of Birth (mm/dd/yyyy) 07/24/1990

5. Gender ☒ Male ☐ Female

6. Marital Status ☐ Single ☒ Married ☐ Divorced ☐ Widowed

7. City/Town/Village of Birth Bogota

8. Country of Birth Colombia

9. Country of Citizenship or Nationality Colombia

Other Names Used

Provide all other names you have ever used, including aliases, maiden name, and nicknames. If you need extra space to complete this section, use the space provided in **Part 8. Additional Information**.

10.a. Family Name (Last Name)

10.b. Given Name (First Name)

10.c. Middle Name

Sample Form I-129F, Petition for Alien Fiancé(e) (as used by married couple) (page 5)

Part 2. Information About Your Beneficiary (continued)

Mailing Address for Your Beneficiary

11.a. In Care Of Name

11.b. Street Number and Name — 123 Calle Centro

11.c. ☐ Apt. ☐ Ste. ☐ Flr.

11.d. City or Town — Bogota

11.e. State

11.f. ZIP Code

11.g. Province — DC

11.h. Postal Code — 11001000

11.i. Country — Colombia

Your Beneficiary's Address History

Provide your beneficiary's physical addresses for the last five years, whether inside or outside the United States. Provide your beneficiary's current address first if it is different from the mailing address in **Item Numbers 11.a. - 11.i.** If you need extra space to complete this section, use the space provided in **Part 8. Additional Information**.

Beneficiary's Physical Address 1

12.a. Street Number and Name

12.b. ☐ Apt. ☐ Ste. ☐ Flr.

12.c. City or Town

12.d. State

12.e. ZIP Code

12.f. Province

12.g. Postal Code

12.h. Country

13.a. Date From (mm/dd/yyyy) — 07/01/2012

13.b. Date To (mm/dd/yyyy) — present

Beneficiary's Physical Address 2

14.a. Street Number and Name

14.b. ☐ Apt. ☐ Ste. ☐ Flr.

14.c. City or Town

14.d. State

14.e. ZIP Code

14.f. Province

14.g. Postal Code

14.h. Country

15.a. Date From (mm/dd/yyyy)

15.b. Date To (mm/dd/yyyy)

Your Beneficiary's Employment History

Provide your employment history for the last five years, whether inside or outside the United States. Provide your current employment first. If you need extra space to complete this section, use the space provided in **Part 8. Additional Information**.

Beneficiary's Employer 1

16. Full Name of Employer — Bogota Motors

17.a. Street Number and Name — 222 Avenida de Arboles

17.b. ☐ Apt. ☐ Ste. ☐ Flr.

17.c. City or Town — Bogota

17.d. State

17.e. ZIP Code

17.f. Province — DC

17.g. Postal Code — 11001000

17.h. Country — Bogota

18. Beneficiary's Occupation (specify) — Mechanic

19.a. Employment Start Date (mm/dd/yyyy) — 01/16/2009

19.b. Employment End Date (mm/dd/yyyy) — 02/01/2020

Sample Form I-129F, Petition for Alien Fiancé(e) (as used by married couple) (page 6)

Part 2. Information About Your Beneficiary (continued)

Beneficiary's Employer 2

20. Full Name of Employer

21.a. Street Number and Name

21.b. ☐ Apt. ☐ Ste. ☐ Flr.

21.c. City or Town

21.d. State ___ 21.e. ZIP Code

21.f. Province

21.g. Postal Code

21.h. Country

22. Beneficiary's Occupation (specify)

23.a. Employment Start Date (mm/dd/yyyy)

23.b. Employment End Date (mm/dd/yyyy)

Information About Your Beneficiary's Parents

Parent 1's Information

24.a. Family Name (Last Name) — Cuevas

24.b. Given Name (First Name) — Jose

24.c. Middle Name — Antonio

25. Date of Birth (mm/dd/yyyy) — 10/11/1962

26. Gender ☒ Male ☐ Female

27. Country of Birth — Colombia

28.a. City/Town/Village of Residence — Bogota

28.b. Country of Residence — Colombia

Parent 2's Information

29.a. Family Name (Last Name) — DeJesus

29.b. Given Name (First Name) — Maria

29.c. Middle Name — Nina

30. Date of Birth (mm/dd/yyyy) — 11/29/1964

31. Gender ☐ Male ☒ Female

32. Country of Birth — Colombia

33.a. City/Town/Village of Residence — Bogota

33.b. Country of Residence — Colombia

Other Information About Your Beneficiary

34. Has your beneficiary ever been previously married? ☐ Yes ☒ No

If you answered "Yes" to **Item Number 34.**, provide the names of each prior spouse and the date each prior marriage ended in **Item Numbers 35.a. - 36.** If you need to provide information for more than one spouse, use the space provided in **Part 8. Additional Information**.

Name of Previous Spouse

35.a. Family Name (Last Name)

35.b. Given Name (First Name)

35.c. Middle Name

36. Date Marriage Ended (mm/dd/yyyy)

37. Has your beneficiary ever been in the United States? ☐ Yes ☒ No

If your beneficiary is currently in the United States, complete **Item Numbers 38.a. - 38.h.**

38.a. He or she last entered as a (for example, visitor, student, exchange alien, crewman, stowaway, temporary worker, without inspection):

38.b. I-94 Arrival-Departure Record Number ▶

38.c. Date of Arrival (mm/dd/yyyy)

Sample Form I-129F, Petition for Alien Fiancé(e) (as used by married couple) (page 7)

Part 2. Information About Your Beneficiary (continued)

38.d. Date authorized stay expired or will expire as shown on Form I-94 or I-95 (mm/dd/yyyy)

38.e. Passport Number

38.f. Travel Document Number

38.g. Country of Issuance for Passport or Travel Document

38.h. Expiration Date for Passport or Travel Document (mm/dd/yyyy)

39. Does your beneficiary have any children?
☐ Yes   ☒ No

If you answered "Yes" to **Item Number 39.**, provide the following information about each child. If you need to provide information for more than one child, use the space provided in **Part 8. Additional Information**.

Children of Beneficiary

40.a. Family Name (Last Name)

40.b. Given Name (First Name)

40.c. Middle Name

41. Country of Birth

42. Date of Birth (mm/dd/yyyy)

43. Does this child reside with your beneficiary?
☐ Yes   ☐ No

If the child does not reside with your beneficiary, provide the child's physical residence.

44.a. Street Number and Name

44.b. ☐ Apt. ☐ Ste. ☐ Flr.

44.c. City or Town

44.d. State   **44.e.** ZIP Code

44.f. Province

44.g. Postal Code

44.h. Country

Address in the United States Where Your Beneficiary Intends to Live

45.a. Street Number and Name | 123 4th Street

45.b. ☒ Apt. ☐ Ste. ☐ Flr. | 2

45.c. City or Town | San Diego

45.d. State | CA   **45.e.** ZIP Code | 92120

46. Daytime Telephone Number | 8582335321

Your Beneficiary's Physical Address Abroad

47.a. Street Number and Name | 123 Calle Centro

47.b. ☐ Apt. ☐ Ste. ☐ Flr.

47.c. City or Town | Bogota

47.d. Province | DC

47.e. Postal Code | 11001000

47.f. Country | Colombia

48. Daytime Telephone Number | 57123557554

Your Beneficiary's Name and Address in His or Her Native Alphabet

49.a. Family Name (Last Name) | n/a

49.b. Given Name (First Name)

49.c. Middle Name

50.a. Street Number and Name

50.b. ☐ Apt. ☐ Ste. ☐ Flr.

50.c. City or Town

50.d. Province

50.e. Postal Code

50.f. Country

Sample Form I-129F, Petition for Alien Fiancé(e) (as used by married couple) (page 8)

Part 2. Information About Your Beneficiary (continued)

51. Is your fiancé(e) related to you?
☐ Yes ☐ No ☒ N/A, beneficiary is my spouse

52. Provide the nature and degree of relationship (for example, third cousin or maternal uncle).
n/a

53. Have you and your fiancé(e) met in person during the two years immediately before filing this petition?
☐ Yes ☐ No ☒ N/A, beneficiary is my spouse

If you answered "Yes" to **Item Number 53.**, describe the circumstances of your in-person meeting in **Item Number 54.** Attach evidence to demonstrate that you were in each other's physical presence during the required two year period.

If you answered "No," explain your reasons for requesting an exemption from the in person meeting requirement in **Item Number 54.** and provide evidence that you should be exempt from this requirement. Refer to **Part 2., Item Numbers 53. - 54.** of the **Specific Instructions** section of the Instructions for additional information about the requirement to meet. If you need extra space to complete this section, use the space provided in **Part 8. Additional Information**.

54. _____

International Marriage Broker (IMB) Information

55. Did you meet your beneficiary through the services of an IMB? ☐ Yes ☒ No

If you answered "Yes" to **Item Number 55.**, provide the IMB's contact information and Website information below. In addition, attach a copy of the signed, written consent form the IMB obtained from your beneficiary authorizing your beneficiary's personal contact information to be released to you.

56. IMB's Name (if any)

57.a. Family Name of IMB (Last Name)

57.b. Given Name of IMB (First Name)

58. Organization Name of IMB

59. Website of IMB

60.a. Street Number and Name

60.b. ☐ Apt. ☐ Ste. ☐ Flr.

60.c. City or Town

60.d. Province

60.e. Postal Code

60.f. Country

61. Daytime Telephone Number

Consular Processing Information

Your beneficiary will apply for a visa abroad at the U.S. Embassy or U.S. Consulate at:

62.a. City or Town
Bogota

62.b. Country
Colombia

Part 3. Other Information

Criminal Information

NOTE: These criminal information questions must be answered even if your records were sealed, cleared, or if anyone, including a judge, law enforcement officer, or attorney, told you that you no longer have a record. If you need extra space to complete this section, use the space provided in **Part 8. Additional Information**.

1. Have you **EVER** been subject to a temporary or permanent protection or restraining order (either civil or criminal)? ☐ Yes ☒ No

Have you EVER been arrested or convicted of any of the following crimes:

2.a. Domestic violence, sexual assault, child abuse, child neglect, dating violence, elder abuse, stalking or an attempt to commit any of these crimes? (See **Part 3. Other Information, Item Numbers 1. - 3.c.** of the Instructions for the full definition of the term "domestic violence.") ☐ Yes ☒ No

Sample Form I-129F, Petition for Alien Fiancé(e) (as used by married couple) (page 9)

Part 3. Other Information (continued)

2.b. Homicide, murder, manslaughter, rape, abusive sexual contact, sexual exploitation, incest, torture, trafficking, peonage, holding hostage, involuntary servitude, slave trade, kidnapping, abduction, unlawful criminal restraint, false imprisonment, or an attempt to commit any of these crimes? ☐ Yes ☒ No

2.c. Three or more arrests or convictions, not from a single act, for crimes relating to a controlled substance or alcohol? ☐ Yes ☒ No

NOTE: If you were ever arrested or convicted of any of the specified crimes, you must submit certified copies of all court and police records showing the charges and disposition for every arrest or conviction. You must do so even if your records were sealed, expunged, or otherwise cleared, and regardless of whether anyone, including a judge, law enforcement officer, or attorney, informed you that you no longer have a criminal record. If you need extra space to complete this section, use the space provided in **Part 8. Additional Information**.

If you have provided information about a conviction for a crime listed in **Item Numbers 2.a. - 2.c.** and you were being battered or subjected to extreme cruelty at the time of your conviction, select all of the following that apply to you:

3.a. ☐ I was acting in self-defense.

3.b. ☐ I violated a protection order issued for my own protection.

3.c. ☐ I committed, was arrested for, was convicted of, or pled guilty to a crime that did not result in serious bodily injury and there was a connection between the crime and me having been battered or subjected to extreme cruelty.

4.a. Have you ever been arrested, cited, charged, indicted, convicted, fined, or imprisoned for breaking or violating any law or ordinance in any country, excluding traffic violations (unless a traffic violation was alcohol- or drug-related or involved a fine of $500 or more)? ☐ Yes ☒ No

4.b. If the answer to **Item Number 4.a.** is "Yes," provide information about each of those arrests, citations, charges, indictments, convictions, fines, or imprisonments in the space below. If you were the subject of an order of protection or restraining order and believe you are the victim, please explain those circumstances and provide any evidence to support your claims. Include the dates and outcomes. If you need extra space to complete this section, use the space provided in **Part 8. Additional Information**.

_____

_____

Multiple Filer Waiver Request Information

Refer to **Part 3. Types of Waivers** in the **Specific Instructions** section of the Instructions for an explanation of the filing waivers.

Indicate which one of the following waivers you are requesting:

5.a. ☐ Multiple Filer, No Permanent Restraining Orders or Convictions for a Specified Offense (**General Waiver**)

5.b. ☐ Multiple Filer, Prior Permanent Restraining Orders or Criminal Conviction for Specified Offense (**Extraordinary Circumstances Waiver**)

5.c. ☐ Multiple Filer, Prior Permanent Restraining Order or Criminal Convictions for Specified Offense Resulting from Domestic Violence (**Mandatory Waiver**)

5.d. ☒ Not applicable, beneficiary is my spouse or I am not a multiple filer

Part 4. Biographic Information

1. Ethnicity (Select **only one** box)
   - ☐ Hispanic or Latino
   - ☒ Not Hispanic or Latino

2. Race (Select **all applicable** boxes)
   - ☒ White
   - ☐ Asian
   - ☐ Black or African American
   - ☐ American Indian or Alaska Native
   - ☐ Native Hawaiian or Other Pacific Islander

3. Height   Feet [5]   Inches [4]

4. Weight   Pounds [1] [2] [2]

5. Eye Color (Select **only one** box)
   - ☐ Black   ☒ Blue   ☐ Brown
   - ☐ Gray   ☐ Green   ☐ Hazel
   - ☐ Maroon   ☐ Pink   ☐ Unknown/Other

6. Hair Color (Select **only one** box)
   - ☐ Bald (No hair)   ☐ Black   ☒ Blond
   - ☐ Brown   ☐ Gray   ☐ Red
   - ☐ Sandy   ☐ White   ☐ Unknown/Other

Sample Form I-129F, Petition for Alien Fiancé(e) (as used by married couple) (page 10)

Part 5. Petitioner's Statement, Contact Information, Declaration, Certification, and Signature

NOTE: Read the **Penalties** section of the Form I-129F Instructions before completing this part.

Petitioner's Statement

NOTE: Select the box for either **Item Number 1.a.** or **1.b.** If applicable, select the box for **Item Number 2.**

1.a. ☒ I can read and understand English, and I have read and understand every question and instruction on this petition and my answer to every question.

1.b. ☐ The interpreter named in **Part 6.** read to me every question and instruction on this petition and my answer to every question in

_____ ,
a language in which I am fluent, and I understood everything.

2. ☐ At my request, the preparer named in **Part 7.**,

_____ ,
prepared this petition for me based only upon information I provided or authorized.

Petitioner's Contact Information

3. Petitioner's Daytime Telephone Number
8582335321

4. Petitioner's Mobile Telephone Number (if any)
8582335321

5. Petitioner's Email Address (if any)
christalee@email.com

Petitioner's Declaration and Certification

Copies of any documents I have submitted are exact photocopies of unaltered, original documents, and I understand that USCIS may require that I submit original documents to USCIS at a later date. Furthermore, I authorize the release of any information from any and all of my records that USCIS may need to determine my eligibility for the immigration benefit that I seek.

I furthermore authorize release of information contained in this petition, in supporting documents, and in my USCIS records, to other entities and persons where necessary for the administration and enforcement of U.S. immigration law .

I understand that USCIS may require me to appear for an appointment to take my biometrics (fingerprints, photograph, and/or signature) and, at that time, if I am required to provide biometrics, I will be required to sign an oath reaffirming that:

1) I reviewed and understood all of the information contained in, and submitted with, my petition; and

2) All of this information was complete, true, and correct at the time of filing.

I certify, under penalty of perjury, that all of the information in my petition and any document submitted with it were provided or authorized by me, that I reviewed and understand all of the information contained in, and submitted with my petition, and that all of this information is complete, true, and correct.

Petitioner's Signature

6.a. Petitioner's Signature
➡ *Christa L. Anderson*

6.b. Date of Signature (mm/dd/yyyy) 02/01/2020

NOTE TO ALL PETITIONERS: If you do not completely fill out this petition or fail to submit required documents listed in the Instructions, USCIS may deny your petition.

Part 6. Interpreter's Contact Information, Certification, and Signature

Provide the following information about the interpreter.

Interpreter's Full Name

1.a. Interpreter's Family Name (Last Name)

1.b. Interpreter's Given Name (First Name)

2. Interpreter's Business or Organization Name (if any)

Interpreter's Mailing Address

3.a. Street Number and Name

3.b. ☐ Apt. ☐ Ste. ☐ Flr.

3.c. City or Town

3.d. State ____ **3.e.** ZIP Code

3.f. Province

3.g. Postal Code

3.h. Country

Sample Form I-751, Petition To Remove Conditions on Residence (page 1)

Petition to Remove Conditions on Residence
Department of Homeland Security
U.S. Citizenship and Immigration Services

USCIS
Form I-751
OMB No. 1615-0038
Expires 12/31/2019

	Receipt	Action Block	Remarks

For USCIS Use Only

Reloc Sent	Reloc Received
Date (mm/dd/yyyy) __/__/__	Date (mm/dd/yyyy) __/__/__
Date (mm/dd/yyyy) __/__/__	Date (mm/dd/yyyy) __/__/__

☐ Petitioner interviewed on (mm/dd/yyyy) __/__/__   ☐ Approved under INA 216(c)(4)(C) Battered Spouse/Child

To be completed by an attorney or accredited representative (if any).	☐ Select this box if Form G-28 is attached.	Attorney State Bar Number (if applicable)	Attorney or Accredited Representative USCIS Online Account Number (if any)

►START HERE - Type or print in black ink.

Part 1. Information About You, the Conditional Resident

1.a. Family Name (Last Name) **Hollis**
1.b. Given Name (First Name) **Nigel**
1.c. Middle Name **Ian**

Other Names Used

List all other names you have ever used, including aliases, maiden name, and nicknames. If you need extra space to complete this section, use the space provided in **Part 11. Additional Information**.

2.a. Family Name (Last Name)
2.b. Given Name (First Name)
2.c. Middle Name

3.a. Family Name (Last Name)
3.b. Given Name (First Name)
3.c. Middle Name

Other Information

4. Date of Birth (mm/dd/yyyy) **09/26/1991**

5. Country of Birth **United Kingdom**

6. Country of Citizenship or Nationality (provide all that apply) **United Kingdom**

7. Alien Registration Number (A-Number) (if any) ► A- 1 2 3 4 5 6 7 8 9

8. U.S. Social Security Number (if any) ► 8 8 8 1 1 8 8 8 8

9. USCIS Online Account Number (if any) ►

Marital Status

10. Marital Status ☐ Single ☒ Married ☐ Divorced ☐ Widowed

11. Date of Marriage (mm/dd/yyyy) **06/23/2020**

12. Place of Marriage **New York NY**

13. If the marriage through which you gained conditional residence has ended, provide the date it ended (date of divorce or date of death) (mm/dd/yyyy)

14. Conditional Residence Expires On (mm/dd/yyyy) **07/01/2021**

Sample Form I-751, Petition To Remove Conditions on Residence (page 2)

Part 1. Information About You, the Conditional Resident (continued)

Mailing Address

15.a. In Care Of Name

15.b. Street Number and Name `114 Fulton Street`

15.c. ☒ Apt. ☐ Ste. ☐ Flr. `6E`

15.d. City or Town `New York`

15.e. State `NY ▼`   **15.f.** ZIP Code `10038`

16. Is your physical address different than your mailing address? ☐ Yes ☒ No

If you answered "Yes" to **Item Number 16.**, provide your physical address below.

Physical Address

17.a. In Care Of Name

17.b. Street Number and Name

17.c. ☐ Apt. ☐ Ste. ☐ Flr.

17.d. City or Town

17.e. State   **17.f.** ZIP Code

Additional Information About You

18. Are you in removal, deportation, or rescission proceedings? ☐ Yes ☒ No

19. Was a fee paid to anyone other than an attorney in connection with this petition? ☐ Yes ☒ No

20. Have you ever been arrested, detained, charged, indicted, fined, or imprisoned for breaking or violating any law or ordinance (excluding traffic regulations), or committed any crime which you were not arrested in the United States or abroad? ☐ Yes ☒ No

If you answered "Yes" to **Item Number 20.**, provide a detailed explanation in **Part 11. Additional Information** or on a separate sheet of paper, and refer to the **What Initial Evidence Is Required** section of the Form I-751 instructions to determine what criminal history document to include with your petition.

21. If you are married, is this a different marriage than the one through which you gained conditional resident status? ☐ Yes ☒ No

22. Have you resided at any other address since you became a permanent resident? ☐ Yes ☒ No

If you answered "Yes" to **Item Number 22.**, provide a list of all addresses where you have resided since becoming a permanent resident and the dates you resided at those locations in the space provided in **Part 11. Additional Information**.

23. Is your spouse or parent's spouse currently serving with or employed by the U.S. Government and serving outside the United States? ☐ Yes ☒ No

Part 2. Biographic Information

1. Ethnicity (Select **only one** box)
   ☐ Hispanic or Latino
   ☒ Not Hispanic or Latino

2. Race (Select **all applicable** boxes)
   ☒ White
   ☐ Asian
   ☐ Black or African American
   ☐ American Indian or Alaska Native
   ☐ Native Hawaiian or Other Pacific Islander

3. Height   Feet `6 ▼` Inches `2 ▼`

4. Weight   Pounds `1` `8` `5`

5. Eye Color (Select **only one** box)
   ☐ Black ☒ Blue ☐ Brown
   ☐ Gray ☐ Green ☐ Hazel
   ☐ Maroon ☐ Pink ☐ Unknown/Other

6. Hair Color (Select **only one** box)
   ☐ Bald (No hair) ☐ Black ☐ Blond
   ☐ Brown ☐ Gray ☐ Red
   ☒ Sandy ☐ White ☐ Unknown/Other

Sample Form I-751, Petition To Remove Conditions on Residence (page 3)

Part 3. Basis for Petition

Joint Filing

My conditional residence is based on my marriage or my parent's marriage to a U.S. citizen or lawful permanent resident, and I am filing this joint petition together with (Select **only one** box):

1.a. ☒ My spouse.

1.b. ☐ My parent's spouse because I am unable to be included in a joint petition filed by my parent and my parent's spouse.

OR (Select **all** applicable boxes in the next section.)

Waiver or Individual Filing Request

My conditional residence is based on my marriage or my parent's marriage to a U.S. citizen or lawful permanent resident, I am unable to file a joint petition with my spouse or my parent's spouse, because:

1.c. ☐ My spouse is deceased.

1.d. ☐ My marriage was entered in good faith, but the marriage was terminated through divorce or annulment.

1.e. ☐ I entered the marriage in good faith, and, during the marriage, I was battered, or was the subject of extreme cruelty, by my U.S. citizen or lawful permanent resident spouse.

1.f. ☐ My parent entered the marriage in good faith, and, during the marriage, I was battered, or was subjected to extreme cruelty, by my parent's U.S. citizen or lawful permanent resident spouse or by my conditional resident parent.

1.g. ☐ The termination of my status and removal from the United States would result in an extreme hardship.

Part 4. Information About the U.S. Citizen or Lawful Permanent Resident Spouse. If Filing as a Child Separately, Information About the U.S. Citizen or Lawful Permanent Resident Stepparent Through Whom You Gained Your Conditional Residence.

Relationship

1.a. ☒ Spouse or Former Spouse

1.b. ☐ Parent's Spouse or Former Spouse

Other Information

2.a. Family Name (Last Name) `Hollis`

2.b. Given Name (First Name) `Sandra`

2.c. Middle Name `Leah`

3. Date of Birth (mm/dd/yyyy) `12/22/1990`

4. U.S. Social Security Number (if any)
▶ `1 2 3 4 5 6 7 8 9`

5. A-Number (if any)
▶ A- ☐☐☐☐☐☐☐☐☐

Physical Address

6.a. Street Number and Name `114 Fulton Street`

6.b. ☒ Apt. ☐ Ste. ☐ Flr. `6E`

6.c. City or Town `New York`

6.d. State `NY ▾`   **6.e.** ZIP Code `10038`

6.f. Province

6.g. Postal Code

6.h. Country `USA`

Part 5. Information About Your Children

Provide information on all of your children. If you need extra space to complete this section, use the space provided in **Part 11. Additional Information**.

Child 1

1.a. Family Name (Last Name) `Hollis`

1.b. Given Name (First Name) `Desmond`

1.c. Middle Name `James`

2. Date of Birth (mm/dd/yyyy) `12/02/2017`

3. A-Number (if any)
▶ A- ☐☐☐☐☐☐☐☐☐

4. Is this child living with you? ☒ Yes ☐ No

5. Is this child applying with you? ☐ Yes ☒ No

Sample Form I-751, Petition To Remove Conditions on Residence (page 4)

Part 5. Information About Your Children (continued)

Physical Address

6.a. Street Number and Name: `114 Fulton Street`

6.b. ☒ Apt. ☐ Ste. ☐ Flr. `6E`

6.c. City or Town: `New York`

6.d. State: `NY` ▼ **6.e.** ZIP Code: `10038`

6.f. Province:

6.g. Postal Code:

6.h. Country: `USA`

Child 2

7.a. Family Name (Last Name):

7.b. Given Name (First Name):

7.c. Middle Name:

8. Date of Birth (mm/dd/yyyy):

9. A-Number (if any): ▶ A-

10. Is this child living with you? ☐ Yes ☐ No

11. Is this child applying with you? ☐ Yes ☐ No

Physical Address

12.a. Street Number and Name:

12.b. ☐ Apt. ☐ Ste. ☐ Flr.

12.c. City or Town:

12.d. State: ▼ **12.e.** ZIP Code:

12.f. Province:

12.g. Postal Code:

12.h. Country:

Child 3

13.a. Family Name (Last Name):

13.b. Given Name (First Name):

13.c. Middle Name:

14. Date of Birth (mm/dd/yyyy):

15. A-Number (if any): ▶ A-

16. Is this child living with you? ☐ Yes ☐ No

17. Is this child applying with you? ☐ Yes ☐ No

Physical Address

18.a. Street Number and Name:

18.b. ☐ Apt. ☐ Ste. ☐ Flr.

18.c. City or Town:

18.d. State: ▼ **18.e.** ZIP Code:

18.f. Province:

18.g. Postal Code:

18.h. Country:

Child 4

19.a. Family Name (Last Name):

19.b. Given Name (First Name):

19.c. Middle Name:

20. Date of Birth (mm/dd/yyyy):

21. A-Number (if any): ▶ A-

22. Is this child living with you? ☐ Yes ☐ No

23. Is this child applying with you? ☐ Yes ☐ No

Sample Form I-751, Petition To Remove Conditions on Residence (page 5)

Part 5. Information About Your Children (continued)

Physical Address

24.a. Street Number and Name

24.b. ☐ Apt. ☐ Ste. ☐ Flr.

24.c. City or Town

24.d. State [▾] **24.e.** ZIP Code

24.f. Province

24.g. Postal Code

24.h. Country

Child 5

25.a. Family Name (Last Name)

25.b. Given Name (First Name)

25.c. Middle Name

26. Date of Birth (mm/dd/yyyy)

27. A-Number (if any)

▶ A-

28. Is this child living with you? ☐ Yes ☐ No

29. Is this child applying with you? ☐ Yes ☐ No

Physical Address

30.a. Street Number and Name

30.b. ☐ Apt. ☐ Ste. ☐ Flr.

30.c. City or Town

30.d. State [▾] **30.e.** ZIP Code

30.f. Province

30.g. Postal Code

30.h. Country

Part 6. Accommodations for Individuals With Disabilities and/or Impairments

NOTE: Read the information in the Form I-751 Instructions before completing this part.

1. Are you requesting an accommodation because of your disabilities and/or impairments? ☐ Yes ☒ No

2. Are you requesting an accommodation because of your spouse's disabilities and/or impairments? ☐ Yes ☒ No

3. Are you requesting an accommodation because of your included children's disabilities and/or impairments? ☐ Yes ☒ No

If you answered "Yes" to **Item Numbers 1. - 3.**, select any applicable box for **Item Numbers 4.a. - 4.c.** Provide information on the disabilities and/or impairments for each person.

4.a. ☐ I am deaf or hard of hearing and request the following accommodation. (If you are requesting a sign-language interpreter, indicate for which language (for example, American Sign Language).):

_____

_____

4.b. ☐ I am blind or have low vision and request the following accommodation:

_____

_____

4.c. ☐ I have another type of disability and/or impairment. (Describe the nature of your disability and/or impairment and the accommodation you are requesting.):

_____

_____

Sample Form I-751, Petition To Remove Conditions on Residence (page 6)

Part 7. Petitioner's Statement, Contact Information, Acknowledgement of Appointment at USCIS Application Support Center, Certification, and Signature

NOTE: Read the information on penalties in the **Penalties** section of the Form I-751 Instructions before completing this part.

NOTE: If you selected **Box 1.a.** in **Part 3.**, your spouse must also read and sign the petition in **Part 8.** Signature of a conditional resident child under 14 years of age is not required; a parent may sign for a child.

Petitioner's Statement

NOTE: Select the box for either **Item Number 1.a.** or **1.b.** If applicable, select the box for **Item Number 2.**

1.a. ☒ I can read and understand English, and have read and understand every question and instruction on this petition, as well as my answer to every question. I have read and understand the **Acknowledgement of Appointment at USCIS Application Support Center.**

1.b. ☐ The interpreter named in **Part 9.** has also read to me every question and instruction on this petition, as well as my answer to every question, in

_____,
a language in which I am fluent. I understand every question and instruction on this petition as translated to me by my interpreter, and have provided complete, true, and correct responses in the language indicated above. The interpreter named in **Part 9.** has also read the **Acknowledgement of Appointment at USCIS Application Support Center** to me, in the language in which I am fluent, and I understand this Application Support Center (ASC) Acknowledgement as read to me by my interpreter.

2. ☐ I have requested the services of and consented to

_____,
who ☐ is ☐ is not an attorney or accredited representative, preparing this petition for me. This person who assisted me in preparing my petition has reviewed the **Acknowledgement of Appointment at USCIS Application Support Center** with me, and I understand the ASC Acknowledgement.

Petitioner's Contact Information

3. Petitioner's Daytime Telephone Number
`2122221111`

4. Petitioner's Mobile Telephone Number (if any)
`2122221111`

5. Petitioner's Email Address (if any)
`nigelh@email.com`

Acknowledgement of Appointment at USCIS Application Support Center

I, `N.I.Hollis`,
understand that the purpose of a USCIS ASC appointment is for me to provide fingerprints, photograph, and/or signature and to re-affirm that all of the information in my petition is complete, true, and correct and was provided by me. I understand that I will sign my name to the following declaration which USCIS will display to me at the time I provide my fingerprints, photograph, and/or signature during my ASC appointment.

By signing here, I declare under penalty of perjury that I have reviewed and understand my application, petition, or request as identified by the receipt number displayed on the screen above, and all supporting documents, applications, petitions, or requests filed with my application, petition, or request that I (or my attorney or accredited representative) filed with USCIS, and that all of the information in these materials is complete, true, and correct.

If conditional residence was based on a marriage, I further certify that the marriage was entered into in accordance with the laws of the place where the marriage took place and was not for the purpose of procuring an immigration benefit.

I also understand that when I sign my name, provide my fingerprints, and am photographed at the USCIS ASC, I will be re-affirming that I willingly submit this petition; I have reviewed the contents of this petition; all of the information in my petition and all supporting documents submitted with my petition were provided by me and are complete, true, and correct; and if I was assisted in completing this petition, the person assisting me also reviewed this **Acknowledgement of Appointment at USCIS Application Support Center** with me.

Sample Form I-751, Petition To Remove Conditions on Residence (page 7)

Part 7. Petitioner's Statement, Contact Information, Acknowledgement of Appointment at USCIS Application Support Center, Certification, and Signature (continued)

Petitioner's Certification

Copies of any documents I have submitted are exact photocopies of unaltered, original documents, and I understand that USCIS may require that I submit original documents to USCIS at a later date. Furthermore, I authorize the release of any information from any and all of my records that USCIS may need to determine my eligibility for the immigration benefit that I seek.

I furthermore authorize release of information contained in this petition, in supporting documents, and in my USCIS records to other entities and persons where necessary for the administration and enforcement of U.S. immigration laws.

I certify under penalty of perjury, that the information in my petition, my responses to each question, and any document submitted with my petition were provided by me and are complete, true, and correct.

Petitioner's Signature

6.a. Petitioner's Signature

> *Nigel J. Hollis*

6.b. Date of Signature (mm/dd/yyyy)   04/15/2021

NOTE TO ALL PETITIONERS: If you do not completely fill out this petition or fail to submit required documents listed in the Instructions, USCIS may deny your petition.

NOTE: If you are filing based on claims of having been battered or subjected to extreme cruelty waiver or individual filing, you are not required to have the spouse's or individual listed in **Part 4's** signature.

Part 8. Spouse's or Individual Listed in Part 4.'s Statement, Contact Information, Acknowledgement of Appointment USCIS Application Support Center, Certification, and Signature (if applicable)

Provide the following information about the spouse or individual listed in **Part 4.**

NOTE: Read the information on penalties in the **Penalties** section of the Form I-751 Instructions before completing this part.

Spouse's or Individual's Statement

NOTE: Select the box for either **Item Number 1.a.** or **1.b.** If applicable, select the box for **Item Number 2.**

1.a. ☒ I can read and understand English, and have read and understand every question and instruction on this petition, as well as the petitioner's answer to every question. I have read and understand the **Acknowledgement of Appointment at USCIS Application Support Center.**

1.b. ☐ The interpreter named in **Part 9.** has also read to me every question and instruction on this petition, as well as the petitioner's answer to every question, in

> _____ ,

a language in which I am fluent. I understand every question and instruction on this petition as translated to me by my interpreter, and have provided complete, true, and correct responses in the language indicated above. The interpreter named in **Part 9.** has also read the **Acknowledgement of Appointment at USCIS Application Support Center** to me, in the language in which I am fluent, and I understand this Application Support Center (ASC) Acknowledgement as read to me by my interpreter.

2. ☐ I have requested the services of and consented to

> _____ ,

who ☐ is ☐ is not an attorney or accredited representative, preparing this petition for me. This person who assisted me in preparing my petition has reviewed the **Acknowledgement of Appointment at USCIS Application Support Center** with me, and I understand the ASC Acknowledgement.

Spouse's or Individual's Contact Information

3. Spouse's or Individual's Daytime Telephone Number

    2122221212

4. Spouse's or Individual's Mobile Telephone Number (if any)

    2122221212

5. Spouse's or Individual's Email Address (if any)

    sandrah@email.com

Sample Form I-751, Petition To Remove Conditions on Residence (page 8)

Part 8. Spouse's or Individual Listed in Part 4.'s Statement, Contact Information, Acknowledgement of Appointment USCIS Application Support Center, Certification, and Signature (if applicable) (continued)

Acknowledgement of Appointment at USCIS Application Support Center

I, S.L.Hollis ,
understand that the purpose of a USCIS ASC appointment is for me to provide my fingerprints, photograph, and/or signature and to re-affirm that all of the information in my petition is complete, true, and correct and was provided by me. I understand that I will sign my name to the following declaration which USCIS will display to me at the time I provide my fingerprints, photograph, and/or signature during my ASC appointment.

> *By signing here, I declare under penalty of perjury that I have reviewed and understand my application, petition, or request as identified by the receipt number displayed on the screen above, and all supporting documents, applications, petitions, or requests filed with my application, petition, or request that I (or my attorney or accredited representative) filed with USCIS, and that all of the information in these materials is complete, true, and correct.*

I also understand that when I sign my name, provide my fingerprints, and am photographed at the USCIS ASC, I will be re-affirming that I willingly submit this petition; I have reviewed the contents of this petition; all of the information in my petition and all supporting documents submitted with my petition were provided by me and are complete, true, and correct; and if I was assisted in completing this petition, the person assisting me also reviewed this **Acknowledgement of Appointment at USCIS Application Support Center** with me.

Spouse's or Individual's Certification

Copies of any documents I have submitted are exact photocopies of unaltered, original documents, and I understand that USCIS may require that I submit original documents to USCIS at a later date. Furthermore, I authorize the release of any information from any and all of my records that USCIS may need to determine my eligibility for the immigration benefit that I seek.

I furthermore authorize release of information contained in this petition, in supporting documents, and in my USCIS records to other entities and persons where necessary for the administration and enforcement of U.S. immigration laws.

I certify under penalty of perjury, that the information in my petition, my responses to each question, and any document submitted with my petition were provided by me and are complete, true, and correct.

Spouse's or Individual's Signature

6.a. Spouse's or Individual's Signature

Sandra L Hollis

6.b. Date of Signature (mm/dd/yyyy) 04/15/2021

NOTE TO ALL SPOUSES OR INDIVIDUALS: If you do not completely fill out this petition or fail to submit required documents listed in the instructions, USCIS may deny your petition.

Part 9. Interpreter's Contact Information, Certification, and Signature

Provide the following information about the interpreter.

Interpreter's Full Name

1.a. Interpreter's Family Name (Last Name)

1.b. Interpreter's Given Name (First Name)

2. Interpreter's Business or Organization Name (if any)

Interpreter's Mailing Address

3.a. Street Number and Name

3.b. ☐ Apt. ☐ Ste. ☐ Flr.

3.c. City or Town

3.d. State ▼ **3.e.** ZIP Code

3.f. Province

3.g. Postal Code

3.h. Country

Interpreter's Contact Information

4. Interpreter's Daytime Telephone Number

5. Interpreter's Email Address (if any)

Your Parents as Immigrants

I f you are a U.S. citizen age 21 or over, but your parents are citizens of another country, your parents are your "immediate relatives" and you may request U.S. green cards for them. They must separately meet the other criteria for green card approval, however.

Another important issue is whether your parents really want to come to the United States. Many are interested in family togetherness, but don't really want to permanently leave the life they've made for themselves elsewhere. Remember that a green card is not just an easy travel pass—unless your parents are ready to settle down in the U.S. permanently, they could lose the green card by spending too much time overseas (and all your hard work could go down the drain).

However, one reason that some parents agree to come is that they can help other family members get green cards; see "Family Immigration Strategies After Your Parents Get Green Cards," below.

A. Who Qualifies to Petition for Their Parents

To petition to get a green card for your parents, you must meet a couple of basic requirements.

> **CAUTION**
> **If the U.S. petitioner has a criminal record, see an attorney.** Under the Adam Walsh Child Protection and Safety Act of 2006, U.S. citizens and lawful permanent residents who have been convicted of any "specified offense against a minor" are prohibited from filing a family-based immigrant petition on behalf of any beneficiary (whether a child or not). USCIS will run security checks on all petitions and may call the petitioner in for fingerprinting. If the petitioner has a conviction for one of the specified offenses against a minor, then the petition will not be approved unless USCIS determines that the U.S. petitioner poses no risk to the beneficiary.

1. You Must Be a U.S. Citizen

You must be a U.S. citizen to file a petition on behalf of your parents. You are a citizen of the United States if you were:

- naturalized (after you applied and passed an exam)
- born in any of the 50 states of the United States or its territories—U.S. Virgin Islands, Puerto Rico, or Guam, or
- born outside the United States or its territories, if one of your parents was a U.S. citizen when you were born. See Chapter 20 for details or contact the U.S. Embassy; if you are not satisfied, consult a lawyer or another experienced naturalization professional. (See Chapter 24.)

2. You Must Be at Least 21 Years Old

As a U.S. citizen, you must be 21 years old or older to bestow the immigration benefit of a green card on your mother and your father as your immediate relatives.

If you were born in the United States to parents who live there illegally, 21 years will be a frustratingly long time to wait. In fact, because your parents may be ineligible to apply for green cards within the U.S. using the procedure called adjustment of status (see Chapter 16) but may instead have to leave the U.S. and apply through a U.S. consulate (see Chapter 17), your citizenship may turn out not to be much help to them.

The reason is that too much time spent in the U.S. illegally can result in bars on returning to the U.S. after they leave (for three or ten years, based on illegal stays of six months or one year or more).

In rare circumstances, your parents might benefit from the newer, "stateside" provisional waiver of unlawful presence, which would allow them to have their unlawful time in the U.S. forgiven before leaving the U.S. for their consular interview. The major difficulty, however, is that your parents will not be able to get a waiver based on any hardship their ban would cause to *you*, the child petitioner.

They would need a "qualifying relative" who is either a U.S. citizen or lawful permanent resident spouse or a parent, and who would suffer extreme hardship if they were denied the green card. This is a tricky area of law, so you'd do best to consult with an attorney before applying for a waiver. See Chapter 4 for more about the provisional waiver.

B. Who Qualifies As Your Parent

If you're from a traditional family—that is, you were born and raised by a married couple—you should have no problem petitioning for your parents to immigrate. However, U.S. immigration law also recognizes some variations on the traditional family. Under certain circumstances, you can also petition for unmarried parents, stepparents, and adoptive parents, as described further below. You'll usually have to provide additional documents to prove the relationship, as also described below.

1. Natural Mother

If your mother was not married to your father when you were born, so that your mother's maiden name appears on your birth certificate, you can prove your relationship by presenting a copy of your birth certificate when you file the petition for your mother.

If your mother has changed her name because she has married someone else, then also present her marriage certificate to show her change of name.

2. Natural Father

If your biological father did not marry your mother either before or after you were born, you can still petition for him as your immediate relative. You must also provide some evidence of your relationship: Make a copy of your birth certificate, baptismal certificate, or other religious records showing his name as your father. USCIS may require both you and your father to take a blood test as proof of your relationship.

> **Proposed Changes to U.S. Immigration Law May Affect Green Cards for Parents**
>
> In early 2017, President Trump proposed changing the law that allows U.S. citizens to petition for green cards for their parents. This was part of an effort to end so-called "chain migration" and cut legal immigration to the United States. Congress considered various proposals, including one that would have eliminated green cards for all immigrating relatives other than spouses and minor children.
>
> Although this particular round of proposals was ultimately defeated, additional calls for changes to U.S. immigration law can be expected in the coming months and years. The good news is that all immigration petitions filed before the law changes would likely be allowed to go forward. To be safe, therefore, if your parent qualifies for legal permanent residency and wishes to live in the U.S., it might be worth submitting a Form I-130 petition as soon as possible.
>
> Stay tuned to the news and Nolo's online immigration updates for announcements about the future of family-based green cards.

If you and your father did not live together before you turned 18, you must present proof that, up to the time you turned 21 years of age, he maintained a father-child relationship with you by providing financial support, writing to you or your mother about your well-being, sending you birthday cards, holiday cards, and photographs, or perhaps naming you as a beneficiary to his life insurance.

If you lived with your father before your 18th birthday, you must present proof that there was a father-child relationship, as evidenced by school records, photographs, letters, civil records, or written statements from friends and relatives.

If You, the Petitioner, Change Names

If you are a married U.S. citizen petitioning for your parents, you may have changed your name after marriage. Therefore, in addition to your birth certificate to prove the parent-child relationship when you send the Petition for Alien Relative, Form I-130, for your mother or father, you must also attach your marriage certificate to show your change of name.

If you have changed your name by petitioning the court, you must attach a final court judgment as proof of that change.

3. Stepmother or Stepfather

If your father or mother marries somebody other than your biological parent before you turn 18 years of age, the person he or she marries becomes your stepmother or stepfather.

When you file a petition for your stepmother or stepfather as your immediate relative (by submitting the usual petition Form I-130), add to it the following documents:

- your birth certificate showing the name of your remarried parent, and
- the marriage certificate of your remarried parent to show the name of the new spouse (your stepparent).

For you to petition for your stepparent, the marriage must have occurred before your 18th birthday. If the marriage happened after your 18th birthday, then say, "I love you, but I cannot claim you as my immediate relative for immigration into the United States."

But all is not lost.

Your natural mother or father, after qualifying as your immediate relative and obtaining a green card, can petition for your stepparent who is now the spouse of a permanent resident—2A, the second preference beneficiary. Unfortunately, however, the stepparent might have to wait a few years until a visa becomes available in this category.

Immigrant Story: Petitioning for a Surviving Stepparent

Luzmaria, originally from El Salvador, married a U.S. citizen at age 25, and became a U.S. citizen herself at age 29. She then filed visa petitions for her father and for her stepmother, who her father married when Luzmaria was 14.

Sadly, Luzmaria's father died a few months later. Luzmaria was doubly heartbroken, thinking that now her stepmother would not be eligible to immigrate.

However, because the stepmother continues to fit the criteria for immediate relative of a U.S. citizen (having married Luzmaria's father when Luzmaria was under 18), she is able to continue with her application and eventually receive a U.S. green card.

4. Adoptive Mother and Father

Suppose you were adopted by a non-U.S. citizen before your 16th birthday. If you are a U.S. citizen and you are now 21 years or older, you can petition for your adoptive mother and father as your immediate relatives.

When you file the petition (Form I-130), you must also submit:

- the court decree of your adoption
- your birth certificate showing the name of your adopting parents as your father and mother, and
- a statement showing the dates and places you have lived together.

CAUTION
Adopted children cannot petition for their natural parents. When you were adopted, your natural parents gave up all parental ties with you. Therefore, you will never be able to petition for your natural parents as your immediate relatives. The adoption decree cuts off all legal ties between you and your natural parents.

C. Quick View of the Application Process

To get a green card for your parent, you must begin the process by preparing a petition (Form I-130, together with certain documents). Form I-130 serves to prove to the immigration authorities that your parents are truly and legally yours. After that petition is approved (in most cases), your parents must complete their half of the process by submitting an immigrant visa application and attending an interview, sometimes but not always with you accompanying them. Their application serves to prove that not only do they qualify as parents of a U.S. citizen, but that they're otherwise eligible for U.S. permanent residence.

However, the details of when and how your parents complete their half of the process depend on whether your parents are living overseas or in the United States, as described next.

D. Detailed Instructions for the Application Process

Now we'll break the application process down into individual procedures, some of which will be covered in this chapter, and others in later chapters—we'll tell you exactly where to turn to for your situation.

1. The I-130 Petition

Let's start by discussing the initial petition that all people seeking to sponsor their parents to immigrate must prepare to begin the process. You'll need to assemble:

☐ Form I-130, Petition for Alien Relative (available at www.uscis.gov/i-130; see the sample at the end of this chapter)

☐ documents showing your U.S. citizenship

☐ a copy of your birth certificate, showing your name as well as your mother's name, if filing for your mother, and the names of both parents, if filing for your father

☐ a copy of the marriage certificate of your parents if you are filing for your father; your stepparents' marriage certificate, if you are filing for either stepparent

☐ a copy of your adoption decree, if you are filing for your adoptive parent

☐ the filing fee, currently $535 in a personal check or money order payable to the Department of Homeland Security. You may also pay by credit card, by filling out Form G-1450, Authorization for Credit Card Transaction (www.uscis.gov/g-1450) along with your application. Place this on top of the other forms and documents you send to USCIS, if you apply by mail. (Online filing is also an option.) Don't send cash.

☐ Form G-1145. This is optional, but filing it is a good idea, so that you'll receive an email and/or text notification from USCIS when your application has been accepted. (Get it from www.uscis.gov/g-1145.) Once USCIS sends you a receipt number, you can use that number to sign up to receive automatic email updates letting you know whenever mail is sent regarding your application.

TIP
How to sign up for automatic email updates: Go to www.uscis.gov and click "Check Case Status." Then under "Why sign up for an account?" click "Sign Up." After accepting the terms and conditions, you can register as an applicant/petitioner.

Once you've assembled all these items, make a copy of everything (including the check or money order) for your records. It's also a good idea to write a cover letter, explaining what type of petition it is (for example, saying "I am a U.S. citizen, filing the enclosed I-130 petition on behalf of my mother"). The letter should include a bulleted list, much like the checklist above, of everything you're sending. This will help USCIS see that you're organized. It will help you, too, to make sure that nothing has been forgotten.

If your parents are not in the United States, apply online at www.uscis.gov by creating an account, or mail all these documents and the fee by Priority Mail to the USCIS Dallas or Phoenix lockbox, which will forward it to the appropriate USCIS office. (See the USCIS website for contact details.) If your parents are in the United States, they might be able to file directly for adjustment of status (see Chapter 16) in which case, you may choose to mail the I-130 along with the required forms and documents.

2. The Green Card Application

The next step in your parents' immigration process depends on where they're located. If they're in the United States, you need to start by figuring out whether they are eligible to adjust status (apply for their green card) here. See Chapter 16, Section A, to determine this. (If they entered on valid visas, then they are probably eligible, even if they remained in the U.S. past the date they were allowed to stay.)

> **CAUTION**
> **Traveling outside the U.S. might trigger penalties.** Even though remaining in the U.S. past the date allowed by USCIS will not prevent your parents' applications from being granted, if they travel outside the U.S. before that time—either with or without USCIS permission—they could trigger a penalty for their unlawful presence and may not be granted permanent residence for three to ten years, depending on the length of their unlawful stay.
>
> Your parents should also know that if they obtained a tourist or another visa with the secret intention of applying for a green card after they got here, that could be visa fraud. They can be denied the green card based on this fraud.

> **NEXT STEP**
> **If your parents are allowed to adjust status in the U.S.** You can mail the I-130 petition in combination with an adjustment of status application to a USCIS office, as also described in Chapter 16. Eventually, they will be fingerprinted, called in for an interview at a local USCIS office, and hopefully approved for U.S. residency. In straightforward cases, where all required paperwork is properly submitted with the application, USCIS may opt to approve the application without an interview.

> **NEXT STEP**
> **If your parents do not qualify to adjust status but are currently in the U.S.** With limited exceptions, if your parents entered the U.S. without inspection, they are not eligible to apply for adjustment of status. If they leave the U.S., however, to apply for a visa at a U.S. consulate, their departure after unlawful presence could result in their being prevented from reentering for three or ten years, depending on the length of their unlawful stay. There is a new provisional waiver of unlawful presence, which allows certain immediate relatives who are in this situation to learn whether or not USCIS will grant them a waiver of the time bar BEFORE they leave the United States. (See Chapter 4 for more on this.) The provisional waiver is difficult to get, however, and they would need a qualifying U.S. citizen spouse or parent who would experience "extreme hardship," in order to apply. Seek the advice of an immigration attorney before applying.

Be Kind to the Elderly

If your mother or father is elderly, take some time to help them get acquainted with U.S. customs and cultural habits.

Introduce them to the nearest senior citizen center. Teach them how to use the public transport system. Alert them to precautions to be taken if you live in a high-crime area. Bring them to cultural or popular entertainment activities.

Pay them a decent amount if they take care of your children. It is unfair to make your parents mere babysitters; they have already done all the childrearing they were responsible for when raising you. Do not take advantage of their presence in your home to do the work you should be doing.

NEXT STEP

If your parents still live in their home country. Their next step is to await USCIS approval of the I-130 petition and then go through consular processing, as described in Chapter 17. Eventually, they will be called in for an interview at their local U.S. consulate, at which time they will hopefully be approved for an immigrant visa to enter the United States and claim their permanent residency.

RELATED TOPIC

See Chapter 23 for important information on how your parents can protect their right to keep the green card.

Family Immigration Strategies After Your Parents Get Green Cards

By becoming U.S. permanent residents, your parents can petition for all their unmarried children—in family second preference Category 2A or 2B. If they become naturalized U.S. citizens, they can petition even for their married children—in the family third preference category.

Although as a U.S. citizen you may have filed for your brothers and sisters (family fourth preference), your mother or father, after becoming U.S. citizens, could secure a green card for them more quickly. It's okay to file more than one visa petition for the same person at the same time. (You can wait to see which Priority Date becomes current first.)

However, your parents must be aware that getting a green card does not automatically mean that their children can get their own green cards. Your parents would also have to live (maintain residence) in the United States until their other children obtain their green cards, which will take years.

The rules on maintaining U.S. residency are complicated and require that the person make the United States his or her home. While the law allows travel overseas, most important family and business ties should be in the United States, and your parents should compile evidence of these, such as:

- a lease, rental agreement, or title to property in the United States
- utility bills
- a driver's license or car registration, or
- state and federal tax returns.

And that's just the minimum for maintaining permanent resident status. The rules for amount of time spent in the U.S. before applying for U.S. citizenship are even stricter. If you or your parents have questions about whether you are properly maintaining permanent residence, consult an immigration attorney.

Sample Form I-130, Petition for Alien Relative (as used for immigrating parents) (page 1)

Petition for Alien Relative

Department of Homeland Security
U.S. Citizenship and Immigration Services

USCIS
Form I-130
OMB No. 1615-0012
Expires 02/28/2021

For USCIS Use Only		
A-Number		

A- [ ][ ][ ][ ][ ][ ][ ][ ][ ]

Initial Receipt

Resubmitted

Relocated	Section of Law/Visa Category		
Received	☐ 201(b) Spouse - IR-1/CR-1	☐ 203(a)(1) Unm. S/D - F1-1	☐ 203(a)(2)(B) Unm. S/D - F2-4
Sent	☐ 201(b) Child - IR-2/CR-2	☐ 203(a)(2)(A) Spouse - F2-1	☐ 203(a)(3) Married S/D - F3-1
Completed	☐ 201(b) Parent - IR-5	☐ 203(a)(2)(A) Child - F2-2	☐ 203(a)(4) Brother/Sister - F4-1

Approved	Petition was filed on (Priority Date mm/dd/yyyy):	☐ Field Investigation	☐ Personal Interview	☐ 204(a)(2)(A) Resolved
Returned	PDR request granted/denied - New priority date (mm/dd/yyyy):	☐ Previously Forwarded	☐ Pet. A-File Reviewed	☐ I-485 Filed Simultaneously
		☐ 203(g) Resolved	☐ Ben. A-File Reviewed	☐ 204(g) Resolved

Remarks

At which USCIS office (e.g., NBC, VSC, LOS, CRO) was Form I-130 adjudicated? _____

To be completed by an attorney or accredited representative (if any).			
☐ **Select this box if Form G-28 is attached.**	**Volag Number** (if any)	**Attorney State Bar Number** (if applicable)	**Attorney or Accredited Representative USCIS Online Account Number** (if any)

▶ **START HERE - Type or print in black ink.**

> If you need extra space to complete any section of this petition, use the space provided in **Part 9. Additional Information.**
> **Complete and submit as many copies of Part 9., as necessary, with your petition.**

Part 1. Relationship (You are the Petitioner. Your relative is the Beneficiary)

1. I am filing this petition for my (Select **only one** box):

   ☐ Spouse ☒ Parent ☐ Brother/Sister ☐ Child

2. If you are filing this petition for your child or parent, select the box that describes your relationship (Select **only one** box):

   ☒ Child was born to parents who were married to each other at the time of the child's birth

   ☐ Stepchild/Stepparent

   ☐ Child was born to parents who were not married to each other at the time of the child's birth

   ☐ Child was adopted (not an Orphan or Hague Convention adoptee)

3. If the beneficiary is your brother/sister, are you related by adoption? ☐ Yes ☒ No

4. Did you gain lawful permanent resident status or citizenship through adoption? ☐ Yes ☒ No

Part 2. Information About You (Petitioner)

1. Alien Registration Number (A-Number) (if any)

   ▶ A- [1][2][3][3][2][1][1][2][3]

2. USCIS Online Account Number (if any)

   ▶ [ ][ ][ ][ ][ ][ ][ ][ ][ ][ ][ ][ ]

3. U.S. Social Security Number (if any)

   ▶ [9][8][7][6][5][4][3][2][1]

Your Full Name

4.a.	Family Name (Last Name)	Solomos
4.b.	Given Name (First Name)	Aphrodite
4.c.	Middle Name	Eleni

Sample Form I-130, Petition for Alien Relative (as used for immigrating parents) (page 2)

Part 2. Information About You (Petitioner) (continued)

Other Names Used (if any)

Provide all other names you have ever used, including aliases, maiden name, and nicknames.

5.a. Family Name (Last Name): Arvanitis

5.b. Given Name (First Name): Aphrodite

5.c. Middle Name: Eleni

Other Information

6. City/Town/Village of Birth: Athens

7. Country of Birth: Greece

8. Date of Birth (mm/dd/yyyy): 07/03/1984

9. Sex: ☐ Male ☒ Female

Mailing Address

10.a. In Care Of Name:

10.b. Street Number and Name: 123 3rd Street

10.c. ☐ Apt. ☐ Ste. ☐ Flr.

10.d. City or Town: Baton Rouge

10.e. State: LA **10.f.** ZIP Code: 70808

10.g. Province:

10.h. Postal Code:

10.i. Country: USA

11. Is your current mailing address the same as your physical address? ☒ Yes ☐ No

If you answered "No" to **Item Number 11.**, provide information on your physical address in **Item Numbers 12.a. - 13.b.**

Address History

Provide your physical addresses for the last five years, whether inside or outside the United States. Provide your current address first if it is different from your mailing address in **Item Numbers 10.a. - 10.i.**

Physical Address 1

12.a. Street Number and Name:

12.b. ☐ Apt. ☐ Ste. ☐ Flr.

12.c. City or Town:

12.d. State: **12.e.** ZIP Code:

12.f. Province:

12.g. Postal Code:

12.h. Country:

13.a. Date From (mm/dd/yyyy): 03/01/2016

13.b. Date To (mm/dd/yyyy): present

Physical Address 2

14.a. Street Number and Name: 188 Crescent Street

14.b. ☐ Apt. ☐ Ste. ☐ Flr.

14.c. City or Town: New Orleans

14.d. State: LA **14.e.** ZIP Code: 70115

14.f. Province:

14.g. Postal Code:

14.h. Country: USA

15.a. Date From (mm/dd/yyyy): 08/01/2011

15.b. Date To (mm/dd/yyyy): 02/28/2016

Your Marital Information

16. How many times have you been married? ▶ 1

17. Current Marital Status

☐ Single, Never Married ☒ Married ☐ Divorced
☐ Widowed ☐ Separated ☐ Annulled

Sample Form I-130, Petition for Alien Relative (as used for immigrating parents) (page 3)

Part 2. Information About You (Petitioner) (continued)

18. Date of Current Marriage (if currently married) (mm/dd/yyyy)   03/17/2010

Place of Your Current Marriage (if married)

19.a. City or Town   New Orleans

19.b. State   LA

19.c. Province

19.d. Country   USA

Names of All Your Spouses (if any)

Provide information on your current spouse (if currently married) first and then list all your prior spouses (if any).

Spouse 1

20.a. Family Name (Last Name)   Solomos

20.b. Given Name (First Name)   Nicholas

20.c. Middle Name   Evangelos

21. Date Marriage Ended (mm/dd/yyyy)

Spouse 2

22.a. Family Name (Last Name)

22.b. Given Name (First Name)

22.c. Middle Name

23. Date Marriage Ended (mm/dd/yyyy)

Information About Your Parents

Parent 1's Information

Full Name of Parent 1

24.a. Family Name (Last Name)   Arvanitis

24.b. Given Name (First Name)   Kiriaki

24.c. Middle Name   Anthe

25. Date of Birth (mm/dd/yyyy)   03/22/1957

26. Sex   ☐ Male   ☒ Female

27. Country of Birth   Greece

28. City/Town/Village of Residence   Athens

29. Country of Residence   Greece

Parent 2's Information

Full Name of Parent 2

30.a. Family Name (Last Name)   Arvanitis

30.b. Given Name (First Name)   Demosthenes

30.c. Middle Name   Mark

31. Date of Birth (mm/dd/yyyy)   02/16/1950

32. Sex   ☒ Male   ☐ Female

33. Country of Birth   Greece

34. City/Town/Village of Residence   Deceased

35. Country of Residence   Deceased

Additional Information About You (Petitioner)

36. I am a (Select only one box):
☒ U.S. Citizen   ☐ Lawful Permanent Resident

If you are a U.S. citizen, complete Item Number 37.

37. My citizenship was acquired through (Select only one box):
☐ Birth in the United States
☒ Naturalization
☐ Parents

38. Have you obtained a Certificate of Naturalization or a Certificate of Citizenship?   ☒ Yes   ☐ No

If you answered "Yes" to **Item Number 38.**, complete the following:

39.a. Certificate Number   32134545

39.b. Place of Issuance   New Orleans, LA

39.c. Date of Issuance (mm/dd/yyyy)   03/17/2017

Sample Form I-130, Petition for Alien Relative (as used for immigrating parents) (page 4)

Part 2. Information About You (Petitioner) (continued)

If you are a lawful permanent resident, complete **Item Numbers 40.a. - 41.**

40.a. Class of Admission

40.b. Date of Admission (mm/dd/yyyy)

Place of Admission

40.c. City or Town

40.d State

41. Did you gain lawful permanent resident status through marriage to a U.S. citizen or lawful permanent resident?

☐ Yes ☐ No

Employment History

Provide your employment history for the last five years, whether inside or outside the United States. Provide your current employment first. If you are currently unemployed, type or print "Unemployed" in **Item Number 42.**

Employer 1

42. Name of Employer/Company

Olympus Travel Agency

43.a. Street Number and Name

1900 Gulfview Lane

43.b. ☐ Apt. ☐ Ste. ☐ Flr.

43.c. City or Town

Baton Rouge

43.d. State LA **43.e.** ZIP Code 70808

43.f. Province

43.g. Postal Code

43.h. Country

USA

44. Your Occupation

Owner

45.a. Date From (mm/dd/yyyy) 01/15/2016

45.b. Date To (mm/dd/yyyy) present

Employer 2

46. Name of Employer/Company

Crescent City Travel

47.a. Street Number and Name 1999 Crescent Street

47.b. ☐ Apt. ☐ Ste. ☐ Flr.

47.c. City or Town New Orleans

47.d. State LA **47.e.** ZIP Code 70115

47.f. Province

47.g. Postal Code

47.h. Country

USA

48. Your Occupation

Travel Agent

49.a. Date From (mm/dd/yyyy) 10/20/2011

49.b. Date To (mm/dd/yyyy) 12/31/2015

Part 3. Biographic Information

NOTE: Provide the biographic information about you, the petitioner.

1. Ethnicity (Select **only one** box)

☐ Hispanic or Latino
☒ Not Hispanic or Latino

2. Race (Select **all applicable** boxes)

☒ White
☐ Asian
☐ Black or African American
☐ American Indian or Alaska Native
☐ Native Hawaiian or Other Pacific Islander

3. Height Feet 5 Inches 5

4. Weight Pounds 1 8 0

5. Eye Color (Select **only one** box)

☐ Black ☐ Blue ☒ Brown
☐ Gray ☐ Green ☐ Hazel
☐ Maroon ☐ Pink ☐ Unknown/Other

Sample Form I-130, Petition for Alien Relative (as used for immigrating parents) (page 5)

Part 3. Biographic Information (continued)

6. Hair Color (Select **only one** box)

- ☐ Bald (No hair)
- ☐ Black
- ☐ Blond
- ☒ Brown
- ☐ Gray
- ☐ Red
- ☐ Sandy
- ☐ White
- ☐ Unknown/Other

Part 4. Information About Beneficiary

1. Alien Registration Number (A-Number) (if any) ▶ A- [ ][ ][ ][ ][ ][ ][ ][ ][ ]

2. USCIS Online Account Number (if any) ▶

3. U.S. Social Security Number (if any) ▶

Beneficiary's Full Name

4.a. Family Name (Last Name): Arvanitis
4.b. Given Name (First Name): Kiriaki
4.c. Middle Name: Anthe

Other Names Used (if any)

Provide all other names the beneficiary has ever used, including aliases, maiden name, and nicknames.

5.a. Family Name (Last Name): Mamalis
5.b. Given Name (First Name): Kiriaki
5.c. Middle Name: Anthe

Other Information About Beneficiary

6. City/Town/Village of Birth: Santorini
7. Country of Birth: Greece
8. Date of Birth (mm/dd/yyyy): 03/22/1957
9. Sex: ☐ Male ☒ Female
10. Has anyone else ever filed a petition for the beneficiary? ☐ Yes ☒ No ☐ Unknown

NOTE: Select "Unknown" *only* if you do not know, and the beneficiary also does not know, if anyone else has ever filed a petition for the beneficiary.

Beneficiary's Physical Address

If the beneficiary lives outside the United States in a home without a street number or name, leave **Item Numbers 11.a.** and **11.b.** blank.

11.a. Street Number and Name: Galanou 25
11.b. ☐ Apt. ☐ Ste. ☐ Flr.
11.c. City or Town: Athens
11.d. State: **11.e.** ZIP Code:
11.f. Province:
11.g. Postal Code: 10553
11.h. Country: Greece

Other Address and Contact Information

Provide the address in the United States where the beneficiary intends to live, if different from **Item Numbers 11.a. - 11.h.** If the address is the same, type or print "SAME" in **Item Number 12.a.**

12.a Street Number and Name: SAME
12.b. ☐ Apt. ☐ Ste. ☐ Flr.
12.c. City or Town:
12.d. State: **12.e.** ZIP Code:

Provide the beneficiary's address outside the United States, if different from **Item Numbers 11.a. - 11.h.** If the address is the same, type or print "SAME" in **Item Number 13.a.**

13.a. Street Number and Name:
13.b. ☐ Apt. ☐ Ste. ☐ Flr.
13.c. City or Town:
13.d. Province:
13.e. Postal Code:
13.f. Country:
14. Daytime Telephone Number (if any):

Sample Form I-130, Petition for Alien Relative (as used for immigrating parents) (page 6)

Part 4. Information About Beneficiary (continued)

15. Mobile Telephone Number (if any)

30142345465565

16. Email Address (if any)

karvanitis@email.com

Beneficiary's Marital Information

17. How many times has the beneficiary been married?   ▶   1

18. Current Marital Status

☐ Single, Never Married   ☐ Married   ☐ Divorced

☒ Widowed   ☐ Separated   ☐ Annulled

19. Date of Current Marriage (if currently married) (mm/dd/yyyy)

Place of Beneficiary's Current Marriage (if married)

20.a. City or Town

20.b. State

20.c. Province

20.d. Country

Names of Beneficiary's Spouses (if any)

Provide information on the beneficiary's current spouse (if currently married) first and then list all the beneficiary's prior spouses (if any).

Spouse 1

21.a. Family Name (Last Name)   None

21.b. Given Name (First Name)

21.c. Middle Name

22. Date Marriage Ended (mm/dd/yyyy)

Spouse 2

23.a. Family Name (Last Name)   Arvanitis

23.b. Given Name (First Name)   Demosthenes

23.c. Middle Name   Mark

24. Date Marriage Ended (mm/dd/yyyy)   11/20/2018

Information About Beneficiary's Family

Provide information about the beneficiary's spouse and children.

Person 1

25.a. Family Name (Last Name)   Solomos

25.b. Given Name (First Name)   Aphrodite

25.c. Middle Name   Eleni

26. Relationship   Child

27. Date of Birth (mm/dd/yyyy)   07/03/1984

28. Country of Birth

Greece

Person 2

29.a. Family Name (Last Name)

29.b. Given Name (First Name)

29.c. Middle Name

30. Relationship

31. Date of Birth (mm/dd/yyyy)

32. Country of Birth

Person 3

33.a. Family Name (Last Name)

33.b. Given Name (First Name)

33.c. Middle Name

34. Relationship

35. Date of Birth (mm/dd/yyyy)

36. Country of Birth

Sample Form I-130, Petition for Alien Relative (as used for immigrating parents) (page 7)

| **Part 4. Information About Beneficiary** (continued) | | |

Person 4

37.a. Family Name (Last Name)

37.b. Given Name (First Name)

37.c. Middle Name

38. Relationship

39. Date of Birth (mm/dd/yyyy)

40. Country of Birth

Person 5

41.a. Family Name (Last Name)

41.b. Given Name (First Name)

41.c. Middle Name

42. Relationship

43. Date of Birth (mm/dd/yyyy)

44. Country of Birth

Beneficiary's Entry Information

45. Was the beneficiary **EVER** in the United States? ☒ Yes ☐ No

If the beneficiary is currently in the United States, complete **Items Numbers 46.a. - 46.d.**

46.a. He or she arrived as a (Class of Admission):

46.b. Form I-94 Arrival-Departure Record Number ▶

46.c. Date of Arrival (mm/dd/yyyy)

46.d. Date authorized stay expired, or will expire, as shown on Form I-94 or Form I-95 (mm/dd/yyyy) or type or print "D/S" for Duration of Status

47. Passport Number
12335444GRE

48. Travel Document Number

49. Country of Issuance for Passport or Travel Document
Greece

50. Expiration Date for Passport or Travel Document (mm/dd/yyyy) 05/10/2023

Beneficiary's Employment Information

Provide the beneficiary's current employment information (if applicable), even if they are employed outside of the United States. If the beneficiary is currently unemployed, type or print "Unemployed" in **Item Number 51.a.**

51.a. Name of Current Employer (if applicable)
Unemployed

51.b. Street Number and Name

51.c. ☐ Apt. ☐ Ste. ☐ Flr.

51.d. City or Town

51.e. State   **51.f.** ZIP Code

51.g. Province

51.h. Postal Code

51.i. Country

52. Date Employment Began (mm/dd/yyyy)

Additional Information About Beneficiary

53. Was the beneficiary **EVER** in immigration proceedings? ☐ Yes ☒ No

54. If you answered "Yes," select the type of proceedings and provide the location and date of the proceedings.

☐ Removal ☐ Exclusion/Deportation
☐ Rescission ☐ Other Judicial Proceedings

55.a. City or Town

55.b. State

56. Date (mm/dd/yyyy)

Sample Form I-130, Petition for Alien Relative (as used for immigrating parents) (page 8)

Part 4. Information About Beneficiary (continued)

If the beneficiary's native written language does not use Roman letters, type or print his or her name and foreign address in their native written language.

57.a. Family Name (Last Name)

57.b. Given Name (First Name)

57.c. Middle Name

58.a. Street Number and Name

58.b. ☐ Apt. ☐ Ste. ☐ Flr.

58.c. City or Town

58.d. Province

58.e. Postal Code

58.f. Country

If filing for your spouse, provide the last address at which you physically lived together. If you never lived together, type or print, "Never lived together" in Item Number 59.a.

59.a. Street Number and Name

59.b. ☐ Apt. ☐ Ste. ☐ Flr.

59.c. City or Town

59.d. State

59.e. ZIP Code

59.f. Province

59.g. Postal Code

59.h. Country

60.a. Date From (mm/dd/yyyy)

60.b. Date To (mm/dd/yyyy)

The beneficiary is in the United States and will apply for adjustment of status to that of a lawful permanent resident at the U.S. Citizenship and Immigration Services (USCIS) office in:

61.a. City or Town

61.b. State

The beneficiary will not apply for adjustment of status in the United States, but he or she will apply for an immigrant visa abroad at the U.S. Embassy or U.S. Consulate in:

62.a. City or Town | Athens

62.b. Province

62.c. Country | Greece

NOTE: Choosing a U.S. Embassy or U.S. Consulate outside the country of the beneficiary's last residence does not guarantee that it will accept the beneficiary's case for processing. In these situations, the designated U.S. Embassy or U.S. Consulate has discretion over whether or not to accept the beneficiary's case.

Part 5. Other Information

1. Have you **EVER** previously filed a petition for this beneficiary or any other alien? ☐ Yes ☒ No

If you answered "Yes," provide the name, place, date of filing, and the result.

2.a. Family Name (Last Name)

2.b. Given Name (First Name)

2.c. Middle Name

3.a. City or Town

3.b. State

4. Date Filed (mm/dd/yyyy)

5. Result (for example, approved, denied, withdrawn)

If you are also submitting separate petitions for other relatives, provide the names of and your relationship to each relative.

Relative 1

6.a. Family Name (Last Name)

6.b. Given Name (First Name)

6.c. Middle Name

7. Relationship

Sample Form I-130, Petition for Alien Relative (as used for immigrating parents) (page 9)

Part 5. Other Information (continued)

Relative 2

8.a. Family Name
(Last Name)

8.b. Given Name
(First Name)

8.c. Middle Name

9. Relationship

WARNING: USCIS investigates the claimed relationships and verifies the validity of documents you submit. If you falsify a family relationship to obtain a visa, USCIS may seek to have you criminally prosecuted.

PENAL TIES: By law , you may be imprisoned for up to 5 years or fined $250,000, or both, for entering into a marriage contract in order to evade any U.S. immigration law. In addition, you may be fined up to $10,000 and imprisoned for up to 5 years, or both, for knowingly and willfully falsifying or concealing a material fact or using any false document in submitting this petition.

Part 6. Petitioner's Statement, Contact Information, Declaration, and Signature

NOTE: Read the **Penalties** section of the Form I-130 Instructions before completing this part.

Petitioner's Statement

NOTE: Select the box for either **Item Number 1.a.** or **1.b.** If applicable, select the box for **Item Number 2.**

1.a. ☒ I can read and understand English, and I have read and understand every question and instruction on this petition and my answer to every question.

1.b. ☐ The interpreter named in **Part 7.** read to me every question and instruction on this petition and my answer to every question in

a language in which I am fluent. I understood all of this information as interpreted.

2. ☐ At my request, the preparer named in **Part 8.**,

prepared this petition for me based only upon information I provided or authorized.

Petitioner's Contact Information

3. Petitioner's Daytime Telephone Number

2255094378

4. Petitioner's Mobile Telephone Number (if any)

2255095599

5. Petitioner's Email Address (if any)

aphrodite@email.com

Petitioner's Declaration and Certification

Copies of any documents I have submitted are exact photocopies of unaltered, original documents, and I understand that USCIS may require that I submit original documents to USCIS at a later date. Furthermore, I authorize the release of any information from any of my records that USCIS may need to determine my eligibility for the immigration benefit I seek.

I further authorize release of information contained in this petition, in supporting documents, and in my USCIS records to other entities and persons where necessary for the administration and enforcement of U.S. immigration laws.

I understand that USCIS may require me to appear for an appointment to take my biometrics (fingerprints, photograph, and/or signature) and, at that time, if I am required to provide biometrics, I will be required to sign an oath reaffirming that:

1) I provided or authorized all of the information contained in, and submitted with, my petition;

2) I reviewed and understood all of the information in, and submitted with, my petition; and

3) All of this information was complete, true, and correct at the time of filing.

I certify, under penalty of perjury, that all of the information in my petition and any document submitted with it were provided or authorized by me, that I reviewed and understand all of the information contained in, and submitted with, my petition, and that all of this information is complete, true, and correct.

Petitioner's Signature

6.a. Petitioner's Signature (sign in ink)

➡ *Aphrodite E. Solomos*

6.b. Date of Signature (mm/dd/yyyy)   05/01/2020

NOTE TO ALL PETITIONERS: If you do not completely fill out this petition or fail to submit required documents listed in the Instructions, USCIS may deny your petition.

Child Immigrants

When Congress writes laws regulating immigration, it aims to keep families together. Foreign-born children of U.S. citizens or permanent residents are eligible to get a green card when a parent files a petition for them. However, you need to look carefully at who qualifies as a "child."

Note: This chapter addresses only children whose parents have already immigrated to the United States. The situation of children accompanying an immigrating parent is covered in other chapters of this book.

A. Who Qualifies

A person is eligible for a green card if he or she is the child of:

- a U.S. citizen, and is under 21 years of age (immediate relative)
- a U.S. citizen, if the child is over 21 and not married (family first preference category)
- a U.S. citizen, if the child is married (family third preference category)
- a lawful permanent resident, if the child is not married and is under 21 (family second 2A preference), or
- a lawful permanent resident, if the child is over 21 years old and not married (family second 2B preference). If the child was formerly married, but is now divorced or a widow or widower, or if the marriage has been annulled, the child can still immigrate in the 2B category.

CAUTION
If the U.S. petitioner has a criminal record, see an attorney. Under the Adam Walsh Child Protection and Safety Act of 2006, U.S. citizens and lawful permanent residents who have been convicted of any "specified offense against a minor" are prohibited from filing a family-based immigrant petition on behalf of any beneficiary (whether a child or not). USCIS will run security checks on all petitions and may call the petitioner in for fingerprinting. If the petitioner has a conviction for one of the specified offenses against a minor, then the petition will not be approved, unless USCIS determines that the U.S. petitioner poses no risk to the beneficiary.

Adult Children of Permanent Residents Wait Longer

Around 88,000 immigrant visas are allowed to be given out each year to the spouses and unmarried children under 21 years of age of green card holders. But only around 26,000 visas per year can go to their unmarried children over 21 years of age. The law places no time limits on processing the applications.

The waiting period for a spouse and unmarried children under the age of 21 (Category 2A) is often up to about two years. Children over 21 (Category 2B) should, however, be prepared to wait seven years or more for their immigrant visas.

The green card–holding parent or spouse might be able to hurry the process along by becoming a U.S. citizen.

CAUTION
Caution for children who get married or turn 21 before receiving their green cards. As a broad rule, the visa categories described above must fit the children not only when the visa application process is begun, but at the very end. This end might be years later, when the child attends the interview at which he or she is approved for the green card, and also, if coming from overseas, when the child actually enters the United States.

There are exceptions to this rule, however, added by the Child Status Protection Act (CSPA). The exceptions depend on whether the child is an immediate relative or is in a preference category. For immediate relatives, as long as the I-130 petition was submitted when the child was less than 21 years old, that child remains an immediate relative child regardless of his or her age at the time of actual immigration. Children in the 2A preference category, however, only get to add to their age the time that it took USCIS to make a decision on their I-130 petition. For details, see Chapter 5. Although CSPA exceptions will prevent some children from "aging out" after their 21st birthday, they won't protect children who marry. If, for example, the child of a permanent resident gets married, his or her green card eligibility will be destroyed (at least until the parent becomes a U.S. citizen and starts the petition process all over again). If you are a permanent resident, explain to your children that if they get married, it could nullify their right to immigrate with you.

B. Definition of "Child"

Immigration law recognizes many different meanings of the word "child" as it relates to obtaining a green card. This definition is important because it determines what kind of documents USCIS will require when the visa petition is filed.

1. Child of Married Parents

When a child is born to a man and a woman who are married to each other, the child is, in legal terms, their legitimate child. If the mother will be filing the visa petition, the only document necessary to establish their relationship is the birth certificate showing the name of the mother and of the child.

If the father will be filing the I-130 petition, to show the relationship of father and child, two documents are necessary:

- the birth certificate, which shows the name of the father and the child, and
- the marriage certificate, which shows that the mother and the father were married before the birth of the child.

2. Child of Unmarried Parents

A woman and a man who conceive a child are that child's natural parents. Proving this relationship for immigration purposes requires extra steps if the woman and man are not married to one another.

Proving through mother. When a child is born of a woman who is not married to the child's father, the child is her natural child.

To establish the relationship of mother and child, the only document necessary is the birth certificate showing the name of the mother and the name of the child.

If the mother's maiden name as shown on the birth certificate of her child differs from her present name, the mother must present the document showing that her name was changed. Usually, she has changed her name after marrying. The marriage certificate will then verify that the mother named on the birth certificate and the mother on the immigration form are the same person.

Proving through father. Even if the father of the child is not married to the mother when the child is born, the father can petition for the child to immigrate into the United States.

But proving the father-child relationship can get complicated. First, the father must establish that he is really the biological father of the child. The birth certificate is the best proof, if his name appears as the father of the child.

If his name is not on the birth certificate, the father should apply to his civil registry requesting that his name be added to the birth certificate as the father of the child. He should do this before the child turns 18.

In some countries, the father might have to acknowledge before a civil court, government agency, or civil registry that he is the father of the child. Doing this "legitimates" the child for purposes of U.S. immigration law. Again, such acknowledgment must occur before the child turns 18 years old.

If none of this is available, a blood test, accompanied by an affidavit from the mother stating that the man is the father of the child, might be acceptable to prove paternity, although it doesn't "legitimate" the child.

In cases where the father did not legitimate the child before the child turned 18, the father must show that he was not simply the biological father, but that there was a father-child relationship in existence before the child turned 21. He must provide documents to prove either of the following:

- The father and child lived together before the child turned 21.
- There was a true father-child relationship before the child turned 21 or got married.

This relationship can be shown by letters written by one to the other; canceled checks or other proof of money sent regularly to support the child; photos of both of them together; school records showing the father's name; sworn statements from at least two people who know of the father-child relationship; U.S. income tax returns showing the child listed as a dependent; birthday cards; or Valentine, Christmas, or other holiday cards sent and received.

In short, almost any evidence can help show that the father did not abandon the child, but kept up paternal ties before the child turned 21 years old.

Some Countries Require No Proof

The governments in some countries, such as China, Haiti, Trinidad and Tobago, and Jamaica, have passed laws erasing the legal distinction between children born to parents who are married to one another and those whose parents are not married.

But if these laws were recently passed, the father has to show USCIS that the law was changed before the child turned 18. If he can show this, he need not submit all those letters, sworn statements, school records, and other proof mentioned above.

---

3. Legitimated Child of Recently Married Parents

When a child is born to a man and a woman who are not married to each other but who marry each other before the child turns 18 years of age, the child is considered to be a legitimated child.

To prove the relationship of mother and child, only the birth certificate is necessary.

To prove the relationship of father and child, two documents are needed: the birth certificate and the marriage certificate.

4. Stepchild

When the mother or the father of a child marries a person who is not the biological parent of that child, a step-relationship is created between the new parent and the child.

For there to be any immigration benefit, the marriage between the child's parent and stepparent must occur before the child turns 18 years of age. A U.S. citizen or green card–holding spouse can petition for a foreign-born spouse's children (as his or her stepchildren) at any time, as long as the children were under 18 years of age at the time of the marriage.

In addition to the birth certificate of the child, a marriage certificate is necessary to show that the step-relationship was created by a marriage that occurred before the child's 18th birthday.

5. Adopted Child

The first thing to know about adopting an immigrant child is that the adoption usually must be finalized before the child turns 16 years of age. An adoption after the age of 16 might benefit the child in ways unrelated to immigration—for example, making inheritance simpler—but it will not usually help the child get a green card.

The next thing that you must know is whether that child lives in a country that has signed onto the

Hague Convention on the Protection of Children. You can find details about all of the countries on the U.S. Department of State's adoption website at http://adoption.state.gov. To search for countries that are included, click "Country Information." At time of publication, 101 countries were listed, some with restrictions on whether U.S. citizens can adopt.

When the child lives in a Hague Convention country. The Hague Convention entered into force in the U.S. in April of 2008, and has significantly changed the rules and procedures for immigrating adopted children. Each country that is a party to the Convention must have an officially designated central authority to safeguard the adoption process, which in the U.S. is the Department of State (DOS).

Only U.S. citizens may petition. The petition must be filed before the child's 16th birthday (no exceptions), and the child must be adopted abroad. One thing that is easier in Hague Convention cases is that, unlike in other cases, there's no requirement that you have two years' legal custody of and joint residence with the child.

CAUTION
Adoptions from Hague Convention countries must be completed in the exact order specified by the Convention, step by step. Even if you otherwise meet all the requirements, failing to meet them in the specified order can result in the child's being unable to immigrate based upon the adoption.

Here are the basic steps for nonorphan adoptions of children from Hague Convention countries:

1. **Choose an adoption service provider (ASP).** The ASP must be authorized to provide adoption services in connection with a Hague adoption, so ask about this before hiring or paying any money to a provider.
2. **Obtain a home study report.** This must come from someone authorized to complete a Hague adoption home study.
3. **File Form I-800A with USCIS.** This form must be filed before you are matched with the child to be adopted. To be eligible to file this form, you must be a U.S. citizen and habitually reside in the United States. If you are married, your spouse must also sign your Form I-800A and must also intend to adopt any child whom you adopt. If you are not married, you must be at least 24 years of age when you file your Form I-800A, and you must be at least 25 years of age when you later file Form I-800.
4. **Once USCIS approves your Form I-800A, work with the ASP to obtain a proposed adoption placement.**
5. **File Form I-800.** This serves to determine the child's eligibility as a Convention adoptee.
6. **Adopt the child.** Or, you can obtain custody in order to adopt the child in the United States.
7. **Obtain an immigrant visa for the child.**
8. **Bring the child to the United States.**

The filing fee for Form I-800A is $775. An $85 fee for biometrics is also required, not only for the applicant but also for each person 18 years of age or older who is living with the applicant. There is no fee required for the first Form I-800 filed for a child on the basis of an approved Form I-800A. If more than one Form I-800 is filed during the approval period for different children, the fee is $775 for the second and each subsequent Form I-800, except that if the children were siblings before the adoption, no additional filing fee is required. See the form instructions for where to file.

Adopting a child from a Hague Convention country is complicated. We recommend that you consult an attorney who is experienced in immigration and adoptions before proceeding.

When the child does not live in a Hague Convention country. An adopted immigrant child from a non-Hague convention country will be considered the child (or adult son or daughter) of the adopting parent as long as there was a full and final adoption before the child's 16th birthday.

There is one exception to this age limit, which applies to a child between the ages of 16 and 18, if the older child is the natural sibling of a younger child you have already adopted or are adopting at the same time as the older one. "Natural sibling" means the children share at least one biological parent. Unlike an orphan child (discussed in Chapter 10), the adopted child is neither orphaned nor abandoned by his or her natural parents.

Additional requirements under this process are that the parent must have had legal and physical custody of the child for at least two years while the child was a minor, and the child must have lived with the adopting parents at least two years before the petition was filed.

When these two periods have occurred, either at the same time or one after the other, the immigrant petition can be filed.

Because of these requirements, the most practical way the adopted child can get an immigrant visa is, in most cases, for one or both of the adopting parents to live in the foreign country with the alien child. But this is, as a practical matter, impossible for lawful permanent resident parents, who must maintain their U.S. residences in order to keep their green cards.

What if you're a U.S. citizen and the child you want to adopt is already living in the United States? This gets complicated, and you'll probably want to get an immigration lawyer's help. But let's take a brief look at the three main possibilities, after first reviewing one bit of good news: A child under 18 can't rack up "unlawful presence" in the U.S., and therefore you probably won't have to worry about the three- and ten-year bars (described in Chapter 4) being used to block the child from returning to the U.S. if, for example, he or she needs to leave and have a visa interview at a U.S. consulate. (But watch the timing carefully if you're adopting a child who's already close to 16.) However, a child who is staying in the U.S. without a visa or other permission from the immigration authorities can still be arrested and removed (deported).

The child entered the U.S. illegally. If the child entered illegally, you can petition a court for legal custody, but that just makes you the rightful parent. It doesn't make the child's U.S. stay legal for immigration purposes. At the end of the two years of legal custody and having the child live with you, you can file the visa petition, but will ultimately have to take the child to a U.S. consulate abroad for the visa interview (which completes the green card application process).

The child entered the U.S. legally but has overstayed. If the child originally came to the U.S. on a visa, but has stayed past the expiration date on his or her I-94 card (either a small white card tucked into the passport or, if the child entered in 2013 or later, the online version of Form I-94), you can petition a court for legal custody. However, being granted custody just makes you the rightful parent. It doesn't make the child's U.S. stay legal for immigration purposes. At the end of the two years' custody and residence, you can file a petition and an adjustment of status application with USCIS. (This is a different procedure than for the child who entered illegally; the combination of your U.S. citizenship and the child's legal entry saves this child from having to do part of the green card application through a U.S. consulate in another country.) However, don't interpret this section to mean that you should go to another country, adopt a child, then use a tourist visa to bring the child back to the U.S. in hopes of completing the application process here. That could probably be interpreted as visa fraud, and destroy the child's chances of immigrating.

The child entered the U.S. legally and is still legal. If the child originally came to the U.S. on a visa, and the expiration date on his or her I-94 card (either a small white card tucked into the passport or, if the child entered in 2013 or later, the online version of Form I-94), hasn't passed, you're in relatively good shape. You can petition a court for legal custody, making you the child's rightful parent. Then the question becomes, when does the I-94 run out? If the child is on a student visa, it might easily run for the two years you'll need before submitting the I-130 petition and green card application (without leaving the U.S.). If not, see the paragraph above this one—and talk to a lawyer. Though certain visa stays can be extended, you wouldn't want to ruin the entire plan by lying about the reasons for the extension.

Another alternative might be to process the immigration papers required for an orphan child. (See Chapter 10.)

C. Quick View of the Application Process

With the exception of children adopted from Hague Convention countries, the standard process for someone to get a green card as a child is as follows. The U.S. citizen or permanent resident parent must begin the process by mailing a petition (Form I-130) to USCIS. We're going to assume that the person reading this is the parent.

Form I-130 serves to prove to the immigration authorities that your children are truly and legally yours. After that petition is approved (in most cases), your children complete their half of the process (with your help, of course) by submitting an immigrant visa application and attending an interview, most likely with you or a close relative accompanying them. Their application serves to prove that not only do they qualify as children of a U.S. citizen or permanent resident, but that they're otherwise eligible for U.S. permanent residence.

However, the details of when and how your children complete their half of the process depend on whether they are living overseas or in the United States, as described next.

D. Detailed Instructions for the Application Process

Now we'll break the application process down into individual procedures, some of which will be covered in this chapter, and others in later chapters—we'll tell you exactly where to turn to for your situation.

1. Preparing the Form I-130 Petition

All U.S. parents of immigrating children must prepare Form I-130 and supporting documents to begin the process. You'll need to assemble:

☐ Form I-130, Petition for Alien Relative (the latest version of which is available at www.uscis.gov/i-130; see sample at the end of this chapter)

☐ birth certificate of child

☐ parents' marriage certificate (if any) and proof that any prior marriages ended. If you are the father petitioning for your child born out of wedlock, provide evidence as described in Section B, above.

☐ documents proving the parent's U.S. citizenship or permanent residence (see Chapter 20)

☐ filing fee for Form I-130, currently $535, payable by check or money order to the U.S. Department of Homeland Security, and

☐ Form G-1145 (www.uscis.gov/g-1145). This is optional, but filing it is a good idea, so that you'll receive an email and/or text notification from USCIS when your petition has been accepted. Once USCIS sends you a receipt number, you can use that number to sign up to receive automatic email updates letting you know whenever mail is sent regarding your case.

> TIP
> **How to sign up for automatic email updates:**
> Go to www.uscis.gov. Click "Check Case Status," then under "Why sign up for an account?" click "Sign Up." After accepting the terms and conditions, you can register as an applicant/petitioner.

In cases where the child is adopted from a non–Hague Convention country, the following documents must also be presented (remember that if the child is from a Hague Convention country, Forms I-800A and I-800 are used instead of Form I-130, and that the legal and procedural requirements are different):

- ☐ the adoption decree showing adoption prior to 16 years of age
- ☐ documents showing legal custody for at least two years
- ☐ documents proving that the adopted child has resided with the adopting parent or parents for at least two years (such as school and medical records)
- ☐ a birth certificate of the child showing the adopting parent as mother or father by reason of the adoption decree, and
- ☐ documents showing the marital status of the petitioning parent.

Once you've assembled all these items, make a copy for your records. It's also a good idea to write a cover letter, explaining what type of petition it is (for example, saying "I am a U.S. citizen, filing the enclosed I-130 petition on behalf of my married daughter"). The letter should include a bulleted list, much like the checklist above, of everything you're sending. This will help USCIS see that you're organized. It will help you, too, to make sure that nothing has been forgotten.

2. Where to Submit the I-130 Petition

Once you've assembled and copied everything, your next step will be applying online or by mail, as detailed below.

NEXT STEP
Next step for unmarried children under age 21 of U.S. citizens (immediate relatives) if the children live overseas. The parent can create an account and file online at www.uscis.gov or mail the visa petition to USCIS's Dallas or Phoenix lockbox (depending on where he or she lives). The lockbox facility will forward it to a USCIS office appropriate for the parent's geographical area. Soon after the visa petition is approved, the U.S. consulate serving the country where the child lives will take over. The child will apply for the immigrant visa and green card through consular processing, described in Chapter 17.

Immigrant Story: Children Nearing Age 21

Rajiv, a U.S. permanent resident, petitioned for his wife and three children to come to the United States from India. When he first filed the I-130 petition, the children were under 21. But with people in Category 2A having to wait about two years for their Priority Dates to become current, the family rightly worried that the children would "age out" before they could be issued their green cards.

When the Priority Date finally became current, the oldest child, Sandip, was already 22 years old and eight months. The middle child, Ayanna, turned 21 years old that month, and the youngest child, Iqbal, was then 19 years old.

Can Sandip and Ayanna immigrate to the U.S. even though they're both now over 21? Under the Child Status Protection Act, the children get to subtract from their age the amount of time it took USCIS to approve the I-130. Although the family waited two years for the Priority Date to become current, they waited only eight months for USCIS to approve the I-130. Unfortunately, eight months is not enough to help Sandip. Eight months will help Ayanna, however, by making her—for purposes of getting a visa—20 years and three months old. To take advantage of this protection, Ayanna will have to file her green card application within one year of the Priority Date becoming current. So long as she acts soon, she doesn't have to worry about turning 21.

The last child, Iqbal, is still only 19 years old, so he does not need to worry (unless he ruins his eligibility by getting married).

NEXT STEP

Next step for unmarried children under age 21 of U.S. citizens (immediate relatives) if the children live in the United States. If the child is eligible for adjustment of status (as explained in Chapter 16), then the parent shouldn't file the visa petition by itself, but should combine it with the adjustment of status application, and then mail it according to the instructions in Chapter 16. If, however, the child is not eligible to adjust status, and has spent any time in the U.S. illegally or out of status, consult an experienced immigration attorney.

NEXT STEP

Next step for all children of U.S. permanent residents, and married or over-21 children of U.S. citizens (preference relatives) if the children live overseas. The parent can create an account and file online at www.uscis.gov or mail the I-130 petition to USCIS's Dallas or Phoenix lockbox (depending on where he or she lives). The lockbox facility will forward it to the USCIS office appropriate for the parent's geographical area. After the petition is approved, the child will be put on a waiting list, based on his or her Priority Date. When the Priority Date becomes "current," the U.S. consulate serving the country where the child lives will take over. The child will apply for the immigrant visa and green card through consular processing, described in Chapter 17.

NEXT STEP

Next step for all children of U.S. permanent residents and married or over-21 children of U.S. citizens (preference relatives) if the children live in the United States. The parent can create an account and file online at www.uscis.gov or mail the I-130 petition to USCIS's Dallas or Phoenix lockbox (depending on where he or she lives). The lockbox facility will forward it to the appropriate USCIS office for the parent's geographical area. After the petition is approved, the child will be put on a waiting list, based on his or her Priority Date.

It could be many years before the Priority Date becomes current, during which time the mere filing of an I-130 petition gives the child no rights to remain in the United States (though many do, illegally). After the child's Priority Date becomes current, then:

- If the child is still living in the U.S. and is eligible for adjustment of status (unlikely), see Chapter 16 for instructions.
- If the child is living in the U.S. and is not eligible for adjustment of status, or has left the U.S. but spent more than six months here illegally before leaving, see an experienced immigration attorney for help.
- If the child left the U.S. without having spent too much time there illegally, you can safely continue the process, and the U.S. consulate serving the country where the child lives will take over. The child will apply for the immigrant visa and green card through consular processing, described in Chapter 17.

Proposed Changes to Law Could Affect Green Cards for Adult and Married Children

In early 2017, citing "chain migration" concerns, President Trump proposed changing the law that allows U.S. citizens to petition for green cards for their adult and married children (both unmarried children over 21 years old in the second preference category and married children in the third preference category, as shown on the *Visa Bulletin*). During Senate debate, one draft bill would have eliminated green cards for all immigrating relatives except spouses and minor children.

Although Congress ultimately voted down this proposal, expect further efforts at changing U.S. immigration law in the months to come. The good news is that all visa petitions before the law changes would likely be allowed to go forward. To be safe, therefore, if your adult or married child qualifies for legal permanent residence and wishes to live in the U.S., it might be worth submitting Form I-130 as soon as possible.

Stay tuned to the news and Nolo's online immigration updates for announcements about the future of family-based green cards.

E. Automatic Citizenship for Some Children

In 2000, Congress passed important new legislation allowing many children living in the U.S. with green cards to become citizens automatically if they have at least one U.S. citizen parent. Natural-born as well as adopted children can benefit from these new laws.

The law is slightly less helpful for children living overseas, who must go through an application process in order to claim their U.S. citizenship.

1. Children Living in the United States

For natural-born children to qualify for automatic citizenship, one parent needs to be a U.S. citizen, the child must have a green card and be living in the legal and physical custody of the U.S. citizen parent, and the child must still be under age 18 when all of these conditions are fulfilled.

For adopted children to qualify, one of the parents must be a U.S. citizen, a full and final adoption must have occurred, the child must be living in the United States after having entered on an immigrant visa (meaning the child is a green card holder), and the child must still be under age 18 at the time that all these things become true.

Though the process is automatic—and USCIS tries to send such children certificates of citizenship within six weeks of when they get their green cards—it's an excellent idea for such children to also apply for U.S. passports as proof of their U.S. citizen status.

> **EXAMPLE:** Lorna is 16 years old and living in Mexico. Some years ago, her father, a U.S. permanent resident, petitioned for her to immigrate. Even before her Priority Date became current, however, he became a U.S. citizen, so the process was speeded up. Lorna successfully applies for an immigrant visa through consular processing, and enters the United States to live with her father.

> Almost as soon as Lorna enters the U.S., she automatically becomes a U.S. citizen, because she (1) has a U.S. citizen parent, (2) has a green card, (3) is living in the citizen parent's legal and physical custody, and (4) was still under 18 when the first three things became true. USCIS should, recognizing her status, automatically send her a citizenship certificate. (Note: If Lorna's father had become a citizen after she got her green card and came to the U.S., but before she turned 18, USCIS wouldn't realize she'd become an automatic citizen, and Lorna would have to request a certificate to prove it.)

Children living in the U.S. can also, if USCIS fails to send a certificate, file for a certificate of citizenship on Form N-600. This form is used for biological and adopted children. For further instructions, see the USCIS website at www.uscis.gov/n-600.

2. Children Living Overseas

For children who are living overseas, the process is somewhat more complex. Either natural-born or adopted children may qualify for automatic citizenship, but they need to have one U.S. citizen parent; that parent or the parent's parent must have been physically present in the U.S. for five years, two of which were after the age of 14; the child must be visiting the U.S. on a temporary visa or other lawful means of entry; the child must live in the legal and physical custody of the U.S. citizen parent in their overseas home; and the child must remain under the age of 18 and in valid visa status until USCIS makes its decision on the citizenship application.

In practice, these conditions are hard to meet. You might wish to consult with a lawyer. The application is made on Form N-600K for biological and adopted children. For a sample of Form N-600K, see the end of the chapter. For further instructions, see the USCIS website at www.uscis.gov/n-600K. You can file online or by mail.

Sample Form I-130, Petition for Alien Relative (as used for immigrating children) (page 1)

Petition for Alien Relative

Department of Homeland Security
U.S. Citizenship and Immigration Services

USCIS
Form I-130
OMB No. 1615-0012
Expires 02/28/2021

For USCIS Use Only	Fee Stamp	Action Stamp

A-Number
A-

Initial Receipt

Resubmitted

Relocated	**Section of Law/Visa Category**	
Received	☐ 201(b) Spouse - IR-1/CR-1 ☐ 203(a)(1) Unm. S/D - F1-1 ☐ 203(a)(2)(B) Unm. S/D - F2-4	
Sent	☐ 201(b) Child - IR-2/CR-2 ☐ 203(a)(2)(A) Spouse - F2-1 ☐ 203(a)(3) Married S/D - F3-1	
Completed	☐ 201(b) Parent - IR-5 ☐ 203(a)(2)(A) Child - F2-2 ☐ 203(a)(4) Brother/Sister - F4-1	

Approved	Petition was filed on (Priority Date mm/dd/yyyy):	☐ Field Investigation ☐ Personal Interview ☐ 204(a)(2)(A) Resolved
Returned	PDR request granted/denied - New priority date (mm/dd/yyyy):	☐ Previously Forwarded ☐ Pet. A-File Reviewed ☐ I-485 Filed Simultaneously ☐ 203(g) Resolved ☐ Ben. A-File Reviewed ☐ 204(g) Resolved

Remarks

At which USCIS office (e.g., NBC, VSC, LOS, CRO) was Form I-130 adjudicated? _____

To be completed by an attorney or accredited representative (if any).			
☐ **Select this box if Form G-28 is attached.**	**Volag Number** (if any)	**Attorney State Bar Number** (if applicable)	**Attorney or Accredited Representative USCIS Online Account Number** (if any)

▶ **START HERE - Type or print in black ink.**

> If you need extra space to complete any section of this petition, use the space provided in **Part 9. Additional Information.**
> **Complete and submit as many copies of Part 9., as necessary, with your petition.**

Part 1. Relationship (You are the Petitioner. Your relative is the Beneficiary)

1. I am filing this petition for my (Select **only one** box):

   ☐ Spouse ☐ Parent ☐ Brother/Sister ☒ Child

2. If you are filing this petition for your child or parent, select the box that describes your relationship (Select **only one** box):

   ☐ Child was born to parents who were married to each other at the time of the child's birth

   ☒ Stepchild/Stepparent

   ☐ Child was born to parents who were not married to each other at the time of the child's birth

   ☐ Child was adopted (not an Orphan or Hague Convention adoptee)

3. If the beneficiary is your brother/sister, are you related by adoption? ☐ Yes ☐ No

4. Did you gain lawful permanent resident status or citizenship through adoption? ☐ Yes ☒ No

Part 2. Information About You (Petitioner)

1. Alien Registration Number (A-Number) (if any)

   ▶ A-

2. USCIS Online Account Number (if any)

   ▶

3. U.S. Social Security Number (if any)

   ▶ 3 3 3 4 4 5 5 5 5

Your Full Name

4.a. Family Name (Last Name) Carlton

4.b. Given Name (First Name) Derek

4.c. Middle Name Andrew

Sample Form I-130, Petition for Alien Relative (as used for immigrating children) (page 2)

Part 2. Information About You (Petitioner) (continued)

Other Names Used (if any)

Provide all other names you have ever used, including aliases, maiden name, and nicknames.

5.a. Family Name (Last Name) [ ]

5.b. Given Name (First Name) [ ]

5.c. Middle Name [ ]

Other Information

6. City/Town/Village of Birth
[Chicago]

7. Country of Birth
[USA]

8. Date of Birth (mm/dd/yyyy) [06/18/1984]

9. Sex ☒ Male ☐ Female

Mailing Address

10.a. In Care Of Name [ ]

10.b. Street Number and Name [575 7th Street]

10.c. ☒ Apt. ☐ Ste. ☐ Flr. [2]

10.d. City or Town [Champaign]

10.e. State [IL] **10.f.** ZIP Code [61820]

10.g. Province [ ]

10.h. Postal Code [ ]

10.i. Country
[USA]

11. Is your current mailing address the same as your physical address? ☒ Yes ☐ No

If you answered "No" to **Item Number 11.**, provide information on your physical address in **Item Numbers 12.a. - 13.b.**

Address History

Provide your physical addresses for the last five years, whether inside or outside the United States. Provide your current address first if it is different from your mailing address in **Item Numbers 10.a. - 10.i.**

Physical Address 1

12.a. Street Number and Name [ ]

12.b. ☐ Apt. ☐ Ste. ☐ Flr. [ ]

12.c. City or Town [ ]

12.d. State [ ] **12.e.** ZIP Code [ ]

12.f. Province [ ]

12.g. Postal Code [ ]

12.h. Country
[ ]

13.a. Date From (mm/dd/yyyy) [ ]

13.b. Date To (mm/dd/yyyy) [ ]

Physical Address 2

14.a. Street Number and Name [290 11th Street]

14.b. ☐ Apt. ☐ Ste. ☐ Flr. [ ]

14.c. City or Town [Chicago]

14.d. State [IL] **14.e.** ZIP Code [60176]

14.f. Province [ ]

14.g. Postal Code [ ]

14.h. Country
[USA]

15.a. Date From (mm/dd/yyyy) [08/02/2013]

15.b. Date To (mm/dd/yyyy) [12/31/2017]

Your Marital Information

16. How many times have you been married? ▶ [1]

17. Current Marital Status

☐ Single, Never Married ☒ Married ☐ Divorced

☐ Widowed ☐ Separated ☐ Annulled

Sample Form I-130, Petition for Alien Relative (as used for immigrating children) (page 3)

Part 2. Information About You (Petitioner) (continued)

18. Date of Current Marriage (if currently married) (mm/dd/yyyy) — 08/20/2019

Place of Your Current Marriage (if married)

19.a. City or Town — Champaign
19.b. State — IL
19.c. Province —
19.d. Country — USA

Names of All Your Spouses (if any)

Provide information on your current spouse (if currently married) first and then list all your prior spouses (if any).

Spouse 1
20.a. Family Name (Last Name) — Srisai
20.b. Given Name (First Name) — Kanya
20.c. Middle Name — Lawan
21. Date Marriage Ended (mm/dd/yyyy) —

Spouse 2
22.a. Family Name (Last Name) —
22.b. Given Name (First Name) —
22.c. Middle Name —
23. Date Marriage Ended (mm/dd/yyyy) —

Information About Your Parents

Parent 1's Information
Full Name of Parent 1
24.a. Family Name (Last Name) — Carlton
24.b. Given Name (First Name) — Frederick
24.c. Middle Name — John
25. Date of Birth (mm/dd/yyyy) — 04/15/1957
26. Sex — ☒ Male ☐ Female

27. Country of Birth — USA
28. City/Town/Village of Residence — Chicago
29. Country of Residence — USA

Parent 2's Information
Full Name of Parent 2
30.a. Family Name (Last Name) — Carlton
30.b. Given Name (First Name) — Shawna
30.c. Middle Name — Marie
31. Date of Birth (mm/dd/yyyy) — 06/08/1959
32. Sex — ☐ Male ☒ Female
33. Country of Birth — USA
34. City/Town/Village of Residence — San Francisco
35. Country of Residence — USA

Additional Information About You (Petitioner)

36. I am a (Select **only one** box):
☒ U.S. Citizen ☐ Lawful Permanent Resident

If you are a U.S. citizen, complete Item Number 37.

37. My citizenship was acquired through (Select **only one** box):
☒ Birth in the United States
☐ Naturalization
☐ Parents

38. Have you obtained a Certificate of Naturalization or a Certificate of Citizenship? ☐ Yes ☒ No

If you answered "Yes" to **Item Number 38.**, complete the following:
39.a. Certificate Number —
39.b. Place of Issuance —
39.c. Date of Issuance (mm/dd/yyyy) —

Sample Form I-130, Petition for Alien Relative (as used for immigrating children) (page 4)

Part 2. Information About You (Petitioner) (continued)

If you are a lawful permanent resident, complete **Item Numbers 40.a. - 41.**

40.a. Class of Admission

[   ]

40.b. Date of Admission (mm/dd/yyyy)

[   ]

Place of Admission

40.c. City or Town

[   ]

40.d State

[   ]

41. Did you gain lawful permanent resident status through marriage to a U.S. citizen or lawful permanent resident?

☐ Yes   ☐ No

Employment History

Provide your employment history for the last five years, whether inside or outside the United States. Provide your current employment first. If you are currently unemployed, type or print "Unemployed" in **Item Number 42.**

Employer 1

42. Name of Employer/Company

[MDH Consulting]

43.a. Street Number and Name

[55 Westlake Drive]

43.b. ☐ Apt. ☒ Ste. ☐ Flr. [2000]

43.c. City or Town [Champaign]

43.d. State [IL]   **43.e.** ZIP Code [61820]

43.f. Province [   ]

43.g. Postal Code [   ]

43.h. Country

[USA]

44. Your Occupation

[Consultant]

45.a. Date From (mm/dd/yyyy) [12/01/2017]

45.b. Date To (mm/dd/yyyy) [present]

Employer 2

46. Name of Employer/Company

[JRR Publishing]

47.a. Street Number and Name [1000 Main Avenue]

47.b. ☐ Apt. ☒ Ste. ☐ Flr. [900]

47.c. City or Town [Chicago]

47.d. State [IL]   **47.e.** ZIP Code [60177]

47.f. Province [   ]

47.g. Postal Code [   ]

47.h. Country

[USA]

48. Your Occupation

[Editor]

49.a. Date From (mm/dd/yyyy) [07/11/2011]

49.b. Date To (mm/dd/yyyy) [11/30/2017]

Part 3. Biographic Information

NOTE: Provide the biographic information about you, the petitioner.

1. Ethnicity (Select **only one** box)

☐ Hispanic or Latino
☒ Not Hispanic or Latino

2. Race (Select **all applicable** boxes)

☐ White
☐ Asian
☒ Black or African American
☐ American Indian or Alaska Native
☐ Native Hawaiian or Other Pacific Islander

3. Height   Feet [6]   Inches [0]

4. Weight   Pounds [2][1][0]

5. Eye Color (Select **only one** box)

☐ Black   ☐ Blue   ☒ Brown
☐ Gray   ☐ Green   ☐ Hazel
☐ Maroon   ☐ Pink   ☐ Unknown/Other

Sample Form I-130, Petition for Alien Relative (as used for immigrating children) (page 5)

Part 3. Biographic Information (continued)

6. Hair Color (Select **only one** box)

☐ Bald (No hair) ☒ Black ☐ Blond
☐ Brown ☐ Gray ☐ Red
☐ Sandy ☐ White ☐ Unknown/Other

Part 4. Information About Beneficiary

1. Alien Registration Number (A-Number) (if any)
   ▶ A-

2. USCIS Online Account Number (if any)
   ▶

3. U.S. Social Security Number (if any)
   ▶

Beneficiary's Full Name

4.a. Family Name (Last Name) — Srisai
4.b. Given Name (First Name) — Achara
4.c. Middle Name — Hom

Other Names Used (if any)

Provide all other names the beneficiary has ever used, including aliases, maiden name, and nicknames.

5.a. Family Name (Last Name)
5.b. Given Name (First Name)
5.c. Middle Name

Other Information About Beneficiary

6. City/Town/Village of Birth — Saraburi

7. Country of Birth — Thailand

8. Date of Birth (mm/dd/yyyy) — 02/02/2016

9. Sex ☐ Male ☒ Female

10. Has anyone else ever filed a petition for the beneficiary?
    ☐ Yes ☒ No ☐ Unknown

NOTE: Select "Unknown" *only* if you do not know, and the beneficiary also does not know, if anyone else has ever filed a petition for the beneficiary.

Beneficiary's Physical Address

If the beneficiary lives outside the United States in a home without a street number or name, leave **Item Numbers 11.a.** and **11.b.** blank.

11.a. Street Number and Name — 14 Sri Ayudayha Road
11.b. ☐ Apt. ☐ Ste. ☐ Flr.
11.c. City or Town — Bangkok
11.d. State   11.e. ZIP Code
11.f. Province
11.g. Postal Code — 10120
11.h. Country — Thailand

Other Address and Contact Information

Provide the address in the United States where the beneficiary intends to live, if different from **Item Numbers 11.a. - 11.h.** If the address is the same, type or print "SAME" in **Item Number 12.a.**

12.a Street Number and Name — SAME
12.b. ☐ Apt. ☐ Ste. ☐ Flr.
12.c. City or Town
12.d. State   12.e. ZIP Code

Provide the beneficiary's address outside the United States, if different from **Item Numbers 11.a. - 11.h.** If the address is the same, type or print "SAME" in **Item Number 13.a.**

13.a. Street Number and Name
13.b. ☐ Apt. ☐ Ste. ☐ Flr.
13.c. City or Town
13.d. Province
13.e. Postal Code
13.f. Country

14. Daytime Telephone Number (if any)

Sample Form I-130, Petition for Alien Relative (as used for immigrating children) (page 6)

Part 4. Information About Beneficiary (continued)

15. Mobile Telephone Number (if any)

    +011646464643585

16. Email Address (if any)

    None

Beneficiary's Marital Information

17. How many times has the beneficiary been married?

    ▶ 0

18. Current Marital Status

    ☒ Single, Never Married ☐ Married ☐ Divorced

    ☐ Widowed ☐ Separated ☐ Annulled

19. Date of Current Marriage (if currently married) (mm/dd/yyyy)

Place of Beneficiary's Current Marriage (if married)

20.a. City or Town

20.b. State

20.c. Province

20.d. Country

Names of Beneficiary's Spouses (if any)

Provide information on the beneficiary's current spouse (if currently married) first and then list all the beneficiary's prior spouses (if any).

Spouse 1

21.a. Family Name (Last Name)

21.b. Given Name (First Name)

21.c. Middle Name

22. Date Marriage Ended (mm/dd/yyyy)

Spouse 2

23.a. Family Name (Last Name)

23.b. Given Name (First Name)

23.c. Middle Name

24. Date Marriage Ended (mm/dd/yyyy)

Information About Beneficiary's Family

Provide information about the beneficiary's spouse and children.

Person 1

25.a. Family Name (Last Name)

25.b. Given Name (First Name)

25.c. Middle Name

26. Relationship

27. Date of Birth (mm/dd/yyyy)

28. Country of Birth

Person 2

29.a. Family Name (Last Name)

29.b. Given Name (First Name)

29.c. Middle Name

30. Relationship

31. Date of Birth (mm/dd/yyyy)

32. Country of Birth

Person 3

33.a. Family Name (Last Name)

33.b. Given Name (First Name)

33.c. Middle Name

34. Relationship

35. Date of Birth (mm/dd/yyyy)

36. Country of Birth

Sample Form I-130, Petition for Alien Relative (as used for immigrating children) (page 7)

Part 4. Information About Beneficiary (continued)

Person 4

37.a. Family Name (Last Name)

37.b. Given Name (First Name)

37.c. Middle Name

38. Relationship

39. Date of Birth (mm/dd/yyyy)

40. Country of Birth

Person 5

41.a. Family Name (Last Name)

41.b. Given Name (First Name)

41.c. Middle Name

42. Relationship

43. Date of Birth (mm/dd/yyyy)

44. Country of Birth

Beneficiary's Entry Information

45. Was the beneficiary **EVER** in the United States?
☐ Yes ☒ No

If the beneficiary is currently in the United States, complete **Items Numbers 46.a. - 46.d.**

46.a. He or she arrived as a (Class of Admission):

46.b. Form I-94 Arrival-Departure Record Number ▶

46.c. Date of Arrival (mm/dd/yyyy)

46.d. Date authorized stay expired, or will expire, as shown on Form I-94 or Form I-95 (mm/dd/yyyy) or type or print "D/S" for Duration of Status

47. Passport Number
S45245423

48. Travel Document Number

49. Country of Issuance for Passport or Travel Document
Thailand

50. Expiration Date for Passport or Travel Document (mm/dd/yyyy)
02/16/2023

Beneficiary's Employment Information

Provide the beneficiary's current employment information (if applicable), even if they are employed outside of the United States. If the beneficiary is currently unemployed, type or print "Unemployed" in **Item Number 51.a.**

51.a. Name of Current Employer (if applicable)
Unemployed

51.b. Street Number and Name

51.c. ☐ Apt. ☐ Ste. ☐ Flr.

51.d. City or Town

51.e. State **51.f.** ZIP Code

51.g. Province

51.h. Postal Code

51.i. Country

52. Date Employment Began (mm/dd/yyyy)
02/02/2016

Additional Information About Beneficiary

53. Was the beneficiary **EVER** in immigration proceedings?
☐ Yes ☒ No

54. If you answered "Yes," select the type of proceedings and provide the location and date of the proceedings.
☐ Removal ☐ Exclusion/Deportation
☐ Rescission ☐ Other Judicial Proceedings

55.a. City or Town

55.b. State

56. Date (mm/dd/yyyy)

Sample Form I-130, Petition for Alien Relative (as used for immigrating children) (page 8)

Part 4. Information About Beneficiary (continued)

If the beneficiary's native written language does not use Roman letters, type or print his or her name and foreign address in their native written language.

57.a. Family Name (Last Name)

57.b. Given Name (First Name)

57.c. Middle Name

58.a. Street Number and Name

58.b. ☐ Apt. ☐ Ste. ☐ Flr.

58.c. City or Town

58.d. Province

58.e. Postal Code

58.f. Country

If filing for your spouse, provide the last address at which you physically lived together. If you never lived together, type or print, "Never lived together" in Item Number 59.a.

59.a. Street Number and Name

59.b. ☐ Apt. ☐ Ste. ☐ Flr.

59.c. City or Town

59.d. State

59.e. ZIP Code

59.f. Province

59.g. Postal Code

59.h. Country

60.a. Date From (mm/dd/yyyy)

60.b. Date To (mm/dd/yyyy)

The beneficiary is in the United States and will apply for adjustment of status to that of a lawful permanent resident at the U.S. Citizenship and Immigration Services (USCIS) office in:

61.a. City or Town

61.b. State

The beneficiary will not apply for adjustment of status in the United States, but he or she will apply for an immigrant visa abroad at the U.S. Embassy or U.S. Consulate in:

62.a. City or Town — Bangkok

62.b. Province

62.c. Country — Thailand

NOTE: Choosing a U.S. Embassy or U.S. Consulate outside the country of the beneficiary's last residence does not guarantee that it will accept the beneficiary's case for processing. In these situations, the designated U.S. Embassy or U.S. Consulate has discretion over whether or not to accept the beneficiary's case.

Part 5. Other Information

1. Have you **EVER** previously filed a petition for this beneficiary or any other alien? ☒ Yes ☐ No

If you answered "Yes," provide the name, place, date of filing, and the result.

2.a. Family Name (Last Name) — Srisai

2.b. Given Name (First Name) — Kanya

2.c. Middle Name — Lawan

3.a. City or Town — Dallas Lockbox

3.b. State — TX

4. Date Filed (mm/dd/yyyy) — 04/01/2020

5. Result (for example, approved, denied, withdrawn) — Pending

If you are also submitting separate petitions for other relatives, provide the names of and your relationship to each relative.

Relative 1

6.a. Family Name (Last Name) — Srisai

6.b. Given Name (First Name) — Kanya

6.c. Middle Name — Lawan

7. Relationship — Spouse

Sample Form I-130, Petition for Alien Relative (as used for immigrating children) (page 9)

Part 5. Other Information (continued)

Relative 2

8.a. Family Name (Last Name)

8.b. Given Name (First Name)

8.c. Middle Name

9. Relationship

WARNING: USCIS investigates the claimed relationships and verifies the validity of documents you submit. If you falsify a family relationship to obtain a visa, USCIS may seek to have you criminally prosecuted.

PENALTIES: By law , you may be imprisoned for up to 5 years or fined $250,000, or both, for entering into a marriage contract in order to evade any U.S. immigration law. In addition, you may be fined up to $10,000 and imprisoned for up to 5 years, or both, for knowingly and willfully falsifying or concealing a material fact or using any false document in submitting this petition.

Part 6. Petitioner's Statement, Contact Information, Declaration, and Signature

NOTE: Read the **Penalties** section of the Form I-130 Instructions before completing this part.

Petitioner's Statement

NOTE: Select the box for either **Item Number 1.a.** or **1.b.** If applicable, select the box for **Item Number 2.**

1.a. ☒ I can read and understand English, and I have read and understand every question and instruction on this petition and my answer to every question.

1.b. ☐ The interpreter named in **Part 7.** read to me every question and instruction on this petition and my answer to every question in
_____ ,
a language in which I am fluent. I understood all of this information as interpreted.

2. ☐ At my request, the preparer named in **Part 8.**,
_____ ,
prepared this petition for me based only upon information I provided or authorized.

Petitioner's Contact Information

3. Petitioner's Daytime Telephone Number
3125489888

4. Petitioner's Mobile Telephone Number (if any)
3125489888

5. Petitioner's Email Address (if any)
dacarlton@email.com

Petitioner's Declaration and Certification

Copies of any documents I have submitted are exact photocopies of unaltered, original documents, and I understand that USCIS may require that I submit original documents to USCIS at a later date. Furthermore, I authorize the release of any information from any of my records that USCIS may need to determine my eligibility for the immigration benefit I seek.

I further authorize release of information contained in this petition, in supporting documents, and in my USCIS records to other entities and persons where necessary for the administration and enforcement of U.S. immigration laws.

I understand that USCIS may require me to appear for an appointment to take my biometrics (fingerprints, photograph, and/or signature) and, at that time, if I am required to provide biometrics, I will be required to sign an oath reaffirming that:

1) I provided or authorized all of the information contained in, and submitted with, my petition;

2) I reviewed and understood all of the information in, and submitted with, my petition; and

3) All of this information was complete, true, and correct at the time of filing.

I certify, under penalty of perjury, that all of the information in my petition and any document submitted with it were provided or authorized by me, that I reviewed and understand all of the information contained in, and submitted with, my petition, and that all of this information is complete, true, and correct.

Petitioner's Signature

6.a. Petitioner's Signature (sign in ink)
➡ *Derek A. Carlton*

6.b. Date of Signature (mm/dd/yyyy) 04/01/2020

NOTE TO ALL PETITIONERS: If you do not completely fill out this petition or fail to submit required documents listed in the Instructions, USCIS may deny your petition.

Sample Form N-600K, Application for Citizen and Issuance of Certificate Under Section 322 (page 1)

Application for Citizenship and Issuance of Certificate Under Section 322

Department of Homeland Security
U.S. Citizenship and Immigration Services

USCIS Form N-600K
OMB No. 1615-0087
Expires 12/31/2018

For USCIS Use Only	Date Stamp	Receipt	Action Block
	Remarks		

To be completed by an Attorney or Accredited Representative (if any).	☐ Select this box if Form G-28 is attached.	Attorney State Bar Number (if applicable)	Attorney or Accredited Representative USCIS Online Account Number (if any)

► **START HERE - Type or print in black ink.**

Part 1. Information About the Child's Eligibility

Child's A-Number:
► A-

1. The application is being filed for a child. The child is under 18 years of age and (Select **only one** box):

   ☒ The BIOLOGICAL child of a qualifying U.S. citizen (USC) parent filing this application.

   ☐ The ADOPTED child of a qualifying USC parent filing this application.

   ☐ The grandchild of a qualifying USC grandparent or the child ward of a USC legal guardian filing this application within five years of the death of the USC parent.

Part 2. Information About the Child (for whom this application is being filed)

1. Current Legal Name (do **not** provide a nickname)

Family Name (Last Name)	Given Name (First Name)	Middle Name
Rossi	Adriana	Suzetta

2. Your Name Exactly As It Appears on the Permanent Resident Card (if applicable)

Family Name (Last Name)	Given Name (First Name)	Middle Name

3. Other Names Used (if applicable)
Provide all other names you have ever used, including nicknames, maiden name, and aliases.

Family Name (Last Name)	Given Name (First Name)	Middle Name

4. U.S. Social Security Number (if applicable)   5. USCIS Online Account Number (if any)
   ►   ►

6. Date of Birth (mm/dd/yyyy)   7. Country of Birth
   02/01/2009   Italy

Sample Form N-600K, Application for Citizen and Issuance of Certificate Under Section 322 (page 2)

Part 2. **Information About the Child** (for whom this application is being filed) (continued)	A-

8. Prior Country of Citizenship or Nationality

Italy

9. Gender
☐ Male ☒ Female

10. Height
Feet **4** ▼ Inches **11** ▼

11. Mailing Address

In Care Of Name (if any)

[ ]

Street Number and Name

Viale Europa 22

Apt. ☐ Ste. ☐ Flr. ☐ Number [ ]

City or Town

Roma

State [ ] ZIP Code [ ]-[ ]

Province

RM

Postal Code

00144

Country

Italy

12. Physical Address (Do **not** provide a PO Box in this space unless it is the **ONLY** address.)

Street Number and Name

Viale Europa 22

Apt. ☐ Ste. ☐ Flr. ☐ Number [ ]

City or Town

Roma

State [ ] ZIP Code [ ]-[ ]

Province

RM

Postal Code

00144

Country

Italy

13. Marital Status

☒ Single, Never Married ☐ Married ☐ Divorced ☐ Widowed ☐ Separated ☐ Marriage Annulled

☐ Other (Explain): [ ]

14. Information About the Admission Into the United States and Current Immigration Status

NOTE: Do **NOT** complete this section. The USCIS officer will complete it during the interview.

A. Arrived in the following manner:

Port-of-Entry

City or Town [ ] State [▼] Date of Entry (mm/dd/yyyy) [ ]

Exact Name Used at Time of Entry

Family Name (Last Name) [ ] Given Name (First Name) [ ] Middle Name [ ]

B. Current Immigration Status [ ]

15. Was there any prior application for citizenship or for a U.S. passport? ☐ Yes ☒ No

---

Sample Form N-600K, Application for Citizen and Issuance of Certificate Under Section 322 (page 3)

Part 2. Information About the Child (for whom this application is being filed) (continued) A- [ ][ ][ ][ ][ ][ ][ ][ ][ ]

16. Was the child adopted? ☐ Yes ☒ No

    A. Date of Adoption (mm/dd/yyyy) [   ] **B.** Date Legal Custody Began (mm/dd/yyyy) [   ] **C.** Date Physical Custody Began (mm/dd/yyyy) [   ]

17. Were the child's parents married to each other when the child was born (or adopted)? ☒ Yes ☐ No

Part 3. Information About the Child's U.S. Citizen Biological or Adoptive Parent

NOTE: Provide information about the U.S. citizen father or mother applying on behalf of the eligible child. **Provide information about the child's U.S. citizen parent in the sections noted** if the U.S. citizen grandparent or legal guardian is filing this form.

1. Current Legal Name of U.S. Citizen Parent

Family Name (Last Name)	Given Name (First Name)	Middle Name
Rossi	John	Paul

2. Date of Birth (mm/dd/yyyy) [03/30/1975] **3.** Country of Birth [United States]

4. U.S. Social Security Number (if applicable) ► [1][2][3][4][5][6][8][9][0]

5. Physical Address

Street Number and Name (Do **not** provide a PO Box in this space unless it is your **ONLY** address.) Apt. Ste. Flr. Number
[Viale Europa 22] ☐ ☐ ☐ [   ]

City or Town	State	ZIP Code
Roma		-

Province	Postal Code	Country
RM	00144	Italy

6. Daytime Telephone Number [0331201129] **7.** Work Telephone Number (if any) [0331201130]

8. Evening Telephone Number [0331201170] **9.** Mobile Telephone Number (if any) [0331201129]

10. Email Address (if any) [jprossi@email.com]

Sample Form N-600K, Application for Citizen and Issuance of Certificate Under Section 322 (page 4)

Part 3. Information About the Child's U.S. Citizen Biological or Adoptive Parent (continued)	A- [ ][ ][ ][ ][ ][ ][ ][ ][ ]

11. The parent is a U.S. citizen by:

[X] Birth in the United States   [ ] Acquisition after birth through naturalization of alien parents

[ ] Birth abroad to U.S. citizen parents

Certificate of Citizenship Number   Alien Registration Number (A-Number) (if known)

[_____]   ▶ A- [ ][ ][ ][ ][ ][ ][ ][ ][ ]

[ ] Naturalization

Place of Naturalization

Name of Court or USCIS Office Location

[_____]

City or Town   State

[_____]   [_____]

Certificate of Naturalization Number   A-Number (if known)   Date of Naturalization (mm/dd/yyyy)

[_____]   ▶ A- [ ][ ][ ][ ][ ][ ][ ][ ][ ]   [_____]

12. Has the U.S. citizen father or mother ever lost U.S. citizenship or taken any action that would cause loss of U.S. citizenship?   [ ] Yes [X] No

If the answer is "Yes" to **Item Number 12.**, provide a full explanation in the space provided in **Part 11. Additional Information.**

13. Marital History

A. How many times has the U.S. citizen father or mother been married (including annulled marriages and marriages to the same person)?   [1]

B. What is the U.S. citizen father or mother's current marital status?

[ ] Single, Never Married [X] Married [ ] Divorced [ ] Widowed [ ] Separated [ ] Marriage Annulled

[ ] Other (Explain): [_____]

C. Information About the U.S. Citizen Father's or Mother's **Current Spouse**

Family Name (Last Name)   Given Name (First Name)   Middle Name

[Rossi]   [Assunta]   [Maria]

Date of Birth (mm/dd/yyyy)   Country of Birth

[10/16/1976]   [Italy]

Country of Citizenship or Nationality

[Italy]

Spouse's Physical Address

Street Number and Name (Do **not** provide a PO Box in this space unless it is your spouse's **ONLY** address.)   Apt. Ste. Flr. Number

[Viale Europa 22]   [ ] [ ] [ ] [_____]

City or Town   State   ZIP Code

[Roma]   [____] [____]-[____]

Province   Postal Code   Country

[RM]   [00144]   [Italy]

Sample Form N-600K, Application for Citizen and Issuance of Certificate Under Section 322 (page 5)

Part 3. Information About the Child's U.S. Citizen Biological or Adoptive Parent (continued)   A- ☐☐☐☐☐☐☐☐☐

Date of Marriage (mm/dd/yyyy)
09/03/2009

Place of Marriage

City or Town: Columbus   State: OH ▼   Country: USA

Spouse's Immigration Status
☐ U.S. Citizen ☐ Lawful Permanent Resident ☒ Other (Explain): Visitor Visa

D. Is the U.S. citizen father's or mother's current spouse also the child's biological (or adoptive) parent?   ☒ Yes ☐ No

14. Member of U.S. Armed Forces

A. Is the sponsoring U.S. citizen parent a member of the U.S. Armed Forces?   ☐ Yes ☒ No

B. If the answer is "Yes," then are there official orders authorizing the child to accompany and reside with the sponsoring U.S. citizen parent who is a member of the U.S. Armed Forces?   ☐ Yes ☐ No

NOTE: If the U.S. citizen biological or adoptive parent is filing this application AND has the required physical presence in the United States, skip Part 4. and go directly to Part 5.

Part 4. Information About the Child's Qualifying U.S. Citizen Grandparent

NOTE: Complete this part **only** if the U.S. citizen parent (or adoptive parent), grandparent, or legal guardian is applying for citizenship for the child, and the U.S. citizen parent **has not** been physically present in the United States for five years; two years of which were after 14 years of age.)

1. Current Legal Name of U.S. Citizen Grandparent

Family Name (Last Name)   Given Name (First Name)   Middle Name

2. Date of Birth (mm/dd/yyyy)   **3.** Country of Birth

4. U.S. Social Security Number (if applicable)
▶ ☐☐☐☐☐☐☐☐☐

5. Physical Address

Street Number and Name (Do **not** provide a PO Box in this space unless it is your **ONLY** address.)   Apt. ☐ Ste. ☐ Flr. ☐ Number

City or Town   State ▼   ZIP Code ☐-☐

Province   Postal Code   Country

6. Daytime Telephone Number   **7.** Work Telephone Number (if any)

Sample Form N-600K, Application for Citizen and Issuance of Certificate Under Section 322 (page 6)

Part 4. Information About the Child's Qualifying U.S. Citizen Grandparent (continued)	A- [ ][ ][ ][ ][ ][ ][ ][ ][ ]

8. Evening Telephone Number

9. Mobile Telephone Number (if any)

10. Email Address (if any)

11. The grandparent is a U.S. citizen by:

☐ Birth in the United States   ☐ Acquisition after birth through naturalization of alien parents

☐ Birth abroad to U.S. citizen parents

   Certificate of Citizenship Number   A-Number (if known)

   ▶ A- [ ][ ][ ][ ][ ][ ][ ][ ][ ]

☐ Naturalization

   Place of Naturalization

   Name of Court or USCIS Office Location

   City or Town   State

   Certificate of Naturalization Number   A-Number (if known)   Date of Naturalization (mm/dd/yyyy)

   ▶ A- [ ][ ][ ][ ][ ][ ][ ][ ][ ]

12. Has the grandparent ever lost U.S. citizenship or taken any action that would cause loss of U.S. citizenship?   ☐ Yes   ☐ No

If the answer is "Yes" to **Item Number 12.**, provide a full explanation in the space provided in **Part 11. Additional Information**.

Part 5. Physical Presence in the United States From Birth Until Filing of Form N-600K

NOTE: Provide the dates that the U.S. citizen parent or grandparent was present in the United States. If the U.S. citizen parent **has not** been physically present in the United States for five years, two years of which were after 14 years of age, then the child must use the physical presence of the U.S. citizen grandparent.

1. Indicate whether this information relates to the U.S. citizen parent or to the qualifying grandparent.
   ☒ U.S. Citizen Parent   ☐ U.S. Citizen Grandparent

2. Physical Presence in the United States

	From (mm/dd/yyyy)	Until (mm/dd/yyyy)		From (mm/dd/yyyy)	Until (mm/dd/yyyy)
A.	03/30/1975	07/15/2007	**B.**		
C.			**D.**		
E.			**F.**		
G.			**H.**		

NOTE: If the U.S. citizen biological/adoptive parent is filing this application, skip Part 6. and go directly to Part 7.

Sample Form N-600K, Application for Citizen and Issuance of Certificate Under Section 322 (page 7)

Part 6. Information About the Legal Guardian	A- [ ][ ][ ][ ][ ][ ][ ][ ][ ]

NOTE: Complete this part **only** if your legal guardian is filing this application in lieu of a deceased U.S. citizen parent.

1. Current Legal Name of the Legal Guardian

Family Name (Last Name)   Given Name (First Name)   Middle Name

2. Date of Birth (mm/dd/yyyy)   3. Country of Birth

4. U.S. Social Security Number (if applicable)

5. Physical Address

Street Number and Name (Do **not** provide a PO Box in this space unless it is your **ONLY** address.) Apt. Ste. Flr. Number

City or Town   State   ZIP Code

Province   Postal Code   Country

6. Daytime Telephone Number   7. Work Telephone Number (if any)

8. Evening Telephone Number   9. Mobile Telephone Number (if any)

10. Email Address (if any)

11. The legal guardian is a U.S. citizen by:

☐ Birth in the United States   ☐ Acquisition after birth through naturalization of alien parents

☐ Birth abroad to U.S. citizen parents

Certificate of Citizenship Number   A-Number (if known) ► A-

☐ Naturalization

Place of Naturalization

Name of Court or USCIS Office Location

City or Town   State

Certificate of Naturalization Number   A-Number (if known) ► A-   Date of Naturalization (mm/dd/yyyy)

Sample Form N-600K, Application for Citizen and Issuance of Certificate Under Section 322 (page 8)

| Part 6. Information About the Legal Guardian (continued) | A- | | | | | | | | |

12. Date of Legal Guardianship (mm/dd/yyyy)

13. Name of Authority that Granted Legal Guardianship

14. Address of Authority that Granted Legal Guardianship

Street Number and Name (Do **not** provide a PO Box in this space unless it is your **ONLY** address.) Apt. Ste. Flr. Number

City or Town   State   ZIP Code

Province   Postal Code   Country

Part 7. Preferred Location and Date for Interview

1. USCIS Office Location

Manhattan

City or Town   State

New York   NY

2. Preferred Date (mm/dd/yyyy)

09/01/2020

USCIS will attempt to accommodate the requested preferences.

NOTE: Interview date should be at least 90 days after filing Form N-600K and before the child's 18th birthday.

Part 8. Applicant's Statement, Contact Information, Certification, and Signature

NOTE: Read the **Penalties** section of the Form N-600K Instructions before completing this part.

Applicant's Statement

NOTE: Select the box for either **Item A.** or **B.** in **Item Number 1.** If applicable, select the box for **Item Number 2.**

1. Applicant's Statement Regarding the Interpreter

    A. [X] I can read and understand English, and I have read and understand every question and instruction on this application and my answer to every question.

    B. [ ] The interpreter named in **Part 9.** read to me every question and instruction on this application and my answer to every question in _____, a language in which I am fluent, and I understood everything.

2. Applicant's Statement Regarding the Preparer

    [ ] At my request, the preparer named in **Part 10.**, _____, prepared this application for me based only upon information I provided or authorized.

Sample Form N-600K, Application for Citizen and Issuance of Certificate Under Section 322 (page 9)

Part 8. Applicant's Statement, Contact Information, Certification, and Signature (continued)	A- [ ][ ][ ][ ][ ][ ][ ][ ][ ]

Applicant's Contact Information

3. Applicant's Daytime Telephone Number

0331201170

4. Applicant's Mobile Telephone Number (if any)

5. Applicant's Email Address (if any)

jpr@email.com

Applicant's Certification

Copies of any documents I have submitted are exact photocopies of unaltered, original documents, and I understand that USCIS may require that I submit original documents to USCIS at a later date. Furthermore, I authorize the release of any information from any of my records that USCIS may need to determine my eligibility for the immigration benefit I seek.

I further authorize release of information contained in this application, in supporting documents, and in my USCIS records to other entities and persons where necessary for the administration and enforcement of U.S. immigration laws.

I understand that USCIS may require me to appear for an appointment to take my biometrics (fingerprints, photograph, and/or signature) and, at that time, if I am required to provide biometrics, I will be required to sign an oath reaffirming that:

> **1)** I reviewed and provided or authorized all of the information in my application;
>
> **2)** I understood all of the information contained in, and submitted with, my application; and
>
> **3)** All of this information was complete, true, and correct at the time of filing.

I certify, under penalty of perjury, that I provided or authorized all of the information in my application, I understand all of the information contained in, and submitted with, my application, and that all of this information is complete, true, and correct.

Applicant's Signature

6. Applicant's Signature (sign in ink)

➡ *John P. Rossi*

Date of Signature (mm/dd/yyyy)

04/01/2020

NOTE TO ALL APPLICANTS: If you do not completely fill out this application or fail to submit required documents listed in the Instructions, USCIS may deny your application.

Part 9. Interpreter's Contact Information, Certification, and Signature

Provide the following information about the interpreter.

Interpreter's Full Name

1. Interpreter's Family Name (Last Name)

Interpreter's Given Name (First Name)

2. Interpreter's Business or Organization Name (if any)

Orphan Immigrants in
Non-Hague Convention Countries

f you're considering adopting a child, and that child might be an orphan, you might not need to read this chapter—it depends entirely on what country the child is from. That's because some but not all countries have signed on to the Hague Convention on the Protection of Children and Cooperation in Respect of Intercountry Adoption. This took effect in the United States in 2008. If you plan to adopt from a country that has signed onto the Hague Convention, it doesn't matter whether the child is an orphan or not—the procedures will essentially be the same as those covered in Chapter 9, rather than this one.

If, however, you plan to adopt from a country that has not signed onto the Hague Convention, keep reading. This chapter describes the special process for adopting orphans who live in countries that have not signed the Hague Convention.

For the list of countries that are parties to the Hague Convention, go to the Department of State's website at https://travel.state.gov and click "Intercountry Adoption" then "Country Information." You'll also find information there about each country's individual requirements, regardless of whether it is a party to the Hague Convention.

The requirements for adopting and immigrating a non-Hague orphan child are less difficult than the requirements for adopting and immigrating a non-Hague nonorphan. Most important is that there is no requirement that you live with an orphan child for two years before the adoption. That is why many U.S. citizens who adopted from overseas in the past chose to adopt orphans.

There are two types of orphan immigrant visas:

- an IR-3 visa classification, for orphans who have met the parents and whose adoptions were completed abroad, and

- an IR-4 classification, for orphans who, although in the legal custody of the U.S. citizen parent or parents, still need to be legally adopted after reaching the United States, or who need to be readopted because the U.S. parents haven't yet seen the child.

In either case, the application process includes a number of complexities. If you're like many Americans, you might find it easiest to use an agency that specializes in international adoptions, although direct adoption is also possible. Even with help from an agency, expect the process to take at least six to twelve months.

A nonprofit called the Intercountry Adoption Accreditation and Maintenance Entity, Inc. (IAAME) collects information on accredited adoption agencies. See www.iaame.net.

Look for an agency that has been doing adoptions for a number of years, successfully completes a comparatively large number per year, serves the countries in which you're interested, and is happy to show you evidence that it's licensed and comes with good references.

CAUTION

If the U.S. petitioner has a criminal record, see an attorney. Under the Adam Walsh Child Protection and Safety Act of 2006, U.S. citizens and lawful permanent residents who have been convicted of any "specified offense against a minor" are prohibited from filing a family-based immigrant petition on behalf of any beneficiary (whether a child or not). USCIS will run security checks on all petitions and may call the petitioner in for fingerprinting. If the petitioner has a conviction for one of the specified offenses against a minor, then the petition will not be approved unless USCIS determines that the U.S. petitioner poses no risk to the beneficiary.

CAUTION
You'll also need to follow the rules of the country you're adopting from. Not every country allows international adoptions, and those that do usually impose various requirements on the parents. For example, some countries refuse to allow single-parent adoptions, or require that adopting parents be of a certain age. This chapter covers only the U.S. requirements; you'll need to research the international requirements with the help of your adoption agency or by going to the DOS website, which provides information about each country's special requirements.

A. Who Qualifies as an Orphan Child

A child under 16 years of age (or under 18, if being adopted along with a brother or sister under 16) is considered an orphan if the child meets any of these conditions:

- Both parents have died or have disappeared.
- The sole or surviving parent is incapable of providing the proper child care and has, in writing, released the child for adoption and emigration.
- Both father and mother have abandoned the child, or have become separated or lost from the child—and the legal authorities in the child's country, recognizing the child as abandoned, have granted legal custody of the child to an orphanage.

However, if the child has been placed with other people or temporarily in the orphanage, or if one or both parents continue to maintain contact—for example, sending gifts, writing letters, or showing that they have not ended their parental obligations to the child—the child will not be considered an orphan by the U.S. government.

You can't get around these requirements by having the overseas parent or parents "abandon" the child into the hands of the adopting U.S. couple or person.

B. Who Can Petition for an Orphan Child

Only U.S. citizens are allowed to file a visa petition for an orphan child; lawful permanent residents may not do so. A number of other regulations also apply:

- If a married couple is adopting, only one of them need be a U.S. citizen (but both have to be age 21 or over and sign the petition).
- A U.S. citizen who is not married must be at least 25 years of age before filing the petition. If citizen is under 25 when a foreign adoption takes place, that adoption will be considered invalid, and the citizen will have to readopt the child after the child reaches the United States (if allowed in their state of residence).
- The orphan child must be less than 16 years of age when the petition is filed (or under 18, if the parents are also petitioning for the child's brother or sister who is under 16).
- The adopting married couple, or single person, must have completed certain preadoption requirements, such as a home study, before filing the petition. (See Section C, below.)
- The adopting married couple, or single person, must have seen the child in the orphan's country before or during the adoption proceedings, or show that they'll be able to "readopt" the child in the United States.

CAUTION
Beware of lawbreakers. In some developing countries, kidnapping poor children and then selling them for adoption to childless couples in the United States and Europe has become rampant.

Your search for a child of your own should not cause the kidnapping or sale of another person's child. Before signing up with any adoption organization, check its references with friends who have worked with the organization—or ask for the names of some former clients, and then call them. Above all, avoid direct arrangements with the surviving parent or private individuals acting as brokers for a fee.

International Adoption for Lesbians and Gays

Many countries prohibit adoption by an openly gay person or a same-sex couple.

People have found ways to adopt from some of these countries nonetheless. If you are proceeding with a foreign adoption, you might opt to keep your sexual orientation—and your relationship with your partner—hidden from the host country. It is a judgment call as to whether to tell the agency helping you with the adoption. Many agencies operate on a wink-and-nod basis— though aware of the nature of your relationship with your partner, they refer to the partner as a "roommate" in reports to the host country, and simply ignore the issue of sexual orientation.

For more about adoption and parenting for same-sex couples, check out *A Legal Guide for Lesbian & Gay Couples,* by Denis Clifford, Frederick Hertz, and Emily Doskow (Nolo).

C. Preadoption Requirements

To protect the child and to ensure that the adopting parent or parents will care for the child properly, U.S. immigration laws require what's called a "home study" before an adoption decree is finalized or before a petition for an orphan child will be approved. Many couples take care of this first, as part of an advance processing application, described below in Section D1.

The purpose of the home study is to allow the state agency handling adoptions to investigate the future home of the child (and any adult living in it) and verify whether the adopting couple, or the single person, is psychologically and economically fit. Most home studies take about three months.

The home study must result in a favorable report recommending the proposed adoption. The report must be signed by an official of a state agency, or an agency licensed by the state in which the child will live with the adopting parent or parents. The home study should be submitted to USCIS within six months of its completion date.

This report must cover:

- the financial ability of the parent or parents to raise and educate the child
- a discussion of possible negative factors, such as a history of substance abuse, child abuse, sexual abuse, domestic violence, criminal behavior, or past denials of adoptions or unfavorable home study reports
- a detailed description of the living accommodations, including any special accommodations for a child with disabilities or medical issues, and
- a factual evaluation of the physical, mental, and moral ability of the adopting parent or parents, including observations made during personal interviews.

In addition to the home study, other preadoption conditions may be required by some states before an adoption petition can be filed with local courts. Therefore, if you are planning to adopt the orphan child in the United States, you must first comply with these state rules.

D. Starting the Adoption Process

The first steps toward adoption depend in part on whether or not the orphan child has been identified (chosen).

1. When the Child Is Not Yet Identified

If a particular child has not yet been singled out and the parents are going abroad to locate an orphan child for adoption, or for adoption after arrival in the United States, they should file an advance processing application, as follows:

- ☐ Form I-600A, Application for Advance Processing of Orphan Petition, signed by the U.S. citizen and, if married, the spouse. (See sample at end of this chapter.)
- ☐ Proof of applicant's U.S. citizenship. (See Chapter 21.)
- ☐ If married, evidence of the spouse's U.S. citizenship or lawful legal status in the United States and citizenship in another country.
- ☐ Marriage certificate, divorce or annulment decree, or death certificate, as evidence of present and previous marital status.
- ☐ Fees for biometrics (fingerprints and so on) of the U.S. citizen and, if married, of the spouse, plus for any other adults aged 18 years or older who live in your household. ($85 per person.) If paying by check or money order, make it out to the U.S. Department of Homeland Security. Your other option is to pay by credit card, using Form G-1450, Authorization for Credit Card Transactions.
- ☐ Evidence of petitioner's age, if unmarried, and if not already shown on other documents.
- ☐ A favorable home study report. If the home study report is not yet available, it must be submitted within one year from the date of filing the advance application. Otherwise, the application will be considered to have been abandoned.
- ☐ Proof of compliance with any preadoption requirements of the state in which the child will live if the adoption is to be completed in the United States (see Section C).
- ☐ A filing fee (currently $775).

After USCIS approves the advance processing application, you have 18 months in which to locate an orphan child and continue with the process. If you're not having any luck finding an orphan child within the one year, you can ask USCIS for a onetime extension. Do so within the 90 days before the USCIS approval notice expires—don't wait until it has already expired. You must make the request in writing, to the same office that approved your Form I-600A. With your letter, you must include an updated or amended home study report. You'll probably also need to request a onetime re-fingerprinting, since the original fingerprints are valid for only 15 months.

If you miss the deadline to ask for an extension, or you still can't find a child even after an extension, you basically need to start over. That means you'll have to submit a new advance processing application (with a new filing fee) if the child has not yet been identified, or a petition as described below (which also requires the filing fee of $775) if the child has been identified.

When you look at the sample I-600A, you'll notice that it assumes you've already figured out which country you plan to adopt a child from, and asks questions about your travel plans. But what if you end up being unable to find a child in that country? If you're still within the 18-month approval period, you can request a onetime change of country, at no extra charge. To do so, send a letter to the same USCIS office that approved the I-600A petition. However, if you later want to change the country of adoption a second time, you'll need to file USCIS Form I-824, Application for Action on an Approved Application or Petition, along with a filing fee (currently $465). The reason for all this paperwork is that by now, USCIS will have notified the U.S. consulate in the country you originally planned to adopt from, and now needs to notify a different consulate instead (you'll specify which one in Part 2 of Form I-824).

Can You Bring the Child to the U.S. First?

It's frustrating for parents eager to bring an orphan child into their home to have to wait for all the immigration procedures to be completed. In light of this, the U.S. government tries to give high priority to orphan petitions. However, the government doesn't smile upon efforts by parents to get around the U.S. immigration laws, for example by bringing the child in on a tourist or student visa, and attempting to complete the adoption and immigration processes afterward. Basically, this won't work. In rare cases, however, USCIS will grant humanitarian parole to allow an orphan into the U.S. even before the immigration procedures have been finished—most often because of a medical or similar emergency. You're best off consulting an experienced immigration attorney for help in requesting humanitarian parole.

---

2. When the Child Is Identified

When the adopting parent or parents have identified the orphan child they wish to adopt, they can immediately file a petition for the child at the appropriate USCIS service center. (See the USCIS website at www.uscis.gov for the exact address.) Or, if the U.S. citizen will be overseas to adopt or locate the orphan, you can file the petition with the U.S. consulate in the country of the child's residence.

This can be done even if the advance processing application has not yet been approved or has not yet been filed. If the advance processing application has been filed but not approved, include a copy of the filing receipt with the petition. If it has already been approved, include a copy of the approval notice.

You must file all the documents listed in Section D1, above (except Form I-600A), as well as:

- ☐ Form I-600, Petition to Classify Orphan as an Immediate Relative
- ☐ birth certificate of the orphan child, who must be under 16 years of age when the petition is filed
- ☐ death certificates of the parents of the child or proof of legal abandonment by both the father and mother
- ☐ the adoption decree or evidence that you have legal custody of the orphan and are working toward adoption, and
- ☐ filing fee (currently $775) unless you're filing based on an approved I-600A filed within the previous 18 months, in which case you don't need to pay the fee.

E. After the Petition Is Approved

If the petition is filed and approved by USCIS in the United States, the entire file is sent to the U.S. consulate in the country in which the child lives.

The consular officer then investigates the child. This can take months. The investigation aims to confirm that the child:

- meets the legal definition of an orphan, and
- does not have an illness or disability that was not described in the orphan petition.

A long delay in the adoption process of an orphan child can cause would-be parents much anxiety. However, keep in mind that the investigation is performed as a service to protect adopting parents from the heartbreaking situation that could develop if the child later proved not to be available for adoption.

Meeting Face-to-Face

The American individual or couple who wishes to adopt need not have seen the child personally before filing the petition if the adoption is to be done in the United States. However, if you are going to adopt a child to raise as your own for the rest of your life, you will likely want to find out what the child looks like, how you react to each other, what the child's physical condition is, and other imperceptible factors that only a face-to-face encounter can provide. Most people prefer to visit the child abroad before beginning adoption proceedings.

F. Filing for a Visa

When the petition is approved, the case will be transferred to the U.S. consulate in the orphan child's country of residence, for immigrant visa processing. (See Chapter 17 for advice and instructions on consular processing.)

In addition to the documents ordinarily required for consular processing, you'll need to bring the child's final adoption decree or proof of custody from the foreign government.

After receiving an immigrant visa, the orphan child can then enter the United States as a permanent resident. If the child has not yet been adopted in the foreign country, the U.S. citizen or couple can proceed to adopt the child according to the laws of the state in which they live.

G. Automatic Citizenship for Adopted Orphans

Under the Child Citizenship Act of 2000, orphans who enter on IR-3 visas (meaning the adoption is legally complete before they enter the U.S.) become citizens as soon as they enter the United States, and should receive a citizenship certificate by mail from USCIS within about six weeks.

Orphans who enter the U.S. on IR-4 visas will become U.S. citizens as soon as their adoptions are complete. To obtain proof of their citizenship, the parents will need to apply to their local USCIS office, using Form N-600K.

Sample Form I-600A, Application for Advance Processing of Orphan Petition (page 1)

Application for
Advance Processing of an Orphan Petition
Department of Homeland Security
U.S. Citizenship and Immigration Services

USCIS
Form I-600A
OMB No. 1615-0028
Expires 12/31/2018

For USCIS Use Only			
The applicant is: ☐ Married ☐ Unmarried **The applicant:** ☐ WILL provide proper care to a child if admitted to the United States. ☐ WILL NOT provide proper care to a child if admitted to the United States.	**The state of the child's proposed residence:** ☐ HAS preadoptive requirements. ☐ DOES NOT HAVE preadoptive requirements. Describe preadoption requirements *(if any)*. _____ _____ _____	**The preadoption requirements:** ☐ WERE met. ☐ HAVE NOT BEEN met.	**Fee Stamp**
		File Number | **DD**	**Remarks**
		Date of Favorable Determination | **District**	
Received	**Trans In**	**Completed**	

▶ **START HERE - Type or print legibly in black ink.** *This application is made by a prospective adoptive parent for advance processing of an orphan petition.*

Part 1. Information About You (Applicant)

1. Family Name (Last Name)   Given Name (First Name)   Middle Name (if applicable)

   | Lerner | Cora | Lynn |

2. Other Names You Have Used (including maiden name, nicknames, and aliases, if any)

   Family Name (Last Name)   Given Name (First Name)   Middle Name (if applicable)

   | Adams | Cora | Lynn |

3. U.S. Mailing Address (if any)

   In Care Of Name

   [ ]

   Street Number and Name   Apt. Ste. Flr. Number

   444 5th Street   ☐ ☐ ☐

   City or Town   State   ZIP Code

   Fremont   CA ▼   94536

4. Is your current U.S. mailing address the same as your U.S. physical address?   ☒ Yes ☐ No

   If you answered "No" to **Item Number 4.**, provide your U.S. physical address in **Item Number 5.** or your address abroad in **Item Number 6.**, as appropriate.

5. U.S. Physical Address (if any)

   Street Number and Name   Apt. Ste. Flr. Number

   [ ]   ☐ ☐ ☐

   City or Town   State   ZIP Code

   [ ]

Sample Form I-600A, Application for Advance Processing of Orphan Petition (page 2)

Part 1. Information About You (Applicant) (continued)

6. Address Abroad (if any)

Street Number and Name

Apt. Ste. Flr. ☐ ☐ ☐ Number

City or Town

State

Province

Postal Code

Country

7. Date of Birth (mm/dd/yyyy)
► 09/06/1981

8. City/Town/Village of Birth
Fort Bragg

9. State or Province of Birth
CA

10. Country of Birth
USA

11. Information About U.S. Citizenship

A. Are you a citizen of the United States? ☒ Yes ☐ No

NOTE: If you answered "No," you may NOT file Form I-600A. See the **What Are the Eligibility Requirements?** section of the Form I-600A instructions for more information.

B. How did you acquire your U.S. citizenship? ☒ Birth ☐ Parents ☐ Naturalization

C. If you acquired your citizenship through your parents, have you obtained a Certificate of Citizenship in your own name? ☐ Yes ☐ No

If "Yes," provide the following information about your Certificate of Citizenship:

Name Under Which the Certificate of Citizenship Was Issued

Family Name (Last Name)

Given Name (First Name)

Middle Name (if applicable)

Alien Registration Number (A-Number) (if any)
► A-

Certificate of Citizenship Number

Date of Issuance (mm/dd/yyyy) ►

Place of Issuance

D. If you acquired your citizenship through naturalization, provide the following information about your Certificate of Naturalization:

Name Under Which the Certificate of Naturalization Was Issued

Family Name (Last Name)

Given Name (First Name)

Middle Name (if applicable)

A-Number (if any)
► A-

Certificate of Naturalization Number

Date of Naturalization (mm/dd/yyyy) ►

Place of Naturalization

Sample Form I-600A, Application for Advance Processing of Orphan Petition (page 3)

Part 1. Information About You (Applicant) (continued)

12. Have you, or any person through whom you claimed citizenship, **EVER** lost U.S. citizenship?   ☐ Yes   ☒ No

NOTE: If you answered "Yes," attach a detailed explanation on a separate sheet of paper; type or print your name and A-Number (if any) at the top of each sheet; indicate the **Page Number, Part Number,** and **Item Number** to which your answer refers; and sign and date each sheet.

13. What is your marital status?   ☒ Married   ☐ Widowed   ☐ Divorced   ☐ Single

14. How many times have you been married (including your current marriage, if applicable)?   `1`

15. Date of Current Marriage (if applicable)   **16.** Place Where Current Marriage Occurred (if applicable)

(mm/dd/yyyy) ▶ `10/04/2013`   `Fremont CA`

17. Information About Your Current Spouse (if applicable)

Family Name (Last Name)	Given Name (First Name)	Middle Name (if applicable)
Lerner	Kenneth	John

Other Names Your Current Spouse Has Used (including maiden name, nicknames, and aliases, if any)

Family Name (Last Name)	Given Name (First Name)	Middle Name (if applicable)

Date of Birth   A-Number (if any)   City/Town/Village of Birth

(mm/dd/yyyy) ▶ `07/08/1981`   ▶ A- ` ` ` ` ` ` ` ` ` ` ` ` ` `   `Buffalo`

State or Province of Birth   Country of Birth

`NY`   `USA`

Spouse's Immigration Status

`US Citizen`

18. How many times has your current spouse been married (including your current marriage, if applicable)?   `1`

19. Does your current spouse reside with you?   ☒ Yes   ☐ No

If you answered "No," provide your current spouse's physical address in **Item Number 20.**

20. Your Current Spouse's Physical Address

Street Number and Name   Apt. Ste. Flr.   Number

` `   ☐ ☐ ☐   ` `

City or Town   State   ZIP Code

` `   ` `   ` `

Province   Postal Code   Country

` `   ` `   ` `

21. How many persons 18 years of age or older, other than your current spouse (if married), reside with you?   `0`

If you answered "1" or more, you **MUST** complete Form I-600A/I-600 Supplement 1, Listing of Adult Member of the Household, for each person.

Sample Form I-600A, Application for Advance Processing of Orphan Petition (page 4)

Part 1. Information About You (Applicant) (continued)

22. Have you ever previously filed Form I-600A, Form I-600, *Petition to Classify Orphan as an Immediate Relative*, Form I-800A, *Application for Determination of Suitability to Adopt a Child From a Convention Country*, or Form I-800, *Petition to Classify Convention Adoptee as an Immediate Relative*?   ☐ Yes ☒ No

    If "Yes," provide the following:

    A. Type of Application/Petition Filed

    [   ]

    B. Result - Check the box that best describes the action taken by USCIS and/or U.S. Department of State on your application and/or petition.

    ☐ Approved - Approval Date *(mm/dd/yyyy)* ▶ [   ]

    ☐ Denied - Denial Date *(mm/dd/yyyy)* ▶ [   ]

    NOTE: A copy of the denial notice must accompany this application.

    ☐ Other - Explain _____

    C. A detailed description of any previous Form I-600 or Form I-800 filing that resulted in a disruption prior to finalization of the adoption or that resulted in a completed adoption that was later dissolved either in the United States or abroad.

    _____

    _____

    _____

    NOTE: If you need extra space to complete this question, attach a separate sheet of paper; type or print your A-Number (if any) at the top of each sheet; include the **Page Number**, **Part Number**, and **Item Number** to which your answer refers; and sign and date each sheet.

Duty of Disclosure

You and your spouse (if married), must answer the following questions. See the **Duty of Disclosure** section in the instructions to Form I-600A concerning your ongoing duty to disclose information in response to these questions. If you or your spouse answer "Yes" to any of these questions, provide a certified copy of the documentation showing the final disposition of each incident which resulted in arrest, indictment, conviction, and/or any other judicial or administrative action and a written statement giving details, including any mitigating circumstances about each arrest, signed by you and/or your spouse (if married) under penalty of perjury under U.S. law. The written statement must show the date of each incident; place incident occurred (city/town, state/province, country); name of police department or other law enforcement administration or other entity involved; date of incarceration and name of facility, if applicable. Provide a description of any type of counseling, rehabilitation, or other information that you and your spouse (if married) would like considered in light of this history on a separate sheet of paper; type or print your name and A-Number (if any) at the top of each sheet; indicate the **Page Number, Part Number,** and **Item Number** to which your answer refers; and sign and date each sheet.

23. Have you **EVER**, whether in or outside the United States:

    A. Been arrested, cited, charged, indicted, convicted, fined, or imprisoned for breaking or violating any law or ordinance, excluding traffic violations, but including driving or operating a vehicle while intoxicated or while impaired by or under the influence of alcohol or other intoxicant, even if the record of the arrest, conviction, or other adverse criminal history was expunged, sealed, pardoned, or the subject of any other amelioration?   ☐ Yes ☒ No

    B. Been the beneficiary of a pardon, amnesty, rehabilitation decree, other act of clemency, or similar action?   ☐ Yes ☒ No

    C. Received a suspended sentence, been placed on probation or parole, or in an alternative sentencing or rehabilitation program, such as diversion, deferred prosecution, deferred or withheld adjudication, or expungement of a criminal charge?   ☐ Yes ☒ No

Sample Form I-600A, Application for Advance Processing of Orphan Petition (page 5)

Part 1. Information About You (Applicant) (continued)

D. At any time been the subject of any investigation by any child welfare agency, court, or other official authority in any state or foreign country concerning the abuse or neglect of any child, *other than* an investigation that has been completed and formally closed based on a finding that the allegation of abuse or neglect was unfounded or unsubstantiated? ☐ Yes ☒ No

24. Has your spouse **EVER,** whether in or outside the United States:

A. Been arrested, cited, charged, indicted, convicted, fined, or imprisoned for breaking or violating any law or ordinance, excluding traffic violations, but including driving or operating a vehicle while intoxicated or while impaired by or under the influence of alcohol or other intoxicant, even if the record of the arrest, conviction, or other adverse criminal history was expunged, sealed, pardoned, or the subject of any other amelioration? ☐ Yes ☒ No

B. Been the beneficiary of a pardon, amnesty, rehabilitation decree, other act of clemency, or similar action? ☐ Yes ☒ No

C. Received a suspended sentence, been placed on probation or parole, or in an alternative sentencing or rehabilitation program, such as diversion, deferred prosecution, deferred or withheld adjudication, or expungement of a criminal charge? ☐ Yes ☒ No

D. At any time been the subject of any investigation by any child welfare agency, court, or other official authority in any state or foreign country concerning the abuse or neglect of any child, *other than* an investigation that has been completed and formally closed based on a finding that the allegation of abuse or neglect was unfounded or unsubstantiated? ☐ Yes ☒ No

Part 2. Information About Your Home Study Preparer and/or Adoption Service Provider

1. Your home study:

A. ☒ **IS** attached to this Form I-600A.

B. ☐ **IS NOT** attached to this Form I-600A because of state requirements necessitating review and documentation. The appropriate state authority has indicated that it will submit the home study directly to U.S. Citizenship and Immigration Services (USCIS). (Do not submit your Form I-600A to USCIS until the state authority is ready to send your home study to USCIS.)

C. ☐ Will be submitted within one year from the date of this Form I-600A filing. (If your home study is not received within one year, your Form I-600A application will be denied under 8 CFR 204.3(c)(2) and (h)(5).)

2. Select one of the following options for which you will provide a name, address, and contact information in **Item Number 3.**:

A. ☒ The adoption service provider that is responsible for your home study (i.e., the accredited agency as defined in 22 CFR 96.2, that prepared your home study or reviewed and approved your home study after it was prepared by another authorized home study preparer, or the public domestic authority, as defined in 22 CFR 96.2, that prepared your home study); **or**

B. ☐ The primary adoption service provider who is responsible in your case, if you have already identified a primary adoption service provider. (A primary adoption service provider is an accredited agency or approved person who is responsible under 22 CFR 96.14 for ensuring the six adoption services defined in 22 CFR 96.2 are provided, supervising and being responsible for supervised providers where used, and developing and implementing a service plan in accordance with 22 CFR 96.44.)

3. Provide the name and contact information of your adoption service provider.

A. Name of Adoption Service Provider

Adopt International

B. Point of Contact Within the Organization

Family Name (Last Name)	Given Name (First Name)
Smith	Allison

Sample Form I-600A, Application for Advance Processing of Orphan Petition (page 6)

Part 2. Information About Your Home Study Preparer and/or Adoption Service Provider (continued)

C. Provider's Mailing Address

Street Number and Name

1000 Brannan Street

Apt. Ste. Flr. ☐ ☒ ☐   Number 301

City or Town

Menlo Park

State CA ▼   ZIP Code 94025

Province

Postal Code

Country USA

D. Provider's Daytime Telephone Number

4159340300

E. Provider's Fax Number (if any)

4159340700

F. Provider's Email Address (if any)

adopt@adoptinter.org

Part 3. General Information

1. Do you or your spouse (if married) plan to travel abroad to locate or adopt a child?   ☒ Yes   ☐ No

2. If you answered "Yes" to **Item Number 1.**, provide the following information (if available):

   A. Your intended departure date
   (mm/dd/yyyy) ▶ 04/10/2020

   Your spouse's intended departure date
   (mm/dd/yyyy) ▶ 04/10/2020

   B. Place to which you or your spouse (if married) are traveling
   City or Town
   Buenos Aires

   Province

   Country
   Argentina

3. Will you and your spouse (if married) adopt the child abroad after either you or your spouse (if married) have personally seen and observed the child?   ☒ Yes   ☐ No

4. Provide a written description of the pre-adoption requirements, if any, of the state of the child's proposed residence if you know that the child will be adopted in the United States. Cite any relevant state statutes and regulations, and describe the steps you have already taken or will take to comply with these requirements. Note and explain any pre-adoption requirements that you cannot meet at this time due to operation of state law.

   See attached statement.

   NOTE: If you need extra space to complete this **Item Number**, attach a separate sheet of paper; type or print your name and Alien Registration Number (A-Number) (if any) at the top of each sheet; indicate the **Page Number**, **Part Number**, and **Item Number** to which your answer refers; and sign and date each sheet.

5. What is the intended country of adoption (if known)?   Argentina

Sample Form I-600A, Application for Advance Processing of Orphan Petition (page 7)

Part 3. General Information (continued)

6. Where do you wish to file your orphan petition? (Complete **one** of the options below)

    A. The USCIS office located at: [   ]

    OR

    B. The U.S. Embassy or U.S. Consulate located at: [Buenos Aires Argentina   ]

7. Do you plan to adopt more than one child? ☐ Yes ☒ No

8. If you answered "Yes" to **Item Number 7.**, enter the number of children you plan to adopt. [   ]

Part 4. Accommodations for Individuals With Disabilities and/or Impairments

1. Are you requesting an accommodation because of disabilities and/or impairments? ☐ Yes ☒ No

2. If you answered "Yes" to **Item Number 1.**, select all applicable boxes below to indicate who has the disabilities and/or impairments.
    ☐ Applicant   ☐ Spouse   ☐ Other Household Member

3. If you answered "Yes" to **Item Number 1.**, select all applicable boxes below. Provide information for each person with the disabilities and/or impairments.

    A. ☐ Deaf or hard of hearing and request the following accommodations (If requesting a sign-language interpreter, indicate for which language (e.g., American Sign Language):

    _____

    _____

    B. ☐ Blind or have low vision and request the following accommodations:

    _____

    _____

    C. ☐ Another type of disability and/or impairment. (Describe the nature of the disability and/or impairment and accommodation you are requesting):

    _____

    _____

Part 5. Applicant's Statement, ASC Acknowledgement (if applicable), Certification, Signature, and Contact Information

Applicant's Statement

Select the box for either **Item Number 1.A.** or **1.B.** If applicable, select the box for **Item Number 2.**

1.A. ☒ I can read and understand English, and have read and understand each and every question and instruction on this application, as well as my answer to each question. I have read and understand the **Acknowledgement of Appointment at USCIS Application Support Center** (if applicable).

1.B. ☐ The interpreter named in **Part 9.** has read to me each and every question and instruction on this application, as well as my answer to each question, in [   ], a language in which I am fluent. I understand each and every question and instruction on this application as translated to me by my interpreter, and have provided complete, true, and correct responses. The interpreter named in **Part 9.** also has read the **Acknowledgement of Appointment at USCIS Application Support Center** (if applicable) to me, in the language in which I am fluent, and I understand this ASC Acknowledgement as read to me by my interpreter.

Sample Form I-600A, Application for Advance Processing of Orphan Petition (page 8)

Part 5. Applicant's Statement, ASC Acknowledgement (if applicable), Certification, Signature, and Contact Information (continued)

2. ☐ I have requested the services of and consented to _____ ,
who is ☐ is not ☐ an attorney or accredited representative, preparing this application for me. This person who assisted me in preparing my application has reviewed the **Acknowledgement of Appointment at USCIS Application Support Center** (if applicable) with me and I understand the ASC Acknowledgement.

Acknowledgement of Appointment at USCIS Application Support Center (if applicable)

I, | Cora Lynn Lerner | ,
understand that the purpose of a USCIS Application Support Center (ASC) appointment is for me to provide my fingerprints, photograph, and/or signature and to reverify that all of the information in my application is complete, true, and correct and was provided by me. I understand that I will sign my name to the following declaration which USCIS will display to me at the time I provide my fingerprints, photograph, and/or signature during my ASC appointment:

By signing here, I declare under penalty of perjury that I have reviewed and understand this application as identified by the receipt number displayed on the screen above, and all supporting documents, applications, petitions, or requests filed with this application that I (or my attorney or accredited representative) filed with USCIS, and that all of the information in these materials is complete, true, and correct.

I also understand that when I sign my name, provide my fingerprints, and am photographed at the USCIS ASC, I will be reverifying that I willingly submit this application; I have reviewed the contents of this application; all of the information in this application and all supporting documents submitted with my application are complete, true, and correct; and if I was assisted in completing this application, the person assisting me also reviewed this **Acknowledgement of Appointment at USCIS Application Support Center** (if applicable) with me.

Applicant's Certification

I certify, under penalty of perjury under the laws of the United States of America, that the information in this application and any document submitted with this application is complete, true, and correct.

Copies of any documents I have submitted are exact photocopies of unaltered, original documents, and I understand that USCIS may require that I submit original documents to USCIS at a later date. Furthermore, I authorize the release of any information from my records that USCIS may need to determine my suitability and eligibility as an adoptive parent.

I furthermore authorize release of information contained in this application, in supporting documents, and in my USCIS records, to other entities and persons where necessary for the administration of U.S. immigration laws.

Applicant's Signature

3. Applicant's Signature
Cora L. Lerner

Date of Signature *(mm/dd/yyyy)* ► 02/01/2020

Applicant's Contact Information

4. Applicant's Daytime Telephone Number
5105551212

5. Applicant's Mobile Telephone Number (if any)
5105550101

6. Applicant's Email Address (if any)
coralern@email.com

Sample Form I-600A, Application for Advance Processing of Orphan Petition (page 9)

Part 6. Applicant's Duty of Disclosure

Certification: I understand the ongoing duty to disclose information concerning my suitability and eligibility as an adoptive parent, as described in the Form I-600A and/or Form I-600 instructions, and I agree to notify the home study preparer and USCIS of any new information that I am required to disclose.

Applicant's Signature

Cora L. Lerner

Date of Signature

(mm/dd/yyyy) ▶ 02/01/2020

Part 7. Spouse's Statement, ASC Acknowledgement (if applicable), Certification, Signature, and Contact Information

Spouse's Statement

Select the box for either **Item Number 1.A.** or **1.B.** If applicable, select the box for **Item Number 2.**

1.A. ☒ I can read and understand English, and have read and understand each and every question and instruction on this application, as well as my answer to each question. I have read and understand the **Acknowledgement of Appointment at USCIS Application Support Center** (if applicable).

1.B. ☐ The interpreter named in **Part 9.** has read to me each and every question and instruction on this application, as well as my

answer to each question, in _____, a language in which I am fluent.

I understand each and every question and instruction on this application as translated to me by my interpreter, and have provided complete, true, and correct responses. The interpreter named in **Part 9.** also has read the **Acknowledgement of Appointment at USCIS Application Support Center** (if applicable) to me, in the language in which I am fluent, and I understand this ASC Acknowledgement as read to me by my interpreter.

2. ☐ I have requested the services of and consented to _____,

who is ☐ is not ☐ an attorney or accredited representative, preparing this application for me. This person who assisted me in preparing this application has reviewed the **Acknowledgement of Appointment at USCIS Application Support Center** (if applicable) with me and I understand the ASC Acknowledgement.

Acknowledgement of Appointment at USCIS Application Support Center (if applicable)

I, | Kenneth John Lerner |,
understand that the purpose of a USCIS Application Support Center (ASC) appointment is for me to provide my fingerprints, photograph, and/or signature and to reverify that all of the information in this application is complete, true, and correct and was provided by me or my spouse. I understand that I will sign my name to the following declaration which USCIS will display to me at the time I provide my fingerprints, photograph, and/or signature during my ASC appointment:

> *By signing here, I declare under penalty of perjury that I have reviewed and understand this application as identified by the receipt number displayed on the screen above, and all supporting documents, applications, petitions, or requests filed with this application that I (or my attorney or accredited representative) filed with USCIS, and that all of the information in these materials is complete, true, and correct.*

I also understand that when I sign my name, provide my fingerprints, and am photographed at the USCIS ASC, I will be reverifying that I willingly submit this application; I have reviewed the contents of this application; all of the information in this application and all supporting documents submitted with my application are complete, true, and correct; and if I was assisted in completing this application, the person assisting me also reviewed this **Acknowledgement of Appointment at USCIS Application Support Center** (if applicable) with me.

Spouse's Certification

I certify, under penalty of perjury under the laws of the United States of America, that the information in this application and any document submitted with this application is complete, true, and correct.

Sample Form I-600A, Application for Advance Processing of Orphan Petition (page 10)

Part 7. Spouse's Statement, ASC Acknowledgement (if applicable), Certification, Signature, and Contact Information (continued)

Copies of any documents I have submitted are exact photocopies of unaltered, original documents, and I understand that USCIS may require that I submit original documents to USCIS at a later date. Furthermore, I authorize the release of any information from my records that USCIS may need to determine my suitability and eligibility as an adoptive parent.

I furthermore authorize release of information contained in this application, in supporting documents, and in my USCIS records, to other entities and persons where necessary for the administration of U.S. immigration laws.

Spouse's Signature

3. Spouse's Signature

Kenneth J. Lerner

Date of Signature
(mm/dd/yyyy) ▶ 02/01/2020

Spouse's Contact Information

4. Spouse's Daytime Telephone Number

5105552222

5. Spouse's Mobile Telephone Number (if any)

5105551010

6. Spouse's Email Address (if any)

kenlern@email.com

Part 8. Spouse's Duty of Disclosure

Certification: I understand the ongoing duty to disclose information concerning my suitability and eligibility as an adoptive parent, as described in the Form I-600A and/or Form I-600 instructions, and I agree to notify the home study preparer and USCIS of any new information that I am required to disclose.

Spouse's Signature

Kenneth J. Lerner

Date of Signature
(mm/dd/yyyy) ▶ 02/01/2020

Part 9. Interpreter's Name, Contact Information, Certification, and Signature

If you and/or your spouse (if married) used an interpreter to read and complete this application, the interpreter must provide the following information:

Interpreter's Full Name

1. Interpreter's Family Name (Last Name)

Interpreter's Given Name (First Name)

2. Interpreter's Business or Organization Name (if any)

Interpreter's Mailing Address

3. Street Number and Name

Apt. Ste. Flr. ☐ ☐ ☐ Number

City or Town

State

ZIP Code

Province

Postal Code

Country

The Diversity Visa Lottery

In 1990, Congress created a new green card category to help balance out the numbers of immigrants coming from different countries, by opening up green card opportunities for people from countries that don't send many immigrants to the United States. Although the official name for this category is the "diversity visa," most people know it as the "visa lottery," because winners—50,000 in total—are selected through a random drawing. (The drawing is done by a computer.)

The visa lottery is held once a year. Every year the U.S. government looks to see which countries have sent the fewest immigrants to the United States in the last five years, and accordingly adds to or subtracts from the list of countries whose natives are allowed to put their names into the drawing. Diversity visas are divided among six geographic regions. No one country can receive more than 7% of the available diversity visas in any year.

You can enter the lottery if you are a native of one of the listed countries and meet certain other requirements. One of the requirements is some technological savvy—all applicants must now submit their applications through the Internet and attach a digital photo. And the newest requirement is that the main applicant possess a valid passport from the home country.

If you win the lottery, you've won the right to apply for green cards for yourself, your spouse, and your unmarried children under age 21—but no more than the right to apply. You can still be refused a green card for many reasons, including because of delays by the U.S. government causing you to miss the deadline, or because you've failed to meet the educational, health, or financial criteria for the diversity visa and green card.

Certain risks come with applying for the lottery. For example, if you win the lottery but are ultimately refused a green card, you've announced to the U.S. government that you're hoping to get a green card. That can make it more difficult to obtain or extend short-term visas to the United States—such as student or visitor visas. (Most short-term visas require you to assure the U.S. government that you have every intention of returning home afterward.) Even entering the lottery and losing is something you must declare on any later applications for U.S. visas, and it may be taken into account in considering whether you'll really return home on time.

Details of the Lottery That Began in 2019

At the time this book went to print, the most recent lottery had begun in 2019 (which the government calls "DV-2019"). Applications were accepted between noon on October 2, 2019 and noon on November 5, 2019. Entrants could check the status of their entries from May 5, 2020 through September 30, 2021, at www.dvlottery.state.gov/ESC. Natives of the following countries were not eligible (meaning that people who were natives of any other country in the world were allowed to enter):

Bangladesh	India
Brazil	Jamaica
Canada	Mexico
China (mainland-born, not including Macau, Taiwan, or Hong Kong)	Nigeria
	Pakistan
	Philippines
Colombia	South Korea
Dominican Republic	United Kingdom (except Northern Ireland) and its dependent territories
El Salvador	
Guatemala	
Haiti	Vietnam

CAUTION

The lottery changes every year and could disappear entirely. It is an annual event, with a slightly different set of rules, including qualifying countries, every year. In 2018, for instance, the U.S. Senate seriously considered eliminating the diversity lottery altogether and instead allocating visas using a points-based system, in which potential immigrants could better their chances of obtaining a visa by demonstrating their education and income levels, English language fluency, existing job offer, and other factors. Keep your eyes on the Legal Updates on Nolo's website, and double-check with the U.S. State Department during the year in which you'll be applying. The rules are usually announced around September, and posted on the State Department website at www. dvlottery.state.gov.

> **CAUTION**
> **Beware of lottery scams.** Every year, fraudulent emails and letters are sent to DV applicants. The scammers pose as the U.S. government—with increasingly sophisticated methods, such as including official-looking images of the U.S. flag, Capitol building, or White House—then attempt to get money from DV applicants. Don't be fooled! The government does *not* personally contact winners. Information about your DV entry will be available only through the official government website. To double-check that it's really a government website look for the ".gov" suffix on the Internet address. The same goes for any visa-related emails you receive. If they're not from an address ending with ".gov," be suspicious.

A. Who Qualifies for the Lottery

Whether or not you're allowed to enter the lottery depends on whether you:
- are a passport-holding native of one of the countries that is eligible that year, and
- meet the educational or work requirements.

It doesn't matter if you've already got an application for a green card underway in another category, for example through a family member or an employer —you can still enter the diversity visa lottery.

1. What Country—or Countries— You're a Native Of

Lottery applicants should make sure that they can actually claim what the law describes as "nativity" in an eligible country. Nativity is usually based on having been born in the country. Living in a country is not enough, even if you have residence rights there.

You may, however, be a native of more than one country. This can be helpful for lottery purposes if you were born in one of the ineligible countries, or if your native country has a lot of people applying for the lottery from it. There are two ways to gain nativity in a country other than having been born there:
- If your spouse was born in an eligible country, you can claim your spouse's country of birth for lottery purposes.
- If neither of your parents was born in your birth country or made a home there at the time of your birth, you might be able to claim nativity in one of your parents' countries of birth.

And remember, the list of eligible countries usually changes slightly every year, so check the State Department's instructions before you apply.

Immigrant Story: Applying Based on Spouse's Country

Azu was born and lives in Nigeria. Although in past years he's been able to enter the visa lottery, he has never won—and Nigeria was recently dropped from the list of eligible countries.

However, Azu's wife Marie is a native of Cameroon. So he submits a lottery application based on her country—and wins!

Assuming the U.S. consulate in Nigeria can process his case quickly enough, Azu, his wife, and their two unmarried children can become U.S. permanent residents.

! **CAUTION**
You must choose on which country to base your application. Even if you're a native of more than one eligible country, you can't apply for the lottery more than once within a single year.

Citizens of Certain Countries May Be Denied Diversity Visas Due to Travel Ban

Nationals of countries affected by Trump travel bans might have difficulty securing diversity visas for the foreseeable future. When this book went to print (mid-2020), no diversity visas were being issued for nationals of the following countries: Iran, Libya, North Korea, Somalia, Syria, Venezuela, and Yemen. This was true even if they had submitted a lottery entry or visa application before the travel ban went into effect. What's more, Trump has suspended participation in the Diversity Visa Lottery for certain nationals of Sudan and Tanzania. These entry restrictions come from a variety of proclamations issued by the Trump administration, and are often referred to collectively as the "Travel Ban" or "Muslim Ban."

Exceptions can be made for some applicants, however. If you were already issued a U.S. visa before the relevant proclamation went into effect, it cannot be revoked under the ban. Or if you are already in the U.S., the ban should not apply to you. The ban does not apply to dual nationals, so if you are a citizen of one of the countries subject to the ban and of another country that is not on the restricted list, you cannot be denied a diversity visa simply because of your "banned country" citizenship.

Additionally, you might be approved for a waiver if the U.S. government finds that it's in the national interest to grant you a diversity visa; if you pose no national security or public safety threat; or if denying you the visa would cause undue hardship.

If you are from one of the barred countries above (but were allowed to enter the lottery), and your name is selected, contact an experienced immigration attorney for help pursuing a green card.

---

2. The Educational Requirements

Applicants from qualifying countries must have either:

- a high school diploma or its equivalent, meaning a successfully completed twelve-year course of elementary plus secondary education that would qualify you to enter a U.S. college or university, or
- a minimum of two years' work experience (within the last five years) in a job that normally requires at least two years' training or experience. American job offers are not necessary. However, you won't be allowed to argue about how much experience your job requires—this judgment will be made based on a list of job titles and descriptions kept by the U.S. government in an online database called O*NET, at www.onetonline.org. (To check this out yourself, go to the website and click "Find Occupations.")

You won't be asked to prove your educational qualifications on the lottery application—but that doesn't mean you can puff up the truth. If you win the lottery, you will have to come up with proof of your education as part of the green card application.

B. How to Apply for the Lottery

A new application period starts every year, usually in early October. You can submit one application—and only one. People who try to apply more than once will have all their lottery visa applications tossed out of the running. Husbands, wives, and children in the same family can, however, submit separate applications if each one who applies separately meets the educational and other eligibility criteria.

No fee is charged for applying, so watch out for websites and consultants who claim that there is, or who charge you a lot of money for supposed "special" handling. The application is fairly simple and can be done by yourself, or with minimal help from another person.

CAUTION
Registrations submitted one year are not held over to the next. So if you are not selected one year, you need to reapply the next year to be considered.

1. The Application

We can't give you a sample application, because the one and only way to apply is online.

The Web address at which to apply is www.dvlottery.state.gov. It doesn't matter what country you're in when you submit the online application. You can start the application and then stop without submitting it, for example if you realize you're missing a piece of information—but you cannot save or download your work. And if you try to submit an application and the system rejects it, you can try again until you succeed.

Once you start your application, the system will give you only an hour in which to submit it before it erases all the information you've entered. So, you'll need to assemble all the needed information ahead of time, and plan for a time when you can complete the entire application within that hour.

Here's what you'll probably be asked when you go to the State Department website to apply:

1. Full name—last name (family or surname), first name, middle name
2. Date of birth—day, month, year
3. Gender—male or female
4. City where you were born
5. Country where you were born (use your country's current name, even if it had a different name when you were born there—for example, Myanmar instead of Burma)
6. Country of eligibility or chargeability—normally, the same as your country of birth. However, if you were born in a country that is not eligible for the DV lottery, you might be able to claim your spouse's country of birth, or your parents' country of birth, if different from your own. See "What

Country—or Countries—You're a Native Of," above.
7. Entry photograph(s)—you'll need to submit digital photographs of you, your spouse, and all your children (unmarried, under age 21), if you have any. See the technical information on the State Department website, https://travel.state.gov.

CAUTION
Get the digital photographs right. Your entry will be rejected—or your visa later refused—if you don't submit all the required photographs or the photographs are not recent, have been manipulated, or fail to meet the specifications on the Department of State website.

8. Mailing address—in care of, address, city/town, district/county/province/state, postal code/zip code, country
9. Country where you live today
10. Phone number (optional)
11. Email address (required)
12. What is the highest level of education you have achieved, as of today? (You don't need to list all your schooling, just the last type of school you completed, for example high school, vocational school, university, or graduate school.)
13. Marital status—unmarried, married, divorced, widowed, or legally separated
14. Number of children that are unmarried and under 21 years of age (no need to mention children who are ineligible either because they are U.S. legal permanent residents or U.S. citizens or are over 21 years old or married)
15. Spouse information—name, date of birth, gender, city/town of birth, country of birth, photograph
16. Children information—name, date of birth, gender, city/town of birth, country of birth, photograph

> **CAUTION**
> **If you are legally married and/or have children, be sure to say so.** This is important even if your spouse or children do not plan to become permanent residents. If you fail to include them on your original DV lottery entry, and they later try to apply for permanent residence based on your DV winning, your entire case will be disqualified. This applies only to people who were family members at the time the original application was submitted, not those acquired at a later date.

After you've successfully completed and submitted your online application, you'll get a confirmation screen, showing your name, other personal information, and a date/time stamp. It can take several minutes before you receive this screen. The confirmation doesn't mean you've won, it simply means your application went through okay. This is the only time you will be sent your confirmation number, so be sure to print out the confirmation screen for your records.

Be extra careful not to make typing errors. If your application contains a typing error, particularly in the spelling of your name, the State Department might throw it out. This is because it believes that people try to cheat the system by submitting more than one application with their name spelled slightly differently.

> **CAUTION**
> **Don't sign off without writing down your confirmation number.** You'll need this number in order to find out whether or not you are selected as a winner. If you forget, the way to retrieve a confirmation number is at the entrant status check page at www.dvlottery. state.gov. Click "Forgot Confirmation Number," select the lottery year, and enter your name (spelled exactly the same as on your lottery entry), your date of birth, and your email address.

2. Notification of Winners

Ever since the DV-2012 lottery, winners are no longer notified by mail. The only way to find out whether or not you have been picked is to check the State Department website at www.dvlottery.state. gov. All entrants, including those not selected, will be able to check the status of their entries through this website. In order to access this information, you must have the confirmation number that was given you when you made your online entry.

C. After You Win—The Green Card Application

Unfortunately, winning the lottery doesn't guarantee you a green card. The government always declares more than 50,000 winners—but gives out only 50,000 green cards. This means if you don't follow up quickly or receive your interview on time, the supply of green cards could run out. You'll have to complete the process and have received your visa or green card by September 30th of the year following your selection. (For example, applicants in 2019, who will be notified in 2020, will lose their chance if they can't complete the process by September 30, 2021.)

This can be a serious problem. You want to be ready to access the Entrant Status Check as soon as winners are posted. Even before learning whether you are a winner, it's worth taking a look at Chapter 16 (if you are already in the U.S. and eligible to adjust your status by filing an application with USCIS) or Chapter 17 (if you are outside the U.S. and will apply for your green card using consular processing) to see what types of documents you will need to collect, prepare, and ultimately submit with your application.

If you are among the lucky winners, you will receive a receipt number for the geographic location of your country, as well as instructions on how to apply for your lawful permanent residence. Winners will be instructed to check the *Visa Bulletin* to learn when their cutoff numbers appear under the appropriate region (or in some instances, country). If you are not immediately eligible to apply, keep checking the *Visa Bulletin* each month.

If you will be consular processing, use your DV case number to fill out Form DS-260, Online Immigrant Visa and Alien Registration Application. This alerts the Kentucky Consular Center (KCC) that your application is time-sensitive. You can also contact the KCC at 606-526-7500 (7:30 a.m. to 4:00 p.m. Eastern Standard Time) or email KCCDV@state.gov.

If you will be adjusting your status, you'll need to submit Form I-485, Application to Register Permanent Residence or Adjust Status along with supporting documents and forms to USCIS, and check the box in Part 2 indicating you are a lottery winner.

It's best to also indicate on the envelope and cover letter that you are a DV applicant and are facing a September 30th deadline. Few immigrants who win the lottery have the opportunity to adjust status in the United States. Find out whether you are eligible at www.uscis.gov/greencard/diversity-visa. Despite taking such precautions, you could encounter delays over which you have little control. Some people's applications get stalled while their security checks are being completed by the FBI (Federal Bureau of Investigation) and CIA (Central Intelligence Agency). Even if you've never done anything wrong, just having a common name can lead to delays, as the FBI and CIA check and double-check your name and fingerprints against various databases.

Given that you are facing the DV cap and deadline, consider hiring an experienced immigration attorney to help make sure your application is complete the first time around and to respond if and when delays occur. Another problem is that, as with all green card applications, if you win the lottery, you still must prove that you are not "inadmissible" to the United States. For example, if you have been arrested for committing certain crimes, are considered a security risk, have spent too much time in the United States illegally, or are afflicted with certain physical or mental illnesses, you might be prevented from receiving a green card. (For more on inadmissibility, see Chapter 4.)

Proving that you'll be able to support yourself financially in the U.S. can be a challenge for lottery winners. If you can't show this, you'll be considered inadmissible as a potential "public charge"—that is, someone who might need government financial assistance. You will need to show that you are either self-supporting, have sufficient skills and/or education to find employment, or have friends or family who will support you once you're living in the United States. In 2019, for example, the U.S. government said that a family of four who were getting their green cards through the visa lottery would be presumed to need government assistance unless their income was $25,750 per year or more.

> **TIP**
> **You'll face less onerous financial requirements than most other green card applicants.** Most people applying for green cards must have a sponsor submit an Affidavit of Support for them on Form I-864, which shows that their sponsor can support them at 125% of the U.S. poverty guidelines. People getting green cards through the visa lottery, however, submit a shorter and simpler Affidavit of Support, on Form I-134. Instead of showing an income that is at least 125% of the poverty guidelines, your sponsor needs only show an income that reaches 100%. You also have the option of filling out this form yourself if your income is sufficient, avoiding the need for a sponsor.

> **SEE AN EXPERT**
> **Don't miss your chance—get professional help.** A good lawyer will know the latest ways to get your application through the system quickly, and when and who to ask for speeded up handling.

> ⚠ **CAUTION**
>
> **Don't forget to pay the extra fees.** Lottery winners must pay a "diversity visa surcharge" in addition to the regular fees for applying for a green card. At the time this book was published, the fee was $330.

D. How to Bring Your Spouse and Children

For the lottery application itself, it's very simple to include your spouse and children—in fact, you're required to name them on your application, unless you and your spouse are legally separated (by court order) or divorced, or your children are U.S. citizens or permanent residents. Simply include your spouse and children's names, and remember to attach a digital photograph of each one to your lottery submission. (And remember that your spouse may, if eligible, submit a separate lottery application for him- or herself, which includes your name and those of your children.)

It doesn't matter whether your spouse and children plan to come with you to the U.S. or not—you must still list their names and provide their photos with your lottery application. If you don't list them, not only will they lose their chance to immigrate with you if you win, but your entire application will be disqualified! In fact, even if you and your spouse are no longer living together, you must provide your spouse's photo unless you're either legally separated (by court order) or divorced—a requirement that causes problems for some applicants.

What if you give birth to a child or get married after submitting the lottery application? That's okay—your new child and spouse will be allowed to immigrate with you if you win. However, you may be asked to provide extra proof that this relationship wasn't created fraudulently, to get the newly added person a green card.

If you win the lottery, the rules and paperwork for your family get more complicated. First, you need to figure out which family members are allowed to immigrate with you. Your spouse will be allowed, so long as you're legally married. Your children will also be allowed, so long as they're under 21 years of age and remain unmarried up to the date you're approved for green cards. Warn your children that they must remain unmarried until they've entered the U.S., or they'll lose their eligibility!

Next, each family member must submit a separate green card application, as described in either Chapter 17 (discussing consular processing for people coming from overseas) or Chapter 16 (discussing adjustment of status for people already in the United States and lucky enough to have a right to apply for a green card without leaving). No matter where you apply, the application will consist of several forms, expensive fees, medical examination results, and more.

Fortunately, only the lead person—the one who won the lottery—is required to meet the educational and work requirements of the lottery. However, each of your family members must separately prove that he or she doesn't have any of the health, criminal, or other problems that make people inadmissible to the United States. And you'll have to show that the family as a whole isn't likely to need government assistance.

You'll also need to pay for your entire family's airfare to the United States, and for housing once you get here. You won't receive any U.S. government assistance with your transition.

> ⚠ **CAUTION**
>
> **Be careful if you have a child about to turn 21.** Getting older is, of course, something your children have no control over. But a child who turns 21 before being approved for a green card is, technically, no longer eligible. Fortunately, the law contains some protections for children in this situation. When and if you are approved for green cards, your child will be allowed to subtract from his or her age the amount of time between the date you could have first applied for the lottery and the date the winners were announced.

CHAPTER

12

Your Brothers and Sisters as Immigrants

If you are a U.S. citizen, whether by birth, naturalization, or some other means, you can petition for your brothers and sisters to immigrate—but you must be at least 21 years old when you file the petition.

What's more, your brothers and sisters will be put in the family fourth preference visa category, which is so overloaded with applicants that they'll face a wait of at least 13 years, and up to around 24 years for applicants from some countries. (See Chapter 5 for more information on waiting periods in visa preference categories.) Nevertheless, the years can pass surprisingly quickly, so it might be worthwhile to get the petition in and reserve your brother or sister a place on the waiting list.

Once a visa number becomes available, your brother or sister will also be able to bring in his or her spouse and any unmarried children under age 21.

CAUTION
Congress might someday eliminate the F4 immigrant preference category for siblings. One of the proposals that Congress regularly brings up when discussing comprehensive immigration reform is to stop allowing U.S. citizens to petition for green cards for their siblings. And President Trump has been pushing for an end to so-called "chain migration" into the U.S., even proposing cutting off visas for all immigrating relatives other than spouses and minor children. Although Congress had made no changes by the time this book went to print, we can expect additional efforts in the upcoming months. The good news is that all family petitions before the law changes would likely be allowed to go forward. To be safe, if your sibling wishes to live in the U.S. permanently, it might be worthwhile to apply for a green card as soon as possible.

A. Who Counts As Your Brother or Sister

The immigration laws contain specific definitions setting out who qualifies as a brother and sister in every family.

When it comes time to submit the paperwork for your brothers or sisters (the Form I-130 petition), you'll need to prove that they fit into one of these relationship categories. The sections below will explain the different possibilities and list the documentation that you'll need to provide as proof.

1. Legitimate Brother and Sister

If your mother and father were married and had other children, all of them are your legitimate brothers and sisters.

Be sure to add the following to your visa petition:
- ☐ your birth certificate, and
- ☐ your brothers' and sisters' birth certificates (to show that you have the same mother and father).

EXAMPLE: Your parents raised your cook's baby as their own child. But to file a petition for that baby, you would have to present proof that your birth certificate and the other child's birth certificate show the same father and mother. Of course, you cannot do this. There is no way you can petition for this person as your brother or sister.

The only way around this strict rule is for someone in the family to legally adopt the child before the child turns 16. If that is not possible, you will have to look for another way for the child to immigrate to the United States, such as an employment visa.

2. Half-Brother and Half-Sister

If you and another person have the same mother or father, but not both parents in common, that other person is your half-brother or half-sister.

It does not matter when the relationship of half-brother or half-sister occurred. As far as the immigration law is concerned, you can petition for them just as if they were your full-blooded brothers or sisters.

Be sure to add the following to your I-130 petition:

- ☐ your birth certificate, and
- ☐ your half-brothers' or -sisters' birth certificates (showing that you have one parent in common).

3. Stepbrother and Stepsister

If your mother or father has married somebody who had children from a previous marriage or relationship, the children of your stepfather or stepmother would be your stepbrothers and stepsisters.

However, for purposes of immigration into the United States, you can file a petition for them only on one condition: Your mother or father must have married your stepparent before your 18th birthday.

Be sure to include the following documents with your visa petition:

- ☐ your birth certificate
- ☐ the birth certificates of your stepbrothers or stepsisters, and
- ☐ the marriage certificate of your mother or father and your stepparent, as well as documents showing that any and all of their prior marriages ended by death, divorce, or annulment.

4. Adopted Brother and Adopted Sister

If your mother and father have adopted a child according to the laws of the state or country they are in, that child is your adopted brother or adopted sister. Or, you might have been adopted by parents who have other legitimate children of their own. Their children became your brothers and sisters when you were adopted into their family.

However, you can petition for your adopted sibling only if the adoption decree occurs before the 16th birthday of your adopted brother or sister if they are the petitioners, or before your own 16th birthday if you were the adopted child.

Be sure to include the following with your visa petition:

- ☐ the adoption decree, and
- ☐ your and your siblings' birth certificates to show you had the same parents.

B. Quick View of the Application Process

To get a green card as a brother or sister, the U.S. citizen must begin the process by submitting USCIS Form I-130, the petition used for family immigrants. We're going to assume that the person reading this is the U.S. citizen.

Form I-130 serves to prove to the immigration authorities that your siblings are truly and legally yours. After that petition is approved, your siblings must complete their half of the process (with your help, of course) by submitting immigrant visa applications and attending interviews, possibly with you accompanying them. Their applications serve to prove that not only do they qualify as the brothers or sisters of a U.S. citizen, but that they're otherwise eligible for U.S. permanent residence.

However, the details of when and how your brothers or sisters complete their half of the process depend on whether they are living overseas or in the United States, as described in Section D, below.

TIP

Other people can petition for your brother and sister at the same time. There's no limit on the number of petitions that can be filed for a person—and it can be good to have more than one pending, in case one petitioner dies, for example. Let's say your parents are or become permanent U.S. residents—in that case, they could file visa petitions for your siblings (if your siblings are unmarried) in the second preference visa category, which moves much faster than the fourth preference. But you could file for your siblings as well, as a backup.

C. Detailed Instructions for the Application Process

Now we'll break the application process down into individual procedures, some of which will be covered in this chapter, and others in later chapters—we'll tell you exactly where to turn for your situation. We'll start by discussing the petition, which the U.S. citizen must always prepare to begin the process.

1. Preparing the Form I-130 Petition

To prepare the immigrant petition, the U.S. citizen will need to assemble and prepare the following:

- ☐ Form I-130, Petition for Alien Relative (available at www.uscis.gov/i-130; see the sample at the end of this chapter).
- ☐ Copy of a document proving your U.S. citizenship, such as a birth certificate, naturalization certificate, or passport.
- ☐ Copy of your birth certificate.
- ☐ Copy of your immigrating brother or sister's birth certificate.
- ☐ Any other required proof of your relationship as detailed in Section A, above.
- ☐ If you or any of your brothers and sisters have changed your name from the name that appears on the birth certificate, a copy of a marriage certificate or court document that explains the change.
- ☐ Filing fee (currently $535, but double-check the USCIS website at www.uscis.gov). Don't send cash. Pay by check or money order to the U.S. Department of Homeland Security. Or pay by credit card, by including Form G-1450, Authorization for Credit Card Transaction, with your application. Place this on top of the other papers you send to USCIS.
- ☐ Form G-1145. This is optional, but filing it is a good idea, so that you'll receive an email and/or text notification from USCIS when your application has been accepted. (Get it at www.uscis.gov/g-1145.) Once USCIS sends you a receipt number, you can use that number to sign up to receive automatic email updates letting you know whenever mail is sent regarding your application.

> **TIP**
> **Here's how to sign up for automatic email updates:** Go to www.uscis.gov and click "Check Case Status" on the home page. Then, click "Sign Up" and follow the prompts.

2. Submitting the Form I-130 Petition

After preparing and assembling all the items on the above list, the U.S. citizen should make a complete copy of everything (even the check or money order—this will be helpful if USCIS loses the application, which happens more often than it should). Then create an account and file online at www.uscis.gov, or send it to USCIS's Dallas or Phoenix lockbox (depending on where the U.S. citizen lives). The lockbox facility will forward it to the appropriate USCIS office—mailing information is on the USCIS website, www.uscis.gov/i-130.

After USCIS receives the I-130 and determines that nothing was left out, it will send the U.S. citizen a receipt notice. In the upper left-hand corner of this notice will be a receipt number, which you can use to track the status of the petition on USCIS's website, www.uscis.gov. There, you can also sign up to have USCIS send you automatic email updates about the petition.

Don't expect a final decision on the petition for many years, however. USCIS often decides to wait until a visa will soon be available to the immigrants before making a decision on the petition—which, in the case of brothers and sisters, could be decades away.

If you move during that wait, be sure to send your change of address to the USCIS office that has the petition. You can change your address online at www.uscis.gov or download Form AR-11.

Immigrant Story:
Reuniting Brother and Sister

Karl, from Sweden, became a U.S. permanent resident after winning the visa lottery. Although most of his family is uninterested in joining him in the United States, his twin sister, Karla, is extremely close to Karl and swears she'll never live more than 20 miles away from him.

Unfortunately, Karl must wait until he is a U.S. citizen to file a visa petition for Karla. As soon as his required five years of permanent residence have passed, he files a petition for naturalization. Within a year, Karl is a U.S. citizen. Now he petitions for Karla in the fourth preference category: But unfortunately, the wait in this category is over ten years long. During that time, Karla marries and has two children.

At last, Karla's Priority Date becomes current. After talking to her husband, they agreed to give life in the U.S. a try. Based on Karl's original application, Karla and her husband and children all apply for and receive U.S. green cards.

D. What Happens After Filing Form I-130

And now, your brothers or sisters must sit back and wait. There is no way to hurry up the process—see Chapter 5 for details on the visa preference system,

and for information on how to track your brothers' or sisters' progress on the waiting list (using their priority dates).

Having a visa petition on file does not give your brothers or sisters any right to stay in the United States. In fact, it could cause them problems when they apply for tourist or other temporary visas, because the State Department will know that they also have plans to stay in the U.S. permanently.

If your brothers or sisters are already in the United States, they cannot become permanent residents unless they remain in legal status during all the time they are in the country. They will probably have to return to their home country and proceed with consular processing (see Chapter 17), unless they're lucky enough to qualify for adjustment of status in the U.S. (see Chapter 16).

If your brothers or sisters are in the U.S. illegally, or have spent six or more months here illegally since 1997, they should talk to a lawyer about whether they'll be found inadmissible and barred from returning.

Once the immigrant visa is available to your brothers or sisters, they can extend the immigration privilege to their spouses and all unmarried children under 21 years of age at the same time, as "accompanying relatives."

CAUTION

A brother or sister who wants to come to the United States to visit during the waiting period must tell the U.S. consul when applying for a tourist or business visa that he or she has an approved I-130 petition. To be silent about this important fact will be looked upon as fraud in an immigrant visa file—and could mean a lost chance for a green card in the future. On the other hand, to be approved for the visa, the sibling will need plenty of evidence of intent to return home after a brief stay in the United States.

Sample Form I-130, Petition for Alien Relative (as used for immigrating siblings of U.S. citizens) (page 1)

<table>
<tr><td></td><td colspan="2">**Petition for Alien Relative**
Department of Homeland Security
U.S. Citizenship and Immigration Services</td><td>**USCIS**
Form I-130
OMB No. 1615-0012
Expires 02/28/2021</td></tr>
</table>

For USCIS Use Only	Fee Stamp	Action Stamp

A-Number

A- ☐☐☐☐☐☐☐☐☐

Initial Receipt

Resubmitted

Relocated	Section of Law/Visa Category
Received	☐ 201(b) Spouse - IR-1/CR-1 ☐ 203(a)(1) Unm. S/D - F1-1 ☐ 203(a)(2)(B) Unm. S/D - F2-4
Sent	☐ 201(b) Child - IR-2/CR-2 ☐ 203(a)(2)(A) Spouse - F2-1 ☐ 203(a)(3) Married S/D - F3-1
Completed	☐ 201(b) Parent - IR-5 ☐ 203(a)(2)(A) Child - F2-2 ☒ 203(a)(4) Brother/Sister - F4-1

Approved	Petition was filed on (Priority Date mm/dd/yyyy):	☐ Field Investigation	☐ Personal Interview	☐ 204(a)(2)(A) Resolved
Returned	PDR request granted/denied - New priority date (mm/dd/yyyy):	☐ Previously Forwarded ☐ 203(g) Resolved	☐ Pet. A-File Reviewed ☐ Ben. A-File Reviewed	☐ I-485 Filed Simultaneously ☐ 204(g) Resolved

Remarks

At which USCIS office (e.g., NBC, VSC, LOS, CRO) was Form I-130 adjudicated? _____

To be completed by an attorney or accredited representative (if any).

☐ Select this box if Form G-28 is attached.	Volag Number (if any)	Attorney State Bar Number (if applicable)	Attorney or Accredited Representative USCIS Online Account Number (if any)
	☐☐☐☐☐☐☐	☐☐☐☐☐☐☐	☐☐☐☐☐☐☐☐☐☐☐

▶ **START HERE - Type or print in black ink.**

If you need extra space to complete any section of this petition, use the space provided in **Part 9. Additional Information.**
Complete and submit as many copies of Part 9., as necessary, with your petition.

Part 1. Relationship (You are the Petitioner. Your relative is the Beneficiary)

1. I am filing this petition for my (Select **only one** box):

   ☐ Spouse   ☐ Parent   ☒ Brother/Sister   ☐ Child

2. If you are filing this petition for your child or parent, select the box that describes your relationship (Select **only one** box):

   ☐ Child was born to parents who were married to each other at the time of the child's birth

   ☐ Stepchild/Stepparent

   ☐ Child was born to parents who were not married to each other at the time of the child's birth

   ☐ Child was adopted (not an Orphan or Hague Convention adoptee)

3. If the beneficiary is your brother/sister, are you related by adoption?   ☐ Yes   ☒ No

4. Did you gain lawful permanent resident status or citizenship through adoption?   ☐ Yes   ☒ No

Part 2. Information About You (Petitioner)

1. Alien Registration Number (A-Number) (if any)

   ▶ A- ☐☐☐☐☐☐☐☐☐

2. USCIS Online Account Number (if any)

   ▶ ☐☐☐☐☐☐☐☐☐☐☐☐

3. U.S. Social Security Number (if any)

   ▶ 7 7 0 0 2 0 4 2 2

Your Full Name

4.a.	Family Name (Last Name)	Gray
4.b.	Given Name (First Name)	Alexandra
4.c.	Middle Name	Elaine

Sample Form I-130, Petition for Alien Relative (as used for immigrating siblings of U.S. citizens) (page 2)

Part 2. Information About You (Petitioner) (continued)

Other Names Used (if any)

Provide all other names you have ever used, including aliases, maiden name, and nicknames.

5.a. Family Name (Last Name): Boffin

5.b. Given Name (First Name): Alexandra

5.c. Middle Name: Elaine

Other Information

6. City/Town/Village of Birth: Brussels

7. Country of Birth: Belgium

8. Date of Birth (mm/dd/yyyy): 03/22/1992

9. Sex ☐ Male ☒ Female

Mailing Address

10.a. In Care Of Name:

10.b. Street Number and Name: 555 Glasgow Road

10.c. ☐ Apt. ☐ Ste. ☐ Flr.

10.d. City or Town: Mission Hills

10.e. State: KS   **10.f.** ZIP Code: 66208

10.g. Province:

10.h. Postal Code:

10.i. Country: USA

11. Is your current mailing address the same as your physical address? ☒ Yes ☐ No

If you answered "No" to **Item Number 11.**, provide information on your physical address in **Item Numbers 12.a. - 13.b.**

Address History

Provide your physical addresses for the last five years, whether inside or outside the United States. Provide your current address first if it is different from your mailing address in **Item Numbers 10.a. - 10.i.**

Physical Address 1

12.a. Street Number and Name:

12.b. ☐ Apt. ☐ Ste. ☐ Flr.

12.c. City or Town:

12.d. State: **12.e.** ZIP Code:

12.f. Province:

12.g. Postal Code:

12.h. Country:

13.a. Date From (mm/dd/yyyy):

13.b. Date To (mm/dd/yyyy):

Physical Address 2

14.a. Street Number and Name: 555 Main Street

14.b. ☒ Apt. ☐ Ste. ☐ Flr. 2

14.c. City or Town: Kansas City

14.d. State: MO   **14.e.** ZIP Code: 64102

14.f. Province:

14.g. Postal Code:

14.h. Country: USA

15.a. Date From (mm/dd/yyyy): 08/10/2014

15.b. Date To (mm/dd/yyyy): 12/05/2017

Your Marital Information

16. How many times have you been married? ▶ 0

17. Current Marital Status

☒ Single, Never Married ☐ Married ☐ Divorced

☐ Widowed ☐ Separated ☐ Annulled

Sample Form I-130, Petition for Alien Relative (as used for immigrating siblings of U.S. citizens) (page 3)

Part 2. Information About You (Petitioner) (continued)

18. Date of Current Marriage (if currently married) (mm/dd/yyyy) [ ]

Place of Your Current Marriage (if married)

19.a. City or Town [ ]

19.b. State [ ]

19.c. Province [ ]

19.d. Country [ ]

Names of All Your Spouses (if any)

Provide information on your current spouse (if currently married) first and then list all your prior spouses (if any).

Spouse 1

20.a. Family Name (Last Name) [ ]

20.b. Given Name (First Name) [ ]

20.c. Middle Name [ ]

21. Date Marriage Ended (mm/dd/yyyy) [ ]

Spouse 2

22.a. Family Name (Last Name) [ ]

22.b. Given Name (First Name) [ ]

22.c. Middle Name [ ]

23. Date Marriage Ended (mm/dd/yyyy) [ ]

Information About Your Parents

Parent 1's Information

Full Name of Parent 1

24.a. Family Name (Last Name) [Boffin]

24.b. Given Name (First Name) [Alexander]

24.c. Middle Name [Nicolas]

25. Date of Birth (mm/dd/yyyy) [10/11/1971]

26. Sex [X] Male [ ] Female

27. Country of Birth [Belgium]

28. City/Town/Village of Residence [Brussels]

29. Country of Residence [Belgium]

Parent 2's Information

Full Name of Parent 2

30.a. Family Name (Last Name) [Boffin]

30.b. Given Name (First Name) [Maxime]

30.c. Middle Name [Elise]

31. Date of Birth (mm/dd/yyyy) [06/29/1971]

32. Sex [ ] Male [X] Female

33. Country of Birth [Belgium]

34. City/Town/Village of Residence [Brussels]

35. Country of Residence [Belgium]

Additional Information About You (Petitioner)

36. I am a (Select **only one** box):
    [X] U.S. Citizen [ ] Lawful Permanent Resident

If you are a U.S. citizen, complete Item Number 37.

37. My citizenship was acquired through (Select **only one** box):

    [ ] Birth in the United States

    [X] Naturalization

    [ ] Parents

38. Have you obtained a Certificate of Naturalization or a Certificate of Citizenship? [X] Yes [ ] No

If you answered "Yes" to **Item Number 38.**, complete the following:

39.a. Certificate Number [1233435]

39.b. Place of Issuance [Kansas City, MO]

39.c. Date of Issuance (mm/dd/yyyy) [12/13/2016]

Sample Form I-130, Petition for Alien Relative (as used for immigrating siblings of U.S. citizens) (page 4)

Part 2. Information About You (Petitioner) (continued)

If you are a lawful permanent resident, complete **Item Numbers 40.a. - 41.**

40.a. Class of Admission

40.b. Date of Admission (mm/dd/yyyy)

Place of Admission

40.c. City or Town

40.d State

41. Did you gain lawful permanent resident status through marriage to a U.S. citizen or lawful permanent resident?

☐ Yes ☐ No

Employment History

Provide your employment history for the last five years, whether inside or outside the United States. Provide your current employment first. If you are currently unemployed, type or print "Unemployed" in **Item Number 42.**

Employer 1

42. Name of Employer/Company

Kansas Media Corporation

43.a. Street Number and Name

1110 High Street

43.b. ☐ Apt. ☒ Ste. ☐ Flr. 120

43.c. City or Town Overland Park

43.d. State KS **43.e.** ZIP Code 66204

43.f. Province

43.g. Postal Code

43.h. Country

USA

44. Your Occupation

Advertising Manager

45.a. Date From (mm/dd/yyyy) 12/01/2017

45.b. Date To (mm/dd/yyyy) present

Employer 2

46. Name of Employer/Company

The Kansas City Star

47.a. Street Number and Name 1729 Grand Boulevard

47.b. ☐ Apt. ☐ Ste. ☐ Flr.

47.c. City or Town Kansas City

47.d. State MO **47.e.** ZIP Code 64108

47.f. Province

47.g. Postal Code

47.h. Country

USA

48. Your Occupation

Digital Editor

49.a. Date From (mm/dd/yyyy) 05/20/2014

49.b. Date To (mm/dd/yyyy) 11/30/2017

Part 3. Biographic Information

NOTE: Provide the biographic information about you, the petitioner.

1. Ethnicity (Select **only one** box)

☐ Hispanic or Latino
☒ Not Hispanic or Latino

2. Race (Select **all applicable** boxes)

☒ White
☐ Asian
☐ Black or African American
☐ American Indian or Alaska Native
☐ Native Hawaiian or Other Pacific Islander

3. Height Feet 5 Inches 7

4. Weight Pounds 1 4 5

5. Eye Color (Select **only one** box)

☐ Black ☐ Blue ☐ Brown
☐ Gray ☐ Green ☒ Hazel
☐ Maroon ☐ Pink ☐ Unknown/Other

Sample Form I-130, Petition for Alien Relative (as used for immigrating siblings of U.S. citizens) (page 5)

Part 3. Biographic Information (continued)

6. Hair Color (Select **only one** box)

☐ Bald (No hair)   ☐ Black   ☐ Blond
☒ Brown   ☐ Gray   ☐ Red
☐ Sandy   ☐ White   ☐ Unknown/Other

Part 4. Information About Beneficiary

1. Alien Registration Number (A-Number) (if any)

▶ A- ☐☐☐☐☐☐☐☐☐

2. USCIS Online Account Number (if any)

▶ ☐☐☐☐☐☐☐☐☐☐

3. U.S. Social Security Number (if any)

▶ ☐☐☐☐☐☐☐☐☐

Beneficiary's Full Name

4.a. Family Name (Last Name) | Boffin
4.b. Given Name (First Name) | Ignace
4.c. Middle Name | Anton

Other Names Used (if any)

Provide all other names the beneficiary has ever used, including aliases, maiden name, and nicknames.

5.a. Family Name (Last Name)
5.b. Given Name (First Name)
5.c. Middle Name

Other Information About Beneficiary

6. City/Town/Village of Birth

Brussels

7. Country of Birth

Belgium

8. Date of Birth (mm/dd/yyyy)   07/29/1987

9. Sex   ☒ Male   ☐ Female

10. Has anyone else ever filed a petition for the beneficiary?

☐ Yes   ☒ No   ☐ Unknown

NOTE: Select "Unknown" *only* if you do not know, and the beneficiary also does not know, if anyone else has ever filed a petition for the beneficiary.

Beneficiary's Physical Address

If the beneficiary lives outside the United States in a home without a street number or name, leave **Item Numbers 11.a.** and **11.b.** blank.

11.a. Street Number and Name   Van Cuppenstraat 85

11.b. ☐ Apt.   ☐ Ste.   ☐ Flr.

11.c. City or Town   Antwerp

11.d. State | 11.e. ZIP Code

11.f. Province

11.g. Postal Code   B222

11.h. Country

Belgium

Other Address and Contact Information

Provide the address in the United States where the beneficiary intends to live, if different from **Item Numbers 11.a. - 11.h.** If the address is the same, type or print "SAME" in **Item Number 12.a.**

12.a Street Number and Name   SAME

12.b. ☐ Apt.   ☐ Ste.   ☐ Flr.

12.c. City or Town

12.d. State | 12.e. ZIP Code

Provide the beneficiary's address outside the United States, if different from **Item Numbers 11.a. - 11.h.** If the address is the same, type or print "SAME" in **Item Number 13.a.**

13.a. Street Number and Name

13.b. ☐ Apt.   ☐ Ste.   ☐ Flr.

13.c. City or Town

13.d. Province

13.e. Postal Code

13.f. Country

14. Daytime Telephone Number (if any)

323334424311

Sample Form I-130, Petition for Alien Relative (as used for immigrating siblings of U.S. citizens) (page 6)

Part 4. Information About Beneficiary (continued)

15. Mobile Telephone Number (if any)

323334424311

16. Email Address (if any)

iaboffin@email.com

Beneficiary's Marital Information

17. How many times has the beneficiary been married?

▶ 0

18. Current Marital Status

☒ Single, Never Married ☐ Married ☐ Divorced

☐ Widowed ☐ Separated ☐ Annulled

19. Date of Current Marriage (if currently married) (mm/dd/yyyy)

Place of Beneficiary's Current Marriage (if married)

20.a. City or Town

20.b. State

20.c. Province

20.d. Country

Names of Beneficiary's Spouses (if any)

Provide information on the beneficiary's current spouse (if currently married) first and then list all the beneficiary's prior spouses (if any).

Spouse 1

21.a. Family Name (Last Name)

21.b. Given Name (First Name)

21.c. Middle Name

22. Date Marriage Ended (mm/dd/yyyy)

Spouse 2

23.a. Family Name (Last Name)

23.b. Given Name (First Name)

23.c. Middle Name

24. Date Marriage Ended (mm/dd/yyyy)

Information About Beneficiary's Family

Provide information about the beneficiary's spouse and children.

Person 1

25.a. Family Name (Last Name)

25.b. Given Name (First Name)

25.c. Middle Name

26. Relationship

27. Date of Birth (mm/dd/yyyy)

28. Country of Birth

Person 2

29.a. Family Name (Last Name)

29.b. Given Name (First Name)

29.c. Middle Name

30. Relationship

31. Date of Birth (mm/dd/yyyy)

32. Country of Birth

Person 3

33.a. Family Name (Last Name)

33.b. Given Name (First Name)

33.c. Middle Name

34. Relationship

35. Date of Birth (mm/dd/yyyy)

36. Country of Birth

Sample Form I-130, Petition for Alien Relative (as used for immigrating siblings of U.S. citizens) (page 7)

Part 4. Information About Beneficiary (continued)

Person 4

37.a. Family Name
(Last Name)

37.b. Given Name
(First Name)

37.c. Middle Name

38. Relationship

39. Date of Birth (mm/dd/yyyy)

40. Country of Birth

Person 5

41.a. Family Name
(Last Name)

41.b. Given Name
(First Name)

41.c. Middle Name

42. Relationship

43. Date of Birth (mm/dd/yyyy)

44. Country of Birth

Beneficiary's Entry Information

45. Was the beneficiary **EVER** in the United States?

☒ Yes   ☐ No

If the beneficiary is currently in the United States, complete **Items Numbers 46.a. - 46.d.**

46.a. He or she arrived as a (Class of Admission):

46.b. Form I-94 Arrival-Departure Record Number

▶ [ ][ ][ ][ ][ ][ ][ ][ ][ ][ ][ ]

46.c. Date of Arrival (mm/dd/yyyy)

46.d. Date authorized stay expired, or will expire, as shown on Form I-94 or Form I-95 (mm/dd/yyyy) or type or print "D/S" for Duration of Status

47. Passport Number

87390279

48. Travel Document Number

49. Country of Issuance for Passport or Travel Document

Belgium

50. Expiration Date for Passport or Travel Document (mm/dd/yyyy)

01/29/2024

Beneficiary's Employment Information

Provide the beneficiary's current employment information (if applicable), even if they are employed outside of the United States. If the beneficiary is currently unemployed, type or print "Unemployed" in **Item Number 51.a.**

51.a. Name of Current Employer (if applicable)

Unemployed

51.b. Street Number and Name

51.c. ☐ Apt. ☐ Ste. ☐ Flr.

51.d. City or Town

51.e. State   **51.f.** ZIP Code

51.g. Province

51.h. Postal Code

51.i. Country

52. Date Employment Began (mm/dd/yyyy)

Additional Information About Beneficiary

53. Was the beneficiary **EVER** in immigration proceedings?

☐ Yes   ☒ No

54. If you answered "Yes," select the type of proceedings and provide the location and date of the proceedings.

☐ Removal   ☐ Exclusion/Deportation
☐ Rescission   ☐ Other Judicial Proceedings

55.a. City or Town

55.b. State

56. Date (mm/dd/yyyy)

Sample Form I-130, Petition for Alien Relative (as used for immigrating siblings of U.S. citizens) (page 8)

Part 4. Information About Beneficiary
(continued)

If the beneficiary's native written language does not use Roman letters, type or print his or her name and foreign address in their native written language.

57.a. Family Name
(Last Name)

57.b. Given Name
(First Name)

57.c. Middle Name

58.a. Street Number
and Name

58.b. ☐ Apt. ☐ Ste. ☐ Flr.

58.c. City or Town

58.d. Province

58.e. Postal Code

58.f. Country

If filing for your spouse, provide the last address at which you physically lived together. If you never lived together, type or print, "Never lived together" in Item Number 59.a.

59.a. Street Number
and Name

59.b. ☐ Apt. ☐ Ste. ☐ Flr.

59.c. City or Town

59.d. State [ ]   **59.e.** ZIP Code

59.f. Province

59.g. Postal Code

59.h. Country

60.a. Date From (mm/dd/yyyy)

60.b. Date To (mm/dd/yyyy)

The beneficiary is in the United States and will apply for adjustment of status to that of a lawful permanent resident at the U.S. Citizenship and Immigration Services (USCIS) office in:

61.a. City or Town

61.b. State

The beneficiary will not apply for adjustment of status in the United States, but he or she will apply for an immigrant visa abroad at the U.S. Embassy or U.S. Consulate in:

62.a. City or Town   Brussels

62.b. Province

62.c. Country   Belgium

NOTE: Choosing a U.S. Embassy or U.S. Consulate outside the country of the beneficiary's last residence does not guarantee that it will accept the beneficiary's case for processing. In these situations, the designated U.S. Embassy or U.S. Consulate has discretion over whether or not to accept the beneficiary's case.

Part 5. Other Information

1. Have you **EVER** previously filed a petition for this beneficiary or any other alien?   ☐ Yes ☐ No

If you answered "Yes," provide the name, place, date of filing, and the result.

2.a. Family Name
(Last Name)

2.b. Given Name
(First Name)

2.c. Middle Name

3.a. City or Town

3.b. State

4. Date Filed (mm/dd/yyyy)

5. Result (for example, approved, denied, withdrawn)

If you are also submitting separate petitions for other relatives, provide the names of and your relationship to each relative.

Relative 1

6.a. Family Name
(Last Name)

6.b. Given Name
(First Name)

6.c. Middle Name

7. Relationship

Sample Form I-130, Petition for Alien Relative (as used for immigrating siblings of U.S. citizens) (page 9)

Part 5. Other Information (continued)

Relative 2

8.a. Family Name
(Last Name)

8.b. Given Name
(First Name)

8.c. Middle Name

9. Relationship

WARNING: USCIS investigates the claimed relationships and verifies the validity of documents you submit. If you falsify a family relationship to obtain a visa, USCIS may seek to have you criminally prosecuted.

PENALTIES: By law , you may be imprisoned for up to 5 years or fined $250,000, or both, for entering into a marriage contract in order to evade any U.S. immigration law. In addition, you may be fined up to $10,000 and imprisoned for up to 5 years, or both, for knowingly and willfully falsifying or concealing a material fact or using any false document in submitting this petition.

Part 6. Petitioner's Statement, Contact Information, Declaration, and Signature

NOTE: Read the **Penalties** section of the Form I-130 Instructions before completing this part.

Petitioner's Statement

NOTE: Select the box for either **Item Number 1.a.** or **1.b.** If applicable, select the box for **Item Number 2.**

1.a. ☒ I can read and understand English, and I have read and understand every question and instruction on this petition and my answer to every question.

1.b. ☐ The interpreter named in **Part 7.** read to me every question and instruction on this petition and my answer to every question in

_____ ,

a language in which I am fluent. I understood all of this information as interpreted.

2. ☐ At my request, the preparer named in **Part 8.**,

_____ ,

prepared this petition for me based only upon information I provided or authorized.

Petitioner's Contact Information

3. Petitioner's Daytime Telephone Number

9136425656

4. Petitioner's Mobile Telephone Number (if any)

9136425656

5. Petitioner's Email Address (if any)

alexboffin@email.com

Petitioner's Declaration and Certification

Copies of any documents I have submitted are exact photocopies of unaltered, original documents, and I understand that USCIS may require that I submit original documents to USCIS at a later date. Furthermore, I authorize the release of any information from any of my records that USCIS may need to determine my eligibility for the immigration benefit I seek.

I further authorize release of information contained in this petition, in supporting documents, and in my USCIS records to other entities and persons where necessary for the administration and enforcement of U.S. immigration laws.

I understand that USCIS may require me to appear for an appointment to take my biometrics (fingerprints, photograph, and/or signature) and, at that time, if I am required to provide biometrics, I will be required to sign an oath reaffirming that:

1) I provided or authorized all of the information contained in, and submitted with, my petition;

2) I reviewed and understood all of the information in, and submitted with, my petition; and

3) All of this information was complete, true, and correct at the time of filing.

I certify, under penalty of perjury, that all of the information in my petition and any document submitted with it were provided or authorized by me, that I reviewed and understand all of the information contained in, and submitted with, my petition, and that all of this information is complete, true, and correct.

Petitioner's Signature

6.a. Petitioner's Signature (sign in ink)

➡ *Alexandra E. Gray*

6.b. Date of Signature (mm/dd/yyyy)   04/01/2020

NOTE TO ALL PETITIONERS: If you do not completely fill out this petition or fail to submit required documents listed in the Instructions, USCIS may deny your petition.

Refugees and Asylees

Since the Refugee Act of 1980 was passed by the U.S. Congress, many people fleeing persecution from their own countries have found a permanent haven in the United States. Those who made it to the U.S. on their own applied for what's called "asylum." (An unlimited number of people can apply for asylum every year.) Others were granted refugee status and a right to come to the U.S. while they were overseas. The U.S. president limits the number of refugees who'll be accepted every year—in recent years, the maximum has been set at between 70,000 and 90,000, but when this book went to print, it was at a historic low: 18,000 per year. People fleeing natural disasters or war who do not receive this permanent protection may receive what is called Temporary Protected Status if they are in the U.S. when their country is designated. (See Section I, below.)

SEE AN EXPERT

You will need more help than what's in this book. This chapter explains the basic procedures and describes the immigration forms required for people claiming status as refugees and asylees. However, the full legal process requires much more than filling out forms. You must present the facts of your case, in detail, in a convincing and compelling manner and if applying for asylum, you must also document the conditions in your country and make the legal argument that your facts qualify you for asylum. What's more, you must deal with a rapidly changing legal landscape, featuring new Trump Administration orders and policies and subsequent lawsuits. If, after reading the chapter, you decide that you might qualify as a refugee or an asylee, it is best to consult an experienced immigration lawyer or other immigration professional. Many nonprofit organizations offer free or low-cost services to people fleeing persecution. The current demand for services has overwhelmed many nonprofits and private attorneys, however, so it will be important to contact many agencies and attorneys in order to find someone to represent you. (See Chapter 24.)

A. Who Qualifies

To qualify as either a refugee or an asylee you must be unable or unwilling to return to your country because of actual persecution or a well-founded fear of persecution on account of your:

- race
- religion
- nationality
- membership in a particular social group, or
- political opinion.

Persecution can include such things as threats, violence, torture, inappropriate and abusive imprisonment, or a failure by the government to protect you from such things.

You do not have to provide evidence that you would be singled out individually for persecution if you can establish the following:

- There is a pattern or practice in your country of persecuting groups of people similarly situated to you.
- You belong to or identify with the groups of people being persecuted so that your fear is reasonable.

The persecution may have been by your government, or you can claim asylum by showing that you were persecuted by a group that your government is unable or unwilling to control, or that you fear such persecution.

For example, these might include guerrilla groups, warring tribes, or organized vigilantes. Again, however, the persecution must have some political or social basis—for example, a member of a criminal network who comes after you just because you haven't paid him off is not persecution according to refugee law unless there is some more specific reason that you in particular are being targeted.

Although the law does not list types of persecution, it does, in one section, specify that refugees and asylees can include people who have undergone or fear a "coercive population control program" (such as forced abortion or sterilization). This provision was directed mainly at mainland China.

The most well-known kind of asylum is "political asylum," where an applicant is given safe haven in the U.S. because of persecution (past or future) based on political opinion. As mentioned earlier, however, asylum is also available if the persecution is based on race, religion, nationality, or membership in a particular social group. The definition of "membership in a particular social group" is ever-evolving. In recent years, this has allowed some applicants to gain protection based on having undergone or fearing cultural practices such as female genital cutting or forced marriage. Another social group recognized only in the last two decades is one based on sexual orientation. In some circumstances, gays, lesbians, and transgendered individuals who were persecuted in their home country, or fear such persecution in the future, have been granted asylum. More recently, however, the Trump administration's Department of Justice has attempted to narrow options for people fleeing nongovernmental actors and for those relying on the particular social group category.

1. The Difference Between Asylees and Refugees

The difference between someone who can claim "asylee" status and someone who can claim "refugee" status has nothing to do with basic eligibility (both must meet the same standards). It simply refers to where you are when you file the application. To apply to be a refugee, you must be outside your country of nationality or country of residence but not within the borders of the United States. In addition, the president of the United States is empowered to recognize as a refugee any person who is still residing in his or her own country.

To apply to be an asylee, you must be either at the border or already inside the United States.

Although the standards are the same, there are major differences in the way that refugee and asylee applications are processed. One difference is that each year the U.S. president designates certain countries and areas of the world as places from

which the U.S. will fill the annual refugee quota. No such designation exists for asylees. What that means is that if a person seeks refugee status from a country that is not designated under that year's quota, a U.S. consular officer can't accept the application, but will instead refer the person to the United Nations High Commissioner for Refugees.

Also, the U.S. government prioritizes the processing of refugee applications based on several factors, including familial relationships in the U.S. and country of origin. No such prioritizing occurs with asylum applications, which are traditionally handled on a first-come, first-served basis although in recent years have been handled on a last-in, first-out basis.

2. Challenges in Proving Your Case

The biggest challenge in applying, especially for asylees, is proving that you were, in fact, persecuted or you reasonably fear that you might be persecuted in the future. You can't just say "I was persecuted" or "I'm afraid" and expect to be approved. But you probably didn't come to the U.S. with a lot of documents to prove what happened, if indeed any such documents exist. Nevertheless, you are required to at least attempt to obtain corroborating evidence of your persecution. (That's a fairly new development in U.S. asylum law, based on the 2005 REAL ID Act.) If you are unable to obtain corroborating evidence, it is important to explain why and describe your attempts or explain that it is unavailable.

Succeeding with your application will depend a great deal on your own ability to tell a detailed, compelling story of what occurred, including names, dates, places, and more. You'll probably need to write down the dates when everything you're talking about happened, and then read them several times to refresh your memory (unless you already have a better memory than most people, who probably couldn't tell you where they were on a particular date last week, much less last year).

Also realize that the person deciding your case is allowed to take into account your demeanor when testifying, as well as any previous statements you made while not under oath. This can create problems for people who, for example, have been culturally trained not to look anyone in the eye. Looking someone straight in the eye is, in the U.S., considered a sign of honesty, and the judge or asylum officer could interpret looking at your hands or at the floor as a sign that you're lying.

If you underwent torture or suffered other medical or psychological stress, it might help to get a written evaluation by a doctor who is trained in this area and can verify that you suffer from the effects of these things.

You'll also need to show that your own story matches up with accounts by independent sources of what goes on in your country. A good asylum application is accompanied by a thick stack of newspaper clippings, human rights reports, and more, all containing information about the kind of human rights violation you're describing. If, for example, you fled because local government officials were threatening to imprison you because you sent a letter to the editor protesting a political matter, you'd need to provide evidence that others who expressed similar political opinions have been imprisoned or threatened with prison. (And you'd definitely want to produce a copy of the newspaper's printing of your letter.)

B. Who Is Barred From Qualifying

A number of people are prohibited from becoming refugees or asylees in the United States.

1. Those Who Have Assisted in Persecution

The opportunity for refugee or asylum status is not open to anyone who has ordered, incited, assisted, or participated in the persecution of any other person owing to that person's race, religion, nationality, membership in a particular social group, or political opinion.

For example, this rule is often used to deny refugee status to military or police officials who assisted in persecuting minority or guerrilla groups (even though they might, indeed, fear for their life because members of those groups are seeking revenge against them).

2. Those Who Threaten U.S. Safety or Security

No one who has been convicted of a "particularly serious crime" and is therefore a danger to the community of the United States will be granted refugee or asylee status. There is no list of particularly serious crimes—the decision is made case by case, depending on the facts surrounding the crime. However, all "aggravated felonies" are considered particularly serious crimes—and, because of the immigration laws' strict definitions of aggravated felonies, some crimes that may have been called misdemeanors when prosecuted will be looked upon as aggravated felonies.

In addition, no person who has been convicted of a serious nonpolitical crime in a country outside the United States will be granted refugee or asylee status. However, people whose crimes were nonserious or political in nature may still qualify.

Furthermore, no person who has been involved in terrorist activity or who can reasonably be regarded as a threat to U.S. security will be granted refugee or asylee status.

As discussed in Chapter 4, the definition of who is a "terrorist" is broader than you might expect. It could, for example, be interpreted to cover people who have provided food or other "material support" to guerrillas or others trying to overthrow the government, or people who have given money to organizations whose aims the U.S. government believes are, at least in part, terrorist in nature.

Asylum applicants who provided material support under duress (for example, at gunpoint) can in some cases overcome this barrier.

3. Those Who Have Resettled

Refugee status is also denied to refugees or asylees who have become "firmly resettled" in another country. A person is regarded as firmly resettled if he or she has been granted permanent residency, citizenship, or some other type of permanent resettlement in a nation other than the one from which he or she is seeking asylum. Other things taken into account are whether that person enjoyed the same kind of rights and privileges as citizens of the nation in which they lived, in areas like housing, employment, permission to hold property, and rights to travel.

The Trump administration is also making agreements with certain other countries to designate them as "safe third countries" so that if you pass through one of those countries and don't apply for asylum there, you won't be eligible to apply in the United States.

4. One-Year Deadline

The law says that in order to qualify for asylum, you must apply within one year of entering the United States. There are some exceptions if you have been in some other lawful status or if exceptional circumstances prevented you from applying (such as severe mental health issues) or if circumstances in your country have recently changed and made it unsafe for you to return.

5. Alternatives to Asylum

Some people who don't qualify for asylum may qualify for Withholding of Removal or protection under the Convention Against Torture (also called CAT). These forms of protection require a higher likelihood of persecution and only result in employment authorization and permission to remain in the United States rather than eligibility to apply for a green card in the future, but they can overcome some of the bars to asylum.

C. How to Apply for Refugee Status

If you are outside the U.S. and believe you qualify as a refugee, you must first receive a referral to the U.S. Refugee Admissions Program (USRAP) for consideration. USRAP refers refugees based upon its priorities, which usually include cases identified by the United Nations High Commissioner for Refugees (UNHCR), a U.S. embassy, or a reputable nonprofit organization, and cases of people from countries with extreme conflict, or who need family reunification. For more information about the process, visit the Immigration section of www.nolo.com.

1. Filing the Application

If you are fortunate enough to get a USRAP referral, you will need to prepare and submit the following:

- Form I-590, Registration for Classification as Refugee
- documentation of persecution or a detailed affidavit supporting your request for classification as a refugee
- an assurance from a sponsor, which can be a responsible person or an organization, that employment and housing on entry will be arranged for you, and that you will be provided transportation to your final destination (usually accomplished through an umbrella organization called the American Council for Voluntary Agencies), and
- a medical examination report to ascertain that you are mentally sound and do not have a serious communicable disease.

2. Refugee Interview

After submitting your application, you will be interviewed by an overseas immigration officer who will decide whether you have been persecuted or have a well-founded fear of persecution because of your race, religion, nationality, political opinion, or membership in a particular social group.

**Refugees Should Expect
Long Waits and Delays**

Beginning in 2017, drastic cuts to both the maximum number of allowed refugees and refugee admissions were initiated by the Trump administration. In 2017, President Trump signed executive orders lowering the maximum number of refugees to 50,000 and introduced extreme vetting procedures. Then for 2019–2020, the number has been lowered even farther, to 18,000.

What this means is that many refugees who already received a referral from USRAP are still waiting in line for U.S. entry. Unfortunately, coming to the U.S. as a refugee is more difficult than ever before.

3. Action on Your Refugee Application

If the overseas immigration officer decides that you meet the requirements and may be designated as a refugee, the application will be granted. You will have four months in which to enter the United States.

If the application is denied, there is no appeal. You have no further recourse because you are outside the United States and its legal mechanism of judicial review.

While this chapter outlines the process for requesting refugee status from outside the U.S., keep in mind you cannot simply "apply" to become a refugee—you must first get a referral. A referral from the UNCHR is your best bet for getting into the USRAP, but even then only 1% of cases are referred for resettlement in a third country such as the United States. If you are referred to USRAP, you still have no guarantee of receiving refugee status.

Next is the refugee application and interview process, which can also be difficult. The good news is that, after you are classified as a refugee, you will be matched with agencies that can support your efforts. After your arrival in the in the U.S., they will provide you with cultural orientation and line you up with low-cost housing, employment options, and English language classes. Asylees do not receive all these benefits.

Once you have been granted status as a refugee, you will be granted work authorization for one year as soon as you enter the United States.

4. When Refugees Can Apply for a Green Card

After one year of physical presence as a refugee in the United States, during which you must not have violated certain laws or regulations, you, your spouse, and your children may apply for permanent residence (a green card).

If you are found to be eligible, you and your family will be given lawful permanent resident status. The date of your permanent residence will be the date that you first arrived in the United States as a refugee. You will be eligible to apply for citizenship five years from that date.

5. If Your Green Card Is Denied

If you are found ineligible for permanent residency, removal proceedings may be started against you and your family, and you will have to present your cases before an Immigration Judge. If this happens, consult with an experienced immigration lawyer who specializes in removal cases. (See Chapter 24.)

D. How to Apply for Asylum

If you are interested in applying for asylum, you must fill out USCIS Form I-589 and explain your case to a USCIS asylum officer or an Immigration Judge.

1. Where to Request Asylum

You can request asylum in the following ways:
- by requesting it upon arrival at the U.S. border or port of entry, if you are an alien stowaway, a crewman, or a passenger seeking

admission into the United States. But at many ports of entry along the southern border, asylum applicants were (as of 2020) being forced to wait in Mexico while waiting for their court date, under the Migrant Protection Protocols, also referred to as the Remain in Mexico policy.

- by presenting asylum as a defense at a removal hearing before the Immigration Judge, or
- by sending an application to USCIS, after which you'll be interviewed at one of the USCIS asylum offices. You can apply for asylum even if you're in the U.S. without status—but understand that if your application is not approved, it will be forwarded to an Immigration Judge. If you cannot persuade the judge that you should be granted asylum, you could find yourself with an order of deportation and removal against you.

> CAUTION
> **Don't delay in preparing your application (if you're already in the U.S. and not in removal proceedings).** The law says that applications for asylum must be submitted within one year of your entry into the United States. If you entered on a visa, USCIS policy is to allow you to proceed with your application within a period of "a reasonable time" after your visa-permitted stay expires (typically a maximum of six months). But this is up to the discretion of the USCIS officer deciding on your case. Similarly, time during which you had Temporary Protected Status (discussed in Section I, below) does not count toward your one year. If you've already spent more than a year here, talk to an immigration attorney as soon as possible. Exceptions are possible in rare cases, based on changed country conditions, changes in your circumstances that affect your eligibility for asylum, or other compelling reasons, such as your having been under the age of 18 when you first arrived in the United States.

2. Asylum Applications at the Border or Port of Entry

If you arrive at a U.S. border or port of entry and the officer says your visa isn't valid or you can't be admitted to the U.S., you can tell the CBP officer that you fear returning to your home country and plan to request asylum. The officer is supposed to refer you to another officer who is trained to understand, based on very little information, whether you have a believable and valid claim. Unfortunately, these officers do not act consistently, and there are many tragic reports of people being turned around and sent back to places where they were physically harmed.

Again, note that if you arrive at the southern border to seek asylum, you might have to wait in Mexico for your court hearing. There are nonprofit organizations that can help you prepare your asylum application. See www.alotrolado.org for help finding a clinic in Mexico.

Immigrant Story: Filing Beyond the One-Year Deadline

Roberto came to the United States alone, without a visa or documents, when he was 14 years old. Three years later, he came out as gay and became publicly and actively involved in gay rights causes. Then, during a demonstration, Roberto was arrested by immigration agents.

Because Roberto had already been in the U.S. for three years, his lawyer had to make a special request to the judge to extend the one-year deadline for filing for political asylum.

Fortunately, the judge agreed to hear the asylum application based on two grounds: 1) that Roberto had entered the U.S. as an unaccompanied minor, and therefore could not have been expected to know about the one-year asylum filing deadline, and 2) that Roberto's circumstances had changed since he publicly came out as gay, which could make him subject to persecution in El Salvador.

Applying for a Work Permit

Some years ago, applicants for asylum were eligible for a work permit as soon as they submitted an I-589—but no more. Now, in order to apply for a work permit, you have to either win your case—which can take anywhere between a few months and several years—or be lucky enough to be left waiting for an unusually long time (180 days or more) with no initial decision by the U.S. government on your application.

This obviously creates hardships for asylum applicants, who have to find money to live on and potentially pay their lawyers with, until the case is won. You may want to find help from lawyers at a nonprofit organization who, if you're financially needy, will charge low or no fees.

While USCIS attempts to issue decisions within 180 days, longer wait times are common. If the 180 days pass with no decision, or if your application for asylum is approved, you'll need to take steps to apply for a work permit (formally known as an Employment Authorization Document, or EAD). You can submit your application once your wait time reaches 150 days, but your work permit can't be granted until your wait time reaches 180 days. Any request for rescheduling or other delay on your part stops the accrual of days toward your ability to apply for a work permit. This is referred to as stopping the clock. The clock will restart once the delay is resolved.

You can apply for a work permit once you are eligible by filling out Form I-765 (available on the USCIS website). Most of this form is self-explanatory. On Question 27, if you've been waiting for 150 days or more with no decision, enter "(c)(8)." If your asylum application has already been approved, enter "(a)(5)." Follow the instructions on the form for what to include and where to send it.

Remember that any steps on your part that delay processing of your application can lead USCIS or the Immigration Court to "stop the clock" on your case. That means that if you request a rescheduled asylum interview, ask the Immigration Judge for more time to find an attorney or prepare your application, or do not accept the next available hearing date with the Immigration Judge, you could hurt your chances of getting a work permit before your asylum case is decided, but not doing so may hurt your chances for winning asylum if you aren't really ready to proceed. For more information about this tricky rule, consult an experienced immigration attorney

---

If the officer denies your entry despite your request for asylum, you won't be allowed to reapply for U.S. entry for five years without a special waiver. You can, however, sometimes avoid this bar by withdrawing your request for entry—in other words, by saying you changed your mind and don't want to enter the U.S. after all. But the border official has the option of deciding whether to allow you to withdraw your request for entry.

If the officer with whom you meet thinks you have a possible asylum case, you'll be placed in removal proceedings, where an Immigration Judge will consider your asylum claim (and any other relevant claims for immigration benefits you want to make). At this point, you'll have to prepare the application described in Section 3, below—and you should, if at all possible, get an attorney's help.

Don't Bow to Pressure From U.S. Officials to Give Up Asylum Case

Disturbing reports have arisen stating that U.S. Customs and Border Protection (CBP) officials have been informing migrants along the U.S.–Mexico border that there is "no right to asylum" or that the U.S. is no longer accepting asylum applications. Despite a change in administration, the right to request asylum upon arrival at the U.S. border still exists. If you have read this far and think that you meet the qualifications for asylum, you do have the right to request asylum at the U.S. border or another port of entry.

Be aware, however, that even if a U.S. asylum officer finds that your asylum claim has merit, you can be kept in immigration detention—a nicer word for prison—for weeks or months or be forced to wait in Mexico or possibly a third country, such as Guatemala, until you are able to see an Immigration Judge. In case you are detained within the U.S., it is good to carry the name of an immigration lawyer and friends and family members with legal status in the U.S., so that you can contact them for help to request that the Immigration Judge authorize your release upon payment of a bond.

3. Preparing and Filing Your Asylum Application

The following documents should be mailed to a USCIS regional service center, if you are not in removal proceedings, or submitted in person to the Immigration Judge (or to the clerk's window or mailed to the court), if you are already in proceedings:

- ☐ Form I-589, Application for Asylum and for Withholding of Removal—one original and one copy. (Available at www.uscis.gov/i-589; see the sample at the end of this chapter.)

Also make one copy of all supplementary documents. There is no filing fee for this form. Your spouse and children may be included in the application, as long as you supply an additional copy of your filled-out Form I-589 and attached documents for each. If you include your family members, they will also be granted asylum if you win or be placed in removal proceedings with you if you lose. (Regardless of whether you take the required steps to officially include them, you must provide their names and other requested information on your Form I-589.)

- ☐ One color passport-style photo of you and each family member applying with you. Write the person's name in pencil on the back.
- ☐ Copies (two) of your passports (if you have them) and any other travel documents (including from USCIS or the border authorities, such as a Form I-94 Arrival-Departure card)
- ☐ Copies (two) of documents to prove your identity, such as a birth certificate, driver's license, or national identity document ("cedula")
- ☐ Copies (two) of documents to prove the relationships between the family members applying, such as birth and marriage certificates
- ☐ Documentation (two copies) of your experience and the human rights situation in your country, showing why you fear to return, supported by your own detailed written statement
- ☐ If possible, also include statements (two copies) by any witnesses, doctors, friends, relatives, or respected leaders of your community, relevant news reports, or letters from people in your country.

CAUTION

Documents not in English must be translated. You'll have to provide a word-for-word English translation of any document in another language. Any capable person can do this, but should, on their translation, add the following text at the bottom: "I certify that I am competent in both English and [*your language*], and that the foregoing is a full and accurate translation into English, to the best of my knowledge and ability." The person should sign his or her name and add the date under this statement.

Not long after receiving your application, USCIS will call you in to have your fingerprints taken (if you're over age 14). This is to make sure that you don't have a record of criminal or terrorist acts and that you haven't applied for asylum before.

4. USCIS Asylum Offices—Where to File

There are four regional service centers that handle all asylum applications. Where you file depends on where you live. To find out which service center to use, go to www.uscis.gov/i-589. If you are submitting your I-589 to USCIS rather than to the Immigration Court, it now requires you to fill in every field on the form even if the answer is just "none" or "not applicable." USCIS can reject the form if even one field is left blank.

5. USCIS Interview

CAUTION

USCIS currently faces an unusually large backlog of asylum applications. The wait for an interview at one of the eight U.S. asylum offices and suboffices is now as long as four years. USCIS often states that it suspects people of applying for asylum solely to receive employment authorization (a temporary work permit, during the wait for an interview). USCIS thus rearranged its interview-scheduling priorities, which are now: 1) rescheduled interviews; 2) applications pending 21 days or less; and 3) all other pending asylum applications in the order received, with the newest cases scheduled first. This fast-tracking means that recent asylum applicants are unlikely to receive work permits (which, by law, are only given out to applicants after they've waited 180 days without a decision).

So, if you have been awaiting an asylum interview, you might expect to wait quite a while longer, while people who are just now applying for asylum might have their cases decided before you. This fast-tracking makes it all the more important for new asylum applicants to get help from an experienced immigration attorney.

The purpose of your interview will be to determine whether you are eligible for asylum. Interviews can last anywhere from one to three hours.

If you aren't comfortable in English, you'll need to bring your own interpreter. This doesn't have to be a hired professional—a family member or friend will do. But if your friends and family aren't truly fluent in both English and your own language, it's worth spending the money on a professional. Many asylum interviews have gone badly because the interpreter wasn't fully competent and the asylum officer, not knowing of the problem, assumed that the applicant couldn't get his or her story straight. For example, we know of a case in which the interpreter repeatedly translated the Spanish word "padres" (which means parents) as "father." The applicant was testifying about the death of both his parents in Guatemala, and the interviewer became very suspicious when the applicant suddenly appeared to be talking about only his father.

The asylum officer will also call a translating service (on contract with the U.S. government), to have a monitor listen in on the interview by telephone. The monitor's job is to interrupt if he or she believes that your interpreter is not being accurate.

Expect the interviewer to begin by reviewing some of the basic items in your application, such as your name, address, date and place of birth, and date of entry into the U.S., then to move quickly into open-ended questions such as "Why are you afraid to return to your country?" The interviewer may interrupt you at any point. He or she may also ask questions you never expected, sometimes to test whether you are who you claim to be. For example, if you claim to be a member of a persecuted Christian minority in a Middle Eastern country, you might be asked questions about Christian doctrine. These interviewers are highly trained in the human rights situations of countries around the globe, and many of them have law degrees, so expect some intelligent, probing questions.

Whether the interviewer will behave courteously is another matter. Many of them are sympathetic people who took this job because they're interested in human rights issues—others are government bureaucrats whose first concern is to ferret out cases of fraud. You won't be able to choose your interviewer. Women who have been raped or experienced similar trauma can, however, request a female interviewer by contacting the office in advance or including the request in writing when submitting the asylum application.

Protection Under the U.N. Convention Against Torture

Even if you don't qualify for asylum, you may be protected from deportation by the United Nations Convention Against Torture. This prohibits deporting anyone who can show that he or she is more likely than not to suffer torture at the hands of his or her home country's government. The asylum application has a place to mention whether you feel you qualify for this protection. However, it won't get you a green card—it will just stop USCIS from deporting you. Whether USCIS will also allow you a work permit is up to its discretion.

6. Comments of the Department of State

When USCIS receives your application, the officer may send a copy to the Bureau of Human Rights and Humanitarian Affairs (BHRHA) of the U.S. Department of State for comments on:

- the accuracy of the assertions on the conditions in the foreign country and the experiences described
- how an applicant who returned to the foreign country would be likely to be treated
- whether people who are similarly situated as the applicant are persecuted in the foreign country and the frequency of such persecution, and
- whether one of the grounds for denial might apply to the applicant.

However, the process usually goes faster than the BHRHA's ability to provide comments. Almost no one receives these comments anymore.

7. Decision by the Asylum Officer

After interviewing you, the asylum officer has discretion to approve or deny your application for asylum. However, you won't be told the decision that day. Normally, you have to return to the USCIS Asylum Office at an appointed time two weeks later to pick up your decision from the front desk. Accomodations can be made if you live especially far from an asylum office. The coronavirus pandemic may also result in changes to this practice. Sometimes, if your case needs further review or if the office falls behind in issuing decisions, you might be told that it will mail you its decision.

If you're approved, you'll be given a document stating this. Take good care of this document, and make copies to keep in safe places. You'll need it to apply for your Social Security card, work permit, and green card (permanent resident status) in a year.

CAUTION
Need to travel after you've been granted asylum? Don't leave the U.S. without first obtaining a refugee travel document allowing you to return. The

application is made on Form I-131; see the USCIS website at www.uscis.gov/i-131 for the form and instructions. Allow several weeks for your fingerprinting appointment and then possibly several additional months for the document to be approved. Also check the website to see the projected processing time, and take into account whether you will need any visas for your trip, to give yourself enough time to apply in advance of your trip. Also, do not return to the country that persecuted you—this will be taken as a sign that you aren't really in danger there after all, and you might not be allowed to return to the United States. If you feel you have no choice but to return to your home country, talk to an experienced immigration attorney before you leave. Even after you receive your green card, you should not travel to your home country even if conditions have changed and it is now safer for you to return. You should not travel to your home country until you have naturalized and become a U.S. citizen.

E. If Your Asylum Application Is Denied

If you are not approved, your case will be referred to the Immigration Court where you will have another chance to convince the Immigration Judge that you should be granted asylum (or Withholding of Removal or protection under the Convention against Torture). It is very important to get an attorney to help you.

> **CAUTION**
>
> **Don't miss the court hearing!** If, after you have been notified orally and in writing of the time, place, and date of the hearing, you fail to attend an asylum hearing before an Immigration Judge, you will be ordered deported in your absence and won't be able to adjust your status, obtain voluntary departure, or be granted cancellation of removal for a period of ten years and you will be subject to immediate removal if ICE finds you.

Only "exceptional circumstances beyond your control," such as your own serious illness or the death of an immediate relative, are considered to be valid excuses for failing to appear before the Immigration Judge. Your lawyer will need to file a motion to reopen the order of your deportation. Even if your circumstances don't seem to qualify for reopening, consult with an attorney in case there is another argument to be made.

If the Immigration Judge denies your case, you are free to appeal the case to the Board of Immigration Appeals (BIA) and from there to the federal circuit court of appeals. In the meantime, while your case or your appeal is pending, you are able to remain in the United States. If you have already received work authorization, it will continue to be granted for one year at a time. If you haven't, you'll have to continue living without a work permit. Be sure to file your notice of appeal within 30 days of the denial. The appeal notice has to be received by the Board of Immigration Appeals within the 30 days, so don't leave it to the last minute.

Some people turn around after they've been denied asylum and try to apply for it again. This won't work. First of all, it's not allowed, and second, USCIS has your fingerprints on file and will check them, so even if you change your name, you'll get caught.

F. Asylees Can Bring Overseas Spouses and Children to the United States

If you're granted asylum and you have a husband, wife, or unmarried children (who were under 21 when you applied for asylum) who are still living in the country that persecuted you, you have the right to request asylum for them, too. But you must act within two years of when you're granted asylum, or they'll miss their chance (at least, until you're a permanent resident or U.S. citizen and can petition for them, but this takes years). No other relatives are eligible—you cannot, for example, bring your parents or grandchildren.

CAUTION
Getting married after you've won asylum won't do it. As an asylee, you can bring in your spouse only if the two of you were already married when you were granted asylum. If, however, your wife gave birth to a child after you won asylum, you can bring the child in so long as it was in the womb when you were granted asylum.

The procedure for bringing your spouse and children to join you is to prepare and assemble the following (use separate forms and documents for each person):

☐ Form I-730, Refugee/Asylee Relative Petition, available at www.uscis.gov/i-730. (See the sample at the end of this chapter.)
☐ a copy of the document granting you asylum
☐ a clear photograph of your family member
☐ a copy of proof of the relationship between you and the person you're applying for—a marriage certificate for your spouse, or a birth certificate for your child (if an adoption certificate, the adoption must have occurred before the child was 16), plus a marriage certificate in your child's petition if you're the child's father or stepparent, and
☐ if your child is adopted, evidence that he or she has been living in your legal custody for the last two years.

There is no filing fee. For more detailed information, see the instructions that come with Form I-730. After you've finished preparing the applications, make a complete copy for your records and send it the USCIS service center indicated on the USCIS website. If you were granted asylee status in court and your spouse or children were in the U.S. but not in removal proceedings with you, you can also use this form to apply for asylee status for them.

Despite your status as an asylee, be aware that your family members can be denied entry to the U.S. if they've committed serious nonpolitical crimes, been affiliated with terrorism, or otherwise violated the provisions of the immigration law in I.N.A. § 208(b)(2), 8 U.S.C. § 1158.

CAUTION
Your children must remain unmarried until they enter the United States. Warn them not to get married, or they'll ruin their chance to claim asylum and join you. Of course, turning 21 is something your children have no control over. Fortunately, a law called the Child Status Protection Act (CSPA) offers them protection. The law says that if your child was under age 21 when you filed your Form I-589 with USCIS, he or she will still be considered 21 years of age when you file the Form I-730 and the child comes to claim U.S. asylee status.

G. Getting a Green Card After Asylum Approval

One year after your asylum application has been approved, you and your family may apply to become permanent residents. (You can also wait more than a year, but it's safest to apply as soon as you can.) You are eligible for a green card if you:

• have been physically in the United States for 365 days after being granted asylum—although the 365 days do not have to be consecutive
• continue to be a refugee or an asylee or the spouse or child of a refugee or an asylee (as defined in Section A, above; if conditions in your country have improved a lot, see an attorney), and
• have not violated certain U.S. criminal laws.

If you meet these criteria, it's time to prepare and submit an application for adjustment of status, as described in Chapter 16. You can skip the sections of that chapter that discuss whether or not you're truly eligible to use the adjustment of status procedure—as an asylee, you are. You also don't need to worry about proving that you entered the U.S. legally, like some applicants do. And unlike most other adjustment of status applicants, you need not submit an Affidavit of Support (Form I-864) or I-944, because you are not subject to the public charge rules.

There is no deadline to submit an application for adjustment of status. There is not even a requirement to ever do so. Asylee status is indefinite. However, the U.S. government has the authority to review your asylee status from time to time, to see if you are still eligible, and to see if conditions in your home country have improved to such an extent that it is no longer dangerous for you to return. Although the government does not often conduct such reviews, your safest course of action is to apply for permanent resident status as soon as you can.

H. Revocation of Asylee Status

Be aware that if your country's political situation has improved or changed so that you are no longer in danger of being persecuted, USCIS may revoke your asylee status. However, it must first notify you and then convince either an asylum officer or an Immigration Judge that you either:

- no longer have a well-founded fear of persecution upon your return, due to a change of conditions in your country
- were guilty of fraud in your application so that you were not eligible for asylum when it was granted, or
- have committed any of the acts that would have caused your asylum application to be denied—such as a serious felony.

I. Temporary Protected Status (TPS)

Temporary Protected Status (TPS) is a legal category that was fashioned by the U.S. Congress to respond to situations when natural disasters, such as earthquakes, volcanic eruptions, or tidal waves occur, or when war is being waged in a foreign country. It is a form of safe haven for aliens whose country is in turmoil. Congress responded with this humanitarian gesture to avoid the deportation of aliens to countries where their personal safety is threatened or in which normal living conditions are substantially disrupted. It does not, however, lead to permanent residence or a green card.

1. TPS Benefits

Temporary Protected Status offers several short-term benefits:

- **Stay of deportation.** You will not be placed in removal proceedings. If a removal case is already underway, you can claim TPS, and the proceedings will be paused until the end of the TPS period.
- **Work authorization.** You will receive work authorization as long as the TPS is in effect.
- **Temporary Treatment (TT).** When you file for TPS, so long as it is complete with such documentary proof as a birth certificate showing that you are a national of the designated country, you'll be granted a stay of deportation immediately and work authorization if the approval of TPS is significantly delayed, and they won't be taken away until either the TPS designation is ended or your application is denied.

2. Who Designates the TPS Aliens

The U.S. attorney general, working through USCIS, will designate the countries whose nationals deserve Temporary Protected Status. The following situations may give rise to this designation:

- ongoing armed conflict and civil war that pose a serious threat to the lives and personal safety of deported aliens who are nationals of that country
- earthquakes, floods, droughts, epidemics, or other environmental disasters, resulting in a substantial disruption of living conditions and an inability to handle the return of its nationals, in a foreign country that has requested a TPS designation, or
- extraordinary and temporary conditions in the foreign country preventing its nationals in the United States from returning safely to their country.

3. Period of Protected Status

The attorney general will designate the initial period of protection as not less than six months or more than 18 months. Sixty days before the end of the period, the attorney general will review the conditions of the foreign country to determine whether to end the TPS, or to extend it for a period of six, 12, or 18 months.

The termination or the extension will be published in the *Federal Register*.

4. Who Qualifies for TPS

Nationals or native-born citizens of the designated foreign countries may apply for Temporary Protected Status if they:

- have been physically present in the United States continuously since the date of the designation
- have continuously resided in the United States since a certain date
- register for TPS during a registration period of not less than 180 days, and
- pay the filing fee.

5. Who Is Not Eligible for TPS

TPS is not available to nationals or native-born citizens of a designated foreign country who are outside the United States. In addition, even if you are already in the United States, your application for TPS will be denied if you:

- have been convicted of any felony, or at least two misdemeanors, in the United States
- have ordered, incited, assisted, or participated in persecuting any person
- have committed a serious nonpolitical crime outside the United States, or
- are regarded as a terrorist or danger to the security of the United States.

TPS-Designated Countries

At the time this book went to print, citizens from the countries on the list below were still eligible for TPS. However, this list changes rapidly, so keep your eyes on the news and USCIS website at www.uscis.gov:

- El Salvador, Haiti, Honduras, Nepal, Nicaragua, and Sudan (terminated, but then extended due to a lawsuit until January 4, 2021)
- Somalia (extended through September 17, 2021)
- South Sudan (through November 2, 2020)
- Syria (recently extended through March 31, 2021)
- Yemen (recently extended through September 3, 2021)

Liberians used to have TPS and then something called DED and now any Liberian who has lived in the U.S. since November 20, 2014 can apply for permanent residence even if they didn't have TPS or DED in the past. This is called the Liberian Refugee Immigration Fairness (LRIF) Act and the application deadline is December 20, 2020.

6. No Departure From the U.S. Allowed Without Advance Parole

If a person who has been granted TPS leaves the United States without getting advance permission from USCIS, the agency may treat the TPS status as having been abandoned.

For humanitarian reasons, USCIS recognizes emergency and extenuating circumstances, and may grant something called advance parole, which is permission to depart for a brief and temporary trip without affecting one's TPS. Use Form I-131 to apply for advance parole. It is a good idea to consult with an immigration attorney or accredited representative before traveling abroad with advance parole. If you leave without first obtaining advance parole, you will not be able to re-enter the U.S. based solely on your TPS status.

7. How to Apply for TPS

The following forms should be sent to the USCIS address indicated for your specific country on the Form I-821 instructions. (You can also check the USCIS website at www.uscis.gov and under the heading "Humanitarian" click "Temporary Protected Status & Deferred Enforced Departure" for contact details.) The forms include:

- Form I-821, Application for Temporary Protected Status. It's available at www.uscis.gov/i-821. The filing fee is $50 for your initial registration, plus an additional $85 for fingerprinting if you are age 14 or older. There is no filing fee to renew the I-821, but if you are over 14 years old and you want to renew your work permit, you must pay the I-765 fee again (currently $410) and the fingerprinting fee ($85). Sometimes, the Department of Homeland Security issues an automatic extension of expiring work permits for TPS beneficiaries from specific countries. For example, as of this book's early 2020 print date, work permits (EADs) had been automatically extended for El Salvador, Haiti, Honduras, Nepal, Nicaragua, and Sudan. For an up-to-date list and more information, go to www.uscis. gov, and search for "Temporary Protected Status."
- Form I-765, Employment Authorization Application. (It's available at www.uscis.gov/i-765.) If you do not want a work permit, you must submit this form for biographic purposes, but you do not need to pay a separate filing fee. If you do want a work permit, submit this form with the fee, which is currently $410. Work authorization, effective until TPS is ended, is granted for the TPS period. The fee must be paid each time.

- For initial applications, copies of documents showing your physical presence during the period designated: passport used in entering the United States, for example, Form I-94 (Arrival-Departure Record), rent receipts, school records, hospital records, pay stubs, banking records, employment records, and affidavits of responsible members of your community (such as a religious officer, school director, or employer).
- For initial applications, two kinds of documents showing personal identity and nationality: birth certificate, a passport, driver's license, employment ID, or school ID.
- For initials and renewals, two photographs, passport style.
- For renewals, a copy of your expiring work permit and previous approval notices.

8. Termination of TPS

After the U.S. government decides that the situation in the foreign country has improved and there is no longer any reason to retain the Temporary Protective Status for nationals of that country, it will announce that the TPS designation will be lifted. Your work authorization will continue until the TPS expiration date.

If you do not have any other legal right to be in the United States, you are expected to leave at that time. However, if there are other immigration options available to you, you might be able to pursue them rather than leave. Consult with an immigration attorney or accredited representative to see if you have any other immigration options available to you.

J. Deferred Enforced Departure (DED)

Another benefit that might be available for people from countries that have political or civil conflicts is known as Deferred Enforced Departure (DED). This is a temporary form of relief that allows designated individuals to work and stay in the United States for a certain period of time, during which the authorities will not try to deport them.

At the time this book went to print, only Liberia was designated under the DED program, and DED status for Liberians was extended through March 30, 2020. But the Trump administration announced that this would be the end of the program.

As mentioned above, Liberians can now apply for permanent residence under the LRIF Act if they entered the U.S. before November 20, 2014 and submit their application before December 20, 2020. Their spouses and unmarried children can also apply for permanent residence regardless of their date of entry or nationality.

The law makes certain people ineligible for DED, including those who have committed certain crimes, persecuted others, or have been previously deported, excluded, or removed from the United States.

If you are already in removal proceedings, you may ask the Immigration Judge to defer action on your case based on DED if your country becomes designated. If your case is already up on appeal after a decision by an Immigration Judge at the Board of Immigration Appeals, you should receive notice automatically about the administrative or temporary closure of your proceeding.

Sample Form I-589, Application for Asylum and for Withholding of Removal (page 1)

Department of Homeland Security
U.S. Citizenship and Immigration Services

U.S. Department of Justice
Executive Office for Immigration Review

OMB No. 1615-0067; Expires 09/30/2022

I-589, Application for Asylum and for Withholding of Removal

START HERE - Type or print in black ink. See the instructions for information about eligibility and how to complete and file this application. There is no filing fee for this application.

NOTE: [X] Check this box if you also want to apply for withholding of removal under the Convention Against Torture.

Part A.I. Information About You

1. Alien Registration Number(s) (A-Number) (if any)	2. U.S. Social Security Number (if any)	3. USCIS Online Account Number (if any)
None	None	None

4. Complete Last Name	5. First Name	6. Middle Name
ROMERO	Luis	Manuel

7. What other names have you used (include maiden name and aliases)?
Luis ROMERO

8. Residence in the U.S. (where you physically reside)

Street Number and Name	Apt. Number
156 Arbol Lane	None

City	State	Zip Code	Telephone Number
Richmond	CA	94666	(510) 555-1212

9. Mailing Address in the U.S. (if different than the address in Item Number 8)

In Care Of (if applicable):	Telephone Number
not applicable - same as physical address	(510) 555-1212

Street Number and Name	Apt. Number
not applicable	None

City	State	Zip Code
not applicable	not applicable	94666

10. Gender: [X] Male [ ] Female   **11.** Marital Status: [ ] Single [X] Married [ ] Divorced [ ] Widowed

12. Date of Birth (mm/dd/yyyy)	13. City and Country of Birth
04/07/1975	Quetzaltenango, Guatemala

14. Present Nationality (Citizenship)	15. Nationality at Birth	16. Race, Ethnic, or Tribal Group	17. Religion
Guatemalan	Guatemalana	Hispanic	Catholic

18. Check the box, a through c, that applies: **a.** [X] I have never been in Immigration Court proceedings.
b. [ ] I am now in Immigration Court proceedings.   **c.** [ ] I am **not** now in Immigration Court proceedings, but I have been in the past.

19. Complete 19 a through c.

a. When did you last leave your country? (mmm/dd/yyyy) 10/04/2019   **b.** What is your current I-94 Number, if any? 02654000102

c. List each entry into the U.S. beginning with your most recent entry. List date (mm/dd/yyyy), place, and your status for each entry. (Attach additional sheets as needed.)

Date	Place	Status	Date Status Expires
10/04/2019	San Francisco CA	B-2	04/04/2020
05/07/2015	Los Angeles CA	B-2	

20. What country issued your last passport or travel document?	21. Passport Number 7758211001	22. Expiration Date (mm/dd/yyyy)
Guatemala	Travel Document Number None	01/15/2021

23. What is your native language (include dialect, if applicable)?	24. Are you fluent in English?	25. What other languages do you speak fluently?
Spanish	[X] Yes [ ] No	None

For EOIR use only.	For USCIS use only.	Action: Interview Date: _____ Asylum Officer ID No.: _____	Decision: Approval Date: _____ Denial Date: _____ Referral Date: _____

Form I-589 (Rev. 09/10/19) N

Sample Form I-589, Application for Asylum and for Withholding of Removal (page 2)

Part A.II. Information About Your Spouse and Children

Your spouse ☐ I am not married. (Skip to **Your Children** below.)

1. Alien Registration Number (A-Number) (if any) **None**	2. Passport/ID Card Number (if any) **850991002**	3. Date of Birth (mm/dd/yyyy) **05/09/1975**	4. U.S. Social Security Number (if any) **None**
5. Complete Last Name **ROMERO**	6. First Name **Maria**	7. Middle Name **Beatriz**	8. Other names used (include maiden name and aliases) **CARCAMO**

9. Date of Marriage (mm/dd/yyyy) **11/07/1999**	10. Place of Marriage **Antigua Guatemala**	11. City and Country of Birth **Panajachel Guatemala**

12. Nationality (Citizenship) **Guatemalan**	13. Race, Ethnic, or Tribal Group **Hispanic**	14. Gender ☐ Male ☒ Female

15. Is this person in the U.S.? ☒ Yes (Complete Blocks 16 to 24.) ☐ No (Specify location): _____

16. Place of last entry into the U.S. **San Francisco CA**	17. Date of last entry into the U.S. (mm/dd/yyyy) **10/04/2019**	18. I-94 Number (if any) **02288001113**	19. Status when last admitted (Visa type, if any) **B-2 Visitor**
20. What is your spouse's current status? **B-2**	21. What is the expiration date of his/her authorized stay, if any? (mm/dd/yyyy) **04/04/2020**	22. Is your spouse in Immigration Court proceedings? ☐ Yes ☒ No	23. If previously in the U.S., date of previous arrival (mm/dd/yyyy) **not previously in US**

24. If in the U.S., is your spouse to be included in this application? (Check the appropriate box.)

☒ Yes (Attach one photograph of your spouse in the upper right corner of Page 9 on the extra copy of the application submitted for this person.)

☐ No

Your Children. List all of your children, regardless of age, location, or marital status.

☒ I do not have any children. (Skip to Part A.III., **Information about your background.**)

☐ I have children.   Total number of children: _____.

(NOTE: Use Form I-589 Supplement A or attach additional sheets of paper and documentation if you have more than four children.)

1. Alien Registration Number (A-Number) (if any) **not applicable**	2. Passport/ID Card Number (if any) **not applicable**	3. Marital Status (Married, Single, Divorced, Widowed) **not applicable**	4. U.S. Social Security Number (if any) **not applicable**
5. Complete Last Name **not applicable**	6. First Name **not applicable**	7. Middle Name **not applicable**	8. Date of Birth (mm/dd/yyyy) **not applicable**
9. City and Country of Birth **not applicable**	10. Nationality (Citizenship) **not applicable**	11. Race, Ethnic, or Tribal Group **not applicable**	12. Gender ☐ Male ☐ Female

13. Is this child in the U.S. ? ☐ Yes (Complete Blocks 14 to 21.) ☐ No (Specify location): _____

14. Place of last entry into the U.S. **not applicable**	15. Date of last entry into the U.S. (mm/dd/yyyy) **not applicable**	16. I-94 Number (If any) **00000000000**	17. Status when last admitted (Visa type, if any) **not applicable**
18. What is your child's current status? **not applicable**	19. What is the expiration date of his/her authorized stay, if any? (mm/dd/yyyy) **not applicable**	20. Is your child in Immigration Court proceedings? ☐ Yes ☐ No	

21. If in the U.S., is this child to be included in this application? (Check the appropriate box.)

☐ Yes (Attach one photograph of your child in the upper right corner of Page 9 on the extra copy of the application submitted for this person.)

☐ No

Sample Form I-589, Application for Asylum and for Withholding of Removal (page 3)

Part A.II. Information About Your Spouse and Children (Continued)

1. Alien Registration Number (A-Number) *(if any)*	**2.** Passport/ID Card Number *(if any)*	**3.** Marital Status *(Married, Single, Divorced, Widowed)*	**4.** U.S. Social Security Number *(if any)*
not applicable	not applicable	not applicable	not applicable

5. Complete Last Name	**6.** First Name	**7.** Middle Name	**8.** Date of Birth *(mm/dd/yyyy)*
not applicable	not applicable	not applicable	not applicable

9. City and Country of Birth	**10.** Nationality *(Citizenship)*	**11.** Race, Ethnic, or Tribal Group	**12.** Gender
not applicable	not applicable	not applicable	☐ Male ☐ Female

13. Is this child in the U.S. ? ☐ Yes *(Complete Blocks 14 to 21.)* ☐ No *(Specify location):* _____

14. Place of last entry into the U.S.	**15.** Date of last entry into the U.S. *(mm/dd/yyyy)*	**16.** I-94 Number *(If any)*	**17.** Status when last admitted *(Visa type, if any)*
not applicable	not applicable	00000000000	not applicable

18. What is your child's current status?	**19.** What is the expiration date of his/her authorized stay, if any? *(mm/dd/yyyy)*	**20.** Is your child in Immigration Court proceedings?
not applicable	not applicable	☐ Yes ☐ No

21. If in the U.S., is this child to be included in this application? *(Check the appropriate box.)*

☐ Yes *(Attach one photograph of your spouse in the upper right corner of Page 9 on the extra copy of the application submitted for this person.)*

☐ No

1. Alien Registration Number (A-Number) *(if any)*	**2.** Passport/ID Card Number *(if any)*	**3.** Marital Status *(Married, Single, Divorced, Widowed)*	**4.** U.S. Social Security Number *(if any)*
not applicable	not applicable	not applicable	not applicable

5. Complete Last Name	**6.** First Name	**7.** Middle Name	**8.** Date of Birth *(mm/dd/yyyy)*
not applicable	not applicable	not applicable	not applicable

9. City and Country of Birth	**10.** Nationality *(Citizenship)*	**11.** Race, Ethnic, or Tribal Group	**12.** Gender
not applicable	not applicable	not applicable	☐ Male ☐ Female

13. Is this child in the U.S. ? ☐ Yes *(Complete Blocks 14 to 21.)* ☐ No *(Specify location):* _____

14. Place of last entry into the U.S.	**15.** Date of last entry into the U.S. *(mm/dd/yyyy)*	**16.** I-94 Number *(If any)*	**17.** Status when last admitted *(Visa type, if any)*
not applicable	not applicable	00000000000	not applicable

18. What is your child's current status?	**19.** What is the expiration date of his/her authorized stay, if any? *(mm/dd/yyyy)*	**20.** Is your child in Immigration Court proceedings?
not applicable	not applicable	☐ Yes ☐ No

21. If in the U.S., is this child to be included in this application? *(Check the appropriate box.)*

☐ Yes *(Attach one photograph of your spouse in the upper right corner of Page 9 on the extra copy of the application submitted for this person.)*

☐ No

1. Alien Registration Number (A-Number) *(if any)*	**2.** Passport/ID Card Number *(if any)*	**3.** Marital Status *(Married, Single, Divorced, Widowed)*	**4.** U.S. Social Security Number *(if any)*
not applicable	not applicable	not applicable	not applicable

5. Complete Last Name	**6.** First Name	**7.** Middle Name	**8.** Date of Birth *(mm/dd/yyyy)*
not applicable	not applicable	not applicable	not applicable

9. City and Country of Birth	**10.** Nationality *(Citizenship)*	**11.** Race, Ethnic, or Tribal Group	**12.** Gender
not applicable	not applicable	not applicable	☐ Male ☐ Female

13. Is this child in the U.S. ? ☐ Yes *(Complete Blocks 14 to 21.)* ☐ No *(Specify location):* _____

14. Place of last entry into the U.S.	**15.** Date of last entry into the U.S. *(mm/dd/yyyy)*	**16.** I-94 Number *(If any)*	**17.** Status when last admitted *(Visa type, if any)*
not applicable	not applicable	00000000000	not applicable

18. What is your child's current status?	**19.** What is the expiration date of his/her authorized stay, if any? *(mm/dd/yyyy)*	**20.** Is your child in Immigration Court proceedings?
not applicable	not applicable	☐ Yes ☐ No

21. If in the U.S., is this child to be included in this application? *(Check the appropriate box.)*

☐ Yes *(Attach one photograph of your spouse in the upper right corner of Page 9 on the extra copy of the application submitted for this person.)*

☐ No

Form I-589 (Rev. 09/10/19) N Page 3

Sample Form I-589, Application for Asylum and for Withholding of Removal (page 4)

Part A.III. Information About Your Background

1. List your last address where you lived before coming to the United States. If this is not the country where you fear persecution, also list the last address in the country where you fear persecution. *(List Address, City/Town, Department, Province, or State and Country.)*
   (NOTE: *Use Form I-589 Supplement B, or additional sheets of paper, if necessary.)*

Number and Street *(Provide if available)*	City/Town	Department, Province, or State	Country	Dates From *(Mo/Yr)*	To *(Mo/Yr)*
123 Avenida 7	Guatemala City	Guatemala	Guatemala	11/1995	10/2019

2. Provide the following information about your residences during the past 5 years. List your present address first.
   (NOTE: *Use Form I-589 Supplement B, or additional sheets of paper, if necessary.)*

Number and Street	City/Town	Department, Province, or State	Country	Dates From *(Mo/Yr)*	To *(Mo/Yr)*
156 Arbol Lane	Richmond	CA	USA	10/2019	present
123 Avenida 7	Guatemala City	Guatemala	Guatemala	11/1995	10/2019

3. Provide the following information about your education, beginning with the most recent school that you attended.
   (NOTE: *Use Form I-589 Supplement B, or additional sheets of paper, if necessary.)*

Name of School	Type of School	Location *(Address)*	Attended From *(Mo/Yr)*	To *(Mo/Yr)*
San Carlos University	College	Guatemala City Guatemala	09/1992	06/1996
Quetzal High School	High School	Quetzaltenango Guatemala	09/1988	06/1992
Santa Maria Academy	Primary School	Quetzaltenango Guatemala	09/1980	06/1988

4. Provide the following information about your employment during the past 5 years. List your present employment first.
   (NOTE: *Use Form I-589 Supplement B, or additional sheets of paper, if necessary.)*

Name and Address of Employer	Your Occupation	Dates From *(Mo/Yr)*	To *(Mo/Yr)*
Jose Torres Ramirez, Attorney, Guatemala City	Legal Assistant	08/2007	10/2019

5. Provide the following information about your parents and siblings (brothers and sisters). Check the box if the person is deceased.
   (NOTE: *Use Form I-589 Supplement B, or additional sheets of paper, if necessary.)*

Full Name	City/Town and Country of Birth	Current Location
Mother **Gloria ALCALA DE ROMERO**	Quetzaltenango Guatemala	☒ Deceased
Father **Jorge ROMERO**	Quetzaltenango Guatemala	☒ Deceased
Sibling **Felipe ROMERO**	Quetzaltenango Guatemala	☒ Deceased
Sibling **Laura ROMERO**	Quetzaltenango Guatemala	☐ Deceased **Antigua Guatemala**
Sibling		☐ Deceased
Sibling		☐ Deceased

Sample Form I-589, Application for Asylum and for Withholding of Removal (page 5)

Part B. Information About Your Application

(**NOTE:** *Use Form I-589 Supplement B, or attach additional sheets of paper as needed to complete your responses to the questions contained in Part B.)*

When answering the following questions about your asylum or other protection claim (withholding of removal under 241(b)(3) of the INA or withholding of removal under the Convention Against Torture), you must provide a detailed and specific account of the basis of your claim to asylum or other protection. To the best of your ability, provide specific dates, places, and descriptions about each event or action described. You must attach documents evidencing the general conditions in the country from which you are seeking asylum or other protection and the specific facts on which you are relying to support your claim. If this documentation is unavailable or you are not providing this documentation with your application, explain why in your responses to the following questions.

Refer to Instructions, Part 1: Filing Instructions, Section II, "Basis of Eligibility," Parts A - D, Section V, "Completing the Form," Part B, and Section VII, "Additional Evidence That You Should Submit," for more information on completing this section of the form.

1. Why are you applying for asylum or withholding of removal under section 241(b)(3) of the INA, or for withholding of removal under the Convention Against Torture? Check the appropriate box(es) below and then provide detailed answers to questions A and B below.

   I am seeking asylum or withholding of removal based on:

☐	Race	☒	Political opinion
☐	Religion	☒	Membership in a particular social group
☐	Nationality	☒	Torture Convention

A. Have you, your family, or close friends or colleagues ever experienced harm or mistreatment or threats in the past by anyone?

☐ No   ☒ Yes

If "Yes," explain in detail:
1. What happened;
2. When the harm or mistreatment or threats occurred;
3. Who caused the harm or mistreatment or threats; and
4. Why you believe the harm or mistreatment or threats occurred.

> From July to September 2019, military vehicles with darkened windows have been circling our law office and have followed me home on at least two occasions on September 5, 2019 and September 30, 2019. I filed police reports with the Guatemala City police on both those dates. (See attached). The neighbors informed me that a military officer knocked on their doors on several occasions in September 2017 asking about me. On September 30, 2019, I received a phone call from an anonymous caller who told me "you and your boss better drop the Diaz case or your wife will be a widow." He was referring to a case of a victim of military human rights abuses that my employer Attorney Jose Torres Ramirez is handling. See attached affidavits and documentation regarding these incidents.

B. Do you fear harm or mistreatment if you return to your home country?

☐ No   ☒ Yes

If "Yes," explain in detail:
1. What harm or mistreatment you fear;
2. Who you believe would harm or mistreat you; and
3. Why you believe you would or could be harmed or mistreated.

> I believe that members of the Guatemalan military would torture, imprison, or kill me because of my work on the Diaz case and assisting victims of military human rights abuses with their court cases. Since I left Guatemala, a law clerk at the office where I worked was detained and beaten by military officers. See attached affidavits and documentation regarding the continued work on the Diaz case, and other relevant cases my employer, Attorney Jose Torres Ramirez, is handling. Attached also find police and hospital reports from my former co-worker detailing the recent incidents with military officers.

Sample Form I-589, Application for Asylum and for Withholding of Removal (page 6)

Part B. Information About Your Application (Continued)

2. Have you or your family members ever been accused, charged, arrested, detained, interrogated, convicted and sentenced, or imprisoned in any country other than the United States (including for an immigration law violation)?

   ☒ No   ☐ Yes

   If "Yes," explain the circumstances and reasons for the action.

3.A. Have you or your family members ever belonged to or been associated with any organizations or groups in your home country, such as, but not limited to, a political party, student group, labor union, religious organization, military or paramilitary group, civil patrol, guerrilla organization, ethnic group, human rights group, or the press or media?

   ☒ No   ☐ Yes

   If "Yes," describe for each person the level of participation, any leadership or other positions held, and the length of time you or your family members were involved in each organization or activity.

3.B. Do you or your family members continue to participate in any way in these organizations or groups?

   ☒ No   ☐ Yes

   If "Yes," describe for each person your or your family members' current level of participation, any leadership or other positions currently held, and the length of time you or your family members have been involved in each organization or group.

---

4. Are you afraid of being subjected to torture in your home country or any other country to which you may be returned?

   ☐ No   ☒ Yes

   If "Yes," explain why you are afraid and describe the nature of torture you fear, by whom, and why it would be inflicted.

   See attached affidavit.

Sample Form I-589, Application for Asylum and for Withholding of Removal (page 7)

Part C. Additional Information About Your Application

(**NOTE:** *Use Form I-589 Supplement B, or attach additional sheets of paper as needed to complete your responses to the questions contained in Part C.*)

1. Have you, your spouse, your child(ren), your parents or your siblings ever applied to the U.S. Government for refugee status, asylum, or withholding of removal?

   ☒ No   ☐ Yes

   If "Yes," explain the decision and what happened to any status you, your spouse, your child(ren), your parents, or your siblings received as a result of that decision. Indicate whether or not you were included in a parent or spouse's application. If so, include your parent or spouse's A-number in your response. If you have been denied asylum by an immigration judge or the Board of Immigration Appeals, describe any change(s) in conditions in your country or your own personal circumstances since the date of the denial that may affect your eligibility for asylum.

2.A. After leaving the country from which you are claiming asylum, did you or your spouse or child(ren) who are now in the United States travel through or reside in any other country before entering the United States?

   ☒ No   ☐ Yes

2.B. Have you, your spouse, your child(ren), or other family members, such as your parents or siblings, ever applied for or received any lawful status in any country other than the one from which you are now claiming asylum?

   ☒ No   ☐ Yes

   If "Yes" to either or both questions (2A and/or 2B), provide for each person the following: the name of each country and the length of stay, the person's status while there, the reasons for leaving, whether or not the person is entitled to return for lawful residence purposes, and whether the person applied for refugee status or for asylum while there, and if not, why he or she did not do so.

3. Have you, your spouse or your child(ren) ever ordered, incited, assisted or otherwise participated in causing harm or suffering to any person because of his or her race, religion, nationality, membership in a particular social group or belief in a particular political opinion?

   ☒ No   ☐ Yes

   If "Yes," describe in detail each such incident and your own, your spouse's, or your child(ren)'s involvement.

Sample Form I-589, Application for Asylum and for Withholding of Removal (page 8)

Part C. Additional Information About Your Application (Continued)

4. After you left the country where you were harmed or fear harm, did you return to that country?

    ☒ No   ☐ Yes

    If "Yes," describe in detail the circumstances of your visit(s) (for example, the date(s) of the trip(s), the purpose(s) of the trip(s), and the length of time you remained in that country for the visit(s).)

5. Are you filing this application more than 1 year after your last arrival in the United States?

    ☒ No   ☐ Yes

    If "Yes," explain why you did not file within the first year after you arrived. You must be prepared to explain at your interview or hearing why you did not file your asylum application within the first year after you arrived. For guidance in answering this question, see Instructions, Part 1: Filing Instructions, Section V. "Completing the Form," Part C.

6. Have you or any member of your family included in the application ever committed any crime and/or been arrested, charged, convicted, or sentenced for any crimes in the United States (including for an immigration law violation)?

    ☒ No   ☐ Yes

    If "Yes," for each instance, specify in your response: what occurred and the circumstances, dates, length of sentence received, location, the duration of the detention or imprisonment, reason(s) for the detention or conviction, any formal charges that were lodged against you or your relatives included in your application, and the reason(s) for release. Attach documents referring to these incidents, if they are available, or an explanation of why documents are not available.

Sample Form I-589, Application for Asylum and for Withholding of Removal (page 9)

Part D. Your Signature

I certify, under penalty of perjury under the laws of the United States of America, that this application and the evidence submitted with it are all true and correct. Title 18, United States Code, Section 1546(a), provides in part: Whoever knowingly makes under oath, or as permitted under penalty of perjury under Section 1746 of Title 28, United States Code, knowingly subscribes as true, any false statement with respect to a material fact in any application, affidavit, or other document required by the immigration laws or regulations prescribed thereunder, or knowingly presents any such application, affidavit, or other document containing any such false statement or which fails to contain any reasonable basis in law or fact - shall be fined in accordance with this title or imprisoned for up to 25 years. I authorize the release of any information from my immigration record that U.S. Citizenship and Immigration Services (USCIS) needs to determine eligibility for the benefit I am seeking.

> Staple your photograph here or the photograph of the family member to be included on the extra copy of the application submitted for that person.

WARNING: Applicants who are in the United States **unlawfully** are subject to removal if their asylum or withholding claims are not granted by an asylum officer or an immigration judge. Any information provided in completing this application may be used as a basis for the institution of, or as evidence in, removal proceedings even if the application is later withdrawn. Applicants determined to have knowingly made a frivolous application for asylum will be permanently ineligible for any benefits under the Immigration and Nationality Act. You may not avoid a frivolous finding simply because someone advised you to provide false information in your asylum application. If filing with USCIS, unexcused failure to appear for an appointment to provide biometrics (such as fingerprints) and your biographical information within the time allowed may result in an asylum officer dismissing your asylum application or referring it to an immigration judge. Failure without good cause to provide DHS with biometrics or other biographical information while in removal proceedings may result in your application being found abandoned by the immigration judge. See sections 208(d)(5)(A) and 208(d)(6) of the INA and 8 CFR sections 208.10, 1208.10, 208.20, 1003.47(d) and 1208.20.

Print your complete name.	Write your name in your native alphabet.
Luis Manuel Romero	n/a

Did your spouse, parent, or child(ren) assist you in completing this application? ☒ No ☐ Yes *(If "Yes," list the name and relationship.)*

NA	NA	NA	NA
(Name)	*(Relationship)*	*(Name)*	*(Relationship)*

Did someone other than your spouse, parent, or child(ren) prepare this application? ☒ No ☐ Yes *(If "Yes," complete Part E.)*

Asylum applicants may be represented by counsel. Have you been provided with a list of persons who may be available to assist you, at little or no cost, with your asylum claim? ☒ No ☐ Yes

Signature of Applicant *(The person in Part. A.I.)*

➡ [*Luis Manuel Romero*]   08/01/2020

Sign your name so it all appears within the brackets   Date *(mm/dd/yyyy)*

Part E. Declaration of Person Preparing Form, if Other Than Applicant, Spouse, Parent, or Child

I declare that I have prepared this application at the request of the person named in Part D, that the responses provided are based on all information of which I have knowledge, or which was provided to me by the applicant, and that the completed application was read to the applicant in his or her native language or a language he or she understands for verification before he or she signed the application in my presence. I am aware that the knowing placement of false information on the Form I-589 may also subject me to civil penalties under 8 U.S.C. 1324c and/or criminal penalties under 18 U.S.C. 1546(a).

Signature of Preparer	Print Complete Name of Preparer
	not applicable

Daytime Telephone Number	Address of Preparer: Street Number and Name
( )	not applicable

Apt. Number	City		State	Zip Code
NA	not applicable		NA	

To be completed by an attorney or accredited representative (if any).	☐ Select this box if Form G-28 is attached.	Attorney State Bar Number (if applicable)	Attorney or Accredited Representative USCIS Online Account Number (if any)
		NA	⬚⬚⬚⬚⬚⬚⬚⬚⬚⬚⬚⬚⬚

Sample Form I-589, Application for Asylum and for Withholding of Removal (page 10)

Part F. To Be Completed at Asylum Interview, if Applicable

NOTE: *You will be asked to complete this part when you appear for examination before an asylum officer of the Department of Homeland Security, U.S. Citizenship and Immigration Services (USCIS).*

I swear (affirm) that I know the contents of this application that I am signing, including the attached documents and supplements, that they are ☐ all true or ☐ not all true to the best of my knowledge and that correction(s) numbered _____ to _____ were made by me or at my request. Furthermore, I am aware that if I am determined to have knowingly made a frivolous application for asylum I will be permanently ineligible for any benefits under the Immigration and Nationality Act, and that I may not avoid a frivolous finding simply because someone advised me to provide false information in my asylum application.

Signed and sworn to before me by the above named applicant on:

_____
Signature of Applicant

_____
Date *(mm/dd/yyyy)*

_____
Write Your Name in Your Native Alphabet

_____
Signature of Asylum Officer

Part G. To Be Completed at Removal Hearing, if Applicable

NOTE: *You will be asked to complete this Part when you appear before an immigration judge of the U.S. Department of Justice, Executive Office for Immigration Review (EOIR), for a hearing.*

I swear (affirm) that I know the contents of this application that I am signing, including the attached documents and supplements, that they are ☐ all true or ☐ not all true to the best of my knowledge and that correction(s) numbered _____ to _____ were made by me or at my request. Furthermore, I am aware that if I am determined to have knowingly made a frivolous application for asylum I will be permanently ineligible for any benefits under the Immigration and Nationality Act, and that I may not avoid a frivolous finding simply because someone advised me to provide false information in my asylum application.

Signed and sworn to before me by the above named applicant on:

_____
Signature of Applicant

_____
Date *(mm/dd/yyyy)*

_____
Write Your Name in Your Native Alphabet

_____
Signature of Immigration Judge

Sample Form I-589, Supplement A

Supplement A, Form I-589

A-Number *(If available)*	Date
None	

Applicant's Name	Applicant's Signature
Luis Manuel ROMERO	

List All of Your Children, Regardless of Age or Marital Status
(NOTE: *Use this form and attach additional pages and documentation as needed, if you have more than four children)*

1. Alien Registration Number (A-Number) *(if any)*	2. Passport/ID Card Number *(if any)*	3. Marital Status *(Married, Single, Divorced, Widowed)*	4. U.S. Social Security Number *(if any)*
not applicable	not applicable	not applicable	not applicable

5. Complete Last Name	6. First Name	7. Middle Name	8. Date of Birth *(mm/dd/yyyy)*
not applicable	not applicable	not applicable	not applicable

9. City and Country of Birth	10. Nationality *(Citizenship)*	11. Race, Ethnic, or Tribal Group	12. Gender
not applicable	not applicable	not applicable	☐ Male ☐ Female

13. Is this child in the U.S. ? ☐ Yes *(Complete Blocks 14 to 21.)* ☐ No *(Specify location):*

14. Place of last entry into the U.S.	15. Date of last entry into the U.S. *(mm/dd/yyyy)*	16. I-94 Number *(If any)*	17. Status when last admitted *(Visa type, if any)*
not applicable	not applicable		not applicable

18. What is your child's current status?	19. What is the expiration date of his/her authorized stay, if any? *(mm/dd/yyyy)*	20. Is your child in Immigration Court proceedings?
not applicable	not applicable	☐ Yes ☐ No

21. If in the U.S., is this child to be included in this application? *(Check the appropriate box.)*

☐ Yes *(Attach one photograph of your child in the upper right corner of Page 9 on the extra copy of the application submitted for this person.)*

☐ No

1. Alien Registration Number (A-Number) *(if any)*	2. Passport/ID Card Number *(if any)*	3. Marital Status *(Married, Single, Divorced, Widowed)*	4. U.S. Social Security Number *(if any)*
not applicable	not applicable	not applicable	not applicable

5. Complete Last Name	6. First Name	7. Middle Name	8. Date of Birth *(mm/dd/yyyy)*
not applicable	not applicable	not applicable	not applicable

9. City and Country of Birth	10. Nationality *(Citizenship)*	11. Race, Ethnic, or Tribal Group	12. Gender
not applicable	not applicable	not applicable	☐ Male ☐ Female

13. Is this child in the U.S. ? ☐ Yes *(Complete Blocks 14 to 21.)* ☐ No *(Specify location):*

14. Place of last entry into the U.S.	15. Date of last entry into the U.S. *(mm/dd/yyyy)*	16. I-94 Number *(If any)*	17. Status when last admitted *(Visa type, if any)*
not applicable	not applicable		not applicable

18. What is your child's current status?	19. What is the expiration date of his/her authorized stay, if any? *(mm/dd/yyyy)*	20. Is your child in Immigration Court proceedings?
not applicable	not applicable	☐ Yes ☐ No

21. If in the U.S., is this child to be included in this application? *(Check the appropriate box.)*

☐ Yes *(Attach one photograph of your child in the upper right corner of Page 9 on the extra copy of the application submitted for this person.)*

☐ No

Sample Form I-589, Supplement B

Supplement B, Form I-589

Additional Information About Your Claim to Asylum

A-Number *(if available)*	Date
None	

Applicant's Name	Applicant's Signature
Luis Manuel ROMERO	

NOTE: *Use this as a continuation page for any additional information requested. Copy and complete as needed.*

Part _____

Question _____

not applicable - see attached declaration and supporting documents.

Sample Form I-730, Refugee/Asylee Relative Petition (page 1)

Department of Homeland Security
U.S. Citizenship and Immigration Services

OMB No. 1615-0037; Expires 09/30/2021

I-730, Refugee/Asylee Relative Petition

FOR USCIS OFFICE ONLY		
Section of Law ☐ 207 (c)(2) Spouse ☐ 207 (c)(2) Child ☐ 208 (b)(3) Spouse ☐ 208 (b)(3) Child	**Action Stamp**	**Receipt**
Reserved		**Remarks**

☐ Beneficiary Not Previously Claimed
☐ Beneficiary Previously Claimed On: _____ (e.g., Form I-590, Form I-589, etc.) CSPA Eligible: ☐ Yes ☐ No ☐ N/A

START HERE - **Type or print legibly in black ink.**

My Status: ☐ Refugee ☐ Lawful Permanent Resident based on previous Refugee status
☒ Asylee ☐ Lawful Permanent Resident based on previous Asylee status

The beneficiary is my: ☒ Spouse
☐ Unmarried child who is a (n): ☐ Biological Child ☐ Stepchild ☐ Adopted Child
Number of relatives for whom I am filing separate Form I-730s: 1 (1 of 1)

Part 1. Information About You, the Petitioner (*USPS ZIP Code Lookup*)

Family Name (Last name), Given Name (First name), Middle Name:
Bera, John Paul

Address of Residence (Where you physically reside)

Street Number and Name: **876 5th Street 14**	Apt. Number
City: **Providence**	State or Province: **RI**
Country: **USA**	Zip/Postal Code: **02901**

Mailing Address (If different from residence) - C/O:

Street Number and Name:	Apt. Number:
City:	State or Province:
Country:	Zip/Postal Code:

Telephone Number including Country and City/Area Code:
4015551212

Your E-Mail Address, if available:
johnpaulbera@email.com

Gender: **a.** ☒ Male **b.** ☐ Female	Date of Birth (mm/dd/yyyy): **12/15/1978**
Country of Birth: **Nigeria**	Country of Citizenship/Nationality: **Nigeria**
U.S. Alien Registration Number: A- **012345678**	U.S. Social Security Number (If applicable): **123456789**

Part 2. Information About Your Alien Relative, the Beneficiary

Family Name (Last name), Given Name (First name), Middle Name:
Bera, Gladys Mary

Address of Residence (Where the beneficiary physically resides)

Street Number and Name: **17 Ozumba Mbadicue Avenue**	Apt. Number **2**
City: **Lagos**	State or Province:
Country: **Nigeria**	Zip/Postal Code: **100001**

Mailing Address (If different from residence) - C/O:

Street Number and Name:	Apt. Number
City:	State or Province:
Country:	Zip/Postal Code:

Telephone Number including Country and City/Area Code:
2341123456

The Beneficiary's E-Mail Address, if available:
none

Gender: **a.** ☐ Male **b.** ☒ Female	Date of Birth (mm/dd/yyyy): **7/24/1980**
Country of Birth: **Nigeria**	Country of Citizenship/Nationality: **Nigeria**
U.S. Alien Registration Number: A-	U.S. Social Security Number (If applicable):

Form I-730 (09/17/19) Page 1

Sample Form I-730, Refugee/Asylee Relative Petition (page 2)

Part 1. Information About You, the Petitioner (Continued)	**Part 2. Information About Your Alien Relative, the Beneficiary (Continued)**
Other Names Used (Including maiden name): **None**	Other Names Used (Including maiden name): **Gladys Mary Amah**
If married, Name of Spouse, Date (mm/dd/yyyy), and Place of Present Marriage: **Gladys Bera 07/18/2000 Lagos Nigeria**	If married, Name of Spouse, Date (mm/dd/yyyy), and Place of Present Marriage: **John Bera 07/18/2000 Lagos Nigeria**
If previously married, names of prior spouses:	If previously married, names of prior spouses:
Dates (mm/dd/yyyy) and Places Previous Marriages Ended: Please provide documentation indicating how marriages ended (e.g., death certificate, divorce certificate, etc.):	Dates (mm/dd/yyyy) and Places Previous Marriages Ended: Please provide documentation indicating how marriages ended (e.g., death certificate, divorce certificate, etc.):
Date (mm/dd/yyyy) and Place Asylee Status was granted in the United States **08/15/2020 Immigration Court Boston MA** **OR** Date (mm/dd/yyyy) and Place you received your approval for Refugee Status while living abroad	☐ Beneficiary is currently in the United States. ☒ Beneficiary is outside the United States and will apply for travel authorization at a USCIS Office or a U.S. Embassy or consulate in: **Lagos Nigeria** City and Country
If You Were Approved for Refugee Status, Date (mm/dd/yyyy) and Place Admitted to the United States as a Refugee:	**To Be Completed By** **Attorney or Representative, if any.** ☐ Fill in box if G-28 is attached to represent the petitioner. Volag Number: [ ] Attorney State License Number: [ ]

Part 2. Information About Your Alien Relative, the Beneficiary (Continued)

Name and **mailing** address of the beneficiary written in the language of the country where he or she now **resides**:

Family Name: **Bera**	Given Name: **Gladys**	Middle Name: **Mary**

Address - C/O:

Street Number and Name: **17 Ozumba Mbadicue Avenue**		Apt. Number: **2**
City/State or Province: **Lagos**	Country: **Nigeria**	Zip/Postal Code: **100001**

Check the box, a. through d., that applies:

a. ☒ The beneficiary has never been in the United States

b. ☐ The beneficiary is now in immigration court proceedings in the United States Where?

c. ☐ The beneficiary has never been in immigration court proceedings in the United States

d. ☐ The beneficiary is not now in immigration court proceedings in the United States, but has been in the past. Where?

What is the beneficiary's native language? **Igbo**	Is the beneficiary fluent in English? ☐ No ☒ Yes	What other languages does the beneficiary speak fluently: **None**

Sample Form I-730, Refugee/Asylee Relative Petition (page 3)

Part 2. Information About Your Alien Relative, the Beneficiary (Continued)

List Each of the beneficiary's entries into the United States, if any, beginning with the most recent entry. Submit a copy of each I-94 and/or copy of the beneficiary's passport showing all the entry and exit stamps for each entry. Attach an additional sheet if the beneficiary has more than two entries into the United States:

Date of Arrival (mm/dd/yyyy):	Place (City and State):		Status:
I-94 Number:	Date Status Expires (mm/dd/yyyy):	Passport Number:	
Travel Document Number:	Expiration Date for Passport or Travel Document:	Country of Issuance for Passport or Travel Document:	

Date of Arrival (mm/dd/yyyy):	Place (City and State):		Status:
I-94 Number:	Date Status Expires (mm/dd/yyyy):	Passport Number:	
Travel Document Number:	Expiration Date for Passport or Travel Document:	Country of Issuance for Passport or Travel Document:	

Part 3. Two-Year Filing Deadline

Are you filing this application more than two years after the date you were admitted to the United States as a refugee or granted asylee status? ☐ Yes ☒ No

If you answered "Yes" to the previous question, explain the delay in filing and submit evidence to support your explanation (Attach additional sheets of paper if necessary):

Part 4. Warning

WARNING: Any beneficiary who is in the United States illegally is subject to removal if Form I-730 is not granted by USCIS. Any information provided in completing this petition may be used as a basis for the institution of, or as evidence in, removal proceedings, even if the petition is later withdrawn. Unexcused failure by the beneficiary to appear for an appointment to provide biometrics (such as fingerprints and photographs) and biographical information within the time allowed may result in denial of Form I-730. Information provided on this form and biometrics and biographical information provided by the beneficiary may also be used in producing an Employment Authorization Document if the beneficiary is granted derivative refugee or asylee status.

Sample Form I-730, Refugee/Asylee Relative Petition (page 4)

Part 5. Petitioner's Statement, Contact Information, Declaration, Certification, and Signature

NOTE: Read the **Penalties** section of the Form I-730 Instructions before completing this part.

Petitioner's Statement

NOTE: Select the box for either **Item Number 1.a.** or **1.b.** If applicable, select the box for **Item Number 2.**

1.a. ☒ I can read and understand English, and I have read and I understand every question and instruction on this petition and my answer to every question.

1.b. ☐ The interpreter named in **Part 7.** read to me every question and instruction on this petition and my answer to every question in _____, a language in which I am fluent, and I understood everything.

2. ☐ At my request, the preparer named in **Part 8.,** _____, prepared this petition for me based only upon information I provided or authorized.

Petitioner's Contact Information

3. Petitioner's Daytime Telephone Number

4015551212

4. Petitioner's Mobile Telephone Number (if any)

4015551234

5. Petitioner's Email Address (if any)

johnpaulbera@email.com

Petitioner's Declaration and Certification

Copies of any documents I have submitted are exact photocopies of unaltered, original documents, and I understand that USCIS may require that I submit original documents to USCIS at a later date. Furthermore, I authorize the release of any information from any of my records that USCIS may need to determine my eligibility for the immigration benefit I seek.

I further authorize release of information contained in this petition, in supporting documents, and in my USCIS records to other entities and persons where necessary for the administration and enforcement of U.S. immigration laws.

I understand that USCIS may require me to appear for an appointment to take my biometrics (fingerprints, photograph, and/or signature) and, at that time, if I am required to provide biometrics, I will be required to sign an oath reaffirming that:

    1) I provided or authorized all of the information contained in, and submitted with, my petition;

    2) I reviewed and understood all of the information in, and submitted with, my petition; and

    3) All of this information was complete, true, and correct at the time of filing.

I certify, under penalty of perjury, that all of the information in my petition and any document submitted with it were provided or authorized by me, that I reviewed and understand all of the information contained in, and submitted with, my petition, and that all of this information is complete, true, and correct.

Petitioner's Signature

6.a. Petitioner's Signature

➡ *John P. Bera*

6.b. Date of Signature (mm/dd/yyyy)

08/30/2020

NOTE TO ALL PETITIONERS: If you do not completely fill out this petition or fail to submit required evidence listed in the Instructions, USCIS may deny your petition.

Sample Form I-730, Refugee/Asylee Relative Petition (page 5)

Part 6. Beneficiary's Statement, Contact Information, Declaration, Certification, and Signature if in the United States

NOTE: Read the information on penalties in the **Penalties** section of the Form I-730 Instructions before completing this part.

NOTE: **If the beneficiary is not currently in the United States, or is not 14 years of age or older, this section should be left blank.**

Beneficiary's Statement

NOTE: Select the box for either **Item Number 1.a.** or **1.b.** If applicable, select the box for **Item Number 2.**

1.a. ☐ I can read and understand English, and I have read and I understand every question and instruction on this petition and my answer to every question.

1.b. ☐ The interpreter named in **Part 7.** read to me every question and instruction on this petition and my answer to every question in [_____], a language in which I am fluent, and I understood everything.

2. ☐ At my request, the preparer named in **Part 8.**, [_____], prepared this petition for me based only upon information I and the petitioner provided or authorized.

Beneficiary's Contact Information

3. Beneficiary's Daytime Telephone Number

4. Beneficiary's Mobile Telephone Number (if any)

5. Beneficiary's Email Address (if any)

Beneficiary's Declaration and Certification

Copies of any documents I have submitted are exact photocopies of unaltered, original documents, and I understand that USCIS may require that I submit original documents to USCIS at a later date. Furthermore, I authorize the release of any information from any of my records that USCIS may need to determine my eligibility for the immigration benefit I seek.

I further authorize release of information contained in this petition, in supporting documents, and in my USCIS records to other entities and persons where necessary for the administration and enforcement of U.S. immigration laws.

I understand that USCIS may require me to appear for an appointment to take my biometrics (fingerprints, photograph, and/or signature) and, at that time, if I am required to provide biometrics, I will be required to sign an oath reaffirming that:

    1) I provided or authorized all of the information contained in, and submitted with, my petition;

    2) I reviewed and understood all of the information in, and submitted with, my petition; and

    3) All of this information was complete, true, and correct at the time of filing.

I certify, under penalty of perjury, that all of the information in my petition and any document submitted with it were provided or authorized by me, that I reviewed and understand all of the information contained in, and submitted with, my petition, and that all of this information is complete, true, and correct.

Beneficiary's Signature

6.a. Beneficiary's Signature

6.b. Date of Signature (mm/dd/yyyy)

NOTE: This petition must be completely filled out and all required evidence submitted or USCIS may deny this petition.

Military Veterans and Enlistees

The immigration laws recognize the patriotism and valor of aliens who have defended the U.S. Constitution by serving in the military. Some veterans can jump directly to becoming U.S. citizens. Others have a path to a U.S. green card.

A. Who Qualifies to Apply for Citizenship Without a Green Card

If you have honorably and actively served the U.S. military in a time of war or conflict, you are exempt from all green card requirements and might qualify for immediate citizenship. (See I.N.A. § 329, 8 U.S.C. § 1440.) This special benefit depends, however, on the war or conflict in which you fought under the U.S. Armed Forces. It includes:

- World War II, specifically between September 1, 1939 and December 31, 1946
- the Korean War, specifically between June 25, 1950 and July 1, 1955
- the Vietnam War, specifically between February 28, 1961 and October 15, 1978
- the Persian Gulf Conflict, specifically between August 2, 1990 and April 11, 1991, and
- the "War on Terror" (also called "Operation Enduring Freedom"), which began on September 11, 2001 and will end on a date to be determined by the U.S. president.

It also depends on where you were when you enlisted. Your enlistment, reenlistment, extension of enlistment, or induction must have been in the United States, the Canal Zone, American Samoa, or Swains Island, or on board a public vessel owned or operated by the U.S. for noncommercial service.

What's more, the government has started requiring that active duty recruits actively serve for at least 180 days and undergo various background and security checks before even beginning basic training, much less being approved for citizenship. (In past years, one could apply right after basic training.) You'll need to submit an application for naturalization in order to become a citizen. Your application will consist of Form N-400, Application for Naturalization; and Form N-426, Request for Certification of Military or Naval Service (certified by the military; or if you've already left the military, with a copy of your DD Form 214, Certificate of Release or Discharge from Active Duty, or NGB Form 22, National Guard Report of Separation and Record of Service). You will need to undergo a security check, including providing fingerprints (biometrics) if USCIS doesn't already have yours. Depending on what's available where you are living, you might need to go to your local military police or perhaps a U.S. consulate or USCIS application support center.

As a member of the military, you are exempt from paying the usual application fee.

> **CAUTION**
> **At one point, your military installation would have a designated point of contact to help you with your application**—but the Trump administration is seemingly doing away with these.

You'll ultimately need to attend an interview and pass a test of your knowledge of the English language and U.S. civics and government. But you won't have to worry about many of the other citizenship requirements, including your age and your period of residence within the United States.

If you're eventually separated from the Armed Forces under other-than-honorable conditions before you've served honorably for a total of five years, your citizenship can be revoked (taken away).

B. Who Qualifies for Permanent Residence

If you were outside the U.S. when you enlisted in the military, or for other reasons don't qualify for immediate U.S. citizenship, you might still be able to apply for a U.S. green card, under the employment-based classification of "special immigrant."

The spouse and minor children under 21 years of age who are joining or accompanying the veteran or enlistee are also entitled to immigrant visas.

In order to have enlisted outside the U.S., you must be in a country that has a treaty with the United States allowing this.

Immigrant Story:
Major Diaz Becomes a U.S. Citizen

Reynaldo Diaz came to the U.S. from Mexico as a four-year-old, with his family. A cousin helped smuggle them across the border near San Diego. After completing high school in the U.S., Reynaldo decided to join the U.S. Army. He was sent to serve in Iraq, where he received many awards and commendations.

As soon as Reynaldo learns of the law permitting him to apply for citizenship, he talks to a superior officer, who helps him fill out the paperwork. Reynaldo attends his naturalization interview while at home in Kansas on leave, and passes the test easily.

As a U.S. citizen, he can now petition for residency for his parents, brothers, and sisters.

RESOURCE

You can call or email for advice. Members of the U.S. military and their families stationed around the world can call USCIS for help with immigration services and benefits by using a dedicated, toll-free telephone help line, at 877-CIS-4MIL (877-247-4645). Alternatively, you can email a customer service representative at militaryinfo@uscis.dhs.gov.

1. Veterans

An alien veteran of the U.S. Armed Forces can apply for permanent residence if he or she:

- has served honorably
- has served on active duty
- has served after October 15, 1978
- is recommended for a special immigrant visa by the U.S. Armed Forces or Navy officer under whom he or she serves
- originally enlisted outside the United States
- has served for an aggregate of 12 years, and
- was honorably discharged when separated from the service.

2. Enlistees on Active Duty

An alien enlistee in the U.S. Armed Forces can apply for permanent residence if he or she:

- originally enlisted outside the United States for six years
- is on active duty when applying for adjustment of status under this law
- has reenlisted for another six years, giving a total of 12 years active duty service, and
- is recommended for a special immigrant visa by the U.S. Armed Forces or Navy officer under whom he or she serves.

A Break for Illegal Workers

Because of this special law for alien members of the U.S. Armed Forces, the Immigration and Nationality Act allows the applicant—and his or her spouse and children—to get permanent residence even if they may have worked illegally in the United States.

3. Iraqi or Afghan Translators for U.S. Armed Forces

In 2008, Congress created a new program to bring Afghan and Iraqi translators and interpreters who worked with the U.S. military to the United States. (See the National Defense Authorization Act Section 1059.) Under this program, you may apply for a U.S. green card if you are a national of Iraq or Afghanistan and you:

- worked directly with the U.S. Armed Forces as a translator for at least 12 months
- received a letter of recommendation from a general or flag officer in your unit, and
- have passed background checks and screening.

Your application process will be similar to the one described below, except that you'll need to provide documents proving the above three things (instead of the certifications required of other members of the military). Also, you must submit a petition (Form I-360) to the USCIS Nebraska Service Center to start the process; you can't combine it with an adjustment of status application even if you're in the United States. You will not need to pay a filing fee.

! CAUTION
Afghan and Iraqi interpreters face long waits for green cards. Since this special immigrant visa program began, more than 50,000 people have applied for green cards, but only 7,000 can be approved in total. What was supposed to be a program to fast-track permanent residence for people who served alongside military personnel in armed conflict at great peril to themselves now has many applicants stuck in "administrative processing" (a bureaucratic term for background checks). Expect to wait a year for approval—or denial.

---

4. How to File for Permanent Residence

To file for permanent residence as a special immigrant, you must complete and file the following forms. The filing fee is $435 (early 2020 figure; it might go up soon), but Afghan and Iraqi translator applicants need not pay the fee. Others must pay either by money order or certified check made payable to U.S. Department of Homeland Security or by credit card, using Form G-1450, Authorization for Credit Card Transaction (preferably placed on top of the paperwork you send USCIS). Submit the following:

- ☐ Form I-360, Petition for Amerasian, Widow(er), or Special Immigrant (available at www.uscis.gov/i-360; see sample at the end of this chapter; note that it includes only the pages relevant to veterans and

enlistees; but you'll still need to submit all the pages, even the ones you don't fill in)
- ☐ Form N-426, Request for Certification for Military or Naval Service
- ☐ certification of past active duty status of 12 years for the veteran, or certified proof of reenlistment after six years of active duty service for the enlistee, issued by an authorized Armed Forces official, and
- ☐ your birth certificate to show that you are a national of the country that has an agreement with the United States allowing the enlistment of its nationals in the U.S. Armed Forces.

These papers have to be filed with either:
- the USCIS office having jurisdiction over the veteran or enlistee's current residence or intended place of residence in the United States, or
- the overseas USCIS office having jurisdiction over the residence abroad.

If you are in the U.S., you may (unless you're an Afghan or Iraqi translator, as described in Section B3, above) apply directly for adjustment of status (see Chapter 16), and so may your spouse and your children under 21 years of age. Form I-360 and accompanying materials should be included with the rest of the adjustment of status application.

If your spouse and children are outside the United States, you may file Form I-824, Application for Action on an Approved Application or Petition, to be sent to the U.S. consulate where they will apply for immigrant visas as derivative relatives of a special immigrant.

! CAUTION
USCIS will automatically revoke the petition and bar the enlistee from getting a green card if he or she:
- fails to complete the period of reenlistment, or
- receives other than an honorable discharge.

The enlistee's spouse and children will also be barred from getting green cards. If any of them already have green cards, USCIS will begin proceedings to have them taken away.

5. Applying for Citizenship After Getting a Green Card

If you got your green card as a veteran or an enlistee, you're only a few short steps away from being eligible for U.S. citizenship. Although most people must wait five years after getting their green card, you are immediately able to apply for citizenship.

Servicepeople who got their green cards in other ways than through their military service can apply for citizenship as soon as they've served honorably for one year; it doesn't matter how long they've had the green card for—one day is enough. However, if they've been discharged, the discharge must have been honorable, and they must apply for citizenship within six months of the discharge date.

To file for naturalization, you must file the following forms and documents with USCIS:

- ☐ Form N-400, Application for Naturalization
- ☐ Form N-426, Request for Certification for Military or Naval Service
- ☐ a copy of your green card
- ☐ two photographs.

There is no fee for filing a naturalization application for servicemembers filing for citizenship on the basis of their military service.

RESOURCE
Want complete information on the application process for U.S. citizenship, including special exceptions applying to members of the military? See *Becoming a U.S. Citizen: A Guide to the Law, Exam & Interview*, by Ilona Bray (Nolo).

Sample Form I-360, Petition for Amerasian, Widow(er), or Special Immigrant (page 1)

Petition for Amerasian, Widow(er), or Special Immigrant

Department of Homeland Security
U.S. Citizenship and Immigration Services

**USCIS
Form I-360**

OMB No. 1615-0020
Expires 04/30/2020

For USCIS Use Only		Fee Stamp	Action Block
Returned			
Resubmitted			
Relocated	Received		
	Sent		

Remarks:

☐ Petitioner/Applicant Interviewed
☐ Interviewed Beneficiary Interviewed
☐ I-485 Filed Concurrently
☐ Bene "A" File Reviewed

Classification

Consulate

Priority Date

To be completed by an Attorney or Accredited Representative (if any).	☐ **Select this box if Form G-28 or G-28I is attached.**	**Attorney State Bar Number** (if applicable)	**Attorney or Accredited Representative USCIS Online Account Number** (if any)

▶ **START HERE** - Type or print in black ink.

Part 1. Information About Person or Organization Filing This Petition

NOTE: You must complete **Part 1.** as the petitioner if you are filing this petition on behalf of another person. If you are a Violence Against Women Act (VAWA) self-petitioner or special immigrant juvenile, skip to **Part 1.**, **Item Number 7.**

1. Your Full Name

   Family Name (Last Name): **Zapato**

   Given Name (First Name): **Dante**

   Middle Name: **Diego**

2. USCIS Online Account Number (if any)
   ▶

3. U.S. Social Security Number (if any)
   ▶ 1 2 4 5 6 7 8 9 0

4. Alien Registration Number (A-Number) (if any)
   ▶ A-

5. Individual IRS Tax Number (if any)
   ▶

6. Mailing Address   *(USPS ZIP Code Lookup)*

   In Care Of Name (if any)

   Organization Name (if applicable)

   Street Number and Name: **122 Juniper Street**

   Apt. Ste. Flr. ☐ ☐ ☐   Number

   City or Town: **Makati**   State   ZIP Code

   Province: **Metro Manila**   Postal Code: **1630**   Country: **Philippines**

Sample Form I-360, Petition for Amerasian, Widow(er), or Special Immigrant (page 2)

Part 1. Information About Person or Organization Filing This Petition (continued)

7. Alternate and/or Safe Mailing Address

If you are a VAWA self-petitioning spouse, child, parent, or a special immigrant juvenile and do not want U.S. Citizenship and Immigration Services (USCIS) to send notices about this petition to your home, you may provide an alternate and/or safe mailing address.

In Care Of Name (if any)

Street Number and Name   Apt. Ste. Flr.   Number
☐ ☐ ☐

City or Town   State   ZIP Code

Province   Postal Code   Country

Part 2. Classification Requested

Select **only one** box.

1. A. ☐ Amerasian

   B. ☐ Widow(er) of a U.S. citizen

   C. ☐ Special Immigrant Juvenile

   D. ☐ Special Immigrant Religious Worker

       (1) Will the beneficiary be working as a minister?   ☐ Yes   ☐ No

   E. ☐ Special Immigrant based on employment with the Panama Canal Company, Canal Zone Government, or U.S. Government in the Canal Zone

   F. ☐ Special Immigrant Physician

   G. ☐ Special Immigrant G-4 International Organization Employee or Family Member or NATO-6 Employee or Family Member

   H. ☒ Special Immigrant Armed Forces Member

   I. ☐ Self-Petitioning Spouse of Abusive U.S. citizen or Lawful Permanent Resident

   J. ☐ Self-Petitioning Child of Abusive U.S. citizen or Lawful Permanent Resident

   K. ☐ VAWA Self-Petitioning Parent of a U.S. citizen son or daughter

   L. ☐ Special Immigrant Afghanistan or Iraq National who worked with the U.S. Armed Forces as a translator

   M. ☐ Special Immigrant Iraq National who was employed by or on behalf of the U.S. Government

   N. ☐ Special Immigrant Afghanistan National who was employed by or on behalf of the U.S. Government or the International Security Assistance Force (ISAF) in Afghanistan

   O. ☐ Broadcasters

   P. ☐ Other
       Provide the name of the classification below.

Sample Form I-360, Petition for Amerasian, Widow(er), or Special Immigrant (page 3)

Part 3. Information About the Person for Whom This Petition Is Being Filed

NOTE: On this petition, the "beneficiary" or "self-petitioner" means the person for whom this petition is being filed. If you provided an alternate and/or safe mailing address above, you must also complete **Part 3.**

1. Your Full Name

Family Name (Last Name)	Given Name (First Name)	Middle Name

2. Mailing Address

In Care Of Name (if any)

Street Number and Name: **122 Juniper Street**   Apt. Ste. Flr. ☐ ☐ ☐   Number

City or Town: **Makati**   State   ZIP Code

Province: **Metro Manila**   Postal Code: **1630**   Country: **Philippines**

Other Information

3. Date of Birth (mm/dd/yyyy): **01/15/1970**

4. Country of Birth: **Philippines**

5. U.S. Social Security Number (if any): ▶

6. A-Number (if any): ▶ A- 1 2 4 5 6 7 8 9 0

7. Marital Status ☐ Single ☐ Married ☒ Divorced ☐ Widowed

Complete **Item Numbers 8. - 15.** if this person is in the United States. If an item number is not applicable or the answer is "none," leave the space blank. Provide information below for the passport or other document used at the time of last arrival to the United States.

8. Date of Last Arrival (mm/dd/yyyy)

9. Form I-94 Number or I-95 Crewman's Landing Permit ▶

10. Passport Number

11. Travel Document Number

12. Country of Issuance for Passport or Travel Document

13. Expiration Date for Passport or Travel Document (mm/dd/yyyy)

14. Current Nonimmigrant Status

15. Date current status expired, or will expire, as shown on Form I-94 or I-95 (mm/dd/yyyy)

Part 4. Processing Information

1. If the person listed in **Part 3.** is outside the U.S., is ineligible to adjust status in the U.S., or does not wish to adjust status in the U.S., provide the following information about the U.S. Consulate at which the person prefers to apply for an immigrant visa.

U.S. Consulate

A. City or Town: **Manila**

B. Country: **Philippines**

Sample Form I-360, Petition for Amerasian, Widow(er), or Special Immigrant (page 4)

Part 4. Processing Information (continued)

2. If a U.S. address was provided in **Part 3.**, type or print the person's foreign address below. If he or she does not maintain a foreign address, list the city or town and country of last foreign residence. If his or her native alphabet does not use Roman letters, type or print his or her name and foreign address in the native alphabet.

   A. Your Full Name

Family Name (Last Name)	Given Name (First Name)	Middle Name

   B. Mailing Address

Street Number and Name	Apt. Ste. Flr. ☐ ☐ ☐	Number

   City or Town

Province	Postal Code	Country

3. Gender of the beneficiary: ☒ Male ☐ Female

4. A. Are you filing any other petitions or applications with this one? ☐ Yes ☒ No

   B. If you answered "Yes" to **Item A.** in **Item Number 4.**, how many? [ ]

If you answer "Yes" to **Item Numbers 5. - 6.**, provide an explanation in the space provided in **Part 15. Additional Information**.

5. Is the beneficiary in removal proceedings? ☐ Yes ☒ No

6. Has the beneficiary ever worked in the U.S. without permission? (If you are applying for a special immigrant juvenile status, you are not required to answer this item number.) ☐ Yes ☒ No

7. Is an application for adjustment of status attached to this petition? ☐ Yes ☒ No

---

Part 5. Information About the Spouse and Children of the Person for Whom This Petition Is Being Filed

NOTE: Depending on the classification you seek, you can either file this petition for another person or for yourself. On this petition, the "beneficiary" or "self-petitioner" means the person for whom this petition is being filed, whether that person is yourself or another person.

1. If you are filing as a self-petitioning spouse, have any of your children filed separate self-petitions? ☐ Yes ☐ No

2. **Person 1**

Family Name (Last Name)	Given Name (First Name)	Middle Name

Date of Birth (mm/dd/yyyy)	Country of Birth

   Relationship   A-Number (if any)

   ☐ Spouse ☐ Child ▶ A-[ ][ ][ ][ ][ ][ ][ ][ ][ ]

Sample Form I-360, Petition for Amerasian, Widow(er), or Special Immigrant (page 14)

Part 10. Complete Only If Filing as a VAWA Self-Petitioning Spouse or Child of a U.S. Citizen or Lawful Permanent Resident or a VAWA Self-Petitioning Parent of a U.S. Citizen Son or Daughter (continued)

8. **A.** When did you and your abuser get married? (If you are a self-petitioning child or self-petitioning parent, type or print "N/A.")
   (mm/dd/yyyy)

   B. Where did you and your abuser get married? (If you are a self-petitioning child or self-petitioning parent, type or print "N/A.")

9. When did you live with your abuser?

   From (mm/dd/yyyy)   To (mm/dd/yyyy)

   Include any other dates you have lived off/on with your abuser in the space provided in **Part 15. Additional Information**.

10. Provide the last address at which you lived together with your abuser.

    Street Number and Name   Apt. Ste. Flr. Number
                                                            ☐ ☐ ☐

    City or Town   State   ZIP Code

    Province   Postal Code   Country

11. Provide the last date that you lived together with your abuser at this address.

    From (mm/dd/yyyy)   To (mm/dd/yyyy)

12. I am currently residing in the United States and I request an Employment Authorization Document.   ☐ Yes ☐ No

Part 11. Petitioner's Statement, Contact Information, Declaration, and Signature (Individual)

IMPORTANT: Complete this section **ONLY** if you are an individual filing this petition for yourself. If you are filing Form I-360 to petition for another person or as an authorized signatory of an organization, complete **Part 12. Statement, Contact Information, Declaration, and Signature of the Petitioner or Authorized Signatory.**

NOTE: Read the **Penalties** section of the Form I-360 Instructions before completing this part.

Petitioner's Statement

NOTE: Select the box for either **Item A.** or **B.** in **Item Number 1.** If applicable, select the box for **Item Number 2.**

1. Petitioner's Statement Regarding the Interpreter
   A. ☒ I can read and understand English, and I have read and understand every question and instruction on this petition and my answer to every question.
   B. ☐ The interpreter named in **Part 13.** read to me every question and instruction on this petition and my answer to every question in _____,
   a language in which I am fluent. I understand all of this information as interpreted.

2. Petitioner's Statement Regarding the Preparer
   ☐ At my request, the preparer named in **Part 14.**, _____,
   prepared this petition for me based only upon information I provided or authorized.

Sample Form I-360, Petition for Amerasian, Widow(er), or Special Immigrant (page 15)

Part 11. Petitioner's Statement, Contact Information, Declaration, and Signature (Individual) (continued)

Petitioner's Contact Information

3. Petitioner's Daytime Telephone Number

6328595300

4. Petitioner's Mobile Telephone Number (if any)

6328237000

5. Petitioner's Email Address (if any)

dzapato@email.com

Petitioner's Declaration and Certification

Copies of any documents I have submitted are exact photocopies of unaltered, original documents, and I understand that USCIS may require that I submit original documents to USCIS at a later date. Furthermore, I authorize the release of any information from any and all of my records that USCIS may need to determine my eligibility for the immigration benefit I seek.

I further authorize release of information contained in this petition, in supporting documents, and in my USCIS records to other entities and persons where necessary for the administration and enforcement of U.S. immigration laws.

I understand that USCIS may require me to appear for an appointment to take my biometrics (fingerprints, photograph, and/or signature) and, at that time, if I am required to provide biometrics, I will be required to sign an oath reaffirming that:

    1) I provided or authorized all of the information contained in, and submitted with, my petition;

    2) I reviewed and understood all of the information in, and submitted with, my petition; and

    3) All of this information was complete, true, and correct at the time of filing.

I certify, under penalty of perjury, that all of the information in my petition and any document submitted with it were provided or authorized by me, that I reviewed and understand all of the information contained in, and submitted with, my petition, and that all of this information is complete, true, and correct.

Petitioner's Signature

6. Petitioner's Signature

➡ *Dante D. Zapato*

Date of Signature (mm/dd/yyyy)

05/01/2020

NOTE TO ALL PETITIONERS: If you do not completely fill out this petition or fail to submit required documents listed in the Instructions, USCIS may deny your petition.

Part 12. Statement, Contact Information, Declaration, and Signature of the Petitioner or Authorized Signatory

IMPORTANT: Complete this section **ONLY** if you are filing Form I-360 to petition for another person or as an authorized signatory of an organization. If you are an individual filing this petition for yourself, complete **Part 11. Petitioner's Statement, Contact Information, Declaration, and Signature (Individual).**

NOTE: Read the **Penalties** section of the Form I-360 Instructions before completing this part.

Petitioner's or Authorized Signatory's Statement

NOTE: Select the box for either **Item A.** or **B.** in **Item Number 1.** If applicable, select the box for **Item Number 2.**

1. Petitioner's Statement Regarding the Interpreter

    A. ☐ I can read and understand English, and I have read and understand every question and instruction on this petition and my answer to every question.

Sample Form I-360, Petition for Amerasian, Widow(er), or Special Immigrant (page 16)

Part 12. Statement, Contact Information, Declaration, and Signature of the Petitioner or Authorized Signatory (continued)

B. ☐ The interpreter named in **Part 13.** read to me every question and instruction on this petition and my answer to every question in [＿＿＿＿＿＿＿＿＿＿],

a language in which I am fluent. I understand all of this information as interpreted.

2. Petitioner's Statement Regarding the Preparer

☐ At my request, the preparer named in **Part 14.**, [＿＿＿＿＿＿＿＿＿＿],

prepared this petition for me based only upon information I provided or authorized.

Authorized Signatory's Contact Information

3. Authorized Signatory's Family Name (Last Name) [＿＿＿＿＿＿＿＿] Authorized Signatory's Given Name (First Name) [＿＿＿＿＿＿＿＿]

4. Authorized Signatory's Title [＿＿＿＿＿＿＿＿] **5.** Authorized Signatory's Daytime Telephone Number [＿＿＿＿＿＿＿＿]

6. Authorized Signatory's Mobile Telephone Number (if any) [＿＿＿＿＿＿＿＿] **7.** Authorized Signatory's Email Address (if any) [＿＿＿＿＿＿＿＿]

Petitioner's or Authorized Signatory's Declaration and Certification

Copies of any documents submitted are exact photocopies of unaltered, original documents, and I understand that, as the petitioner, I may be required to submit original documents to USCIS at a later date.

I authorize the release of any information from my records, or from the petitioning organization's records, to USCIS or other entities and persons where necessary to determine eligibility for the immigration benefit sought or where authorized by law. I recognize the authority of USCIS to conduct audits of this petition using publicly available open source information. I also recognize that any supporting evidence submitted in support of this petition may be verified by USCIS through any means determined appropriate by USCIS, including but not limited to, on-site compliance reviews.

If filing this petition on behalf of an organization, I certify that I am authorized to do so by the organization.

I certify, under penalty of perjury, that I have reviewed this petition, I understand all of the information contained in, and submitted with, my petition, and all of this information is complete, true, and correct.

Petitioner's or Authorized Signatory's Signature

8. Petitioner's or Authorized Signatory's Signature | Date of Signature (mm/dd/yyyy)

➡ *Dante D. Zapato* | **05/01/2020**

NOTE TO ALL PETITIONERS AND AUTHORIZED SIGNATORIES: If you do not completely fill out this petition or fail to submit required documents listed in the Instructions, USCIS may delay a decision on or deny your petition.

Cancellation of Removal:
Do Ten Illegal Years Equal One Green Card?

mmigration law does provide a green card as a form of relief from removal (deportation) to a person who has been in the United States for more than ten years. However, the process can normally be started only if you're already in Immigration Court proceedings, facing removal from the United States. This relief is called "cancellation of removal," formerly known as "suspension of deportation." When granted, an alien immediately becomes a lawful permanent resident—and receives a green card soon after the court hearing.

This area of immigration law has changed drastically over the years. Some people can still qualify under more flexible, pre-1996 rules; others will qualify only if they meet later, more restrictive rules.

A. Applying in Court Proceedings

You cannot file an application to begin cancellation of removal directly with USCIS, as you can with other immigration applications. This process is available only when you are already in Immigration Court (EOIR) proceedings, as a defense against deportation and removal. (The only exception to this rule is for people who qualify for benefits under the Nicaraguan Adjustment and Central American Relief Act.)

Unlike the other kinds of applications discussed in this book, the decision on your case will be made by the Immigration Judge. USCIS will not be part of the decision making. However, a branch of the Department of Homeland Security (DHS) called Immigration and Customs Enforcement (ICE) will serve as "opposing counsel" in your case.

Being in removal proceedings means that DHS has learned of your illegal status and has served you with a summons called a Notice to Appear or NTA (once called an Order to Show Cause). The NTA gives you the time, date, and place to appear for a court hearing on whether or not you should be deported.

If DHS has not started removal proceedings against you, and you want to apply for cancellation of removal, your sole possibility is to turn yourself in to DHS—and it might then start removal proceedings against you. But consult an experienced immigration attorney before taking this risk. The attorney can help evaluate whether you qualify for relief and the chances of DHS's cooperating with you. More often, DHS just lets applications sit in its files for years, perhaps waiting for the laws to turn harsher.

B. Who Qualifies for Cancellation

If you have been in the United States for ten years or more and you are of good moral character, and your deportation would cause hardship to certain close family members who are either U.S. citizens or permanent residents, there is a chance that your application for cancellation of removal will be granted.

SEE AN EXPERT

It is very risky to ask to be placed in removal proceedings solely to request cancellation. If you are contemplating turning yourself in to DHS, discuss your situation first with an immigration attorney who specializes in cancellation issues or with an immigration law clinic or a group that specializes in counseling on immigration matters.

CAUTION

Watch out for scammers. Unscrupulous immigration practitioners (also sometimes called notarios) have spread a myth that after you live in the U.S. for ten years, you automatically qualify for permanent residence. That's wrong: There's no "ten-year green card" you can apply to USCIS for. Rather, ten years' continuous presence in the U.S. provides the possibility of deportation relief, which could result in a green card. But this relief is totally discretionary. Some immigration judges won't grant cancellation of removal except in the most dire of circumstances, while others are more generous.

C. Who Is Not Eligible for Cancellation

A number of people are not allowed to apply for cancellation of removal. They include:

- aliens who entered the United States as crewmen after June 30, 1964
- J-1 visa holders who have not fulfilled a two-year home country residency requirement (if they are required to do so), and those who came to the U.S. to receive graduate medical education or training
- certain categories of inadmissible aliens, including those who the U.S. government believes are coming to the U.S. to engage in espionage, unlawful activities to overturn the U.S. government, or terrorist activities, and those who have been members of totalitarian or some communist parties
- people who are deportable for offenses involving national security, espionage, or terrorism
- people who have participated in persecuting others
- certain people previously given relief from removal or deportation
- people who have been convicted of certain crimes involving morally bad conduct or illegal drugs
- people convicted of crimes involving morally bad conduct in the five years after being admitted to the U.S. if the crimes are punishable by a sentence of one year or more (regardless of the sentence actually handed down)
- people who have been convicted of certain offenses involving failure to comply with alien registration or change of address requirements, or certain offenses involving document fraud, and
- people convicted of aggravated felonies. This includes murder, rape, sexual abuse of a minor, illegal trafficking in drugs or firearms, money laundering, crimes of violence, some theft crimes, burglary, or other offenses, including some misdemeanors. If you have been convicted of a crime, get advice from an experienced attorney.

D. Preparing a Convincing Case

If you decide that your best approach is to file for cancellation of removal, know that you will have some difficult times ahead. Nationwide, Immigration Judges are not allowed to grant more than 4,000 cancellation of removal cases per year, so applicants are effectively competing against each other to show who is most worthy of this relief—usually by showing whose family will be most devastated by their removal from the United States.

What's more, if you appear in court after the 4,000 annual limit has been reached for that year, the Immigration Judge is likely to continue (postpone) your case until the following year, perhaps without holding a full hearing. Or the judge might allow the hearing to go forward but then, if inclined to grant your case, "reserve judgement" (put off issuing a decision) until a green card becomes available. Your first task will be to find a lawyer. (See Chapter 24 for advice on finding a good one.) Together, you will figure out what kinds of evidence you can submit to show that you should be granted cancellation of removal. The following three sections will get you started.

1. Proof of Good Moral Character

You must show that you've been a person of good moral character for at least the last ten years. You might be able to secure a certificate of good conduct from your local police station. This certificate will attest that, according to computer records, you have never been in trouble with the police. Although DHS will also send your fingerprints to the Federal Bureau of Investigation in Washington, DC, submitting your own record from the local police will help prove to the court that you are a person of good moral character.

You can also submit declarations from relatives, friends, and community members verifying that you have participated in religious institutions, volunteered at schools or other civic places, or in any other way demonstrated that you are a good person.

If you have committed any serious crime during the ten years you were in the United States, the Immigration Judge may find that you lack good moral character. Ten years must pass from the time you committed the crime until the time you can apply for a suspension of deportation. However, committing certain serious crimes will make you ineligible forever.

2. Proof That You Stayed in the U.S. Ten Years

You must show also that you have lived in the United States continuously for at least ten years. Copies of your passport and I-94 (Arrival-Departure Record) from when you first arrived in the United States are the best proof of this.

In addition, copies of your apartment lease, bank statements, and income tax returns are good evidence that you have been in the United States for ten years. School and medical records, subscriptions and memberships, and statements from friends, landlords, or coworkers are also useful.

3. Proof of Hardship

You must convince the court that if you are deported from the United States, it would cause "exceptional and extremely unusual hardship" to your spouse, child, or parent who is a U.S. citizen or a permanent resident. (The law in effect before 1996 allowed an individual to qualify by showing extreme hardship to himself or herself as well as to one of those family members, but this no longer works.)

Of course, if your spouse, parent, or adult child (21 or over) is a U.S. citizen, you qualify as a candidate for an immigrant visa as an immediate relative or as a family preference beneficiary (see Chapter 4). Cancellation of removal is considered a remedy of last resort, so if you are able to adjust your status based on an I-130 petition filed by any of those family members, you are expected to do so. If for some reason you are not able to adjust your status, however, cancellation of removal might be your only available avenue.

Because cancellation of removal depends almost completely on the discretion of the judge, you can only hope for a judge who is compassionate and humane. You and your lawyer must convince the judge that leaving the United States and returning to your own country would cause exceptional and extremely unusual hardship for your family members due to any combination of personal, economic, sociocultural, and psychological reasons.

What Does "Continuous Physical Presence" Mean?

The court will consider that you have been continuously present in the U.S. even if you departed from the country, as long as your absences did not exceed more than 90 days per trip or 180 days total. There are exceptions for individuals who served honorably in the Armed Forces for at least two years. Also, the time that can be used toward the ten-year presence period will be cut short if you commit an act that makes you deportable or inadmissible, or when DHS issues you a Notice to Appear.

Personal reasons. The Immigration Court will need the birth certificate of your child, your marriage certificate, and your own birth certificate (if your parents are the U.S. citizens or permanent residents who will suffer hardship should you leave the United States).

For starters, your relatives should be prepared to testify in court about how much you mean to them, how much they depend on you, and how disastrous it would be for them if you were not allowed to remain in the United States. Since nearly every family would face some similar pain, the judge wants to see that the hardship your family would face is "exceptional and extremely unusual."

If your American-born children are under 14, the judge will normally not ask to hear their testimony. However, the testimony of such young children, detailing their affection for you and the hardships they would endure if they accompanied you to your native country—problems with language, problems being uprooted from friends and schools—could strengthen your case.

Although testimony by your young children that, as Americans, they would rather stay in the United States with their grandparents or with a foster family than leave for a country they don't know could be hurtful for you to hear, such testimony would be further evidence that your deportation would cause them hardship.

Proof that any illness for which you or a family member is being treated in the United States, and evidence that the same treatment or medicine is either lacking or too expensive in your own country should also be given to the judge, supported by letters from doctors and pharmacists in the United States and the foreign country.

Provided they are either U.S. citizens or permanent residents, more distant relatives—including the grandparents or the biological parents of your child, their aunts, uncles, or cousins, or your own brothers and sisters—may all testify that your departure would also be an extreme hardship to them and to the family in general.

Whether or not these people testify, they should all submit letters of support for you. Letters that are sworn under penalty of perjury are usually given more weight than other letters.

If you have a boyfriend or girlfriend who is married to somebody else, it is not recommended that he or she testify either on your behalf, or on behalf of the child he or she had with you. Although adultery has been repealed from immigration law as proof of the lack of good moral character, many judges will not look with favor upon such situations.

Economic reasons. Although you might be earning much more in the United States than you would earn in your own country, economic reasons are the least persuasive arguments against deportation. Economic hardship by itself has never been considered by the Immigration Court as

sufficient reason to cancel deportation. If you would be completely unable to support yourself and your family in your home country, however, the judge may consider that as a hardship factor.

If you are receiving welfare, government subsidies, or any form of public assistance, you may have a more difficult time receiving mercy from the judge. A judge is unlikely to grant you permission to stay in the United States permanently if you may be seen as a burden to the government.

Proof of regular and continuous employment is very important. Letters from your employers, past and present, detailing your employment history and your value as an employee, your most current pay stubs, and evidence of your work product, in the form of photos or newspaper articles, are all useful in demonstrating your contribution to the economic life of the nation. Try to contrast this to how different your employment opportunities would be in your home country.

You should have filed income tax returns for the past ten years, so submit copies as proof. These will show that, except for your illegal immigration status, you have been law-abiding. If you have not filed any tax returns because you do not have a Social Security number or because you have always been paid in cash, consult a tax expert at once. You might have to pay back taxes.

If you are in business for yourself, submit copies of documents demonstrating this. These could include your business license, your business checking account showing activity, a financial statement from an accountant to the court, and incorporation papers showing you as the major or sole stockholder. Also consider providing photos of your business in operation, payroll records for any employees, and a letter from your bank giving your account history and the average balance of your business account. Letters from your business partners and testimony in court explaining how the business would be affected if you were forced to leave it should also be presented during the hearing.

If you have invested in real estate, present proof of ownership, mortgage papers, and a letter from a real estate broker concerning how much your property would be worth if sold in the present market and especially how much financial loss this would cause you.

Sociocultural reasons. Convince the court that you are in good standing in your community in the United States. Present letters from your church, temple, or mosque about your active membership, from your block or village association, from the Parent-Teacher Association, from volunteer organizations, and from people you have cared for or helped. All are important to show that your life has been intimately entwined with U.S. society and that you have been a useful member of your community.

Letters from the union supervisor or from your coworkers explaining the kind of person you are and how valuable you are to them, personally and in terms of work, are also persuasive documents to present to the judge.

The judge will want to know whether you have any other possible forms of relief from deportation available to you, whether you have any pending petitions submitted on your behalf by a relative or an employer, and why it is advantageous for the U.S. government to grant you permanent residence through an immediate cancellation of removal instead of waiting for the Priority Date of any other immigration petition that might be pending.

Psychological reasons. You will have to acquaint the judge with the social, cultural, and political situation in your country and how your family may be subjected to prejudice, bigotry, or ostracism.

If you have a child born outside of marriage, or who is of a different race or is physically handicapped, provide evidence of how such children are treated in your country. Explain how going back to your country would affect your emotional and psychological health, thereby affecting your U.S. citizen and permanent resident family members. Also explain how going back would directly affect the emotional or psychological health of any relative who is a U.S. citizen or permanent resident. Testimony from an expert witness, such as a psychiatrist or a psychologist, would bolster your case.

If you have a child who is a U.S. citizen, explain how the child's inability to fluently speak the language of your native country would be harmful to the child's education, and how removal from relatives, friends, and classmates could cause the child great psychological trauma.

E. How to File

You and your lawyer must submit the following documents to the Immigration Judge, along with a filing fee of $100:

- Form EOIR-42B, Application for Cancellation of Removal and Adjustment of Status for Certain Nonpermanent Residents
- Form G-325A, Biographical Information
- Documentary evidence as described in Section D, above
- A color photograph taken within 30 days of submitting the application, and
- Proof that you paid the $85 biometrics (fingerprinting) fee; DHS will provide instructions on how to do this.

Notice that we don't provide sample, filled-in forms in this chapter. That's because you'd be foolish to go into Immigration Court without the help of an attorney; and the attorney will help you fill out the forms. You must also submit a copy to the Assistant Chief Counsel for DHS.

You can apply for a work permit once you have filed Form EOIR-42B, by filing Form I-765 at the address indicated on the form's instructions, along with the filing fee ($410 in early 2020, but expected to go up).

Your answer to Question 27 (eligibility category) is "(c)(10)."

The Immigration Judge will set a hearing date for your case—giving enough time for you and your lawyer to prepare and for USCIS to investigate your case. In the meantime, USCIS should issue you a work permit.

The hearing might not finish the first day. In fact, it could be postponed one or more times because the Immigration Court devotes only a few hours at a time to each case on its calendar. Unless you are being detained at the immigration jail, your case could easily take one or two years before it is fully heard and a decision is reached.

F. Approving Your Application

If the Immigration Judge approves your application for cancellation of removal, you will be granted permanent residence that day (if there are still visa numbers available for the current year).

Winning Is Not Enough

Remember, even if an Immigration Judge decides to cancel your removal order, you could face a delay. Only 4,000 people each year are granted formal cancellation of removal. Immigration Judges have the power to grant conditional or temporary cancellation of removal orders until the person becomes eligible. The removal proceedings will not be formally ended, and permanent residence will not be formally granted, until your waiting number is reached.

G. Additional Types of Cancellation of Removal

There are two additional varieties of cancellation of removal. One is for permanent residents (green card holders) who have become deportable or removable. The other is for people who have been subjected to extreme cruelty or battery by a spouse or parent who is a U.S. citizen or permanent resident while in the United States.

1. Permanent Residents

An Immigration Judge may cancel the removal of, and regrant a green card to, a permanent resident if the person:

- has five years as a permanent resident
- has lived continuously in the U.S. for at least seven years after having been admitted in any status, and
- has not been convicted of an aggravated felony.

This relief will serve as a waiver of removal for many permanent residents who commit acts that make them deportable. See a lawyer for help with this (and Chapter 24).

2. Abused Spouse or Child

An abused spouse or child of a U.S. citizen or permanent resident may apply for cancellation of removal under different rules provided by the Violence Against Women Act, or VAWA. In this case, the applicant must show that he or she:

- suffered physical abuse or extreme mental cruelty in the U.S. at the hands of a permanent resident or U.S. citizen who is or was the applicant's parent or spouse—or the applicant is the parent of such an abused child
- has been physically present in the U.S. for a continuous period of at least three years at the time of the application
- has had good moral character for at least the three-year period, and
- is not inadmissible due to a conviction for a crime involving moral turpitude or drugs, or on national security or terrorism grounds or other specified grounds, and has not been convicted of an aggravated felony.

The applicant must also show that the removal would result in extreme hardship to the applicant, or to his or her child or parent (if the applicant is a child).

Congress added this provision so that spouses and children who are victims of abuse by their petitioning relative would have a way to obtain status if they left the household of the abuser.

Again, seek a lawyer's help with this type of application. Many nonprofits offer free or low-cost help.

Adjustment of Status

Are you ready for the final step toward getting a green card while you're living in the United States? By now, you should have already completed some preliminary steps, such as winning the visa lottery, receiving approval of a petition on Form I-130 filed by a member of your family, or having spent one year in the U.S. as an asylee or a refugee. Or you should have figured out that, because of special circumstances (most likely that you're the immediate relative of a U.S. citizen and entered the U.S. legally), you don't need to get advance approval of a Form I-130 before continuing with your application. In any case, it's now your turn, as the immigrant, to file your application for a green card.

The procedure for obtaining a green card while you're in the United States is called adjustment of status. It involves submitting forms to USCIS and attending an interview at a local USCIS office. It literally means you're changing your status from that of an undocumented person or a nonimmigrant visa holder to that of permanent resident. The alternate way to obtain a green card is through what's called "consular processing" (discussed in Chapter 17), in which you correspond with and attend interviews at an overseas U.S. embassy or consulate.

If you're living or staying in the United States right now, you might prefer the convenience of applying for your green card without leaving, using the adjustment of status process. Unfortunately, it's not always that easy. Many people who are eligible for green cards—because they're family members of U.S. citizens or permanent residents, or fall into other immigration categories—are nevertheless not allowed to stay in the United States to get their green card. Read on to find out the possibilities and potential problems that surround adjustment of status.

This chapter will discuss:

- who is allowed to use the adjustment of status procedure (Section A)
- who doesn't qualify, and what effect this has on the person's efforts to immigrate (Section B), and
- if you qualify, what forms and application procedures you'll need to use (Section C).

How Do You Decide?

If you are eligible for both adjustment of status in the United States and consular processing abroad, it is often best to choose adjustment of status because:

- You will save the expense of traveling back to your home country.
- If your application to adjust your status is denied, you can remain and work in the U.S. while you appeal that decision.
- If you go for consular processing and your application is denied, there is no right to appeal.
- When adjusting status, there is no risk of being kept out for three or ten years due to past illegal stays in the United States.

Nevertheless, adjustment of status is not the best choice for everyone. For example, if you don't face any problems with the time bars, and are planning to visit your home country anyway—you might want to choose consular processing for a less expensive green card.

A. Who Is Allowed to Use the Adjustment of Status Procedure

You are allowed to choose adjustment of status as your green card application method only if you fall into one of the following three categories:

- You are the immediate relative of a U.S. citizen and your last entry into the U.S. was done legally (see Section 1, below).
- Your last entry into the U.S. was done legally and you have remained in legal status ever since (see Section 2, below).
- You are "grandfathered in" under certain old laws because you had a visa petition on file before the laws changed (unlikely; see Section 3, below).

In addition, you must not be inadmissible based on the "permanent bar." This bar applies to people who lived in the United States illegally for more than a year and then left or were deported, but who returned to the United States illegally (or were caught trying to). Such people might never be allowed to get a green card. See a lawyer if you believe this bar might apply to you.

1. Immediate Relatives Who Entered Legally

If you meet the following two criteria, you are one of the lucky few allowed to use the adjustment of status procedure:

- You are the immediate relative (spouse, parent, or minor, unmarried child) of a U.S. citizen.
- Your most recent entry to the United States was done legally, most likely using a visa (such as a tourist or a student visa), a visa waiver (in which you simply showed your passport and were admitted for a 90-day tourist stay), or some other entry document like a border crossing card. There are exceptions, however: You cannot adjust under this category if you entered as a crewman on a boat or plane, regardless of what visa you had, or you were in transit to another country without a visa (for example, changing planes in a U.S. airport).

CAUTION

Remember, this chapter discusses only procedures, not your underlying eligibility for a green card. Unless you've already completed the steps explained in another chapter—most likely one describing family- or lottery-based visas—you shouldn't be in this chapter. It's only for people with approved immigrant petitions—or immediate relatives who are filing an I-130 petition with their application for adjustment of status—or for people with winning lottery letters who are now completing their green card application process.

EXAMPLE: Katerina is a foreign student from Germany who has used her student visa to enter the United States many times, most recently on her return trip after summer vacation. She is engaged to marry a fellow student named Mark, a U.S. citizen. Once they're married, Katerina will be an immediate relative, whose last entry to the U.S. was done legally. (In fact, it wouldn't matter if she let her student visa expire before applying to adjust status, though we don't recommend this method, since it means spending time in the U.S. illegally.) Katerina will be able to apply for her green card without leaving the U.S., using the adjustment of status procedure.

However, there's one major, and common, difficulty for some immediate relatives: Your use of the visa or visa waiver to enter the U.S. has to have been an innocent one, merely to study, travel, or whatever it was your visa was meant for. If instead you used the visa specifically for the purpose of getting yourself to the U.S. so you could adjust status, that's visa fraud, and will make you ineligible for a green card. Visas are meant to be used only for the limited purpose of coming to the U.S. for a temporary stay—any secret plans to stay permanently can be seen as a big problem.

EXAMPLE: While Sally was a foreign student in the Netherlands, she met Joost, and they became engaged. After Sally's studies ended, she returned to the United States. Joost stayed behind for a few months, to finish an architecture project. Because citizens of the Netherlands are not required to obtain visas to visit the U.S., Joost simply picked up his passport when he was ready, and flew to New York. He told the border official he was there to visit friends for a few months, and was let in. They got married at city hall the next week, and Joost immediately began preparing his green card application. Joost's actions could easily be considered visa fraud. Although, technically, Joost would be able to use the adjustment of status procedure—in fact, he would probably have no problem submitting his full green card application—when the time comes for Joost's interview, the USCIS officer will likely question him closely about whether he purposely lied when he entered the U.S. and told the border official that he would stay here for only a few months. If Joost can't come up with a good answer, his application will be denied. (There is a waiver Joost can apply for, with the help of an attorney, but it's hard to get.)

DOS Makes It Easier to Accuse Applicants of Visa Fraud (Changes 30/60-Day Rule)

In late 2017, the DOS made changes to its *Foreign Affairs Manual*, specifically to what was commonly called the "30/60 rule." This concerns a ground of inadmissibility under I.N.A. 212(a)(6)(C) applying to any alien "who, by fraud or willfully misrepresenting a material fact, seeks to procure (or has sought to procure or has procured) a visa, other documentation, or admission into the United States." (For more information on inadmissibility, see Chapter 4.)

Under the former 30/60 rule, consular and USCIS officials presumed that the immigrant lied if he or she did something inconsistent with the terms of the visa (such as take a job while on a student visa or come to the U.S. to get married and stay permanently while on a tourist visa) within 30 days of U.S. entry. Any such actions after 30 days but before 60 days were typically not considered fraud unless separate evidence showed otherwise. If the relevant conduct took place after 60 days of U.S. entry, there was no presumption of misrepresentation.

However, this has been replaced with the "90-day rule," under which a consular officer may presume misrepresentation for actions within 90 days of entry and may also make a determination that fraud existed long after 90 days have passed if enough evidence supports it. This policy is much broader and gives immigration officials far more discretion in determining whether immigrants lied in obtaining a visa or immigration benefit.

Although USCIS (which operates separately from DOS) has not yet updated its own policy manual to include the new 90-day rule, it will likely follow suit. This is a huge issue for adjustment of status based upon marriage after entering the U.S. on a tourist visa, the Visa Waiver Program, or another short-term visa. Note the example below.

married or submit the green card application—hopefully three months, at least—you'll face fewer questions, because USCIS might presume you were thinking your plans over in between. And some people are able to convincingly explain that their intentions when entering the U.S. were truly just to visit (or do whatever their visa was intended for), but while here, they talked it over with their relative (or soon-to-be spouse) and decided that the immigrant should stay and apply for a green card.

EXAMPLE: John, a U.S. citizen living near Washington DC, and Fernando, a citizen of Spain, are engaged. They know about the K-1 visa that would allow Fernando to travel to the U.S. to be married and stay permanently; and that they have the option of getting married and later applying for an immigrant visa at a consulate abroad. However, they decide it will be less expensive and inconvenient for Fernando to simply travel to the U.S. on the Visa Waiver Program (VWP), which allows nationals of certain countries to enter without a visa and stay for a maximum of 90 days; then to marry and file for adjustment of status afterwards. Fernando travels to the U.S. and tells the border official at the airport that he is staying with a friend and plans to sightsee but does not mention any wedding plans. Two weeks later, the couple is married at a reception with 100 of their friends and family attending.

While it's not against the law to get married in U.S. while on a tourist visa or using the VWP, it is a violation of law to misrepresent your intentions to a border official in order to gain U.S. admission. If Fernando decides to stay in the U.S. and adjust status rather than returning to Spain, he might have difficulty convincing USCIS he did not commit visa fraud by failing to mention that he was going to get married and planned to live in the U.S. permanently. This is especially true since the couple will need to submit marriage evidence with their adjustment application, which will show that they planned a big wedding reception months before Fernando came to the U.S.—and got married two weeks later! Best-case scenario is that the USCIS officer overlooks the indiscretion and approves Fernando's green

An unbelievable number of married couples make the same mistake that Sally and Joost did. A few get lucky and the immigration official who interviews them simply overlooks the problem. If you wait long enough after your entry to either get card, but there is the possibility that his green card will be denied, a fraud finding made, and he will be returned to Spain with diminished hopes for ever again living in the United States.

The safest thing for Fernando to do is return to Spain within 90 days and obtain his green card through consular processing rather than applying using adjustment of status procedures. While he might face questions about why he told the border official that he was coming to the U.S. to sightsee when he actually got married, he will be able to sidestep any questions about lying about his intentions to live in the U.S. permanently after his travel on the VWP.

Additional difficulties can occur if you entered the U.S. on the Visa Waiver Program. In this situation, you should submit a complete adjustment application to USCIS and, ideally, submit it before the expiration of the 90-day period of your visa-waiver–authorized stay. USCIS may approve your I-485 application even if you overstayed, but in most jurisdictions, if your application is denied, you won't get a "second bite at the apple" by asking an Immigration Judge to consider your application.

2. People Who Entered Legally and Remain Legal

Even if you're not the immediate relative of a U.S. citizen, you're allowed to get a green card using the adjustment of status procedure if you meet all the following criteria:

- You entered the U.S. legally, most likely using a visa (such as a tourist or a student visa) or some other entry document like a border crossing card. There are exceptions, however: You cannot adjust under this rule if you entered using a visa waiver, you entered as a crewman on a boat or plane (regardless of what visa you had), or you were in transit to another country without a visa (for example, changing planes in a U.S. airport).
- You have never been out of legal status (your right to stay, as most likely shown on your I-94, hasn't expired).

- You have never worked without INS or USCIS authorization.

Whether or not your permitted stay has expired is an important issue. If you were granted a tourist visa (B-2), for example, the visa itself might be valid for many years and allow multiple entries. However, the important issue is how long the border officials said you could stay on this particular trip. You'll find this information on your I-94, which you must obtain online, and will show the expiration date of your authorized stay. You might also find this date stamped on your passport. If you've overstayed that date, and didn't get any extension or change of status, your status is now illegal, no matter how long your visa is good for.

Note to students: Your I-94 might not have an expiration date, but instead simply say "D/S," which means "duration of status." In other words, you're allowed to stay in the U.S. as long as you continue your studies (and don't violate the other terms of your student visa).

Working without authorization is also a troublesome issue for many would-be immigrants. Tourist and student visa holders, for example, are frequent violators of the work permit rules (tourists aren't allowed to work at all, and students can work only under limited circumstances).

> **EXAMPLE:** Ahmed and Ali, two brothers age 24 and 26, come to visit their mother in the United States, where she lives as a permanent resident. A month into their six-month stay, their mother's U.S. citizenship finally comes through. Because the mother petitioned for the brothers some years ago, they can use their old Priority Date, and they find that they're immediately eligible for green cards in the family first preference category (see Chapter 9). But can they apply for adjustment of status? They entered legally, and their stay is still legal. However, Ali has picked up a part-time job in a local restaurant. Only Ahmed will be able to adjust status. Ali will have to return home and try to get his green card through consular processing (where he might face questions about his illegal work).

Another problem that comes up for some applicants is the use of visa fraud to enter the United States. After waiting outside the United States for many years for their Priority Date to become current, many applicants figure they can simply get a visa to the U.S. and submit an adjustment of status application once they're here. Many of them are disappointed to find out they've just committed visa fraud. Again, visas are meant to be used only for the limited purpose of coming to the U.S. for a temporary stay, and your activities on that visa must remain within its purposes—visitor visa holders must act like tourists, student visa holders must act like students, and so on. Although immigration officials will sometimes look the other way, it's best to avoid the problem, stay in your home country, and finish your application through the local consulate.

> **EXAMPLE:** Meijin is a U.S. permanent resident who filed visa petitions for her two children, aged 26 and 28, in the second preference category, many years ago. Their Priority Date finally becomes current, and they receive forms and information from the U.S. consulate in Beijing, China, near where they live. The older child, Guofeng, can't wait—he uses a tourist visa he already happens to have to enter the United States. He tells the border officials in San Francisco he's just coming to sightsee (otherwise they would have turned Guofeng around and sent him home). Guofeng submits a green card application. The application is denied, because Guofeng inappropriately used a tourist visa when his real intention was to stay permanently. His sister, Jinqing, stays home and files her paperwork with the U.S. consulate, and she succeeds in getting an immigrant visa and a green card.

SEE AN EXPERT

Not sure whether you can adjust status under these rules? If you have any doubts at all about whether you qualify to adjust status, consult a qualified immigration attorney. See Chapter 24 for advice on finding a good one.

3. People Who Qualify Under Old Laws

As you've seen, a number of people are barred from adjusting status, including those who entered the U.S. illegally; overstayed their visa or other permitted time; worked without authorization; entered while in transit without a visa; or entered as crew on planes or boats. However, there are two exceptions, based on changes in the laws over the years.

At one time, a law called "245(i)" allowed all people who were otherwise unable to adjust status to do so by paying a penalty fee. That law is now gone, but a few people who were around when the law was still in effect are allowed to make use of it. You can apply to adjust status under § 245(i) if you:

- had an approvable immigrant petition or labor certification filed on your behalf before January 14, 1998 (it doesn't matter whether it was filed by the same person or employer as the one through whom you're now immigrating)
- had an approvable immigrant petition or labor certification filed on your behalf before April 30, 2001, as long as you were physically in the U.S. on December 21, 2000 (again, it doesn't matter whether it was filed by the same person or employer as the one through whom you're now immigrating), or
- in certain circumstances, are the spouse or child of someone described above.

There is a financial catch to using these old laws to adjust status, however: You'll have to pay a penalty fee, currently $1,000.

B. People Who Can't Adjust Status at All

If you don't fall into any of the categories described above, you do not qualify to use adjustment of status as your green card application method. This means that many people who only recently became eligible to immigrate—for example, by marrying a U.S. citizen—but who entered the U.S. without being inspected and admitted by a border official, and had no immigrant petitions filed for them by any of the important 1998 or 2001 dates, will be ineligible to adjust status.

Unfortunately, this is a difficult trap, because if a person has spent more than 180 days in the U.S. illegally, leaving the U.S. to try to apply through an overseas U.S. consulate could result in being barred from returning for three or ten years. Some, but not all people facing this trap might be able to get around it by applying for a provisional waiver of unlawful presence, allowing them to receive an answer before leaving the United States. (Review Chapter 4 for details.) See a lawyer if you're in this or a similar situation.

C. How to File

If you are one of the lucky people who can adjust status in the U.S., a number of picky rules control how and when you can submit your various application forms. Follow them exactly, to be sure that your paperwork can be processed quickly and properly.

1. Whether You Need to Wait for Approval of Form I-130

Most people who are eligible to adjust status can do so only after receiving some official government statement about their basic eligibility for a green card—for example, USCIS receipt or approval of their Form I-130 petition, a State Department letter indicating they won the lottery, or a grant of political asylum (which can be used as the basis for a green card after one year). However, one exception allows certain applicants applying through family to turn this two-step application process into one step.

If you are the spouse, parent, or minor child of a U.S. citizen (an immediate relative), then you can file the I-130 and adjustment of status paperwork at the same time. If you've already filed the I-130, file your adjustment application with either the approval or with a request for USCIS to request that the pending file be transferred.

If you are applying through a family member but do not match the description in the paragraph above, then your family member must file Form I-130 and accompanying documents at a USCIS service center first. (The procedures for I-130 submissions are explained in the various chapters of this book that apply to different types of eligibility for family members.) Only after the I-130 is approved and your Priority Date is current can you continue with your application.

2. Adjustment of Status Forms and Documents

To apply for adjustment of status, you must submit the following forms to USCIS:

☐ **Copy of government document proving your basic green card eligibility.** This might be an approval or receipt notice for an I-130 petition (unless you're a family member who can submit this petition together with the adjustment of status application as described in Section 1, above), a State Department letter notifying you that you've won the lottery, a grant of political asylum or refugee status, or, if you entered on a K-1 or K-2 fiancé visa, copies of the I-129F fiancé petition approval notice, your marriage certificate, and your Form I-94 (which is either a card tucked into your passport or a page you've printed from the U.S. Customs and Border Protection (CBP) website).

TIP
Getting a copy of your I-94. Until 2013, all nonimmigrants (such as students and tourists) entering the U.S. needed to complete Form I-94, Arrival/Departure Record, a small white piece of paper. The border agent would then indicate the date by which the entrant would need to depart the U.S., and staple the form to the person's passport. Now, paper I-94s have been mostly phased out. You will, however, still need your I-94 number for your adjustment of status application. To find and print it, go to https://i94.cbp.dhs.gov/I94/#/home. If you can't locate your information on the first try, try different variations of your name. For example, include your middle name along with your first name, or both last names, if applicable. Still

out of luck? Call a Customs and Border Patrol Deferred Inspection Site for more information. Some adjustment applicants have had luck by simply submitting a statement that they were unable to locate their I-94 number on the CBP website. Otherwise, USCIS will likely instruct you to file Form I-102, Application for Replacement/Initial Nonimmigrant Arrival-Departure Document, along with the $445 filing fee. Another possibility for locating your I-94 (especially if it was a paper document) is to submit a Freedom of Information Act (FOIA) request online with CBP at www.cbp.gov/site-policy-notices/foia.

☐ **Proof that you're eligible to use the adjustment of status procedure.** What you use as proof depends on the reason you're able to adjust status. For example, if you're an immediate relative who entered the U.S. legally, a copy of your Form I-94 would be sufficient. If you're an asylee or a refugee and have been present in the U.S. for one year or more, submit proof of the day your status started. This could be your I-94, the Asylum Office approval letter, or the order of the Immigration Judge. If you entered the U.S. on a fiancé visa (K-1, K-2, K-3, or K-4) and got married or met your other visa requirements, submit a copy of your visa and I-94. If you're claiming eligibility because you fall under the Section 245(i) law from 1998, you'll need to submit a copy of your I-130 petition or labor certification approval notice, with proof that your application was received by the January 14, 1998 deadline. If you are claiming eligibility under the Section 245(i) law from 2001, you'll need to submit the Approval Notice with proof that the application was received by April 30, 2001, as well as proof that you were in the U.S. on December 21, 2000. Such proof might include medical or dental records from that date, a pay stub, or even a traffic ticket. If you don't have a document issued exactly on December 21,

2000—and most people don't—submit documents that are close in time to that date.

☐ **Form I-485, Application to Register Permanent Resident or Adjust Status.** This is the primary form used to adjust status, which collects information on who you are, where you live, how you're eligible for a green card, and whether any of the grounds of inadmissibility (disqualification) apply to you. (See the sample at the end of this chapter.)

☐ **Form I-485 Supplement A.** Use this form only if you're applying to adjust status based on old laws (245(i)). Also remember to pay the penalty fee.

☐ **If you want permission to work, Form I-765.** (See the sample at the end of this chapter.) Several months could pass before you're approved for a green card, during which time you can't work without getting permission. Use this form to ask permission (the current filing fee is $410). If for some reason you submit your work permit application later, you'll have to submit a copy of your Form I-797C Notice of Action receipt showing you filed the I-485, in order to show you're eligible for the work permit. You'll be given an Employment Authorization Document (EAD), which is an identification card with your photo. Even if you don't plan to work, this card is a handy way to prove who you are. The last question on the form, Number 16, can be confusing (and the instructions list many ways that different types of applicants must answer it). As an adjustment applicant, you simply answer it "(c)(9)," regardless of how you became eligible for your green card.

☐ **Form I-131, Application for Travel Document.** This is optional, but very handy. Submitting it will result in your obtaining an "Advance Parole" (AP) document, which you'll need if you leave the U.S. before your green card application has been approved. Even if you don't have plans to leave the U.S. anytime soon, having this AP document will save a lot of time and worry if circumstances arise requiring you to leave before you receive your green card (such as an emergency in your home country or a required trip abroad for work). See the sample at the end of this chapter; and ignore the part of the form that says you have to supply a separate explanation as to why you deserve Advance Parole. Approval is fairly automatic for adjustment of status applicants who haven't already left the U.S., so you really don't need to explain anything. Leaving the U.S. without Advance Parole will lead to your adjustment of status application being canceled. The current filing fee is $575. As with the EAD application, if you apply after submitting your I-485 application, be sure to submit a copy of your I-797 Receipt Notice to show you have a pending I-485. If you also apply for an EAD and are approved, you will receive an "EAD-AP" combo card, which both serves as your work permission and enables you to leave the U.S. while you await a decision on Form I-485.

TIP

Advance Parole does NOT guarantee readmission into the U.S. You can still be denied reentry at the discretion of Customs and Border Protection (CBP) or if you're inadmissible. This was, in the past, a particular problem for people who'd been unlawfully present in the U.S. for 180 days or more. Fortunately, the Board of Immigration Appeals (BIA) ruled in *Matter of Arrabally Yerrabelly*, 25 I&N Dec. 771 (BIA 2012) that people with a pending permanent residency application who leave the U.S. with Advance Parole do not trigger the three- and ten-year unlawful presence bars. However, to be cautious, you might want to consult an immigration attorney before leaving.

☐ **Form I-864, Affidavit of Support.** (See the sample in Chapter 17.) If you're applying through a family member (not through an employer or as an asylee or a refugee, nor if you're a self-petitioning widow(er) or a battered spouse or child), you must submit this sworn statement from the petitioner (the U.S. citizen or lawful permanent resident who submitted the visa petition for you, who has sufficient income and who promises to support you and to reimburse the U.S. government if you must receive public assistance after receiving your permanent residence).

☐ **Form I-864W (if you fall within an exception to Form I-864 requirement).** Certain exceptions apply: The petitioner need not submit a Form I-864 if either the immigrant or the immigrant's spouse or parent has already worked in the U.S. for 40 quarters as defined by the Social Security system—about ten years. Nor do you need the Form I-864 if the beneficiary is a child (adopted or natural born) who will become a U.S. citizen automatically upon entering the U.S. If you're exempt from the affidavit of support requirement due to one of these exceptions, fill out Form I-864W instead of the regular Form I-864.

☐ **Documents to support Form I-864.** The latest year's tax returns (or IRS transcripts) of the citizen or permanent resident should be attached to the affidavit as proof of financial capacity (or up to three years' worth if it will strengthen your case). Proof of the sponsor's employment should also be attached.

☐ **Additional Form I-864 or I-864A (Contract Between Sponsor and Household Member) if getting help with sponsorship.** If your petitioner doesn't earn enough to meet the government requirements, you'll have to find an additional financial sponsor or another member of the sponsor's household who can add income and assets to the mix.

Sample Sponsor's Job Letter

ABC Company
123 Main Street
Anytown, Anystate 12345

April 24, 20xx

U.S. Citizenship and Immigration Services
26 Federal Plaza
New York, NY 10278

Dear Sir or Madam:

This letter is to certify that Jon Fratellanza has been employed by this company since March 2005 as a widget inspector.

His salary is $850 per week and he is employed on a full-time, permanent basis. His prospects for continued employment with this company are excellent.

Our personnel records indicate that this employee is married. In case of emergency, his spouse, Danielle Fratellanza, must be notified at their home telephone: 111-222-3456.

Sincerely,

Milton Mutter
Milton Mutter
Personnel Director, ABC Company

☐ **Form I-864EZ (for simple cases).** If you are the only person that your petitioner is sponsoring, and your petitioner can meet the sponsorship requirements based upon his or her income alone, it's okay to instead use a shorter version of the form called I-864EZ.

☐ **Job letter for immigrant.** If you are working (with USCIS authorization), you can submit a job letter from your employer in the United States stating your work history, when you started to work, whether your employment is permanent, and how much you earn, along with a payroll statement confirming your earnings.

If you are applying for a green card based on marriage, ask your employer whether it's willing to add to this job letter basic information about your marital status, such as name of spouse and confirmation that he or she is listed as the person to be notified in case of an emergency.

☐ **Form I-944, Declaration of Self-Sufficiency, and accompanying financial information.** (See sample at end of this chapter.) Under new rules, anyone subject to the public charge ground of inadmissibility must fill this form out and provide extensive evidence of the entire household's financial situation and resources, including credit score. Chapter 4 has more on dealing with this requirement. (The main categories of applicants who need not submit it are refugees and asylees, VAWA applicants, and U visa applicants.)

☐ **Form I-693, Medical Examination of Aliens Seeking Adjustment of Status.** This must be filled out by a USCIS-approved doctor and submitted in an unopened envelope. To find a USCIS-approved doctor, go to https://my.uscis.gov/findadoctor and enter your zip code or call the USCIS Contact Center (800-375-5283). You can submit the Form I-693 with your I-485 Application or later, either in response to a USCIS Request for Evidence or when appearing at the local office for your interview.

☐ **Refugees, take note:** If you are a refugee and you had your medical exam overseas, a USCIS-approved doctor will need to complete only the Part 9. Vaccination Record and Parts 1–4 and 6 of Form I-693, as long as your earlier exam didn't turn up any medical grounds of inadmissibility. Your state or local refugee health coordinator might be able to complete Part 9 of the form for you.

☐ **Derivative asylum applicants, take note:** If you had your medical exam overseas, a USCIS-approved doctor will need to complete only the Part 9. Vaccination Record and Parts 1–4 and 6 of Form I-693, as long as no medical grounds of inadmissibility were noted during your exam and you are applying for adjustment of status within one year of becoming eligible to file.

☐ **K nonimmigrant visa holders, take note:** You are not required to have another medical exam, so long as no medical grounds of inadmissibility were noted during your exam (or you received a waiver) and if the Form DS 3025 vaccination record was properly completed and included. Carefully check your overseas medical exam and vaccination record. If you did not have the vaccinations before traveling to the U.S., you will need to have a USCIS-approved doctor complete the Part 9 Vaccination Record and Parts 1–4 and 6 of Form I-693.

☐ **If applying as an asylee or a refugee, proof that you've been physically present in the U.S. for at least a year.** This could be a letter verifying your employment, an apartment lease, or school records. You'll also need to include evidence of any trips you've made outside the U.S. since gaining asylum. (Remember, if you've made any trips to the country you fled from, you might have canceled your eligibility and should see a lawyer.)

☐ **A copy of your birth certificate.** Include a word-for-word translation, if it is not in English. Be sure the translator is not related to you and have him or her sign an attached statement confirming that the translation is complete and accurate and that the translator is competent to translate from the foreign language into English.

☐ **Passport-style color photographs.** If requesting Advance Parole and an EAD, submit six passport-style, color photographs. USCIS requires two for each of Forms I-485, I-765, and I-131. It's good idea to put your name and A number (if any) on the back of the photos. If filing Form I-130 along with your adjustment package based on marriage to a U.S. citizen, also include two photos of the U.S. citizen petitioner.

☐ **Filing fee.** USCIS charges fees for handling applications, based on which forms you submit and the applicant's age. Check www.uscis.gov/i-485 for a current list of fees. As of the date that this book went to print, the fee to file Form I-485 is $1,140 (with the exception of refugees, who pay no fee, and applicants under age 14 who are filing with at least one parent, who owe a fee total of $750). There is an additional fingerprinting ("biometrics") fee of $85 for people between ages 14 and 78, which can be paid with the filing fee. Make checks or money orders payable to the U.S. Department of Homeland Security. You can also pay by credit card, using Form G-1450, Authorization for Credit Card Transactions and placing this on top of the other paperwork you send. Keep in mind that the few applicants who will file Form I-485, Supplement A with their applications will also need to pay a penalty fee of $1,000.

☐ **Form G-1145.** While not required, it is a good idea to also file Form G-1145, so as to receive an email and/or text notification from USCIS letting you know that your application has been accepted.

3. Submission Procedures

Years ago, people could walk the application right into a local USCIS office. Now, however, you'll have to mail your application to a service center or an out-of-state processing office. See the chart below for the appropriate address.

D. After You Apply

After you've submitted your adjustment of status application, USCIS should send you a receipt notice (on Form I-797C). This will confirm that your application contained everything it should have, and that you're now in line for an adjustment of status interview.

You can use the number on your receipt notice to sign up for automatic email and/or text updates letting you know when mail is sent regarding your application. To sign up for these, go to the USCIS website, www.uscis.gov, and click "Check Your Case Status." Enter your receipt number, then click "Check Status." On this page, you can also create an account to get case status updates about your application.

If your application was incomplete, you will receive a letter indicating what's missing, and you should reply as soon as possible. How long you'll have to wait for your adjustment of status interview depends on how backed up your local USCIS office is. (These interviews are held locally, at a different office than the one you submitted your application to.) Several months is typical, but it's not unheard of for it to take a year or longer.

Some weeks after you submit your application, you'll be called in to have your fingerprints taken for your security checks.

During this wait, it's best not to take any long trips or move to a different address. USCIS won't give you much advance notice of your interview date, usually about a month or so.

Travel Outside the U.S. While Awaiting Your Interview

As discussed earlier, you or your minor children should not leave the United States while waiting for your adjustment of status interview without first applying for and receiving Advance Parole. If you didn't apply for Advance Parole when you filed your adjustment of status application, you can do so later, by submitting Form I-131 to the designated lockbox for the office handling your file. Check the USCIS website for the current address. The current filing fee is $575.

If you leave without this permission, USCIS will cancel your adjustment of status application. It will assume that your departure shows your lack of interest in receiving your green card in the United States and that you have abandoned your application.

E. Interview and Approval

Although USCIS makes some exceptions, it requires most applicants to attend an interview at a local USCIS office before approving them for permanent residence and a green card. You'll get a form letter (see the sample below) advising you of the interview date and location, and telling you what to bring along.

The required documents normally include a photo identification; recent financial records from whoever signed the affidavit of support, to show continuing employment and ownership of assets; documents updating other information in your application, for example if you've changed your name; and originals of your birth certificate, passport, visas, and other documents you've submitted copies of in connection with your application (these are for the USCIS officer to view, not keep); and documents showing any changes in the information on your application, such as a new employer.

Where to Send an Adjustment of Status Application

If you're applying based on:	Send your adjustment of status application to:
A family relationship (for example, you're the spouse, widow, parent, or child of a U.S. citizen, or the spouse or child of a U.S. permanent resident); as a winner of the diversity visa lottery; as someone eligible for registry; as a special immigrant member of the Armed Forces; or as an Amerasian	USCIS P.O. Box 805887, Chicago, IL 60680-4120 (if you're using the U.S. Postal Service) or USCIS, Attn: FBAS 131 South Dearborn—3rd Floor, Chicago, IL 60603-5517 (if you're using a private courier)
Having held asylum or refugee status for at least one year and you live in one of the following states: AK, AZ, CA, CO, Commonwealth of Northern Mariana Islands, Guam, HI, IA ID, IL, IN, KS, MI, MN, MO, MT, ND, NE, NV, OH, OR, SD, UT, WA, WI, or WY	USCIS, P.O. Box 21281, Phoenix, AZ 85036 (if you're using the U.S. Postal Service) or USCIS, Attn: AOS, 1820 E. Skyharbor Circle S, Suite 100, Phoenix, AZ 85034 (if you're using a private courier)
Having held asylum or refugee status for at least one year and you live in one of the following states: AL, AR, CT, DE, FL, GA, KY, LA, MA, MD, ME, MS, NC, NH, NJ, NM, NY, OK, PA, Puerto Rico, RI, SC, TN, TX, VA, VT, U.S. Virgin Islands, WV, or Washington, DC	USCIS, P.O. Box 660867, Dallas, TX 75266 (if you're using the U.S. Postal Service) or USCIS, Attn: AOS, 2501 S State Hwy. 121 Business, Suite 400, Lewisville, TX 75067 (if you're using a private courier)
Having an approved petition as an Afghan or Iraqi translator	USCIS, Nebraska Service Center, P.O. Box 87485, Lincoln, NE 68501-7485
As a battered spouse or child or a T or U visa applicant	USCIS, Vermont Service Center, Attn: CRU, 75 Lower Welden Street, St. Albans, VT 05479-0001

If you're applying based on marriage, you'll also need to bring documents proving that your marriage is the real thing, such as copies of your home mortgage or lease, joint credit card statements, children's birth certificates, and more.

Then there's the question of whom to bring along. Everyone who submitted a green card application and is mentioned in the interview notice should go along, including children. And if the green cards are based on marriage, the U.S. petitioner needs to be there as well. For other family relationships, however—for example if you're getting a green card as the brother, sister, parent, or child of a U.S. citizen—the rules are less strict. USCIS would prefer to see the petitioner there, first off to make sure that he or she is still alive, and in case questions arise about the affidavit of support. But if that's inconvenient, for example if the petitioner lives in another part of the U.S., you can go to your appointment without the petitioner. However, it's best to bring a recent, signed, sworn statement by the petitioner explaining the situation and providing a phone number in case USCIS wants to follow up.

When bringing new documents, be sure to make copies of any that you don't want to leave with USCIS—they're usually happy with copies, particularly if they can view the original when you bring it. They're often unable or unwilling, however, to make photocopies for you, so you must either bring a copy or lose your original to the USCIS file.

If you don't speak English, you'll need to bring your own interpreter. You don't need to spend money on a professional—a friend or family member over 18 who is a legal U.S. resident will do. But it's worth spending the money if you don't know anyone who's truly fluent in both English and your native language—your future is at stake here, and a little confusion could delay or destroy your hopes of getting a green card.

> **! CAUTION**
> **Arrive on time—and follow the rules.** Leave extra time for parking and passing through the security guard post at the USCIS office. Remember, this is a federal government building, so they'll X-ray your possessions and confiscate pocket knives or other illegal materials. They may also prohibit other items, such as cell phones and food. If you arrive late, you will probably lose your chance to be interviewed that day, and go through major hassles getting USCIS to reschedule you.

At your interview, a USCIS officer will review your application, ask you some questions, and presumably approve you for a green card. Most of the questions will relate to what's already on your application,

such as your current address, how you last entered the United States, and whether you have a criminal record or are otherwise ineligible for a green card.

If you're applying based on marriage, be prepared to answer additional questions to prove that your marriage is the real thing, such as how you met, details of your wedding, and details about your house and your life together.

Interview Tips for Spouses

If you are requesting an adjustment of status as the spouse of a U.S. citizen or permanent resident, USCIS will require a personal interview with you both before granting your application.

Bring copies of all the forms relevant to your application, along with evidence of a bona fide marriage—such as wedding pictures, joint bank statements, rental agreements, children's birth certificates, health insurance contracts, and more. (See Chapter 7.)

If you've got solid documentary evidence of your real marriage, the officer is likely to ask only a few questions. If, on the other hand, the documents are weak, or you and your spouse don't seem able to answer the questions about your marriage, you may be sent for what's called a "fraud interview." This means that you and your spouse will each separately meet with the USCIS officer, who will ask each of you the same set of questions, and then check whether your answers match up. If you don't already have an attorney, this is a good time to ask that the interview be postponed, so that you can return with legal help.

Most interviews last 20 to 30 minutes. Answer the questions courteously and honestly—but don't volunteer extra information. Saying too much wastes the officer's time and might bring to light information that would have been better left unsaid.

If everything is in order, your application for adjustment of status should be approved. If you are not approved at your interview, you will later be notified of the approval by mail.

Your green card—which resembles a driver's license in size and format—will be sent by mail to your address within several weeks after approval. Be sure to inform USCIS of any change of address, because your green card might not be forwarded to you by the post office. Even after you get your green card, you are obligated to send USCIS written word every time your address changes—see Chapter 23 for this and other important rules on keeping your right to a green card.

You are now a lawful permanent resident who is authorized to work and stay in the United States legally.

SEE AN EXPERT

If your application is denied, consult an experienced immigration attorney. Unless you have some other visa or legal status in the United States, your file will be transferred to the Immigration Court for removal proceedings. See Chapter 24 for advice on finding a good attorney.

Immigrant Story: Proving a Real Marriage

Brian, a U.S. citizen, and Toshi, from Japan, met and fell in love while they were in college in Champaign, Illinois. Brian graduated two years ahead of Toshi, and got a great job in Atlanta. They corresponded long distance, and the next year got married and applied for Toshi's green card.

However, by the time Toshi got called for her adjustment of status interview, the couple was still not living together. They were worried that the immigration officer would not believe that their marriage was the real thing. After much thought, here are the documents they came up with to prove their relationship:

- college receipts showing that Brian was helping pay for Toshi's education
- sworn statements from Toshi's dormmates attesting to Brian's frequent visits
- documents showing that Toshi is the beneficiary of Brian's life insurance policy and 401(k)
- letter from a fertility specialist that Brian and Toshi had consulted about her difficulty in getting pregnant, and
- copies of emails, texts, and phone bills showing their frequent communication.

Brian and Toshi easily answered all the officer's questions at the interview, and Toshi was granted U.S. permanent residence.

Sample Interview Appointment Notice

Department of Homeland Security U.S. Citizenship and Immigration Services	**Form I-797C, Notice of Action**

THIS NOTICE DOES NOT GRANT ANY IMMIGRATION STATUS OR BENEFIT.

REQUEST FOR APPLICANT TO APPEAR FOR INITIAL INTERVIEW		**Notice Date** November 07, 2019
Case Type FORM I485, APPLICATION TO REGISTER PERMANENT RESIDENCE OR ADJUST STATUS		**A#** 099 909 909
Receipt Number MSC1912345678	**Received Date** September 09, 2019	**Priority Date** September 09, 2019
		Page 1 of 2

```
HAI-ZI ZHANG                                          A Number
c/o ILONA BRAY
950 PARKER ST.                                    A 099 909 909
BERKELEY, CA 94710
                                                  Receipt Number

                                                  MSC 191 234 5678
```

You are hereby notified to appear for the interview appointment, as scheduled below, for the completion of your Application to Register Permanent Residence or Adjust Status (Form I-485) and any supporting applications or petitions. *Failure to appear for this interview and/or failure to bring the below listed items will result in the denial of your application. (8 CFR 103.2(b)(13))*

Who should come with you?

- *If your eligibility is based on your marriage, your husband or wife must come with you to the interview.*
- If you do not speak English fluently, you should bring an interpreter.
- Your attorney or authorized representative may come with you to the interview.
- If your eligibility is based on a parent/child relationship and the child is a minor, the petitioning parent and the child must appear for the interview.

NOTE: Every adult (over 18 years of age) who comes to the interview must bring Government-issued photo identification, such as a driver's license or ID card, in order to enter the building and to verify his/her identity at the time of the interview. You do not need to bring your children unless otherwise instructed. Please be on time, but do not arrive more than 30 minutes early. We may record or videotape your interview.

YOU MUST BRING THE FOLLOWING ITEMS WITH YOU: (Please use as a checklist to prepare for your interview)

- This Interview Notice and your Government issued photo identification.
- A completed medical examination (Form I-693) and vaccination supplement in a sealed envelope (unless already submitted).
- A completed Affidavit(s) of Support (Form I-864) with all required evidence, including the following, for each of your sponsors (unless already submitted):
  - Federal Income Tax returns and W-2's, or certified IRS printouts, for the most recent tax year;
  - Letters from each current employer, verifying current rate of pay and average weekly hours, and pay stubs for the past 2 months;
  - Evidence of your sponsor's and/or co-sponsor's United States Citizenship or Lawful Permanent Resident status.
- All documentation establishing your eligibility for Lawful Permanent Resident status.
- Any immigration-related documentation ever issued to you, including any Employment Authorization Document (EAD) and any Authorization for Advance Parole (Form I-512).
- All travel documents used to enter the United States, including Passports, Advance Parole documents (I-512) and I-94s (Arrival/Departure Document).
- Your Birth Certificate.
- Your petitioner's Birth Certificate and your petitioner's evidence of United States Citizenship or Lawful Permanent Resident Status.
- If you have children, bring a Birth Certificate for each of your children.
- If your eligibility is based on your marriage, in addition to your spouse coming to the interview with you, bring:
  - A certified copy of your Marriage Document issued by the appropriate civil authority;
  - Your spouse's Birth Certificate and your spouse's evidence of United States Citizenship or Lawful Permanent Resident status;
  - If either you or your spouse were ever married before, all divorce decrees/death certificates for each prior marriage/former spouse;
  - Birth Certificates for all children of this marriage, and custody papers for your children and for your spouse's children not living with you;
- Supporting evidence of your relationship, such as copies of any documentation regarding joint assets or liabilities you and your spouse may have together. This may include: tax returns, bank statements, insurance documents (car, life, health), property documents (car, house, etc.), rental agreements, utility bills, credit cards, contracts, leases, photos, correspondence and/or any other documents you feel may substantiate your relationship.
- Original and copy of each supporting document that you submitted with your application. Otherwise, we may keep your originals for our records.
- If you have ever been arrested, bring the related Police Report and the original or certified Final Court Disposition for each arrest, even if the charges have been dismissed or expunged. If no court record is available, bring a letter from the court with jurisdiction indicating this.

If you have questions, please call the USCIS Contact Center at 1-800-375-5283 (hearing impaired TDD service is 1-800-767-1833)

PLEASE COME TO: U.S. Citizenship and Immigration Services 550 MAIN STREET JW PECK FEDERAL BLDG, ROOM 4-001 CINCINNATI, OH 45202	**ON:** Friday, December 20, 2019 **AT:** 10:30AM
1	

If this is an interview or biometrics appointment notice, please see the back of this notice for important information.   Form I-797C 04/01/19

Sample Form I-485, Application to Register Permanent Residence or Adjust Status (page 1)

Application to Register Permanent Residence or Adjust Status

Department of Homeland Security
U.S. Citizenship and Immigration Services

**USCIS
Form I-485**
OMB No. 1615-0023
Expires 10/31/2021

For USCIS Use Only

Preference Category:

Country Chargeable:

Priority Date:

Date Form I-693 Received:

☐ Applicant Interviewed	☐ Interview Waived

Date of Initial Interview: _____

Lawful Permanent Resident as of: _____

Receipt

Action Block

Section of Law
☐ INA 209(a)　☐ INA 249
☐ INA 209(b)　☐ Sec. 13, Act of 9/11/57
☐ INA 245(a)　☐ Cuban Adjustment Act
☐ INA 245(i)　☐ Other _____
☐ INA 245(m)

To be completed by an attorney or accredited representative (if any).

☐ Select this box if Form G-28 is attached.

Volag Number (if any)

Attorney State Bar Number (if applicable)

Attorney or Accredited Representative USCIS Online Account Number (if any)

▶ **START HERE - Type or print in black ink.**

A-Number ▶ A- 1 2 3 4 5 6 7 8 9

NOTE TO ALL APPLICANTS: If you do not completely fill out this application or fail to submit required documents listed in the Instructions, U.S. Citizenship and Immigration Services (USCIS) may deny your application.

Part 1. Information About You (individual applying for lawful permanent residence)

Your Current Legal Name (do not provide a nickname)

1.a. Family Name (Last Name) **Michelski**
1.b. Given Name (First Name) **Anda**
1.c. Middle Name

Other Names You Have Used Since Birth (if applicable)

NOTE: Provide all other names you have ever used, including your family name at birth, other legal names, nicknames, aliases, and assumed names. If you need extra space to complete this section, use the space provided in **Part 14. Additional Information**.

2.a. Family Name (Last Name)
2.b. Given Name (First Name)
2.c. Middle Name

3.a. Family Name (Last Name)
3.b. Given Name (First Name)
3.c. Middle Name

4.a. Family Name (Last Name)
4.b. Given Name (First Name)
4.c. Middle Name

Other Information About You

5. Date of Birth (mm/dd/yyyy) **06/28/1986**

NOTE: In addition to providing your actual date of birth, include any other dates of birth you have used in connection with any legal names or non-legal names in the space provided in **Part 14. Additional Information**.

6. Gender ☐ Male ☒ Female

7. City or Town of Birth **Sofia**

Form I-485 Edition 10/15/19

Sample Form I-485, Application to Register Permanent Residence or Adjust Status (page 2)

A-Number ▶ A- 1 2 3 4 5 6 7 8 9

Part 1. Information About You (Person applying for lawful permanent residence) (continued)

8. Country of Birth
Bulgaria

9. Country of Citizenship or Nationality
Bulgaria

10. Alien Registration Number (A-Number) (if any)
▶ A- 1 2 3 4 5 6 7 8 9

NOTE: If you have **EVER** used other A-Numbers, include the additional A-Numbers in the space provided in **Part 14. Additional Information**.

11. USCIS Online Account Number (if any) ▶

12. U.S. Social Security Number (if any) ▶

U.S. Mailing Address

13.a. In Care Of Name (if any)

13.b. Street Number and Name
68 Waterton Boulevard

13.c. ☒ Apt. ☐ Ste. ☐ Flr. 12

13.d. City or Town Erie

13.e. State PA **13.f.** ZIP Code 19380

Alternate and/or Safe Mailing Address

If you are applying based on the Violence Against Women Act (VAWA) or as a special immigrant juvenile, human trafficking victim (T nonimmigrant), or victim of qualifying criminal activity (U nonimmigrant) and you do not want USCIS to send notices about this application to your home, you may provide an alternative and/or safe mailing address.

14.a. In Care Of Name (if any)

14.b. Street Number and Name

14.c. ☐ Apt. ☐ Ste. ☐ Flr.

14.d. City or Town

14.e. State **14.f.** ZIP Code

Recent Immigration History

Provide the information for **Item Numbers 15. - 19.** if you last entered the United States using a passport or travel document.

15. Passport Number Used at Last Arrival
S1343944

16. Travel Document Number Used at Last Arrival

17. Expiration Date of this Passport or Travel Document (mm/dd/yyyy) 08/09/2022

18. Country that Issued this Passport or Travel Document
Bulgaria

19. Nonimmigrant Visa Number from this Passport (if any)
K1234567

Place of Last Arrival into the United States

20.a. City or Town New York

20.b. State NY

21. Date of Last Arrival (mm/dd/yyyy) 12/06/2019

When I last arrived in the United States, I:

22.a. ☒ Was inspected at a port of entry and admitted as (for example, exchange visitor; visitor, waived through; temporary worker; student):
K-1 Fiance

22.b. ☐ Was inspected at a port of entry and paroled as (for example, humanitarian parole, Cuban parole):

22.c. ☐ Came into the United States without admission or parole.

22.d. ☐ Other:

If you were issued a Form I-94 Arrival-Departure Record Number:

23.a. Form I-94 Arrival-Departure Record Number
▶ 9 9 2 5 5 5 7 6 6 A 1

23.b. Expiration Date of Authorized Stay Shown on Form I-94 (mm/dd/yyyy) 03/06/2020

23.c. Status on Form I-94 (for example, class of admission, or paroled, if paroled)
K-1

Sample Form I-485, Application to Register Permanent Residence or Adjust Status (page 3)

A-Number ▶ A- | 1 | 2 | 3 | 4 | 5 | 6 | 7 | 8 | 9 |

Part 1. Information About You (Person applying for lawful permanent residence) (continued)

24. What is your current immigration status (if it has changed since your arrival)?

Provide your name exactly as it appears on your Form I-94 (if any)

25.a. Family Name (Last Name) | Michelski

25.b. Given Name (First Name) | Anda

25.c. Middle Name |

Part 2. Application Type or Filing Category

1. I am filing this Form I-485 as a (select **only one** box):

☐ Principal applicant

☐ Derivative applicant

NOTE: Attach a copy of the Form I-797 receipt or approval notice for the underlying petition or application, as appropriate.

I am applying as a principal or derivative applicant to register lawful permanent residence or adjust status to that of a lawful permanent resident based on the following immigrant category (select **only one** category). (See the Form I-485 Instructions for more information, including any **Additional Instructions** that relate to the immigrant category you select.):

Family-based

2.a. ☐ Immediate relative spouse of a U.S. citizen, parent of a U.S. citizen if the U.S. citizen is 21 years of age or older, and unmarried child under 21 years of age of a U.S. citizen, Form I-130

2.b. ☐ Other relative of a U.S. citizen or relative of a lawful permanent resident under the family-based preference categories, Form I-130

2.c. ☒ Individual admitted to the United States as a fiancé(e) or child of a fiancé(e) of a U.S. citizen, Form I-129F (K-1/K-2 Nonimmigrant)

2.d. ☐ Widow or widower of a U.S. citizen, Form I-360

2.e. ☐ VAWA self-petitioner, Form I-360

2.f. ☐ Spouse, child, or parent of a deceased U.S. active duty service member in the armed forces under the National Defense Authorization Act (NDAA), Form I-130 or Form I-360

Employment-based

3.a. ☐ Alien worker, Form I-140 (if you select this box, you must answer **Item Number 9.a.**)

3.b. ☐ Alien entrepreneur, Form I-526

Special Immigrant

4.a. ☐ Religious worker, Form I-360

4.b. ☐ Special immigrant juvenile, Form I-360

4.c. ☐ Certain Afghan or Iraqi national, Form I-360

4.d. ☐ Certain international broadcaster, Form I-360

4.e. ☐ Certain G-4 international organization or family member or NATO-6 employee or family member, Form I-360

4.f. ☐ Certain U.S. armed forces members (also known as the Six and Six program), Form I-360

4.g. ☐ Panama Canal Zone employees, Form I-360

4.h. ☐ Certain Physicians, Form I-360

4.i. ☐ Certain employee or former employee of the U.S. Government abroad, Form I-360

Asylee or Refugee

5.a. ☐ Asylum status (INA section 208), Form I-589 or Form I-730

5.b. ☐ Refugee status (INA section 207), Form I-590 or Form I-730

Human Trafficking Victim or Victim of Qualifying Criminal Activity

6.a. ☐ Human trafficking victim (T Nonimmigrant), Form I-914 or derivative family member, Form I-914A

6.b. ☐ Victim of Qualifying Criminal Activity (U Nonimmigrant), Form I-918, derivative family member, Form I-918A, or qualifying family member, Form I-929

Sample Form I-485, Application to Register Permanent Residence or Adjust Status (page 4)

A-Number ▶ A- | 1 | 2 | 3 | 4 | 5 | 6 | 7 | 8 | 9 |

Part 2. Application Type or Filing Category (continued)

Special Programs Based on Certain Public Laws

7.a. ☐ Applicant adjusting under the Cuban Adjustment Act

7.b. ☐ Applicant adjusting under the Cuban Adjustment Act for battered spouses and children

7.c. ☐ Applicant adjusting based on dependent status under the Haitian Refugee Immigrant Fairness Act

7.d. ☐ Applicant adjusting based on dependent status under the Haitian Refugee Immigrant Fairness Act for battered spouses and children

7.e. ☐ Lautenberg Parolees

7.f. ☐ Diplomats or high ranking officials unable to return home (Section 13 of the Act of September 11, 1957)

7.g. ☐ Applicant adjusting under the Indochinese Parole Adjustment Act of 2000

7.h. ☐ Applicant adjusting under the Amerasian Act (October 22, 1982), Form I-360

Additional Options

8.a. ☐ Diversity Visa program

8.b. ☐ Continuous residence in the United States since before January 1, 1972 ("Registry")

8.c. ☐ Individual born in the United States under diplomatic status

8.d. ☐ S nonimmigrants and qualifying family members (only law enforcement agencies can file Form I-485 for someone in this category.)

8.e. ☐ Other eligibility (see the Form I-485 Instructions, **Who May Form I-485, Item Number 3. Other Immigrant Categories** for examples)

[   ]

Additional Alien Worker Information

Answer **Item Number 9.a.** only if you selected **Item Number 3.a.** "Alien worker, Form I-140."

9.a. Did a relative file the associated Form I-140 for you or does a relative have a significant ownership interest (five percent or more) in the business that filed Form I-140 for you? (The relative must be your husband, wife, father, mother, child, adult son, adult daughter, brother, or sister.)

☐ Yes ☐ No

If you answered "Yes" to **Item Number 9.a.**, answer **Item Numbers 9.b. - 9.c.** If you answered "No," skip to **Item Number 10.**

9.b. How is your relative related to you?

☐ Brother or sister

☐ Husband, wife, father, mother, child, adult son, or adult daughter

9.c. This relative is a:

☐ U.S. citizen

☐ U.S. national

☐ Lawful permanent resident

☐ None of the above

10. Regardless of the immigrant category you are adjusting under, do you hold:

VAWA self-petitioner status ☐ Yes ☐ No

Victim of Qualifying Criminal Activity (U nonimmigrant) status ☐ Yes ☐ No

Human trafficking victim (T nonimmigrant) status ☐ Yes ☐ No

INA Section 245(i)

11. Are you applying for adjustment based on the Immigration and Nationality Act (INA) section 245(i)?

☐ Yes ☒ No

NOTE: If you answered "Yes" to **Item Number 11.**, you must have selected a family-based, employment-based, special immigrant, or Diversity Visa immigrant category listed above in **Item Numbers 2.a. - 8.e.** as the basis for your application for adjustment of status. Fill out the rest of this application **AND** Supplement A to Form I-485, Adjustment of Status Under Section 245(i) (Supplement A). For detailed filing instructions, read the Form I-485 Instructions (including any **Additional Instructions** that relate to the immigrant category that you selected in **Item Numbers 2.a. - 8.e.**) and Supplement A Instructions.

Information About Your Immigrant Category

If you are the **principal applicant**, provide the following information.

12. Receipt Number of Underlying Petition (if any)

[WAC1990012345]

13. Priority Date from Underlying Petition (if any) (mm/dd/yyyy)

[n/a]

Sample Form I-485, Application to Register Permanent Residence or Adjust Status (page 5)

A-Number ▶ A- 1 2 3 4 5 6 7 8 9

Part 2. Application Type or Filing Category (continued)

If you are a **derivative applicant** (the spouse or unmarried child under 21 years of age of a principal applicant), provide the following information for the **principal applicant**.

Principal Applicant's Name

14.a. Family Name (Last Name)

14.b. Given Name (First Name)

14.c. Middle Name

15. Principal Applicant's A-Number (if any)

▶ A-

16. Principal Applicant's Date of Birth (mm/dd/yyyy)

17. Receipt Number of Principal's Underlying Petition (if any)

▶

18. Priority Date of Principal Applicant's Underlying Petition (if any) (mm/dd/yyyy)

Part 3. Additional Information About You

1. Have you ever applied for an immigrant visa to obtain permanent resident status at a U.S. Embassy or U.S. Consulate abroad? ☐ Yes ☒ No

If you answered "Yes" to **Item Number 1.**, complete **Item Numbers 2.a. - 4.** below. If you need extra space to complete this section, use the space provided in **Part 14. Additional Information**.

Location of U.S. Embassy or U.S. Consulate

2.a. City

2.b. Country

3. Decision (for example, approved, refused, denied, withdrawn)

4. Date of Decision (mm/dd/yyyy)

Address History

Provide physical addresses for everywhere you have lived during the last five years, whether inside or outside the United States. Provide your current address first. If you need extra space to complete this section, use the space provided in **Part 14. Additional Information**.

Physical Address 1 (current address)

5.a. Street Number and Name | 68 Waterton Boulevard

5.b. ☒ Apt. ☐ Ste. ☐ Flr. | 12

5.c. City or Town | Erie

5.d. State | PA **5.e.** ZIP Code | 19380

5.f. Province

5.g. Postal Code

5.h. Country | USA

Dates of Residence

6.a. From (mm/dd/yyyy) | 12/06/2019

6.b. To (mm/dd/yyyy) | Present

Physical Address 2

7.a. Street Number and Name | 500 Hladilnika

7.b. ☒ Apt. ☐ Ste. ☐ Flr. | 4

7.c. City or Town | Sofia

7.d. State | **7.e.** ZIP Code

7.f. Province

7.g. Postal Code | 1113

7.h. Country | Bulgaria

Sample Form I-485, Application to Register Permanent Residence or Adjust Status (page 6)

A-Number ▶ A- | 1 | 2 | 3 | 4 | 5 | 6 | 7 | 8 | 9 |

Part 3. Additional Information About You (continued)

Dates of Residence

8.a. From (mm/dd/yyyy) `06/01/2011`

8.b. To (mm/dd/yyyy) `12/05/2019`

Provide your most recent address outside the United States where you lived for more than one year (if not already listed above).

9.a. Street Number and Name

9.b. ☐ Apt. ☐ Ste. ☐ Flr.

9.c. City or Town

9.d. State   **9.e.** ZIP Code

9.f. Province

9.g. Postal Code

9.h. Country

Dates of Residence

10.a. From (mm/dd/yyyy)

10.b. To (mm/dd/yyyy)

Employment History

Provide your employment history for the last five years, whether inside or outside the United States. Provide the most recent employment first. If you need extra space to complete this section, use the space provided in **Part 14. Additional Information**.

Employer 1 (current or most recent)

11. Name of Employer or Company
`Unemployed`

Address of Employer or Company

12.a. Street Number and Name

12.b. ☐ Apt. ☐ Ste. ☐ Flr.

12.c. City or Town

12.d. State   **12.e.** ZIP Code

12.f. Province

12.g. Postal Code

12.h. Country

13. Your Occupation

Dates of Employment

14.a. From (mm/dd/yyyy) `12/01/2019`

14.b. To (mm/dd/yyyy) `Present`

Employer 2

15. Name of Employer or Company
`National Museum of History`

Address of Employer or Company

16.a. Street Number and Name `1618 Rezodemtsia Boyana`

16.b. ☐ Apt. ☐ Ste. ☐ Flr.

16.c. City or Town `Sofia`

16.d. State   **16.e.** ZIP Code

16.f. Province

16.g. Postal Code `1073`

16.h. Country
`Bulgaria`

17. Your Occupation
`Curator`

Dates of Employment

18.a. From (mm/dd/yyyy) `05/01/2011`

18.b. To (mm/dd/yyyy) `11/30/2019`

Sample Form I-485, Application to Register Permanent Residence or Adjust Status (page 7)

A-Number ▶ A- | 1 | 2 | 3 | 4 | 5 | 6 | 7 | 8 | 9 |

Part 3. Additional Information About You (continued)

Provide your most recent employment outside of the United States (if not already listed above).

19. Name of Employer or Company

Address of Employer or Company

20.a. Street Number and Name

20.b. ☐ Apt. ☐ Ste. ☐ Flr.

20.c. City or Town

20.d. State [   ]   **20.e.** ZIP Code

20.f. Province

20.g. Postal Code

20.h. Country

21. Your Occupation

Dates of Employment

22.a. From (mm/dd/yyyy)

22.b. To (mm/dd/yyyy)

Part 4. Information About Your Parents

Information About Your Parent 1

Parent 1's Legal Name

1.a. Family Name (Last Name)   Michelski

1.b. Given Name (First Name)   Anastasia

1.c. Middle Name

Parent 1's Name at Birth (if different than above)

2.a. Family Name (Last Name)   Antov

2.b. Given Name (First Name)

2.c. Middle Name

3. Date of Birth (mm/dd/yyyy)   04/19/1962

4. Gender   ☐ Male   ☒ Female

5. City or Town of Birth   Sofia

6. Country of Birth   Bulgaria

7. Current City or Town of Residence (if living)   Sofia

8. Current Country of Residence (if living)   Bulgaria

Information About Your Parent 2

Parent 2's Legal Name

9.a. Family Name (Last Name)   Michelski

9.b. Given Name (First Name)   Liski

9.c. Middle Name

Parent 2's Name at Birth (if different than above)

10.a. Family Name (Last Name)

10.b. Given Name (First Name)

10.c. Middle Name

11. Date of Birth (mm/dd/yyyy)   07/25/1961

12. Gender   ☒ Male   ☐ Female

13. City or Town of Birth   Sofia

14. Country of Birth   Bulgaria

15. Current City or Town of Residence (if living)   Sofia

16. Current Country of Residence (if living)   Bulgaria

Sample Form I-485, Application to Register Permanent Residence or Adjust Status (page 8)

A-Number ▶ A- 1 2 3 4 5 6 7 8 9

Part 5. Information About Your Marital History

1. What is your current marital status?

☐ Single, Never Married ☒ Married ☐ Divorced

☐ Widowed ☐ Marriage Annulled

☐ Legally Separated

2. If you are married, is your spouse a current member of the U.S. armed forces or U.S. Coast Guard?

☐ N/A ☐ Yes ☒ No

3. How many times have you been married (including annulled marriages and marriages to the same individual)?

1

Information About Your Current Marriage (including if you are legally separated)

If you are currently married, provide the following information about your current spouse.

Current Spouse's Legal Name

4.a. Family Name (Last Name): Brown

4.b. Given Name (First Name): Andrew

4.c. Middle Name: Brian

5. A-Number (if any) ▶ A-

6. Current Spouse's Date of Birth (mm/dd/yyyy): 11/11/1984

7. Date of Marriage to Current Spouse (mm/dd/yyyy): 02/03/2020

Current Spouse's Place of Birth

8.a. City or Town: Erie

8.b. State or Province: PA

8.c. Country: USA

Place of Marriage to Current Spouse

9.a. City or Town: Erie

9.b. State or Province: PA

9.c. Country: USA

10. Is your current spouse applying with you?

☐ Yes ☒ No

Information About Prior Marriages (if any)

If you have been married before, whether in the United States or in any other country, provide the following information about your prior spouse. If you have had more than one previous marriage, use the space provided in **Part 14. Additional Information** to provide the information below.

Prior Spouse's Legal Name (provide family name before marriage)

11.a. Family Name (Last Name):

11.b. Given Name (First Name):

11.c. Middle Name:

12. Prior Spouse's Date of Birth (mm/dd/yyyy):

13. Date of Marriage to Prior Spouse (mm/dd/yyyy):

Place of Marriage to Prior Spouse

14.a. City or Town:

14.b. State or Province:

14.c. Country:

15. Date Marriage with Prior Spouse Legally Ended (mm/dd/yyyy):

Sample Form I-485, Application to Register Permanent Residence or Adjust Status (page 9)

A-Number ▶ A- 1 2 3 4 5 6 7 8 9

Part 5. Information About Your Marital History (continued)

Place Where Marriage with Prior Spouse Legally Ended

16.a. City or Town

16.b. State or Province

16.c. Country

Part 6. Information About Your Children

1. Indicate the total number of ALL living children (including adult sons and daughters) that you have.

   NOTE: The term "children" includes all biological or legally adopted children, as well as current stepchildren, of any age, whether born in the United States or other countries, married or unmarried, living with you or elsewhere and includes any missing children and those born to you outside of marriage.

   `0`

Provide the following information for each of your children. If you have more than three children, use the space provided in **Part 14. Additional Information**.

Child 1

Current Legal Name

2.a. Family Name (Last Name)

2.b. Given Name (First Name)

2.c. Middle Name

3. A-Number (if any) ▶ A-

4. Date of Birth (mm/dd/yyyy) 11/11/1984

5. Country of Birth

6. Is this child applying with you? ☐ Yes ☐ No

Child 2

Current Legal Name

7.a. Family Name (Last Name)

7.b. Given Name (First Name)

7.c. Middle Name

8. A-Number (if any) ▶ A-

9. Date of Birth (mm/dd/yyyy)

10. Country of Birth

11. Is this child applying with you? ☐ Yes ☐ No

Child 3

Current Legal Name

12.a. Family Name (Last Name)

12.b. Given Name (First Name)

12.c. Middle Name

13. A-Number (if any) ▶ A-

14. Date of Birth (mm/dd/yyyy)

15. Country of Birth

16. Is this child applying with you? ☐ Yes ☐ No

Part 7. Biographic Information

1. Ethnicity (Select **only one** box)
   ☐ Hispanic or Latino
   ☒ Not Hispanic or Latino

2. Race (Select **all applicable** boxes)
   ☒ White
   ☐ Asian
   ☐ Black or African American
   ☐ American Indian or Alaska Native
   ☐ Native Hawaiian or Other Pacific Islander

Sample Form I-485, Application to Register Permanent Residence or Adjust Status (page 10)

A-Number ▶ A- 1 2 3 4 5 6 7 8 9

Part 7. Biographic Information (continued)

3. Height — Feet 5 — Inches 2

4. Weight — Pounds 1 0 0

5. Eye Color (Select **only one** box)
   - ☐ Black   ☒ Blue   ☐ Brown
   - ☐ Gray   ☐ Green   ☐ Hazel
   - ☐ Maroon   ☐ Pink   ☐ Unknown/Other

6. Hair Color (Select **only one** box)
   - ☐ Bald (No hair)   ☐ Black   ☒ Blond
   - ☐ Brown   ☐ Gray   ☐ Red
   - ☐ Sandy   ☐ White   ☐ Unknown/Other

Part 8. General Eligibility and Inadmissibility Grounds

1. Have you **EVER** been a member of, involved in, or in any way associated with any organization, association, fund, foundation, party, club, society, or similar group in the United States or in any other location in the world including any military service?   ☒ Yes   ☐ No

If you answered "Yes" to **Item Number 1.**, complete **Item Numbers 2. - 13.b.** below. If you need extra space to complete this section, use the space provided in **Part 14. Additional Information**. If you answered "No," but are unsure of your answer, provide an explanation of the events and circumstances in the space provided in **Part 14. Additional Information**.

Organization 1

2. Name of Organization
   National Curators Committee

3.a. City or Town
   Sofia

3.b. State or Province

3.c. Country
   Bulgaria

4. Nature of Group
   Museum professionals group

Dates of Membership or Dates of Involvement

5.a. From (mm/dd/yyyy)   05/01/2011

5.b. To (mm/dd/yyyy)   12/01/2019

Organization 2

6. Name of Organization

7.a. City or Town

7.b. State or Province

7.c. Country

8. Nature of Group

Dates of Membership or Dates of Involvement

9.a. From (mm/dd/yyyy)

9.b. To (mm/dd/yyyy)

Organization 3

10. Name of Organization

11.a. City or Town

11.b. State or Province

11.c. Country

12. Nature of Group

Dates of Membership or Dates of Involvement

13.a. From (mm/dd/yyyy)

13.b. To (mm/dd/yyyy)

Sample Form I-485, Application to Register Permanent Residence or Adjust Status (page 11)

A-Number ▶ A- |1|2|3|4|5|6|7|8|9|

Part 8. General Eligibility and Inadmissibility Grounds (continued)

Answer **Item Numbers 14. - 80.b.** Choose the answer that you think is correct. If you answer "Yes" to any questions **(or if you answer "No," but are unsure of your answer)**, provide an explanation of the events and circumstances in the space provided in **Part 14. Additional Information**.

14. Have you **EVER** been denied admission to the United States? ☐ Yes ☒ No

15. Have you **EVER** been denied a visa to the United States? ☐ Yes ☒ No

16. Have you **EVER** worked in the United States without authorization? ☐ Yes ☒ No

17. Have you **EVER** violated the terms or conditions of your nonimmigrant status? ☐ Yes ☒ No

18. Are you presently or have you **EVER** been in removal, exclusion, rescission, or deportation proceedings? ☐ Yes ☒ No

19. Have you **EVER** been issued a final order of exclusion, deportation, or removal? ☐ Yes ☒ No

20. Have you **EVER** had a prior final order of exclusion, deportation, or removal reinstated? ☐ Yes ☒ No

21. Have you **EVER** held lawful permanent resident status which was later rescinded? ☐ Yes ☒ No

22. Have you **EVER** been granted voluntary departure by an immigration officer or an immigration judge but failed to depart within the allotted time? ☐ Yes ☒ No

23. Have you **EVER** applied for any kind of relief or protection from removal, exclusion, or deportation? ☐ Yes ☒ No

24.a. Have you **EVER** been a J nonimmigrant exchange visitor who was subject to the two-year foreign residence requirement? ☐ Yes ☒ No

If you answered "Yes" to **Item Number 24.a.**, complete **Item Numbers 24.b. - 24.c.** If you answered "No" to **Item Number 24.a.**, skip to **Item Number 25.**

24.b. Have you complied with the foreign residence requirement? ☐ Yes ☐ No

24.c. Have you been granted a waiver or has Department of State issued a favorable waiver recommendation letter for you? ☐ Yes ☐ No

Criminal Acts and Violations

For **Item Numbers 25. - 45.**, you must answer "Yes" to any question that applies to you, even if your records were sealed or otherwise cleared, or even if anyone, including a judge, law enforcement officer, or attorney, told you that you no longer have a record. You must also answer "Yes" to the following questions whether the action or offense occurred here in the United States or anywhere else in the world. If you answer "Yes" to **Item Numbers 25. - 45.**, use the space provided in **Part 14. Additional Information** to provide an explanation that includes why you were arrested, cited, detained, or charged; where you were arrested, cited, detained, or charged; when (date) the event occurred; and the outcome or disposition (for example, no charges filed, charges dismissed, jail, probation, community service).

25. Have you **EVER** been arrested, cited, charged, or detained for any reason by any law enforcement official (including but not limited to any U.S. immigration official or any official of the U.S. armed forces or U.S. Coast Guard)? ☐ Yes ☒ No

26. Have you **EVER** committed a crime of any kind (even if you were not arrested, cited, charged with, or tried for that crime)? ☐ Yes ☒ No

27. Have you **EVER** pled guilty to or been convicted of a crime or offense (even if the violation was subsequently expunged or sealed by a court, or if you were granted a pardon, amnesty, a rehabilitation decree, or other act of clemency)? ☐ Yes ☒ No

NOTE: If you were the beneficiary of a pardon, amnesty, a rehabilitation decree, or other act of clemency, provide documentation of that post-conviction action.

28. Have you **EVER** been ordered punished by a judge or had conditions imposed on you that restrained your liberty (such as a prison sentence, suspended sentence, house arrest, parole, alternative sentencing, drug or alcohol treatment, rehabilitative programs or classes, probation, or community service)? ☐ Yes ☒ No

29. Have you **EVER** been a defendant or the accused in a criminal proceeding (including pre-trial diversion, deferred prosecution, deferred adjudication, or any withheld adjudication)? ☐ Yes ☒ No

30. Have you **EVER** violated (or attempted or conspired to violate) any controlled substance law or regulation of a state, the United States, or a foreign country? ☐ Yes ☒ No

Sample Form I-485, Application to Register Permanent Residence or Adjust Status (page 12)

A-Number ▶ A- | 1 | 2 | 3 | 4 | 5 | 6 | 7 | 8 | 9 |

Part 8. General Eligibility and Inadmissibility Grounds (continued)

31. Have you **EVER** been convicted of two or more offenses (other than purely political offenses) for which the combined sentences to confinement were five years or more? ☐ Yes ☒ No

32. Have you **EVER** illicitly (illegally) trafficked or benefited from the trafficking of any controlled substances, such as chemicals, illegal drugs, or narcotics? ☐ Yes ☒ No

33. Have you **EVER** knowingly aided, abetted, assisted, conspired, or colluded in the illicit trafficking of any illegal narcotic or other controlled substances? ☐ Yes ☒ No

34. Are you the spouse, son, or daughter of a foreign national who illicitly trafficked or aided (or otherwise abetted, assisted, conspired, or colluded) in the illicit trafficking of a controlled substance, such as chemicals, illegal drugs, or narcotics and you obtained, within the last five years, any financial or other benefit from the illegal activity of your spouse or parent, although you knew or reasonably should have known that the financial or other benefit resulted from the illicit activity of your spouse or parent? ☐ Yes ☒ No

35. Have you **EVER** engaged in prostitution or are you coming to the United States to engage in prostitution? ☐ Yes ☒ No

36. Have you **EVER** directly or indirectly procured (or attempted to procure) or imported prostitutes or persons for the purpose of prostitution? ☐ Yes ☒ No

37. Have you **EVER** received any proceeds or money from prostitution? ☐ Yes ☒ No

38. Do you intend to engage in illegal gambling or any other form of commercialized vice, such as prostitution, bootlegging, or the sale of child pornography, while in the United States? ☐ Yes ☒ No

39. Have you **EVER** exercised immunity (diplomatic or otherwise) to avoid being prosecuted for a criminal offense in the United States? ☐ Yes ☒ No

40. Have you **EVER**, while serving as a foreign government official, been responsible for or directly carried out violations of religious freedoms? ☐ Yes ☒ No

41. Have you **EVER** induced by force, fraud, or coercion (or otherwise been involved in) the trafficking of persons for commercial sex acts? ☐ Yes ☒ No

42. Have you **EVER** trafficked a person into involuntary servitude, peonage, debt bondage, or slavery? Trafficking includes recruiting, harboring, transporting, providing, or obtaining a person for labor or services through the use of force, fraud, or coercion. ☐ Yes ☒ No

43. Have you **EVER** knowingly aided, abetted, assisted, conspired, or colluded with others in trafficking persons for commercial sex acts or involuntary servitude, peonage, debt bondage, or slavery? ☐ Yes ☒ No

44. Are you the spouse, son or daughter of a foreign national who engaged in the trafficking of persons and have received or obtained, within the last five years, any financial or other benefits from the illicit activity of your spouse or your parent, although you knew or reasonably should have known that this benefit resulted from the illicit activity of your spouse or parent? ☐ Yes ☒ No

45. Have you **EVER** engaged in money laundering or have you **EVER** knowingly aided, assisted, conspired, or colluded with others in money laundering or do you seek to enter the United States to engage in such activity? ☐ Yes ☒ No

Security and Related

Do you intend to:

46.a. Engage in any activity that violates or evades any law relating to espionage (including spying) or sabotage in the United States? ☐ Yes ☒ No

46.b. Engage in any activity in the United States that violates or evades any law prohibiting the export from the United States of goods, technology, or sensitive information? ☐ Yes ☒ No

46.c. Engage in any activity whose purpose includes opposing, controlling, or overthrowing the U.S. Government by force, violence, or other unlawful means while in the United States? ☐ Yes ☒ No

46.d. Engage in any activity that could endanger the welfare, safety, or security of the United States? ☐ Yes ☒ No

46.e. Engage in any other unlawful activity? ☐ Yes ☒ No

47. Are you engaged in or, upon your entry into the United States, do you intend to engage in any activity that could have potentially serious adverse foreign policy consequences for the United States? ☐ Yes ☒ No

Sample Form I-485, Application to Register Permanent Residence or Adjust Status (page 13)

A-Number ▶ A- | 1 | 2 | 3 | 4 | 5 | 6 | 7 | 8 | 9

Part 8. General Eligibility and Inadmissibility Grounds (continued)

Have you **EVER**:

48.a. Committed, threatened to commit, attempted to commit, conspired to commit, incited, endorsed, advocated, planned, or prepared any of the following: hijacking, sabotage, kidnapping, political assassination, or use of a weapon or explosive to harm another individual or cause substantial damage to property? ☐ Yes ☒ No

48.b. Participated in, or been a member of, a group or organization that did any of the activities described in **Item Number 48.a.**? ☐ Yes ☒ No

48.c. Recruited members or asked for money or things of value for a group or organization that did any of the activities described in **Item Number 48.a.**? ☐ Yes ☒ No

48.d. Provided money, a thing of value, services or labor, or any other assistance or support for any of the activities described in **Item Number 48.a.**? ☐ Yes ☒ No

48.e. Provided money, a thing of value, services or labor, or any other assistance or support for an individual, group, or organization who did any of the activities described in **Item Number 48.a.**? ☐ Yes ☒ No

49. Have you **EVER** received any type of military, paramilitary, or weapons training? ☐ Yes ☒ No

50. Do you intend to engage in any of the activities listed in any part of **Item Numbers 48.a. - 49.**? ☐ Yes ☒ No

NOTE: If you answered "Yes" to any part of **Item Numbers 46.a. - 50.**, explain what you did, including the dates and location of the circumstances, or what you intend to do in the space provided in **Part 14. Additional Information**.

Are you the spouse or child of an individual who **EVER**:

51.a. Committed, threatened to commit, attempted to commit, conspired to commit, incited, endorsed, advocated, planned, or prepared any of the following: hijacking, sabotage, kidnapping, political assassination, or use of a weapon or explosive to harm another individual or cause substantial damage to property? ☐ Yes ☒ No

51.b. Participated in, or been a member or a representative of a group or organization that did any of the activities described in **Item Number 51.a.**? ☐ Yes ☒ No

51.c. Recruited members, or asked for money or things of value, for a group or organization that did any of the activities described in **Item Number 51.a.**? ☐ Yes ☒ No

51.d. Provided money, a thing of value, services or labor, or any other assistance or support for any of the activities described in **Item Number 51.a.**? ☐ Yes ☒ No

51.e. Provided money, a thing of value, services or labor, or any other assistance or support to an individual, group, or organization who did any of the activities described in **Item Number 51.a.**? ☐ Yes ☒ No

51.f. Received any type of military, paramilitary, or weapons training from a group or organization that did any of the activities described in **Item Number 51.a.**? ☐ Yes ☒ No

NOTE: If you answered "Yes" to any part of **Item Number 51.**, explain the relationship and what occurred, including the dates and location of the circumstances, in the space provided in **Part 14. Additional Information.**

52. Have you **EVER** assisted or participated in selling, providing, or transporting weapons to any person who, to your knowledge, used them against another person? ☐ Yes ☒ No

53. Have you **EVER** worked, volunteered, or otherwise served in any prison, jail, prison camp, detention facility, labor camp, or any other situation that involved detaining persons? ☐ Yes ☒ No

54. Have you **EVER** been a member of, assisted, or participated in any group, unit, or organization of any kind in which you or other persons used any type of weapon against any person or threatened to do so? ☐ Yes ☒ No

55. Have you **EVER** served in, been a member of, assisted, or participated in any military unit, paramilitary unit, police unit, self-defense unit, vigilante unit, rebel group, guerilla group, militia, insurgent organization, or any other armed group? ☐ Yes ☒ No

56. Have you **EVER** been a member of, or in any way affiliated with, the Communist Party or any other totalitarian party (in the United States or abroad)? ☐ Yes ☒ No

57. During the period from March 23, 1933 to May 8, 1945, did you ever order, incite, assist, or otherwise participate in the persecution of any person because of race, religion, national origin, or political opinion, in association with either the Nazi government of Germany or any organization or government associated or allied with the Nazi government of Germany? ☐ Yes ☒ No

Sample Form I-485, Application to Register Permanent Residence or Adjust Status (page 14)

A-Number ▶ A- | 1 | 2 | 3 | 4 | 5 | 6 | 7 | 8 | 9 |

Part 8. General Eligibility and Inadmissibility Grounds (continued)

Have you **EVER** ordered, incited, called for, committed, assisted, helped with, or otherwise participated in any of the following:

58.a. Acts involving torture or genocide? ☐ Yes ☒ No

58.b. Killing any person? ☐ Yes ☒ No

58.c. Intentionally and severely injuring any person? ☐ Yes ☒ No

58.d. Engaging in any kind of sexual contact or relations with any person who did not consent or was unable to consent, or was being forced or threatened? ☐ Yes ☒ No

58.e. Limiting or denying any person's ability to exercise religious beliefs? ☐ Yes ☒ No

59. Have you **EVER** recruited, enlisted, conscripted, or used any person under 15 years of age to serve in or help an armed force or group? ☐ Yes ☒ No

60. Have you **EVER** used any person under 15 years of age to take part in hostilities, or to help or provide services to people in combat? ☐ Yes ☒ No

NOTE: If you answered "Yes" to any part of **Item Numbers 52. - 60.**, explain what occurred, including the dates and location of the circumstances, in the space provided in **Part 14. Additional Information.**

Public Charge

Those who are subject to the public charge ground of inadmissibility under INA section 212(a)(4) must complete Form I-944, Declaration of Self-Sufficiency, and may also have to submit Form I-864, Affidavit of Support Under Section 213A of the INA. Answer the questions below to determine whether you need to submit these forms together with this Form I-485.

Declaration of Self-Sufficiency (Form I-944)

61. Are you exempt from the public charge ground of inadmissibility? ☐ Yes ☒ No

To determine if you are exempt from the public charge ground of inadmissibility, and therefore exempt from filing Form I-944, read the Form I-485 Instructions, **What Evidence Must You Submit, Item Number 9. Public Charge: Declaration of Self-Sufficiency (Form I-944) and Affidavit of Support Under Section 213A of the INA (Form I-864).** If you answered "Yes" to **Item Number 61.**, proceed to **Item Number 63.a.** If you answered "No," complete Form I-944 and include it with your Form I-485 filing, and proceed to **Item Number 62.a.**

Affidavit of Support Under Section 213A of the INA (Form I-864)

You may need to file Form I-864. For more information, read the Form I-485 Instructions, **What Evidence Must You Submit, Item Number 9. Public Charge: Declaration of Self-Sufficiency (Form I-944) and Affidavit of Support Under INA section 213A (Form I-864).**

I am EXEMPT from filing Form I-864 because:

62.a. ☐ I have earned or can receive credit for 40 qualifying quarters (credits) of work in the United States (as defined by the Social Security Act (SSA). (Attach your SSA earnings statements. Do not count any quarters during which you received a means-tested public benefit).

62.b. ☐ I am under 18 years of age, unmarried, immigrating as the child of a U.S. citizen, and will automatically become a U.S. citizen under the Child Citizenship Act of 2000 upon my admission to the United States.

62.c. ☐ I am applying under the widow or widower of a U.S. citizen (Form I-360) immigrant category.

62.d. ☐ I am applying under an alien worker (Form I-140) employment-based preference immigrant category and both of the following apply:

   (1) I am not a relative of the Form I-140 petitioner; and

   (2) I do not have a relative with a significant ownership interest (at least five percent) in the business that filed Form I-140.

62.e. ☐ I am applying under the alien entrepreneur (Form I-526) immigrant category.

62.f. ☐ I am applying under the human trafficking victim (T nonimmigrant) immigrant category (INA section 245(l)).

62.g. ☐ I am applying under a category other than the human trafficking victim (T nonimmigrant) category (INA section 245(l)), or as an alien worker under the employment-based preference categories where a relative filed Form I-140 for me or has a five percent or more ownership interest in the business that filed Form I-140, and I either have a pending application for T nonimmigrant status or I am an individual who is in valid T nonimmigrant status.

NOTE: If, when USCIS adjudicates your adjustment application, your Form I-914 is no longer pending a decision or you are no longer in valid T nonimmigrant status, you may have to submit a Form I-944 and Form I-864.

62.h. ☐ I am applying under the victim of qualifying criminal activity (U nonimmigrant) immigrant category (INA section 245(m)).

Sample Form I-485, Application to Register Permanent Residence or Adjust Status (page 15)

A-Number ▶ A- 1 2 3 4 5 6 7 8 9

Part 8. General Eligibility and Inadmissibility Grounds (continued)

62.i. ☐ I am applying under a category other than the victim of qualifying criminal activity (U nonimmigrant) category under INA section 245(m) or as an alien worker under the employment-based preference categories where a relative filed Form I-140 for me or has a five percent or more ownership interest in the business that filed Form I-140, but I either have a pending petition for U nonimmigrant status or I am an individual who is granted U nonimmigrant status.

NOTE: If, at the time of the adjudication of the Form I-485, your Form I-918 is no longer pending a decision or you are no longer in valid U nonimmigrant status, you may be required to submit Form I-944 and Form I-864.

62.j. ☐ I am applying under the diplomat or high ranking official unable to return home (Section 13 of the Act of September 11, 1957) immigrant category.

62.k. ☐ I am a law enforcement officer filing this Form I-485 for an S nonimmigrant immigrant (or a qualifying family member).

62.l. ☐ I am applying under the Diversity Visa program immigrant category.

62.m. ☐ I am applying under one of the following special immigrant categories (select one):

☐ Armed forces (also known as the Six and Six program)

☐ Panama Canal Zone

☐ Certain broadcasters

☐ G-4 or NATO-6 employees and their family members

☐ International employees of the U.S. Government abroad

☐ Religious workers

☐ Certain physicians

☐ Employed by or on behalf of the U.S. Government

62.n. ☐ I am applying under the Amerasian Act (October 22, 1982).

Illegal Entries and Other Immigration Violations

63.a. Have you **EVER** failed or refused to attend or to remain in attendance at any removal proceeding filed against you on or after April 1, 1997? ☐ Yes ☒ No

63.b. If your answer to **Item Number 63.a.** is "Yes," do you believe you had reasonable cause? ☐ Yes ☐ No

63.c. If your answer to **Item Number 63.b.** is "Yes," attach a written statement explaining why you had reasonable cause.

64. Have you **EVER** submitted fraudulent or counterfeit documentation to any U.S. Government official to obtain or attempt to obtain any immigration benefit, including a visa or entry into the United States? ☐ Yes ☒ No

65. Have you **EVER** lied about, concealed, or misrepresented any information on an application or petition to obtain a visa, other documentation required for entry into the United States, admission to the United States, or any other kind of immigration benefit? ☐ Yes ☒ No

66. Have you **EVER** falsely claimed to be a U.S. citizen (in writing or any other way)? ☐ Yes ☒ No

67. Have you **EVER** been a stowaway on a vessel or aircraft arriving in the United States? ☐ Yes ☒ No

68. Have you **EVER** knowingly encouraged, induced, assisted, abetted, or aided any foreign national to enter or to try to enter the United States illegally (alien smuggling)? ☐ Yes ☒ No

69. Are you under a final order of civil penalty for violating INA section 274C for use of fraudulent documents? ☐ Yes ☒ No

Removal, Unlawful Presence, or Illegal Reentry After Previous Immigration Violations

70. Have you **EVER** been excluded, deported, or removed from the United States or have you ever departed the United States on your own after having been ordered excluded, deported, or removed from the United States? ☐ Yes ☒ No

71. Have you **EVER** entered the United States without being inspected and admitted or paroled? ☐ Yes ☒ No

Since April 1, 1997, have you been unlawfully present in the United States:

72.a. For more than 180 days but less than a year, and then departed the United States? ☐ Yes ☒ No

72.b. For one year or more and then departed the United States? ☐ Yes ☒ No

NOTE: You were unlawfully present in the United States if you entered the United States without being inspected and admitted or inspected and paroled, or if you legally entered the United States but you stayed longer than permitted.

Sample Form I-485, Application to Register Permanent Residence or Adjust Status (page 16)

A-Number ▶ A- 1 2 3 4 5 6 7 8 9

Part 8. General Eligibility and Inadmissibility Grounds (continued)

Since April 1, 1997, have you **EVER** reentered or attempted to reenter the United States without being inspected and admitted or paroled after:

73.a. Having been unlawfully present in the United States for more than one year in the aggregate? ☐ Yes ☒ No

73.b. Having been deported, excluded, or removed from the United States? ☐ Yes ☒ No

Miscellaneous Conduct

74. Do you plan to practice polygamy in the United States? ☐ Yes ☒ No

75. Are you accompanying another foreign national who requires your protection or guardianship but who is inadmissible after being certified by a medical officer as being helpless from sickness, physical or mental disability, or infancy, as described in INA section 232(c)? ☐ Yes ☒ No

76. Have you **EVER** assisted in detaining, retaining, or withholding custody of a U.S. citizen child outside the United States from a U.S. citizen who has been granted custody of the child? ☐ Yes ☒ No

77. Have you **EVER** voted in violation of any Federal, state, or local constitutional provision, statute, ordinance, or regulation in the United States? ☐ Yes ☒ No

78. Have you **EVER** renounced U.S. citizenship to avoid being taxed by the United States? ☐ Yes ☒ No

Have you **EVER**:

79.a. Applied for exemption or discharge from training or service in the U.S. armed forces or in the U.S. National Security Training Corps on the ground that you are a foreign national? ☐ Yes ☒ No

79.b. Been relieved or discharged from such training or service on the ground that you are a foreign national? ☐ Yes ☒ No

79.c. Been convicted of desertion from the U.S. armed forces? ☐ Yes ☒ No

80.a. Have you **EVER** left or remained outside the United States to avoid or evade training or service in the U.S. armed forces in time of war or a period declared by the President to be a national emergency? ☐ Yes ☒ No

80.b. If your answer to **Item Number 80.a.** is "Yes," what was your nationality or immigration status immediately before you left (for example, U.S. citizen or national, lawful permanent resident, nonimmigrant, parolee, present without admission or parole, or any other status)?

Part 9. Accommodations for Individuals With Disabilities and/or Impairments

NOTE: Read the information in the Form I-485 Instructions before completing this part.

1. Are you requesting an accommodation because of your disabilities and/or impairments? ☐ Yes ☒ No

If you answered "Yes" to **Item Number 1.**, select any applicable box in **Item Numbers 2.a. - 2.c.** and provide an answer.

2.a. ☐ I am deaf or hard of hearing and request the following accommodation. (If you are requesting a sign-language interpreter, indicate for which language (for example, American Sign Language).):

2.b. ☐ I am blind or have low vision and request the following accommodation:

2.c. ☐ I have another type of disability and/or impairment. (Describe the nature of your disability and/or impairment and the accommodation you are requesting.)

Part 10. Applicant's Statement, Contact Information, Certification, and Signature

NOTE: Read the **Penalties** section of the Form I-485 Instructions before completing this part. You must file Form I-485 while in the United States.

Sample Form I-485, Application to Register Permanent Residence or Adjust Status (page 17)

A-Number ▶ A- | 1 | 2 | 3 | 4 | 5 | 6 | 7 | 8 | 9 |

Part 10. Applicant's Statement, Contact Information, Certification, and Signature (continued)

Applicant's Statement

NOTE: Select the box for either **Item Number 1.a.** or **1.b.** If applicable, select the box for **Item Number 2.**

1.a. ☒ I can read and understand English, and I have read and understand every question and instruction on this application and my answer to every question.

1.b. ☐ The interpreter named in **Part 11.** read to me every question and instruction on this application and my answer to every question in

[   ],

a language in which I am fluent, and I understood everything.

2. ☐ At my request, the preparer named in **Part 12.**,

[   ],

prepared this application for me based only upon information I provided or authorized.

Applicant's Contact Information

3. Applicant's Daytime Telephone Number

    8142223344

4. Applicant's Mobile Telephone Number (if any)

    8142223344

5. Applicant's Email Address (if any)

    andam@email.com

Applicant's Certification

Copies of any documents I have submitted are exact photocopies of unaltered, original documents, and I understand that USCIS may require that I submit original documents to USCIS at a later date. Furthermore, I authorize the release of any information from any and all of my records that USCIS may need to determine my eligibility for the immigration benefit that I seek.

I understand that if I am a male who is 18 to 26 years of age, submitting this application will automatically register me with the Selective Service System as required by the Military Selective Service Act.

I furthermore authorize release of information contained in this application, in supporting documents, and in my USCIS records, to other entities and persons where necessary for the administration and enforcement of U.S. immigration law.

I understand that USCIS may require me to appear for an appointment to take my biometrics (fingerprints, photograph, and/or signature) and, at that time, if I am required to provide biometrics, I will be required to sign an oath reaffirming that:

1) I reviewed and understood all of the information contained in, and submitted with, my application; and

2) All of this information was complete, true, and correct at the time of filing.

I certify , under penalty of perjury , that all of the information in my application and any document submitted with it were provided or authorized by me, that I reviewed and understand all of the information contained in, and submitted with, my application and that all of this information is complete, true, and correct.

Applicant's Signature

6.a. Applicant's Signature (sign in ink)

➡ *Anda Michelski*

6.b. Date of Signature (mm/dd/yyyy)   04/01/2020

NOTE TO ALL APPLICANTS: If you do not completely fill out this application or fail to submit required documents listed in the Instructions, USCIS may deny your application.

Part 11. Interpreter's Contact Information, Certification, and Signature

Provide the following information about the interpreter.

Interpreter's Full Name

1.a. Interpreter's Family Name (Last Name)

[   ]

1.b. Interpreter's Given Name (First Name)

[   ]

2. Interpreter's Business or Organization Name (if any)

[   ]

Sample Form I-765, Application for Employment Authorization (page 1)

Application For Employment Authorization

Department of Homeland Security

U.S. Citizenship and Immigration Services

USCIS
Form I-765

OMB No. 1615-0040
Expires 05/31/2020

For USCIS Use Only	
☐ **Authorization/Extension Valid From** _____	
☐ **Authorization/Extension Valid Through** _____	
Alien Registration Number A- ☐☐☐☐☐☐☐	
Remarks	

Fee Stamp

Action Block

To be completed by an attorney or Board of Immigration Appeals (BIA)-accredited representative (if any).	☐ Select this box if Form G-28 is attached.	**Attorney or Accredited Representative USCIS Online Account Number** (if any) ☐☐☐☐☐☐☐☐☐☐☐☐☐

▶ **START HERE - Type or print in black ink.**

Part 1. Reason for Applying

I am applying for (select **only one** box):

1.a. ☒ Initial permission to accept employment.

1.b. ☐ Replacement of lost, stolen, or damaged employment authorization document, or correction of my employment authorization document **NOT DUE** to U.S. Citizenship and Immigration Services (USCIS) error.

NOTE: Replacement (correction) of an employment authorization document due to USCIS error does not require a new Form I-765 and filing fee. Refer to **Replacement for Card Error** in the **What is the Filing Fee** section of the Form I-765 Instructions for further details.

1.c. ☐ Renewal of my permission to accept employment. (Attach a copy of your previous employment authorization document.)

Part 2. Information About You

Your Full Legal Name

1.a. Family Name (Last Name) | Michelski

1.b. Given Name (First Name) | Anda

1.c. Middle Name |

Other Names Used

Provide all other names you have ever used, including aliases, maiden name, and nicknames. If you need extra space to complete this section, use the space provided in **Part 6. Additional Information**.

2.a. Family Name (Last Name) |

2.b. Given Name (First Name) |

2.c. Middle Name |

3.a. Family Name (Last Name) |

3.b. Given Name (First Name) |

3.c. Middle Name |

4.a. Family Name (Last Name) |

4.b. Given Name (First Name) |

4.c. Middle Name |

Sample Form I-765, Application for Employment Authorization (page 2)

Part 2. Information About You (continued)	**13.b.** Provide your Social Security number (SSN) (if known).

Your U.S. Mailing Address

5.a. In Care Of Name (if any)

5.b. Street Number and Name `68 Waterton Boulevard`

5.c. ☒ Apt. ☐ Ste. ☐ Flr. `12`

5.d. City or Town `Erie`

5.e. State `PA` **5.f.** ZIP Code `19380`

6. Is your current mailing address the same as your physical address? ☒ Yes ☐ No

NOTE: If you answered "No" to **Item Number 6.**, provide your physical address below.

U.S. Physical Address

7.a. Street Number and Name

7.b. ☐ Apt. ☐ Ste. ☐ Flr.

7.c. City or Town

7.d. State **7.e.** ZIP Code

Other Information

8. Alien Registration Number (A-Number) (if any)

► A- `1` `2` `3` `4` `5` `6` `7` `8` `9`

9. USCIS Online Account Number (if any)

►

10. Gender ☐ Male ☒ Female

11. Marital Status
☐ Single ☒ Married ☐ Divorced ☐ Widowed

12. Have you previously filed Form I-765?
☐ Yes ☒ No

13.a. Has the Social Security Administration (SSA) ever officially issued a Social Security card to you?
☐ Yes ☒ No

NOTE: If you answered "No" to **Item Number 13.a.**, skip to **Item Number 14.** If you answered "Yes" to **Item Number 13.a.**, provide the information requested in **Item Number 13.b.**

13.b. Provide your Social Security number (SSN) (if known).

►

14. Do you want the SSA to issue you a Social Security card? (You must also answer "Yes" to **Item Number 15.**, **Consent for Disclosure**, to receive a card.)
☒ Yes ☐ No

NOTE: If you answered "No" to **Item Number 14.**, skip to **Part 2.**, **Item Number 18.a.** If you answered "Yes" to **Item Number 14.**, you must also answer "Yes" to **Item Number 15.**

15. **Consent for Disclosure:** I authorize disclosure of information from this application to the SSA as required for the purpose of assigning me an SSN and issuing me a Social Security card. ☒ Yes ☐ No

NOTE: If you answered "Yes" to **Item Numbers 14. - 15.**, provide the information requested in **Item Numbers 16.a. - 17.b.**

Father's Name

Provide your father's birth name.

16.a. Family Name (Last Name) `Michelski`

16.b. Given Name (First Name) `Liski`

Mother's Name

Provide your mother's birth name.

17.a. Family Name (Last Name) `Antov`

17.b. Given Name (First Name) `Anastasia`

Your Country or Countries of Citizenship or Nationality

List all countries where you are currently a citizen or national. If you need extra space to complete this item, use the space provided in **Part 6. Additional Information**.

18.a. Country `Bulgaria`

18.b. Country

Sample Form I-765, Application for Employment Authorization (page 3)

Part 2. Information About You (continued)

Place of Birth

List the city/town/village, state/province, and country where you were born.

19.a. City/Town/Village of Birth

> Sofia

19.b. State/Province of Birth

19.c. Country of Birth

> Bulgaria

20. Date of Birth (mm/dd/yyyy) `06/28/1986`

Information About Your Last Arrival in the United States

21.a. Form I-94 Arrival-Departure Record Number (if any)

> ► `9 9 2 5 5 5 7 6 6 A 1`

21.b. Passport Number of Your Most Recently Issued Passport

> S1343944

21.c. Travel Document Number (if any)

21.d. Country That Issued Your Passport or Travel Document

> Bulgaria

21.e. Expiration Date for Passport or Travel Document (mm/dd/yyyy) `08/09/2022`

22. Date of Your Last Arrival Into the United States, On or About (mm/dd/yyyy) `12/06/2019`

23. Place of Your Last Arrival Into the United States

> New York

24. Immigration Status at Your Last Arrival (for example, B-2 visitor, F-1 student, or no status)

> K-1

25. Your Current Immigration Status or Category (for example, B-2 visitor, F-1 student, parolee, deferred action, or no status or category)

> K-1

26. Student and Exchange Visitor Information System (SEVIS) Number (if any)

> ► N-

Information About Your Eligibility Category

27. **Eligibility Category.** Refer to the **Who May File Form I-765** section of the Form I-765 Instructions to determine the appropriate eligibility category for this application. Enter the appropriate letter and number for your eligibility category below (for example, (a)(8), (c)(17)(iii)).

(`c`) (`9`) ( )

28. **(c)(3)(C) STEM OPT Eligibility Category.** If you entered the eligibility category **(c)(3)(C)** in **Item Number 27.**, provide the information requested in **Item Numbers 28.a - 28.c.**

28.a. Degree

28.b. Employer's Name as Listed in E-Verify

28.c. Employer's E-Verify Company Identification Number or a Valid E-Verify Client Company Identification Number

29. **(c)(26) Eligibility Category.** If you entered the eligibility category (c)(26) in **Item Number 27.**, provide the receipt number of your H-1B spouse's most recent Form I-797 Notice for Form I-129, Petition for a Nonimmigrant Worker.

> ►

30. **(c)(8) Eligibility Category.** If you entered the eligibility category (c)(8) in **Item Number 27.**, have you **EVER** been arrested for and/or convicted of any crime?

☐ Yes ☐ No

NOTE: If you answered "Yes" to **Item Number 30.**, refer to **Special Filing Instructions for Those With Pending Asylum Applications (c)(8)** in the **Required Documentation** section of the Form I-765 Instructions for information about providing court dispositions.

31.a. **(c)(35) and (c)(36) Eligibility Category.** If you entered the eligibility category (c)(35) in **Item Number 27.**, please provide the receipt number of your Form I-797 Notice for Form I-140, Immigrant Petition for Alien Worker. If you entered the eligibility category (c)(36) in **Item Number 27.**, please provide the receipt number of your spouse's or parent's Form I-797 Notice for Form I-140.

> ►

31.b. If you entered the eligibility category (c)(35) or (c)(36) in **Item Number 27.**, have you **EVER** been arrested for and/or convicted of any crime? ☐ Yes ☐ No

NOTE: If you answered "Yes" to **Item Number 31.b.**, refer to **Employment-Based Nonimmigrant Categories, Items 8. - 9.**, in the **Who May File Form I-765** section of the Form I-765 Instructions for information about providing court dispositions.

Sample Form I-765, Application for Employment Authorization (page 4)

Part 3. Applicant's Statement, Contact Information, Declaration, Certification, and Signature

NOTE: Read the **Penalties** section of the Form I-765 Instructions before completing this section. You must file Form I-765 while in the United States.

Applicant's Statement

NOTE: Select the box for either **Item Number 1.a.** or **1.b.** If applicable, select the box for **Item Number 2.**

1.a. [X] I can read and understand English, and I have read and understand every question and instruction on this application and my answer to every question.

1.b. [ ] The interpreter named in **Part 4.** read to me every question and instruction on this application and my answer to every question in

[   ] ,

a language in which I am fluent, and I understood everything.

2. [ ] At my request, the preparer named in **Part 5.**,

[   ] ,

prepared this application for me based only upon information I provided or authorized.

Applicant's Contact Information

3. Applicant's Daytime Telephone Number

[8142223344]

4. Applicant's Mobile Telephone Number (if any)

[8142223344]

5. Applicant's Email Address (if any)

[andam@email.com]

6. [ ] Select this box if you are a Salvadoran or Guatemalan national eligible for benefits under the ABC settlement agreement.

Applicant's Declaration and Certification

Copies of any documents I have submitted are exact photocopies of unaltered, original documents, and I understand that USCIS may require that I submit original documents to USCIS at a later date. Furthermore, I authorize the release of any information from any and all of my records that USCIS may need to determine my eligibility for the immigration benefit that I seek.

I furthermore authorize release of information contained in this application, in supporting documents, and in my USCIS records, to other entities and persons where necessary for the administration and enforcement of U.S. immigration law.

I understand that USCIS may require me to appear for an appointment to take my biometrics (fingerprints, photograph, and/or signature) and, at that time, if I am required to provide biometrics, I will be required to sign an oath reaffirming that:

1) I reviewed and understood all of the information contained in, and submitted with, my application; and

2) All of this information was complete, true, and correct at the time of filing.

I certify, under penalty of perjury, that all of the information in my application and any document submitted with it were provided or authorized by me, that I reviewed and understand all of the information contained in, and submitted with, my application and that all of this information is complete, true, and correct.

Applicant's Signature

7.a. Applicant's Signature

➡️ 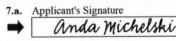 *Anda Michelski*

7.b. Date of Signature (mm/dd/yyyy) [04/01/2020]

NOTE TO ALL APPLICANTS: If you do not completely fill out this application or fail to submit required documents listed in the Instructions, USCIS may deny your application.

Part 4. Interpreter's Contact Information, Certification, and Signature

Provide the following information about the interpreter.

Interpreter's Full Name

1.a. Interpreter's Family Name (Last Name)

[   ]

1.b. Interpreter's Given Name (First Name)

[   ]

2. Interpreter's Business or Organization Name (if any)

[   ]

Sample Form I-131, Application for Travel Document (page 1)

Application for Travel Document
Department of Homeland Security
U.S. Citizenship and Immigration Services

**USCIS
Form I-131**

OMB No. 1615-0013
Expires 04/30/2022

For USCIS Use Only	Receipt	Action Block	To Be Completed by an *Attorney/ Representative,* if any.

☐ **Document Hand Delivered**

By: _____ Date: _____ / _____ / _____

☐ Fill in box if G-28 is attached to represent the applicant.

Document Issued

☐ Re-entry Permit *(Update " Mail To" Section)*   ☐ Refugee Travel Document *(Update " Mail To" Section)*

☐ Single Advance Parole   ☐ Multiple Advance Parole *Valid Until:* _____ / _____ / _____

Mail To *(Re-entry & Refugee Only)*

☐ Address in *Part 1*
☐ US Consulate at: _____
☐ Intl DHS Ofc at: _____

Attorney State License Number:

_____

▶ **Start Here.** Type or Print in Black Ink

Part 1. Information About You

1.a. Family Name *(Last Name)* | Michelski

1.b. Given Name *(First Name)* | Anda

1.c. Middle Name |

Physical Address

2.a. In Care of Name |

2.b. Street Number and Name | 68 Waterton Boulevard

2.c. Apt. ☒   Ste. ☐   Flr. ☐   12

2.d. City or Town | Erie

2.e. State | PA   **2.f.** Zip Code | 19380

2.g. Postal Code |

2.h. Province |

2.i. Country | USA

Other Information

3. Alien Registration Number (A-Number)

▶ A- | 1 | 2 | 3 | 4 | 5 | 6 | 7 | 8 | 9 |

4. Country of Birth | Bulgaria

5. Country of Citizenship | Bulgaria

6. Class of Admission | K-1

7. Gender ☐ Male ☒ Female

8. Date of Birth *(mm/dd/yyyy)* ▶ | 06/28/1986

9. U.S. Social Security Number *(if any)*

▶ | | | | | | | | | |

Form I-131 04/24/19

Sample Form I-131, Application for Travel Document (page 2)

Part 2. Application Type

1.a. ☐ I am a permanent resident or conditional resident of the United States, and I am applying for a reentry permit.

1.b. ☐ I now hold U.S. refugee or asylee status, and I am applying for a Refugee Travel Document.

1.c. ☐ I am a permanent resident as a direct result of refugee or asylee status, and I am applying for a Refugee Travel Document.

1.d. ☒ I am applying for an Advance Parole Document to allow me to return to the United States after temporary foreign travel.

1.e. ☐ I am outside the United States, and I am applying for an Advance Parole Document.

1.f. ☐ I am applying for an Advance Parole Document for a person who is outside the United States.

If you checked box "1.f." provide the following information about that person in 2.a. through 2.p.

2.a. Family Name *(Last Name)*

2.b. Given Name *(First Name)*

2.c. Middle Name

2.d. Date of Birth *(mm/dd/yyyy)* ▶

2.e. Country of Birth

2.f. Country of Citizenship

2.g. Daytime Phone Number (☐☐☐) ☐☐☐ - ☐☐☐☐

Physical Address (If you checked box 1.f.)

2.h. In Care of Name

2.i. Street Number and Name

2.j. Apt. ☐ Ste. ☐ Flr. ☐

2.k. City or Town

2.l. State ☐ **2.m.** Zip Code

2.n. Postal Code

2.o. Province

2.p. Country

Part 3. Processing Information

1. Date of Intended Departure
(mm/dd/yyyy) ▶ 06/01/2020

2. Expected Length of Trip *(in days)* 14

3.a. Are you, or any person included in this application, now in exclusion, deportation, removal, or rescission proceedings? ☐ Yes ☒ No

3.b. If "Yes", Name of DHS office:

4.a. Have you ever before been issued a reentry permit or Refugee Travel Document? *(If "Yes" give the following information for the last document issued to you):*
☐ Yes ☒ No

4.b. Date Issued *(mm/dd/yyyy)* ▶

4.c. Disposition *(attached, lost, etc.)*:

If you are applying for a non-DACA related Advance Parole Document, skip to Part 7; *DACA recipients must complete Part 4 before skipping to Part 7.*

Sample Form I-131, Application for Travel Document (page 3)

Part 3. Processing Information *(continued)*

Where do you want this travel document sent? *(Check one)*

5. ☒ To the U.S. address shown in **Part 1 (2.a through 2.i.)** of this form.

6. ☐ To a U.S. Embassy or consulate at:

6.a. City or Town _____

6.b. Country _____

7. ☐ To a DHS office overseas at:

7.a. City or Town _____

7.b. Country _____

If you checked "6" or "7", where should the notice to pick up the travel document be sent?

8. ☐ To the address shown in **Part 2 (2.h. through 2.p.)** of this form.

9. ☐ To the address shown in **Part 3 (10.a. through 10.i.)** of this form.:

10.a. In Care of Name _____

10.b. Street Number and Name _____

10.c. Apt. ☐ Ste. ☐ Flr. ☐ _____

10.d. City or Town _____

10.e. State _____ **10.f.** Zip Code _____

10.g. Postal Code _____

10.h. Province _____

10.i. Country _____

10.j. Daytime Phone Number (___) ___ - ____

Part 4. Information About Your Proposed Travel

1.a. Purpose of trip. *(If you need more space, continue on a separate sheet of paper.)*

_____
_____
_____
_____

1.b. List the countries you intend to visit. *(If you need more space, continue on a separate sheet of paper.)*

_____
_____
_____
_____

Part 5. Complete Only If Applying for a Re-entry Permit

Since becoming a permanent resident of the United States (or during the past 5 years, whichever is less) how much total time have you spent outside the United States?

1.a. ☐ less than 6 months   **1.d.** ☐ 2 to 3 years
1.b. ☐ 6 months to 1 year   **1.e.** ☐ 3 to 4 years
1.c. ☐ 1 to 2 years   **1.f.** ☐ more than 4 years

2. Since you became a permanent resident of the United States, have you ever filed a Federal income tax return as a nonresident or failed to file a Federal income tax return because you considered yourself to be a nonresident? *(If "Yes" give details on a separate sheet of paper.)*

☐ Yes   ☐ No

Sample Form I-131, Application for Travel Document (page 4)

Part 6. Complete Only If Applying for a Refugee Travel Document

1. Country from which you are a refugee or asylee:

[ ]

If you answer "Yes" to any of the following questions, you must explain on a separate sheet of paper. Include your Name and A-Number on the top of each sheet.

2. Do you plan to travel to the country named above? [ ] Yes [ ] No

Since you were accorded refugee/asylee status, have you ever:

3.a. Returned to the country named above? [ ] Yes [ ] No

3.b. Applied for and/or obtained a national passport, passport renewal, or entry permit of that country? [ ] Yes [ ] No

3.c. Applied for and/or received any benefit from such country (for example, health insurance benefits)? [ ] Yes [ ] No

Since you were accorded refugee/asylee status, have you, by any legal procedure or voluntary act:

4.a. Reacquired the nationality of the country named above? [ ] Yes [ ] No

4.b. Acquired a new nationality? [ ] Yes [ ] No

4.c. Been granted refugee or asylee status in any other country? [ ] Yes [ ] No

Part 7. Complete Only If Applying for Advance Parole

On a separate sheet of paper, explain how you qualify for an Advance Parole Document, and what circumstances warrant issuance of advance parole. Include copies of any documents you wish considered. *(See instructions.)*

1. How many trips do you intend to use this document? [ ] One Trip [X] More than one trip

If the person intended to receive an Advance Parole Document is outside the United States, provide the location (City or Town and Country) of the U.S. Embassy or consulate or the DHS overseas office that you want us to notify.

2.a. City or Town

2.b. Country

If the travel document will be delivered to an overseas office, where should the notice to pick up the document be sent?:

3. [ ] To the address shown in **Part 2 (2.h. through 2.p.)** of this form.

4. [ ] To the address shown in **Part 7 (4.a. through 4.i.)** of this form.

4.a. In Care of Name

4.b. Street Number and Name

4.c. Apt. [ ] Ste. [ ] Flr. [ ]

4.d. City or Town

4.e. State [ ] **4.f.** Zip Code

4.g. Postal Code

4.h. Province

4.i. Country

4.j. Daytime Phone Number ( ) -

Sample Form I-131, Application for Travel Document (page 5)

Part 8. Signature of Applicant *(Read the information on penalties in the Form instructions before completing this Part.)* If you are filing for a Re-entry Permit or Refugee Travel Document, you must be in the United States to file this application.

1.a. I certify, under penalty of perjury under the laws of the United States of America, that this application and the evidence submitted with it is all true and correct. I authorize the release of any information from my records that U.S. Citizenship and Immigration Services needs to determine eligibility for the benefit I am seeking.

Signature of Applicant

➡ *Anda Michelski*

1.b. Date of Signature *(mm/dd/yyyy)* ▶ 04/01/2020

2. Daytime Phone Number (8 1 4) 2 2 2 - 3 3 4 4

NOTE:If you do not completely fill out this form or fail to submit required documents listed in the instructions, your application may be denied.

Part 9. Information About Person Who Prepared This Application, If Other Than the Applicant

NOTE:If you are an attorney or representative, you must submit a completed Form G-28, Notice of Entry of Appearance as Attorney or Accredited Representative, along with this application.

Preparer's Full Name

Provide the following information concerning the preparer:

1.a. Preparer's Family Name *(Last Name)*

1.b. Preparer's Given Name *(First Name)*

2. Preparer's Business or Organization Name

Preparer's Mailing Address

3.a. Street Number and Name

3.b. Apt. ☐ Ste. ☐ Flr. ☐

3.c. City or Town

3.d. State ___ **3.e.** Zip Code

3.f. Postal Code

3.g. Province

3.h. Country

Preparer's Contact Information

4. Preparer's Daytime Phone Number   Extension

(___) ___ - ___

5. Preparer's E-mail Address *(if any)*

Declaration

To be completed by all preparers, including attorneys and authorized representatives: I declare that I prepared this benefit request at the request of the applicant, that it is based on all the information of which I have knowledge, and that the information is true to the best of my knowledge.

6.a. Signature of Preparer

6.b. Date of Signature *(mm/dd/yyyy)* ▶

NOTE:If you require more space to provide any additional information, use a separate sheet of paper. You must include your Name and A-Number on the top of each sheet.

Form I-131 04/24/19   Page 5 of 5

Sample Form I-944, Declaration of Self-Sufficiency (page 1)

Declaration of Self-Sufficiency

Department of Homeland Security

U.S. Citizenship and Immigration Services

**USCIS
Form I-944**
OMB No. 1615-0142
Expires 10/31/2021

To be completed by an attorney or accredited representative (if any).			
☐ **Select this box if Form G-28 is attached.**	**Volag Number** (if any)	**Attorney State Bar Number** (if applicable)	**Attorney or Accredited Representative USCIS Online Account Number** (if any)

▶ **START HERE** - Type or print in black ink.

Part 1. Information About You

1. Your Current Legal Name (do not provide a nickname)

Family Name (Last Name)	Given Name (First Name)	Middle Name
Michelski	Anda	

2. U.S. Mailing Address

   In Care Of Name (if any)

Street Number and Name	Apt.	Ste.	Flr.	Number
68 Waterton Boulevard	☐	☐	☐	12

City or Town	State	ZIP Code
Erie	PA	19380

3. Alien Registration Number (A-Number) (if any)

   ▶ A- 1 2 3 4 5 6 7 8 9

4. USCIS Online Account Number (if any)

   ▶

5. Date of Birth (mm/dd/yyyy)

   06/28/1986

6. Place of Birth

City or Town of Birth	Country of Birth
Sofia	Bulgaria

7. Country of Citizenship or Nationality

   Bulgaria

Sample Form I-944, Declaration of Self-Sufficiency (page 2)

Part 2. Family Status (Your Household)

In this Part, you will be providing information about the individuals in your household. If you need additional space to complete any Item Number in this Part, use the space provided in **Part 9. Additional Information**. Please see the Instructions for who is included in your household. If not already provided with your Form I-485, provide evidence of your relationship to each individual (such as a birth certificate or marriage certificate). If you do not have evidence of a relationship to one or more members of the household, please submit a signed statement from such household member(s) or his or her legal guardian, if applicable.

1. Below, list yourself and all the individuals who are part of your household.

A. Family Name (Last Name): Michelski

Given Name (First Name): Anda

Middle Name:

Date of Birth (mm/dd/yyyy): 06/28/1986

Relationship to you: Self

Alien Registration Number (A-Number) (if any): ► A- 1 2 3 4 5 6 7 8 9

Does this individual live with you? ☐ Yes ☐ No

Is this individual filing an application for an immigration benefit with you or has this individual already filed an application? ☐ Yes ☐ No

B. Family Name (Last Name): Brown

Given Name (First Name): Andrew

Middle Name: Brian

Date of Birth (mm/dd/yyyy): 11/11/1984

Relationship to you: Spouse

Alien Registration Number (A-Number) (if any): ► A-

Does this individual live with you? ☒ Yes ☐ No

Is this individual filing an application for an immigration benefit with you or has this individual already filed an application? ☐ Yes ☒ No

C. Family Name (Last Name):

Given Name (First Name):

Middle Name:

Date of Birth (mm/dd/yyyy):

Relationship to you:

Alien Registration Number (A-Number) (if any): ► A-

Does this individual live with you? ☐ Yes ☐ No

Is this individual filing an application for an immigration benefit with you or has this individual already filed an application? ☐ Yes ☐ No

D. Family Name (Last Name):

Given Name (First Name):

Middle Name:

Date of Birth (mm/dd/yyyy):

Relationship to you:

Alien Registration Number (A-Number) (if any): ► A-

Does this individual live with you? ☐ Yes ☐ No

Is this individual filing an application for an immigration benefit with you or has this individual already filed an application? ☐ Yes ☐ No

E. Total number of household members (including yourself): 2

Sample Form I-944, Declaration of Self-Sufficiency (page 3)

Part 3. Your and Your Household Members' Assets, Resources, and Financial Status

In this Part, you will be providing information about your assets, resources, and financial status, as well as the assets, resources, and financial status of all other household members. If you need additional space to complete any Item Number in this Part, use the space provided in **Part 9. Additional Information**.

Household Income

1. List your and your household members', listed in **Part 2.**, total income from the most recent federal income tax returns, if any. See the Instructions for additional information.

   A. Name (self or household member)

Family Name (Last Name)	Given Name (First Name)	Middle Name
Michelski	Anda	

   Did you or your household member(s), whose income is being included, file a federal tax return? ☐ Yes ☒ No

   If you and your household members did not file, select the reason for not filing, and provide an explanation.

   ☐ Plan to file the tax return before the due date for this year.

   ☒ Not required to file a tax return. (Provide an explanation.)

   ☐ Filed for an extension.

   ☐ Not going to file. (Provide an explanation.)

   ☐ Other _____

   Federal Tax Year | n/a | Total income from tax return or Item 1 on W-2 "Wages, tips, other compensation" (U.S. dollars) (if applicable) $ | n/a

   Explanation for Not Filing:

   No income in U.S. for 2019.

   B. Name (self or household member)

Family Name (Last Name)	Given Name (First Name)	Middle Name
Brown	Andrew	Brian

   Did you or your household member, whose income is being included, file a Federal Tax Return? ☒ Yes ☐ No

   If you and your household members did not file, select the reason for not filing, and provide an explanation.

   ☐ Plan to file the tax return before the due date for this year.

   ☐ Not required to file a tax return. (Provide an explanation.)

   ☐ Filed for an extension.

   ☐ Not going to file. (Provide an explanation.)

   ☐ Other _____

   Federal Tax Year | 2019 | Total income from tax return or Item 1 on W-2 "Wages, tips, other compensation" (U.S. dollars) (if applicable) $ | 75,000

   Explanation for Not Filing:

Sample Form I-944, Declaration of Self-Sufficiency (page 4)

Part 3. Your and Your Household Member(s)'s Assets, Resources, and Financial Status (continued)

C. Name (self or household member)

Family Name (Last Name)   Given Name (First Name)   Middle Name

Did you or your household member, whose income is being included, file a Federal Tax Return? ☐ Yes ☐ No

If you and your household members did not file, select the reason for not filing, and provide an explanation.

☐ Plan to file the tax return before the due date for this year.

☐ Not required to file a tax return. (Provide an explanation.)

☐ Filed for an extension.

☐ Not going to file. (Provide an explanation.)

☐ Other

Federal Tax Year [ ]   Total income from tax return or Item 1 on W-2 "Wages, tips, other compensation" (U.S. dollars) (if applicable) $ [ ]

Explanation for Not Filing:

2. Does any of the income from your or your household members' federal tax return(s) come from an illegal activity or source (such as proceeds from illegal gambling or illegal drug sales)? ☐ Yes ☒ No

3. If you answered "Yes" to **Item Number 2.**, what amount of income from your or your household members' federal tax returns is from an illegal activity? $ n/a

4. Does any of the income from your or your household members' federal tax return(s) come from public benefits as listed in the Instructions? ☐ Yes ☒ No

5. If you answered "Yes" to **Item Number 4.**, what amount of income from your or your household members' federal tax returns is from public benefits as listed in the Instructions? $ n/a

6. If you or your household members received additional income on a continuing weekly, monthly, or annual basis during the most recent tax year, and the income is **NOT** listed on the tax return, provide the amount of additional income (for example, child support). Attach evidence of the additional income. In addition, if you are a child, list any additional income or support available from your parent(s), legal guardian, or other individual providing at least 50 percent of your financial support that is not listed in their tax return.

A. Name of recipient (You or your household member's name):

Family Name (Last Name)   Given Name (First Name)   Middle Name
n/a

Type of Additional Income   Annual Amount Received
                                                   $

Will you or your household member continue to receive this income in the future? ☐ Yes ☐ No

When do you anticipate you or your household member will stop receiving this additional income? (mm/dd/yyyy) [ ]   Total annual amount of additional income received (at the time of filing) $ [ ]

Sample Form I-944, Declaration of Self-Sufficiency (page 5)

Part 3.	Your and Your Household Member(s)'s Assets, Resources, and Financial Status (continued)

B. Name of recipient (You or your household member's name)

Family Name (Last Name)

Given Name (First Name)

Middle Name

Type of Additional Income

Annual Amount Received
$

Will you or your household member continue to receive this income in the future? ☐ Yes ☐ No

If you answered "No," when will you or your household member stop receiving this additional income? (mm/dd/yyyy)

Total annual amount of additional income received (at the time of filing)
$

C. Name of recipient (You or your household member's name):

Family Name (Last Name)

Given Name (First Name)

Middle Name

Type of Additional Income

Annual Amount Received
$

Will you or your household member continue to receive this income in the future? ☐ Yes ☐ No

If you answered "No," when will you or your household member stop receiving this additional income? (mm/dd/yyyy)

Total annual amount of additional income received (at the time of filing)
$

D. Name of recipient (You or your household member's name):

Family Name (Last Name)

Given Name (First Name)

Middle Name

Type of Additional Income

Annual Amount Received
$

Will you or your household member continue to receive this income in the future? ☐ Yes ☐ No

If you answered "No," when will you or your household member stop receiving this additional income? (mm/dd/yyyy)

Total annual amount of additional income received (at the time of filing)
$

7. Is any of the additional income listed above from an illegal activity or source? (such as proceeds from illegal gambling or illegal drug sales) ☐ Yes ☐ No

8. If you answered "Yes" to **Item Number 7.**, what amount of additional annual income listed above is from an illegal activity?
$

Sample Form I-944, Declaration of Self-Sufficiency (page 6)

Part 3. Your and Your Household Member(s)'s Assets, Resources, and Financial Status (continued)

Your Household's Assets and Resources

For more information on what are considered assets and how you can demonstrate their value, please see the Form I-944 Instructions.

9. Provide the amount of assets and resources available to you and your household members in the table below. Attach evidence as provided in the Instructions.

If you are a child, provide any assets available from your parent(s), legal guardian, or other individual providing at least 50 percent of your financial support.

Name of Asset Holder (you or your household member)	Type of Asset (cash value)	Amount (U.S. dollars)
Myself	Savings - Bank Account	10,000
Andrew Brown, spouse/household member	Savings - Bank Account	20,000
Andrew Brown, spouse/household member	Other	10,000
Current Cash Value (U.S. dollars) $		40,000
TOTAL (U.S. dollars) $		40,000

Liabilities/Debts

10. Provide a list of your liabilities and/or debts in the table below. Attach evidence showing these liabilities or debts.

Type of Liability or Debt		Amount (U.S. dollars)
Mortgages	$	0
Car Loans	$	0
Credit Card Debt	$	500
Education Related Loans	$	2,000
Tax Debts	$	0
Liens	$	0
Personal Loans	$	0
Other	$	0
TOTAL (U.S. dollars) $		2,500

Credit Report and Score

Provide the information about your credit history. Provide documentation as provided in the Instructions.

11. Do you have a U.S. credit report?

☐ Yes. Provide a U.S. credit report generated within the last 12 months prior to the date of filing.

☒ No. Provide a credit agency report that demonstrates that you do not have a credit record or score.

Sample Form I-944, Declaration of Self-Sufficiency (page 7)

Part 3. Your and Your Household Member(s)'s Assets, Resources, and Financial Status (continued)

12. Do you have a U.S. credit score? ☐ Yes ☒ No

If you answered "Yes," enter a credit score within the last 12 months and attach the credit score document.

n/a

13. If you have negative credit history or a low credit score in the United States reflected on your credit report, provide an explanation. For guidance on what constitutes negative credit history, please see the Instructions.

n/a

14. Have you **EVER** filed for bankruptcy, either in the United States or in a foreign country? ☐ Yes ☒ No

If you answered "Yes" to **Item Number 14.**, provide the information about each bankruptcy filing in **Item A. - C.** and provide evidence of the resolution of each bankruptcy.

A. Place of Filing

City | State or Country

Date (mm/dd/yyyy) | Type of Bankruptcy

☐ Chapter 7 ☐ Chapter 11 ☐ Chapter 13

B. Place of Filing

City | State or Country

Date (mm/dd/yyyy) | Type of Bankruptcy

☐ Chapter 7 ☐ Chapter 11 ☐ Chapter 13

C. Place of Filing

City | State or Country

Date (mm/dd/yyyy) | Type of Bankruptcy

☐ Chapter 7 ☐ Chapter 11 ☐ Chapter 13

Health Insurance

15. Do you currently have health insurance? ☒ Yes ☐ No

If you answered "Yes" to **Item Number 15.**, attach evidence of health insurance.

If you answered "No" to **Item Number 15.**, proceed to **Item D.**

A. If you answered "Yes" to **Item Number 15.**, did you receive a Premium Tax Credit or Advanced Premium Tax Credit under the Affordable Care Act, for the health insurance? ☐ Yes ☒ No

B. If you answered "Yes" to **Item Number 15.**, what is your total annual deductible or annual premium?

$ | 7,000

C. If you answered "Yes" to **Item Number 15.**, when does your health insurance terminate or date that it must be renewed?

(mm/dd/yyyy) | 12/31/2020

Sample Form I-944, Declaration of Self-Sufficiency (page 8)

Part 3. Your and Your Household Member(s)'s Assets, Resources, and Financial Status (continued)

D. Have you enrolled or will soon enroll in health insurance but your health coverage has not started yet?

☒ Yes, I am enrolled ☐ I will soon enroll ☐ No

If you answered "Yes," attach a letter or other evidence from the insurance company showing that you have enrolled in or have a future enrollment date for health insurance and when your coverage begins.

If you receive federally-funded Medicaid, please list those benefits in **Items Numbers 15.** and **16.**

If you answered "No" to **Item Number 15.**, you may provide information on how you plan to pay for reasonably anticipated medical costs. If you need extra space to complete this section, use the space provided in **Part 9. Additional Information**.

Public Benefits

Provide the requested information and submit documentation, as outlined in the Instructions. If you need additional space to complete any **Item Number** in this Part, use the space provided in **Part 9. Additional Information**.

16. Have you **EVER** received, or are currently certified to receive in the future any of the following public benefits? (select **all** that apply).

☐ Yes, I have received, or I am currently certified to receive in the future the following benefits:

☐ Any Federal, State, local or tribal cash assistance for income maintenance

☐ Supplemental Security Income (SSI)

☐ Temporary Assistance for Needy Families (TANF)

☐ General Assistance (GA)

☐ Supplemental Nutrition Assistance Program (SNAP, formerly called "Food Stamps")

☐ Section 8 Housing Assistance under the Housing Choice Voucher Program

☐ Section 8 Project-Based Rental Assistance (including Moderate Rehabilitation)

☐ Public Housing under the Housing Act of 1937, 42 U.S.C. 1437 et seq.

☐ Federal-funded Medicaid

☒ No, I have not received any public benefits.

☐ No, I am not certified to receive in the future any of the above public benefits.

17. Have you disenrolled, withdrawn from, or requested to be disenrolled from the public benefit(s)? ☐ Yes ☐ No

Expected date of disenrollment (mm/dd/yyyy) [n/a]

Sample Form I-944, Declaration of Self-Sufficiency (page 9)

Part 3. Your and Your Household Member(s)'s Assets, Resources, and Financial Status   (continued)

18. If you selected one or more public benefits in **Item Number 16.**, provide information about the public benefits in the space below. If you need additional space to complete any Item Number in this Part, use the space provided in **Part 9. Additional Information**. If a question does not apply, please enter N/A.

   A.   Type of Public Benefit

           n/a

          Agency that Granted the Public Benefit

   Date You Started Receiving the Benefit or if Certified, Date You Will Start Receiving the Benefit or Date Your Coverage Starts

   (mm/dd/yyyy)

   Date Benefit or Coverage Ended or Expires or is Expected to Expire

   (mm/dd/yyyy)

   Amount Received $

   B.   Type of Public Benefit

          Agency that Granted the Public Benefit

   Date You Started Receiving the Benefit or if Certified, Date You Will Start Receiving the Benefit or Date Your Coverage Starts

   (mm/dd/yyyy)

   Date Benefit or Coverage Ended or Expires or is Expected to Expire

   (mm/dd/yyyy)

   Amount Received $

   C.   Type of Public Benefit

          Agency that Granted the Public Benefit

   Date You Started Receiving the Benefit or if Certified, Date You Will Start Receiving the Benefit or Date Your Coverage Starts

   (mm/dd/yyyy)

   Date Benefit or Coverage Ended or Expires or is Expected to Expire

   (mm/dd/yyyy)

   Amount Received $

19. If you answered "Yes" to **Item Number 16.**, do any of the following apply to you? (select all that apply) Provide the evidence listed in the Instructions if any of the following apply to you.

   ☐ I am enlisted in the U.S. Armed Forces, or am serving in active duty or in the Ready Reserve Component of the U.S. Armed Forces.

   ☐ I am the spouse or the child of an individual who is enlisted in the U.S. Armed Forces, or is serving in active duty or in the Ready Reserve Component of the U.S. Armed Forces.

   ☐ At the time I received the public benefits, I (or my spouse or parent) was enlisted in the U.S. Armed Forces, or was serving in active duty or in the Ready Reserve Component of the U.S. Armed Forces.

   ☐ At the time I received the public benefits, I was present in the United States in a status exempt from the public charge ground of inadmissibility and I received the public benefits during that time.

   ☐ At the time I received public benefits, I was present in the United States after being granted a waiver from the public charge ground of inadmissibility.

   ☐ I am the child of U.S. citizens whose lawful admission for permanent residence and subsequent residence in the legal and physical custody of my U.S. citizen parent will result in me automatically acquiring U.S. citizenship upon meeting the eligibility under INA 320.

Sample Form I-944, Declaration of Self-Sufficiency (page 10)

Part 3.	Your and Your Household Member(s)'s Assets, Resources, and Financial Status (continued)

☐ I am the child of U.S. citizens whose lawful admission for permanent residence will result automatically in my acquisition of citizenship upon finalization of adoption (and I satisfied the requirements applicable to adopted children under INA 101(b)(1)), in the United States by the U.S. citizen parent(s), upon meeting the eligibility criteria under INA 320.

☐ None of the above statements apply to me.

20. Have you received, applied for, or have been certified to receive federally-funded Medicaid in connection with any of following? (select all that apply)

Submit evidence as outlined in the Instructions.

☐ An emergency medical condition

☐ For a service under the Individuals with Disabilities Education Act (IDEA)

☐ Other school-based benefits or services available up to the oldest age eligible for secondary education under State law

☐ While you were under the age of 21

☐ While you were pregnant or during the 60-day period following the last day of pregnancy

☒ None of the above apply to me

21. Provide the applicable dates (mm/dd/yyyy) `n/a` to (mm/dd/yyyy) `n/a`

22. Have you ever applied for any of the following public benefits and the application is currently pending or was denied?

☐ Yes   ☒ No

23. If you answered "Yes" to **Item Number 22.**, provide the following information (select all that apply).

☐ I have a pending application for the following public benefits (select all that apply):

    ☐ Any Federal, State, local or tribal cash assistance for income maintenance

    ☐ Supplemental Security Income (SSI)

    ☐ Temporary Assistance for Needy Families (TANF)

    ☐ General Assistance (GA)

    ☐ Supplemental Nutrition Assistance Program (SNAP, formerly called "Food Stamps")

    ☐ Section 8 Housing Assistance under the Housing Choice Voucher Program

    ☐ Section 8 Project-Based Rental Assistance (including Moderate Rehabilitation)

    ☐ Public Housing under the Housing Act of 1937, 42 U.S.C. 1437 et seq.

    ☐ Federally-funded Medicaid

☐ I applied for and the application was denied (select all that apply):

    ☐ Any Federal, State, local or tribal cash assistance for income maintenance

    ☐ Supplemental Security Income (SSI)

    ☐ Temporary Assistance for Needy Families (TANF)

    ☐ General Assistance (GA)

    ☐ Supplemental Nutrition Assistance Program (SNAP, formerly called "Food Stamps")

    ☐ Section 8 Housing Assistance under the Housing Choice Voucher Program

    ☐ Section 8 Project-Based Rental Assistance (including Moderate Rehabilitation)

    ☐ Public Housing under the Housing Act of 1937, 42 U.S.C. 1437 et seq.

    ☐ Federally-funded Medicaid

Sample Form I-944, Declaration of Self-Sufficiency (page 11)

Part 3. Your and Your Household Member(s)'s Assets, Resources, and Financial Status (continued)

24. Date you applied for any of the above listed public benefits (mm/dd/yyyy)   `n/a`

25. Did you withdraw your application(s) before being certified to receive the public benefit(s)?   ☐ Yes ☐ No

26. Have you applied for or received a fee waiver when applying for an immigration benefit from USCIS?   ☐ Yes ☒ No

If you answered "Yes" to **Item Number 26.**, provide the information below. Explain the circumstances that caused you to apply for a fee waiver and if those circumstances have changed in **Part 9. Additional Information**.

A. Date Fee Waiver Received (If you did not receive the fee waiver, write N/A) (mm/dd/yyyy)   `n/a`

Type of Immigrant Benefit (Form Number)   Receipt Number
►

B. Date Fee Waiver Received (If you did not receive the fee waiver, write N/A) (mm/dd/yyyy)

Type of Immigrant Benefit (Form Number)   Receipt Number
►

C. Date Fee Waiver Received (If you did not receive the fee waiver, write N/A) (mm/dd/yyyy)

Type of Immigrant Benefit (Form Number)   Receipt Number
►

Part 4. Your Education and Skills

1. Do you have an approved Form I-140 as an alien worker?   ☐ Yes ☒ No

If you answered "Yes" to **Item Number 1.**, provide the receipt number and skip to **Part 5.**

Receipt Number
►

If you answered "No," proceed to **Item Number 2.**

Provide information about your education, occupational skills, and other related information. If you need additional space to complete any Item Number in this Part, use the space provided in **Part 9. Additional Information**.

2. Have you graduated high school or earned a high school equivalent diploma?   ☒ Yes ☐ No

3. List your educational history below. Include all degrees attained (high school diploma, college degrees or equivalent, etc.). If you answered "No" to **Item Number 2.**, then list the highest grade completed. Provide documentation as provided in the Instructions.

A.

Program/School Name	Degree/Certificate
Sofia High School	Diploma

Field of Study (if applicable)	Date Started (mm/dd/yyyy)	Date Ended (mm/dd/yyyy)
n/a	08/2000	06/2004

Credit Hours/Hours of Study Completed (if no degree or certificate completed)   `Diploma`

Sample Form I-944, Declaration of Self-Sufficiency (page 12)

Part 4. Your Education and Skills (continued)

B. Program/School Name

Sofia University

Degree/Certificate

Bachelor

Field of Study (if applicable)

Art History

Date Started (mm/dd/yyyy)

08/2004

Date Ended (mm/dd/yyyy)

05/2008

Credit Hours/Hours of Study Completed (if no degree or certificate completed)   Bachelor

C. Program/School Name

Degree/Certificate

Field of Study (if applicable)

Date Started (mm/dd/yyyy)

Date Ended (mm/dd/yyyy)

Credit Hours/Hours of Study Completed (if no degree or certificate completed)

D. Program/School Name

Degree/Certificate

Field of Study (if applicable)

Date Started (mm/dd/yyyy)

Date Ended (mm/dd/yyyy)

Credit Hours/Hours of Study Completed (if no degree or certificate completed)

4. Do you have any occupational skills?   ☐ Yes   ☒ No

If you answered "Yes" to **Item Number 4.**, provide the information below. If you answered "No," skip to **Item Number 5.** Provide documentation as provided in the Instructions.

A. Certification/License Type/Occupational Skill

Date Obtained (mm/dd/yyyy)

Who Issued Your License or Certification? (if any)

License Number (if any)

Expiration/Renewal Date (mm/dd/yyyy) (if any)

B. Certification/License Type/Occupational Skill

Date Obtained (mm/dd/yyyy)

Who Issued Your License or Certification? (if any)

License Number (if any)

Expiration/Renewal Date (mm/dd/yyyy) (if any)

C. Certification/License Type/Occupational Skill

Date Obtained (mm/dd/yyyy)

Who Issued Your License or Certification? (if any)

License Number (if any)

Expiration/Renewal Date (mm/dd/yyyy) (if any)

Sample Form I-944, Declaration of Self-Sufficiency (page 13)

Part 4. Your Education and Skills (continued)

5. Provide the following information about your skill with English and any other language in **Item A. - C.** below.

   Provide documentation as provided in the Instructions.

   A. Language

   English

   Certification/Courses Attended or Currently Attending (if any)

   University

   Date Certificate Obtained or Date Course Completed (mm/dd/yyyy)

   n/a

   Who Issued the Certification? (if any)

   n/a

   B. Language

   Bulgarian

   Certification/Courses Attended or Currently Attending (if any)

   Native speaker

   Date Certificate Obtained or Date Course Completed (mm/dd/yyyy)

   n/a

   Who Issued the Certification? (if any)

   n/a

   C. Language

   Certification/Courses Attended or Currently Attending (if any)

   Date Certificate Obtained or Date Course Completed (mm/dd/yyyy)

   Who Issued the Certification? (if any)

6. Retirement

   A. Are you currently retired? ☐ Yes ☒ No

   B. If you are retired, since when have you been retired? (mm/dd/yyyy)   n/a

7. Are you the primary caregiver, who is over the age of 18, for a child, or an elderly, ill or disabled individual in your household?

   ☐ Yes ☒ No

Part 5. Declarant's Statement, Contact Information, Certification, and Signature

NOTE: Read the **Penalties** section of the Form I-944 Instructions before completing this section. You must file Form I-944 while in the United States.

Declarant's Statement

NOTE: Select the box for either **Item A.** or **B.** in **Item Number 1.** If applicable, select the box for **Item Number 2.**

1. Declarant's Statement Regarding the Interpreter

   A. ☒ I can read and understand English, and I have read and understand every question and instruction on this declaration and my answer to every question.

   B. ☐ The interpreter named in **Part 6.** read to me every question and instruction on this declaration and my answer to every question in _____, a language in which I am fluent, and I understood everything.

2. Declarant's Statement Regarding the Preparer

   ☐ At my request, the preparer named in **Part 7.,** _____, prepared this declaration for me based only upon information I provided or authorized.

Sample Form I-944, Declaration of Self-Sufficiency (page 14)

Part 5. Declarant's Statement, Contact Information, Certification, and Signature (continued)

Declarant's Contact Information

3. Declarant's Daytime Telephone Number

8142223344

4. Declarant's Mobile Telephone Number (if any)

8142223344

5. Declarant's Email Address (if any)

andam@email.com

Federal Agency Disclosure and Authorizations

I authorize, as applicable, the Social Security Administration (SSA) to verify my Social Security number (to match my name, Social Security number, and date of birth with information in SSA records and provide the results of the match) to USCIS. I authorize SSA to provide explanatory information to USCIS as necessary.

I authorize, as applicable, the SSA, U.S. Department of Agriculture (USDA), U.S. Department of Health and Human Services (HHS), U.S. Department of Housing and Urban Development (HUD), and any other government agency that has received and/or adjudicated a request for a public benefit, as defined in 8 C.F.R. 212.21(b), submitted by me or on my behalf, and/or granted one or more public benefits to me, to disclose to USCIS that I have applied for, received, or have been certified to receive, a public benefit from such agency, including the type and amount of benefit(s), date(s) of receipt and any other relevant information provided to the agency for the purpose of obtaining such public benefit, to the extent permitted by law. I also authorize SSA, USDA, HHS, HUD, and any other U.S. Government agency to provide any additional data and information to USCIS, to the extent permitted by law.

I authorize, as applicable, custodians of records and other sources of information pertaining to my request for or receipt of public benefits to release information regarding my request for and/or receipt of public benefits, upon the request of the investigator, special agent, or other duly accredited representative of any federal agency authorized above, regardless of any previous agreement to the contrary.

I understand that the information released by records custodians and sources of information is for official use by the federal government, that the U.S. Government will use it only to review if I have received public benefits in regards to my eligibility for immigration benefits and to enforce immigration laws, and that the U.S. Government may disclose the information only as authorized by law.

Credit Reports and Scores Disclosure and Authorization

USCIS may require information from one or more consumer reporting agencies in order to obtain information, including credit reports and scores, in connection with a background investigation regarding your eligibility for immigration benefits.

I authorize USCIS to request, and any consumer reporting agency to provide, such reports.

NOTE: If you have a security freeze on your consumer or credit report file, we may not be able to access the information necessary to complete your investigation. To avoid any delays, you should expeditiously respond to any requests made to release the credit freeze.

Declarant's Certification

Copies of any documents I have submitted are exact photocopies of unaltered, original documents, and I understand that USCIS may require that I submit original documents to USCIS at a later date. Furthermore, I authorize the release of any information from any and all of my records that USCIS may need to determine my eligibility for the immigration benefit that I seek.

I furthermore authorize release of information contained in this declaration, in supporting documents, and in my USCIS records, to other entities and individual where necessary for the administration and enforcement of U.S. immigration law.

I understand that USCIS may require me to appear for an appointment to take my biometrics (fingerprints, photograph, and/or signature) and, at that time, if I am required to provide biometrics, I will be required to sign an oath reaffirming that:

1) I reviewed and understood all of the information contained in, and submitted with, my declaration; and

2) All of this information was complete, true, and correct at the time of filing.

Sample Form I-944, Declaration of Self-Sufficiency (page 15)

Part 5. Declarant's Statement, Contact Information, Certification, and Signature (continued)

I certify, under penalty of perjury, that all of the information in my declaration and any document submitted with it were provided or authorized by me, that I reviewed and understand all of the information contained in, and submitted with, my declaration and that all of this information is complete, true, and correct.

Declarant's Signature

6. Declarant's Signature

➡ *Anda Michelski*

Date of Signature (mm/dd/yyyy)

04/01/2020

NOTE TO ALL DECLARANTS: If you do not completely fill out this declaration or fail to submit required documents listed in the Instructions, USCIS may deny your declaration.

Part 6. Interpreter's Contact Information, Certification, and Signature

Provide the following information about the interpreter.

Interpreter's Full Name

1. Interpreter's Family Name (Last Name)

Interpreter's Given Name (First Name)

2. Interpreter's Business or Organization Name (if any)

Interpreter's Mailing Address

3. Street Number and Name

Apt. Ste. Flr. Number

☐   ☐   ☐

City or Town

State ZIP Code

Province

Postal Code

Country

Interpreter's Contact Information

4. Interpreter's Daytime Telephone Number

5. Interpreter's Mobile Telephone Number (if any)

6. Interpreter's Email Address (if any)

Interpreter's Certification

I certify, under penalty of perjury, that:

I am fluent in English and   which is the same language specified in **Part 5.**,

Item B. in **Item Number 1.**, and I have read to this declarant in the identified language every question and instruction on this declaration and his or her answer to every question. The declarant informed me that he or she understands every instruction, question, and answer on the declaration, including the **Declarant's Certification**, and has verified the accuracy of every answer.

Consular Processing

The second type of government procedure for getting a green card (other than adjustment of status) is "consular processing." It means that the immigrant goes to a U.S. embassy or consulate to complete the green card application. Only after the consulate interviews and approves the immigrant for an immigrant visa can he or she enter the United States and claim permanent resident status.

Most immigrants will have no choice but to use consular processing as their application method. Immigrants who are overseas are almost all required to use consular processing, though many would love to enter the U.S. and finish their application there. However, with the exception of fiancés and people immigrating based on marriage (who can use a K-3 fiancé visa to enter the U.S. and then adjust status) most immigrants will only get themselves in trouble (for example, accused of visa fraud) if they try to enter the U.S. to finish their green card application.

Immigrants who are already in the United States might be required to use consular processing if they are not eligible to use the adjustment of status procedure described in Chapter 16. Unfortunately, this lack of choice creates a potential trap for immigrants who have lived illegally in the U.S. for 180 days or more. By leaving the U.S., they become subject to penalties for their illegal stay. Even if they otherwise qualify for a green card, the consulate must, under the law, bar them from reentering the U.S. for three years (if their illegal stay was between 180 days and one year) or ten years (for illegal stays over one year). See an attorney if you're in this situation—there are waivers you can apply for, including a "provisional waiver" that allows some applicants to receive an answer before they actually leave the U.S., but it's hard to get one approved.

This chapter will discuss the paperwork and other requirements involved in consular processing.

> **CAUTION**
>
> **Remember, this chapter discusses only procedures, not your underlying eligibility for a green card.** Unless you've already completed the steps explained in another chapter—most likely one describing family- or lottery-based visas—you shouldn't be in this chapter. It's only for people with approved immigrant petitions or winning lottery letters who are now completing their green card application process.

If You Have a Choice of Procedure

While the requirements for adjustment of status (getting a green card at a USCIS office) are rather restrictive, if you qualify, there are a number of advantages to that procedure over consular processing. If you are currently in the U.S., read Chapter 16 carefully to see whether you qualify to get a green card through adjustment of status.

> **TIP**
>
> **Are you a K-3 spouse applying for a green card by applying for a fiancé visa and later using adjustment of status procedure?** The consular processing procedures and fee amounts outlined in this chapter apply only to spouses applying for immigrant visas who will not have to adjust status after arriving in the United States. If USCIS approves your Form I-130 prior to or at the same as your Form I-129F, your application will be converted to consular processing and will be subject to the procedures (and fees) in this chapter. This is because your main reason for applying for a K-3 visa—the shorter processing times—is now no longer a concern for you. See Chapters 6, 7, and 16 for more information about using the K-3 visa and adjusting status in the United States.

A. How Your Case Gets to the Consulate

When your relative filled out your I-130 immigrant petition, or when you filled out your lottery application, your address or other information will have indicated to the U.S. government which consulate would be most convenient for you. After your immigrant petition has been approved or you've won the lottery, a central office known as the National Visa Center (NVC) will take care of transferring your file to the appropriate consulate. (Remember that if you're not an immediate relative but a "preference relative," you might have to wait several years before your Priority Date becomes current and your case is transferred to a consulate—see Chapter 5 for details.)

A lot has to happen, however, before the NVC transfers your case. You will have to visit the Consular Electronic Application Center (CEAC) at http://ceac.state.gov/ceac and complete DS-261, Online Choice of Address and Agent. Log in using the case number that the NVC sent you either by mail or email. It's a fairly simple form, but keep in mind that by choosing an "agent," you are essentially deciding where and how all the important notices from the U.S. government will be sent—to your overseas address or to the petitioner or via email. If mail service from the U.S. has been at all unreliable where you live, or if you might be moving before your visa interview, it's safest to choose the petitioner (in the U.S.) as your agent or to indicate that you'd rather be contacted by email. Since the majority of the steps you need to take on your I-130 petition are online, it makes sense to enroll in email notifications.

After you submit the DS-261, you will receive some information about filing fees. If you are immigrating through a family member, the NVC will send the U.S. family member petitioner a bill for the Affidavit of Support review and send either you or your agent a bill for the immigrant visa processing fee (currently $325). If any family members who are included on your petition are immigrating with you, a separate filing fee for each will also be required. However, all family members can be included on the one $120 filing fee for the Affidavit of Support.

The NVC prefers that you pay these fees online, by entering your checking account number and bank routing number. That's also the best way to ensure that your fees get credited to your account, all your documents are kept together, and that the NVC doesn't lose your paper check. The affidavit of support and the immigrant visa processing fees may be paid online at https://ceac.state.gov/IV/Login.aspx.

If you don't have a checking account, you will need to pay by mail using a bank check or money order. Make sure to have your visa bill handy, because it contains a bar code that the NVC will need in order to credit your fee to your application.

After paying your fees, you will need to submit DS-260, the online immigrant visa application. This form will ask you a number of biographical questions, such as all names used, all addresses where you have lived, work and educational history, and family member information. You will also be asked questions to determine your admissibility to the United States.

The DS-260 application can be submitted only online. You will again need your NVC invoice number and receipt number in order to complete it. You can save your DS-260 and come back to it later if you need to. Keep in mind that you do need to complete this form in English using English characters only, so have someone ready to help if you aren't confident in your English ability.

This online form requires a lot of detail. You'll be asked for all your addresses since the age of 16 and the exact dates that you lived there. Make sure that all your answers correspond with the answers given on the petitioner's Form I-130. If an answer does not apply to you (such as U.S. Social Security number), you will be given the option to choose "Does Not Apply." See more tips for filling out immigration forms in Chapter 21.

After you submit the DS-260, print the confirmation page and bring it to your interview. Although you are not required to do so, it doesn't hurt to print out a copy of the entire form as well, so that you can refer to it when needed.

TIP
Got questions? The Department of State website has an outline of the entire process. At https:// travel.state. gov, click "U.S. Visas," then "Immigrate," then "Learn About Immigrating to the United States." To learn more about the NVC, click "National Visa Center" on the right side of the page. There, you'll find ways to contact the NVC, including its Public Inquiry Form. Be sure to have your USCIS receipt number or NVC case number ready when you call or inquire online.

You will receive further instructions and a checklist on what else the NVC needs from you before your interview. See the next section for our own checklist of the forms and documents you'll need. For consulate-specific information on what you will be required to bring, visit https://travel.state.gov/content/travel/en/us-visas/visa-information-resources/list-of-posts.html. And there's a list of U.S. embassies and consulates at www.usembassy.gov. Many consulate-specific websites offer information in the country's native language.

All foreign-language documents must be translated as well. For more information on the requirements, see Chapter 21.

After the NVC is satisfied that you have submitted the necessary documentation and have paid all your fees, it will schedule an interview date and transfer your visa file to the appropriate U.S. consulate or embassy.

Fees for Visa Services

The following chart shows the fees required for immigrant visa processing (as of the date this book went to print in mid-2020) after your Form I-130 is approved by USCIS. For an updated list of fee amounts, go to https://usvisas.state.gov and click "Fees/Reciprocity" then "Fees-Visa Services." These fees are required only for immigrant visas, not nonimmigrant visas.

Fee Type	Fee Amount	Payment Details
Affidavit of Support Review Fee	$120	Only one fee is required for the applicant and all family members included in the visa application
Immediate Family and Family Preference Applications Immigrant Visa Fee	$325	Separate filing fee is required for each family member included in the visa application
Diversity Lottery Visa Fee	$330	Only required for diversity lottery visa applicants
USCIS Immigrant Fee	$220	Separate filing fee is required for each family member after the consulate interview and visa approval. You may pay this fee after you receive your visa to enter the U.S., but you will not receive a green card until the fee is paid. It's best to pay this fee after receiving your visa packet from the U.S. consulate.

Before your interview, you will need to attend a medical examination with an authorized physician. To find one in your country and learn more about the required medical examination, go to https://travel. state.gov. Click "U.S. Visas," then "Immigrate," and finally "Prepare for Your Interview."

Medical exam fees vary among doctors, so it's best to call around to inquire. Bringing your vaccination records and any recent chest X-rays will help you to avoid additional costs for shots and X-rays (if necessary).

This exam is not like the ordinary one you'd have with your own doctor. Its sole purpose is to spot any grounds of inadmissibility that might prevent you from getting a green card. See Chapter 4 for a discussion of the grounds of inadmissibility. If you do have a medical ground of inadmissibility, you could be eligible for a waiver (also discussed in Chapter 4), and should consult an immigration lawyer. See Chapter 24 for tips on finding a good lawyer.

B. Forms and Documents You'll Need to Provide

Here's a summary of the forms and documents that you'll need to give to either the NVC or the consulate between now and the end of the process:

☐ Confirmation page for Form DS-260, which you'll fill out online (as described above)

☐ Copies of current passports. You'll be asked to send in a copy of the key pages of your family members' passports—but not the originals. You'll bring the original passports to your interview at the U.S. consulate.

☐ Birth certificates or adoption records for you and for your spouse or children, with English translations if they are not in the language of the country in which you are interviewed

☐ A police clearance certificate for each person over 16 years of age from the country of nationality or current residence if he or she has lived there for more than six months, and from any other country where the applicant lived for more than one year

☐ Marriage certificate, death certificate, divorce or annulment decree—whichever shows your current marital status and history

☐ Military record of any service in your country, or any country, including certified proof of military service and of honorable or dishonorable discharge

☐ Certified copy of court and prison records if you have been convicted of a crime

☐ Form I-864 or I-864EZ, Affidavit of Support. (See the sample Form I-864 at the end of this chapter. Notice that in our sample, the sponsor didn't have enough income, and therefore had to add a Form I-864A in which his daughter, who lives with him, also promised to add her income to help the immigrant.) Which form you must submit depends on your situation. You must file Form I-864 if your petition is family based (except K-1 fiancé visas). But if you are the only person that your petitioner is sponsoring, and your petitioner can meet the sponsorship requirements based upon his or her income alone, he or she can use a shorter version of the form, called I-864EZ. On both Form I-134 and I-864, a U.S. citizen or permanent resident promises to repay the U.S. government if you become impoverished and go on public assistance after you arrive in the United States.

☐ Documents to support form I-864. Your sponsor who fills out the form must also include financial documents, including an employment verification letter or other proof of income such as a "year-to-date" pay stub, the sponsor's latest U.S. income tax transcript and W-2s (or the last three years', if it will strengthen the case). If the sponsor is relying on assets to meet the poverty guidelines, then proof of those assets—such as bank statements—must be submitted.

□ Form I-864W (in cases where an I-864 is not required). In certain exceptional cases, a Form I-864 need not be filed. One of these is where the beneficiary is a child (adopted or natural born) who will become a U.S. citizen automatically upon entering the United States (see Chapter 20 for details). The other is where the beneficiary, or the beneficiary's spouse or parent, has worked 40 "quarters" (about ten years, as defined by the Social Security Administration) in the United States. If you're exempt from the affidavit of support requirement due to one of these exceptions, you should fill out and sign Form I-864W.

□ Form DS-5540, Public Charge Questionnaire. (See sample at end of chapter.) This asks about financial issues like household size, assets, and whether you will have health insurance coverage in the United States. Documents to accompany Form DS-5540, depending on your answers to the questions. You might, for instance, need to provide an IRS tax transcript if you've paid taxes in the United States; and should document any health insurance that you'll have. Be ready for the consulate to request additional documents, as well.

You will also be required to submit to fingerprinting, for a background check by the FBI and CIA. (See Chapter 21, Section F, for more about these security checks.)

The final set of documents you'll normally need to prepare for your interview include:

□ Two color photographs, passport style

□ Current passports for you and for everyone in your family who is getting an immigrant visa (they must not expire earlier than six months after your interview date)

□ Medical examination report. During the exam, your blood will be tested and you will be X-rayed. You may be barred from immigrating if these tests show that you have a contagious disease of public health concern such as tuberculosis, or if you have a severe mental disorder. If any of these bars apply to you, you could be eligible for a waiver (see Chapter 4), and should consult an immigration lawyer.

□ U.S. income tax transcripts. If you have worked in the U.S., you must present proof that you filed income tax returns for every year you worked.

□ Visa fees, if not already paid or a receipt showing you paid the fees online.

For a printable checklist of this information, go to https://travel.state.gov and click "U.S. Visas," then "Immigrate," then "The Immigrant Visa Process," then "Prepare for the Interview," then "Items You Must Bring to Your Visa Interview."

! CAUTION

Unmarried children beware. If you are an unmarried son or daughter of a permanent resident or a U.S. citizen, and you marry before you have your immigration visa interview, be prepared for a shock: Your visa will be denied because you are no longer in the immediate relative or second preference category under which you were petitioned.

If you married after your visa interview but before you entered the U.S. with your immigrant visa, you could also be in serious trouble. Although you might be admitted into the United States (because USCIS has no way of knowing that you are no longer eligible), the agency could discover this fact if you later apply to bring your spouse or try to become a U.S. citizen.

It will not matter that you have been admitted as a permanent resident. Removal proceedings will be started against you, you and your spouse will not be reunited in the United States, and you will eventually have to go back to your country and start all over again in the preference category of the married son or daughter of a U.S. citizen. You could completely lose your immigrant eligibility if your parent is only a green card holder.

If you fall into this category, see an experienced attorney. (Chapter 24 offers tips on finding one.)

C. Attending Your Visa Interview

The final step in obtaining your visa is to attend an interview with a U.S. consular official. Until the date of your interview, it's quite possible that neither you nor your petitioning spouse or family members (if any) will have had any personal contact with any immigration official. At last, you can deal with a real human being—for better and for worse.

With all the paperwork you've submitted by now, you might wonder why the interview is even necessary. However, the government regards the interview as its opportunity to confirm the contents of your application after you've sworn to tell the truth. If you're applying based on marriage, it also allows them to ask personal questions designed to reveal whether your marriage is the real thing or a sham.

Tips for the Interview

The most important thing to do is relax. Wear conservative but comfortable clothes. The interviewer will ask you mostly about information you have already given in response to questions on your immigration forms and other documents.

Answer all questions truthfully. If you cannot understand a question, be brave and ask for an interpreter. It is better to be embarrassed about not understanding English very well than to be denied your immigrant visa because you misunderstood the question.

If you're being petitioned by a spouse or another family member, they're not expected to attend the interview—although it can help to have them there. If yours is a marriage case, your spouse's willingness to travel and be with you at the interview is a good sign that your marriage is not a sham. Some, but not all, consulates also allow you to bring a lawyer, if you feel you need one.

To prepare for your interview, the most important thing is to review all your paperwork. Look at all the questions and answers on all the forms, including any that were submitted for you by your U.S. family member. Though boring, this information is all important to the consular officials. Be alert for any inconsistencies and mistakes, and bring along any documents that will help correct them.

If you're applying through a spouse or fiancé, spend some time together reviewing the details of how you met, how you've corresponded and visited each other or each other's families, and when and why you decided to get married. If already married, review the details of the wedding—number of guests, where it was held, what food and drink was served, and the like.

If you don't live in the same city as the consulate, it's a good idea to get there a few days in advance, particularly for purposes of getting your medical exam and photos done. Some consulates require a longer waiting period, to ensure that the medical exam results are complete before the interview. (In Indonesia, for example immigrant visa interviews are done at the consulate in Jakarta, which requires that the medical exam be completed ten days before the interview. Applicants who do not live nearby have the choice of either visiting Jakarta for longer than ten days or going there a month before the interview just to do the medical exam.) This is why it's important to review the consulate-specific instructions carefully.

Arrive at the consulate early, in case there's a line. Consulates often schedule applicants in large groups, telling them all to arrive at the same time. The interview itself will probably last 30 minutes. And be careful of personal security outside the consulate—it's a common place for pickpockets and con artists to hang around.

CAUTION

Expect delays due to coronavirus pandemic. Many consulates are canceling or limiting visa interviews. Even after they resume normal functions, there will be a backlog of past cases to catch up on.

D. Approval of Your Immigrant Visa

If the U.S. consulate or embassy needs more information, it will tell you that further administrative processing is necessary and what types of documents it needs. If it denies your case, it will give you a letter detailing the reasons. In any case, you are unlikely to receive the visa at the end of the interview.

The consulate will let you know the method by which you can check on your case status, submit any required documents, and after you're approved, receive your visa (either by mail or in-person pickup). It will give you back your passport with your immigrant visa, a sealed packet (DO NOT open this), and an envelope with your X-rays, all of which you will need to carry with you when you arrive at the U.S. border and are inspected by Customs and Border Protection.

Check the visa for any spelling or other factual errors. Immigrants will also have to pay one additional fee, the USCIS immigrant fee, in order to receive their actual green card after entering the United States. You can do so at www.my.uscis.gov/uscis-immigrant-fee.

Your immigrant visa is valid for six months, and you must arrive in the United States within those six months. Keep in mind that your permanent resident status does not start until you actually enter the United States.

If you are unable to leave for the United States and your visa is about to expire, you may apply for an extension of your immigrant visa by means of an affidavit, or written statement signed before a notary public, explaining why you are unable to leave on time. But unless you have a very good reason, the U.S. consulate will be reluctant to approve an extension.

E. Arriving in the United States

When you arrive at your U.S. port of entry, the U.S. citizens who were on the plane with you will be admitted in one line, while all the noncitizens will be queuing in another line.

When it is your turn, the immigration officer will take your immigrant documents and keep them—all but your X-rays—and make them part of your permanent record in the USCIS office. Your passport will be stamped to show that you have entered as a lawful permanent resident.

Your green card will be mailed to you within several weeks to months. You must inform USCIS if you change addresses within ten days of your move (or you can be deported). Besides, if you don't tell them, you may not receive your green card until you have made several trips to the USCIS office and filled out countless forms. See Chapter 23 for more information on changing addresses and keeping your right to a green card.

At last! You are now a bona fide immigrant—able to live and work legally in the United States. Welcome.

Sample Form I-864, Affidavit of Support Under Section 213A of the Act (page 1)

Affidavit of Support Under Section 213A of the INA

Department of Homeland Security
U.S. Citizenship and Immigration Services

**USCIS
Form I-864**

OMB No. 1615-0075
Expires 10/31/2021

	Affidavit of Support Submitter	Section 213A Review	Number of Support Affidavits in File
For USCIS Use Only	☐ Petitioner ☐ 1st Joint Sponsor ☐ 2nd Joint Sponsor ☐ Substitute Sponsor ☐ 5% Owner	☐ MEETS requirements ☐ DOES NOT MEET requirements Reviewed By: _____ Office: _____ Date (mm/dd/yyyy): _____	☐ 1 ☐ 2 **Remarks**

To be completed by an attorney or accredited representative (if any).	☐ Select this box if Form G-28 or G-28I is attached.	Attorney State Bar Number (if applicable)	Attorney or Accredited Representative USCIS Online Account Number (if any)

▶ **START HERE** - Type or print in black ink.

Part 1. Basis For Filing Affidavit of Support

I, [Alberto Ilario Mancini] ,
am the sponsor submitting this affidavit of support because (Select **only one** box):

1.a. ☒ I am the petitioner. I filed or am filing for the immigration of my relative.

1.b. ☐ I filed an alien worker petition on behalf of the intending immigrant, who is related to me as my
_____

1.c. ☐ I have an ownership interest of at least 5 percent in
_____
which filed an alien worker petition on behalf of the intending immigrant, who is related to me as my
_____

1.d. ☐ I am the only joint sponsor.

1.e. ☐ I am the ☐ first ☐ second of two joint sponsors.

1.f. ☐ The original petitioner is deceased. I am the substitute sponsor. I am the intending immigrant's
_____

NOTE: If you are filing this form as a sponsor, you must include proof of your U.S. citizenship, U.S. national status, or lawful permanent resident status.

Part 2. Information About the Principal Immigrant

1.a. Family Name (Last Name) [Mancini]

1.b. Given Name (First Name) [Terese]

1.c. Middle Name [Maria]

Mailing Address

2.a. In Care Of Name
_____

2.b. Street Number and Name [108 Piazza D'Azaglio]

2.c. ☐ Apt. ☐ Ste. ☐ Flr. _____

2.d. City or Town [Venice]

2.e. State ___ **2.f.** ZIP Code _____

2.g. Province _____

2.h. Postal Code [99999]

2.i. Country [Italy]

Other Information

3. Country of Citizenship or Nationality [Italy]

4. Date of Birth (mm/dd/yyyy) [02/15/1985]

5. Alien Registration Number (A-Number) (if any)
▶ A- _____

6. USCIS Online Account Number (if any)
▶ _____

7. Daytime Telephone Number [3951676464]

Sample Form I-864, Affidavit of Support Under Section 213A of the Act (page 2)

Part 3. Information About the Immigrants You Are Sponsoring

1. I am sponsoring the principal immigrant named in **Part 2.**

   ☒ Yes ☐ No (Applicable only if you are sponsoring family members in **Part 3.** as the second joint sponsor or if you are sponsoring family members who are immigrating more than six months after the principal immigrant)

2. ☒ I am sponsoring the following family members immigrating at the same time or within six months of the principal immigrant named in **Part 2.** (Do not include any relative listed on a separate visa petition.)

3. ☐ I am sponsoring the following family members who are immigrating more than six months after the principal immigrant.

Family Member 1

4.a. Family Name (Last Name) Moreno

4.b. Given Name (First Name) Giovana

4.c. Middle Name Anna

5. Relationship to Principal Immigrant Daughter

6. Date of Birth (mm/dd/yyyy) 06/01/2015

7. Alien Registration Number (A-Number) (if any) ▶ A-

8. USCIS Online Account Number (if any) ▶

Family Member 2

9.a. Family Name (Last Name)

9.b. Given Name (First Name)

9.c. Middle Name

10. Relationship to Principal Immigrant

11. Date of Birth (mm/dd/yyyy)

12. Alien Registration Number (A-Number) (if any) ▶ A-

13. USCIS Online Account Number (if any) ▶

Family Member 3

14.a. Family Name (Last Name)

14.b. Given Name (First Name)

14.c. Middle Name

15. Relationship to Principal Immigrant

16. Date of Birth (mm/dd/yyyy)

17. Alien Registration Number (A-Number) (if any) ▶ A-

18. USCIS Online Account Number (if any) ▶

Family Member 4

19.a. Family Name (Last Name)

19.b. Given Name (First Name)

19.c. Middle Name

20. Relationship to Principal Immigrant

21. Date of Birth (mm/dd/yyyy)

22. Alien Registration Number (A-Number) (if any) ▶ A-

23. USCIS Online Account Number (if any) ▶

Family Member 5

24.a. Family Name (Last Name)

24.b. Given Name (First Name)

24.c. Middle Name

25. Relationship to Principal Immigrant

26. Date of Birth (mm/dd/yyyy)

27. Alien Registration Number (A-Number) (if any) ▶ A-

28. USCIS Online Account Number (if any) ▶

Sample Form I-864, Affidavit of Support Under Section 213A of the Act (page 3)

Part 3. Information About the Immigrants You Are Sponsoring (continued)

29. Enter the total number of immigrants you are sponsoring on this affidavit which includes the principal immigrant listed in **Part 2.**, any immigrants listed in **Part 3., Item Numbers 1. - 28.** and (if applicable), any immigrants listed for these questions in **Part 11. Additional Information**. Do not count the principal immigrant if you are only sponsoring family members entering more than 6 months after the principal immigrant.

| 2 |

Part 4. Information About You (Sponsor)

Sponsor's Full Name

1.a.	Family Name (Last Name)	Mancini
1.b.	Given Name (First Name)	Alberto
1.c.	Middle Name	Ilario

Sponsor's Mailing Address

2.a. In Care Of Name

2.b. Street Number and Name | 800 Broadway

2.c. ☐ Apt. ☐ Ste. ☐ Flr.

2.d. City or Town | Lindenhurst

2.e. State | NY   2.f. ZIP Code | 11757

2.g. Province

2.h. Postal Code

2.i. Country | USA

3. Is your current mailing address the same as your physical address? ☒ Yes ☐ No

If you answered "No" to **Item Number 3.**, provide your physical address in **Item Numbers 4.a. - 4.h.**

Sponsor's Physical Address

4.a. Street Number and Name

4.b. ☐ Apt. ☐ Ste. ☐ Flr.

4.c. City or Town

4.d. State   4.e. ZIP Code

4.f. Province

4.g. Postal Code

4.h. Country

Other Information

5. Country of Domicile | USA

6. Date of Birth (mm/dd/yyyy) | 03/10/1967

7. City or Town of Birth | Los Angeles

8. State or Province of Birth | CA

9. Country of Birth | USA

10. U.S. Social Security Number (Required) ▶ | 2 | 0 | 0 | 5 | 5 | 8 | 8 | 8 | 8 |

Citizenship or Residency

11.a. ☒ I am a U.S. citizen.

11.b. ☐ I am a U.S. national.

11.c. ☐ I am a lawful permanent resident.

12. Sponsor's A-Number (if any) ▶ A-

13. Sponsor's USCIS Online Account Number (if any) ▶

Military Service (To be completed by petitioner sponsors only.)

14. I am currently on **active duty** in the U.S. Armed Forces or U.S. Coast Guard. ☐ Yes ☒ No

Sample Form I-864, Affidavit of Support Under Section 213A of the Act (page 4)

For USCIS Use Only	

Part 5. Sponsor's Household Size

NOTE: Do not count any member of your household more than once.

Persons you are sponsoring in this affidavit:

1. Provide the number you entered in **Part 3., Item Number 29.** `2`

Persons NOT sponsored in this affidavit:

2. Yourself. `1`

3. If you are currently married, enter "1" for your spouse.

4. If you have dependent children, enter the number here.

5. If you have any other dependents, enter the number here.

6. If you have sponsored any other persons on Form I-864 or Form I-864EZ who are now lawful permanent residents, enter the number here.

7. **OPTIONAL:** If you have siblings, parents, or adult children with the same principal residence who are combining their income with yours by submitting Form I-864A, enter the number here. `1`

8. Add together **Part 5., Item Numbers 1. - 7.** and enter the number here.

    Household Size: `4`

Part 6. Sponsor's Employment and Income

I am currently:

1. ☒ Employed as a/an
   `Cook`

2. Name of Employer 1
   `Bob's Diner`

3. Name of Employer 2 (if applicable)

4. ☐ Self-Employed as a/an (Occupation)

5. ☐ Retired Since (mm/dd/yyyy)

6. ☐ Unemployed Since (mm/dd/yyyy)

7. My current individual annual income is:
   $ `21000`

Income you are using from any other person who was counted in your household size, including, in certain conditions, the intending immigrant. (See Form I-864 Instructions.) Please indicate name, relationship, and income.

Person 1

8. Name
   `Beatrice Stella Mancini`

9. Relationship
   `Daughter`

10. **Current Income** $ `50000`

Person 2

11. Name

12. Relationship

13. **Current Income** $

Person 3

14. Name

15. Relationship

16. **Current Income** $

Person 4

17. Name

18. Relationship

19. **Current Income** $

Sample Form I-864, Affidavit of Support Under Section 213A of the Act (page 5)

<table>
<tr>
<td rowspan="4">For
USCIS
Use
Only</td>
<td colspan="2">Household Size</td>
<td>Poverty Guideline</td>
<td>Remarks</td>
</tr>
<tr>
<td colspan="2">☐ 1   ☐ 2   ☐ 3
☐ 4   ☐ 5   ☐ 6
☐ 7   ☐ 8   ☐ 9
☐ Other _____</td>
<td>Year: _2 0___

Poverty Line:
$ _____</td>
<td></td>
</tr>
</table>

Part 6. Sponsor's Employment and Income (continued)

20. **My Current Annual Household Income** (Total all lines from **Part 6. Item Numbers 7., 10., 13., 16.,** and **19.**; the total will be compared to Federal Poverty Guidelines on Form I-864P.) $ [71000]

21. ☒ The people listed in **Item Numbers 8., 11., 14.,** and **17.** have completed Form I-864A. I am filing along with this affidavit all necessary Form I-864As completed by these people.

22. ☐ One or more of the people listed in **Item Numbers 8., 11., 14.,** and **17.** do not need to complete Form I-864A because he or she is the intending immigrant and has no accompanying dependents.

Name
[   ]

Federal Income Tax Return Information

23.a. Have you filed a Federal income tax return for each of the three most recent tax years?   ☒ Yes   ☐ No

NOTE: You **MUST** attach a photocopy or transcript of your Federal income tax return for only the most recent tax year.

23.b. ☐ (Optional) I have attached photocopies or transcripts of my Federal income tax returns for my second and third most recent tax years.

My total income (adjusted gross income on Internal Revenue Service (IRS) Form 1040EZ) as reported on my Federal income tax returns for the most recent three years was:

	Tax Year	Total Income
24.a. Most Recent	2018	$ 21000
24.b. 2nd Most Recent	2017	$ 20000
24.c. 3rd Most Recent	2016	$ 19500

25. ☐ I was not required to file a Federal income tax return as my income was below the IRS required level and I have attached evidence to support this.

Part 7. Use of Assets to Supplement Income (Optional)

If your income, or the total income for you and your household, from **Part 6., Item Numbers 20.** or **24.a. - 24.c**, exceeds the Federal Poverty Guidelines for your household size, **YOU ARE NOT REQUIRED** to complete this **Part 7.** Skip to **Part 8.**

Your Assets (Optional)

1. Enter the balance of all savings and checking accounts.
$ [   ]

2. Enter the net cash value of real-estate holdings. (Net value means current assessed value minus mortgage debt.)
$ [   ]

3. Enter the net cash value of all stocks, bonds, certificates of deposit, and any other assets not already included in **Item Number 1.** or **Item Number 2.**
$ [   ]

4. Add together **Item Numbers 1. - 3.** and enter the number here.   **TOTAL:** $ [   ]

Assets from Form I-864A, Part 4., Item Number 3.d., for:

5.a. Name of Relative
[   ]

5.b. Your household member's assets from Form I-864A (optional).
$ [   ]

Assets of the principal sponsored immigrant (optional).

The principal sponsored immigrant is the person listed in **Part 2., Item Numbers 1.a. - 1.c.** Only include the assets if the principal immigrant is being sponsored by this affidavit of support.

6. Enter the balance of the principal immigrant's savings and checking accounts.
$ [   ]

7. Enter the net cash value of all the principal immigrant's real estate holdings. (Net value means investment value minus mortgage debt.)
$ [   ]

8. Enter the current cash value of the principal immigrant's stocks, bonds, certificates of deposit, and other assets not included in **Item Number 6.** or **Item Number 7.**
$ [   ]

Sample Form I-864, Affidavit of Support Under Section 213A of the Act (page 6)

For USCIS Use Only	Household Size	Poverty Guideline	Sponsor's Household Income *(Page 5, Line 10)*	Remarks
	☐ 1 ☐ 2 ☐ 3 ☐ 4 ☐ 5 ☐ 6 ☐ 7 ☐ 8 ☐ 9 ☐ Other _____	Year: 2 0 ____ Poverty Line: $ _____	$ _____ *The total value of all assets, line 10, must equal 5 times (3 times for spouses and children of USC's, or 1 time for orphans to be formally adopted in the U.S.) the difference between the poverty guidelines and the sponsor's household income, line 10.*	

Part 7. Use of Assets to Supplement Income (Optional) (continued)

9. Add together **Item Numbers 6. - 8.** and enter the number here. $ [_____]

Total Value of Assets

10. Add together **Item Numbers 4., 5.b., and 9.** and enter the number here.

    TOTAL: $ [_____]

Part 8. Sponsor's Contract, Statement, Contact Information, Declaration, Certification, and Signature

NOTE: Read the **Penalties** section of the Form I-864 Instructions before completing this part.

Sponsor's Contract

Please note that, by signing this Form I-864, you agree to assume certain specific obligations under the Immigration and Nationality Act (INA) and other Federal laws. The following paragraphs describe those obligations. Please read the following information carefully before you sign Form I-864. If you do not understand the obligations, you may wish to consult an attorney or accredited representative.

What is the Legal Effect of My Signing Form I-864?

If you sign Form I-864 on behalf of any person (called the intending immigrant) who is applying for an immigrant visa or for adjustment of status to a lawful permanent resident, and that intending immigrant submits Form I-864 to the U.S. Government with his or her application for an immigrant visa or adjustment of status, under INA section 213A, these actions create a contract between you and the U.S. Government. The intending immigrant becoming a lawful permanent resident is the consideration for the contract.

Under this contract, you agree that, in deciding whether the intending immigrant can establish that he or she is not inadmissible to the United States as a person likely to become a public charge, the U.S. Government can consider your income and assets as available for the support of the intending immigrant.

What If I Choose Not to Sign Form I-864?

The U.S. Government cannot make you sign Form I-864 if you do not want to do so. But if you do not sign Form I-864, the intending immigrant may not become a lawful permanent resident in the United States.

What Does Signing Form I-864 Require Me To Do?

If an intending immigrant becomes a lawful permanent resident in the United States based on a Form I-864 that you have signed, then, until your obligations under Form I-864 terminate, you must:

A. Provide the intending immigrant any support necessary to maintain him or her at an income that is at least 125 percent of the Federal Poverty Guidelines for his or her household size (100 percent if you are the petitioning sponsor and are on active duty in the U.S. Armed Forces or U.S. Coast Guard, and the person is your husband, wife, or unmarried child under 21 years of age); and

B. Notify U.S. Citizenship and Immigration Services (USCIS) of any change in your address, within 30 days of the change, by filing Form I-865.

What Other Consequences Are There?

If an intending immigrant becomes a lawful permanent resident in the United States based on a Form I-864 that you have signed, then, until your obligations under Form I-864 terminate, the U.S. Government may consider (deem) your income and assets as available to that person, in determining whether he or she is eligible for certain Federal means-tested public benefits and also for state or local means-tested public benefits, if the state or local government's rules provide for consideration (deeming) of your income and assets as available to the person.

This provision does **not** apply to public benefits specified in section 403(c) of the Welfare Reform Act such as emergency Medicaid, short-term, non-cash emergency relief; services provided under the National School Lunch and Child Nutrition Acts; immunizations and testing and treatment for communicable diseases; and means-tested programs under the Elementary and Secondary Education Act.

What If I Do Not Fulfill My Obligations?

If you do not provide sufficient support to the person who becomes a lawful permanent resident based on a Form I-864 that you signed, that person may sue you for this support.

Sample Form I-864, Affidavit of Support Under Section 213A of the Act (page 7)

Part 8. Sponsor's Contract, Statement, Contact Information, Declaration, Certification, and Signature (continued)

If a Federal, state, local, or private agency provided any covered means-tested public benefit to the person who becomes a lawful permanent resident based on a Form I-864 that you signed, the agency may ask you to reimburse them for the amount of the benefits they provided. If you do not make the reimbursement, the agency may sue you for the amount that the agency believes you owe.

If you are sued, and the court enters a judgment against you, the person or agency that sued you may use any legally permitted procedures for enforcing or collecting the judgment. You may also be required to pay the costs of collection, including attorney fees.

If you do not file a properly completed Form I-865 within 30 days of any change of address, USCIS may impose a civil fine for your failing to do so.

When Will These Obligations End?

Your obligations under a Form I-864 that you signed will end if the person who becomes a lawful permanent resident based on that affidavit:

- **A.** Becomes a U.S. citizen;
- **B.** Has worked, or can receive credit for, 40 quarters of coverage under the Social Security Act;
- **C.** No longer has lawful permanent resident status and has departed the United States;
- **D.** Is subject to removal, but applies for and obtains, in removal proceedings, a new grant of adjustment of status, based on a new affidavit of support, if one is required; or
- **E.** Dies.

NOTE: Divorce **does not** terminate your obligations under Form I-864.

Your obligations under a Form I-864 that you signed also end if you die. Therefore, if you die, your estate is not required to take responsibility for the person's support after your death. However, your estate may owe any support that you accumulated before you died.

Sponsor's Statement

NOTE: Select the box for either **Item Number 1.a.** or **1.b.** If applicable, select the box for **Item Number 2.**

1.a. ☒ I can read and understand English, and I have read and understand every question and instruction on this affidavit and my answer to every question.

1.b. ☐ The interpreter named in **Part 9.** read to me every question and instruction on this affidavit and my answer to every question in
_____,
a language in which I am fluent, and I understood everything.

2. ☐ At my request, the preparer named in **Part 10.**,
_____,
prepared this affidavit for me based only upon information I provided or authorized.

Sponsor's Contact Information

3. Sponsor's Daytime Telephone Number
2122224444

4. Sponsor's Mobile Telephone Number (if any)
2122225555

5. Sponsor's Email Address (if any)
amancini@email.com

Sponsor's Declaration and Certification

Copies of any documents I have submitted are exact photocopies of unaltered, original documents, and I understand that USCIS or the U.S. Department of State (DOS) may require that I submit original documents to USCIS or DOS at a later date. Furthermore, I authorize the release of any information from any and all of my records that USCIS or DOS may need to determine my eligibility for the benefit that I seek.

I furthermore authorize release of information contained in this affidavit, in supporting documents, and in my USCIS or DOS records, to other entities and persons where necessary for the administration and enforcement of U.S. immigration law.

I certify, under penalty of perjury, that all of the information in my affidavit and any document submitted with it were provided or authorized by me, that I reviewed and understand all of the information contained in, and submitted with, my affidavit and that all of this information is complete, true, and correct.

- **A.** I know the contents of this affidavit of support that I signed;
- **B.** I have read and I understand each of the obligations described in **Part 8.**, and I agree, freely and without any mental reservation or purpose of evasion, to accept each of those obligations in order to make it possible for the immigrants indicated in **Part 3.** to become lawful permanent residents of the United States;
- **C.** I agree to submit to the personal jurisdiction of any Federal or state court that has subject matter jurisdiction of a lawsuit against me to enforce my obligations under this Form I-864;

Sample Form I-864, Affidavit of Support Under Section 213A of the Act (page 8)

Part 8. Sponsor's Contract, Statement, Contact Information, Declaration, Certification, and Signature (continued)

D. Each of the Federal income tax returns submitted in support of this affidavit are true copies, or are unaltered tax transcripts, of the tax returns I filed with the IRS;

E. I understand that, if I am related to the sponsored immigrant by marriage, the termination of the marriage (by divorce, dissolution, annulment, or other legal process) will not relieve me of my obligations under this Form I-864; and

F. I authorize the Social Security Administration to release information about me in its records to USCIS and DOS.

Sponsor's Signature

6.a. Sponsor's Signature

Alberto Ilario Mancini

6.b. Date of Signature (mm/dd/yyyy)   03/06/2020

NOTE TO ALL SPONSORS: If you do not completely fill out this affidavit or fail to submit required documents listed in the Instructions, USCIS or DOS may deny your affidavit.

Part 9. Interpreter's Contact Information, Certification, and Signature

Provide the following information about the interpreter.

Interpreter's Full Name

1.a. Interpreter's Family Name (Last Name)

1.b. Interpreter's Given Name (First Name)

2. Interpreter's Business or Organization Name (if any)

Interpreter's Mailing Address

3.a. Street Number and Name

3.b. ☐ Apt. ☐ Ste. ☐ Flr.

3.c. City or Town

3.d. State   **3.e.** ZIP Code

3.f. Province

3.g. Postal Code

3.h. Country

Interpreter's Contact Information

4. Interpreter's Daytime Telephone Number

5. Interpreter's Mobile Telephone Number (if any)

6. Interpreter's Email Address (if any)

Interpreter's Certification

I certify, under penalty of perjury, that:

I am fluent in English and _____, which is the same language specified in **Part 8., Item Number 1.b.**, and I have read to this sponsor in the identified language every question and instruction on this affidavit and his or her answer to every question. The sponsor informed me that he or she understands every instruction, question, and answer on the affidavit, including the **Sponsor's Declaration and Certification**, and has verified the accuracy of every answer.

Interpreter's Signature

7.a. Interpreter's Signature

7.b. Date of Signature (mm/dd/yyyy)

2020 Poverty Guidelines Chart for Immigrants

For the 48 Contiguous States, the District of Columbia, Puerto Rico, the U.S. Virgin Islands, Guam, and the Commonwealth of the Northern Mariana Islands:		
Sponsor's Household Size	**100% of HHS Poverty Guidelines**	**125% of HHS Poverty Guidelines**
	For sponsors on active duty in the U.S. armed forces who are petitioning for their spouse or child	*For all other sponsors*
2	$17,240	$21,550
3	$21,720	$27,150
4	$26,200	$32,750
5	$30,680	$38,350
6	$35,160	$43,950
7	$39,640	$49,550
8	$44,120	$55,150
	Add $4,480 for each additional person	**Add $5,600 for each additional person**

Alaska		
Sponsor's Household Size	**100% of HHS Poverty Guidelines**	**125% of HHS Poverty Guidelines**
	For sponsors on active duty in the U.S. armed forces who are petitioning for their spouse or child	*For all other sponsors*
2	$21,550	$26,937
3	$27,150	$33,937
4	$32,750	$40,937
5	$38,350	$47,937
6	$43,950	$54,937
7	$49,550	$61,937
8	$55,150	$68,937
	Add $5,600 for each additional person	**Add $7,000 for each additional person**

Hawaii		
Sponsor's Household Size	**100% of HHS Poverty Guidelines**	**125% of HHS Poverty Guidelines**
	For sponsors on active duty in the U.S. armed forces who are petitioning for their spouse or child	*For all other sponsors*
2	$19,830	$24,787
3	$24,980	$31,225
4	$30,130	$37,662
5	$35,280	$44,100
6	$40,430	$50,537
7	$45,580	$56,975
8	$50,730	$63,412
	Add $5,150 for each additional person	**Add $6,437 for each additional person**

Sample Form I-864A, Contract Between Sponsor and Household Member (page 1)

Contract Between Sponsor and Household Member
Department of Homeland Security
U.S. Citizenship and Immigration Services

USCIS
Form I-864A
OMB No. 1615-0075
Expires 10/31/2021

For Government Use Only

This Form I-864A relates to a household member who:

☐ **IS** the intending immigrant   ☐ **IS NOT** the intending immigrant

Reviewed By: _____

Location: _____   Date (mm/dd/yyyy): _____

To be completed by an attorney or accredited representative (if any).	☐ Select this box if Form G-28 or G-28I is attached.	Attorney State Bar Number (if applicable)	Attorney or Accredited Representative USCIS Online Account Number (if any)

▶ **START HERE - Type or print in black ink.**

Part 1. Information About You (the Household Member)

Full Name

1.a. Family Name (Last Name) — Mancini

1.b. Given Name (First Name) — Beatrice

1.c. Middle Name — Stella

Mailing Address
(USPS ZIP Code Lookup)

2.a. In Care Of Name

2.b. Street Number and Name — 800 Broadway

2.c. ☐ Apt. ☐ Ste. ☐ Flr.

2.d. City or Town — Lindenhurst

2.e. State — NY   **2.f.** ZIP Code — 11757

2.g. Province

2.h. Postal Code

2.i. Country — USA

3. Is your current mailing address the same as your physical address?   ☒ Yes   ☐ No

If you answered "No" to **Item Number 3.**, provide your physical address.

Physical Address

4.a. Street Number and Name

4.b. ☐ Apt. ☐ Ste. ☐ Flr.

4.c. City or Town

4.d. State   **4.e.** ZIP Code

4.f. Province

4.g. Postal Code

4.h. Country

Other Information

5. Date of Birth (mm/dd/yyyy) — 03/06/1990

Place of Birth

6.a. City or Town — Horseheads

6.b. State or Province — NY

6.c. Country — USA

7. U.S. Social Security Number (if any) ▶ 2 0 6 4 5 6 7 8 9

8. USCIS Online Account Number (if any) ▶

Sample Form I-864A, Contract Between Sponsor and Household Member (page 2)

Part 2. Your (the Household Member's) Relationship to the Sponsor

Select **Item Number 1.a., 1.b.,** or **1.c.**

1.a. ☐ I am the intending immigrant and also the sponsor's spouse.

1.b. ☐ I am the intending immigrant and also a member of the sponsor's household.

1.c. ☒ I am **not** the intending immigrant. I am the sponsor's household member. I am related to the sponsor as his/her:

☐ Spouse

☒ Son or Daughter (at least 18 years of age)

☐ Parent

☐ Brother or Sister

☐ Other Dependent (Specify)

Part 3. Your (the Household Member's) Employment and Income

I am currently:

1. ☒ Employed as a/an

Legal Secretary

2. Name of Employer Number 1

Wynken, Blynken & Nodd

3. Name of Employer Number 2 (if applicable)

4. ☐ Self employed as a/an

5. ☐ Retired from (Company Name)

Since (mm/dd/yyyy)

6. ☐ Unemployed since (mm/dd/yyyy)

7. **My current individual annual income is:**
$ 50000

Part 4. Your (the Household Member's) Federal Income Tax Information and Assets

1.a. Have you filed a Federal income tax return for each of the three most recent tax years? ☒ Yes ☐ No

NOTE: You **MUST** attach a photocopy or transcript of your Federal income tax return for only the most recent tax year.

1.b. ☐ (Optional) I have attached photocopies or transcripts of my Federal income tax returns for my second and third most recent tax years.

My total income (adjusted gross income on IRS Form 1040EZ) as reported on my Federal income tax returns for the most recent three years was:

		Tax Year		Total Income
2.a.	Most Recent	2018	$	50000
2.b.	2nd Most Recent	2017	$	48000
2.c.	3rd Most Recent	2016	$	47000

My assets (complete only if necessary).

3.a. Enter the balance of all cash, savings, and checking accounts. $

3.b. Enter the net cash value of real-estate holdings. (Net value means assessed value minus mortgage debt.) $

3.c. Enter the cash value of all stocks, bonds, certificates of deposit, and other assets not listed on **Item Numbers 3.a.** or **3.b.** $

3.d. Add together **Item Numbers 3.a.**, **3.b.**, and **3.c.** and enter the number here. $

Part 5. Sponsor's Promise, Statement, Contact Information, Declaration, Certification, and Signature

NOTE: Read the **Penalties** section of the Form I-864A Instructions before completing this part.

I, THE SPONSOR,

Alberto Ilario Mancini   ,

(Print Name)

in consideration of the household member's promise to support the following intending immigrants and to be jointly and severally liable for any obligations I incur under the affidavit of support, promise to complete and file an affidavit of support on behalf of the following named intending immigrants.

2

(Indicate Number)

Sample Form I-864A, Contract Between Sponsor and Household Member (page 3)

Part 5. Sponsor's Promise, Statement, Contact Information, Declaration, Certification, and Signature (continued)

Intending Immigrant Number 1

Name

1.a. Family Name
(Last Name) `Mancini`

1.b. Given Name
(First Name) `Terese`

1.c. Middle Name `Maria`

2. Date of Birth (mm/dd/yyyy) `02/15/1985`

3. Alien Registration Number (A-Number, if any)
▶ A- ☐☐☐☐☐☐☐☐☐

4. U.S. Social Security Number (if any)
▶ ☐☐☐☐☐☐☐☐☐

5. USCIS Online Account Number (if any)
▶ ☐☐☐☐☐☐☐☐☐☐☐☐

Intending Immigrant Number 2

Name

6.a. Family Name
(Last Name) `Moreno`

6.b. Given Name
(First Name) `Giovana`

6.c. Middle Name `Anna`

7. Date of Birth (mm/dd/yyyy) `06/01/2015`

8. Alien Registration Number (A-Number, if any)
▶ A- ☐☐☐☐☐☐☐☐☐

9. U.S. Social Security Number (if any)
▶ ☐☐☐☐☐☐☐☐☐

10. USCIS Online Account Number (if any)
▶ ☐☐☐☐☐☐☐☐☐☐☐☐

Intending Immigrant Number 3

Name

11.a. Family Name
(Last Name)

11.b. Given Name
(First Name)

11.c. Middle Name

12. Date of Birth (mm/dd/yyyy)

13. Alien Registration Number (A-Number, if any)
▶ A- ☐☐☐☐☐☐☐☐☐

14. U.S. Social Security Number (if any)
▶ ☐☐☐☐☐☐☐☐☐

15. USCIS Online Account Number (if any)
▶ ☐☐☐☐☐☐☐☐☐☐☐☐

Intending Immigrant Number 4

Name

16.a. Family Name
(Last Name)

16.b. Given Name
(First Name)

16.c. Middle Name

17. Date of Birth (mm/dd/yyyy)

18. Alien Registration Number (A-Number, if any)
▶ A- ☐☐☐☐☐☐☐☐☐

19. U.S. Social Security Number (if any)
▶ ☐☐☐☐☐☐☐☐☐

20. USCIS Online Account Number (if any)
▶ ☐☐☐☐☐☐☐☐☐☐☐☐

Intending Immigrant Number 5

Name

21.a. Family Name
(Last Name)

21.b. Given Name
(First Name)

21.c. Middle Name

22. Date of Birth (mm/dd/yyyy)

23. Alien Registration Number (A-Number, if any)
▶ A- ☐☐☐☐☐☐☐☐☐

24. U.S. Social Security Number (if any)
▶ ☐☐☐☐☐☐☐☐☐

25. USCIS Online Account Number (if any)
▶ ☐☐☐☐☐☐☐☐☐☐☐☐

Sponsor's Statement

NOTE: Select the box for either **Item Number 26.a.** or **26.b.** If applicable, select the box for **Item Number 27.**

26.a. ☒ I can read and understand English, and I have read and understand every question and instruction on this contract and my answer to every question.

Sample Form I-864A, Contract Between Sponsor and Household Member (page 4)

Part 5. Sponsor's Promise, Statement, Contact Information, Declaration, Certification, and Signature (continued)

26.b. ☐ The interpreter named in **Part 7.** read to me every question and instruction on this contract and my answer to every question in

[_____] ,

a language in which I am fluent, and I understood everything.

27. ☐ At my request, the preparer named in **Part 8.**,

[_____] ,

prepared this contract for me based only upon information I provided or authorized.

Sponsor's Contact Information

28. Sponsor's Daytime Telephone Number
2122224444

29. Sponsor's Mobile Telephone Number (if any)
2122225555

30. Sponsor's Email Address (if any)
amancini@email.com

Sponsor's Declaration and Certification

Copies of any documents I have submitted are exact photocopies of unaltered, original documents, and I understand that U.S. Citizenship and Immigration Services (USCIS) or the U.S. Department of State (DOS) may require that I submit original documents to USCIS or DOS at a later date. Furthermore, I authorize the release of any information from any and all of my records that USCIS or DOS may need to determine my eligibility for the immigration benefit that I seek.

I furthermore authorize release of information contained in this contract, in supporting documents, and in my USCIS or DOS records, to other entities and persons where necessary for the administration and enforcement of U.S. immigration law.

I certify, under penalty of perjury, that all of the information in my contract and any document submitted with it were provided or authorized by me, that I reviewed and understand all of the information contained in, and submitted with, my contract and that all of this information is complete, true, and correct.

Sponsor's Signature

31.a. Sponsor's Signature
Beatrice Stella Mancini

31.b. Date of Signature (mm/dd/yyyy) 03/06/2020

NOTE TO ALL SPONSORS: If you do not completely fill out this contract or fail to submit required documents listed in the Instructions, USCIS may deny your contract.

Part 6. Your (the Household Member's) Promise, Statement, Contact Information, Declaration, Certification, and Signature

NOTE: Read the **Penalties** section of the Form I-864A Instructions before completing this part.

I, THE HOUSEHOLD MEMBER,

Beatrice Stella Mancini ,
(Print Name)

in consideration of the sponsor's promise to complete and file an affidavit of support on behalf of the above named intending immigrants.

2

(Print number of intending immigrants noted in **Part 5. Sponsor's Promise, Statement, Contact Information, Declaration, Certification and Signature.**)

A. Promise to provide any and all financial support necessary to assist the sponsor in maintaining the sponsored immigrants at or above the minimum income provided for in the Immigration and Naturalization Act (INA) section 213A(a)(1)(A) (not less than 125 percent of the Federal Poverty Guidelines) during the period in which the affidavit of support is enforceable;

B. Agree to be jointly and severally liable for payment of any and all obligations owed by the sponsor under the affidavit of support to the sponsored immigrants, to any agency of the Federal Government, to any agency of a state or local government, or to any other private entity that provides means-tested public benefits;

C. Certify under penalty under the laws of the United States that the Federal income tax returns submitted in support of the contract are true copies or unaltered tax transcripts filed with the Internal Revenue Service;

D. Consideration where the household member is also the sponsored immigrant: I understand that if I am the sponsored immigrant and a member of the sponsor's household that this promise relates only to my promise to be jointly and severally liable for any obligation owed by the sponsor under the affidavit of support to any of my dependents, to any agency of the Federal Government, to any agency of a state or local government, or to any other private entity that provides means-tested public benefits and to provide any and all financial support necessary to assist the sponsor in maintaining any of my dependents at or above the minimum income provided for in INA section 213A (a)(1)(A) (not less than 125 percent of the Federal Poverty Guideline) during the period which the affidavit of support is enforceable.

Sample Form I-864A, Contract Between Sponsor and Household Member (page 5)

Part 6. Your (the Household Member's) Promise, Statement, Contact Information, Declaration, Certification, and Signature (continued)

E. I understand that, if I am related to the sponsored immigrant or the sponsor by marriage, the termination of the marriage (by divorce, dissolution, annulment, or other legal process) will not relieve me of my obligations under this Form I-864A.

F. I authorize the Social Security Administration to release information about me in its records to the Department of State and U.S. Citizenship and Immigration Services (USCIS).

Your (the Household Member's) Statement

NOTE: Select the box for either **Item Number 1.a.** or **1.b.** If applicable, select the box for **Item Number 2.**

1.a. ☒ I can read and understand English, and I have read and understand every question and instruction on this contract and my answer to every question.

1.b. ☐ The interpreter named in **Part 7.** read to me every question and instruction on this contract and my answer to every question in

_____,

a language in which I am fluent, and I understood everything.

2. ☐ At my request, the preparer named in **Part 8.**,

_____,

prepared this contract for me based only upon information I provided or authorized.

Your (the Household Member's) Contact Information

3. Your (the Household Member's) Daytime Telephone Number

2122226666

4. Your (the Household Member's) Mobile Telephone Number (if any)

2122227777

5. Your (the Household Member's) Email Address (if any)

bmancini@email.com

Your (the Household Member's) Declaration and Certification

Copies of any documents I have submitted are exact photocopies of unaltered, original documents, and I understand that USCIS or DOS may require that I submit original documents to USCIS or DOS at a later date. Furthermore, I authorize the release of any information from any and all of my records that USCIS or DOS may need to determine my eligibility for the immigration benefit that I seek.

I furthermore authorize release of information contained in this contract, in supporting documents, and in my USCIS or DOS records, to other entities and persons where necessary for the administration and enforcement of U.S. immigration law.

I certify, under penalty of perjury, that all of the information in my contract and any document submitted with it were provided or authorized by me, that I reviewed and understand all of the information contained in, and submitted with, my contract and that all of this information is complete, true, and correct.

Your (the Household Member's) Signature

6.a. Your (the Household Member's) Printed Name

Beatrice Stella Mancini

6.b. Your (the Household Member's) Signature

Beatrice Stella Mancini

6.c. Date of Signature (mm/dd/yyyy) 03/06/2020

NOTE TO ALL HOUSEHOLD MEMBERS: If you do not completely fill out this contract or fail to submit required documents listed in the Instructions, USCIS may deny your contract.

Part 7. Interpreter's Contact Information, Certification, and Signature

Provide the following information about the interpreter.

Interpreter's Full Name

1.a. Interpreter's Family Name (Last Name)

1.b. Interpreter's Given Name (First Name)

2. Interpreter's Business or Organization Name (if any)

Sample Form DS-5540, Public Charge Questionnaire (page 1)

U.S. Department of State

PUBLIC CHARGE QUESTIONNAIRE

OMB CONTROL NO. 1405-0234
EXPIRES: 08/31/2020
ESTIMATED BURDEN: 4.5 hours

PART 1 - INFORMATION ABOUT YOU

1. Your Current Legal Name (Do not provide a nickname)

Family Name (Last Name) Mancini   Given Name (First Name) Terese   Middle Name Maria

2. Date of Birth (mm-dd-yyyy)

02/15/1985

3. Have you ever been to the United States before?

☐ Yes   ☒ No

PART 2 - YOUR HEALTH

4. Do you currently have health insurance coverage in the United States?

☐ Yes   ☒ No

If you answered "Yes" to Item number 4, attach evidence of health insurance and skip to Part 3.
If you answered "No" to Item number 4, proceed to Item A.

4A. Will you be covered by health insurance in the United States within 30 days of your entry into the United States?

☒ Yes   ☐ No

If you answered "yes" to Item A, identify the specific health insurance plan and date coverage will begin.

Blue Health Insurance, 04/01/2020

PART 3 - YOUR HOUSEHOLD SIZE

List the expected members of your household in the United States.

Name	Age	Relationship to you	Current Job	United States Citizen (yes / no)	Was he or she on active duty, other than training, in the U.S. Armed Forces or Ready Reserve while receiving a public benefit? (yes / no)
Alberto Mancini	53	Father	Cook	Yes	No
Beatrice Mancini	35	Sister	Manager	Yes	No
Giovana Moreno	4	Daughter	n/a	n/a	n/a

PART 4 - YOUR ASSETS, RESOURCES, AND FINANCIAL STATUS

6. List below all U.S. federal tax returns you have filed within the last three years and attach your IRS transcript (or copy of the complete, filed tax return) for your most recent U.S. federal tax return.

Federal Tax Year	Did you file a Federal tax return?		Gross Income (U.S. dollars)
n/a	☐ Yes	☐ No	
	☐ Yes	☐ No	
	☐ Yes	☐ No	
	☐ Yes	☐ No	

7. Did you work in the United States in the last three years but not file a U.S. federal tax return?

☐ Yes   ☒ No

If you answered "yes", explain.

DS-5540
01-2020

Page 1 of 4

Sample Form DS-5540, Public Charge Questionnaire (page 2)

8. Income		
8A. What is your current yearly compensation in U.S. dollars? $65,000	8B. If you currently have a job awaiting your arrival in the United States, who is the employer and what is the yearly compensation in U.S. dollars? Yes. Accountants Inc., $70,000	

8C. List below any income not listed above that you will continue to receive after your arrival in the United States (for example, rent, stock dividends, foreign pension, child support). Consular Officers may request additional information or evidence for confirmation.

Type of Income	How often do you receive this income? (annually, monthly, etc.)	Amount (U.S. Dollars)
n/a		
	Total	

9. List the assets available to you in the table below. For example, cash assets may include checking and savings accounts, etc. Non-cash assets may include equity in real estate, annuities, securities, etc.

Type of Asset	Location of Asset	Amount (U.S. Dollars)
Savings - Bank Account	Italy	50,000
	Total	

10. List your liabilities and/or debts in the table below.

Type of Liability or Debt	Amount (U.S. Dollars)
Other (Please Specify in Part 5 - Additional Information)"	n/a - no debts
	Total

Sample Form DS-5540, Public Charge Questionnaire (page 3)

11. For purposes of this form, a public benefit means any of the following forms of assistance received on or after February 24, 2020: 1) Any Federal, state, local, or tribal cash assistance for income maintenance, including supplemental security income (SSI) and Temporary Assistance for Needy Families (TANF); 2) Supplemental Nutrition Assistance Program (SNAP); 3) Housing Choice Voucher Program; 4) Project-Based Rental Assistance (including Moderate Rehabilitation); 5) Subsidized Housing; or 6) Medicaid, except for benefits received for an emergency medical condition, services or benefits funded by Medicaid but provided under the Individuals with Disabilities Education Act (IDEA), school-based services or benefits provided to individuals of secondary school age, benefits received by an alien under 21 years of age, or benefits received by a woman during pregnancy or during the 60-day period beginning on the last day of the pregnancy.

Have you or any of the individuals applying with you covered by this form requested or received public benefits in the United States from a Federal, state, local, or tribal government entity on or after February 24, 2020?

___ Yes   **X** No   If you answered "Yes," provide the information below.

11A.	Type of Benefit n/a		Agency That Grants The Benefit
	Date Benefit Was Granted (mm-dd-yyyy)	Date Benefit Ended or Expires (mm-dd-yyyy)	Reason For Requesting or Receiving The Benefit

11B.	Type of Benefit		Agency That Grants The Benefit
	Date Benefit Was Granted (mm-dd-yyyy)	Date Benefit Ended or Expires (mm-dd-yyyy)	Reason For Requesting or Receiving The Benefit

11C.	Type of Benefit		Agency That Grants The Benefit
	Date Benefit Was Granted (mm-dd-yyyy)	Date Benefit Ended or Expires (mm-dd-yyyy)	Reason For Requesting or Receiving The Benefit

12. If you or your family requested or received a public benefit, were you or your family members exempt from public charge during that period?
___ Yes   **X** No

If you answered "Yes," provide an explanation.

13. Are you likely to request or receive any of the public benefits described in Question 11 in the future in the United States from any Federal, state, local, or tribal government entity?
___ Yes   **X** No

If you answered "Yes," provide an explanation.

14. Have you ever received a fee waiver when applying for an immigration benefit from USCIS?
___ Yes   **X** No

If you answered "Yes," provide the information in the table below. In Part 8 - Additional Information, explain the circumstances that caused you to apply for a fee waiver and if those circumstances have changed.

Date Fee Waiver Received (mm/dd/yyyy)	Type of Immigrant Benefit (Form Number)	Receipt Number

PART 5 - YOUR EDUCATION AND SKILLS

15. Have you graduated high school or earned a high school equivalent diploma?
X Yes   ___ No   If you answered "No," then list the highest grade completed. _____

If you answered "Yes," list any other educational degrees you have earned..   Bachelor in Accounting

16. Do you have any occupational skills?
X Yes   ___ No   If you answered "Yes," provide the information below.

16A.	Certification/License Type/Occupational Skill Chartered Accountant		Date Obtained (mm/dd/yyyy) 05/01/2009
	Who issued your license? (if any) Italian Accountancy Board	License Number (if any) 001	Expiration/Renewal Date (if any) n/a

16B.	Certification/License Type/Occupational Skill		Date Obtained (mm/dd/yyyy)
	Who issued your license? (if any)	License Number (if any)	Expiration/Renewal Date (if any)

Sample Form DS-5540, Public Charge Questionnaire (page 4)

16C.	Certification/License Type/Occupational Skill		Date Obtained (mm/dd/yyyy)
	Who issued your license? (if any)	License Number (if any)	Expiration/Renewal Date (if any)

PART 6 - TRANSLATOR

17. Did you use a translator to help you complete this form? (If yes, provide the following information about the translator you used.)

___ Yes **[X]** No

17A. Translator's Name

Family Name (Last Name)   Given Name (First Name)   Middle Name

17B. Translator's Business or Organization name? (if any)

17C. Translator's Street Address	17D. Translator's City
	17E. Translator's State/Province
	17F. Translator's Postal/Zip Code 17G. Translator's Country

17H. Translator's Phone Number	17I. Translator's Email Address

PART 7 - PREPARER

18. Did anyone, other than a translator, help you complete this form? (If yes, provide the following information about the preparer you used.)

___ Yes **[X]** No

18A. Preparer's Name

Family Name (Last Name)   Given Name (First Name)   Middle Name

18B. Preparer's Business or Organization name? (if any)

18C. Preparer's Street Address	18D. Preparer's City
	18E. Preparer's State/Province
	18F. Preparer's Postal/Zip Code 18G. Preparer's Country

18H. Preparer's Phone Number	18I. Preparer's Email Address

PART 8 - ADDITIONAL INFORMATION (if needed)

If further space is required, attach additional sheets. Please ensure you specify to what question(s) you are responding.

PART 9 - DECLARANT'S SIGNATURE

I understand all the information I have provided in, or in support of, this application may be provided to other U.S. government agencies authorized to use such information for purposes including enforcement of the laws of the United States. I understand all of the information contained in this form and I certify under penalty of perjury under the laws of the United States of America that the foregoing is complete, true, and correct. I understand that any willfully false or misleading statement or willful concealment of a material fact made by me herein may result in refusal of the visa, denial of admission to the United States, and may subject me to criminal prosecution and/or removal from the United States.

Terese Mancini   03/06/2020

Signature   Date

Terese Mancini

Name (Printed)

Federal Agency Disclosure and Authorizations

PAPERWORK REDUCTION ACT STATEMENT:

Public reporting burden for this collection of information is estimated to average 4.5 hours per response, including time required for searching existing data sources, gathering the necessary documentation, providing the information and/or documents required, and reviewing the final collection. You do not have to supply this information unless this collection displays a currently valid OMB control number. If you have comments on the accuracy of this burden estimate and/or recommendations for reducing it, please send them to: PRA_BurdenComments@state.gov.

CONFIDENTIALITY STATEMENT:

INA Section 222(f) provides that visa issuance and refusal records shall be considered confidential and shall be used only for the formulation, amendment, administration, or enforcement of the immigration, nationality, and other laws of the United States. Visa records may be disclosed in certain situations, as described in INA Section 222(f), including disclosure to a court as needed in a case pending before the court.

DS-5540   Page 4 of 4

Deferred Action for Childhood Arrivals

n June 2012, the Obama administration created a new remedy for young immigrants in the U.S. with no legal status. Called "Deferred Action for Childhood Arrivals" or "DACA," it allows noncitizens who were brought to the U.S. as children and who meet various other requirements to apply for two years' protection from deportation (removal), as well a work permit.

In September 2017, President Trump announced that he would be ending DACA, after a wind-down phase. Immigration advocates then filed lawsuits in several states to stop DHS from ending DACA. They alleged, among other things, that the U.S. government failed to follow the necessary procedural requirements under federal law when it abruptly announced it would terminate the program. At the time this book went to print in mid-2020, DACA renewals were still being accepted, due to temporary injunctions issued by federal courts. A temporary injunction, however, just buys time before the final court ruling.

How long DACA holders will be able to submit renewals is thus an open question. On November 12, 2019, the U.S. Supreme Court heard oral arguments on the Trump administration's rescission of DACA. A decision is expected in 2020. So, DACA's ultimate outcome now depends on what the federal courts do on the merits of this case and on whether Congress acts to replace DACA with actual legislation.

Despite Trump's actions to end DACA, he and dozens of members of Congress have publicly expressed openness to enacting legislation giving permanent residency to young, DACA-holding or eligible immigrants. This would open a path to U.S. citizenship after a certain number of years.

Legislators have considered various forms of similar legislation in the past, once referred to as the "DREAM Act." These proposals failed, however, to get enough votes to pass. Still, hope remains that DACA recipients ("DREAMers") could receive green cards in the future. DACA is a turbulent and contentious topic in immigration law, and it's worth paying attention to the news in order to stay up to date.

A. Who Are the DREAMers?

Despite being called "DACA kids" by some, there are DACA recipients who are in their mid-30s and have children of their own, and others who are just teenagers.

Noncitizens were considered DACA eligible if they:

- had not yet turned age 31 as of June 15, 2012
- had not yet turned age 16 upon entering the United States
- continuously lived in the U.S. after at least June 15, 2007 (excluding brief casual, and innocent departures)
- were physically present in the U.S. on June 12, 2012 and at the time of submitting a DACA application
- were in school, had graduated from high school or received a general education development (GED) certificate; or were honorably discharged from the Coast Guard or U.S. Armed Forces
- had not been convicted of a felony, significant misdemeanor, or three or more other misdemeanors, and
- did not otherwise present a threat to U.S. national security or public safety (such as by being a member of a gang).

B. How to Renew DACA

If you currently hold DACA, you will likely want to renew your deportation protection and extend your work permit if you are so eligible. Although no one can predict whether or when Congress will pass a law giving green cards to DREAMers or how long the DACA program will last, the best hope for benefitting from any upcoming legislation is to maintain your DACA approval. It's true that DACA is temporary, but you will be able to renew it in additional two-year increments for as long as court actions requiring the government to continue accepting DACA renewals remain in effect.

1. Timing Your DACA Renewal Application

When this book went to print in mid-2020, USCIS was accepting DACA renewals only from people whose DACA expired one year ago or less.

You can submit a DACA renewal application 150 days before your work permit (employment authorization document or EAD) is due to expire. For example, if your work permit expires on September 15, 2020, you should submit your DACA renewal on or after April 18, 2020. But if you were to submit your application before April 18, 2020, USCIS could reject it.

2. Making Sure You Are Still DACA Eligible

The basic criteria for DACA eligibility are detailed in the previous section of this chapter. In order to renew your DACA and work permit, you must continue to meet the criteria stated there. There are also additional criteria you'll need to meet for DACA renewal, including that you:

- haven't left the U.S. since August 15, 2012 (at least, not without first obtaining permission from USCIS, in the form of what's called Advance Parole)
- have continuously lived ("resided") in the U.S. since submitting your initial DACA application
- haven't been convicted of a felony, significant misdemeanor, or three or more other misdemeanors, and
- haven't done anything suggesting that you present a threat to U.S. national security or public safety (such as being a known member of a gang).

Age requirements are irrelevant now; it does not matter how old you are when you renew DACA. Even if you are now in your mid-30s, if you were initially granted DACA, you have met the age requirements, and don't have to worry about them again.

If you think you might no longer qualify for DACA because of any of the factors listed above, see a qualified immigration attorney to evaluate whether you should apply for a renewal. Absolutely see an attorney if you have been convicted of any crime or you no longer meet the educational requirements; for example, you failed to continue on your path to a GED. In such a case, you might no longer be DACA eligible. Although USCIS doesn't actually require you to show that you're still in school or have otherwise met the educational criteria when renewing, the agency does want to be told if you've failed to do so.

3. DACA Renewal Forms

The forms to submit to USCIS to renew your DACA include:

- ☐ Form I-821D, Consideration of Deferred Action for Childhood Arrivals, and
- ☐ Form I-765, Application for Employment Authorization, accompanied by a worksheet called Form I-765WS. The eligibility category for purposes of Question 20 is "(c)(33)."

These are available as free downloads on the USCIS website, www.uscis.gov/forms. DACA renewal applicants do not need to complete Part 3 of the application.

4. Documentation and Fees for DACA Renewal

You need not submit all the sorts of documentation that you did in support of your initial I-821D DACA application. That's because USCIS has a copy of your original file.

You may submit a copy of your passport biographic page or another photo ID to establish your identity. Other than that, you will need to provide only documentation of anything that has changed since your last DACA application.

If you have received new documentation from an Immigration Court or evidence concerning any criminal issues, include copies in the renewal application. But be sure to discuss such developments with an attorney before filing to renew.

For the Form I-765 employment authorization, submit a copy of the front and back of your current EAD (work permit) card and two passport-style photographs of yourself, with your name and alien registration number ("A number") written on the back. Your A number is on your EAD; it starts with A and has 9 numbers.

The fee for the DACA renewal application is $495, which includes the standard $85 biometrics (fingerprinting) fee for a background check and the fee for a work permit. You may pay the fee with a money order, personal check, or cashier's check made payable to "U.S. Department of Homeland Security." Or, you can pay by credit card, using USCIS Form G-1450, Authorization for Credit Card Transactions (available on the USCIS website).

5. After Submitting Your DACA Renewal Application

After you have mailed your DACA renewal application to USCIS, you will be able to keep your DACA only until its original expiration date, unless you receive an approval notice before it expires.

Unlike with some other types of immigration applications, submitting Form I-821D will not extend your work authorization while USCIS reviews your case. If, therefore, you do not receive your approval notice and an EAD before that time, you will unfortunately not have DACA protection, and your work permit will expire (even if the delay is the fault of USCIS).

While immigration authorities such as Immigration and Customs Enforcement (ICE) don't typically arrest people with lapsed DACA, you are always vulnerable if do not have proof that you are legally authorized to remain in the United States.

You might want to carry your receipt notice with you as proof of your pending DACA renewal, just in case.

Do Not Leave the U.S. After Your DACA Renewal

USCIS is no longer accepting applications for Advance Parole, which allowed DACA recipients to travel outside the U.S. for short trips. While you might have traveled internationally in the past, you should not leave the U.S. unless you have a valid, unexpired Advance Parole document—and even then, it's best to get an attorney's advice before making travel plans.

U Visas for Crime Victims Assisting Law Enforcement

The Victims of Trafficking and Violence Protection Act of 2000 authorized a new visa for immigrant victims of serious crimes, called the "U" visa. The legislation was enacted in response to rising public safety concerns, with the idea that foreign victims of crimes in the U.S. should be allowed to remain here so as to provide law enforcement officials with information helpful in apprehending and prosecuting criminal offenders.

Although the U visa is temporary in nature, it can eventually lead to a U.S. green card, albeit after a long wait. It has, in fact, become an important option for many noncitizens in the United States. (The same legislation also created a "T" visa for victims of severe human trafficking, but because this is used less commonly, we will not cover it within this book.) However, the U visa program is not without potential risk to the applicant.

If you are approved for a U visa, you will be granted legal status in the U.S. for up to four years (which may be extended in "exceptional circumstances"). After you have held your U status for three years, you may be eligible to apply for a green card.

As with all U.S. visas, you will need to take several steps to prove that you qualify for it. In other words, it is not enough to simply claim that you have been a victim of a serious crime. You will need to provide a "certificate of helpfulness" from a qualifying government agency and also prove that you suffered mental or physical abuse by the U.S. criminal perpetrator.

Additionally, if you are "inadmissible" to the U.S. due to past immigration violations or for other reasons, you will need to apply for a waiver of these grounds.

This chapter will discuss the eligibility criteria for a U visa and how to apply. A final note: Although we use the term "U visa" throughout this chapter, only the applicants who come from outside the U.S. will, in literal terms, receive a visa in their passport. (A visa is an entry document.) Applicants from within the U.S. will receive "U status," and will, if they leave the U.S., need to go to a U.S. consulate to get an actual visa stamp in their passport before returning.

A. Who Is Eligible for a U Visa

In order to qualify for a U visa or U status in the U.S., you must meet the following criteria:

- ☐ You must have been a victim of a "qualifying criminal activity," and this crime must have occurred in the U.S. or violated U.S. law. Indirect and bystander victims are also eligible to apply in certain circumstances, though approvals are increasingly rare.
- ☐ In the course of—or as a result of—this criminal activity, you must have suffered substantial physical or mental abuse.
- ☐ You can provide useful information about the criminal activity (or if under age 16, your parent, guardian, or "next friend" such as a counselor or social worker can provide this information for you).
- ☐ You (or your parent, guardian, or next friend) are cooperating with U.S. law enforcement in order to bring the perpetrator of the crime to justice.
- ☐ You are admissible to the U.S. or you are applying for a waiver using Form I-192, Application for Advance Permission to Enter as a Non-Immigrant.

You can apply for a U visa either from within the U.S. or abroad (at a U.S. consulate).

1. What Crimes Qualify Their Victims for a U Visa

In a typical U visa case, you will have been the victim of a serious crime that took place in the United States. In some cases, however, the crime might have violated U.S. laws overseas (such as a human trafficking or kidnapping crime). Examples of qualifying crimes are:

- **Violent crimes:** murder, manslaughter, vehicular homicide, robbery, felonious assault (which usually involves the use of a deadly weapon, and can include statutory rape and other offenses), domestic violence, or stalking
- **Enslavement crimes:** criminal restraint, kidnapping, abduction, being held hostage, forced labor, slavery, human trafficking, indentured or debt servitude, or false imprisonment
- **Sex crimes:** rape, incest, sexual trafficking, sexual assault and abusive sexual contact, prostitution, sexual exploitation, or female genital mutilation, and
- **Obstruction of justice crimes:** perjury, witness tampering, blackmail, extortion, or withholding evidence.

The crime need not have been "completed" in order for it to qualify. An attempt, solicitation, or conspiracy to commit one of the above-mentioned crimes is enough. For example, obviously a murder victim wouldn't be applying for a U visa. But if you are the victim of attempted murder, you may qualify for a U visa.

2. When Indirect and Bystander Victims May Be Eligible for U Status

In limited circumstances, USCIS may grant U status to people who are not the direct victims of crime. The two examples of this are close family members of the direct victim who suffer indirectly, or bystander victims. In either instance, however, the applicant must meet all the other requirements for a U visa, meaning that they: have been helpful, are being helpful, or will be helpful in the investigation, suffered substantial harm as a result of the crime, and are either admissible to the U.S. or qualify for a waiver of inadmissibility.

Certain family members can apply for U visas as indirect victims if the primary victim died due to murder or manslaughter or was rendered incompetent or incapacitated and therefore cannot help authorities with the criminal investigation. For crime victims who are age 21 or older, their spouse, as well as their children under 21 years of age, may be considered indirect victims. For victims under age 21, their parents and unmarried siblings under 18 can be considered indirect victims.

> **EXAMPLE:** Leticia's son Rodrigo was murdered when he was 20 years old. The mother, from Mexico, had a nervous breakdown soon after hearing the news. She helped the police investigation by providing information about her son and the events that happened on the day of the murder. Leticia would qualify as an indirect victim because she is the parent of a deceased victim under 21, she suffered harm as a result of the crime, and she helped in the investigation. She may still qualify even if several years have passed since the murder, because USCIS looks at the age of the victim when the murder took place to determine whether parents were indirect victims, and Rodrigo was 20.

USCIS ordinarily considers minors to be "incapacitated," and therefore their family members often qualify as indirect victims.

> **EXAMPLE:** Minjun, who overstayed a visa from Korea, has a four-year-old daughter, born in the United States. The daughter became the victim of child molestation by a nanny. As soon as Minjun realized his daughter was being abused, he reported the incident to the police, and assisted with the investigation. He suffered serious emotional harm because of what the daughter went through, especially because he was also the victim of abuse as a child. Because the daughter was born in the U.S., she does not need to apply for immigration relief. Minjun therefore could not be a derivative on her U status application. However, he may qualify for U status as an indirect victim, because his daughter was incapacitated (by definition, due to her young age), he helped the investigation, and he suffered harm as a result of the crime.

In both the above examples of indirect victims, the noncitizen would also have to meet the other requirements for eligibility for U status or a U visa, by showing admissibility to the U.S. or qualifying for a waiver of inadmissibility.

USCIS can also grant U visa status to noncitizen bystanders to crimes who suffered unusually severe harm as a result of having witnessed the criminal activity. The example most often used is that of a pregnant woman who suffers a miscarriage as a result of witnessing a criminal activity.

3. Satisfying the Requirement That You Suffered Substantial Physical or Mental Abuse

It is not enough to merely be the victim of a qualifying crime. You must have also suffered "substantial" physical injury or mental anguish as a result of this criminal activity and must provide USCIS with supporting evidence of this, such as medical records and affidavits. The burden of proof is on you to prove that your suffering is "substantial."

In determining whether the injury was "substantial," USCIS reviews applications on a case-by-case basis. USCIS will consider the nature of the injury inflicted; the severity of the perpetrator's conduct; the severity of the harm suffered; the duration of the infliction of the harm; and the extent to which there is permanent or serious harm to the appearance, health, or physical or mental soundness of the victim.

You will need to provide a personal statement detailing the physical or mental harm you suffered, as well as medical records or statements from treating physicians and psychologists, photographs of physical injuries, and affidavits from social workers. Question 6 of Part 3 on the law enforcement certification, Form I-918B, asks the law enforcement officer to detail injuries to the victim, as well. Ensuring that law enforcement is aware of the extent of your injuries can therefore strengthen your case.

4. Satisfying the Requirement That You Are Helping Law Enforcement

One of the reasons that Congress authorized U visas was out of concern that many U.S. immigrants refuse to provide information to U.S. police and other law enforcement authorities, due to cultural differences, language barriers, and fear of deportation. The unfortunate result is that many perpetrators of serious crimes view immigrants as easy targets.

In order to further the public safety objectives of the U visa, your visa petition must be certified by a police officer or another law enforcement official. Obtaining a strong certification is absolutely necessary for a successful U visa application. The official must attest that you were a victim of a qualifying crime and that you are likely to be helpful to an investigation or prosecution of the crime.

The chances of your getting a law enforcement official to cooperate with your U visa application are greatly improved if you are forthcoming with information that could lead to the identification, arrest, and conviction of a serious criminal. This could include (but is not limited to) your providing:

- [ ] an identification of the criminals involved, such as their names and addresses, or by your choosing the correct person in a lineup identification
- [ ] information that helps apprehend the perpetrators, such as your tips as to where they may be "hiding out," names of their friends and family who might give information about their whereabouts, or identifying details about their vehicle (make, color, license plate number)
- [ ] descriptive details that help the prosecution convince a jury that the accused is guilty of the crime, rebut the criminal's alibi, support a motive for committing the crime, or determine what penalty (or sentencing) it should request

☐ evidence that could help law enforcement classify the crime as more serious or charge the criminals with additional crimes. (This might be the situation if, for example, the officer is investigating a felony assault but you have evidence that could lead to an attempted murder charge, or you have information that might lead to an additional charge of sexual assault.)

☐ agreement to testify as a witness if the case goes to trial.

Proving helpful to law enforcement has become more important than ever. In 2019, USCIS issued a new law enforcement resource guide. It encouraged law enforcement agencies to limit their issuance of certifications of helpfulness and said they can choose not to issue certifications at their own discretion. The guidelines also encourage the agencies to conduct their own background checks on victims, impose time limitations on U visa certifications (even though there are no time limits under the law), and withdraw or disavow certification at their discretion.

5. Available Waiver If You Are Inadmissible

To be eligible for a U visa, you must not be "inadmissible" to the United States. This means that you are not barred from U.S. entry due to factors such as multiple criminal convictions, immigration violations (including entering without inspection), certain medical conditions, or any of several other reasons.

Most potential U visa applicants are inadmissible, especially if they entered the U.S. without a visa or other official permission. Luckily, a waiver of inadmissibility is available. In order to apply for the waiver, you must submit to USCIS Form I-192, Application for Advance Permission to Enter as a Nonimmigrant. Unlike many other immigration waivers, this one does not require a showing of "extreme hardship." Almost all grounds of inadmissibility may be waived in conjunction with a U visa application (the only

exceptions being for national-security or terrorism-related grounds). However, just because a ground of inadmissibility can be waived doesn't mean that USCIS will do so. U visa waiver applications are reviewed on a case-by-case basis. You'll definitely want to get a lawyer's help, in order to identify and prove the reasons you deserve the waiver.

If USCIS approves your waiver, the same grounds of inadmissibility will also be waived for your future application for adjustment of status (if any).

6. Qualifying Family Members May Receive Derivative U Visas

Certain family members may be eligible to become derivative U visa recipients if the principal petitioner's application is approved. These include your:

- unmarried children under age 21
- spouse
- parents (if principal petitioner is under age 21), and
- unmarried siblings under 18 years old (if principal petitioner is under age 21).

To obtain derivative status for family members, you (as the primary petitioner) would submit Form I-918, Supplement A, Petition for Qualifying Family Member of U Visa Recipient, along with your own petition or after your U visa is approved. Any derivative relatives that you include must also be "admissible" to the U.S. (or apply for a waiver) and have good moral character.

B. How to Apply for a U Visa

Applying for a U visa involves the following steps:

1. Prepare USCIS Form I-918, Petition for U Nonimmigrant Status (see sample at end of this chapter).
2. Have a qualifying agency provide certification of your helpfulness, to accompany this I-918 petition.

3. Gather evidence to substantiate your eligibility and claim of substantial injury.

4. If you have derivative family members who wish to work in the U.S., prepare Form I-765 for a work permit.

5. Submit your petition and supporting documents to USCIS.

6. Attend an interview at a USCIS office or your local U.S. consulate, if required.

> **CAUTION**
> **Don't follow these instructions if you're in removal proceedings.** This chapter discusses only how to apply for a U visa if you are not in removal proceedings in immigration court. If you are, or if you have a final order of removal, the process is considerably more complex. Filing for a U visa might not prevent your removal at all, due to the long wait times for your case to be decided. Although in the past, one could receive a stay of removal (temporarily blocking deportation) while a U visa was pending, several 2019 ICE and USCIS enforcement policy changes made receiving a stay of removal while in removal proceedings or with a final order of removal much less likely. Consult an immigration attorney for help with a U visa application if your case is being handled by the immigration courts.

We'll explain each of the normal application steps below. Here is a summary of the items you will need to assemble:

- ☐ Form I-918 (No fee is required with this form.)
- ☐ Form I-918, Supplement A (if you want derivative status for a qualifying family member)
- ☐ Form I-918, Supplement B (completed and certified by a qualifying law enforcement agency)
- ☐ supporting documents, as described in Section 2
- ☐ Evidence that you have helpful information about the crime. Form I-918, Supplement B should be sufficient, but if you have any further information about how you are being helpful to authorities in providing information about the crime, you should submit it.
- ☐ Evidence that the crime violated U.S. laws. Again, Form I-918, Supplement B should cover this, but if you have any additional information about the crime, especially if it occurred outside of the U.S. (but violated federal law), you should provide this.
- ☐ Waiver of Grounds of Inadmissibility, if applicable. Submit Form I-192, Application for Advance Permission to Enter as a Nonimmigrant, with check or money order ($930 as of this book's print date), made payable to "U.S. Department of Homeland Security." If you cannot afford this amount, you may apply for a fee waiver.
- ☐ Information to prove relationship of derivative family members. Provide documentation to prove that your family member qualifies for derivative U status (for example, birth or marriage certificates). Make sure that any foreign language documents are accompanied by a full English translation that is certified as complete and accurate by a translator competent to translate from the foreign language into English.
- ☐ Form I-765, Application for Employment Authorization Document (EAD), with appropriate filing fees (or fee waivers), for any derivative family members who wish to work and are currently in the United States. Principal U visa holders will automatically be sent a work permit when approved.

1. Preparing the Petition

A sample Form I-918 is included at the end of this chapter. As a general caution when preparing Form I-918 or the Form I-918 Supplement A for a derivative, realize that you must fill out all fields, unless they are optional. USCIS has been issuing denials for "incomplete" U visa applications when any fields are left blank. For example, a petitioner who does not have children should not leave the question about children blank, but instead enter "N/A" (not applicable) in the appropriate space. Out of an abundance of caution, since the forms do not always clearly indicate which fields are "optional," applicants should complete all fields.

2. Obtaining a Certification of Helpfulness

As part of your application for a U visa, you will need to show USCIS that a law enforcement official has "vouched" for your petition. A judge, police officer, prosecutor, or other law enforcement official must complete a "certification of helpfulness" (I-918 Supplement B, U Nonimmigrant Status Certification) on your behalf. This document is a vital part of your application. It shows that you have been a victim of qualifying criminal activity, have information that will be useful to law enforcement, and are cooperating in order to bring the perpetrator to justice.

The agencies that will most commonly certify a U visa petition are local, state, and federal police departments and prosecutors. Even a judge may sign a U visa certification, although many will refuse to do so in order to avoid a showing of bias for the prosecution. However, any state or federal agency that has "responsibility for the investigation or prosecution of a qualifying crime or criminal activity" may complete the certification of helpfulness. For example, if you are the victim of a crime that requires the involvement of Child Protective Services (CPS), you could bypass the police and justice departments and instead have CPS help you with your application.

USCIS states that people who are in a supervisory role and have responsibility for issuing certificates of helpfulness must sign the petition, but it allows the agency to designate another certifying official if it chooses to do so.

Ultimately, it's up to the law enforcement authorities acting in your case to decide whether or not you are "helpful" to them and whether they should fill out the certification of helpfulness for you. You must file the Supplement B within six months of the date the certifying official signed this, or it will no longer be valid.

TIP

Get to work on obtaining the certification of helpfulness as soon as possible. Not only is it a vital part of your application, but by showing interest and providing helpful evidence to authorities, you will help show that you are eager to participate in the investigation. Also, if the criminals involved are arrested and plead guilty to the criminal charges before you contact police or answer a request for cooperation from law enforcement, your evidence and testimony may not be as useful, since the case will not go to trial.

3. Preparing Documents to Support Your U Visa Petition

Filling out the required forms will not be enough, by itself, to qualify you for a U visa. You will also need to prepare or gather various documents to support your claim, such as:

☐ a personal narrative statement, describing how you are a victim of criminal activity and the circumstances surrounding the crime. You can use this statement to show that you were not at fault in the criminal activity and that you were helpful (if you called the authorities to report the crime, for example). Also describe the extent of your injuries.

☐ evidence that you are the victim of a qualifying criminal activity. This could include trial transcripts, newspaper articles, police reports, affidavits, or orders of protection (restraining orders).

☐ evidence that you suffered substantial physical or mental abuse. This could include affidavits from case or social workers, medical personnel, and police; photographs of injuries; and affidavits from people who have personal knowledge of the criminal activity.

An attorney can help you gather these documents, but you will still need to play a role in considering what the best sources might be, and in talking to friends, doctors, and others who might help.

4. Filling Out Form I-765

You will not be eligible to work while your U visa application is pending, unless you receive deferred action (discussed more in "How Long Does It Take to Get a U Visa?"). The principal petitioner does not need to worry about applying for a work permit (EAD). If the I-918 is approved, he or she will be sent an EAD automatically. Any derivative family member who wants to work must, however, separately submit Form I-765 to request an EAD. They can do so either by including their form with the I-918 petition or by sending in a separate Form I-765 after USCIS has approved the I-918 petition. Derivatives likewise cannot work while the U visa is pending, unless they receive deferred action.

Form I-765 is fairly short and self-explanatory. For Question 27, the applicant's eligibility category, you would fill in "(a)(19)" for the principal applicant and "(a)(20)" for any derivative family members.

Your family members will also need to pay the Form I-765 fee ($410 as of this book's print date) or request a fee waiver.

5. Submitting Your U Visa Petition to USCIS

After you have completed the application, make a copy for your files. Then send the packet of forms and documents to the following USCIS address:

USCIS Vermont Service Center
75 Lower Welden Street
St. Albans, VT 05479

6. Attending a U Visa Interview

If you are applying from within the U.S., chances are you will not be required to attend an interview at a local USCIS office, which is why it is important to provide a strong statement with your I-918 applications. However, it's always possible that you may be required to attend an in-person interview at a local USCIS office. If you (or your family members) are applying from overseas, this interview would be held at the U.S. embassy or consulate in your home country.

The purpose of the interview will be for U.S. officials to review your file and talk with you personally about your eligibility for a U visa or your relationship with the principal applicant (if you are a family member applying for derivative status) and to make sure you are not inadmissible to the United States.

C. No Legal Status While U Visa Is Pending

Until you have received a U visa or deferred action, you do not have legal status. That means that during your long wait, you could be picked up by Immigrations and Customs Enforcement (ICE) and placed into detention or removal proceedings.

What's more, if your U visa is ultimately denied, USCIS may refer your case to ICE for enforcement. This makes applying for a U visa a calculated risk, particularly for people who have significant grounds of inadmissibility. If your U visa is denied, you might be able to appeal that denial, but will need to consult with an immigration attorney. If deported, you have the option of appealing or filing again from overseas.

D. Green Card Possibilities After U Visa Approval

If you have received a U visa or U status as a victim of a serious crime assisting law enforcement, you might be able to adjust your status (receive a green card) after three years of continuous presence in the United States. This does not include time spent in deferred action status. If interested, you should apply for a green card as soon you can, because you must continue to be eligible as a U visa crime victim at the time you apply.

How Long Does It Take to Get a U Visa?

There is an annual limit of 10,000 U visas per year, which means that demand far outpaces supply. To give you an idea of how long the waitlist is, there were 47,225 applications made in Fiscal Year 2019 and 255,495 applications still awaiting a decision as of December 31, 2019.

The backlog has become so bad that all available visas each year are typically allocated to people on the waiting list, which has processed only three months of U visa applications in the last two years. As of February 2020, the Vermont Service Center was processing U visa applications from September 2015.

USCIS will take biometrics (photographs and fingerprints) and process all forms and supporting information (such as the certification of helpfulness by a qualifying agency). After that time, USCIS will add an "approvable" application to the waitlist—which is known as "deferred action." It normally takes about three years from the time you apply to be placed on the U visa waitlist. Once you receive notice that you are on the waitlist, you can apply for a work permit while waiting for a U visa to become available. Your eligibility category in Form I-765 would be (c)(14) if you have deferred action. Unfortunately, this period of time does not count towards the three years of continuous presence required for adjustment of status and to receive a green card.

---

1. Which U Nonimmigrants Are Eligible for a Green Card

Here's a breakdown of the requirements you must meet in order to apply for a U.S. green card:

- You must continue to be eligible for U nonimmigrant status. This means that you must continue to assist law enforcement by providing helpful information used to investigate and prosecute the criminals who victimized you.
- You must not have abandoned this status (for example, by refusing to cooperate with government agencies or by living outside the U.S. for an extended period of time).
- You have been physically present in the U.S. continuously for at least three years.
- You have not unreasonably refused to cooperate with the law enforcement officials investigating and prosecuting the crime against you.
- Your continued presence in the U.S. is justified either on humanitarian grounds, to ensure family unity, or because it is in the public interest.

You will have a difficult time showing USCIS that you are eligible for a green card if your help is no longer necessary to investigate and prosecute the crime against you (for example, the criminal case is now closed and a government official will not vouch for your "helpfulness"). For this reason, you might want to maintain contact with your certifying law enforcement agency while in U status.

2. You Have Continuous U.S. Physical Presence of at Least Three Years

In order to successfully apply for permanent residence, you must show that you have lived in the U.S. continuously for three years. "Continuous" presence for immigration purposes means that you have not taken a trip outside the U.S. for 90 days or more or spent more than 180 days abroad during your time in U status.

You can demonstrate your continuous presence by documenting each trip outside the U.S. (to show that you were abroad only briefly) and providing proof that you now make your life in the United States. This can include pay stubs, tax transcripts, school records, and affidavits from people who know you and can attest to your U.S. presence.

If you can't show continuous presence, you will need to provide a written explanation by a government official who is working on your case, stating that your presence outside the U.S. was necessary in order to assist the investigation or prosecution of the crime or that it was otherwise justified.

3. You Must Continue to Cooperate With Law Enforcement

In order to be eligible for a green card, you must continue to provide helpful information to law enforcement officials, and you cannot have "unreasonably refused" to provide requested assistance.

Ideally, you will submit another certification of helpfulness (Form I-918 Supplement B, U Nonimmigrant Status Certification) with your green card application. This will prove that you are a willing participant in the investigation and prosecution of the crime (or crimes) against you.

If you are unable to obtain another certification of helpfulness, contact an experienced immigration attorney to help, because you will need to instead submit an affidavit and other supporting evidence showing all of your contacts and meetings with law enforcement officials. You will also need to explain that you attempted to obtain a certification from a qualifying agency, but were unable to for good reason.

Additionally, if you ever refused a request for cooperation, you must explain your reasons. USCIS will determine whether the request was "unreasonable" given a variety of factors. Its decision will depend on the nature of the crime, your circumstances, and the extent of the assistance required.

For example, if you are a rape victim and a police investigator asked you to meet with your attacker, USCIS would likely consider this to be an unreasonable request, and would excuse you for refusing it. However, if a police officer asked you to identify your attacker in a lineup where he would not see you and you refused, your denial might cost you a green card.

4. Your Residence Is Justified on Humanitarian, Family Unity, or Public Interest Grounds

Unlike many other green card applicants, U visa holders do not have to apply for a waiver of any applicable inadmissibility grounds. The only ground of inadmissibility that applies to U adjustment applicants concerns participants in Nazi persecution, genocide, or extrajudicial killings. There is no waiver available for these grounds.

However, adjustment of status to permanent residence from a U visa is a discretionary benefit, which means it is completely up to the USCIS officer handling your case whether or not to grant it. Therefore, you should submit evidence with your application to show USCIS that you "deserve" a green card. For example, your family ties in the U.S., achievements and accomplishments, and any reasons why you would be subjected to hardship if you were to return to your home country will be relevant. This is especially true if there are any negative factors in your record (such as arrests or criminal convictions).

5. Your Immediate Relatives May Also Apply for Green Cards

If you have qualifying family members in the U.S. in derivative U status, the procedures to apply for adjustment of status are the same as for the principal U applicant.

However, if you have an immediate family member—spouse, child, or parents (if you are under age 21)—who has never received U derivative status, that person can also apply for adjustment of status or an immigrant visa at the same time you apply or after your approval. To bring this about, file Form I-929, Petition for Qualifying Family Member of U-1 Nonimmigrant, with USCIS. The filing fee as of February 2020 is $230.

You must show that you or your family member would be subjected to "extreme hardship" if he or she was not permitted to reside with you in the United States. This is not an easy task, so you would do best to consult an immigration attorney to help you.

Keep in mind that these relatives (unlike you) WILL be subject to the inadmissibility grounds that prevent many noncitizens from entering the United States.

6. How to File for a U.S. Green Card

If you meet all the requirements, the next step is to file for adjustment of status. You (and each of your derivative family members) will need to assemble:

- ☐ Form I-485, Application to Register Permanent Residence or to Adjust Status
- ☐ the filing fee or, or if you cannot afford it, a waiver request filed on Form I-912, Request for Fee Waiver
- ☐ Form I-693, Report of Medical Examination and Vaccination Record
- ☐ Form I-765, Application for Employment Authorization and supporting documentation (optional; your I-797 Receipt notice can also be used as verification of your employment authorization)
- ☐ Form I-131, Application for Travel Document and supporting documentation (optional)
- ☐ a copy of Form I-797, Notice of Action, showing that USCIS approved you for U nonimmigrant status
- ☐ a copy of your I-94, Arrival/Departure Record. All arriving foreign visitors had this white card stapled into their passports until this form was automated in April 2013; subsequent visitors can obtain a copy of their I-94 from the U.S. Customs and Border Protection (CBP) website at https://i94.cbp.dhs.gov.
- ☐ if any of your family members has not yet obtained derivative status, Form I-929,

Petition for Qualifying Family Member of U-1 Nonimmigrant, as described in Section C5, above
- ☐ a copy of all pages of your passport, including the U nonimmigrant visa page. If you do not have a U visa, because you have not departed the U.S. since you were granted U status, make copies of all of your passport pages regardless. If you don't have a passport, provide an explanation as to why you do not have one, such as loss or theft.
- ☐ a copy of your birth certificate (along with an English translation)
- ☐ two passport-style photos for each of Forms I-485, I-765, and I-131
- ☐ evidence that you have three years of continuous physical presence in the U.S. This can include tax transcripts, pay stubs, leases, receipts, and utility bills for a U.S. residence, a letter from your school or employer, and affidavits from people who can vouch for your U.S. presence.
- ☐ evidence that you complied with requests for assistance from law enforcement officials. The best evidence of this is a new Form I-918 Supplement B. Second-best would be your affidavit, describing your attempts to contact law enforcement officials during your time in U status and reasons for any failure to comply with a request for cooperation.
- ☐ evidence that you "deserve" permanent residence. U visa holders are not subject to a majority of the inadmissibility grounds that others face when applying for a green card. However, because adjustment of status for U visa holders depends on whether USCIS believes it is justified, be prepared to submit evidence that you should be granted a green card on humanitarian, public interest, or family unity grounds.

> **CAUTION**
> **What if your U status will expire before you can apply for a green card?** Your U status, as the principal applicant, will likely last four years. To be eligible to adjust status, you must be in valid U visa status. If your U visa expires before you file to adjust status, immigration law allows for an extension of status based on law enforcement need or upon a determination that the extension is warranted due to exceptional circumstances.

Derivative U visa holders can also find themselves at risk of having their status expire before they can file to adjust status. Due to consular processing delays, many derivative U visa holders are authorized to stay in the U.S. for only three years or less. If your U status will expire before you are able to accrue the continuous presence needed, you might able to extend the time to a period not exceeding four years.

Whether you are a principal applicant or a derivative U visa holder, you can apply to extend your U status by filling out and submitting USCIS Form I-539. Provide the documents described on the USCIS instructions to the form (available at www.uscis.gov/i-539. You should consult with an attorney before preparing an I-539 to extend your U status, because the process is complex and the stakes are high. If your U visa expires before you file for adjustment of status, you risk being deported.

7. What Happens After Submitting Adjustment of Status Application

After you file Form I-485, you should first receive a receipt notice. Later, you will be sent a biometrics appointment notice, requiring you to appear to have your photograph, fingerprints, and signature taken. You are allowed to work while your adjustment of status application is pending. Following that, USCIS will normally schedule you for interview at a local USCIS field office. Bring a copy of everything you sent to USCIS and an interpreter if you are not fluent in English.

Sample Form I-918, Petition for U Nonimmigrant Status (page 1)

Petition for U Nonimmigrant Status

Department of Homeland Security

U.S. Citizenship and Immigration Services

USCIS
Form I-918

OMB No. 1615-0104
Expires 04/30/2021

	Remarks	Receipt	Action Block
For USCIS Use Only			

		Validity Dates (mm/dd/yyyy)	**Wait Listed**
	U.S. Embassy Consulate	From:____/____/____	
		To:____/____/____	Stamp Number Date (mm/dd/yyyy)

To be completed by an attorney or accredited representative (if any).	☐ **Select this box if Form G-28 is attached.**	**Attorney State Bar Number** (if applicable)	**Attorney or Accredited Representative USCIS Online Account Number** (if any)

► **START HERE** - Type or print in black or blue ink.

Part 1. Information About You (Person filing this petition as a victim)

1.a. Family Name (Last Name)   `Chen`

1.b. Given Name (First Name)   `Xing`

1.c. Middle Name   `Mei`

Other Names Used (Include maiden name, nicknames, and aliases, if applicable)

2.a. Family Name (Last Name)   `Chen`

2.b. Given Name (First Name)   `Sally`

2.c. Middle Name

Home Address   *(USPS ZIP Code Lookup)*

3.a. Street Number and Name   `812 142nd St`

3.b. ☐ Apt. ☐ Ste. ☐ Flr.

3.c. City or Town   `Puyallup`

3.d. State `WA`   **3.e.** ZIP Code `98371`

3.f. Province

3.g. Postal Code

3.h. Country   `USA`

Safe Mailing Address *(if other than Home Address)*

4.a. In Care Of Name   `Jia Mei Chen`

4.b. Street Number and Name   `125 C St`

4.c. ☒ Apt. ☐ Ste. ☐ Flr.   `2`

4.d. City or Town   `Tacoma`

4.e. State `WA`   **4.f.** ZIP Code `98402`

4.g. Province

4.h. Postal Code

4.i. Country   `USA`

Other Information

5. Alien Registration Number (A-Number) (if any)
► A- `N/A`

6. U.S. Social Security Number (if any)
► `N/A`

7. USCIS Online Account Number (if any)
► `N/A`

8. Marital Status
☒ Single ☐ Married ☐ Divorced ☐ Widowed

Sample Form I-918, Petition for U Nonimmigrant Status (page 2)

Part 1. Information About You (continued)

9. Gender ☐ Male ☒ Female

10. Date of Birth (mm/dd/yyyy) `08/13/1994`

11. Country of Birth
`China`

12. Country of Citizenship or Nationality
`China`

13. Form I-94 Arrival-Departure Record Number
▶ `1 2 3 2 5 5 3 4 6 7 7`

14. Passport Number `1543446`

15. Travel Document Number `N/A`

16. Country of Issuance for Passport or Travel Document
`China`

17. Date of Issuance for Passport or Travel Document (mm/dd/yyyy) `01/08/2011`

18. Expiration Date for Passport or Travel Document (mm/dd/yyyy) `01/08/2021`

Place and Date of Last Entry into the United States and Date Authorized Stay Expired

19.a. City or Town `Seattle`

19.b. State `WA` ▼

20. Date of Last Entry into the United States (mm/dd/yyyy) `08/12/2019`

21. Date Authorized Stay Expired (mm/dd/yyyy) `09/19/2019`

22. Current Immigration Status
`Student`

Part 2. Additional Information About You

Answering "Yes" to the following questions below requires explanations and supporting documentation. Attach relevant documents in support of your claims that you are a victim of criminal activity listed in the Immigration and Nationality Act (INA) section 101(a)(15)(U)(iii). You must also attach a personal narrative statement describing the criminal activity of which you are a victim. If you are only petitioning for U derivative status for qualifying family members subsequent to your (the principal petitioner) initial filing, you are not required to submit evidence supporting the original petition with the new Form I-918.

If you need extra space to complete **Part 2.**, use the space provided in **Part 8. Additional Information**.

Select "Yes" or "No," as appropriate, for each of the following questions.

1. I am a victim of criminal activity listed in the INA at section 101(a)(15)(U)(iii). ☒ Yes ☐ No

2. I have suffered substantial physical or mental abuse as a result of having been a victim of this criminal activity. ☒ Yes ☐ No

3. I possess information concerning the criminal activity of which I was a victim. ☒ Yes ☐ No

4. I am submitting Form I-918, Supplement B, U Nonimmigrant Status Certification, from a certifying official. ☒ Yes ☐ No

5. The crime of which I am a victim occurred in the United States (including Indian country and military installations) or violated the laws of the United States. ☒ Yes ☐ No

6. I am under 16 years of age. ☐ Yes ☒ No

7.a. I was or am in immigration proceedings. ☐ Yes ☒ No

If you answered "Yes," select the type of proceedings. If you were in proceedings in the past and are no longer in proceedings, provide the date of action. If you are currently in proceedings, type or print "Current" in the appropriate date field. Select **all applicable** boxes. Use the space provided in **Part 8. Additional Information** to provide an explanation.

7.b. ☐ Removal Proceedings
Removal Date (mm/dd/yyyy)

7.c. ☐ Exclusion Proceedings
Exclusion Date (mm/dd/yyyy)

7.d. ☐ Deportation Proceedings
Deportation Date (mm/dd/yyyy)

7.e. ☐ Rescission Proceedings
Rescission Date (mm/dd/yyyy)

7.f. ☐ Judicial Proceedings
Judicial Date (mm/dd/yyyy)

Sample Form I-918, Petition for U Nonimmigrant Status (page 3)

Part 2. Additional Information About You (continued)

Provide the date of entry, place of entry, and status under which you entered the United States for each entry during the five years preceding the filing of this petition.

8.a. Date of Entry (mm/dd/yyyy) `08/12/2019`

Place of Entry into the United States

8.b. City or Town `Seattle`

8.c. State `WA ▼`

8.d. Status at the Time of Entry (for example, F-1 student, B-2 tourist, entered without inspection)
`F-1 Student`

9.a. Date of Entry (mm/dd/yyyy) `01/15/2019`

Place of Entry into the United States

9.b. City or Town `Seattle`

9.c. State `WA ▼`

9.d. Status at the Time of Entry (for example, F-1 student, B-2 tourist, entered without inspection)
`F-1 Student`

10.a. Date of Entry (mm/dd/yyyy) `08/20/2018`

Place of Entry into the United States

10.b. City or Town `Seattle`

10.c. State `WA ▼`

10.d. Status at the Time of Entry (for example, F-1 student, B-2 tourist, entered without inspection)
`F-1 Student`

If you are outside of the United States, provide the U.S. Consulate or inspection facility or a safe foreign mailing address you want notified if this petition is approved.

11.a. Type of Office (Select **only one** box):

☐ U.S. Consulate ☐ Pre-Flight Inspection
☐ Port-of-Entry

11.b. City or Town _____

11.c. State ▼

11.d. Country
_____

Safe Foreign Address Where You Want Notification Sent
(if other than U.S. Consulate, Pre-Flight Inspection, or Port-of-Entry)

12.a. Street Number and Name _____

12.b. ☐ Apt. ☐ Ste. ☐ Flr. _____

12.c. City or Town _____

12.d. Province _____

12.e. Postal Code _____

12.f. Country
_____

Part 3. Processing Information

Answer the following questions about yourself. For the purposes of this petition, you must answer "Yes" to the following questions, if applicable, even if your records were sealed or otherwise cleared or if anyone, including a judge, law enforcement officer, or attorney, told you that you no longer have a record.

NOTE: If you answer "Yes" to **ANY** question in **Part 3.**, provide an explanation in the space provided in **Part 8. Additional Information**.

NOTE: Answering "Yes" does not necessarily mean that U.S. Citizenship and Immigration Services (USCIS) will deny your Petition for U Nonimmigrant Status.

Have you **EVER**:

1.a. Committed a crime or offense for which you have not been arrested? ☐ Yes ☒ No

1.b. Been arrested, cited, or detained by any law enforcement officer (including Department of Homeland Security (DHS), former Immigration and Naturalization Service (INS), and military officers) for any reason? ☐ Yes ☒ No

1.c. Been charged with committing any crime or offense? ☐ Yes ☒ No

1.d. Been convicted of a crime or offense (even if the violation was subsequently expunged or pardoned)? ☐ Yes ☒ No

1.e. Been placed in an alternative sentencing or a rehabilitative program (for example, diversion, deferred prosecution, withheld adjudication, deferred adjudication)? ☐ Yes ☒ No

Sample Form I-918, Petition for U Nonimmigrant Status (page 4)

Part 3. Processing Information (continued)

1.f. Received a suspended sentence, been placed on probation, or been paroled? ☐ Yes ☒ No

1.g. Been in jail or prison? ☐ Yes ☒ No

1.h. Been the beneficiary of a pardon, amnesty, rehabilitation, or other act of clemency or similar action? ☐ Yes ☒ No

1.i. Exercised diplomatic immunity to avoid prosecution for a criminal offense in the United States? ☐ Yes ☒ No

Information About Arrests, Citations, Detentions, or Charges

If you answered "Yes" to any of the above questions, respond to the questions below to provide additional details. If you need extra space, use the space provided in **Part 8. Additional Information**.

2.a Why were you arrested, cited, detained, or charged?

N/A

2.b. Date of arrest, citation, detention, or charge (mm/dd/yyyy)

Where were you arrested, cited, detained, or charged?

2.c. City or Town

2.d. State

2.e. Country

2.f. Outcome or disposition (for example, no charges filed, charges dismissed, jail, probation)

3.a Why were you arrested, cited, detained, or charged?

3.b. Date of arrest, citation, detention, or charge (mm/dd/yyyy)

Where were you arrested, cited, detained, or charged?

3.c. City or Town

3.d. State

3.e. Country

3.f. Outcome or disposition (for example, no charges filed, charges dismissed, jail, probation)

Have you **EVER**:

4.a. Engaged in, or do you intend to engage in, prostitution or procurement of prostitution? ☐ Yes ☒ No

4.b. Engaged in any unlawful commercialized vice, including, but not limited to, illegal gambling? ☐ Yes ☒ No

4.c. Knowingly encouraged, induced, assisted, abetted, or aided any alien to try to enter the United States illegally? ☐ Yes ☒ No

4.d. Illicitly trafficked in any controlled substance or knowingly assisted, abetted, or colluded in the illicit trafficking of any controlled substance? ☐ Yes ☒ No

Have you **EVER** committed, planned or prepared, participated in, threatened to, attempted to, conspired to commit, gathered information for, or solicited funds for any of the following:

5.a. Hijacking or sabotage of any conveyance (including an aircraft, vessel, or vehicle)? ☐ Yes ☒ No

5.b. Seizing or detaining, and threatening to kill, injure, or continue to detain, another individual in order to compel a third person (including a governmental organization) to do or abstain from doing any act as an explicit or implicit condition for the release of the individual seized or detained? ☐ Yes ☒ No

5.c. Assassination? ☐ Yes ☒ No

5.d. The use of any firearm with intent to endanger, directly or indirectly, the safety of one or more individuals or to cause substantial damage to property? ☐ Yes ☒ No

5.e. The use of any biological agent, chemical agent, nuclear weapon or device, explosive, or other weapon or dangerous device, with intent to endanger, directly or indirectly, the safety of one or more individuals or to cause substantial damage to property? ☐ Yes ☒ No

Have you **EVER** been a member of, solicited money or members for, provided support for, attended military training (as defined in section 2339D(c)(1) of Title 18, United States Code) by or on behalf of, or been associated with any other group of two or more individuals, whether organized or not, which has been designated as, or has engaged in or has a subgroup which has been designated as, or has engaged in:

6.a. A terrorist organization under section 219 of the INA? ☐ Yes ☒ No

6.b. Hijacking or sabotage of any conveyance (including an aircraft, vessel, or vehicle)? ☐ Yes ☒ No

Sample Form I-918, Petition for U Nonimmigrant Status (page 5)

Part 3. Processing Information (continued)

6.c. Seizing or detaining, and threatening to kill, injure, or continue to detain, another individual in order to compel a third person (including a governmental organization) to do or abstain from doing any act as an explicit or implicit condition for the release of the individual seized or detained? ☐ Yes ☒ No

6.d. Assassination? ☐ Yes ☒ No

6.e. The use of any firearm with intent to endanger, directly or indirectly, the safety of one or more individuals or to cause substantial damage to property? ☐ Yes ☒ No

6.f. The use of any biological agent, chemical agent, nuclear weapon or device, explosive, or other weapon or dangerous device, with intent to endanger, directly or indirectly, the safety of one or more individuals or to cause substantial damage to property? ☐ Yes ☒ No

6.g. Soliciting money or members or otherwise providing material support to a terrorist organization? ☐ Yes ☒ No

Do you intend to engage in the United States in:

7.a. Espionage? ☐ Yes ☒ No

7.b. Any unlawful activity, or any activity the purpose of which is in opposition to, or the control, or overthrow of the government of the United States? ☐ Yes ☒ No

7.c. Solely, principally, or incidentally in any activity related to espionage or sabotage or to violate any law involving the export of goods, technology, or sensitive information? ☐ Yes ☒ No

8. Have you **EVER** been or do you continue to be a member of the Communist or other totalitarian party, except when membership was involuntary? ☐ Yes ☒ No

9. Have you **EVER**, during the period of March 23, 1933 to May 8, 1945, in association with either the Nazi Government of Germany or any organization or government associated or allied with the Nazi Government of Germany, ordered, incited, assisted or otherwise participated in the persecution of any person because of race, religion, nationality, membership in a particular social group, or political opinion? ☐ Yes ☒ No

Have you **EVER** ordered, incited, called for, committed, assisted, helped with, or otherwise participated in any of the following:

10.a. Acts involving torture or genocide? ☐ Yes ☒ No

10.b. Killing any person? ☐ Yes ☒ No

10.c. Intentionally and severely injuring any person? ☐ Yes ☒ No

10.d. Engaging in any kind of sexual conduct or relations with any person who was being forced or threatened? ☐ Yes ☒ No

10.e. Limiting or denying any person's ability to exercise religious beliefs? ☐ Yes ☒ No

10.f. The persecution of any person because of race, religion, national origin, membership in a particular social group, or political opinion? ☐ Yes ☒ No

10.g. Displacing or moving any person from their residence by force, threat of force, compulsion, or duress? ☐ Yes ☒ No

NOTE: If you answered "Yes" to any question in **Item Numbers 10.a. - 10.g.**, please describe the circumstances in **Part 8. Additional Information.**

11. Have you **EVER** advocated that another person commit any of the acts described in the preceding question, urged, or encouraged another person, to commit such acts? ☐ Yes ☒ No

Have you **EVER** been present or nearby when any person was:

12.a. Intentionally killed, tortured, beaten, or injured? ☒ Yes ☐ No

12.b. Displaced or moved from his or her residence by force, compulsion, or duress? ☒ Yes ☐ No

12.c. In any way compelled or forced to engage in any kind of sexual contact or relations? ☒ Yes ☐ No

Have you **EVER:**

13.a. Served in, been a member of, assisted in, or participated in any military unit, paramilitary unit, police unit, self-defense unit, vigilante unit, rebel group, guerilla group, militia, or other insurgent organization? ☐ Yes ☒ No

Sample Form I-918, Petition for U Nonimmigrant Status (page 6)

Part 3. Processing Information (continued)

13.b. Served in any prison, jail, prison camp, detention facility, labor camp, or any other situation that involved detaining persons? ☐ Yes ☒ No

13.c. Served in, been a member of, assisted in, or participated in any group, unit, or organization of any kind in which you or other persons transported, possessed, or used any type of weapon? ☐ Yes ☒ No

NOTE: If you answered "Yes" to any question in **Item Numbers 13.a. - 13.c.**, please describe the circumstances in **Part 8. Additional Information**.

Have you **EVER**:

14.a. Received any type of military, paramilitary, or weapons training? ☐ Yes ☒ No

14.b. Been a member of, assisted in, or participated in any group, unit, or organization of any kind in which you or other persons used any type of weapon against any person or threatened to do so? ☐ Yes ☒ No

14.c. Assisted or participated in selling or providing weapons to any person who to your knowledge used them against another person, or in transporting weapons to any person who to your knowledge used them against another person? ☐ Yes ☒ No

NOTE: If you answered "Yes" to any question in **Item Numbers 14.a. - 14.c.**, please describe the circumstances in **Part 8. Additional Information**.

Have you **EVER**:

15.a. Recruited, enlisted, conscripted, or used any person under 15 years of age to serve in or help an armed force or group? ☐ Yes ☒ No

15.b. Used any person under 15 years of age to take part in hostilities, or to help or provide services to people in combat? ☐ Yes ☒ No

16. Are you **NOW** in removal, exclusion, rescission, or deportation proceedings? ☐ Yes ☒ No

17. Have you **EVER** had removal, exclusion, rescission, or deportation proceedings initiated against you? ☐ Yes ☒ No

18. Have you **EVER** been removed, excluded, or deported from the United States? ☐ Yes ☒ No

19. Have you **EVER** been ordered to be removed, excluded, or deported from the United States? ☐ Yes ☒ No

20. Have you **EVER** been denied a visa or denied admission to the United States? ☐ Yes ☒ No

21. Have you **EVER** been granted voluntary departure by an immigration officer or an immigration judge and failed to depart within the allotted time? ☐ Yes ☒ No

22. Are you **NOW** under a final order or civil penalty for violating section 274C of the INA (producing and/or using false documentation to unlawfully satisfy a requirement of the INA)? ☐ Yes ☒ No

23. Have you **EVER**, by fraud or willful misrepresentation of a material fact, sought to procure or procured a visa or other documentation, for entry into the United States or any immigration benefit? ☐ Yes ☒ No

24. Have you **EVER** left the United States to avoid being drafted into the U.S. Armed Forces or U.S. Coast Guard? ☐ Yes ☒ No

25. Have you **EVER** been a J nonimmigrant exchange visitor who was subject to the 2-year foreign residence requirement and not yet complied with that requirement or obtained a waiver of such? ☐ Yes ☒ No

26. Have you **EVER** detained, retained, or withheld the custody of a child, having a lawful claim to United States citizenship, outside the United States from a United States citizen granted custody? ☐ Yes ☒ No

27. Do you plan to practice polygamy in the United States? ☐ Yes ☒ No

28. Have you **EVER** entered the United States as a stowaway? ☐ Yes ☒ No

29.a. Do you **NOW** have a communicable disease of public health significance? ☐ Yes ☒ No

29.b. Do you **NOW** have or have you **EVER** had a physical or mental disorder and behavior (or a history of behavior that is likely to recur) associated with the disorder which has posed or may pose a threat to the property, safety, or welfare of yourself or others? ☐ Yes ☒ No

29.c. Are you **NOW** or have you **EVER** been a drug abuser or drug addict? ☐ Yes ☒ No

Sample Form I-918, Petition for U Nonimmigrant Status (page 7)

Part 4. Information About Your Spouse and/or Children

If you need extra space to complete **Part 4.**, use the space provided in **Part 8. Additional Information.**

1.a. Family Name (Last Name) N/A

1.b. Given Name (First Name)

1.c. Middle Name

2. Date of Birth (mm/dd/yyyy)

3. Country of Birth

4. Relationship

5. Current Location

6.a. Family Name (Last Name)

6.b. Given Name (First Name)

6.c. Middle Name

7. Date of Birth (mm/dd/yyyy)

8. Country of Birth

9. Relationship

10. Current Location

11.a. Family Name (Last Name)

11.b. Given Name (First Name)

11.c. Middle Name

12. Date of Birth (mm/dd/yyyy)

13. Country of Birth

14. Relationship

15. Current Location

16.a. Family Name (Last Name)

16.b. Given Name (First Name)

16.c. Middle Name

17. Date of Birth (mm/dd/yyyy)

18. Country of Birth

19. Relationship

20. Current Location

21.a. Family Name (Last Name)

21.b. Given Name (First Name)

21.c. Middle Name

22. Date of Birth (mm/dd/yyyy)

23. Country of Birth

24. Relationship

25. Current Location

Filing On Behalf of Family Members

26. I am petitioning for one or more qualifying family members. ☐ Yes ☒ No

NOTE: If you answered "Yes" to **26.**, you must complete and include Supplement A for each family member for whom you are petitioning.

Sample Form I-918, Petition for U Nonimmigrant Status (page 8)

Part 5. Petitioner's Statement, Contact Information, Declaration, and Signature

NOTE: Read the **Penalties** section of the Form I-918 Instructions before completing this part.

Petitioner's Statement

NOTE: Select the box for either **1.a.** or **1.b.** If applicable, select the box for **2.**

1.a. ☒ I can read and understand English, and I have read and understand every question and instruction on this petition and my answer to every question.

1.b. ☐ The interpreter named in **Part 6.** read to me every question and instruction on this petition and my answer to every question in

[   ],

a language in which I am fluent, and I understood everything.

2. ☐ At my request, the preparer named in **Part 7.**,

[   ],

prepared this petition for me based only upon information I provided or authorized.

Petitioner's Contact Information

3. Petitioner's Daytime Telephone Number

[2535551313]

4. Petitioner's Mobile Telephone Number (if any)

[2535551313]

5. Petitioner's Email Address (if any)

[sallychen@email.com]

Petitioner's Declaration and Certification

Copies of any documents I have submitted are exact photocopies of unaltered, original documents, and I understand that USCIS may require that I submit original documents to USCIS at a later date. Furthermore, I authorize the release of any information from any of my records that USCIS may need to determine my eligibility for the immigration benefit I seek.

I further authorize release of information contained in this petition, in supporting documents, and in my USCIS records to other entities and persons where necessary for the administration and enforcement of U.S. immigration laws.

I understand that USCIS may require me to appear for an appointment to take my biometrics (fingerprints, photograph, and/or signature) and, at that time, if I am required to provide biometrics, I will be required to sign an oath reaffirming that:

1) I provided or authorized all of the information contained in, and submitted with, my petition;
2) I reviewed and understood all of the information in, and submitted with, my petition; and
3) All of this information was complete, true, and correct at the time of filing.

I certify, under penalty of perjury, that all of the information in my petition and any document submitted with it were provided or authorized by me, that I reviewed and understand all of the information contained in, and submitted with, my petition, and that all of this information is complete, true, and correct.

Petitioner's Signature

6.a. Petitioner's Signature

➡ *Sally Chen*

6.b. Date of Signature (mm/dd/yyyy) [04/01/2020]

NOTE TO ALL PETITIONERS: If you do not completely fill out this petition or fail to submit required documents listed in the Instructions, USCIS may deny your petition.

NOTE: A parent or legal guardian may sign for a person who is less than 14 years of age. A legal guardian may sign for a mentally incompetent person.

Part 6. Interpreter's Contact Information, Certification, and Signature

Provide the following information about the interpreter.

Interpreter's Full Name

1.a. Interpreter's Family Name (Last Name)

[   ]

1.b. Interpreter's Given Name (First Name)

[   ]

2. Interpreter's Business or Organization Name (if any)

[   ]

Sample Form I-918, Petition for U Nonimmigrant Status (page 11)

Part 8. Additional Information

If you need extra space to provide any additional information within this petition, use the space below. If you need more space than what is provided, you may make copies of this page to complete and file with this petition or attach a separate sheet of paper. Include your name and A-Number (if any) at the top of each sheet; indicate the **Page Number**, **Part Number**, and **Item Number** to which your answer refers; and sign and date each sheet.

1.a. Family Name (Last Name) | Chen

1.b. Given Name (First Name) | Xing

1.c. Middle Name | Mei

2. A-Number (if any) ▶ A-

3.a. Page Number | 5
3.b. Part Number | 12
3.c. Item Number | a

3.d. My boyfriend, Oliver Ross, intentionally struck me on my face and body and held a knife to my neck on several occasions during our relationship and after it ended. The last incident was on 09/19/2019, when I was a victim of battery, kidnapping, and sexual assault. Mr. Ross was arrested, and I am assisting the police with the criminal prosecution.

4.a. Page Number | 5
4.b. Part Number | 12
4.c. Item Number | b

4.d. On 09/19/19, on my college campus, my ex-boyfriend, Oliver Ross, forced me into his vehicle at knife point and drove me to his apartment. I was a victim of battery, kidnapping, and sexual assault. I was forced to abandon my apartment and leave school. Mr. Ross was arrested, and I am assisting the police with the criminal prosecution.

5.a. Page Number | 5
5.b. Part Number | 12
5.c. Item Number | c

5.d. I was a victim of battery, kidnapping, and sexual assault on 09/19/19. Please see my Declaration, police reports, court filings, and medical records for more details.

6.a. Page Number
6.b. Part Number
6.c. Item Number

6.d.

7.a. Page Number
7.b. Part Number
7.c. Item Number

7.d.

Acquiring Citizenship Through U.S. Citizen Parents

Okay, we know it's unlikely, but every so often someone struggling to qualify for a U.S. green card discovers that he or she was a U.S. citizen all along. How? Because the person's parents or even grandparents held U.S. citizenship at the time of the person's birth in another country. This is called "acquisition" of citizenship. This chapter will describe who qualifies for acquisition of citizenship, how to prove you're a U.S. citizen, and how to figure out whether you qualify for dual citizenship (simultaneous citizenship in the United States and your home country).

RESOURCE
This book does not describe how people who have already gotten their green card can apply to become naturalized citizens. For complete information on your eligibility and the application process, see *Becoming a U.S. Citizen: A Guide to the Law, Exam & Interview*, by Ilona Bray (Nolo).

A. Who Qualifies for Acquisition of Citizenship

In many circumstances, even though a child is born outside the U.S., if at least one parent was a U.S. citizen at the time of the child's birth, the child automatically "acquires" U.S. citizenship. When this child marries and has children, those children may also acquire U.S. citizenship at birth.

The laws governing whether or not a child born outside U.S. boundaries acquires U.S. citizenship from his or her parents have changed several times. The law that was in effect on the date of the child's birth determines whether the child acquired U.S. citizenship from a parent or grandparent. If there is anyone in your direct line of ancestry whom you believe might be a U.S. citizen, it is worth your time to read what the U.S. laws were on the date of your birth and that of your ancestor.

Most laws controlling the passing of U.S. citizenship from parent to child require that the parent, the child, or both have had a period of living in the United States ("residence"). Sometimes the residence is required to be for a specified length of time (for example, five years) and sometimes it is not. When the law doesn't say exactly how long the residence period must be, you can assume that even a brief time, such as a month, might be enough. The key element is often not the amount of time but whether or not USCIS or the State Department believes it was a residence and not a visit. If the period of stay has the character of a residence, the length of time doesn't matter.

1. Birth Prior to May 24, 1934

If you were born before May 24, 1934, the law originally provided that only your U.S. citizen father (not mother) could pass citizenship on to you. The rules were very simple. In order to pass on U.S. citizenship, the father must have resided in the U.S. at some time before the child's birth. The law didn't require any particular length of time or dates when the residence took place. Technically, a day or a week would be enough if it could be regarded as a residence and not just a visit. Once a child obtained U.S. citizenship at birth through a U.S. citizen father, there were no conditions to retaining it. These rules also applied to so-called illegitimate children (children born to unmarried parents), provided the U.S. citizen father had at some time legally legitimated the child (acknowledged his paternal responsibility). U.S. citizenship was then acquired at the time of legitimation, without regard to the child's age.

This law has been challenged several times as discriminatory, with some courts holding that citizenship could also be passed by the mother to the children. Congress finally addressed this issue in 1994 and amended the law, retroactively, to provide that either parent could pass his or her U.S. citizenship to children.

Consider that if you were born before May 24, 1934, and either of your parents was a U.S. citizen, that citizenship might have been passed on to you. Consider also that if either of your parents was born before May 24, 1934, they might have acquired U.S. citizenship from either of their parents, which they then passed on to you under laws in existence at a later date. A check of the family tree could well be worth your while.

2. Birth Between May 25, 1934 and January 12, 1941

If you were born between May 25, 1934 and January 12, 1941, you acquired U.S. citizenship at birth on the conditions that both your parents were U.S. citizens and at least one had resided in the U.S. prior to your birth. The law at this time placed no additional conditions on retaining U.S. citizenship acquired in this way.

You could also get U.S. citizenship if only one of your parents was a U.S. citizen, as long as that parent had a prior U.S. residence. If your U.S. citizenship came from only one parent, you too would have been required to reside in the U.S. for at least two years between the ages of 14 and 28 in order to retain the citizenship you got at birth. Alternatively, you could retain citizenship if your noncitizen parent naturalized before you turned 18 and you began living in the U.S. permanently

What If You Were Born "Out of Wedlock" to a U.S. Citizen Father?

In many cases, your right to U.S. citizenship may depend on your relationship to a U.S. citizen father. However, if your parents weren't married at the time you were born, the laws of the time may refer to you as "illegitimate," meaning in legal terms that you have no recognized father. As you'll see in the sections below, your right to claim citizenship may depend on your providing evidence that your father took the actions necessary to satisfy the legitimation law of your birth country. Legitimation laws require fathers to legally acknowledge their children.

Change might be on the horizon, however. In June 2017, the U.S. Supreme Court declared in a case called *Sessions v. Morales-Santana* that such gender-based distinctions, specifically in § 309(c) of the I.N.A., violate the U.S. Constitution. The case concerned the laws in effect in 1962, the year Mr. Morales-Santana was born in the Dominican Republic. To acquire citizenship through his unmarried father, he needed to show that the father had lived in the U.S. for at least ten years, with five of those years occurring after he turned 14, and the father must have either been listed on the birth certificate or taken other steps to acknowledge paternity, such as "legitimating" him prior to his 21st birthday and before he married.

Meanwhile, to acquire U.S. citizenship through an unmarried mother in and around 1962, the law required only that the mother had U.S. nationality when the child was born, and have previously been physically present in the U.S. or one of its outlying possessions for a continuous period of only one year. Justice Ruth Bader Ginsburg, who wrote the opinion, called this law's variation in treatment of mothers versus fathers "stunningly anachronistic," and found that it fails to achieve its supposed purpose of ensuring that children born overseas have a strong connection to the United States in order to be allowed U.S. citizenship.

Unfortunately for Mr. Morales-Santana (facing deportation from the U.S. for a criminal conviction), the Supreme Court did not feel it had the power to extend the shorter period of required physical presence to children of unwed citizen fathers. Such a move, it said, was up to the U.S. Congress. Perhaps Congress will, at some point, act to create a uniform prescription for acquisition of citizenship that's not based on gender. Until then, however, the Court said that the longer residency requirement should continue to apply to everyone seeking to acquire U.S. citizenship under this (and of course, any other) section of U.S. law.

before age 18. Otherwise, your citizenship would be lost.

If the one U.S. citizen parent was your father and your birth was illegitimate (took place while your parents weren't married), the same rules applied provided your father legally legitimated you (acknowledged paternal responsibility). Citizenship was passed at the time of legitimation without regard to your age, as long as you had met the retention requirements.

3. Birth Between January 13, 1941 and December 23, 1952

If you were born between January 13, 1941 and December 23, 1952, both your parents were U.S. citizens, and at least one had a prior residence in the U.S., you automatically acquired U.S. citizenship at birth, with no conditions to retaining it.

If only one parent was a U.S. citizen, that parent must have resided in the U.S. for at least ten years prior to your birth, and at least five of those years must have been after your parent reached the age of 16. With a parent thus qualified, you then acquired U.S. citizenship at birth, but with conditions for retaining it. To keep your citizenship, you must have resided in the U.S. for at least two years between the ages of 14 and 28. Alternately, you could retain citizenship if your noncitizen parent naturalized before you turned 18 and you began living in the U.S. permanently before age 18. As a result of a U.S. Supreme Court decision, if you were born after October 9, 1952, your parent still had to fulfill the residence requirement in order to confer citizenship on you, but your own residence requirements for retaining U.S. citizenship were abolished—you need not have lived in the U.S. at all.

The law during this time period also contained easier U.S. presence requirements for parents who served honorably in the U.S. armed forces. From December 7, 1941 to December 31, 1946, the parent still needed ten years' U.S. residence, but could count five years of that beginning at age 12. And between January 1, 1947 and December 24, 1952, the parent needed ten years' physical presence in the U.S., at least five years of which were after the age of 14.

If your one U.S. citizen parent was your father and your birth was illegitimate (took place while your parents weren't married), the same rules apply provided you were legally legitimated (your father acknowledged paternal responsibility) prior to your 21st birthday and you were unmarried at the time of legitimation.

4. Birth Between December 24, 1952 and November 13, 1986

If at the time of your birth both your parents were U.S. citizens and at least one had a prior residence in the U.S., you automatically acquired U.S. citizenship, with no other conditions for retaining it.

If only one parent was a U.S. citizen at the time of your birth, that parent must have resided in the U.S. for at least ten years, and at least five of those years must have been after your parent reached the age of 14. If your one U.S. citizen parent is your father and your birth was illegitimate (took place while your parents weren't married), the same rules apply provided you were legally legitimated (your father acknowledged paternal responsibility) prior to your 21st (or 18th if you were born between November 15, 1971 and November 13, 1986) birthday and you were unmarried at the time of legitimation.

5. Birth Between November 14, 1986 and the Present

If at the time of your birth both your parents were U.S. citizens and at least one had a prior residence in the U.S., you automatically acquired U.S. citizenship, with no conditions for retaining it.

If only one parent was a U.S. citizen at the time of your birth, that parent must have resided in the U.S. for at least five years and at least two of those years must have been after your parent reached the age of 14. Even with only one U.S. citizen parent, there are still no conditions to retaining your citizenship. If your one U.S. citizen parent is your father and your birth was illegitimate (took place while your parents weren't married), the same rules apply provided you were legally legitimated (your father acknowledged paternal responsibility) prior to your 18th birthday. Additionally, your father must have established paternity prior to your 18th birthday either by acknowledgment or by court order, and must have stated, in writing, that he would support you financially until your 18th birthday.

> CAUTION
> **The situation is more complicated for children born through assisted reproductive technology or ART (intrauterine insemination and in vitro fertilization).** Before such children can be recognized as U.S. citizens, the U.S. citizen parents must show a biological link with the child. In the past, this was held to mean solely a genetic link, thus excluding children whose U.S. mother carried the child after donation of both sperm and egg. In 2014, however, the U.S. State Department changed its policy so as to acknowledge a biological connection based on gestation, as well.

6. Exception to Requirements for Retaining Citizenship

It is not unusual for a child born and raised outside the U.S. to have acquired U.S. citizenship at birth from parents or grandparents without knowing it. The child, ignorant of the laws and circumstances affecting his or her birthright, then proceeds to lose U.S. citizenship by failing to fulfill U.S. residency requirements.

Congress sought to address this by adding a law for people who once held U.S. citizenship but lost it by failing to fulfill the residency requirements that were in effect before 1978. Such persons can regain their citizenship by simply taking the oath of allegiance to the United States. It is not necessary that the person apply for naturalization. Contact a U.S. consulate or USCIS office for more information. The relevant statute is 8 U.S.C. § 1435(d)(1), I.N.A. § 324(d)(1).

B. Obtaining Proof of U.S. Citizenship

If you have a legitimate claim to U.S. citizenship, in order to establish that claim you must apply for some kind of citizenship document, either a:

- U.S. passport
- certificate of citizenship, or
- certificate of consular registration of birth.

1. U.S. Passport

If you were born abroad to U.S. citizen parents, you can apply for a U.S. passport in the same way as someone born in the United States. However, you will have the added requirement of establishing your citizenship claim. Passports are available from passport offices in the U.S. (run by the U.S. Department of State) and at U.S. consulates outside the U.S., but experience shows that you have a better chance at a U.S. consulate. Wherever you apply, you will be required to present proof of your parents' U.S. citizenship and evidence that they—and you—complied with any applicable U.S. residency requirements. Review the sections on birth to a U.S. citizen for what you must prove under these circumstances. You will need to present documents such as birth or citizenship records of your parent or grandparent and work or tax records establishing U.S. residency for your parent or grandparent.

2. Certificate of Citizenship

Certificates of citizenship are issued only inside the U.S. by USCIS. Anyone with a claim to U.S. citizenship can apply for a certificate of citizenship. In most cases, it is more difficult and takes much longer to get a certificate of citizenship than a U.S. passport.

Certificates of citizenship must be applied for on Form N-600. The current fee is $1,170. Copies of the form and detailed instructions are available on the USCIS website, www.uscis.gov.

We recommend that you also prepare a cover letter explaining the basis of your claim to U.S. citizenship and describing the documents you are offering as proof. These should include your parents' birth certificates, marriage certificate, and citizenship or naturalization certificates.

You should also present your own birth certificate, as well as marriage certificates and any divorce decrees to show legal changes in your name since birth. Your letter should also list whatever evidence you will be presenting to show that you have met any residency requirements as described in this chapter.

Form N-600, the documents, and the cover letter can be submitted online by creating an account at www.uscis.gov or by mail by sending your application package to the USCIS Service Center address noted under Form N-600 on the website. You will most likely be called in for an interview on your application. In the busier USCIS offices, it can take a year or longer to get a decision on an application for certificate of citizenship.

3. Certificate of Consular Report of Birth

Your parents might have registered your birth with a U.S. consulate to establish your right to U.S. citizenship and create an official birth record. If so, the consulate would have issued proof that you are a U.S. citizen, most likely either as as:

- FS-545, Certification of Birth (issued by the Department of State prior to November 1, 1990)
- DS-1350, Certification of Report of Birth (issued by the Department of State prior to December 31, 2010), or
- FS-240, Consular Report of Birth Abroad (currently issued by all U.S. embassies and consulates).

Such documents can be prepared only at U.S. consular offices overseas, and only while the child is under the age of 18. Replacement copies can be obtained at any time, either overseas or in the United States. If an application for a replacement is made in the U.S., a Certification of Report of Birth (DS-1350) is issued, rather than a replacement consular report.

C. Dual Citizenship

Whenever a child is born to U.S. citizen parents but the birth takes place outside U.S. territory, the child may acquire dual citizenship. In this situation, the child will, depending on the laws of the country where the birth took place, usually have the nationality of the country in which he or she was actually born, in addition to U.S. citizenship through the nationality of the parents. U.S. law recognizes dual citizenship under these circumstances, and if you have acquired dual citizenship in this manner, under U.S. law, you will be entitled to maintain dual status for your lifetime.

Filling Out and Submitting Immigration Applications

The most important part of obtaining a green card is the paperwork. The key is to pay very close attention to the immigration forms and other documents you submit as evidence to the U.S. government.

A. Don't Give False Answers

There is one primary rule to keep in mind while answering the questions on the immigration forms: Honesty Is the Best Policy.

For example, if you have been previously married, admit this and provide the documents to prove that your previous marriage ended by divorce, annulment, or the death of your spouse.

If you have children by a previous marriage, or you have had any children while you were unmarried, list all of them on the immigration form, together with their correct names and dates of birth as shown on their birth certificates.

If the immigration form requests such information, be sure to list all your brothers and sisters, whether they are full-blood siblings, half-siblings, or step-brothers or stepsisters.

Once you submit the immigration forms, it is very difficult to change your answers. If you attempt later changes, you run the risk of having your petition denied.

> **EXAMPLE:** Suppose you never told your American husband that you had an illegitimate child. For this reason, you do not mention this child in your immigration papers. Later on, you decide to reveal the truth to your husband. If you want to petition for an immigrant visa for the child you left behind in your country, you will have a hard time convincing USCIS that you had a child prior to your marriage.

1. Criminal Penalties

Lying or failing to mention things on your immigration paperwork can have consequences beyond your immigration case. You also run the risk of being prosecuted criminally for obtaining U.S. entry by a "willfully false or misleading representation or willful concealment of a material fact." This can also affect U.S. citizens or permanent residents who file petitions for an immigrant.

If you are found guilty of committing these offenses, you may be imprisoned for as long as five years or fined as much as $10,000, or receive both forms of punishment. If you received your green card by a fraudulent marriage, the punishment is more severe.

2. Civil Penalties

There are also civil (noncriminal) penalties for people who "forge, counterfeit, alter, or falsely make any document" to satisfy a requirement of immigration law.

If found guilty, you can be fined $250 to $5,000 for each fraudulent document that you have in your possession or have already submitted to USCIS. In addition, if you are an alien, you may be excluded from entering the United States or, if you are already there, you may be removed or deported.

B. Get the Latest Forms and Fee Amounts

The law and the rules on immigration procedures change frequently. Using old, outdated forms can cause your immigration petition to be delayed or, worse, denied. And if your immigration papers are filed with the wrong fee, they will be returned; this will further delay your legal entry as an immigrant. Therefore, before submitting any immigration applications, take the time to obtain the most recent forms and to double-check the filing fees on the USCIS website at www.uscis.gov/fees, or on the State Department website at https://travel.state.gov or with an American consulate in your country of residence, whichever is most convenient.

When mailing USCIS applications, you must pay the fees by personal check or money order made payable to "U.S. Department of Homeland Security," or you can pay by credit card by using Form G-1450, Authorization for Credit Card Transactions. Do not mail cash! Some USCIS and State Department fees (such as the immigrant visa fee) can or must be paid online.

C. Tips for Filling Out Forms

A number of immigration forms ask for the same kinds of identifying information—your name, address, and identification numbers. While the answers often seem obvious, USCIS requires that they be phrased in specific ways.

1. Your Family Name

When an immigration form asks you to fill in your name, write the complete name that you were given on your birth certificate or the name written in your passport, to match whichever document is required.

If the name on your birth certificate is not your name at present, explain the difference in a letter and submit the corresponding court papers or other documents that show the change.

> **EXAMPLE:** If you are a woman named Jane and you're using the surname of your husband, John Smith, as your family name, write your husband's surname—that is, Jane Smith.
>
> On the space that says "other names used," write your maiden name and any other names you have used—that is, Jane Doe.
>
> If you were married previously, write your previous married name on that space. Attach your marriage certificate or divorce decree.

2. Your Address

Your address, as far as USCIS is concerned, is the place where you receive mail. The post office is very important in your immigration relationship because everything from USCIS will come by mail—notice of approval of petition, notice of incomplete submission, notice of interview, notice of proceedings, and your green card.

Do I Need to Answer Every Question?

Try to obtain all the information necessary to fully and completely answer every question on any USCIS or Department of State form. This might, at times, require extra research—or be entirely impossible.

For example, you will be asked for your parents' biographical information, including the city/town and country where your father was born. What if you don't know the answer? Try asking relatives, or obtaining a birth certificate or other relevant records. If your search is fruitless, type "Unknown" in the space provided. However, if you know that your father was born in Ecuador, but are unsure of the city where he was born, write "Unknown City, Ecuador."

If, continuing with the above example, your father is no longer alive and you are asked "Country of Residence," type "Deceased" in the space provided. Or if you do not know your father's identity and it is impossible to obtain his name, write "Unknown" if asked. You may also want to attach a sworn statement informing the immigration officials about how you tried to obtain this information and why it is not available.

It was previously advisable to write "None" or "Not applicable" (or "N/A") when asked a question on a USCIS form that doesn't apply to you, in order to avoid leaving any lines blank. However, with the introduction of new automated USCIS barcoded online forms, this is no longer necessary in most cases.

For example, many forms ask for a USCIS online account number or an Alien Registration Number, and you may not have these numbers. It's okay to leave them blank. Or, if you are applying for a green card based upon marriage to a U.S. citizen, it could ask for the U.S. citizen's date of naturalization. If your U.S. citizen spouse was born in the U.S., this question will not apply, and you should leave it blank. Some questions in the online forms will become inaccessible if you click "yes" or "no," or you may be asked to skip to a different section of the form. As a result, many of the sample forms in this book have blank spaces. When in doubt, double-check the USCIS form instructions, which usually provide line-by-line guidance about which questions need to be answered.

If the mail carrier does not deliver mail in your locality, rent a post office box. However, some USCIS forms ask not only for your mailing address but also for your actual address. In that case, write the exact address or location of your home or indicate c/o—meaning "in care of"—if another person at that address will be receiving your mail.

3. Your Social Security and Alien Registration Numbers

The Social Security number requested on immigration forms is issued by the U.S. government, not by your country's own Social Security administration. You should have one only if you've lived in the U.S. and had a legal right to work there.

An alien registration number, also called your "A#," is issued by USCIS (or, formerly, the INS), usually to people who have applied for an immigration benefit or been in deportation proceedings.

4. Technical Difficulties Filling Out USCIS Forms Online

The latest version of many USCIS forms allows you to save them as PDF documents and fill them out on your computer before printing and mailing them. However, a lot of kinks have yet to be worked out. In fact, you might find that some of your answers will be changed or erased after you save and print the form.

Ironically, this was all part of a USCIS effort to ensure the accurate transfer of information into its databases, by creating new versions of certain forms with a bar code at the bottom that can be scanned. Unfortunately, USCIS released many of these forms without working out all the technical glitches first.

You might find that some answer boxes are impossible to place a check mark in, or that checking one box will erase the answer in another. What's more, some of the blanks are too short to include accurate information in (such as long names and foreign addresses). And because the forms cannot tell the difference between numbers and letters, writing "N/A" or "none" in the blanks

for things like Social Security number (which was once the best practice) is often not allowed.

Our advice? Do your best until the kinks are eventually worked out, but double- (and triple-) check everything before you send it to USCIS, to make sure it is accurate and unchanged from what you entered.

Many forms now have an addendum to provide information that does not fit in other sections of the form. Use the addendum, which normally is the last page of the form, or attach your own page and reference the page, section, and item number for which you're providing extra details.

You also might need to manually write an "X" in your boxes using black ink after printing the form. Although it could be USCIS's fault that its online system changed or deleted your entry, that excuse won't do you much good if USCIS rejects or delays your application as a result.

D. When Additional Proof Is Required

USCIS requires specific proof to be submitted along with the answers on many of its forms. This is because you are entitled to a green card only when you can prove by convincing documentation that you meet specific qualifications. You can go a long way toward eliminating delays and confusion if you take the time to make sure your additional proof is accurate and complete.

1. Proving a Family Relationship

As requested on the immigration forms, you must provide copies of documents to prove that a relationship permits you to apply as a family-based immigrant. If you do not submit the right documents, your materials will be returned and the whole process will be delayed. In some cases, harsh new guidance concerning "required initial evidence" allows USCIS simply to cash your check and deny your application or petition. Check the USCIS website for "required initial evidence" under the form you're submitting.

Do Not Send Your Originals to USCIS

Whenever possible, make a copy of your original document—and send the copy to USCIS. Things often get lost in the mail. And added to that, USCIS offices are busy places crowded with people and documents, so things can get lost there. USCIS often makes no effort to return originals to their owners, and takes no responsibility if they are lost. Keep the originals of your documents in a safe place—one that's fireproof if possible. Then show them to the USCIS officer at your interview.

If you are consular processing, however, you may be required to send your original documents to the National Visa Center. Whenever you send original documents, use a form of delivery that comes with a receipt, so you have proof of delivery and can track your documents through the system.

You must have the official documents. To prove a family relationship, you must have the original birth certificate, marriage certificate, or death certificate issued by the civil registry of your country with the official government seal, stamp, or ribbon attached, depending on how official documents are marked in your country. Nongovernmental documents, such as church or hospital certificates, are usually not sufficient. Although you won't mail the originals in—unless you are processing through the National Visa Center and are instructed to send the NVC the originals—you'll probably be asked to show them to USCIS or a consular officer at your interview.

Use your fingers to verify the indentation of the government seal that is embossed or pressed into the paper. USCIS will often assume that a document without such a seal is fraudulent.

If you have lost the documents, you can request certified copies from your government for an additional charge. Be sure these copies also have the official government seal. Because some unscrupulous people create counterfeit documents, USCIS has to carefully examine the documents presented.

You should write or type the following statement on the back of each photocopy:

Copies of documents submitted are exact photocopies of unaltered original documents, and I understand that I may be required to submit original documents to an immigration or consular official at a later date.

Include your signature and the date. There is no need to have your signature verified by a notary public.

Using the Department of State Documents Finder

Ever wonder how to get a birth certificate in Belarus or a divorce certificate in Djibouti? Go to https://travel.state.gov to find out. (Click "U.S. Visas" then "U.S. Visa: Reciprocity and Civil Documents by Country.")

This tremendously helpful Web page tells you how to get documents you need for immigration cases (like proof of military service or lack of a police record) or replace documents you thought you had but can't lay your hands on. If you really can't get a certain document (such as a birth certificate), the website will give you suggestions on alternatives.

If you don't have the official document. Sometimes, you cannot get your original documents because of war, destruction of the civil registry, your government's prohibition on emigration, or simple oversight or ignorance. Even if you cannot get the particular document, you still likely will need a "non-availability certificate" or another statement from the office that should have the record saying that a search was conducted but no record found.

In such cases, family relationships, such as parent-child, brother-sister, or husband-wife, can be proved by what is called secondary evidence—a combination of documents that do not come from the civil registry, but which nevertheless prove a relationship. These may include:

- Church records, for example, can sometimes be submitted. A baptismal certificate will show the parents' names and the date and place of birth of the child.
- Annotations in a family Bible, old letters, school records, or data from a relevant government census are other types of secondary evidence.
- USCIS might also accept the sworn statements, or affidavits, of two people who have witnessed your birth, your marriage, the death of a spouse, or whatever event you need to prove. The statement should include the witnesses' names and addresses, their relationship to you or your family, and why and how they know about the alleged event. The strongest evidence is from witnesses who were present at the event you need to prove.

For example, if you've never had a birth certificate or you could not obtain a copy, a sworn statement written by your sister could read as the sample below.

Sample Sworn Statement

My name is Jane Doe, and I am the older sister of John Doe.

I live at 123 Middle Abbey Street, Dublin, Ireland.

I was seven years old when my brother, John Doe, was born to our mother, Carolyn Doe, on July 4, 1952, at our home in Cork, Ireland. I remember the midwife coming to our house and I was sent outside to play. After it got dark, my brother was born and they called me inside to see him.

This affidavit is submitted because the civil registry in Cork was burned in 1954 and my brother's birth certificate was lost when the family moved to Dublin in the same year.

Signature: _____

Signed and sworn to before me on March 1, 20xx

[Notary Stamp]

The witnesses have to swear to the truth of their statements before a notary public—a person who is authorized by the state to verify signatures.

You can search for a notary online, or check with your bank—many have one on staff.

Most notaries will charge around $15 for their services, so it might be worthwhile to shop around for the one with the most reasonable fee (unless it's set by state law). If required by the U.S. embassy in your country, the affidavits might have to be sworn to before the U.S. consular official, who will also charge a fee for the service.

You might need to submit your own affidavit stating why you cannot obtain the original documents and what efforts you have made to try to do so.

USCIS might further investigate your family relationship, or request that you and your relative undergo DNA tests or give additional testimony. An investigation could even be conducted in the neighborhood in which you lived in your native country.

Before it confers an immigration benefit, the U.S. government must be certain that the person immigrating is truly the child, brother, sister, husband, or wife—and not the niece, nephew, aunt, uncle, cousin, or friend—of the U.S. citizen or permanent resident petitioner.

2. Proving an INS or USCIS Approval

In some situations, you might have an application or petition that has been approved by USCIS (or the formerly named INS) but need further action because:

- You lost the approval notice or you need a duplicate.
- The U.S. embassy or consulate that originally received the approval notice closed down or you simply could not go to your home country, and another U.S. consulate is willing to process your immigration visa and needs to be officially notified.

- You need USCIS to notify the U.S. consulate in your country that you became a green card holder in the United States so that your spouse and children can receive visas to join you.

In any of these circumstances, you must file Form I-824, Application for Action on an Approved Application or Petition, with the USCIS office that approved the original application or petition. The filing fee was $465 at the time this book went to print.

If you have a copy of the approval, make a copy of that and attach it to your Form I-824.

Documents in Languages Other Than English

If the documents you are submitting are not in English, have them translated accurately. The only exception to this is if you are consular processing, and the document is in the language of the country where the consulate is located. In that situation, the document does not need to be translated. Any translations should be word for word. An English summary of the main points in the document is usually not enough. However, you do not have to hire a professional translator to do the job. Somebody who has competent knowledge of both English and the language in which the documents are written should be able to do the translation.

The translator must attach the following statement to the translated document and sign and date it:

I hereby certify that I am competent to translate this document from [the foreign language] to English and that this translation is accurate and complete to the best of my knowledge and ability.

The translator should also include an address and contact number.

---

3. Proving U.S. Citizenship

U.S. citizens have the right to petition for their spouse, parent, child, brother, sister, fiancée or fiancé, so that their relative can apply for permanent resident status. The widow or widower of a U.S. citizen can sometimes derive status from their deceased spouse. But in all of these situations, USCIS must first see documents proving the petitioning person's U.S. citizenship.

The following are accepted as proof:

- a birth certificate showing the place of birth to be any of the 50 U.S. states, Puerto Rico, the U.S. Virgin Islands, or Guam
- a valid U.S. passport. (You can get a U.S. passport even if the petitioner's birth certificate or baptismal certificate cannot be obtained, by including Form DS-10 with the DS-11 passport application. On the DS-10, a U.S. citizen with firsthand information about the petitioner's birth in the U.S. can sign an affidavit providing relevant details.)
- if the birth certificate cannot be obtained, a baptismal certificate with the seal of the church showing the place of birth and date of baptism, which must have occurred within two months after birth
- a certificate of naturalization
- a Department of State-issued form reporting on the birth abroad of a U.S. citizen, or
- a certificate of citizenship issued by the INS or USCIS, which is also adequate proof that someone is a U.S. citizen born abroad.

U.S. Passport

4. Proving U.S. Lawful Permanent Residence

As a green card holder, you have the right to petition for your spouse and unmarried children, by submitting proof that you are a permanent resident. Although USCIS has your file and alien registration number in its records, you must still submit a copy of your green card.

The official name of your green card is Permanent Resident Card (also sometimes called Form I-551). The Form I-551 is the best form of proof of lawful permanent residence.

If your green card is lost or not available, your "home country" passport—bearing the USCIS rubber stamp showing lawful admission for permanent residence and your alien registration number—is acceptable proof of your permanent resident status. You should also file Form I-90 with USCIS to request a replacement green card, as described in Chapter 23.

E. Submitting Photographs for Identification

The immigration authorities are quite strict about photo requirements. The style and specifications for USCIS photos are the same ones used for U.S. passport photos.

While it is not essential to hire a professional photographer to take USCIS photos, it can be tough to comply with the picky requirements for size, lighting, clarity, and digital resolution. If you or a friend attempt to take the photos on your own, be sure to take many pictures and to read the requirements first. Vending machine photos won't be accepted, but many pharmacies offer passport-photo services for around $10 to $15.

If, as is normally the case, you're asked to submit more than one photo, the photos must be identical—you can't just take a few photos that look quite similar and submit them.

 RESOURCE
Want more detail on the photo requirements? Visit the State Department website at https://travel.state. gov. Click "U.S. Visas," then "Photo Requirements."

1. The Photographs

The overall size of the picture, including the background, must be at least 5 cm (2 inches) square.

The photographs must be in color—with no shadows, marks, or discolorations on them. The background must be white or off-white; it is not acceptable to be photographed against a patterned or colored background. There must be good lighting; the photo must not appear too light or too dark. And the final image must be original, not retouched in any way, and printed on photo-quality paper.

2. Your Image Within the Photo

The image on the photo—the total size of the head—must be centered and sized between 1 inch and 1⅜ inches (2.5 to 3.5 cm) from the top of the hair to the bottom of the chin.

Make sure the eye height is between 1⅛ inches to 1⅜ inches (2.8 cm to 3.5 cm) from the bottom of the photo. You must be facing forward and a neutral or natural smile is preferred.

Although eyewear was once allowed to be worn in passport photos, new regulations no longer permit wearing glasses unless it's a medical requirement for you to wear them at all times. In such a situation, include a note from your physician with your application.

Do not wear jewelry. You may not wear a hat or head covering unless it's required by your religion or for medical reasons. If so, provide a signed statement detailing that the headwear is customarily worn continuously in public for religious reasons or a medical note discussing why a continual head covering is necessary for medical reasons.

Be sure to face the camera directly, keep your eyes open, and submit a photo taken within the last six months.

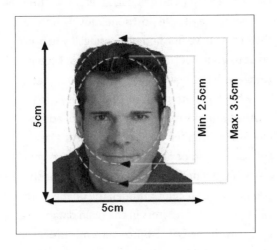

Before You Put Anything in the Mail

Most applications can be filed only by mail. Before mailing any immigration documents, make copies for your own records.

We recommend using U.S. Postal Service Priority Mail, which comes with tracking. This way, you will get confirmation that your papers were received.

F. Fingerprinting Requirements

USCIS requires fingerprinting (also called "biometrics") to accompany a variety of applications, including permanent residence, asylum, and naturalization, among others. Fingerprints are normally reviewed by the FBI and CIA to determine an applicant's actual identity and to determine whether the person has a criminal background that would make him or her inadmissible or ineligible for immigration benefits. USCIS will also check to see whether you've submitted previous applications under a different name.

If the application you are filing requires biometrics, you should include a fee (currently $85) as a check or money order made out to USCIS. This is in addition to any fees for the application itself.

USCIS will usually contact you within 45 days by letter, telling you when you should go to a USCIS-authorized site for fingerprinting. You will be given an address and a specific date and time at which you must appear.

If you cannot make it during your appointed time, you can ask to be rescheduled.

If you live abroad and are filing your application outside the United States, in some cases, you may be fingerprinted at a U.S. consulate or military installation. Whether or not you will be fingerprinted abroad depends on the type of application you submit and the particular U.S. consulate.

G. Keep Your Own File

For your own records, make copies of everything that you submit to the U.S. government, including the immigration forms and the supporting documents. Also make a copy of the receipt USCIS issues to you after you pay any filing fee.

Keep your own copies and original documents in a safe place. You will need them again when you are called to receive your immigrant visa at the U.S. embassy or when you attend your personal interview for your green card at USCIS.

Also, like any other bureaucracy, USCIS does sometimes misplace files. It will save you a lot of headache and heartache if you can show that you have already filed the application with USCIS by presenting a copy of the documents filed and the receipt from USCIS.

H. Tips for Filing Applications

USCIS loses a surprising number of applications, or the documents and checks that came with them. To protect yours, and to make sure they get through the system as smoothly as possible, follow the tips below.

1. Submitting Applications by Mail or Courier

After you've filled out your application forms, assembled the needed documents, and written the checks, you'll be eager to submit everything to USCIS. Most applications must be submitted by mail. But don't just pop yours in the nearest mailbox. First, make complete copies for your files—even copy the checks. Next, you'll want to choose a mailing method that includes tracking. One option is to take your applications or other immigration papers to the post office, and send by Priority Mail or certified mail with return receipt requested. Sending your application via couriers such as FedEx or DHL is another good way to make sure you have proof of its arrival.

However, make sure the USCIS office is equipped to accept this form of delivery. A few never do, because a live person has to be there to sign for the package. Most designate a special address for such deliveries, which you can find on the USCIS website (www.uscis.gov/forms).

When your application arrives at a USCIS office, the clerical staff will first examine your papers to see if everything is in order. Your papers will likely be returned to you if you:

- did not enter your full name, including middle name
- did not sign your application or other papers requiring a signature
- signed a name different from that shown on your attached birth certificate

---

Moving to a New Place? Take Precautions

When files must be transferred between USCIS field offices, they can get lost, at least for a time. No wonder some people postpone moving until after their cases have finished processing! If you don't want to go to such an extreme, at least keep in touch with the new people living at your place, to see whether anything from USCIS arrives.

Also, you must report any change of address to USCIS within ten days. Use Form AR-11, either the paper form or online; go to www.uscis.gov/ar-11. The online form is easiest for most people. If you have your receipt number, the online system will update your address in the main database as well as with the USCIS office currently processing your application. Select the form that you filed with USCIS and enter the zip code used when filed (if any). Then enter the applicant/petitioner information, citizenship information, old and new addresses, and location and date of your U.S. entry (if any). You can also elect to receive email confirmation of the address change. Keep this email handy in case you have trouble with your address change. You might also want to send a letter to the USCIS office processing your application—just in case. Include your receipt number on the letter.

Applicants in a limited number of visa categories (including self-petitioners under the Violence Against Women Act and serious crime and human trafficking victims) can't use the online address system. They will have to send a letter to the USCIS Vermont Service Center.

If you file a paper AR-11 and have no pending applications, you don't need to do anything else. Otherwise, you also need to call 1-800-375-5283 to update your address.

- used an outdated version of the form(s)
- did not enclose the correct filing fee
- left some questions unanswered, or
- forgot to include some documents.

When your papers are returned, there should be a letter included with them, telling you what information was incorrect or missing. You will usually have a chance to correct what was wrong and send back your documents and check or money order. When your documents are in order, USCIS will accept your submission and will send you a receipt notice on Form I-797C.

> **TIP**
> **Will faster, "premium" processing become available?** With USCIS's Premium Processing Service, 15-calendar-day processing is available to people filing certain applications who are willing to pay the premium processing fee (currently $1,440). Unfortunately, only a few kinds of cases are currently eligible for premium processing, and none of them are covered in this book. (It's mainly available for petitions by companies on behalf of important workers.) However, USCIS might someday make the service more widely available.

2. Some Applications Can Be Filed Online ("e-Filing")

USCIS allows online filing for a growing number of applications. While the technology continues to improve and allows you to upload documents, it can be easier to just mail everything together, as a paper application. The main advantage to e-filing is that you will receive an instant confirmation.

As of the date this book went to print, USCIS was allowing e-filing of 11 types of cases. Common applications eligible for e-filing are Form I-90, Application to Replace Permanent Resident Card, Form I-130, Petition for Alien Relative,

Form I-131, Application for Travel Document, Form I-539, Application to Extend/Change Nonimmigrant Status, Form N-400, Application for Naturalization, and Form AR-11, Alien's Change of Address. You also can pay the USCIS immigrant fee online.

3. Always Use Your Alien Number

There are two kinds of numbers by which the Department of Homeland Security identifies every person who comes in contact with it. The first one, an A followed by nine numbers—for example: A093 465 345—is given to those who apply for or receive permanent residence (see Chapter 18) or who have a removal case. It's called an "Alien Registration Number" or "A number."

Until recently, A numbers were issued with only eight numbers. That means that when USCIS needs to enter an "old" A number into its current system, it automatically adds a zero to the beginning. For example, "A93 465 345" becomes "A093 465 345."

Once you have an A number, it never changes. It is even recorded on your Naturalization Certificate if you become a U.S. citizen. However, if you file immigration applications for relatives after becoming a U.S. citizen, you no longer need to use your A number on immigration forms.

The second type of number USCIS assigns is the receipt number, which changes with each application you submit. It starts with the initials of your district or regional service center followed by ten numbers—for example: SRC 1822334455 or EAC 1712345678. Such numbers are given to applications submitted to the various service centers, to track them through processing.

Once your immigration papers are accepted by USCIS, its computer system verifies whether you have ever been assigned an alien number or whether the alien number you wrote on your application is the right one for you.

The clerk then checks the computer files, looking for all the names you may have used, your date and place of birth, and your parents' names. The clerk will confirm the alien number you wrote on your application, or if you have other alien numbers previously assigned, will note them on your application so that all your files can be consolidated under one alien number. If you do not have a previous alien number, the clerk will give your file a new one.

Keep a record of your immigration case number, because any time you pose a question to USCIS, it will ask you first for your number. And if you send letters—for example, asking why your case is taking so long—you must include your A number or processing number.

4. Use One Check for Each Filing Fee

Occasionally, you might find yourself submitting more than one petition or application at the same time. For example, in a marriage case where your spouse is here in the U.S., you can file Form I-130 and Form I-485 simultaneously. Or, you can file applications for your spouse and your stepchild in the same envelope. In any of these situations, resist the temptation to combine all the filing fees into a single check.

If you submit separate, individual checks for each filing fee, then if you make a mistake on a check (for example, you forget to sign it, or you make it for the wrong amount), USCIS will reject only the filing that is affected by that check. But if you submit a single check covering all fees, and you've made a mistake, you will ruin all of the filings at once.

It's a pain to have to write more than one check for forms and applications being submitted in the same package, but most of the time it's worth it.

5. Looking at Your USCIS File

If you need to see your immigration records or to have a copy of a document you submitted, you can do so by filing Form G-639, Freedom of Information/Privacy Act Request, downloadable from the USCIS website (www.uscis.gov/g-639). You can submit the request online by creating an account on the website. Or, if you prefer to mail it, mark your envelope "Freedom of Information Request" and send it to the following address: National Records Center, FOIA/PA Office, P.O. Box 648010, Lee's Summit, MO 64064-8010. Another option is to fax your FOIA request to 816-350-5785, or email www.uscis.foia@uscis.dhs.gov.

You can submit this request without using Form G-639, but it will be harder to get right. First, you'll need to be sure to include the same information as requested on that form, such as your full name, mailing address, date of birth, and place of birth. Then, you'll need to have your signature notarized or executed under penalty of perjury (see the form for the appropriate language).

Expect a long wait. It's not unheard of for a FOIA request to sit at USCIS for longer than a year.

Tracking Your Application Through the System

When you submit an application to U.S. Citizenship and Immigration Services, you probably expect to receive an official reply within a few weeks. But a month might pass, then two—and still no reply arrives. You would like to find out why your application is delayed, but each time you contact the USCIS office, you are simply told to be patient and wait—that your paperwork is "being processed" or "pending."

There are a number of things you can do to be sure that your dealings with USCIS move as smoothly and efficiently as possible. Those options are explained in this chapter.

A. Understanding USCIS Culture

USCIS is just one branch of a huge agency, the Department of Homeland Security (DHS). The people working there reflect the workforce of any other government bureaucracy. They can generally be divided into two types: those who are earnest and conscientious in doing their jobs, and those who are at their posts in body but not in spirit. You take the luck of the draw as to which kind of bureaucrat will be handling your application or answering your questions.

Although USCIS is governed by law (the Immigration and Nationality Act, Code of Federal Regulations, and Operational Instructions), how these controlling rules and laws are applied depends upon USCIS office workers, who have their own cultural and social biases.

For example, you could be confronted with an immigration officer who is anti-immigrant, and who detests dealing on a daily basis with people who do not speak English, who speak with an accent, or who look, dress, or even smell differently from what he or she thinks of as "normal" Americans. This bias might make the worker grumpy, officious, intimidating, unhelpful, unreasonable, discourteous, or downright infuriating.

Furthermore, USCIS is not very phone accessible, and the people at its national information line aren't well-informed about local office procedures. Some of them might give you wrong information.

B. How to Track Your Application Online

It's wise to check your case status online before taking further measures, such as picking up the phone or scheduling an in-person appointment. Here are the most helpful case status websites:

- **USCIS:** At https://egov.uscis.gov/casestatus, you can enter your receipt number to receive an update on your application. You can also sign up for automatic email updates by signing up for a myUSCIS account.
- **Department of State:** Check your visa application status by visiting https://ceac.state.gov and entering your Immigrant Visa Case Number.

Visiting USCIS Offices in Person

The only USCIS offices that you can visit in person are the district or field offices, and even those have restricted entry systems. Each U.S. state usually has one or two such offices (though in a few areas, you'll have to travel to another state). To find the office that serves you, go to www.uscis.gov and click "Find an Office." Click "Field Offices" and follow the prompts.

Until recently, USCIS had an online system, called Infopass, which allowed you to schedule your own appointment. After a staggered transition for all USCIS offices around the U.S., however, USCIS eliminated that useful, self-service system. The stated goal was to reduce the number of people showing up at their offices, so they could get work done and direct people to other resources for help, such as the website and toll-free number. Now, you need to call the USCIS Contact Center at 800-375-5283. A representative will determine whether you qualify for an appointment and schedule it or direct you to other resources.

C. Where to Go

If you're actually at a USCIS office and you feel an immigration officer is being unreasonable, go up the chain of command and appeal to the worker's supervisor. Insist on speaking with the supervisor personally. You can even do this in the middle of an appointment or interview. If that's not possible, try to obtain the supervisor's telephone number and call and explain what happened—or write a detailed letter. Be clear on what action was taken by the worker and what you want the supervising officer to do.

Because the DHS is a bureaucracy with many departments and branches, it is easy to get mixed up in a game of finger-pointing in which each person with whom you speak claims that the problem is not his or her fault.

The most important bit of knowledge you can learn is the exact section where your application is pending and where you need to be directing your inquiry. Here are the offices you'll most likely deal with:

- The USCIS district or field office is open to the public by appointment only and also schedules and handles green card interviews. Most states have at least one. It is rarely possible for a member of the public to talk to someone at the District or Field Office by telephone, but you might be able to speak to someone face-to-face by making an appointment via the phone Contact Center.

- The USCIS regional service center is a processing facility that you cannot normally visit, but to which you may be required to send certain applications. There are six service centers nationwide. You can check on the status of applications that you've filed with them by telephone (see the phone number on your receipt notice) or online at the USCIS website (www.uscis.gov), where you'll click "Check Case Status" and enter your receipt number.

- The National Benefits Center (NBC) was created to handle administrative case processing burdens formerly borne by local USCIS district or field offices. Many kinds of petitions and applications that used to be filed directly with local offices are now filed with a lockbox facility located either in Chicago, Illinois, Dallas, Texas, or Phoenix, Arizona. The lockbox performs fee deposits, issues receipts, and handles initial data entry. After receiving cases from the lockbox, the NBC completes all necessary pre-interview processing of Form I-485 applications (including conducting background security checks, performing initial evidence review, and other tasks). Then the NBC forwards the case files to local field offices for a final interview.

- The National Visa Center (NVC) is not actually part of USCIS or the Department of Homeland Security. It is an arm of the Department of State, and is an intermediary that steps in after your initial visa petition has been approved. It collects visa fees and gets cases ready for transfer to a U.S. consulate in one's home country. If you will be processing your case in the U.S. rather than abroad, the NVC will transfer your file to a USCIS office upon your request. As NVC is not part of DHS/USCIS, however, it will not accept the adjustment of status fees, and if you send it money for consular processing, those fees will not be transferred to your adjustment case or refunded. Depending upon your basis for green card eligibility, your case file might be kept at the NVC for a number of years. The NVC used to be remarkably accessible, but has switched contractors, leading to a huge lag in communication times. There is a customer service hotline at 603-334-0700 for immigrant visa inquiries, but expect long wait times during peak hours. Try calling between 7 p.m. and 11 p.m. Eastern Standard Time.

In addition, there's a Public Inquiry Form, by which customers can request online updates on their immigration petitions: From https://travel.state.gov, click "Contact Us," then "U.S. Visas Contacts," then one of the links to the NVC's Public Inquiry Form, then "Public Inquiry Form" once again. You will need your receipt number, the applicant's and the petitioner's full names and dates of birth, and a valid email address. Don't expect a speedy response. With luck you will get at least some information about your case within six to eight weeks.

- Immigration and Customs Enforcement (ICE) is the enforcement arm of the DHS. Its investigators check on whether both employers and employees have complied with the immigration laws. They do surveillance, make arrests, and issue orders to show up for removal hearings—previously called deportation or exclusion hearings—before the Immigration Court.

- The detention section is run by Enforcement and Removal Operations (ERO), which is part of Immigration and Customs Enforcement (ICE), and comes under DHS. Its job is to find removable people, determine whether to hold them in custody, and execute final removal orders. ICE has an online system that allows the public to find out where a particular detainee is being held: Go to www.ice.gov, and click "Detainee Locator," then search either by entering the detainee's A number and country of birth, or the detainee's name, birth date, and country of birth.

- The Naturalization Section is part of DHS/USCIS, and is responsible for deciding which aliens are eligible for citizenship and who qualifies as a citizen of the United States.

- The Adjustment of Status Section is part of DHS/USCIS, and is responsible for adjudicating applications for permanent residence.

- The Litigation Section is called the Office of the Chief Counsel. It is under the direction of DHS and Immigration and Customs Enforcement (ICE). It is the legal arm of the DHS and represents the government during hearings involving an alien before the Immigration Court and the federal and state courts. It also counsels the other sections of the DHS on legal matters.

- The Immigration Court (also called the Executive Office of Immigration Review), was part of the INS until 1987. Now separate from DHS, it is under the direction of the Department of Justice.

D. Inquiring About Delays

If you're waiting for an appointment or a decision on an immigration petition or application, you're likely to be frustrated. Action by USCIS and the State Department usually takes longer than anyone thinks it should. The question is, how long is too long? To some extent, this depends on the office you're dealing with.

For U.S. consulates, you'll have to ask other people in your country, or contact the consulate directly, to find out its normal schedule. Some consulates post such information on their websites, which you can locate via www.usembassy.gov.

You can find out just how backed up the various USCIS offices are by going to USCIS's online service at www.uscis.gov. Click "Check Processing Times" to find out the dates of applications filed by other people like you. Or, if you have a receipt notice from a service center, click "Check Case Status" and follow the prompts to at least see whether USCIS is still dealing with people who applied before you, or seem to have skipped over you and are dealing with people who applied after you.

In general, if you are waiting for an initial receipt, such as one for an I-129F or I-130 petition filed with a USCIS service center, a month or two is the longest you should wait. After that, there is a good chance that something is wrong. If you sent your application by Priority or certified mail, or with some other delivery confirmation, you might be able to find it that way. If you sent a check with your application, find out from your bank whether the check cleared. If it did, get a copy of the back of the canceled check, which should be stamped with the USCIS receipt number that will help you track your application.

For live assistance, call the USCIS Contact Center at 800-375-5283 (Monday through Friday, 8 a.m. to 8 p.m. Eastern).

Have as much information as possible on hand. The USCIS receipt number will make it easier for them to find your application, but they also may be able to find it with the other information contained in the application, which you will provide on the telephone. USCIS also offers automated information via the same phone line, 24 hours a day.

Make a note of the referral number or the name of the person with whom you speak, as well as the date of the call. It will help to have this information if further inquiries are needed.

Although the USCIS Contact Center will rarely answer your question while you are on the telephone, it can usually make sure that your inquiry gets to someone who can answer it, and you will often get a response later. They customarily ask you to wait 45 days for a response, although the response will hopefully come more quickly than that.

The other good way to inquire about a delay in your case is to submit an online inquiry at www.uscis.gov. Click "Check Case Status" and then scroll down to click "Submit a Case Inquiry." Choose the option that fits your situation. For the "Case outside normal processing times" option, you'll first need to make sure your case receipt date is prior to USCIS's stated "Receipt date for

a case inquiry" under the processing times for your type of case. (That date indicates that they're already making decisions on cases filed later than yours, in which case something has gone awry.)

If your application is at a District or Field Office, or at the National Visa Center, you can send that office a letter of inquiry. If your case is at any of the service centers, however, the only response, if any, that you are likely to get to an inquiry letter is a standard form letter recommending that you call the 1-800 number for the USCIS Contact Center.

> **CAUTION**
> **Avoid the temptation to be rude.** Be courteous, clear, and to the point. Demonstrate that you're well organized, and that you know exactly when USCIS or the State Department received your materials, and when you should have gotten an answer.

Attorneys can't always get results any faster than you could on your own, but they know how to navigate the bureaucracy and can be a valuable resource.

E. Speeding Up Processing in Emergencies

An emergency may arise where you need an action expedited or your immigration papers approved very quickly. For example, your wife might still be abroad because your petition for her is not yet approved, when she is stricken with a rare disease for which the only treatment is found in the United States.

In this type of situation, you might need to speak with an information officer face-to-face. Call the USCIS Contact Center to explain your situation. The representative will escalate your call to an information officer. (Note that the Contact Center is staffed by government contractors who merely read from scripts that USCIS prepared for them. In other words, they're just "order takers.")

Once you talk with the information officer however, you will find that USCIS is extremely reluctant to bend its rules and act outside the standard operating procedures. But if your case truly deserves an exception from the general rule, and you approach the right USCIS worker in the right way, you might get a satisfactory resolution because there is a humanitarian reason to grant your request. It enables USCIS to show its human side.

Unfortunately, it is sometimes difficult to locate USCIS's human side.

For your best chance of success with your expedite request, write a letter explaining your situation and have documents showing why immediate action is necessary. Where appropriate, bring the originals of documents, as well as copies to personally leave with USCIS. The letter you have written gives the information officer something to show supervisors in trying to advocate on your behalf. However, do not expect the officer to read the letter before you have explained your urgent situation. In some cases, you'll simply mail or email the documents to USCIS.

Again, be resigned to the fact that there are varying kinds of USCIS workers. Some make decisions strictly according to the letter of the law, while others exercise discretion when appropriate and make decisions according to the spirit of the law.

If the USCIS worker fails to respond to your inquiry or denies your request, try to go up the chain of command and speak with the supervisor.

If your request for immediate action is still denied unjustly, you could hire a lawyer to help put the pressure on. As a last resort, the lawyer might file a case of mandamus in the federal district court to force USCIS to act on your request.

Sample Letter to Supervisor

Leona Burgett, Supervisor
USCIS Office
Anytown, Anystate 12345

August 12, 20xx

Dear Ms. Burgett:

My file number is A12345678 and I have an adjustment of status application pending in your office.

I received a letter from my mother, with a certification from the hospital, that my father suffered a heart attack and his prognosis is dim. I filed for advance parole two days ago, but my application was denied. The USCIS worker said he believed that the certification from the hospital was fraudulently obtained, and did not accept my mother's letter because it was not translated into English.

Yesterday, I returned with a translation of the letter and my affidavit explaining that in our remote hometown, the most modern equipment available is a manual typewriter, on which some letters might be crooked or spaces might be skipped. The USCIS worker said that my advance parole will still be denied regardless of my explanations that my father is truly very ill.

I am married to a U.S. citizen and have been law-abiding—except for overstaying in this country until submitting my adjustment of status application.

Please help me with my advance parole request.

Sincerely,

Max Haxsim

Max Haxsim

F. Reporting Wrongdoing

In rare cases, a USCIS worker's actions might be truly reprehensible, perhaps involving gross incompetence, immoral conduct, or unlawful behavior. It's not the normal course of business, but there have even been reports of USCIS workers asking for a bribe. If you encounter anything like this, don't just go along with it. Report the misdeed to the head of the particular USCIS office.

Your letter should specify the name of the USCIS worker, if known. If you did not ask for the name or the USCIS worker refused to answer, describe him or her. Also indicate the time, date, and manner of misconduct and the names of any witnesses.

Sometimes, They Surprise You

While it's important to make your dissatisfaction known about a USCIS officer's bad or abusive behavior, the contrary should also be true. If you are served by a USCIS worker who goes the extra mile to be helpful, by all means write to the worker's office and let it know that there is an outstanding worker in their midst.

It might encourage more workers to deliver superlative service to the public.

Although your complaint could lead to an investigation where you may be asked to repeat your facts in front of an investigator or an administrative judge, do not be afraid or unwilling to get involved. The officer's abusive behavior is not likely to stop, and many more people could be injured by it unless you take action.

Keeping, Renewing, and Replacing Your Green Card

Now that you have finally obtained that plastic card giving you the right to stay and work in the United States without major hassles, and to leave and return without applying for a visa, make sure you don't you lose the card—or your right to it. If all goes as it should, your green card will give you the right to live in the United States for as long as you want to. However, you need to protect this right by taking such measures as telling USCIS when you move, not remaining too long outside the United States, and not becoming inadmissible or deportable. You should also make sure to renew your green card on time and replace it if it's lost.

CAUTION

Think about applying for U.S. citizenship. After a certain number of years with a green card (usually five, but fewer for some people), you can apply for U.S. citizenship. This is a much more secure status—you'll be able to travel for longer periods of time, be safe from deportation, and will gain the right to vote. Start planning now: If you wait until five years go by to start thinking about citizenship, you might discover that there was something you needed to do (or something you did that you shouldn't have done) while you were waiting. For complete guidance, see *Becoming a U.S. Citizen: A Guide to the Law, Exam & Interview*, by Ilona Bray (Nolo).

A. Renewing or Replacing Your Green Card

Whether your green card is lost, mutilated, or expires and needs to be renewed, U.S. Citizenship and Immigration Services (USCIS) requires that you file Form I-90, Application to Replace Permanent Resident Card. (See the sample at the end of this chapter.)

The filing fee is currently $455, plus $85 for fingerprints (biometrics). (However, you don't need to pay the filing fee if you're getting a replacement green card because of a mistake by USCIS, for example if it misspelled your name on the card.) For where to file, visit USCIS's website at www.uscis.gov/i-90. Consider e-filing this form in order to avoid any confusion about addresses. You can e-file Form I-90 at www.uscis.gov/i-90, as long as you are not applying for a fee waiver based on financial hardship or paying by money order. E-filing requires you to enter your bank account or credit card information in order to pay the filing fee.

You can also use Form I-90 to get a new green card when:

- Your name has been changed, due to marriage or divorce, in which case you must include a copy of your marriage or divorce certificate and your old card.
- You turn 14 years of age; USCIS requires that you change your green card for a new one.
- You receive an incorrect card with an erroneous name, birth date, photo, or date of entry.
- You never received your green card.
- Your green card is blue, Form I-151; these old cards were issued during the 1960s and 1970s and expired on August 2, 1996, because of their lack of security features, giving opportunities for fraud.

You must swear that all the answers you give when applying for a green card are correct. If you knowingly falsify or conceal a material fact, or use any false document in submitting the application, you may be fined up to $10,000, imprisoned for up to five years, or both. Try to renew your green card shortly after six months before its expiration date. This way, if an unanticipated processing delay occurs, you'll still have a card for work authorization and travel purposes.

You should receive your new green card (Form I-551) within three to six months after USCIS receives your paperwork and filing fee.

B. When the Immigration Authorities Can Take Away Your Card

As a green card holder, you are expected to be law-abiding. Because you were not born with the right to stay in the United States and have not yet been naturalized, the immigration laws put certain restrictions on you that do not apply to U.S. citizens.

1. Failing to Report a Change of Address

The immigration law says that an alien who fails to give written notice to USCIS of a change of address can be deported or removed from the United States. Not only that, the alien could be charged with a misdemeanor and if found guilty, fined up to $200, imprisoned up to 30 days, or both.

The person would have to convince the Immigration Judge during removal hearings that failure to notify USCIS of an address change was reasonably excusable or was not willful.

To avoid any possible problem whenever you move to a new address, submit Form AR-11. To submit by mail, get the form from the USCIS website at www.uscis.gov and send it to:

U.S. Department of Homeland Security
Citizenship and Immigration Services
Attn: Change of Address
1344 Pleasants Drive
Harrisonburg, VA 22801

However, you can also submit the form online, by going to www.uscis.gov/AR-11 and clicking "Online Change of Address." You'll need:

- your USCIS receipt number (if you have a pending case with USCIS)
- your A number
- your new and old addresses, and
- the names and biographical information for any family members for whom you have filed a petition.

The advantage to submitting online is that you'll receive confirmation that your message got through.

There is no fee for filing Form AR-11.

2. Failing to Maintain a Residence in the United States

You become a permanent resident presumably because you intend to live in the United States. Sometimes things happen, however, that require you to spend long periods of time outside the United States. To make sure that you do not unintentionally lose your permanent residence, it's important to keep certain things in mind.

First, if you are outside the U.S. for one year or more without getting advance permission, the law will presume that you abandoned your permanent residence. Like any legal presumption, you can show that it is wrong in your particular case, but it is not easy to make this showing, and you might be required to prove your case in Immigration Court. If you are not successful, your right to U.S. residence and green card will be taken away.

To avoid this situation, if you know that you may be out of the U.S. for one year or more, apply for advance permission (a reentry permit) before you leave. Do this by filing Form I-131 (available at www.uscis.gov/i-131). This form is used for several different purposes, so you want to check off the box in Part 2 that shows you are a permanent (or conditional) resident applying for a reentry permit. Be sure to include a copy of your permanent resident card. (Only copy the back of the card if you have the old style card with information written on the back.) The filing fee for this is currently $575 (plus an $85 biometrics fee if you are between age 14 and 79). There is a sample Form I-131 at the end of this chapter.

A few weeks after USCIS receives your Form I-131, it will send you a receipt notice, and then a fingerprinting notice. You must attend this fingerprinting appointment (where your photo will also be taken) before you leave the United States. However, once that's taken care of, USCIS doesn't mind if you leave the U.S. before your reentry permit is actually approved and sent to you.

a. Six-Plus-Month Departures and Inadmissibility

Apart from the one-year rule that we just discussed, another important thing to know about traveling as a permanent resident is that an absence from the U.S. of more than six months at a time is treated differently than an absence of less than six months. An absence of less than six months at a time is not considered to be a legally significant departure. What this means is that USCIS will not consider whether any of the grounds of inadmissibility apply to you when you return. (See Chapter 4 for a discussion of the grounds of inadmissibility.)

If you are out of the U.S. for more than six months at a time, however, the immigration authorities consider this a legally significant departure and when you (attempt to) return, they will consider whether any of the grounds of inadmissibility now apply to you. If they think you are inadmissible, you will have a chance to show that they are wrong, but you might be required to prove your case in Immigration Court. If you are not successful, your green card (permanent residence) can be taken away.

b. Residence Can Be "Abandoned" After Departures of Any Length

There is one more thing to keep in mind to make sure that you do not unintentionally abandon your U.S. permanent resident status. It is not enough to be sure that you are never outside the U.S. more than one year at a time; it is not even enough to be sure that you are not outside the U.S. more than six months at a time. Even if you take only short trips outside the U.S., if, over the space of several years, you are spending more time outside the U.S. than inside the U.S., at some point border officials

will wonder if you are acting more like a tourist in the U.S. than a permanent resident. In a situation like this, you should be ready to demonstrate your strong ties to the United States. The things that the border official will consider are:

- your purpose in leaving the U.S.
- whether your purpose is consistent with a temporary absence
- whether you have been filing U.S. tax returns as a resident
- whether you still have a job, home, or family in the United States, and
- the duration of your trip.

Even if you are not going to be outside the U.S. for one year or more, if you know that you will be away on so many short trips that you will be outside the U.S. much more than inside over the course of several years, getting a reentry permit (using Form I-131, as described above) could be a good idea. It creates good evidence that you intend to continue living in the United States as a permanent resident. It means that the authorities cannot rely solely on the length of your absences to determine whether you have lost your permanent residence status. However, since they can still look at other facts in your life, you should maintain as many ties to the United States as possible—even if you get a reentry permit.

If you have to go abroad before you receive the permit, you can request that the permit be delivered to your address overseas or, if the mail in your country is not reliable, through the United States embassy or consulate in your country.

If a reentry permit is issued, it is good for two years. However, if you have been outside of the U.S. for four out of the past five years, the permit will be issued for only one year. And if you have been out of the U.S. for that amount of time, you can also expect to receive intense questions at the airport about whether you have maintained your legal residence in the United States.

3. Explaining Your Failure to Reenter the United States

If you stay longer than the two years allowed by the reentry permit, or if you stay longer than one year without applying for the reentry permit, you will jeopardize your lawful permanent resident status.

Upon arriving at the port of entry, the officials will question you about your right to return as a green card holder. You must be ready to present proof of why you did not return to the United States within the time expected.

Illness. A permissible delay could be due to your own serious illness or that of a close relative, especially if the illness started after you left. Convincing evidence of the illness would be copies of a doctor's written diagnosis, medical bills, prescriptions, and letters to you from friends.

Death. A death in the family could be another reason for delay. Bring with you copies of the death certificate, letters from the court or a lawyer on settlement of the estate, life insurance letters concerning distribution of the insurance proceeds, and a court order dividing property of the deceased.

Business reasons. Setting up or closing down a business enterprise could also be a valid reason for delay. Be ready to show bank statements, a contract of sale, invoices, letters from the bank, and letters from your business partners, your lawyer, and your accountant.

In other words, if you are detained at the airport for a more thorough questioning, you must be ready to convince the officer that you had a very good reason for not returning to the United States when expected. If the immigration officer is still not convinced, you will have another chance to explain your case before the Immigration Judge at your hearing.

Insist on your right to a hearing. Too often, the officer acts intimidating, and the scared green card holder signs away all green card rights. Once you do this, it is very difficult to get a second chance to explain your side before the Immigration Court. Your status will most likely automatically revert to that of a nonimmigrant—and you will have to repeat the process of getting a green card all over again.

However, if you were coerced or forced to sign away your rights, contact an immigration attorney, who may be able to help you fight to keep your green card. Above all else, never, ever sign Form I-407, Record of Abandonment of Lawful Permanent Resident Status, without first consulting an immigration attorney.

4. Becoming Inadmissible

Grounds of inadmissibility are conditions that U.S. immigration authorities can legally use to keep you from entering the United States. You had to prove that you weren't inadmissible (that is, hadn't committed any crimes, didn't have any serious illnesses, and weren't likely to need public assistance) in order to get your green card in the first place. But these same grounds apply to you every time you leave the United States for more than six months at a time and try to return. Even with your green card, you could be refused reentry. If one of these grounds of inadmissibility applies to you, however, you might be able to get it waived. (See Chapter 4.)

5. Becoming Removable

In addition to the grounds of inadmissibility described above, the U.S. immigration laws list grounds of removability. These are actions or circumstances that can cause you to lose your right to the green card and be placed in removal proceedings in the United States. If you lose, you could be deported back to the country you came from.

The grounds of removability are too complex to explain in detail here. We have already discussed one of them, namely your obligation to report your changes of address to USCIS. In general, however, you need to make sure not to violate any immigration or criminal laws and not to get involved with any organizations that the U.S. government believes to be terrorist.

For a complete list of the grounds of removability, see I.N.A. § 237 or 8 U.S.C. § 1227.

C. Planning to Apply for U.S. Citizenship

You can avoid all the hassles and worries about losing your green card by applying for U.S. citizenship as soon as you're eligible. Citizenship is the highest benefit available under the U.S. immigration laws, and once you're a citizen, your status can't be taken away (unless you committed fraud in your citizenship application). You're not eligible for U.S. citizenship just yet—most people must wait between three and five years after getting their green card. But it's not too early to start thinking about citizenship and planning to apply.

The basic requirements for U.S. citizenship include:

- You've had permanent residence (a green card) for the required number of years—usually five, but three years if you've been married to and living with a U.S. citizen all that time. Also, asylees will receive green cards that are backdated one year to give them credit for some of their time spent in the U.S. as an asylee before actually getting approved for permanent residence, so in effect they don't need to wait a full five years after the approval. Similarly, refugees can, after receiving a green card, count all their time in the U.S. since their date of entry toward the required five years of permanent residence.
- You've been "physically present," that is, lived in the U.S., for at least half your required years of permanent residence.
- You've been "continuously present" in the United States since being approved for your green card.
- You've lived in the same U.S. state or USCIS district for three months before applying to the USCIS there.
- You're at least 18 years old at the time of filing the application.
- You've demonstrated good moral character over the years leading up to your application for citizenship—for example, by paying your taxes and child support and not committing any crimes.
- You can speak, read, and write English.
- You pass a brief test covering U.S. history and government.
- You're willing to affirm loyalty to the U.S. and serve in its military if necessary.

For now, the important message is to think twice before taking any long trips outside the U.S., do your best to learn English, and be a responsible member of society. You can start worrying about the details of your eligibility, and start studying for the test, closer to the time when you're allowed to apply.

RESOURCE
Need complete instructions on the eligibility criteria and how to apply for U.S. citizenship? See *Becoming a U.S. Citizen: A Guide to the Law, Exam & Interview*, by Ilona Bray (Nolo).

Sample Form I-90, Application to Replace Permanent Resident Card (page 1)

Application to Replace Permanent Resident Card

Department of Homeland Security
U.S. Citizenship and Immigration Services

USCIS
Form I-90
OMB No. 1615-0082
Expires 07/31/2019

For USCIS Use Only	☐ Applicant Interviewed Date: _____	Receipt	Action Block
	Class of Admission		
	Remarks		

▶ **START HERE - Type or print in black ink.**

Part 1. Information About You

1. Alien Registration Number (A-Number)

   A- 2 4 0 7 0 5 0 2 3

2. USCIS Online Account Number (if any)

   ▶ [ ][ ][ ][ ][ ][ ][ ][ ][ ][ ][ ][ ]

Your Full Name

NOTE: Your card will be issued in this name.

3.a. Family Name (Last Name) — Cosmin

3.b. Given Name (First Name) — Mihaita

3.c. Middle Name — Alin

4. Has your name legally changed since the issuance of your Permanent Resident Card?

   ☐ Yes (Proceed to **Item Numbers 5.a. - 5.c.**)

   ☒ No (Proceed to **Item Numbers 6.a. - 6.i.**)

   ☐ N/A - I never received my previous card. (Proceed to **Item Numbers 6.a. - 6.i.**)

Provide your name exactly as it is printed on your current Permanent Resident Card.

NOTE: Attach all evidence of your legal name change with this application.

5.a. Family Name (Last Name) — Cosmin

5.b. Given Name (First Name) — Mihaita

5.c. Middle Name — Alin

Mailing Address

6.a. In Care Of Name — [ ]

6.b. Street Number and Name — 8383 Kew Gardens

6.c. ☒ Apt. ☐ Ste. ☐ Flr. — 401

6.d. City or Town — Queens

6.e. State — NY   6.f. ZIP Code — 11415-1212

6.g. Province — [ ]

6.h. Postal Code — [ ]

6.i. Country — USA

Physical Address

Provide this information only if different than mailing address.

7.a. Street Number and Name — [ ]

7.b. ☐ Apt. ☐ Ste. ☐ Flr. — [ ]

7.c. City or Town — [ ]

7.d. State — [ ]   7.e. ZIP Code — [ ]

7.f. Province — [ ]

7.g. Postal Code — [ ]

7.h. Country — [ ]

Sample Form I-90, Application to Replace Permanent Resident Card (page 2)

Part 1. Information About You (continued)

Additional Information

8. Gender   ☒ Male   ☐ Female

9. Date of Birth   (mm/dd/yyyy)   `10/02/1961`

10. City/Town/Village of Birth

    `Bucharest`

11. Country of Birth

    `Romania`

Mother's Name

12. Given Name
    (First Name)   `Silvia`

Father's Name

13. Given Name
    (First Name)   `Claudius`

14. Class of Admission

    `IR1`

15. Date of Admission

    (mm/dd/yyyy)   `10/31/2016`

16. U.S. Social Security Number (if any)

    ▶ `1 1 2 6 4 5 7 9 3`

Part 2. Application Type

NOTE: If your conditional permanent resident status (for example: CR1, CR2, CF1, CF2) is expiring within the next 90 days, then do **not** file this application. (See the **What is the Purpose of This Application** section of the Form I-90 Instructions for further information.)

My status is (Select **only one** box):

1.a. ☒ Lawful Permanent Resident (Proceed to **Section A.**)

1.b. ☐ Permanent Resident - In Commuter Status
      (Proceed to **Section A.**)

1.c. ☐ Conditional Permanent Resident
      (Proceed to **Section B.**)

Reason for Application (*Select only one box*)

Section A. (To be used **only** by a lawful permanent resident or a permanent resident in commuter status.)

2.a. ☒ My previous card has been lost, stolen, or destroyed.

2.b. ☐ My previous card was issued but never received.

2.c. ☐ My existing card has been mutilated.

2.d. ☐ My existing card has incorrect data because of Department of Homeland Security (DHS) error. (Attach your existing card with incorrect data along with this application.)

2.e. ☐ My name or other biographic information has been legally changed since issuance of my existing card.

2.f. ☐ My existing card has already expired or will expire within six months.

2.g.1. ☐ I have reached my 14th birthday and am registering as required. My existing card will expire AFTER my 16th birthday. (See **NOTE** below for additional information.)

2.g.2. ☐ I have reached my 14th birthday and am registering as required. My existing card will expire BEFORE my 16th birthday. (See **NOTE** below for additional information.)

NOTE: If you are filing this application before your 14th birthday, or more than 30 days after your 14th birthday, you must select reason **2.j.** However, if your card has expired, you must select reason **2.f.**

2.h.1. ☐ I am a permanent resident who is taking up commuter status.

2.h.1.a. **My Port-of-Entry (POE) into the United States will be:**

City or Town and State

2.h.2. ☐ I am a commuter who is taking up actual residence in the United States.

2.i. ☐ I have been automatically converted to lawful permanent resident status.

2.j. ☐ I have a prior edition of the Alien Registration Card, or I am applying to replace my current Permanent Resident Card for a reason that is not specified above.

Sample Form I-90, Application to Replace Permanent Resident Card (page 3)

Part 2. Application Type (continued)

Section B. (To be used only by a conditional permanent resident.)

3.a. ☐ My previous card has been lost, stolen, or destroyed.

3.b. ☐ My previous card was issued but never received.

3.c. ☐ My existing card has been mutilated.

3.d. ☐ My existing card has incorrect data because of DHS error. (Attach your existing permanent resident card with incorrect data along with this application.)

3.e. ☐ My name or other biographic information has legally changed since the issuance of my existing card.

Part 3. Processing Information

1. Location where you applied for an immigrant visa or adjustment of status:

> U.S. Consulate, Bucharest, Romania

2. Location where your immigrant visa was issued or USCIS office where you were granted adjustment of status:

> U.S. Consulate, Bucharest, Romania

Complete **Item Numbers 3.a.** and **3.a1.** if you entered the United States with an immigrant visa. (If you were granted adjustment of status, proceed to **Item Number 4.**)

3.a. Destination in the United States at time of admission

> Queens, NY

3.a.1. Port-of-Entry where admitted to the United States:
City or Town and State

> New York, NY

4. Have you ever been in exclusion, deportation, or removal proceedings or ordered removed from the United States?
☐ Yes ☒ No

5. Since you were granted permanent residence, have you ever filed Form I-407, Abandonment by Alien of Status as Lawful Permanent Resident, or otherwise been determined to have abandoned your status?
☐ Yes ☒ No

NOTE: If you answered **"Yes"** to **Item Numbers 4.** or **5.** above, provide a detailed explanation in the space provided in **Part 8. Additional Information**.

Biographic Information

6. Ethnicity (Select **only one** box)
☐ Hispanic or Latino
☒ Not Hispanic or Latino

7. Race (Select **all applicable** boxes)
☒ White
☐ Asian
☐ Black or African American
☐ American Indian or Alaska Native
☐ Native Hawaiian or Other Pacific Islander

8. Height — Feet `6` Inches `1`

9. Weight — Pounds `2` `0` `1`

10. Eye Color (Select **only one** box)
☐ Black ☐ Blue ☐ Brown
☐ Gray ☒ Green ☐ Hazel
☐ Maroon ☐ Pink ☐ Unknown/Other

11. Hair Color (Select **only one** box)
☐ Bald (No hair) ☐ Black ☐ Blond
☒ Brown ☐ Gray ☐ Red
☐ Sandy ☐ White ☐ Unknown/Other

Part 4. Accommodations for Individuals with Disabilities and/or Impairments (Read the information in the Form I-90 Instructions before completing this part.)

NOTE: If you need extra space to complete this section, use the space provided in **Part 8. Additional Information**.

1. Are you requesting an accommodation because of your disabilities and/or impairments?
☐ Yes ☒ No

If you answered "Yes," select any applicable boxes:

1.a. ☐ I am deaf or hard of hearing and request the following accommodation (If you are requesting a sign-language interpreter, indicate for which language (for example, American Sign Language)):

_____
_____
_____
_____

Sample Form I-90, Application to Replace Permanent Resident Card (page 4)

Part 4. Accommodations for Individuals with Disabilities and/or Impairments (continued)

1.b. ☐ I am blind or have low vision and request the following accommodation:

_____

_____

_____

1.c. ☐ I have another type of disability and/or impairment (Describe the nature of your disability and/or impairment and the accommodation you are requesting):

_____

_____

_____

Part 5. Applicant's Statement, Contact Information, Certification, and Signature

NOTE: Read the **Penalties** section of the Form I-90 Instructions before completing this part.

Applicant's Statement

NOTE: Select the box for either **Item Number 1.a.** or **1.b.** If applicable, select the box for **Item Number 2.**

1.a. ☒ I can read and understand English, and I have read and understand every question and instruction on this application and my answer to every question.

1.b. ☐ The interpreter named in **Part 6.** read to me every question and instruction on this application and my answer to every question in

[_____],

a language in which I am fluent and I understood everything.

2. ☐ At my request, the preparer named in **Part 7.**,

[_____],

prepared this application for me based only upon information I provided or authorized.

Applicant's Contact Information

3. Applicant's Daytime Telephone Number

[7186754892]

4. Applicant's Mobile Telephone Number (if any)

[7185551213]

5. Applicant's Email Address (if any)

[mcosmin@email.com]

Applicant's Certification

Copies of any documents I have submitted are exact photocopies of unaltered, original documents, and I understand that USCIS may require that I submit original documents to USCIS at a later date. Furthermore, I authorize the release of any information from any of my records that USCIS may need to determine my eligibility for the immigration benefit I seek.

I further authorize release of information contained in this application, in supporting documents, and in my USCIS records to other entities and persons where necessary for the administration and enforcement of U.S. immigration laws.

I understand that USCIS will require me to appear for an appointment to take my biometrics (fingerprints, photograph, and/or signature) and, at that time, I will be required to sign an oath reaffirming that:

> 1) I reviewed and provided or authorized all of the information in my application;
> 2) I understood all of the information contained in, and submitted with, my application; and
> 3) All of this information was complete, true, and correct at the time of filing.

I certify, under penalty of perjury, that I provided or authorized all of the information in my application, I understand all of the information contained in, and submitted with, my application, and that all of this information is complete, true, and correct.

Applicant's Signature

6.a. Applicant's Signature (sign in ink)

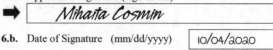 *Mihaita Cosmin*

6.b. Date of Signature (mm/dd/yyyy) [10/04/2020]

NOTE TO ALL APPLICANTS: If you do not completely fill out this application or fail to submit required documents listed in the Instructions, USCIS may deny your application.

Sample Form I-131, Application for Travel Document (page 1)

Application for Travel Document

Department of Homeland Security
U.S. Citizenship and Immigration Services

**USCIS
Form I-131**

OMB No. 1615-0013
Expires 04/30/2022

For USCIS Use Only	**Receipt**	**Action Block**	**To Be Completed by an *Attorney/ Representative,* if any.**

☐ **Document Hand Delivered**

By: _____ Date: _____ / _____ / _____

☐ Fill in box if G-28 is attached to represent the applicant.

Document Issued

☐ Re-entry Permit *(Update " Mail To" Section)*   ☐ Refugee Travel Document *(Update " Mail To" Section)*

☐ Single Advance Parole   ☐ Multiple Advance Parole *Valid Until:* _____ / _____ / _____

Mail To *(Re-entry & Refugee Only)*

☐ Address in *Part 1*

☐ US Consulate at: _____

☐ Intl DHS Ofc at: _____

Attorney State License Number:

_____

▶ **Start Here.** Type or Print in Black Ink

Part 1. Information About You

1.a. Family Name *(Last Name)* — Cosmin

1.b. Given Name *(First Name)* — Mihaita

1.c. Middle Name — Alin

Physical Address

2.a. In Care of Name — [blank]

2.b. Street Number and Name — 8283 Kew Gardens

2.c. Apt. ☒ Ste. ☐ Flr. ☐ 401

2.d. City or Town — Queens

2.e. State — NY   **2.f.** Zip Code — 11415

2.g. Postal Code — [blank]

2.h. Province — [blank]

2.i. Country — USA

Other Information

3. Alien Registration Number (A-Number)

▶ A- 2 4 0 7 0 5 0 2 3

4. Country of Birth — Romania

5. Country of Citizenship — Romania

6. Class of Admission — IR1

7. Gender ☒ Male ☐ Female

8. Date of Birth *(mm/dd/yyyy)* ▶ 10/02/1961

9. U.S. Social Security Number *(if any)*

▶ 1 1 2 6 4 5 7 9 3

Sample Form I-131, Application for Travel Document (page 2)

Part 2. Application Type

1.a. ☒ I am a permanent resident or conditional resident of the United States, and I am applying for a reentry permit.

1.b. ☐ I now hold U.S. refugee or asylee status, and I am applying for a Refugee Travel Document.

1.c. ☐ I am a permanent resident as a direct result of refugee or asylee status, and I am applying for a Refugee Travel Document.

1.d. ☐ I am applying for an Advance Parole Document to allow me to return to the United States after temporary foreign travel.

1.e. ☐ I am outside the United States, and I am applying for an Advance Parole Document.

1.f. ☐ I am applying for an Advance Parole Document for a person who is outside the United States.

If you checked box "1.f." provide the following information about that person in 2.a. through 2.p.

2.a. Family Name *(Last Name)*

2.b. Given Name *(First Name)*

2.c. Middle Name

2.d. Date of Birth *(mm/dd/yyyy)* ▶

2.e. Country of Birth

2.f. Country of Citizenship

2.g. Daytime Phone Number (☐☐) ☐☐ - ☐☐☐☐

Physical Address (If you checked box 1.f.)

2.h. In Care of Name

2.i. Street Number and Name

2.j. Apt. ☐ Ste. ☐ Flr. ☐

2.k. City or Town

2.l. State

2.m. Zip Code

2.n. Postal Code

2.o. Province

2.p. Country

Part 3. Processing Information

1. Date of Intended Departure *(mm/dd/yyyy)* ▶ 06/15/2020

2. Expected Length of Trip *(in days)* 395

3.a. Are you, or any person included in this application, now in exclusion, deportation, removal, or rescission proceedings? ☐ Yes ☒ No

3.b. If "Yes", Name of DHS office:

4.a. Have you ever before been issued a reentry permit or Refugee Travel Document? *(If "Yes" give the following information for the last document issued to you):* ☐ Yes ☒ No

4.b. Date Issued *(mm/dd/yyyy)* ▶

4.c. Disposition *(attached, lost, etc.):*

If you are applying for a non-DACA related Advance Parole Document, skip to Part 7; *DACA recipients must complete Part 4 before skipping to Part 7.*

Sample Form I-131, Application for Travel Document (page 3)

Part 3. Processing Information *(continued)*

Where do you want this travel document sent? *(Check one)*

5. ☒ To the U.S. address shown in **Part 1 (2.a through 2.i.)** of this form.

6. ☐ To a U.S. Embassy or consulate at:

6.a. City or Town _____

6.b. Country _____

7. ☐ To a DHS office overseas at:

7.a. City or Town _____

7.b. Country _____

If you checked "6" or "7", where should the notice to pick up the travel document be sent?

8. ☐ To the address shown in **Part 2 (2.h. through 2.p.)** of this form.

9. ☐ To the address shown in **Part 3 (10.a. through 10.i.)** of this form.:

10.a. In Care of Name _____

10.b. Street Number and Name _____

10.c. Apt. ☐ Ste. ☐ Flr. ☐ _____

10.d. City or Town _____

10.e. State _____ **10.f.** Zip Code _____

10.g. Postal Code _____

10.h. Province _____

10.i. Country _____

10.j. Daytime Phone Number (___) ___ - ____

Part 4. Information About Your Proposed Travel

1.a. Purpose of trip. *(If you need more space, continue on a separate sheet of paper.)*

To care for my terminally ill brother and likely assist with

the settlement of his estate.

_____

_____

1.b. List the countries you intend to visit. *(If you need more space, continue on a separate sheet of paper.)*

Romania

_____

_____

_____

Part 5. Complete Only If Applying for a Re-entry Permit

Since becoming a permanent resident of the United States (or during the past 5 years, whichever is less) how much total time have you spent outside the United States?

1.a. ☒ less than 6 months **1.d.** ☐ 2 to 3 years
1.b. ☐ 6 months to 1 year **1.e.** ☐ 3 to 4 years
1.c. ☐ 1 to 2 years **1.f.** ☐ more than 4 years

2. Since you became a permanent resident of the United States, have you ever filed a Federal income tax return as a nonresident or failed to file a Federal income tax return because you considered yourself to be a nonresident? *(If "Yes" give details on a separate sheet of paper.)*

☐ Yes ☒ No

Sample Form I-131, Application for Travel Document (page 5)

Part 8. Signature of Applicant *(Read the information on penalties in the Form instructions before completing this Part.)* If you are filing for a Re-entry Permit or Refugee Travel Document, you must be in the United States to file this application.

1.a. I certify, under penalty of perjury under the laws of the United States of America, that this application and the evidence submitted with it is all true and correct. I authorize the release of any information from my records that U.S. Citizenship and Immigration Services needs to determine eligibility for the benefit I am seeking.

Signature of Applicant

➡️ | *Mihaita Cosmin* |

1.b. Date of Signature *(mm/dd/yyyy)* ▶ | 10/04/2020 |

2. Daytime Phone Number (7 1 8) 6 7 5 - 4 8 9 2

NOTE: If you do not completely fill out this form or fail to submit required documents listed in the instructions, your application may be denied.

Part 9. Information About Person Who Prepared This Application, If Other Than the Applicant

NOTE: If you are an attorney or representative, you must submit a completed Form G-28, Notice of Entry of Appearance as Attorney or Accredited Representative, along with this application.

Preparer's Full Name

Provide the following information concerning the preparer:

1.a. Preparer's Family Name *(Last Name)*

1.b. Preparer's Given Name *(First Name)*

2. Preparer's Business or Organization Name

Preparer's Mailing Address

3.a. Street Number and Name

3.b. Apt. ☐ Ste. ☐ Flr. ☐

3.c. City or Town

3.d. State | | **3.e.** Zip Code

3.f. Postal Code

3.g. Province

3.h. Country

Preparer's Contact Information

4. Preparer's Daytime Phone Number   Extension

(| | |) | | | - | | | | | |

5. Preparer's E-mail Address *(if any)*

Declaration

To be completed by all preparers, including attorneys and authorized representatives: I declare that I prepared this benefit request at the request of the applicant, that it is based on all the information of which I have knowledge, and that the information is true to the best of my knowledge.

6.a. Signature of Preparer

6.b. Date of Signature *(mm/dd/yyyy)* ▶

NOTE: If you require more space to provide any additional information, use a separate sheet of paper. You must include your Name and A-Number on the top of each sheet.

How to Find and Work With a Lawyer

Although this book's philosophy is to help you understand the immigration law and procedures, your situation could be too complicated for you to handle on your own—particularly if you've spent time in the U.S. illegally, have a history of drug use or criminal activity, or fit any of the other problem scenarios described in this book. Or you might be unable to get USCIS to respond to a request for action on your application. It could become necessary to hire a lawyer for help. This chapter gives you valuable tips on where to find help—and what to do once you find it.

A. Where to Look for a Lawyer

Look carefully to find a good, competent, honest lawyer who will assist you with your immigration problems without charging you a hefty fee up front and a huge hourly fee as your case proceeds.

There are a number of good places to begin your search.

1. Immigration Groups

Organizations that specialize in helping low-income people with immigration problems might be able to answer your questions, represent you in your case, or refer you to an experienced immigration lawyer if the group does not take on individual cases. Ask your local USCIS office or a church, mosque, or temple whether they know of any such immigration groups.

Many of these organizations are what are called "nonprofits," meaning they exist to help the public, not for anyone's personal gain. They raise money from individuals, businesses, and charitable foundations.

Unfortunately, because the U.S. government gives almost no money to nonprofits that help immigrants, and because other funding is rarely enough to meet the community's need, you'll need to be patient with these groups. They might be understaffed and have difficulties returning your phone calls within a reasonable time or spending time with you at all. Also realize that they can legally charge you market-rate fees for their services, although most try to offer lower fees for low-income immigrants.

> **CAUTION**
> **Don't rely on advice from someone who is not a lawyer, or at least supervised by a lawyer.** For example, some church groups try to have volunteers help immigrants with their legal problems. Though their efforts might be well meant, immigration law is too complex to be puzzled out by nonlawyers.

2. Friends and Relatives

Ask your friends and relatives about their own experiences with their immigration lawyers—whether they were satisfied with the representation, the competency, and the fees charged, and about their personal rapport with their attorney. Never choose a lawyer simply because he or she was the relative or classmate or friend of your brother or sister or best friend, without having an idea of the lawyer's competency or track record.

3. Embassies or Consulates

Your own embassy or consulate might have a list of immigration lawyers to recommend to you. Normally, your country's consular officers have your interests at heart and would not recommend a lawyer who is incompetent, a rogue, or a cheat.

4. Ads in Ethnic Newspapers

Your own ethnic newspapers and journals probably have an array of immigration lawyers offering their services directly through advertisements. But beware—anyone can buy ad space. Be sure to investigate the lawyer's reputation on your own.

5. Lawyer Referral Groups

Local bar association and other lawyer groups may offer referral services. Here are some worth checking:

- **The American Immigration Lawyers Association (www.aila.org).** The lawyers who participate in the service are usually competent and knowledgeable, and have access to lots of resources to help them keep up on what's new.
- **Nolo's Lawyer Directory (www.nolo.com/lawyers).** Nolo has an easy-to-use online directory of lawyers, organized by location and area of expertise, and offering comprehensive individual profiles.
- **Lawyers.com.** Here, you'll find a user-friendly search tool that allows you to tailor results by area of law and geography. You can also search for attorneys by name. Attorney profiles prominently display contact information, list topics of expertise, and show ratings—by both clients and other legal professionals.
- **Martindale.com.** This site has an advanced search option allowing you to sort not only by practice area and location, but also by criteria, like law school. Whether you look for lawyers by name or expertise, you'll find listings with detailed background information, peer and client ratings, and profile visibility.

6. State Bar Associations

You can check with the bar association in your state to see whether it maintains a list of Certified Specialists in Immigration and Nationality Law. This is someone who has passed state requirements demonstrating knowledge of and experience in immigration law, often by taking a written exam, completing extra coursework, and being favorably evaluated by other attorneys and judges. Not all states certify specialists, however.

Beware of the Bad Guys

Nonattorney practitioners, visa consultants, immigration pseudo-experts, travel agents, people posing as attorneys, and nonprofit organizations not authorized by U.S. Citizenship and Immigration Services (USCIS) to represent aliens before USCIS—all of them litter the immigration marketplace.

Some of them provide good advice. But for the most part, be wary—especially if they promise you a green card without any hassle for a certain amount of money. Aside from the fact that it is unlawful to practice immigration law without being admitted by a state bar association, there is no way you can check on these individuals' expertise, and nowhere to complain if their services are poor. Many incompetent consultants prey on immigrants and then simply pack up and move when too many people catch on to them.

Report wrongdoers to the attorney general's office in your state so that they will be forced to stop victimizing unsuspecting immigrants.

B. Deciding on a Particular Lawyer

Once you have a referral to a lawyer—or even better, several referrals—contact each to see which one you like best.

A law firm might have a good reputation for its immigration practice, but the lawyer assigned to handle your case is the lawyer responsible for the success or failure of your case. Base your decision about whether to hire an individual lawyer on the rapport you feel with him or her—not just on the law firm's reputation.

1. The Initial Interview

Start by asking for an appointment. The office might ask you to first discuss your immigration problem over the phone, because the lawyer might not handle cases such as yours.

When you do find a lawyer who agrees to meet with you, go to the meeting with the thought in mind that you are interviewing him or her—not the other way around. It will be you who decides whether or not you want to hire that particular lawyer to handle your case.

Rely on your instincts. Does the lawyer seem competent, knowledgeable, fair, efficient, courteous, and personable? It would be unfortunate and unwise for you to feel uneasy every time you are in contact with your lawyer while paying your hard-earned money.

Find out in which state (or states) the attorney is licensed to practice law. Because immigration law is based on federal law, an attorney is allowed to practice it in any state, as long as he or she is licensed to practice in some state. Then you'll need to check the bar association of the attorney's licensing state to see whether any complaints have been filed against the attorney.

2. Consultation Fees

Some lawyers might not charge you an initial consultation fee, but most immigration lawyers charge between $100 and $350, depending on the city where you live, the expertise of the lawyer, and how long the interview lasts. When you call for an appointment, ask whether a consultation fee is charged and how much it is. Also ask how long the lawyer has been in immigration law practice and how many cases like yours he or she has handled.

If you take a few minutes to get organized beforehand, 30 minutes to an hour should be enough time to explain your situation and get at least a basic opinion of what the lawyer can do for you and what that help is likely to cost. Bring with you:

- your passport
- Form I-94 (if you entered the U.S. legally; you might have received a small green or white card or you may need to go to the U.S. Customs and Border Protection (CBP) website at www.cbp.gov and click "Need Your I-94 Number?")
- records of any arrests
- a copy of any immigration forms you may have filled out and correspondence received from the INS or USCIS, and
- certificates and documents you may need to prove family relationships, such as husband and wife or parent and child.

3. Dealing With Paralegals and Assistants

Because the practice of immigration law usually involves filling out a great number of forms, the lawyer might hire a paralegal or secretary who interviews you to get many of the answers needed to complete your paperwork.

The paralegal or secretary becomes your contact person. At the initial interview, ask to meet the paralegal who will be working on your case, too, so that you have an idea of how comfortable you will be in dealing with him or her. Ask whether this person is closely supervised and whether the lawyer normally reviews the forms before submitting them to the U.S. government.

C. Paying the Lawyer

Some law firms or organizations specializing in immigration might take your case *pro bono*, meaning they will provide a lawyer to handle your case without asking for any money or for only a small amount to cover expenses.

However, due to limited resources and great demand, they might not be able to accept your immigration case and might only be able to tell you what your legal options are and advise you about whether you seem to have a strong case. These groups might refer you to a list of attorneys they feel would be representing you in the same spirit of service as they do and whose fees would be reasonable.

1. Types of Fee Arrangements

Many immigration attorneys charge a "flat fee" for their work. Flat fees are set amounts for specific types of cases. The attorney's hourly rate could be specified in the contract and would become important if you decide to end the attorney's representation before the work is completed. (See "Firing a Lawyer," below.) Most lawyers are guided by the principle that time is money.

Since you are being charged a flat fee for a specific job, be sure you know what that job is. For example, if you are hiring an attorney for an adjustment of status case, does the flat fee include filling out the forms (including the forms for the work permit and travel document), making sure that USCIS receives the forms, preparing you for the interview, and attending the interview with you? If you are among the few people who get called back for a second or third interview, does the attorney charge for those interviews separately from the quoted flat fee? If USCIS does not decide your case in a timely fashion, are additional inquiries charged for separately? What are the "incidental" charges that you will be expected to pay in addition to the flat fee? For example, you should know whether you will be paying the USCIS filing fees separately from the attorneys' fee, and whether you will be responsible for mail or courier charges and copying costs.

Many lawyers will agree to let you pay a flat fee in installments during the period it takes to process your immigration papers.

Some immigration lawyers do not charge a flat fee. They will charge for their work based on quarter-hours, so that if you call and spend seven minutes on the telephone, you will be charged for a minimum of 15 minutes of work. Unless you are completely satisfied that your lawyer is honest, you could be opening yourself up to paying into a bottomless money pit when you agree to pay the lawyer according to an hourly charge.

If you agree to the per-hour billing rate—usually unwise unless you are in a removal proceeding due to grave criminal conduct or some other complicated case—request a schedule of legal work to be done and a maximum you will pay for each task.

2. Get It in Writing

Most disagreements between lawyers and clients involve fees, so be sure to get all the details involving money in writing—the per-hour billing rate or flat maximum fee, how often you will be billed, and how the attorney will handle any funds you may have deposited in advance to cover expenses.

D. Managing the Lawyer

A great many complaints against lawyers have to do with their failure to communicate with their clients. Your lawyer might be the one with the legal expertise, but the rights that are being pursued are yours—and you are the most important person involved in your case. You have the right to demand that your lawyer be reasonably available to answer your questions and to keep you posted on your case.

You might need to put some energy into managing your lawyer.

1. Carefully Check Every Statement

Each statement or bill should list costs that the lawyer has paid or that you are expected to pay. If any one lacks sufficient detail, call your lawyer and politely demand that a new, more detailed version be sent before you pay it. Don't feel as though you're being too pushy: The laws in many states actually require thorough detail in lawyers' billing statements.

2. Educate Yourself

By learning the most you can about immigration laws and what to expect during the procedure, you'll be able to monitor your lawyer's work and might even be able to do some legwork, make a suggestion, or provide information that will move your case along faster.

Unfortunately, USCIS and the State Department are bureaucracies and oftentimes a case is simply held up until the slow-grinding wheels of procedure get through it. Many people unfairly blame their lawyers for delays that are actually the government's fault—or just a natural result of how the immigration laws are structured.

However, if an immigration application is proceeding much more slowly than your lawyer initially told you it would, then ask your lawyer whether it would make sense to contact the appropriate office and find out the reason for the delay.

3. Keep Your Own Calendar

Note when papers and appearances are due in court or for responses to so-called "Requests for Evidence." If you rely on your lawyer to keep your case on schedule, you could be unpleasantly surprised to find that an important deadline has been missed. This could put your immigration status in jeopardy. Call or write to your lawyer at least a week before any important deadline in your case to inquire about plans to meet it.

Of course, you need to do your part, by showing up for appointments with your lawyer on time, so that your case can be adequately prepared.

And you must be especially careful to arrive on time—or better yet, early—for any appointments with immigration officials. If you're not in the room when you're scheduled to be there, your case could be delayed for weeks or months, or, in the case of Immigration Court, you might receive an immediate order of removal (deportation).

Your lawyer will be unable to help you out of this mess, even if he or she was in the courtroom at the time.

4. Maintain Your Own File

Try never to give away original documents connected with your case; keep the originals for your own files and give only copies to your lawyer. USCIS will, in most cases, accept copies of the original documents. Also, ask for a copy of every letter and application your lawyer sends to USCIS. By having a well-organized file of your own, you'll be able to discuss your case with your lawyer intelligently and efficiently—even over the telephone.

Being well-informed will help keep your lawyer's effectiveness up and your costs down, especially if your lawyer is working on an hourly basis, in which case telephone consultations are less expensive than office visits.

Also, your lawyer cannot hold your immigration files ransom in case you decide to change legal counsel, because you have copies of everything the office file has on your case.

In any event, you have a right to promptly receive a copy of your file. The attorney might ask you to sign or produce a written authorization and transfer request before turning the file over to you.

E. Firing a Lawyer

Change lawyers if you feel that's necessary. If the relationship between you and the lawyer you chose doesn't seem to be working, or if you feel that your case isn't progressing as it should, think about asking another lawyer to take over.

If you get upset every time you talk to your lawyer because he or she does not seem to understand what you are saying about your case, or will not take the time to listen, you will save yourself both money and mental anguish if you look for someone else to represent you.

But be clear with the first lawyer that you are taking your business elsewhere, and immediately put your decision in writing. At that point, your first lawyer should stop working on your case. The lawyer can then give you an accounting of how much time was spent working on your case. If you have paid the lawyer a lot of money up front, and he or she did not yet spend much time on your case, you will probably be due a refund.

If you were paying in installments and the lawyer spent more time working on your case than you have so far paid for, you might still owe money for the work that was performed, even though you are firing the lawyer.

Do not expect your first lawyer to share any of the fee you've paid with your new lawyer. Unless you have a contingency fee arrangement where the lawyer takes a share of the damages won—and very few immigration cases are structured that way— your fee agreement with your new lawyer will be completely separate from your fee agreement with your first lawyer. Between the two lawyers, you might end up paying more than you would have if you had only one lawyer. Both lawyers could claim they handled the lion's share of the work in your case. Do not be embarrassed to negotiate with the lawyers.

Also, be sure that your new lawyer understands whether you have an application or other matter pending with USCIS or a related agency, and quickly advises that agency of the change in attorneys.

What to Do About Bad Legal Advice

Take prompt action against any behavior by a lawyer that appears to be deceptive, unethical, or otherwise illegal. A call to the local bar association, listed in the telephone directory under "Attorneys," should provide you with guidance on what types of lawyer behavior are prohibited and how to file a complaint.

Still, in most states, groups that regulate attorneys are biased toward them. Unless the lawyer's conduct is plainly dishonest or he or she has abandoned your case, you will probably not get much satisfaction. However, sometimes the threat of filing a complaint can move your lawyer into action. And if worst comes to worst, filing a formal complaint will create a document that you'll need should you end up later filing a malpractice lawsuit against a lawyer.

Index

E

NOLO

More from Nolo

Nolo.com offers a large library of legal solutions and forms, created by Nolo's in-house legal editors. These reliable documents can be prepared in minutes.

Create a Document Online

Incorporation. Incorporate your business in any state.

LLC Formation. Gain asset protection and pass-through tax status in any state.

Will. Nolo has helped people make over 2 million wills. Is it time to make or revise yours?

Living Trust (avoid probate). Plan now to save your family the cost, delays, and hassle of probate.

Provisional Patent. Preserve your right to obtain a patent by claiming "patent pending" status.

Download Useful Legal Forms

Nolo.com has hundreds of top quality legal forms available for download:

- bill of sale
- promissory note
- nondisclosure agreement
- LLC operating agreement
- corporate minutes
- commercial lease and sublease
- motor vehicle bill of sale
- consignment agreement
- and many more.

Nolo's Bestselling Books

Becoming a U.S. Citizen
A Guide to the Law, Exam & Interview
$29.99

Fiance & Marriage Visas
A Couple's Guide to U.S. Immigration
$39.99

U.S. Immigration Made Easy
$44.99

Legal Research
How to Find & Understand the Law
$49.99

Nolo's Encyclopedia of Everyday Law
$34.99

Every Nolo title is available in print and for download at Nolo.com.

www.nolo.com

⚖ NOLO *Save 15%* off your next order

Register your Nolo purchase, and we'll send you a **coupon for 15% off** your next Nolo.com order!

Nolo.com/customer-support/productregistration

On Nolo.com you'll also find:

Books & Software

Nolo publishes hundreds of great books and software programs for consumers and business owners. Order a copy, or download an ebook version instantly, at Nolo.com.

Online Forms

You can quickly and easily make a will or living trust, form an LLC or corporation, apply for a provisional patent, or make hundreds of other forms—online.

Free Legal Information

Thousands of articles answer common questions about everyday legal issues, including wills, bankruptcy, small business formation, divorce, patents, employment, and much more.

Plain-English Legal Dictionary

Stumped by jargon? Look it up in America's most up-to-date source for definitions of legal terms, free at Nolo.com.

Lawyer Directory

Nolo's consumer-friendly lawyer directory provides in-depth profiles of lawyers all over America. You'll find information you need to choose the right lawyer.